Lecture Notes in Computer Science 4418

Commenced Publication in 1973
Founding and Former Series Editors:
Gerhard Goos, Juris Hartmanis, and Jan van Leeuwen

T0189748

André Gagalowicz   Wilfried Philips (Eds.)

Computer Vision/
Computer Graphics
Collaboration Techniques

Third International Conference, MIRAGE 2007
Rocquencourt, France, March 28-30, 2007
Proceedings

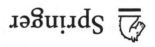 Springer

Volume Editors

André Gagalowicz
INRIA Rocquencourt
MIRAGES project
Domaine de Voluceau, 78153 Le Chesnay Cedex 1, France
E-mail: Andre.Gagalowicz@inria.fr

Wilfried Philips
Ghent University
Department of Telecommunication and Information Processing
St.-Pietersnieuwstraat 41, 9000 Ghent, Belgium
E-mail: philips@telin.UGent.be

Library of Congress Control Number: 2007922974

CR Subject Classification (1998): I.4, I.5, I.2.10, I.3.5, I.3.7, F.2.2

LNCS Sublibrary: SL 6 – Image Processing, Computer Vision, Pattern Recognition, and Graphics

ISSN   0302-9743
ISBN-10 3-540-71456-1 Springer Berlin Heidelberg New York
ISBN-13 978-3-540-71456-9 Springer Berlin Heidelberg New York

Springer is a part of Springer Science+Business Media

springer.com

© Springer-Verlag Berlin Heidelberg 2007

Typesetting: Camera-ready by author, data conversion by Scientific Publishing Services, Chennai, India
Printed on acid-free paper   SPIN: 12037131   06/3142   5 4 3 2 1 0

Preface

This volume contains the papers accepted for presentation at MIRAGE 2007.

The Mirage conference is becoming recognized internationally, with presentations coming from 31 countries. South Korea proved to be the most active scientifically with a total of 73 submitted papers, far above China (27 submitted papers), Taiwan (10) and India (9), which proves the strong domination of Asia in the development of this new technology.

We received a total of 198 submissions. Reviewing was very selective as the Program Committee accepted only 42 oral presentations and 17 posters. We had to extend the conference period from two to three days, as the number of submissions was mutiplied by three compared to the previous conference, which proves that this conference attracts more and more researchers. All papers were reviewed by two to four members of the Program Committee. The final selection was carried out by the Conference Chairs.

We wish to thank the Program Committee and additional referees for their timely and high-quality reviews. We also thank the invited speakers Peter Eisert and Adrian Hilton for kindly accepting to present very interesting talks.

Mirage 2007 was organized by INRIA Rocquencourt and took place at INRIA, Rocquencourt, close to Versailles Castle. We believe that the conference proved to be a stimulating experience, and we hope readers will enjoy these proceedings.

January 2007

A. Gagalowicz
W. Philips

Organization

Mirage 2007 was organized by INRIA and Ghent University.

Conference Chair

André Gagalowicz (INRIA Rocquencourt, Le Chesnay, France)

Conference Co-chairs

Cédric Guiard (THALES, Paris, France)
Emanuele Trucco (Heriot-Watt University, Edinburgh, UK)

Organizing Committee

Florence Barbara (INRIA Rocquencourt, Le Chesnay, France)
André Gagalowicz (INRIA Rocquencourt, Le Chesnay, France)
Chantal Girodon (INRIA Rocquencourt, Rocquencourt, France)
Wilfried Philips (Ghent University, Ghent, Belgium)

Program Committee

Ken Anjyo (OLM Digital, Inc., Tokyo, Japan)
Bruno Arnaldi (IRISA, Rennes, France)
Yuri Bayakovski (Moscow State University, Moscow, Russia)
Jacques Blanc-Talon (DGA, France, Arcueil, France)
Volker Blanz (Max-Planck-Institut für Informatik, Saarbrücken, Germany)
José Braz (Polytechnic Institute of Setúbal, Setúbal, Portugal)
Antonio Camurri (University of Genova, Genova, Italy)
Adrian Clark (University of Essex, Colchester, UK)
Ernst Dickmanns (University of the Bundeswehr, Munich, Hofolding,
    Germany)
Peter Eisert (Heinrich-Hertz-Institut, Berlin, Germany)
Reyes Enciso (USC, Los Angeles, USA)
Alexandre Francois (University of Southern California, Los Angeles, USA)
Andrea Fusiello (Università degli Studi di Verona, Verona, Italy)
André Gagalowicz (INRIA Rocquencourt, Le Chesnay, France)
Sidharta Gautama (TELIN, Ghent University, Ghent, Belgium)
Andrew Glassner (Coyote Wind, Seattle, USA)
Michael Gleicher (University of Wisconsin, Madison, USA)
Michael Goesele (University of Washington, Seattle, USA)

Oliver Grau (BBC, Tadworth, UK)
Radek Grzeszczuk (Nokia Research Lab, Palo Alto, USA)
Cédric Guiard (THALES, Paris, France)
Peter Hall (University of Bath, Bath, UK)
Adrian Hilton (University of Surrey, Guildford, UK)
Hyung Soo Kim (Seoul National University, Seoul, Korea)
Reinhard Koch (Christian-Albrechts-Universität Kiel, Kiel, Germany)
Ivana Kolingerova (University of West Bohemia, Plzen, Czech Republic)
Tosiyasu Kunii (Kanazawa Institute of Technology, Tokyo, Japan)
Hendrik Lensch (Max-Planck-Institut für Informatik, Saarbrücken,
    Germany)
Ales Leonardis (Ljubljana University, Ljubljana, Slovenia)
J.P. Lewis (Stanford University, Stanford, USA)
Zicheng Liu (Microsoft, Redmond, USA)
Takashi Matsuyama (Kyoto University, Kyoto, Japan)
Wojciech Mokrzycki (University of Podlasie, Siedlce, Poland)
Toshio Moriya (Hitachi, Ltd., Kawasaki, Japan)
Vittorio Murino (Università degli Studi di Verona, Verona, Italy)
Heinrich Niemann (University of Erlangen-Nuremberg, Erlangen, Germany)
Kazunori Okada (San Francisco State University, San Francisco, USA)
Joern Ostermann (University of Hannover, Hannover, Germany)
Jean-Claude Paul (Tsinghua University, Peking, China)
Dietrich Paulus (University of Koblenz, Koblenz, Germany)
Wilfried Philips (Ghent University, Ghent, Belgium)
Dan Popescu (CSIRO, Sidney, Australia)
John Robinson (University of York, Heslington, UK)
Christian Roessl (INRIA Sophia-Antipolis, Sophia-Antipolis, France)
Bodo Rosenhahn (Max Planck Institute, Saarbrücken, Germany)
Robert Sablatnig (Vienna University of Technology, Vienna, Austria)
Wladislaw Skarbek (Warsaw University of Technology, Warsaw, Poland)
Franc Solina (University of Ljubljana, Ljubljana, Slovenia)
Daniel Thalmann (EPFL, Lausanne, Switzerland)
Holger Theisel (Max-Planck-Institut für Informatik, Saarbrücken,
    Germany)
Christian Theobalt (Max-Planck-Institut für Informatik, Saarbrücken,
    Germany)
Emanuele Trucco (Heriot-Watt University, Edinburgh, UK)
Thomas Vetter (Basel University, Basel, Switzerland)
Wenping Wang (The University of Hong Kong, Hong Kong, China)
Harry Wechsler (George Mason University, Fairfax, USA)
Konrad Wojciechowski (Institute of Automation, Gliwice, Poland)
Hau San Wong (City University of Hong Kong, Kowloon Hong Kong,
    China)
Geoff Wyvill (University of Otago, New Zealand)
Cha Zhang (Microsoft Research, Redmond, USA)
Tatjana Zrimec (University of South Wales, Australia)

Reviewers

Ken Anjyo (OLM Digital, Inc., Tokyo, Japan)
Bruno Arnaldi (IRISA, Rennes, France)
William Baxter (OLM Digital, Tokyo, Japan)
Jacques Blanc-Talon (DGA, France, Arcueil, France)
Volker Blanz (Max-Planck-Institut für Informatik, Saarbrücken, Germany)
José Braz (Polytechnic Institute of Setúbal, Setúbal, Portugal)
Antonio Camurri (University of Genova, Genova, Italy)
Adrian Clark (University of Essex, Colchester, UK)
Ernst Dickmanns (University of the Bundeswehr, Munich, Hofolding, Germany)
Peter Eisert (Heinrich-Hertz-Institut, Berlin, Germany)
Reyes Enciso (USC, Los Angeles, USA)
Alexandre Francois (University of Southern California, Los Angeles, USA)
Andrea Fusiello (Università degli Studi di Verona, Verona, Italy)
André Gagalowicz (INRIA Rocquencourt, Le Chesnay, France)
Sidharta Gautama (TELIN, Ghent University, Ghent, Belgium)
Andrew Glassner (Coyote Wind, Seattle, USA)
Michael Gleicher (University of Wisconsin, Madison, USA)
Michael Goesele (University of Washington, Seattle, USA)
Oliver Grau (BBC, Tadworth, UK)
Radek Grzeszczuk (Nokia Research Lab, Palo Alto, USA)
Cédric Guiard (THALES, Paris, France)
Peter Hall (University of Bath, Bath, UK)
Adrian Hilton (University of Surrey, Guildford, UK)
Hyung Soo Kim (Seoul National University, Seoul, Korea)
Reinhard Koch (Christian-Albrechts-Universität Kiel, Kiel, Germany)
Ivana Kolingerova (University of West Bohemia, Plzen, Czech Republic)
Tosiyasu Kunii (Kanazawa Institute of Technology, Tokyo, Japan)
Hendrik Lensch (Max-Planck-Institut für Informatik, Saarbrücken, Germany)
Ales Leonardis (Ljubljana University, Ljubljana, Slovenia)
J.P. Lewis (Stanford University, Stanford, USA)
Zicheng Liu (Microsoft, Redmond, USA)
Takashi Matsuyama (Kyoto University, Kyoto, Japan)
Wojciech Mokrzycki (University of Podlasie, Siedlce, Poland)
Toshio Moriya (Hitachi, Ltd., Kawasaki, Japan)
Vittorio Murino (Università degli Studi di Verona, Verona, Italy)
Heinrich Niemann (University of Erlangen-Nuremberg, Erlangen, Germany)
Kazunori Okada (San Francisco State University, San Francisco, USA)
Joern Ostermann (University of Hannover, Hannover, Germany)
Jean-Claude Paul (Tsinghua University, Peking, China)
Dietrich Paulus (University of Koblenz, Koblenz, Germany)
Wilfried Philips (Ghent University, Ghent, Belgium)
Dan Popescu (CSIRO, Sidney, Australia)
John Robinson (University of York, Heslington, UK)
Christian Roessl (INRIA Sophia-Antipolis, Sophia-Antipolis, France)

Table of Contents

Published Papers

An Improved Color Mood Blending Between Images Via Fuzzy Relationship

Ming-Long Huang, Yi-Cai Zhou, and Chung-Ming Wang

Institute of Computer Science, National Chung Hsing University,
Taichung, Taiwan, R.O.C.
{s9456045, s9556050, cmwang}@cs.nchu.edu.tw

Abstract. This paper presents an improved color mood blending between images via fuzzy relationship. We take into consideration the weighted influences of the source as well as the target image. Our algorithm automatically calculates the weights according to the fuzzy relations of images with Gaussian Membership Function, derived from both the statistical features of the source and target image. As the experimental results shown, the visual appearance of the resulting image is more natural and vivid. Our algorithm can offer users another selection for perfecting their work. It has four advantages. First, it is a general approach where previous methods are special cases of our method. Second, it produces a new style and feature. Third, the quality of the resultant image is visually plausible. Finally, it is simple and efficient, with no need to generate swatches.

1 Introduction

In daily life, each object we see or touch has a set of colors to describe it. When the object's colors are reflected into our vision system and the color information is sent to the cerebrum, our cerebrum tells us what the color is. Due to the complex architecture of the cerebrum, our vision is sensitive to colors even if there is only a subtle change in hue. In addition, everyone has different tastes and experiences that affect their perception and identification of colors. For example, we commonly use a vivid green to represent spring and summer. Winter is described by white or silver gray. Moreover, everyone has different reactions to colors and even some perceptual differences, which can affect their responses.

Since colors are ubiquitous and crucial for human perception, the transformation of color features is very important for digital image processing. Reinhard et al. proposed an algorithm to apply the colors of one image to another [10], attempting to make the colors of the source image look more like that of the target image. Their algorithm is simple and effective and the result is impressive. Thereafter, many varied techniques have been presented to achieve the same goal of color transfer. In addition, Welsh et al. [16] and Chen et al. [6] extended Reinhard's work to coloring grayscale images.

As mentioned in [10], given two suitable images for producing a pleasing result, the color distributions of two given images should be similar. Otherwise it may produce a grotesque and unnatural result. Such phenomena occur because the relation of

A. Gagalowicz and W. Philips (Eds.): MIRAGE 2007, LNCS 4418, pp. 1–11, 2007.

Fig. 1. Leaves. (a) is the source image and (b) is the target image. (c) is the result produced by using Reinhard's method [10]. Their work only takes into consideration the colors of the target image, attempting to make the color appearance of the source image look more like that of the target image. We extend Reinhard's work, and consider the influence of both source and target images, blending colors of both images via their fuzzy relationship with Gaussian Membership Function, as shown in (d). The visual appearance of the resulting image is more natural and vivid, producing a new style.

color distribution between two given images are not taken into consideration. For this reason, we think that color transfer should not only involve the target image's color features. It should also include some color characteristics of the source image. A simple linear interpolation method is $Rc = \alpha Sc + (1-\alpha)Tc$, where Rc, Sc, and Tc respectively indicate the resultant, source, and target images' colors; α and $(1-\alpha)$ determine the degrees of source and target image colors transferred. However, as mentioned above, two suitable images must be given to produce a pleasing result by using Reinhard's work [10]. This implies that when the transformation is manipulated the relationship between the two given images should be taken into consideration. As a result, the immediate linear interpolation method is insufficient.

In [15], two user parameters are introduced to attempt to yield a natural and reasonable result, in which the idea is similar to [11]. Even though this operates well, it is still not convenient to use due to the manually adjustment of those two parameters. The relation between images is not taken into account in their work. As a result, we design an automatic way to form an improved color transfer operation based on the relationship between images, resulting in color blending effects. To achieve this goal, in this paper, we are interested in devising an efficient method to provide users another choice for color transfer. Therefore, based on the previous work [10], a new transformation scheme is defined as Eq. (1) in which two parameters, l and m, are individually calculated depending on the fuzzy relation between given images with a Gaussian Membership Function. As the experimental results in Fig. 1, show, our algorithm produces a new style.

We review related work in Section 2 and describe our algorithm in Section 3. We demonstrate results and exhibit those produced by Reinhard's original method in Section 4. The conclusion and future work are given in the final section.

2 Related Works

The initial paper on color transfer between images was proposed by Reinhard et al. [10]. A number of similar papers were then presented [2-5, 13], some of them intending to colorize grayscale images [6, 7, 13, 16, 19], while others intended to improve the efficiency of the colorization [9, 18].

The color transfer algorithm proposed by Reinhard et al. provides an easy and effective approach to transfer color characteristics from the target image to the source image. The operation employs a de-correlation color space $l\alpha\beta$ which was developed by Ruderman [12] for transferring colors. The l channel corresponds to an achromatic luminance channel, and α as well as β channels separately correspond to the yellow-blue and red-green opponent channels. Reinhard et al. did color transformation using a simple statistical method which involves scaling and shifting calculations. Their method performs well. No artistic talent is required, and the outcome is impressive. However, their method may sometimes produce unnatural results where the source and target images do not match as shown in Fig. 4(c). The result reveals an unnatural appearance, which is particularly prominent when the source and target images are unsuitable, either in luminance or in color aspects. To solve this drawback, Reinhard et al. further presented a swatch approach. However, a user has to first generate swatches, and then manually determine swatch pairs to perform the color transfer. As a result, their method requires much user intervention when an unnatural appearance is produced.

Recently, Chang et al. presented an alternative method to deliver the colors from the target image to the source image [2-5]. The method relies on only transferring similar colors between source and target images. It does not catch image colors entirely, but catches some color features for each color unit. A color unit is a perceptually agreeable color category. In their work, they provided eleven basic color categories which were developed by Berlin and Kay [1]. Then, according to psycho-physiological experiments, they transform the relational colors between images and the results are natural and attractive. Unfortunately, their algorithm is not efficient because each pixel value has to be classified into one of the basic color categories before the color transfer. Moreover, their algorithm is limited, since it transfers colors within the same color categories, regardless of possible cross-category color transfer. In addition, if a pixel in the source image has no corresponding colors in the target image, their algorithm needs extra computations to estimate suitable color distributions for transferring such a pixel. Other extra computations are needed for eliminating the pseudo-contour artifacts which occurs at the boundary between two colors.

Based upon Reinhard et al.'s work, Wang et al. generated an image sequence for simulating the atmospheric variations of a scene [14, 15]. In their framework, four images, one simulated source image and three different atmospheric target images are used, and then two statistical values, the mean and the variance, are separately computed in the de-correlation color space [12]. The mean and variance used for image transfer in an image sequence are then interpolated with a color variation curve (CVC) to produce in-between color transfers. The algorithm can produce an image sequence using color mood variation and generates visually plausible effects.

3 Proposed Algorithm

We think that color transfer should involve not only the color characteristics of the target image but also those of the source image. This will allow us to balance the influence between two images, which will result in the appearances of color mood blending. Balance is particularly important when the target image has many abnormal characteristics, such as low luminance, or has a very limited color spectrum. Based on the above concept, different transformation weights should exist for the source and target images in color manipulation. As a result, we define a formula as expressed in Eq. (1),

$$B_i = \frac{\sigma_t}{\sigma_s}(S_i - \mu_s) + l\mu_t + m\mu_s,$$ (1)

where B_i is the ith blended pixel, S_i is the ith pixel in source image, and l and m represent the transformation weights. μ_s and μ_t are the means and σ_s and σ_t are the standard deviations, respectively, where s indicates the source image and t indicates the target image. Clearly, we need to calculate the relations of the transformation weights, l and m. We first express the mean value of the blended result, as shown in Eq. (2).

$$\mu_{new} = \frac{1}{n}\sum_{i=1}^{n} B_i = \frac{1}{n}\sum_{i=1}^{n}\left(\frac{\sigma_t}{\sigma_s}(S_i - \mu_s) + l\mu_t + m\mu_s\right)$$ (2)

In [8], Gaussian Membership Function, Eq. (3), has the ability to measure the distributions of two data sets to interpret their fuzzy relationship. F indicates the degree of similarity between the two data sets.

$$F = exp\left[-\left(\frac{\mu_s - \mu_t}{\sigma_s + \sigma_t}\right)^2\right]$$ (3)

We refer to such a fuzzy value as *matching value*. A large matching value, which is close to one, means that the source and target images are compatible as indicated by the similar mean values. This leads to the final blending result which appears similar to the source image. Note that σ_t and μ_t do not change during the transformation. Now, we further assume that σ_s does not change. Referring to Eq. (2) with a given matching value F, the new mean value μ_{new} can be expressed as Eq. (4).

$$\mu_{new} = \mu_t \pm (\sigma_s + \sigma_t)\left(\sqrt{-lnF}\right) \tag{4}$$

The new mean value should be equal to that shown in Eq. (2). Thus, we derive an Eq. (5), where n is the total number of pixels in the source image.

$$\mu_t \pm (\sigma_s + \sigma_t)\left(\sqrt{-lnF}\right) = \frac{1}{n}\sum_{i=1}^{n}\left(\frac{\sigma_t}{\sigma_s}(S_i - \mu_s) + l\mu_t + m\mu_s\right) \tag{5}$$

Now, let k represent the mean ratio between the source and target images. Then, we can represent the relation of the transformation weights l and m in Eq. (6):

$$l = -(m+c)/k, \quad k = \mu_t/\mu_s, \tag{6}$$

where the constant c is expressed in Eq. (7).

$$c = \frac{\frac{1}{n}\left(\sum_{i=1}^{n}\frac{\sigma_t}{\sigma_s}(S_i - \mu_s)\right) - \mu_t \pm (\sigma_s + \sigma_t)\left(\sqrt{-lnF}\right)}{\mu_s} \tag{7}$$

Comparing our formula, in Eq. (1), with Reinhard et al.'s [10], in Eq. (8), we can derive the boundaries of the transformation weights.

$$R_i = \frac{\sigma_t}{\sigma_s}(S_i - \mu_s) + \mu_t \tag{8}$$

Considering the marginal values where $(l, m) = (1, 0)$ and $(l, m) = (0, \varepsilon)$, we have the following two cases.

Case A: (l, m) = (1, 0)

$$1 = \frac{-\mu_s(0+c)}{\mu_t} = \frac{-\mu_s c}{\mu_t} \implies \mu_t = -\mu_s c \implies \frac{\mu_t}{\mu_s} = -c = k$$

Case B: (l, m) = (0, ε)

$$0 = \frac{-\mu_s(\varepsilon + c)}{\mu_t} \implies 0 = -\mu_s(\varepsilon + c), \text{ and } \mu_s \neq 0$$

$$\implies \varepsilon + c = 0 \implies \varepsilon = -c = k$$

From the cases A and B, we know the relation between the transformation parameters l and m is $m = cl - c$. We plot this relation as a line passing through two end points as shown in Fig. 2. Recalling that when the source and target images are compatible, their mean values are very similar, the matching value is close to one (see Eq. 3).

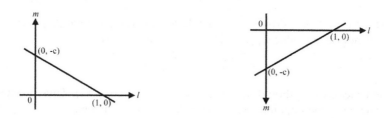

Fig. 2. The relation diagram between the transformation weights l and m. The diagram has two different cases because the constant value c may be positive or negative.

In the extreme case, when the matching value is one, the target image provides no contribution to the final results. For this reason, once we adopt a fixed matching value at each channel, we can compute the maximum value of the transformation parameters. In our experience, we adopt the fixed matching value 0.999999975 in three color channels, and the maximum value of the transformation parameter m equals the ratio k.

Recalling that in Eq. (3), the parameters, l and m, should have a relationship, we rely on using the m value to estimate the l value. When the source and target images are compatible, the matching value will be near one, and thus the target image's color features will be transformed. However, when the matching value is small due to the incompatibility, the transferring operator will yield an unnatural result when we employ Reinhard et al.'s algorithm. Hence, we estimate the m value through the matching value, and we deliver the computed value m into a weighted space, as shown in Eq. (9). Therefore, the final transformation weights for each channel of the source image are estimated depending on the fuzzy relationships between two given images.

$$w(m) = \frac{1.0}{1.0 + e^{-m}} \ , \quad m = \frac{k}{1.0 + F} \tag{9}$$

We do not use the equation $m = cl - c$ to determine the l value. Instead, we employ an approach to prove our idea is correct. Comparing our operation with Reinhard's, we define an error E between the results of these two algorithms, as shown in Eq. 10. If the distributions of the two given images are well matched, the error value equals zero.

$$E = R_i - B_i = \mu_t - l\mu_t - m_s \ , \text{ and } \mu_t = k\mu_s \implies E = \mu_s(k - lk - m) \tag{10}$$

This way, the l value can be resolved by this equation. Similarly, l must be delivered at a similar weighted space, as shown in Eq. (11). The final transformation weights for each channel of the target image are also estimated depending on the fuzzy relationships between the two given images.

$$w(l) = 1.0 - \frac{1.0}{1.0 + e^{-l}} \ , \quad l = \frac{F}{1.0 + F} \tag{11}$$

Finally, $w(m)$ and $w(l)$ are substituted for l and m within Eq. (1) as the final transformation weights, as shown in Eq. (12). This equation is used for the three color channels, respectively.

$$B_i = \frac{\sigma_i}{\sigma_s}(S_i - \mu_s) + w(l)\mu_t + w(m)\mu_s \tag{12}$$

By estimating $w(l)$ and $w(m)$, we obtain three pairs of transformation weights for each color channel of the source and target images. The algorithm has several steps which are presented as follows:

Step1. Convert the source and target images from RGB to CIE L*a*b* color space [17].

Step2. Calculate and estimate arguments for $w(l)$ and $w(m)$.

Step2.1   Compute the means μ and the standard deviations σ of the three CIE Lab channels.

Step2.2   Calculate the fuzzy relation values F between the source and target images for each axis separately in CIE L*a*b* color space using Eq. (3).

Step2.3   Estimate the weight values $w(m)$ and $w(l)$ for each axis separately in CIE L*a*b* color space using Eq. (9) and (11).

Step3. Transform the colors between the source and target images using Eq. (12) to transform the colors.

Step4. Finally, we convert the result back to RGB from CIE L*a*b* color space.

According to the relationships between two given images, our algorithm has the ability to offer another style for users. We will now show the results of our algorithm and exhibit them with Reinhard et al.'s method.

4 Results

In this section we show the results of our and Reinhard's methods. Fig. 3 shows the photograph's appearance against the rendered images. We see that the rendered images and the photo have similar scenes with different colors. Fig. 3(c) shows the result processed by Reinhard et al.'s method, which shows unnatural situations such as the sea, sun and clouds which contain a more reddish orange. Fig. 3(d) shows the result of our new method. Compared with Fig. 3(b), the mood of the sea, sun and clouds are more similar to the appearance in the real world.

Figure 4 shows another result which transfers the color of the flower to a riverside. In Fig. 4(c), the atmosphere of the entire image is yellowish, which is unnatural. In Fig. 4(d), the yellowish appearance is eliminated. The transferred atmosphere is more attractive after processing with our method, as shown in Fig. 4.

Figure 5(c) shows that the result is unnatural without using swatches because the source and target images are incompatible. There is serious over-transformation because the colors are out of the color gamut. Fig. 5(d) is processed by our method, and it shows that the unnatural appearance is gone.

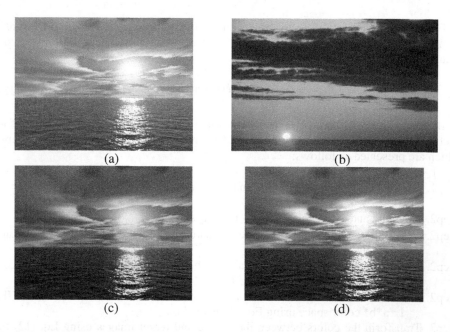

Fig. 3. Transferring the sunset to an ocean view [10]. (a) Rendered image. (b) Photograph image. (c) Result transferred by Reinahrd et al.'s method. (d) Result processed by our method.

Fig. 4. Transferring the color of flowers to a riverside. (a) Source image [2, 3, 4, 5]. (b) Target image. (c) Result transferred by Reinahrd et al.'s method. (d) Result processed by our method.

(a) Source Image

(b) Target Image

(c) Reinhard et al.'s Result

(d) Our Result

Fig. 5. In this case, Reinhard et al.'s work produces an unnatural result, whereas our operation produces a better result according to the fuzzy relations between two given images

(a) Source Image

(b) Target Image

(c) Reinhard et al.'s Result

(d) Our Result

Fig. 6. Another experimental result for color transfer. With our algorithm, we can offer a different color appearance for users.

Figure 6 shows another experimental result. It demonstrates that our proposed algorithm can make the final image appear more natural and attractive.

5 Conclusion

Based on pervious color transfer schemes [10], this paper introduces an improved color mood blending between images via fuzzy relationship. We take into consideration the influences of the source and target images as transformation weights for the three components of the images. Our method automatically calculates those weights according to the fuzzy relations of images, which are computed by Gaussian membership function.

Our approach offers a new style for users. Furthermore, we conclude that our algorithm has four advantages. First, it is a general approach where previous methods are special cases of our method. Second, the proposed algorithm has the ability to balance two images via the fuzzy relations, and the resultant effect often differs from the previous work. Third, the quality of the resultant images is more visually plausible. Finally, it is simple, efficient as well as automatic. No swatches are needed, which are used in Reinhard et al.'s work.

In the future, a better color measuring method is needed to refine the transformation weights. It can aid this proposed algorithm to obtain a more objective result.

Acknowledgements

This research was supported by the National Science Council (NSC) of Taiwan under the grant numbers NSC 95-2221-E-005-046, 94-2218-E-164-001, 94-2213-E-005-022.

References

1. Berlin, B. and Kay, P.: Basic Color Terms: Their Universality and Evolution. University of California Press, Berkeley (1969)
2. Chang, Y., Saito, S., and Nakajima, M.: A Framework for Transfer Colors Based on the Basic Color Categories. Computer Graphics International, Tokyo, Japan, July 09-11 (2003) 176-183
3. Chang, Y., Saito, S., Uchikawa, K., and Nakajima, M.: Example-Based Color Stylization Based on Categorical Perception. in Proc. 1st Symposium on Applied Perception in Graphics and Visualization, Los Angeles, California August 07-08 (2004) 91-98
4. Chang, Y., Saito, S., Uchikawa, K., and Nakajima, M.: Example-Based Color Stylization of Images. ACM Trans. on Applied Perception, 2: 3 (2005) 322-345
5. Chang, Y., Saito, S., Uchikawa, K., and Nakajima, M.: Example-Based Color Transformation for Image and Video. in Proc. 3th International Conference on Computer Graphics and Interactive Techniques in Australasia and South East Asia (2005) 347-353
6. Chen, T., Wang, Y., Schillings, V., and Meinel C.: Grayscale Image Matting and Colorization, in Proc. Asian Conference on Computer Vision (2004) 1164-1169

7. Hertzmann, A., Jacobs, C.E., Oliver, N., Curless, B., and Salesin, D.H.: Image Analogies. in Proc. ACM SIGGRAPH 2001, Los Angeles, California, USA, August 12-17 (2001) 327-340
8. Friedman, M. and Kandel, A.: Introduction to Pattern Recognition: Statistical, Structural, Neural, and Fuzzy Logic Approaches. World Scientific, New York (1999)
9. Levin, A., Lischinski, E., and Weiss, Y.: Colorization using Optimization. ACM Trans. on Graphics, 23:3 (2004) 689-694
10. Reinhard, E., Ashikhmin, M., Gooch, B., and Shirley, P.: Color Transfer between Images. IEEE Computer Graphics and Applications, 21:5 (2001) 34-41
11. Reinhard, E., Akyuz, A.O., Colbert, M., Hughes, C.E, and O'Connor, M.: Real-Time Color Blending of Rendered and Captured Video. in Proc. I/ITSEC 2004, Orlando, December 6-9 (2004)
12. Ruderman, D.L., Cronin, T.W., and Chiao, C.C.: Statistics of Cone Responses to Natural Images: Implications for Visual Coding. Journal of Optical Society of America A, 15:8 (1998) 2036-2045
13. Tai, Y.W., Jia, J., and Tang, C.K.: Local Color Transfer via Probabilistic Segmentation by Expectation-Maximization. in Proc. IEEE Conference on Computer Vision and Pattern Recognition. San Diego, CA, USA, June 20-25 (2005) 747-754
14. Wang, C.M. and Huang, Y.H.: A Novel Color Transfer Algorithm for Image Sequences. Journal of Information Science and Engineering, 20:6 (2004) 1039-1056
15. Wang, C.M., Huang, Y.H., and Huang, M.L.: An Effective Algorithm for Image Sequence Color Transfer. Mathematical and Computer Modelling, 44:7-8 (2006) 608-627
16. Welsh, T., Ashikhmin, M., and Mueller, K.: Transferring Color to Greyscale Images. ACM Trans. on Graphics, 21:3 (2002) 277-280
17. Wyszecki, G. and Stiles, W.S.: Color Science: Concepts and Methods, Quantitative Data and Formulae. 2nd Ed. Wiley-Interscience, New York (2000)
18. Yatziv, L. and Sapiro, G.: Fast Image and Video Colorization using Chrominance Blending. IEEE Trans. on Image Processing, 15:5 (2006) 1120-1129
19. Ying, J. and Ji, L.: Pattern Recognition Based Color Transfer. in Proc. Computer Graphics, Imaging and Visualization. Beijing, China, July 26-29 (2005) 55-60

Evaluation of Alzheimer's Disease by Analysis of MR Images Using Multilayer Perceptrons, Polynomial Nets and Kohonen LVQ Classifiers

Wellington P. dos Santos[1,2], Ricardo E. de Souza[3], Ascendino F.D. e Silva[1], and Plínio B. Santos Filho[4]

[1] Universidade Federal de Pernambuco, Departamento de Eletrônica e Sistemas, Cidade Universitária, Recife, PE, 50740-530, Brazil
wellington@df.ufpe.br,afds@ufpe.br
[2] Universidade de Pernambuco, Departamento de Sistemas Computacionais, Madalena, Recife, PE, 50.720-001, Brazil
wps@dsc.upe.br
[3] Universidade Federal de Pernambuco, Departamento de Física, Cidade Universitária, Recife, PE, 50670-901, Brazil
res@df.ufpe.br
[4] North Carolina State University, Department of Physics, Raleigh, NC, 8202, USA
c2511@terra.com.br

Abstract. Alzheimer's disease is the most common cause of dementia, yet hard to diagnose precisely without invasive techniques, particularly at the onset of the disease. This work approaches image analysis and classification of synthetic multispectral images composed by diffusion-weighted magnetic resonance (MR) cerebral images for the evaluation of cerebrospinal fluid area and its correlation with the advance of Alzheimer's disease. The MR images were acquired from an image system by a clinical 1.5 T tomographer. The classification methods are based on multilayer perceptrons, polynomial nets and Kohonen LVQ classifiers. The classification results are used to improve the usual analysis of the apparent diffusion coefficient map.

1 Introduction

Alzheimer's disease is the most common cause of dementia, both in senile and presenile individuals, observing the gradual progress of the disease as the individual becomes older [1,2]. The major manifestation of Alzheimer's disease is the falling of the cognitive functions with gradual loss of memory, including psychological, neurological and behavioral symptoms indicating the declining of the diary life activities as a whole [3].

Alzheimer's disease is characterized by the reduction of gray matter and the growth of cerebral sulci. The gray matter is responsible by memory. Its reduction explains the gradual loss of memory in senile individuals affected by such disease. However, the white matter is also affected, although the relation between Alzheimer's disease and white matter is still unknown [4,5,6].

A. Gagalowicz and W. Philips (Eds.): MIRAGE 2007, LNCS 4418, pp. 12–22, 2007.

The acquisition of magnetic resonance diffusion-weighted images turns possible the visualization of the dilation of the lateral ventriculi temporal corni, enhancing the augment of sulci, which are related to the advance of Alzheimer's disease [7].

Therefore, the volumetrical measuring of cerebral structures is very important for the diagnosis and evaluation of the progress of diseases like Alzheimer's [1,8,9,10], especially the measuring of the areas occupied by sulci and lateral ventriculi, because such measuring turns possible the addition of quantitative information to the qualitative information expressed by the magnetic resonance diffusion-weighted images [11].

The evaluation of the progress of Alzheimer's disease using image analysis of diffusion-weighted magnetic resonance images is performed after the acquisition of at least three images of each slice of interest, where each image is acquired using the spin-echo sequence with different diffusion exponents, where one of the exponents copes to 0 s/mm^2. In other words, one of them is a T_2-weighted spin-echo image [4,7].

Using such acquired images, a fourth image is calculated, called Apparent Diffusion Coefficient Map, or ADC map, where each pixel is associated to the corresponding apparent diffusion coefficient of the associated voxel. The brighter the pixels of the ADC map, the greater the corresponding apparent diffusion coefficients [7].

This work proposes a new approach to evaluate the progress of Alzheimer's disease: once the ADC map usually presents pixels with considerable intensities in regions not occupied by the sample, a degree of uncertainty can also be considered in the pixels inside the sample. Furthermore, the ADC map is very sensitive to noisy images [7].

Therefore, in this case study, the images are used to compose a multispectral image, where each diffusion-weighted image is considered as a spectral band in a synthetic multispectral image.

The classification results furnish us with a better qualitative and quantitative evaluation of the set of acquired images, turning possible the measuring of the areas of interest, especially the rate between the area occupied by cerebrospinal fluid and the total area occupied by gray and white matter, correlating such rate with the advance of Alzheimer's disease.

2   Materials and Methods

The diffusion-weighted magnetic resonance (MR) images were acquired from the clinical images database of the Laboratory of MR Images, at the Physics Department of the Universidade Federal de Pernambuco, Recife, Brazil. The database is composed by real clinical images acquired from a clinical MR tomographer of 1.5 T.

In this work we used three diffusion-weighted cerebral MR images corresponding to a 70-year-old male patient with Alzheimer's disease, with the following

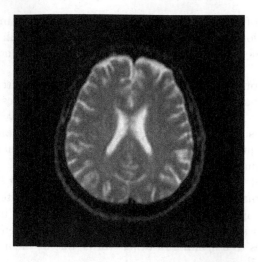

Fig. 1. Axial diffusion-weighted image with exponent diffusion of 0 s/mm^2

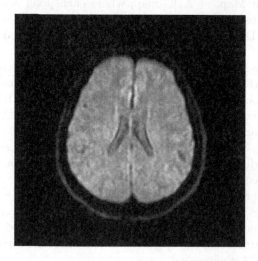

Fig. 2. Axial diffusion-weighted image with exponent diffusion of 500 s/mm^2

diffusion exponents: 0 s/mm^2, 500 s/mm^2 and 1000 s/mm^2, shown in the figures 1, 2 and 3, respectively.

To perform the proposed analysis, we have chosen MR images corresponding to slices showing the temporal corni of the lateral ventriculi, to furnish a better evaluation for the specialist and facilitate the correlation between the data generated by the computational tool and the *a priori* knowledge of the specialist.

The images can be considered as mathematical functions, where their domain is a region of the plain of integers, called a *grid*, and their codomain is the set of the possible values occupied by the pixels corresponding to each position of the grid.

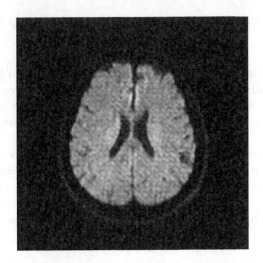

Fig. 3. Axial diffusion-weighted image with exponent diffusion of 1000 s/mm^2

Let $f_i : S \to W$ be the set of the diffusion-weighted MR images, where $1 \le i \le 3$, $S \subseteq \mathbf{Z}^2$ is the grid of the image f_i, where $W \subseteq \mathbf{R}$ is its codomain. The synthetic multispectral image $f : S \to W^3$ composed by the MR images of the figures 1, 2 and 3 is given by:

$$f(\mathbf{u}) = (f_1(\mathbf{u}), f_2(\mathbf{u}), f_3(\mathbf{u}))^T, \tag{1}$$

where $\mathbf{u} \in S$ is the position of the pixel in the image f, and f_1, f_2 and f_3 are the diffusion-weighted MR images with diffusion exponents of $b_1 = 0$ s/mm^2, $b_2 = 500$ s/mm^2, and $b_3 = 1000$ s/mm^2, respectively.

The analysis of diffusion-weighted MR images is often performed using the resulting ADC map. Considering that each pixel $f_i(\mathbf{u})$ is approximately proportional to the signal of the corresponding voxel as follows:

$$f_i(\mathbf{u}) = K\rho(\mathbf{u})e^{-T_E/T_2(\mathbf{u})}e^{-b_i D_i(\mathbf{u})}, \tag{2}$$

where $D_i(\mathbf{u})$ is the diffusion coefficient associated to the voxel mapped in the pixel in the position $\mathbf{u}$, $\rho(\mathbf{u})$ is the nuclear spin density in the voxel, K is a constant of proportionality, $T_2(\mathbf{u})$ is the transversal relaxation in the voxel, T_E is the echo time and b_i is the diffusion exponent, given by [7,12]:

$$b_i = \gamma^2 G_i^2 T_E^3/3, \tag{3}$$

where γ is the gyromagnetic ratio and G_i is the gradient applied during the experiment i; the ADC map $f_{\text{ADC}} : S \to W$ is calculated as follows:

$$f_{\text{ADC}}(\mathbf{u}) = \frac{C}{b_2} \ln\left(\frac{f_1(\mathbf{u})}{f_2(\mathbf{u})}\right) + \frac{C}{b_3} \ln\left(\frac{f_1(\mathbf{u})}{f_3(\mathbf{u})}\right), \tag{4}$$

where C is a constant of proportionality. Thus, the ADC map is given by:

$$f_{ADC}(\mathbf{u}) = CD(\mathbf{u}).\qquad(5)$$

Therefore, the pixels of the ADC map are proportional to the diffusion co-efficients in the corresponding voxels. However, as the images are acquired at different moments, we must consider the occurrence of noise in all the experiments. Furthermore, the presence of noise is amplified by the use of the logarithm (see equation 4).

Such factors leave us to the following conclusion: the pixels of the ADC map not necessarily correspond to the diffusion coefficients, because several pixels indicate high diffusion rates in voxels where the sample are not present or in very solid areas like bone in the cranial box, as can be seen in figure 4. This is the reason why such map indicates *apparent* diffusion coefficients, and not *real* diffusion coefficients.

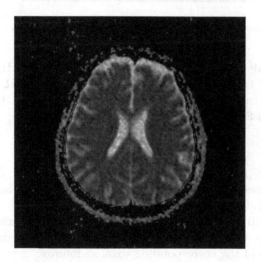

Fig. 4. ADC map calculated from the three diffusion images

In this work we propose an alternative to the analysis of the ADC map: the multispectral analysis of the image $f : S \rightarrow W^3$ using methods based on neural networks.

3   Multispectral Analysis Using Neural Networks

Let the universe of classes of interest be defined as $\Omega = \{C_1, C_2, C_3, C_4\}$, C_1 represents cerebrospinal fluid; C_2, white and gray matter, once they cannot be distinguished using diffusion images, because their diffusion coefficients are very close; C_3 corresponds to the image background and C_4 is the rejection class.

For the multispectral analysis using neural networks, the inputs are associated to the vector $\mathbf{x} = (x_1, x_2, x_3)^T$, where $x_i = f_i(\mathbf{u})$, for $1 \leq i \leq 3$. The network outputs represent the classes of interest and are associated to the vector $\mathbf{y} = (y_1, y_2, y_3, y_4)^T$, where each output corresponds to the class with the same index. The decision criterion employed in such analysis is the Bayes criterion: the output with greater value indicates the more probable class [13,14]. The training set and the test set are built using specialist knowledge at the selection of the regions of interest [15].

The synthetic multispectral image is classified using the following methods:

1. *Multilayer perceptron* (MLP): Learning rate $\eta = 0.2$, training error $\epsilon = 0.05$, maximum of 1000 training iterations, 3 inputs, 3 outputs, 2 layers, 60 neurons in layer 1 [15];
2. *Kohonen LVQ classifier* (LVQ): 3 inputs, 3 outputs, maximum of 200 iterations, learning rate $\eta = 0.01$ [15];
3. *Polynomial net* (PO): Two-layer net: the first layer is a multiplicative net that generates the terms of the 2-degree polynomy from the 3 inputs, and the second layer consists on an one-layer perceptron with learning rate $\eta = 0.1$ and training error $\epsilon = 0.05$, maximum of 200 training iterations, responsible for the calculation of the coefficients of the polynomy that models the discriminant polynomial function of each class [13,14].

These three methods were chosen to evaluate the behavior and the performance of a classical neural network, a clustering-based network and a polynomial approximator of the discriminant functions executing the taks of classification of the synthetic multispectral image.

The multilayer perceptron was selected to evaluate the performance of the multispectral classification based on classical two-layered neural networks. The number of inputs and outputs copes to the number of bands and classes of interest, respectively. The training error was chosen considering the maximum estimated noise in diffusion-weighted images. The number of neurons in layer 1 and the learning rate were empirically determined.

The Kohonen LVQ classifier was selected to evaluate the performance of clustering-based neural networks. The number of inputs and outputs copes to the number of bands and classes of interest, respectively. The learning rate was empirically determined.

The polynomial net is used as a polynomial approximator. Its learning rate and training error were empirically determined.

To implement such methods and other neural networks-based methods, we developed a software tool called *AnImed*, built using the object-oriented programming language *Object Pascal* at the programming environment *Delphi 5*.

4   Results

To evaluate objectively the classification results, we used three methods: the index κ, the *overall accuracy* and the *confusion matrix*. The subjective evaluation was performed by the specialist knowledge of a pathologist. Image background

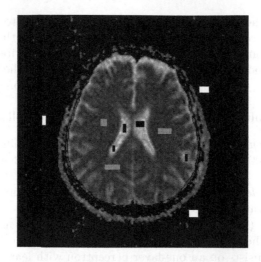

Fig. 5. Training set

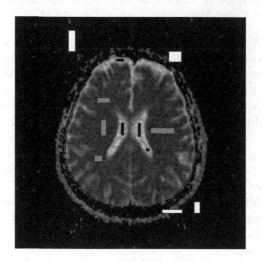

Fig. 6. Test set

(C_3), gray and white matter (C_2) and cerebrospinal fluid (C_1) were associated to the following colors: white, gray and black, respectively. The training set is shown in figure 5, where figure 6 shows the test set. The regions of interest of both the training set and the test set were selected using the ADC map.

The *confusion matrix* for the universe of classes of interest Ω is an $m \times m$ matrix $\mathbf{T} = [t_{i,j}]_{m \times m}$ where each element $t_{i,j}$ represents the number of objects belonging to class C_j but classified as C_i, where $\Omega = \{C_1, C_2, \ldots, C_m\}$ [13,16].

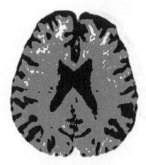

Fig. 7. Classification result by the multilayer perceptron

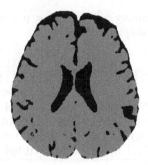

Fig. 8. Classification result by the polynomial net

The *overall accuracy* ϕ is the rate between the number of objects correctly classified and the total number of objects, defined as follows [13,16]:

$$\phi = \rho_v = \frac{\sum_{i=1}^{m} t_{i,i}}{\sum_{i=1}^{m} \sum_{j=1}^{m} t_{i,j}}. \tag{6}$$

The *index* κ is an statistical correlation rate defined as follows [13]:

$$\kappa = \frac{\rho_v - \rho_z}{1 - \rho_z}, \tag{7}$$

where

$$\rho_z = \frac{\sum_{i=1}^{m} (\sum_{j=1}^{m} t_{i,j})(\sum_{j=1}^{m} t_{j,i})}{(\sum_{i=1}^{m} \sum_{j=1}^{m} t_{i,j})^2}. \tag{8}$$

Figures 7, 8 and 9 show the results of the classification of the synthetic multi-spectral image composed by images 1, 2 and 3 using the methods MLP, PO and LVQ, respectively. Table 4 shows the index κ, the overall accuracy ϕ, and the percentage areas A_1, A_2 and A_3 occupied by the classes of interest C_1, C_2 and C_3, respectively, as well as the ratio between the cerebrospinal fluid area and the gray and white matter total area, simply called fluid-matter rate, expressed by A_1/A_2.

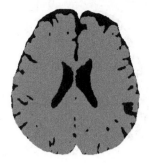

Fig. 9. Classification result by the Kohonen LVQ classifier

Table 1. Percentage overall accuracy ϕ (%), index κ, percentage areas and fluid-matter rate by the classification methods

	MLP	PO	LVQ
ϕ (%)	97.4755	99.9742	99.9742
κ	0.9589	0.9996	0.9996
A_1 (%)	8.558	5.308	4.598
A_2 (%)	18.507	22.546	23.216
A_3 (%)	72.935	72.147	72.186
A_1/A_2	0.462	0.235	0.198

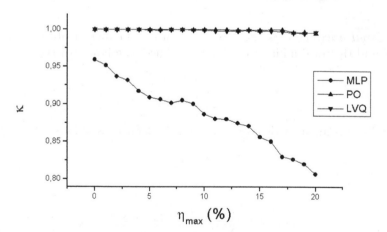

Fig. 10. Behavior of the index κ with the variation of maximum Gaussian noise η_{max}

The experiments were extended by adding artificial Gaussian noise η, with $\bar{\eta} = 0$ and $1\% \leq \eta_{max} \leq 20\%$, generating more 60 images. Such images were used to compose 20 synthetic multispectral images and were classified using the proposed methods. Figure 10 shows the behavior of the index κ versus the maximum Gaussian noise η_{max}.

5   Discussion and Conclusions

From the obtained results, it is clear that the classification results obtained by the use of the multilayer perceptron (figure 7) overestimated the area occupied by cerebral fluid. When this result is compared to the diffusion image with diffusion exponent of 0 (figure 1), we can see that left and right ventriculi are separated. Furthermore, the sulci were also overestimated, which could leave the specialist to evaluate this Alzheimer's case as more advanced than it really is.

The overestimation can also be verified from the data on table 4, where the fluid-matter rate (A_1/A_2) copes to 0.462 for the multilayer perceptron. It is practically twice the rate obtained by the 2-degree polynomial net, with $A_1/A_2 = 0.235$.

In this case, we can consider the result obtained by the PO method as true because, in this case, according to a specialist, its classification result is closer to the expected anatomical result associated to the level of progress of Alzheimer's disease. Furthermore, since the polynomial nets can be considered universal approximators and they are not affected by problems of local convergence at the training process as multilayer perceptrons are, in this case we can expect more confident results [15].

The classification result obtained by the LVQ method and the fluid-matter rate $A_1/A_2 = 0.198$ were very close to the ones obtained by the PO method. Using the specialist knowledge of a pathologist, we can also affirm the correctness of LVQ against MLP, since the lateral ventriculi are shown separated by LVQ classification results.

The classification of the multispectral images generated by artificial Gaussian noise were performed to evaluate the robustness of the proposed methods. The behavior of the index κ, according to the maximum Gaussian noise η_{max}, demonstrated that the PO and the LVQ method are more robust than the MLP classification. The index κ of the MLP method rapidly decays as the maximum level of noise increases.

Consequently, we can discharge the result by the MLP method and consider a good estimation for the real fluid-matter rate as the arithmetic average among the rates obtained by the other methods, which furnishes $A_1/A_2 = 0.217$. The proposed fluid-matter rate is not intended to be a general index for Alzheimer's analysis applications. It is a local index to aid objectively the analysis of the progress of Alzheimer's disease on an individual basis, where its present value should be compared only with past values calculated using exams of the same individual, at approximately the same cerebral slice.

The multispectral classification of diffusion-weighted MR images furnishes a good alternative to the analysis of the ADC map, consisting on a very reasonable mathematical tool useful to perform qualitative (classification results) and quantitative (fluid-matter rate) analysis of the progress of Alzheimer's disease for the medical specialist.

References

1. Ewers, M., Teipel, S. J., Dietrich, O., Schönberg, S. O., Jessen, F., Heun, R., Scheltens, P., van de Pol, L., Freymann, N. R., Moeller, H. J. and Hampela, H., Multicenter assessment of reliability of cranial MRI. *Neurobiology of Aging*, (2006), (27):1051–1059.
2. Mega, M. S., Dinov, I. D., Mazziotta, J. C., Manese, M., Thompson, P. M., Lindshield, C., Moussai, J., Tran, N., Olsen, K., Zoumalan, C. I., Woods, R. P. and Toga, A. W., Automated brain tissue assessment in the elderly and demented population: Construction and validation of a sub-volume probabilistic brain atlas. *NeuroImage*, (2005), (26):1009–1018.
3. Xie, S., Xiao, J. X., Bai, J. and Jiang, X. X., Patterns of brain activation in patients with mild Alzheimer's disease during performance of subtraction: An fMRI study. *Clinical Imaging*, (2005), (29):94–97.
4. Naggara, O., Oppenheim, C., Rieu, D., Raoux, N., Rodrigo, S., Barba, G. D. and Meder, J. F., Diffusion tensor imaging in early Alzheimer's disease. *Psychiatry Research Neuroimaging*, (2006), (146):243–249.
5. Bozzali, M., Falini, A., Franceschi, M., Cercignani, M., Zuffi, M., Scotti, G., Comi, G. and Filippi, M., White matter damage in Alzheimer's disease assessed in vivo using diffusion tensor magnetic resonance imaging. *Journal of Neurology, Neurosurgery and Psychiatry*, (2002), 72:742–746.
6. Du, A. T., Schuff, N., Chao, L. L., Kornak, J., Ezekiel, F., Jagust, W. J., Kramer, J. H., Reed, B. R., Miller, B. L., Norman, D., Chui, H. C. and Weiner, M. W., White matter lesions are associated with cortical atrophy more than entorhinal and hippocampal atrophy. *Neurobiology of Aging*, (2005), (26):553–559.
7. Haacke, E. M., Brown, R. W., Thompson, M. R. and Venkatesan, R., *Magnetic Resonance Imaging: Physical Principles and Sequence Design*. Wiley-Liss, (1999).
8. Carmichael, O. T., Aizenstein, H. A., Davis, S. W., Becker, J. T., Thompson, P. M., Meltzer, C. C. and Liu, Y., Atlas-based hippocampus segmentation in Alzheimer's disease and mild cognitive impairment. *NeuroImage*, (2005), (27):979–990.
9. Hirata, Y., Matsuda, H., Nemoto, K., Ohnishi, T., Hirao, K., Yamashita, F., Asada, T., Iwabuchi, S. and Samejima, H., Voxel-based morphometry to discriminate early Alzheimer's disease from controls. *Neuroscience Letters*, (2005), (382):269–274.
10. Pannacciulli, N., Del Parigi, A., Chen, K., Le, D. S. N. T., Reiman, E. M. and Tataranni, P. A., Brain abnormalities in human obesity: A voxel-based morphometric study. *NeuroImage*, (2006), (31):1419–1425.
11. Hayasaka, S., Du, A. T., Duarte, A., Kornak, J., Jahng, G. H., Weiner, M. W. and Schuff, N., A non-parametric approach for co-analysis of multi-modal brain imaging data: Application to Alzheimer's disease. *NeuroImage*, (2006), (30):768–779.
12. Liang, Z. P. and Lauterbur, P. C., *Principles of Magnetic Resonance Imaging: A Signal Processing Perspective*. IEEE Press, New York, (2000).
13. Duda, R., Hart, P. and Stork, D. G., *Pattern Classification*. John Wiley and Sons, (2001).
14. Sklansky, J. and Wassel, G. N., *Pattern Classifiers and Trainable Machines*. Springer-Verlag, 1st edition, (1981).
15. Haykin, S., *Neural Networks: A Comprehensive Foundation*. Prentice Hall, New York, (1999).
16. Landgrebe, D., Hyperspectral image analysis. *IEEE Signal Processing Magazine*, Jan., (2002).

Joint Bayesian PET Reconstruction Algorithm Using a Quadratic Hybrid Multi-order Prior

Yang Chen[1, 2], Wufan Chen[1], Pengcheng Shi[1], Yanqiu Feng[1], Qianjin Feng[1], Qingqi Wang[2], and Zhiyong Huang[2]

[1] Institute of Medical Information&Technology, School of Biomedical Engineering
Southern Medical University, Guangzhou, 510515, China
{kshzh,chenwf,shipch,foree,fqianjin}@fimmu.com
[2] The 113 Hospital of People's Liberation Army, Ningbo, 315040, China
{wangqingqi,jd21}@163.com

Abstract. To overcome the ill-posed problem of image reconstruction with noisy detected data in PET reconstruction, Bayesian reconstruction or maximum a posteriori (MAP) method has its superiority over others with regard to image quality and convergence. Based on Markov Random Fields (MRF) and Bayesian reconstruction theory, quadratic membrane (QM) prior and quadratic plate (QP) prior function differently for different objective surfaces with different properties. It is reasonable to believe that a hybrid prior which combines the two quadratic prior can work better than just using one prior alone. In this paper, a MRF quadratic hybrid prior multi-order model is proposed. A threshold estimation method based on statistical classification is devised to facilitate a selectively utilization of QM prior, QP prior in the quadratic hybrid multi-order (QHM) prior. Application of the proposed QHM prior in PET reconstruction with joint estimation algorithm is also given. Visional and quantitative comparisons of the results of experiments prove the new hybrid prior's good performance in lowering noise effect and preserving edges for PET reconstruction.

Keywords: Bayesian Reconstruction, Positron Emission Tomography, QM prior, QP prior, QHM prior, mixed gamma distribution.

1 Introduction

As is well known, positron emission tomography (PET) [1] is an ill-posed inverse problem because the observed projection data are contaminated by noise due to low count rate and physical effects. Bayesian methods or equivalently MAP methods, which incorporating Markov Random Fields (MRF) prior information of objective data through regularization or prior terms into the ML-EM algorithm, have been proved theoretically correct and more effective than other methods, such as stopping rules, sieves or post-smoothness [2-4]. However, the space-invariant quadratic membrane (QM) prior has the tendency to smooth both high-frequency edge regions and low-frequency background and often displays an over-smoothing effect in edge regions. And some edge-preserving nonquadratic priors are blamed for their prior

A. Gagalowicz and W. Philips (Eds.): MIRAGE 2007, LNCS 4418, pp. 23–35, 2007.

energy functions' non-convexity which might impair the whole concavity of the Bayesian posterior energy function. In addition, the often needed annealing methods for reconstruction using nonconvex priors will make the solution of the posterior energy function a more difficult and complex problem [5].

It is reasonable to believe that an ideal prior should have following three qualities: 1, quadratic energy function, at least convex; 2, noise-removing which produces smooth images; 3, edge-preserving which preserves important detail information.

Based on MRF theory, quadratic membrane (QM) prior and quadratic plate (QP) prior both have energy functions with quadratic form and have different adaptabilities for the reconstruction of surfaces with different properties. And considering the complexity of the properties of PET images and the noise effect, a hybrid prior model combining QM prior and QP prior can be built to better regularize emission reconstruction in PET. In this article, a quadratic hybrid multi-order (QHM) prior model is proposed, and a statistical classification estimation method for the threshold parameter, which is capable of facilitating an adaptive utilization of QM prior and QP prior, is also devised. The theory of the new QHM prior model and the estimation method for the threshold parameter in the proposed QHM prior are illustrated in Section 2. In Section 3, we further illustrate Bayesian reconstruction using QHM prior. A joint estimation algorithm for both threshold parameter and the objective image is described. In Section 4, we apply the proposed hybrid prior to PET reconstruction. Experiments using both synthetic and real data are presented. Visional and quantitative comparisons with the reconstructions using solely QM prior, QP prior are demonstrated. In Section 5, conclusions and plans for possible future work are given.

2   Quadratic MRF Hybrid Prior

Based on Bayesian or MRF theorem, the posterior probability $P(f \mid g)$ for image reconstruction is simply given by:

$$P(f \mid g) \infty P(g \mid f)P(f). \tag{1}$$

$$P(f) = Z^{-1} \times e^{-\beta U(f)}. \tag{2}$$

where g and f denote the measurement data and the image to be reconstructed, respectively. For PET image reconstruction problem, f represents objective emitter concentrations and g represents the detected projection sinogram data. $P(f)$ is a Gibbs prior distribution, with Z , the partition function, a normalizing constant, and $U(f)$ the MRF prior energy, and β the hyperparameter that controls the degree of the MRF prior's influence on the image f . We can build the posterior energy function as follows:

$$\psi_\beta(f) = \log P(f/g) = L(g,f) - \beta U(f). \tag{3}$$

As we know, smoothness is a generic contextual constraint in this world. For example, the surface of quiet sea is flat and the windy sea presents a texture of waves. Smoothness assumes that physical properties in a neighborhood of space or an interval of time present some coherence and generally do not change abruptly. The MRF prior energy term, or the smoothness constraint, measures the extent to which the smoothness assumption is violated by the surface. In ideal situation when the image f completely meets the prior assumptions, the energy function $U(f)$ has its minimum and the prior distribution (2) attains its maximum. For spatially continuous MRFs, the smoothness prior often involves derivatives and the forms of derivatives depend on the properties of continuity of the surface [7].

Let's firstly define two kinds of surfaces:

The first one is flat surface which has equation $f(x, y) = a_0$ and should have zero first-order derivatives. So for Bayesian reconstruction of this kind of flat surface, we should choose first order QM prior as the prior with the prior energy being

$$U_{QM}(f) = \sum_{x,y} \left\{ [f_h(x, y)]^2 + [f_v(x, y)]^2 \right\}. \tag{4}$$

$$f_h(x, y) = f_{x-1,y} - f_{x,y}. \tag{5}$$

$$f_v(x, y) = f_{x,y-1} - f_{x,y}. \tag{6}$$

where (x, y) represents the pixel position in the surface f. $f_v(x, y)$ and $f_h(x, y)$ are the first partial derivatives at position (x, y) of the surface in the vertical and horizontal directions, respectively.

The second one is planar surface whose equation is $f(x, y) = a_0 + a_1 x + b_0 + b_1 y$ and should have zero second-order derivatives. In this case second order QP prior should be selected, and the prior energy $U(f)$ has the form:

$$U_{QP}(f) = \sum_{x,y} \left\{ [f_{hh}(x, y)]^2 + 2[f_{hv}(x, y)]^2 + [f_{vv}(x, y)]^2 \right\}. \tag{7}$$

$$f_{hh}(x, y) = f_{x-1,y} + f_{x+1,y} - 2f_{x,y}. \tag{8}$$

$$f_{vv}(x, y) = f_{x,y-1} + f_{x,y+1} - 2f_{x,y}. \tag{9}$$

$$f_{hv}(x, y) = f_{x+1,y+1} + f_{x,y} - f_{x+1,y} - f_{x,y+1}. \tag{10}$$

where $f_{hh}(x, y)$ and $f_{vv}(x, y)$ are the second partial derivatives at position (x, y), and $f_{hv}(x, y)$ is the second partial cross derivative at position (x, y).

Above two priors perform well in their according types of surfaces and relatively poorer in other types of surfaces [7]. Often, the property of objective images is not unitary. And, noise and physical factors make the situation even much more complicated. So it is better to regard the objective image f as a combination of the above two types of surfaces than simply consider the objective image to be only one type of surface. Therefore, the building of a hybrid Membrane-Plate prior, which adaptively emphasizes the strengths of QM prior and QP prior, is validated. We name the hybrid prior quadratic hybrid multi-order (QHM) prior.

Now we face the problem of how to highlight the effects of QM prior and QP prior for the hybrid QHM prior adaptively and effectively. From above definitions of the two MRF quadratic priors, we know that QM prior is best suitable for reconstruction or restoration of an ideal surface with zero first-order derivatives everywhere, and QP prior is best suitable for reconstruction of an ideal surface with nonzero first-order derivatives but zero second-order derivatives everywhere. However, considering the complicate characteristics of objective image and the ineluctable noise effects, we can never use nonzero derivatives or zero derivatives to control the usage of QM prior and QP prior. In [8], a simple hybrid quadratic prior with identical weights for QM prior and QP prior was suggested to obtain a compromise of the two priors. However, by now, no efficient way for building of such a hybrid prior model, which is able to realize a selective and adaptive usage of QM prior and QP prior, has been reported.

Our approach is motivated by following assumption deduced from the definitions of above two kinds of surfaces and quadratic priors: value $\sqrt{f_h^2(x,y) + f_v^2(x,y)}$ of the points belonging to flat surface tends to be smaller than the value $\sqrt{f_h^2(x,y) + f_v^2(x,y)}$ of those points belonging to planar surface. So we use a thresholds, named KG, to distinguish the points belong to flat surface from the points belong to planar surface. After obtaining such a threshold KG, we can realize an automatic switching between the two quadratic priors in the Bayesian reconstruction using the QHM prior.

We implement the estimations of threshold KG by the method of Hensick and Chelberg, who used a method of histogram statistical classification to obtain the

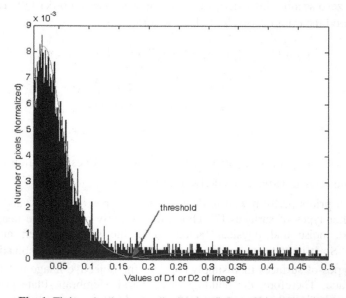

Fig. 1. Finite mixed gamma distribution fitting of histogram data

threshold for edge detection [9]. Based on such threshold determination method, we model the histogram of the map $\sqrt{f_h^2 + f_v^2}$ of the objective image f as a mixture of two gamma probability density functions (pdf), which respectively represent those points belonging to flat surface and those points belonging to planar surface. We denote such two-dimensional map $\sqrt{f_h^2 + f_v^2}$ as D. After estimating the parameters of above mentioned four gamma distributions, we can find threshold KG in the abscissa of the histogram graph to distinguish the points belonging to the two respectively kinds of surfaces. This scheme is clearly expressed by Fig. 1.

So, with the estimated threshold KG, we can build following new pixelwise hybrid prior energy $U_{QHM-xy}(f)$ for QHM prior at position (x, y):

$$U_{QHM-xy}(f) = \omega_{xy}U_{QM}(f) + (1 - \omega_{xy})\rho_{QP}U_{QP}(f). \tag{11}$$

$$\omega_{xy} = \begin{cases} 0 & \varphi_{xy} > KG \\ 1 & otherwise \end{cases}. \tag{12}$$

$$\varphi_{xy} = \sqrt{f_h^2(x, y) + f_v^2(x, y)} . \tag{13}$$

Here parameter KG, and ρ_{QP} are the two parameters needed to be estimated. The estimation for the threshold KG can be implemented through a joint Bayesian reconstruction algorithm process which will be illustrated in next section. Parameter ρ_{QP} is needed to balance the value levels of the two prior energies in the hybrid prior energy.

3   Bayesian Reconstruction Using QHM Prior

With the proposed hybrid prior model and the estimation method for threshold parameter, we apply the proposed QHM prior model in Bayesian image reconstruction and put forward a joint Bayesian estimation algorithm for simultaneously updating objective image f, the parameters of the mixed gamma distributions.

3.1   Joint Bayesian Estimation Strategy

The pdf of a gamma distribution is given by

$$P(\mu / \alpha, \beta) = \frac{\alpha^\alpha}{\beta^\alpha \Gamma(\alpha)} \mu^{\alpha-1} e^{-\frac{\alpha}{\beta}\mu}. \tag{14}$$

with random variable $\mu > 0$, β the mean and β^2/α the variance of the gamma distribution. As is manifested in last section, to estimate threshold KG, we need to fit the histogram of D by a convex combination of two Gamma distributions:

$$\pi_1 P(D/\theta_1) + (1 - \pi_1) P(D/\theta_2). \tag{15}$$

where $D_j > 0$, $\theta = (\alpha, \beta)$. Using such a mixed gamma distribution models to fit the histograms of map D of image f, we can uniquely obtain the threshold KG once the parameters of the relevant two gamma distributions are determined [9-11]. Therefore, for Bayesian reconstruction using our proposed new QHM prior, five additional parameters, denoted by $\alpha_1, \beta_1, \alpha_2, \beta_2, \pi_1$, are needed to be estimated to determine threshold KG for the reconstruction using the proposed QHM prior.

With the including of above new parameters, we build following new posterior probability formula other than (1) from Bayesian theorem:

$$P(f, \theta_1, \theta_2, \pi_1 / g) \propto P(g/f) P(f, \theta_1, \theta_2, \pi_1) \propto P(g/f) P(f/\theta_1, \theta_2, \pi_1) P(\theta_1, \theta_2, \pi_1). \quad (16)$$

Here we use the fact that the objective image data f depends on detected sinogram data g only.

To obtain a full estimation for the parameters of such posterior probability, our strategy is to perform a joint Bayesian estimation which simultaneously solves both the reconstruction of objective image f and the estimation of the parameters for the mixed gamma distributions. We use an alternating iterative coordinate descent procedure, updating, at iteration n, the image f holding parameters $(\theta_1, \theta_2, \pi_1)$ fixed, then updating the parameters $(\theta_1, \theta_2, \pi_1)$ holding image f fixed. The joint Bayesian reconstruction procedure can be summarized as:

$$f^n = \arg \max_f P(g/f) P(f/\theta_1^n, \theta_2^n, \pi_1^n) P(\theta_1^n, \theta_2^n, \pi_1^n) \quad (17)$$

$$(\theta, \pi) = \arg \max_{(\theta, \pi)} P(g/f^n) P(f^n/\theta_1, \theta_2, \pi_1) P(\theta_1, \theta_2, \pi_1)$$

$$= \arg \max_{(\theta, \pi)} P(f^n/\theta_1, \theta_2, \pi_1) P(\theta_1, \theta_2, \pi_1). \quad (18)$$

We define function $histogram(D)$ that returns the relevant histogram information of D $histogram\_info$. Because the gamma parameters can be totally determined by the information of $histogram\_info$ which can also be totally determined by image f^n, we can transform formula (18) into:

$$(\theta, \pi) = \arg \max_{(\theta, \pi)} P(histogram/\theta_1, \theta_2, \pi_1) P(\theta_1, \theta_2, \pi_1). \quad (19)$$

$$histogram\_info = [x, histo] = histogram(D). \quad (20)$$

where x is the one-dimensional sorted $\sqrt{f_h^2 + f_v^2}$ array data in D and $histo$ has the according normalized frequency counts for each data in x, and they all have the same number of elements as two-dimensional map D.

We adopt paraboloidal surrogate coordinate ascent (PSCA) iterative algorithm whose idea is proposed by Fessler and Erdoğan [12] to resolve the maximization problem of (17). In order to obtain the estimation of parameters $\alpha_1, \beta_1, \alpha_2, \beta_2, \pi_1$, we apply a ML-EM (maximum likelihood-expectation maximization) method, which is similar to the method proposed in [9-11].

3.2 Determination of Thresholds KG and Parameter ρ_{QP}

Given all the estimated parameters $(\theta_1, \theta_2, \pi_1)$, the two gamma pdfs are uniquely determination. Having knowing histogram information $[x, histo]$ and starting from the $x(t)$ in origin of coordinates, we choose the threshold KG to be the first $x(t)$ that satisfies inequation $\pi_1 p\left(x(t)_j / \theta_1\right) > (1 - \pi_1) p\left(x(t)_j / \theta_2\right)$, which can be seen in Fig. 1.

In the practical iterative process, parameter ρ_{QP} is set to balance the value levels of the two derivatives $\partial U_{QM}(\hat{f}) / \partial \hat{f}_{x,y}$ and $\partial U_{QP}(\hat{f}) / \partial \hat{f}_{x,y}$. For every j or position (x, y) in image f, each of the above two derivatives can be generalized into the form $\{W(f_s - f_d)\}_{s,d \in (1,...M)}$ ($W = W_{QM} = 8$ for the first derivative and $W = W_{QP} = 64$ for the other). So we set ρ_{QP} to be W_{QM} / W_{QP} (=0.125) in our study.

So for every pixel in image f, values of ρ_{QP} always lie between 0 and 1, thus the QHM prior energy $U_{QHM-xy}(f)$ is always the convex combination of $U_{QM}(f)$ and $U_{QP}(f)$. Therefore, second order derivatives of hybrid prior energy functional (6) must be positive definite, which is important for maintaining the concavity of the according posterior energy function (3).

4 Experimentation and Analyses

4.1 Simulated Emission Data

In this experiment, two 128×128 synthetic simulated phantom data, phantom1 (Fig. 2(a)) and phantom2 (Fig. 2(b)), are used for reconstruction. Phantom1 is a Zubal phantom. Phantom2 comprises a constant background region, a square hot region, blobby hot region and another square cold region. The relevant parameter settings for the simulated sonogram data is listed in Table. 1. The two transition probability matrixes used in the reconstructions of above two phantoms both correspond to parallel strip-integral geometries with 128 radial samples and 128 angular samples distributed uniformly over 180 degrees. And the two simulated sinograms data for the two phantom are both Poisson distributed, and generated by the ASPIRE software system [13]. A PC with Intel P4 CPU and 512 Mb RAM is used as the workstation for reconstructions. In the experiments for Bayesian iterative reconstruction, poisson ML-EM method is used and above convergent iterative PSCA algorithm is used in the updatings of objective image f. The number of iteration is set to be 150.

(a)   (b)

Fig. 2. The synthetic phantom image data used in experiments. (a): phantom 1; (b): phantom 2.

Table 1. Parameter settings for the two simulated phantoms and corresponding sinograms

	Size of sinogram	Number of counts	Percentage of coincidences	Region of pixel values
Phantom1	128×128	4×10^5	10%	$\begin{bmatrix} 0 & 5 \end{bmatrix}$
Phantom2	128×128	3.5×10^5	10%	$\begin{bmatrix} 0 & 8 \end{bmatrix}$

For each phantom, we perform analytic reconstructions using FBP method and four iterative Bayesian reconstructions using QM prior, QP prior and the proposed QHM prior, respectively. With the incorporation of parameter ρ_{QP}, same global parameter β can be used for different Bayesian reconstructions using the same phantom data. We fix β to 5.5 and 2.8 to obtain images with best SNRs (signal to noise ratios) for the two different phantom data, respectively. The images from FBP reconstruction are used as the initial mages in the iteration. The SNRs are computed by following formula:

$$SNR = 10\log_{10}\left(\frac{\sum_{x,y}(f(x,y)-\overline{f})^2}{\sum_{x,y}(f(x,y)-f_{phantom}(x,y))^2}\right). \tag{21}$$

where $f(x,y)$ is the reconstructed image, $\overline{f}$ denoted the mean of intensities of all the pixels in f, $f_{phantom}(x,y)$ is the phantom image data.

Table 2. The SNRs for above reconstructed images with respect to their respective phantom

	FBP	QM	QP	QHM
SNR_phantom1	10.561	11.604	11.310	12.857
SNR_phantom2	11.679	12.595	11.814	13.934

Fig. 3 and Fig. 4 demonstrate the according reconstructed results for the two phantoms respectively. In Fig. 3 and Fig. 4, (a) is the reconstructed image using FBP method, and (b), (c), (d) are the results from Bayesian iterative reconstruction using the above three priors respectively. From Fig. 3 and Fig. 4 we can see that the images produced by reconstructions using the proposed QHM prior are more smooth in background region than those using QP prior, and also show better performance in preserving edges than those using QM prior. The QHM prior realizes an efficient switching between QM prior and QP prior according to different properties of different surfaces in the objective image. Table.2 shows that the SNRs of the reconstructed images from the reconstructions using the proposed QHM prior is higher than those of the reconstructed images from the reconstructions using QM prior, QP prior.

In the reconstruction process using QHM prior, it is observed that the estimate of threshold KG become stable as the iteration proceeds and the ultimate estimate are 0.1895 and 0.1423 for the two phantom data, respectively. The CPU time costs for reconstructions using QM prior, QP prior and QHM prior are respectively 14.41 seconds, 15.35 seconds and 17.22 seconds.

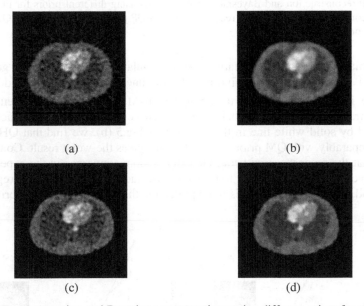

(a)   (b)

(c)   (d)

Fig. 3. FBP reconstruction and Bayesian reconstructions using different priors for phantom 1: (a) FBP reconstruction (b) QM prior reconstruction (c) QP prior reconstruction (d) QHM prior reconstruction

We choose the reconstruction of phantom2 to test the bias-variance trade-offs for reconstruction using QM prior, QP prior and QHM prior. The two plots in Fig.5 show the bias-variance trade-offs of interest region and background for above Bayesian reconstructions using the three priors. The values of β are regulated for different

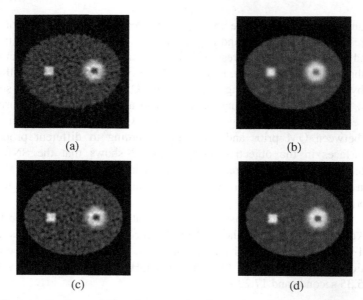

(a)   (b)

(c)   (d)

Fig. 4. FBP reconstruction and Bayesian reconstructions using different priors for phantom 2:
(a) FBP reconstruction (b) QM prior reconstruction (c) QP prior reconstruction (d) QHM prior
reconstruction

values of biases and standard deviations. Fifty simulated sinogram data are generated
for each β. From Fig.5 (a), we find that, for the interest region surrounded by solid
white line in Fig.5 (a), reconstruction using QHM prior produces a better bias-
variance trade-off than the other two reconstructions. As to the background
surrounded by solid white line in the second plot Fig.5 (b), we find that QHM prior
works comparably with QM prior, while QP prior gives the worst result. Considering
the fact that the reconstruction using QP prior seldom converges in the experiments,
we can conclude that, with regard to bias-variance trade-off for the interest region and
background, the new QHM prior is more preferable than QM prior and QP prior.

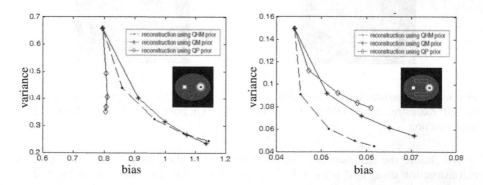

(a) Bias vs variance trade-off of interest region   (b) Bias vs variance trade-off of background

Fig. 5. Bias-variance trade-offs for reconstructions using QM, QP and QHM priors

4.2 Real Emission Data

In the study, 10 minute real patient PET precorrected data obtained from cardiac perfusion imaging using Tc-99m sestamibi are used. For each slice, 128 projections were taken at 120 uniformly spaced angles between 0 and 2π. And the 9th 2D slice

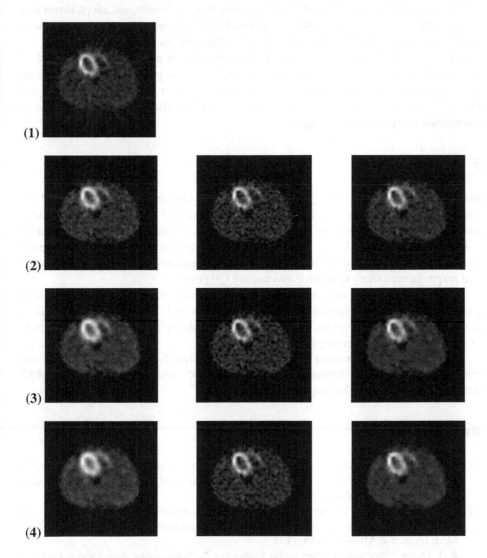

(1)

(2)

(3)

(4)

Fig. 6. FBP reconstruction and Bayesian reconstructions using different priors with different global parameters for real emission data: The first row is FBP reconstruction. In every other row (the second, third, and fourth row), QM prior reconstruction, QP prior reconstruction and QHM prior reconstruction are listed from left to right, respectively. The second row lists Bayesian reconstructions with $\beta = 25$. The third row lists the Bayesian reconstructions with $\beta = 50$. The fourth row lists the Bayesian reconstructions with $\beta = 70$.

data of the total 39 slices is chosen. The reconstruction is done at 128 by 128 with 0.356cm pixel resolution. The reconstruction environment for real data is the same as that for above simulated data. The image from FBP reconstruction is used as the initial mage in the iteration. The number of iteration is set to be 50. The CPU time costs for reconstructions using QM prior, QP prior and QHM prior are respectively 8.29 seconds, 10.05 seconds and 12.28 seconds. In experiments, we adopt Bayuesian data-weighted least squares (WLS) approach for the reconstruction. And above mentioned iterative PSCA algorithm is used in the iteration processes.

Fig.6 show the Bayesian reconstruction using different priors and different global parameters, we can also see that reconstructions using the proposed QHM prior, suppressing noise in background region more effectively than those using QP prior and preserve edge information more effectively than those using QM prior, are able to reconstruct more appealing images.

5 Conclusions

Stemming from Markov theory, the hybrid prior is theoretically reasonable and the joint estimation strategy can be effectively implemented in practice. From above analyses and experiments, for PET reconstruction, despite little more computation cost, the proposed QHM prior is able to emphasize the effects of QM prior, QP prior adaptively according to different properties of different positions in objective image, and outperforms unitary QM prior and unitary QP prior.

Through estimation approach based on statistical classification for threshold parameter, an effective switching between QM prior and QP prior in QHM prior is realized. In addition, the proposed hybrid prior avoids the problem of non-convexity of some other edge-preserving priors.

Further work includes more quantitative comparisons for both simulated data and real data, incorporating higher order priors into the hybrid prior and MRF-MAP image restoration using the proposed the QHM prior.

References

1. T. F. Budinger, G. T. Gullberg, and R. H. Huesman, "Emission computed tomography," in Image Reconstruction from Projections: Implementation and applications, G. T. Herman, Ed. Berlin: Springer Verlag, ch. 5(1979) 147-246
2. E. Levitan and G. T. Herman, "A maximum a posteriori probability expectation maximization algorithm for image reconstruction in emission tomography," IEEE Trans. Med. Imag., vol. MI-6(1987) 185-192
3. P. J. Green, "Bayesian reconstruction from emission tomography data using a modified EM algorithm," IEEE Trans. Med. Imag., vol. 9 (1990) 84-93
4. K. Lange, "Convergence of EM image reconstruction algorithms with Gibbs smoothness," IEEE Trans. Med. Imag., vol .9 (1990) 439-446
5. V. Johnson, W. H. Wong, X. Hu, and C.T. Chen, "Image restoration using Gibbs prior: Boundary modeling, treatment of blurring, and selection of hyperparameter," IEEE Trans. Pattern Anal Machine Intell., vol. 13 (1991) 413-425

6. G. Gindi, A. Rangarajan, M. Lee, P. J. Hong, and G. Zubal, "Bayesian Reconstruction for Emission Tomography via Deterministic Annealing", In H. Barrett and A. Gmitro, editors, Information Processing in Medical Imaging, Springer–Verlag (1993) 322–338
7. Stan Z. Li, Markov Random Field Modeling in image Analysis,: Springer-Verlag, Tokyo (2001) 1-40
8. S. J Lee, Y Choi, GR Gindi, "Validation of new Gibbs priors for Bayesian tomographic reconstruction using numerical studies and physically acquired data," *IEEE Trans Nucl Sci* vol 46 (1999) 2154-2161
9. Peter V. Hensick and David M. Chelberg, "Automatic gradient threshold determination for edge detection," IEEE Trans. Imag Processing , vol. 5 (1996) 784-787
10. G. J. McLachlan and K.E. Basford, Mixture Models, Marcel Dekker (1987)
11. I.-T. Hsiao, A. Rangarajan, and G. Gindi, "Joint-MAP Reconstruction/Segmentation for Transmission Tomography Using Mixture-Models as Priors", Proc. IEEE Nuclear Science Symposium and Medical ImagingConference, II (1998) 1689–1693
12. J. A. Fessler and H. Erdoğan, "A paraboloidal surrogates algorithm for convergent penalized-likelihood emission reconstruction," in Proc. IEEE Nuc. Sci. Symp. Med. Im. Conf., volume 2 (1998) 1132-5
13. J. A. Fessler, " Aspire 3.0 user's guide: A sparse reconstruction library," Communication & Signal Processing Laboratory Technical Report No. 293, Department of Electrical and Computer Engineering, University of Michigan, Ann Arbor(1998)

Automatic Combination of Feature Descriptors for Effective 3D Shape Retrieval

Biao Leng and Zheng Qin

Department of Computer Science & Technology, Tsinghua University, 100084,
Beijing, China
School of Software, Tsinghua University, 100084, Beijing, China
lengb04@mails.tsinghua.edu.cn,qingzh@tsinghua.edu.cn

Abstract. We focus on improving the effectiveness of content-based 3D shape retrieval. Motivated by retrieval performance of several individual 3D model feature vectors, we propose a novel method, called prior knowledge based automatic weighted combination, to improve the retrieval effectiveness. The method dynamically determines the weighting scheme for different feature vectors based on the prior knowledge. The experimental results show that the proposed method provides significant improvements on retrieval effectiveness of 3D shape search with several measures on a standard 3D database. Compared with two existing combination methods, the prior knowledge weighted combination technique has gained better retrieval effectiveness.

1   Introduction

With the rapid development of 3D scanner technology, graphic hardware, and the World-Wide Web, there has been an explosion in the number of 3D models available on the Internet. In order to make use of these 3D models, the techniques of effective 3D shape retrieval become increasingly significant. 3D models can be annotated by keywords at first, facilitating the text-based retrieval. However, this is not a promising approach, because generally annotations are manually created, which is prohibitively expensive and subject to some factors. To overcome the disadvantages of annotation-based approach, the so-called content-based 3D shape retrieval, using the 3D model itself, has been proposed as an alternative mechanism [9]. In [17], Min compared four text annotation-based matching methods and four content-based retrieval approaches, and the experiments showed that the relatively simple solution of using only associated text for retrieval of 3D model was not as effective as using their shape.

As a promising approach applied in many fields, the content-based 3D shape retrieval has attracted many researchers in recent years. In the computer aided design [23], the similar search for standard parts is handy in helping to reach at higher speed with lower cost. In bioinformatics [11], the detection and retrieval of similar protein molecules is applied. Other cases of using this method can be found in the entertainment industry, visual reality, and so forth.

A. Gagalowicz and W. Philips (Eds.): MIRAGE 2007, LNCS 4418, pp. 36–46, 2007.
© Springer-Verlag Berlin Heidelberg 2007

In this paper, we experimentally compare a range of different 3D feature vectors, and the experimental results show that the relative ordering of feature vectors by retrieval effectiveness depends on query models or model classes, which means that no single feature vector can always outperform other feature vectors on all query models. To address the issue and improve the effectiveness of content-based 3D shape retrieval, we propose a novel method, called prior knowledge based automatic weighted combination, which provides significant improvements on retrieval effectiveness of content-based 3D shape search. Compared with two existing methods, one is using entropy impurity, the other is based on purity-weighted, our method achieves better 3D shape retrieval performance.

The rest of this paper is organized as follows. Section 2 introduces the similarity search of 3D objects about feature-based approaches and some feature vectors. Effectiveness measures and retrieval performance for single feature vectors are described in Section 3. Section 4 presents the prior knowledged based automatic weighted combination technique. Results of extensive experiments compared with several single feature vectors and two existing approaches utilizing several standard measures are given in Section 5. Finally, the conclusion and future work are showed in Section 6.

2   Similarity Search of 3D Objects

The 3D shape retrieval problem can be described as follows: Given a 3D model database and a query object, the system returns the models in the database that are most similar, according to the similarity distance in descending order, to the query object.

2.1   Feature-Based Approaches

Having defined certain object aspects, numerical values are extracted from a 3D object. These values describe the 3D object and form a *feature vector* of usually high dimensionality [3]. Thus, 3D model shape descriptors or feature extraction methods are replaced by the *feature vector*.

Nowadays, a variety of feature vectors have been proposed. They are generally classified into geometry-based approach and shape-based approach. Geometry-based method matches 3D models according to the information and distribution of vertices and mesh triangles [20,14,13,15]. While shape-based method matches 3D models by taking the rendering projected images into account [8,19,12]. For the latest developments in content-based 3D shape retrieval technique, please refer to [16,22,3].

Early stage of content-based 3D shape retrieval seems to focus on exploring various single feature vectors, hoping to find the "best" one to represent 3D models. Recently, some composite feature vectors [6] and combination methods [1,2] are presented to improve the retrieval effectiveness. In [2], Bustos proposed a method for the prior estimation of individual feature vector performance based on the entropy impurity measure. Bustos [1] introduced another method, applying the purity concept, to use a dynamically weighted combination of feature vectors.

2.2   Studied Feature Vectors

While we have implemented many different feature vectors in our 3D shape retrieval system, for clarity reason, we just focus on a set of four feature vectors which provides good retrieval performance in our experiments.

Silhouette feature vector [5] characterizes 3D models in terms of their silhouettes that are obtained from canonical renderings. *Depth buffer (D-buffer)* [5] is another shape-based feature vector, in which six gray-scale images are rendered and then transformed using the standard 2D discrete Fourier transform. *Ray-based (Ray)* [7] feature vector is the spherical harmonics transform of samples taken from a combination of model extension and surface orientation properties. Another geometry-based algorithm *Gaussian Euclidean Distance Transform (GEDT)* [14] is a 3D function whose value at each point is given by composition of a Gaussian with the Euclidean Distance Transform of the surface.

3   Measuring Retrieval Effectiveness

In this section, we first introduce the 3D model repositories, and several standard measures, such as precision vs. recall figures, nearest neighbor, first-tier, and second-tier. Then experimental results among four single feature vectors and some detailed discussions are presented.

3.1   Retrieval Evaluation

Our experiments are based on the standard 3D model repositories *Princeton Shape Benchmark (PSB)* [18], containing 1814 3D objects of general categories, like furniture, animal, building, vehicle, etc. All models in the database is divided as evenly as possible into two sets, one is train set with 907 models partitioned into 90 classes, and the other is test set with 907 models partitioned into 92 classes, yielding the ground truth. In our experiment, each classified model in test set was used as a query object, and the models belonging to the same class were taken as relevant objects.

To evaluate the effectiveness of 3D shape retrieval, we use *precision vs. recall figures*, a standard evaluation technique for retrieval systems [4]. Precision indicates the ability to retrieve the relevant models based on the retrieved models. Recall indicates the ability to retrieve the relevant models based on the whole relevant models. In addition to the precision at different recall levels, we employ the widely used *nearest neighbor, first-tier and second-tier* measures [18] for each query. Nearest neighbor is defined as the percentage of the closest match that belongs to the same class as the query model. First-tier and second-tier are associated with the percentage of models in the query model class that appear within the top G matches. Specially, for the query model class with $|C|$ members (excluding the query model), when $G = |C|$ it is for the first-tier, and $G = 2*|C|$ for the second-tier. For all measures, only the precision vs. recall figures regard the query object as relevant model. With the choice of similarity measure, we employ the l_1 (Manhattan) distance, as the experiments show that l_1 acquires the best retrieval results compared with other Minkowski distances.

3.2 Results for Individual Feature Vectors

In our experiments, we compare retrieval performance of four feature vectors using the ground truth. Figure 1 shows the average effectiveness performance (precision vs. recall curves, nearest neighbor, first-tier and second-tier)of four feature vectors. The most precise feature vector among them is D-buffer, followed by GEDT, Silhouette and Ray. Between the first and the second best feature vectors, the differences of retrieval performance are very small, even can be negligible, implying that in practice the two feature vectors have the same average retrieval capabilities.

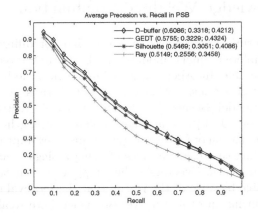

Fig. 1. Average precision vs. recall figures for D-buffer, GEDT, Silhouette and Ray (the legend includes nearest neighbor, first-tier and second-tier values)

Then we evaluate the four feature vectors with two specific model classes. Figure 2 left shows the average retrieval performance for the covered_wagon vehicle model class. In this case, the best effectiveness is obtained by D-buffer, and the performance ordering for this model class is the same with that of performance on average. Figure 2 right shows the average precision vs. recall figures and other measure values for the flying_saucer spaceship model class. For this class, the best feature vectors are Ray and Silhouette. It is concluded that for some model classes, the worst average feature vector Ray performs well.

The experimental results indicate that for some model classes the best average feature vector does not seem to perform well. Generally speaking, we've observed this phenomenon that for many query classes the corresponding rankings of four feature vectors are quite different from the average ranking.

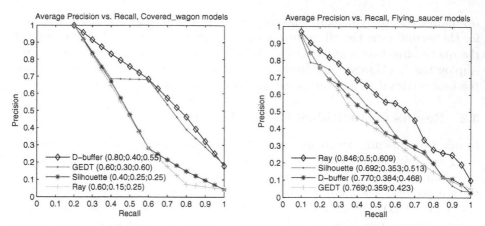

Fig. 2. Average precision vs. recall figures for the covered_wagon vehicle model class (left) and the flying_saucer spaceship model class (right)

4   Prior Knowledge Weighted Combination

The previous experimental analysis indicates that for different query model classes, even for different query models, the best feature vector is quite different and unpredictable. In other words, it implies that the best feature vector achieves good average retrieval effectiveness, but there is no clear predictable winner for a query model. Because the individual feature vectors capture different characteristics of 3D objects, and have different strengths and weaknesses. Therefore, the combination of feature vectors seems to be improving the retrieval effectiveness, avoiding the disadvantages of using a single feature vector. How to combine different feature vectors? The simple concatenation of all feature vectors is not feasible because of the reason that the retrieval effectiveness may degrade with the inclusion of feature vectors which have weak descriptions to the query. To overcome these problems, a novel method, called prior knowledge based automatic weighted combination, is proposed to dynamically determine weighting scheme for different feature vectors based on prior knowledge.

Let U be the universe of 3D objects, $Train \subset U$ be a set of training objects, while $Test \subset U$ be the testing objects. $Train$ and $Test$ are disjoint unions, that is, $Train \cap Test = \emptyset$, and $Train \cup Test = U$. In $Train$, $Train = \uplus_{i=1}^{m} Q_i$, where Q_i is a model class, i.e., a set of similar models. Given a set of feature vectors $\{f_1, \ldots, f_l\}$, l is the total number of feature vectors.

For a query object $q \in Test$, we generate l similarity distance rankings, one for each feature vector, consisting of the distance between q and every object of $Train$ sorted in ascending order. Let $D_{q,k}^{j}$ be the first k positions of the ranking using f_j, and k is a constant value $k \in N^+$. For each Q_i in $Train$, $R_j^i = D_{q,k}^{j} \cap Q_i$ represents the objects in the first k positions belonging to the model class Q_i. The similar class in $Train$ for the query object q by f_j is defined as:

$$SimilarClass(f_j, q, k) = arg \max_{1 \leq i \leq m} (|R_j^i|) \qquad (1)$$

The similar class indicates that the model class in $Train$ has the maximum number of models that belong to the same model class in the first k positions of each ranking. In case of ties, we select the model class whose best model in the first k positions is better (near the front of the ranking) than that of the other model class.

The first k positions $D_{q,k}^{j}$ is converted to a list G, where element G_i has value 1 if its corresponding element in $D_{q,k}^{j}$ is in the similar class, and value 0 otherwise. In the list G, the element near the front should weights more than that later in the list. Then the cumulative gain statistic (CGS) is defined as follows.

$$CGS_i = \begin{cases} G_1, & i=1 \\ CGS_{i-1} + \frac{G_i}{\lg_2(i)}, & \text{otherwise} \end{cases} \tag{2}$$

$$CGS(f_j, q, k) = CGS_k \tag{3}$$

The CGS is regarded as prior knowledge, and it can be taken as the weight of each feature vector for combination. Because the value of CGS is dynamically determined by the query object, the weight of each feature vector is dependable on the query object. The normalization of CGS is defined as follows.

$$CGS(f_j, q, k) = \frac{CGS(f_j, q, k)}{\sum_{j=1}^{l} CGS(f_j, q, k)} \tag{4}$$

Let d_j be the distance function using f_j, and let $d_{max,j}$ be the maximum distance between query object q and every object in $Test$ by feature vector f_j. The prior knowledge weighted distance between the query object q and an object $o \in Test$ is defined as:

$$d(q, o) = \sum_{j=1}^{l} CGS(f_j, q, k) \frac{d_j(q, o)}{d_{max,j}} \tag{5}$$

5   Experiments

Figure 3 shows the average precision versus recall figures for prior knowledge weighted combination method and four single feature vectors. For the prior knowledge weighted combination, we show the results using $k = 10$ (results using value between 6 and 10 are all similar). It is obvious that the prior knowledge weighted combination method has better precision for all recall levels compared with the best single feature vector. The improvement in nearest neighbor between the proposed method and the best single feature vector is about 9.42%, which is significant in terms of quality of the retrieval answer. Compared with D-buffer, one can observe a large effectiveness improvement of 18.38% in terms of first-tier using the prior knowledge weighted combination technique. For the second-tier, the combination method provides a retrieval performance 19.37% better than the best single feature vector.

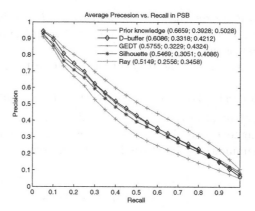

Fig. 3. Average precision vs. recall figures for prior knowledge weighted combination and four single feature vectors

Figure 4 shows the detailed retrieval results for a specific object in biplane airplane model class(1139.off in PSB) with prior knowledge weighted combination and four single feature vectors. The retrieval effectiveness of feature vector Silhouette is the worst, as there are only one object which is relevant in the first eight similar models. D-buffer is the best among the four single feature vector, but there are four objects which are irrelevant in the first eight similar models. For the single feature vectors, the retrieval effectiveness is undesirable. The retrieval performance of the proposed prior knowledge weighted combination method is perfect, as the first eight similar models are relevant. It shows a proof-of-concept of how a retrieval effectiveness of 3D shape search can benefit from the proposed combination technique.

Now, we compare the proposed combination technique with two existing methods, entropy impurity weighted combination [2] and purity weighted method [1]. Figure 5 shows precision vs. recall curves for the prior knowledge weighted combination, entropy impurity weighted method, purity weighted approach and the best single feature vector D-buffer. Our combination method does the best retrieval performance, while the D-buffer does the worst. The entropy impurity weighted method does better than the purity weighted approach, but its retrieval effectiveness, including four standard measures, such as the precision at different recall levels, nearest neighbor, first-tier and second-tier, is a little lower than that of the prior knowledge weighted combination technique.

Table 1 summarizes the improvements in terms of first-tier obtained with different methods. From the table, it is concluded that three combination methods provides better retrieval effectiveness than the best single feature vector, and it indicates that the weighted combination technique improves the retrieval effectiveness of content-based 3D shape search. Note that an improvement of 18.39% in effectiveness is very significant compared with the improvements acquired by the other two combination methods.

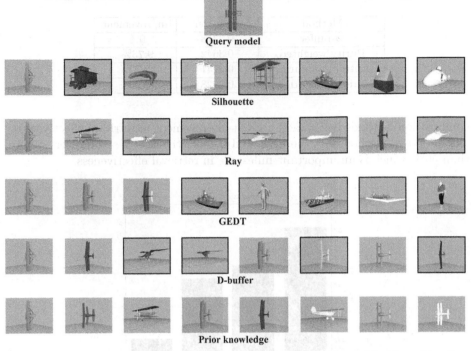

Query model

Silhouette

Ray

GEDT

D-buffer

Prior knowledge

Fig. 4. Retrieval results for a specific model with prior knowledge weighted combination and four single feature vectors. Irrelevant models retrieved are highlighted.

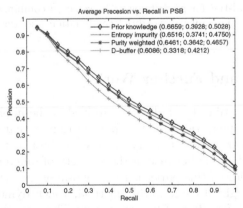

Fig. 5. Average precision vs. recall figures for prior knowledge weighted combination, entropy impurity weighted combination, purity weighted combination and the best single feature vector

Figure 6 compares the average second-tier among prior knowledge weighted technique, entropy impurity weighted method, purity weighted approach and the best single feature vector. From the figure, it is obvious that three different

Table 1. Improvements in effectiveness obtained with different methods

Method	First-tier	Improvement
D-buffer	0.3318	0%
Purity weighted	0.3642	9.73%
Entropy impurity	0.3741	12.72%
Prior knowledge	0.3928	18.39%

combination methods has gained a great improvement in retrieval effectiveness. The proposed method does the best, and the effectiveness of second-tier is more than 50%, which is an important milestone in retrieval effectiveness.

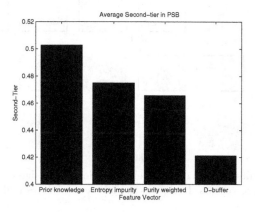

Fig. 6. Average second-tier for prior knowledge weighted combination, entropy impurity weighted combination, purity weighted combination and the best single feature vector

6   Conclusion and Further Work

In this paper, we describe the challenges involved in the implementation of the content-based 3D shape retrieval. It is important to note that for different query model classes, even for different query models, the best feature vector is quite different and unpredictable because of the strength of different feature vectors. The main contribution of this paper is the proposal of the new prior knowledge based automatic weighted combination method, which dynamically determine the weighting scheme for different feature vectors. The experimental results show that the proposed method has gained a significant improvement on retrieval effectiveness of content-based 3D shape search. Compared with two existing combination techniques, the prior knowledged combination method does better retrieval performance with different standard measures.

For further study, we plan to study the interactive mechanism [21] as well as the relevance feedback technique [10] hoping that the retrieval performance can be improved by dynamically assigning different weighs or by training through the classified 3D models.

Acknowledgement

This work is supported by the National Grand Fundamental Research 973 Program of China (No. 2004CB719401), the National Research Foundation for the Doctoral Program of Higher Education of China (No. 20060003060), and the National Natural Science Foundation of China (No. 60542004).

References

1. Bustos B., Keim D., Saupe D., Schreck T., and Vranic D. Automatic selection and combination of descriptors for effective 3d similarity search. In *Proceedings of IEEE Sixth International Symposium on Multimedia Software Engineering (SME2004)*, pages 514–521, Miami, USA, December 2004.
2. Bustos B., Keim D.A., Saupe D., Schreck T., and Vranic D.V. Using entropy impurity for improved 3d object similarity search. In *Proceedings of IEEE International Conference on Multimedia and Expo (ICME)*, pages 1303–1306, Taipeh, Taiwan, June 2004.
3. Bustos B., Keim D.A., Saupe D., Schreck T., and Vranic D.V. Feature-based similarity search in 3d object databases. *ACM Computing Surveys*, 37(4):345–387, 2005.
4. Ricardo B.Y. and Berthier R.N. *Modern Information Retrieval*. Addison-Wesley, Cambridge, 1999.
5. Vranic D.V. *3D Model Retrieval*. PhD thesis, University of Leipzig, Leipzig, Germany, 2004.
6. Vranic D.V. Desire: a composite 3d-shape descriptor. In *Proceedings of IEEE International Conference on Multimedia and Expo (ICME)*, pages 962–965, Amsterdam, Holand, July 2005.
7. Vranic D.V. and Saupe D. Description of 3d-shape using a complex function on the sphere. In *Proceedings of IEEE International Conference on Multimedia and Expo (ICME)*, pages 177–180, Lausanne, Switzerland, Augest 2002.
8. Chen D.Y., Tian X.P., Shen Y.T., and Ouhyoung M. On visual similarity based 3d model retrieval. *Computer Graphics Forum*, 22(3):223–232, 2003.
9. Paquet E. and Rioux M. Nefertiti: a query by content software for three-dimensional models databases management. *Image and Vision Computing*, 17(2):157–166, 1999.
10. Leifman G., Meir R., and Tal A. Semantic-oriented 3d shape retrieval using relevance feedback. *The Visual Computer*, 21(8-10):865–875, 2005.
11. Yeh J.S., Chen D.Y., Chen B.Y., and Ouhyoung M. A web-based three-dimensional protein retrieval system by matching visual similarity. *Bioinformatics*, 21:3056–3057, July 2005.
12. Pu J.T. and Ramani K. On visual similarity based 2d drawing retrieval. *Computer-Aided Design*, 38(3):249–259, 2006.
13. Kazhdan M., Chazelle B., Dobkin D., Funkhouser T., and Rusinkiewicz S. A reflective symmetry descriptor for 3d models. *Algorithmica*, 38(1):201–225, 2003.

14. Kazhdan M., Funkhouser T., and Rusinkiewicz S. Rotation invariant spherical harmonic representation of 3d shape descriptors. In *Proceedings of the 2003 Eurographics symposium on Geometry processing*, pages 156–164, Aachen, Germany, June 2003.
15. Kazhdan M., Funkhouser T., and Rusinkiewicz S. Shape matching and anisotropy. *ACM Transactions on Graphics*, 23(3):623–629, 2004.
16. Iyer N., Jayanti S., Lou K.Y., Kalyanaraman Y., and Ramani K. Three-dimensional shape searching: state-of-the-art review and future trends. *Computer-Aided Design*, 37(5):509–530, 2005.
17. Min P., Kazhdan M., and Funkhouser T. A comparison of text and shape matching for retrieval of online 3d models. In *Proceedings of European Conference on Digital Libraries (ECDL)*, pages 209–220, Bath, UK, September 2004.
18. Shilane P., Min P., Kazhdan M., and Funkhouser T. The princeton shape benchmark. In *Proceedings of Shape Modeling and Applications (SMI)*, pages 167–178, Palazzo Ducale, Genova, Italy, June 2004.
19. Ohbuchi R., Nakazawa M., and Takei T. Retrieving 3d shapes based on their appearance. In *Proceedings of the 5th ACM SIGMM international workshop on Multimedia information retrieval*, pages 39–45, Berkeley, California, USA, November 2003.
20. Osada R., Funkhouser T., Chazelle B., and Dobkin D. Shape distributions. *ACM Transactions on Grgphics*, 21(4):807–832, 2002.
21. Hou S.Y. and Lou K.Y. Ramani K. Svm-based semantic clustering and retrieval of a 3d model dababase. *Journal of Computer Aided Design and Application*, 2:155–164, 2005.
22. Funkhouser T., Kazhdan M., Min P., and Shilane P. Shape-based retrieval and analysis of 3d models. *Communications of the ACM*, 48(6):58–64, 2005.
23. Regli W.C. and Cicirello V.A. Managing digital libraries for computer-aided design. *Computer-Aided Design*, 32(2):119–132, 2000.

Spatio-temporal Reflectance Sharing for Relightable 3D Video

Naveed Ahmed, Christian Theobalt, and Hans-Peter Seidel

MPI Informatik, Saarbrücken, Germany
{nahmed,theobalt,hpseidel}@mpi-inf.mpg.de
http://www.mpi-inf.mpg.de/

Abstract. In our previous work [21], we have shown that by means of a model-based approach, relightable free-viewpoint videos of human actors can be reconstructed from only a handful of multi-view video streams recorded under calibrated illumination. To achieve this purpose, we employ a marker-free motion capture approach to measure dynamic human scene geometry. Reflectance samples for each surface point are captured by exploiting the fact that, due to the person's motion, each surface location is, over time, exposed to the acquisition sensors under varying orientations. Although this is the first setup of its kind to measure surface reflectance from footage of arbitrary human performances, our approach may lead to a biased sampling of surface reflectance since each surface point is only seen under a limited number of half-vector directions. We thus propose in this paper a novel algorithm that reduces the bias in BRDF estimates of a single surface point by cleverly taking into account reflectance samples from other surface locations made of similar material. We demonstrate the improvements achieved with this spatio-temporal reflectance sharing approach both visually and quantitatively.

1 Introduction

The capturing of relightable dynamic scene descriptions of real-world events requires the proper solution to many different inverse problems. First, the dynamic shape and motion of the objects in the scene have to be captured from multi-view video. Second, the dynamic reflectance properties of the visible surfaces need to be estimated. Due to the inherent computational complexity, it has not been possible yet to solve all these problems for general scenes. However, in previous work [21] we have demonstrated that the commitment to an adaptable a priori shape model enables us to reconstruct relightable 3D videos of one specific type of scene, namely of human actors. By means of a marker-free optical motion capture algorithm, it becomes possible to measure both the shape and the motion of a person from multiple synchronized video streams [2]. If the video footage has, in addition, been captured under calibrated lighting conditions, the video frames showing the moving person not only represent texture samples, but actually reflectance samples. Since a description of time-varying scene geometry

A. Gagalowicz and W. Philips (Eds.): MIRAGE 2007, LNCS 4418, pp. 47–58, 2007.

is at our disposition, we know under what different incoming light and outgoing viewing directions each point on the body surface is seen while the person is moving. It thus becomes feasible to fit to each point on the body surface a static parametric BRDF to describe the material properties, and a time-varying normal to describe the dynamic change in surface geometry. Although we have shown in our previous work that it is feasible to reconstruct dynamic surface reflectance properties using only eight cameras and a static set of light sources, this type of sensor arrangement leads to a biased sampling of the reflectance space. Due to the fixed relative arrangement of lights and cameras, each surface point is only seen under a limited number of half-vector directions. Furthermore, even if an actor performs very expressive motion, surface points will never be seen under all possible relative orientations to the cameras. This bias in the reflectance data leads to a bias in the measured reflectance models which may lead to an unnatural appearance if the 3D videos are rendered under virtual lighting conditions that are starkly different from the measurement setup. We thus propose spatio-temporal reflectance sharing, a method to cleverly combine dynamic reflectance samples from different surface points of similar material during BRDF estimation of one specific surface point. The guiding idea behind the approach is to exploit spatial coherence on the surface to obtain more samples for each texel while not compromising the estimation of spatially-varying details in surface appearance. Temporal coherence is also exploited, since samples are collected by combining measurements from subsequent time steps.

We continue with a review of the most relevant related work in Sect. 2. The acquisition setup, the model-based motion estimation approach, as well as the basic principles of dynamic reflectance estimation are described in Sect. 3. In Sect. 4, we describe the nuts and bolts of our proposed dynamic reflectance sharing approach and show how it fits into the original pipeline. Finally, in Sect. 5 we demonstrate both visually and quantitatively that our novel sampling strategy leads to improved results. We conclude in Sect. 6 and give an outlook to possible future work.

2   Related Work

There is a huge body of literature on the estimation of reflectance properties of static scenes from images that are captured under calibrated setups of light source and camera. Typically, parameters of a BRDF model are fitted to the data [18,11] or appearance under novel lighting conditions is created via interpolation between the images themselves [15]. A combination of reflectance estimation and shape-from-shading to refine the geometry of static scenes is also feasible [25,17,1,4,5]. In an independent line of research, many methods to capture and render 3D videos of real-world scenes have been developed in recent years. A popular category of algorithms employs the shape-from-silhouette principle to reconstruct dynamic scene geometry by means of voxels, polyhedrals or point primitives [14,24,13,6,12]. By finding temporal correspondences between per-time-step reconstructions, it becomes feasible to generate novel animations as well [19]. Another category of approaches reconstructs dynamic scene geometry by means of multi-view stereo [27,9,22]. In any case, time-varying textures for rendering are assembled from the input video streams. In contrast, the authors in their previous work have proposed a model-based approach to free-viewpoint video of human actors that jointly employs a marker-free motion capture method and a dynamic multi-view texture generation approach to produce novel viewpoint renditions [2,20]. Unfortunately, none of the aforementioned methods can correctly reproduce 3D video appearance under novel simulated lighting conditions.

Only few papers have been published so far that aim at relighting of dynamic scenes. In [8], a method to generate animatable and relightable face models from images taken with a special light stage is described. Wenger et al. [23] extend the light stage device such that it enables capturing of dynamic reflectance fields. Their results are impressive, however it is not possible to change the viewpoint in the scene. Einarsson et. al. [3] extends it further by using a large light stage, a trade-mill where the person walks on, and light field rendering for display. Eventually, human performances can be rendered from novel perspectives and relit. Unfortunately the method can only present single periodic motion, such as walking, and is only suitable for low frequency relighting.

In contrast, the authors have proposed a model-based method for reconstructing relightable free-viewpoint videos that extends measurement principles for static parametric reflectance models to dynamic scenes [21]. For our 3D video scenario, we prefer a compact scene description based on parametric BRDFs that can be reconstructed in a fairly simple acquisition facility. This paper proposes a novel solution to one important subproblem in the overall process, namely the clever sampling of surface reflectance in order to minimize the bias in the estimated BRDFs. This work has been inspired by the reflectance sharing method of Zickler et al. to reconstruct appearance of static scenes [26]. By regarding reflectance estimation as a scattered interpolation problem, they can exploit spatial coherence to obtain more reliable surface estimate. Our algorithm exploits both spatial and temporal coherence to reliably estimate dynamic reflectance. However, since a full-blown scattered data interpolation would be illusive with our huge sets of samples, we propose a faster heuristic approach to reflectance sharing.

3   Relightable Free-Viewpoint Video of Human Actors–Preliminaries

The algorithm presented in this paper is a methodical improvement of one important step within a larger framework to reconstruct and render relightable free-viewpoint videos of human actors [21]. Although the algorithmic details of this framework, as a whole, are not the subject of this paper, for better understanding in the following we briefly elaborate on the acquisition setup used, as well as the employed model-based marker-less motion capture algorithm. Thereafter, we describe the basic principles of dynamic reflectometry that was used in

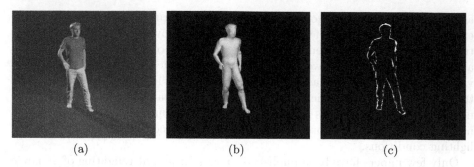

Fig. 1. (a) Input frame, (b) body model in same pose, and (c) silhouette matching

the original pipeline in order to motivate where the novel algorithm described in Sect. 4 comes into play.

3.1 Acquisition

Inputs to our method are synchronized multi-view video sequences captured with eight calibrated cameras that feature 1004x1004 pixel image sensors and record at 25 fps. The cameras are placed in an approximately circular arrangement around the center of the scene which is illuminated by two calibrated spot lights. Since we conceptually separate the BRDF estimation from the estimation of the dynamic normal maps, we record two types of multi-view video sequence for each person and each type of apparel. In the first type of sequence, the so-called reflectance estimation sequence (RES), the person performs a simple rotation if front of the acquisition setup. One RES is recorded for each actor and each type of apparel, and it is later used to reconstruct the per-texel BRDF models. In the second type of sequence, the so-called dynamic scene sequence (DSS), the actor performs arbitrary movements. Several DSS are recorded, and from each of them, one relightable free-viewpoint video clip is reconstructed. Also the second component of our dynamic reflectance model, the dynamic normal maps, are reconstructed from each DSS.

3.2 Reconstructing Dynamic Human Shape and Motion

We employ an analysis-through-synthesis approach to capture both shape and motion of the actor from multi-view video footage without having to resort to optical markers in the scene. It employs a template human body model consisting of a kinematic skeleton and a single-skin triangle mesh surface geometry [2,20]. In an initialization step, the shape and proportions of the template are matched to the recorded silhouettes of the actor. After shape initialization, the model is made to follow the motion of the actor over time by inferring optimal pose parameters at each time step of video using the same silhouette matching principle, Fig. 1. We apply this dynamic shape reconstruction framework to every time step of each captured sequence, i.e. both RES and DSS. This way, we know for each time step of video the orientation of each surface point with respect to the

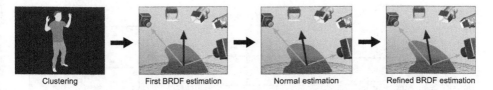

Clustering   First BRDF estimation   Normal estimation   Refined BRDF estimation

Fig. 2. Steps to estimate per-texel BRDFs

acquisition setup which is a precondition for the subsequent dynamic reflectometry procedure.

3.3   Dynamic Reflectometry

Our dynamic reflectance model consists of two components, a static parametric isotropic BRDF for each surface point [16,10], as well as a description of the time-varying direction of the normal at each surface location. The first component of the reflectance model is reconstructed from the video frames of the reflectance estimation sequence, the second component is reconstructed from each dynamic scene sequence. We formulate BRDF reconstruction as an energy minimization problem in the BRDF parameters [21]. This minimization problem has to be solved for each surface point separately.

The energy functional measures the error between the recorded reflectance samples of the point under consideration and the predicted surface appearance according to the current BRDF parameters. Given estimates of the BRDF parameters, we can also refine our knowledge about surface geometry by keeping the reflectance parameters fixed and minimizing the same functional in the normal direction, Fig 2. Once the BRDF parameters have been recovered from the RES, a similar minimization procedure is used to reconstruct the time-varying normal field from each DSS.

Before estimation commences, the surface model is parameterized over the plane and all video frames are transformed into textures. The estimation process is complicated by the fact that our shape model is only an approximation. Furthermore, potential shifting of the apparel over the body surface while the person is moving contradicts our assumption that we can statically assign material properties to individual surface points. We counter the first problem by means of an image-based warp correction step, and solve the latter problem by detecting and compensating textile shift in the texture domain. For details on each of these steps, please refer to [21].

In the original pipeline, as it was summarized above, we have estimated BRDF parameters for each surface point by taking only reflectance samples of this particular point itself into account [21]. In the following, we present a novel spatio-temporal sampling scheme that reduces the risks of a bias in the BRDF estimates by also taking into account dynamic reflectance samples from other surface points with similar material properties.

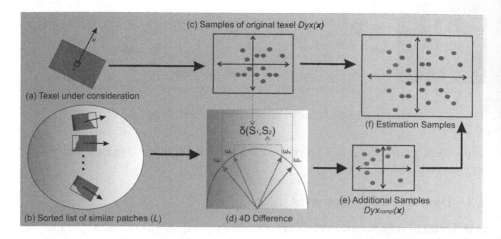

Fig. 3. Weighted selection of samples. Samples from the similar patches are added to the samples from the original texel. Additional samples are selected according to a weighting criteria that is based on their maximum angular difference from the samples of original texel.

4   Spatio-temporal Reflectance Sharing

By looking at its appearance from each camera view over time, we can generate for each surface point, or equivalently, for each texel x a set of N appearance samples

$$\text{Dyx}(x) = \{S_i \mid S_i = (I_i, \hat{l}_i, \hat{v}_i), i \in \{1, \dots, N\}\} \qquad (1)$$

Each sample S_i stores a tuple of data comprising of the captured image intensity I_i (from one of the cameras), the direction to the light source $\hat{l}_i$, and the viewing direction $\hat{v}_i$. Please note that only if a point has been illuminated by exactly one light source, a sample is generated. If a point is totally in shadow, illuminated by two light sources, or not seen from the camera, no sample is created. Our acquisition setup comprising of only 8 cameras and 2 light sources is comparably simple and inexpensive. However, the fixed relative arrangement of cameras and light sources may induce a bias in $\text{Dyx}(x)$. There are two primary reasons for this:

– Due to the fixed relative arrangement of cameras and light sources, each surface point is only seen under a fixed number of half vector directions $\hat{h} = \hat{l} + \hat{v}$.
– Even if the person performs a very expressive motion in the RES, samples lie on "slices" of the hemispherical space of possible incoming light and outgoing viewing directions.

Both of these factors possibly lead to BRDF estimates that may not generalize well to lighting conditions that are very different to the acquisition setup.

By means of a novel spatio-temporal sampling strategy, called spatio-temporal reflectance sharing, we can reduce the bias, Fig. 3. The guiding idea behind this

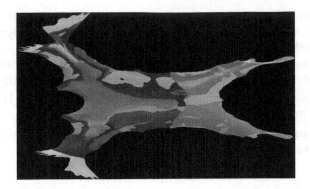

Fig. 4. Texture-space layout of surface patches. Patches of same material are clustered according to the average normal direction. For this illustration, patches of the same material are colored in the same overall tone (e.g. blue for the shirt) but different intensities.

novel scheme is to use more than the samples $\text{Dyx}(x)$ that have been measured for the point x itself while the BRDF parameters for the point x are estimated. The additional samples, combined in a set $\text{Dyx}_{\text{compl}}(x)$, stem from other locations on the surface that are made of similar material. These additional samples have potentially been seen under different lighting and viewing directions than the samples from $\text{Dyx}(x)$ and can thus expand the sampling range. It is the main challenge to incorporate these samples into the reflectance estimation at x in a way that augments the generality of the measured BRDFs but does not compromise the ability to capture spatial variation in surface appearance.

By explaining each step that is taken to draw samples for a particular surface point x, we illustrate how we attack this challenge:

In a first step, the surface is clustered into patches of similar average normal directions and same material, Fig. 4. Materials are clustered by means of a simple k-means clustering using average diffuse colors [21]. The normal direction $\hat{n}$ of x defines the reference normal direction, Fig. 3a. Now, a list L of patches consisting of the same material as x is generated. L is sorted according to increasing angular deviation of average patch normal direction and reference normal direction, Fig. 3b. Now, n_p many patches $P_0, ..., P_{n_p}$ are drawn from L by choosing every lth list element. From each patch, a texel is selected at random, resulting in a set of texels, $T = x_{P_0}, ..., x_{P_{n_p}}$. The set of texels T has been selected in a way that maximizes the number of different surface orientations. From the reflectance samples associated with texels in T, we now select a subset $\text{Dyx}_{\text{compl}}(x)$ that maximizes the coverage of the 4D hemispherical space of light and view directions. In order to decide which samples from T are potential candidates for this set, we employ the following selection mechanism.

A weighting function $\delta(S_1, S_2)$ is applied that measures the difference of two samples $S_1 = (\hat{l}_1, \hat{v}_1)$ and $S_2 = (\hat{l}_2, \hat{v}_2)$ in the 4D sample space as follows:

$$\delta(S_1, S_2) = \Delta(\hat{l}_1, \hat{l}_2) + \Delta(\hat{v}_1, \hat{v}_2) \tag{2}$$

where Δ denotes the angular difference between two vectors. We employ δ to select for each sample S_r in T its closest sample S_{closest} in $\text{Dyx}(x)$, i.e. the sample for which $\omega_{S_r} = \delta(S_r, S_{\text{closest}})$ is minimal, Fig. 3d. Each sample S_r is now weighted by ω_{S_r}. Only the $\lceil \alpha N \rceil$ samples from T with the highest weights eventually find their way into $\text{Dyx}_{\text{compl}}(x)$, Fig. 3e. The BRDF parameters for x are estimated by taking all of the samples from $\text{Dyx}(x) \bigcup \text{Dyx}_{\text{compl}}(x)$ into account, Fig. 3f. Through experiments we have found out that a value of $\alpha = 0.66$ represents a good compromise between estimation robustness and increase in computation time.

5   Results

We have tested our spatio-temporal reflectance sharing method on several input sequences. The sequences of 150-300 frames cover two different human subjects with different types of apparel. The method integrates seamlessly in the original pipeline and no modifications of any kind are required for the rendering system. We have verified both visually and quantitatively that our novel reflectance sampling method leads to BRDF estimation that generalizes better to lighting conditions different from the acquisition setup. Fig. 5 shows a side-by-side comparison between the results obtained with and without spatio-temporal reflectance sharing. Both human subjects are rendered under real world illumination using HDR environment maps. Importance sampling is used to obtain direction light sources that approximate the lighting from the static environment map [7]. Relightable free-viewpoint videos can be rendered from arbitrary viewpoints and under arbitrary lighting conditions at 6 fps if 16 approximating lights are employed. One can see that with the exploitation of spatial coherence, more surface detail is preserved under those lighting conditions which are strongly different from acquisition setup. A small comparison video demonstrating only the relighting can be seen here: http://www.mpi-inf.mpg.de/~nahmed/Mirage2007.avi.

In addition to visual comparison, we also validated the method by comparing the average peak-signal-to-noise-ratio with respect to input video stream obtained under different lighting conditions. We have recorded one of our male test subjects under two different calibrated lighting setups, henceforth termed LC A and LC B. In each of the lighting setups, just one spot light has been employed. The positions of the light sources in LC A and LC B are (angularly) approximately 45° apart with respect to the center of the scene. We reconstructed the BRDF of the test subject under lighting setup LC B with and without our new reflectance sampling. Subsequently, we calculated the PSNR with the ground truth images of the person illuminated under setup LC A. Using our novel sampling method, we have estimated surface reflectance using different percentages of additional samples. For each case, we computed the PSNR with respect to the ground truth. Fig. 6 shows the results that we obtained. Note that the graph of the original method (green line) is constant over the increasing number of samples just for the illustration purpose because it only considers the samples from a single texel. With spatio-temporal reflectance sharing (red line) both results

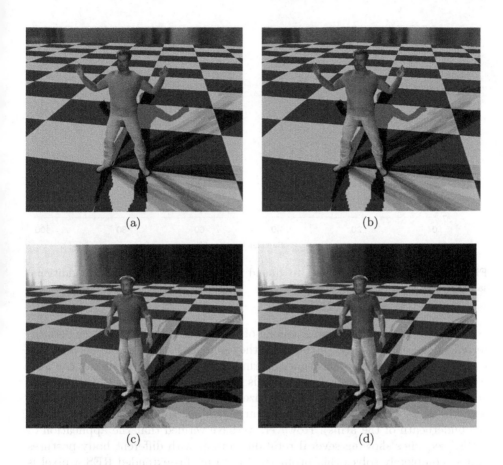

(a)   (b)

(c)   (d)

Fig. 5. Comparison of renditions under captured real-world illumination such as the St Peter's Basilica environment map (a),(b) and the Grace Cathedral environment (c),(d) provided by Paul Debevec. One can see that compared to renditions obtained without spatio-temporal reflectance sharing ((a) (c)), subtle surface details are much better reproduced in the renditions obtained with spatio-temporal reflectance sharing ((b) (d)).

are exactly the same in the beginning as no additional samples are considered, but it can be seen that the PSNR improves as additional samples are taken into account. We get a peak at around 30%-40% of additional samples. With the inclusion of more samples the PSNR gradually decreases as the ever increasing number of additional samples compromises the estimation of the reflectance's spatial variance. At maximum, we obtain a PSNR improvement of 0.75 dB. Although we have performed the PSNR evaluation only for one sequence, we are confident that for others it will exhibit similar results. This assumption is further supported by the more compelling visual appearance obtained for all the other test data that we have used.

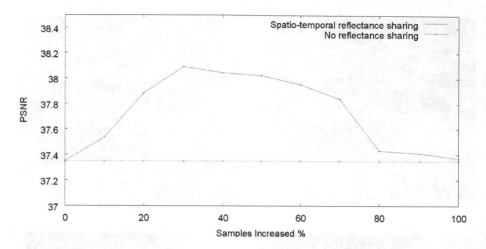

Fig. 6. PSNR values with respect to ground truth for different numbers of additional samples $Dyx_{compl}(x)$

Our approach is subject to a couple of limitations. We currently neglect interreflections on the body. In the RES, they potentially play a role between the wrinkles in clothing. For reflectance sharing, samples from the wrinkles can lead to erroneous estimation. To prevent this effect from degrading the estimation accuracy, we have taken care to minimize the number of wrinkles in the RES. Sometimes, we observe small rendering artefacts due to undersampling (e.g. on the underneath of the arms). However, we have verified that the application of a RES sequence showing several rotation motions with different body postures almost completely solves this problem. If even in this extended RES a pixel is never seen by any of the cameras, we fill in reflectance properties from neighboring regions in texture space.

Despite the limitations, our results show that spatio-temporal reflectance sharing enable faithful estimation of dynamic reflectance models with only a handful of cameras.

6   Conclusions

We have presented a spatio-temporal reflectance sharing method that reduces the bias in BRDF estimation for dynamic scenes. Our algorithm exploits spatial coherence by pooling samples of different surface location to robustify reflectance estimation. In addition, it exploits temporal coherence by taking into consideration samples from different steps of video. Despite the spatial-temporal resampling, our algorithm is capable of reliably capturing spatially-varying reflectance properties. By means of spatio-temporal reflectance sharing, we obtain convincing 3D video renditions in real-time even under lighting conditions which differ strongly from the acquisition setup.

Acknowledgements

This project has been supported by EU 3DTV NoE project No 511568.

References

1. Fausto Bernardini, Ioana M. Martin, and Holly Rushmeier. High-quality texture reconstruction from multiple scans. *IEEE TVCG*, 7(4):318–332, 2001.
2. J. Carranza, C. Theobalt, M.A. Magnor, and H.-P. Seidel. Free-viewpoint video of human actors. In *Proc. of SIGGRAPH'03*, pages 569–577, 2003.
3. Per Einarsson, Charles-Felix Chabert, Andrew Jones, Wan-Chun Ma, Bruce Lamond, im Hawkins, Mark Bolas, Sebastian Sylwan, and Paul Debevec. Relighting human locomotion with flowed reflectance fields. In *Rendering Techniques*, pages 183–194, 2006.
4. Athinodoros S. Georghiades. Recovering 3-d shape and reflectance from a small number of photographs. In *Eurographics Symposium on Rendering*, pages 230–240, 2003.
5. D. Goldman, B. Curless, A. Hertzmann, and S. Seitz. Shape and spatially-varying brdfs from photometric stereo. In *Proc. of ICCV*, pages 341–448, 2004.
6. Markus H. Gross, Stephan Würmlin, Martin Näf, Edouard Lamboray, Christian P. Spagno, Andreas M. Kunz, Esther Koller-Meier, Tomás Svoboda, Luc J. Van Gool, Silke Lang, Kai Strehlke, Andrew Vande Moere, and Oliver G. Staadt. blue-c: a spatially immersive display and 3d video portal for telepresence. *ACM Trans. Graph. (Proc. of SIGGRAPH'03)*, 22(3):819–827, 2003.
7. Vlastimil Havran, Miloslaw Smyk, Grzegorz Krawczyk, Karol Myszkowski, and Hans-Peter Seidel. Importance Sampling for Video Environment Maps. In *ACM SIGGRAPH 2005 Full Conference DVD-ROM*, Los Angeles, USA, August 2005. ACM SIGGRAPH, ACM. Sketches & Applications.
8. T. Hawkins, A. Wenger, C. Tchou, A. Gardner, F. Göransson, and P. Debevec. Animatable facial reflectance fields. In *Proc. of Eurographics Symposium on Rendering*, pages 309–319, 2004.
9. Takeo Kanade, Peter Rander, and P. J. Narayanan. Virtualized reality: Constructing virtual worlds from real scenes. *IEEE MultiMedia*, 4(1):34–47, 1997.
10. E. Lafortune, S. Foo, K. Torrance, and D. Greenberg. "non-linear approximation of reflectance functions". In *Proceedings of SIGGRAPH'97*, pages 117–126, August 1997.
11. Hendrik P. A. Lensch, Jan Kautz, Michael Goesele, Wolfgang Heidrich, and Hans-Peter Seidel. Image-based reconstruction of spatial appearance and geometric detail. *ACM Transactions on Graphics*, 22(2):27, 2003.
12. Ming Li, Hartmut Schirmacher, Marcus Magnor, and Hans-Peter Seidel. Combining stereo and visual hull information for on-line reconstruction and rendering of dynamic scenes. In *Proc. of IEEE Multimedia and Signal Processing*, pages 9–12, 2002.
13. T. Matsuyama and T. Takai. Generation, visualization, and editing of 3D video. In *Proc. of 1st International Symposium on 3D Data Processing Visualization and Transmission (3DPVT'02)*, page 234ff, 2002.
14. W. Matusik, C. Buehler, R. Raskar, S.J. Gortler, and L. McMillan. Image-based visual hulls. In *Proceedings of ACM SIGGRAPH 00*, pages 369–374, 2000.

15. W. Matusik, H. Pfister, M. Brand, and L. McMillan. A data-driven reflectance model. *ACM Trans. Graph. (Proc. SIGGRAPH'03)*, 22(3):759–769, 2003.
16. B.-T. Phong. Illumnation for computer generated pictures. *Communications of the ACM*, pages 311–317, 1975.
17. H. Rushmeier, G. Taubin, and A. Guéziec. Applying Shape from Lighting Variation to Bump Map Capture. In *Eurographics Workshop on Rendering*, pages 35–44, June 1997.
18. Yoichi Sato, Mark D. Wheeler, and Katsushi Ikeuchi. Object Shape and Reflectance Modeling from Observation. In *Proc. of SIGGRAPH'97*, pages 379–388, 1997.
19. J. Starck, G. Miller, and A. Hilton. Video-based character animation. In *Proc. ACM Symposium on Computer Animation*, 2005.
20. C. Theobalt, J. Carranza, M. Magnor, and H.-P. Seidel. Combining 3d flow fields with silhouette-based human motion capture for immersive video. *Graphical Models*, 66:333–351, September 2004.
21. Christian Theobalt, Naveed Ahmed, Hendrik P. A. Lensch, Marcus Magnor, and Hans-Peter Seidel. Seeing people in different light - joint shape, motion and reflectance capture. *IEEE Transactions on Visualization and Computer Graphics*, to appear.
22. M. Waschbüsch, S. Würmlin, D. Cotting, F. Sadlo, and M. Gross. Scalable 3D video of dynamic scenes. In *Proc. of Pacific Graphics*, pages 629–638, 2005.
23. A. Wenger, A. Gardner, C. Tchou, J. Unger, T. Hawkins, and P. Debevec. Performance relighting and reflectance transformation with time-multiplexed illumination. In *ACM TOG (Proc. of SIGGRAPH'05)*, volume 24(3), pages 756–764, 2005.
24. S. Würmlin, E. Lamboray, O.G. Staadt, and M.H. Gross. 3d video recorder. In *Proc. of IEEE Pacific Graphics*, pages 325–334, 2002.
25. Ruo Zhang, Ping-Sing Tsai, James Cryer, and Mubarak Shah. Shape from Shading: A Survey. *IEEE Trans. PAMI*, 21(8):690–706, 1999.
26. Todd Zickler, Sebastian Enrique, Ravi Ramamoorthi, and Peter N. Belhumeur. Reflectance sharing: Image-based rendering from a sparse set of images. In *Proc. of Eurographics Symposium on Rendering*, pages 253–264, 2005.
27. C. Lawrence Zitnick, Sing Bing Kang, Matthew Uyttendaele, Simon Winder, and Richard Szeliski. High-quality video view interpolation using a layered representation. *ACM TOC (Proc. SIGGRAPH'04)*, 23(3):600–608, 2004.

Interactive Hierarchical Level of Detail Level Selection Algorithm for Point Based Rendering

XueMei Lu, Ki-Jung Lee, and Taeg-Keun Whangbo

Dept. of Computer Science, Kyungwon University,
Sujung-Gu, Songnam, Kyunggi-Do, 461-701, Korea
bingqing@ku.kyungwon.ac.kr,
{lkj9731,tkwhangbo}@kyungwon.ac.kr

Abstract. As the sampling data is getting tremendous, more than one sampling points will project into a pixel. This makes point based rendering (PBR) popular. For PBR, the main steps that prominently affect the rendering result are hierarchical data structure, LOD selection method and rendering primitives (triangle, point, surfel [1]). In this paper, we generate a hierarchical structure with tight-octree, and store the vertex and bounding box information for each level. Then we propose a new method to do LOD selection based on the distance between the model and the viewer and the pre-calculated bounding box information. We have tested different polygonal models with million vertices on our system and the results demonstrate that the method is interactive in real time.

1 Introduction

Point based rendering has become more and more popular these days. As the development of 3D scanning technologies, the sampling data has come to million or even larger amount. When rendering such large models, more than one sampling points will project into a pixel. In this case, rendering point directly instead of generating other rendering primitive will achieve better performance, because of its simplicity and efficiency.

Benefiting of three situations: more than one sampling points will project into a pixel; large datasets will occupy too much memory; and when the user transforms the object, or changes the viewer position, the model position is changed and we need to do LOD level selection again, we generate a system with tight-octree data structure and a new LOD level selection method.

Firstly, we use DFS method to construct a hierarchical data structure using tight-octree. Then using BFS to traverse the tree, the representative vertices of each node in the same level will compose one level of detail of the model. Then we write the level information back into file. When the model position has changed, by recalculating the pixel size, and comparing with the bounding box information in each level, we can decide to add or remove the data to the rendering vertex list and re-rendering the model. The algorithm sequence is shown in Fig.1.

A. Gagalowicz and W. Philips (Eds.): MIRAGE 2007, LNCS 4418, pp. 59–69, 2007.

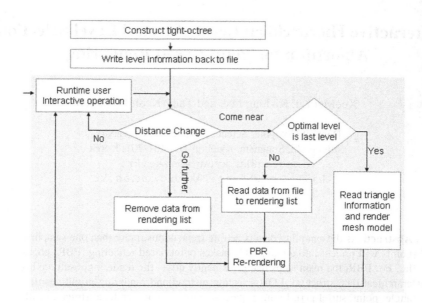

Fig. 1. Algorithm Sequence

Experimenting on models with a million points, we get high quality rendering result. In addition, switching between levels is interactive in real-time display. Normal and color information is added to the rendering model. In order to avoid occupying too much memory, we write back the hierarchical data structure only adds 42 Bytes information for each level to the original data, and it is constructed once and can be used in various.

Our paper contributes to the following two areas: 1. appropriate hierarchical data structure for PBR; 2. efficient method for selecting the proper LOD level in hierarchical structure.

The remainder of this paper is organized as follows. Section 2 gives the related works on PBR and LOD level selection. Part 3 introduces the pre-process of our system. Part 4 explains how to choose the optimal LOD level in detail. Part 5 shows the experiment data and comparison with other method. Part 6 is the conclusion and future work.

2 Related Works

Advances in scanning technology have allowed researchers to acquire models with millions of points and triangles. There have been many methods developed for representing and accelerating rendering of large data.

2.1 Point and Triangle Based Rendering

Polygonal model, especially triangle is the de facto standard geometry representation in computer graphics [12-14]. This is chiefly because of their mathematical simplicity: polygonal models lend themselves to simple, regular rendering algorithms that embed well in hardware, which has in turn led to widely available polygon rendering accelerators for every platform. Polygonal simplification techniques offer one solution for developers grappling with complex models.

Compared with traditional primitives like triangle mesh, points have shown their advantage such as rendering efficiency and freedom from connectivity. Using points as display primitives was first suggested by Marc Levoy [2] in 1985. In 1994, Hoppe [3] gave a raw point set data with no other information to reconstruct the surface. P.Grossman and others [4] detected the fundamental problem in point based rendering: closing any holes to correctly reconstruct the surface. In most recent days, a multi-resolution point rendering system called QSplat was developed by Szymon et.al. [5]. H.Pfister et.al [1] proposed a surfel as rendering primitives to produce high quality pictures. In addition, many efforts have been made to contribute to the point based rendering by improving hardware acceleration [6].

2.2 Simplification Method

There have been many simplification methods both based on polygonal mesh and directly based on point cloud. One of them is iterative simplification. It iteratively contracts point pairs. Contractions are arranged in priority queue according to quadric error metric [8] or energy function Hoppe [9]. Another simplification method is clustering vertices and filtering degenerate triangle. First proposed by Rossignac and Borrel in 1992[10], vertex clustering remains one of the most useful LOD algorithms to date because of its robust, fast and simple to implement. Other researchers have extended the original clustering method [10]. Multiple graphics packages and toolkits have implemented vertex clustering for simple and efficient LOD generation. Another simplification method is particle simulation [11], it resample surface by distributing particles on the surface. Particles move on surface according to repulsion force, and particle relaxation terminates when equilibrium is reached.

2.3 LOD Selection

The most important issue in rendering any model with LOD (levels-of-detail) is to find a criterion by which the system can automatically select a proper level of detail for rendering [16]. A distance-based framework needs a data structure to store the different levels of detail for each object, and a list of distance thresholds to indicate when each LOD should be used. Then it compares the distance from observer to object with the threshold and select the appropriate level. Size-based LOD selection uses the entire object projected size on screen space. This method is particularly popular in continuous and view-dependent LOD systems, such as in the area of terrain visualization. A priority-based solution is proposed to rank object, this is particularly important for preserving the illusion of the scene and the user's acceptance of that illusion. Many other LOD selections are discussed in [7]. Interactive LOD level selection has been introduced in [18] with different data structure supporting. A compact data structure call half-edge tree was introduced in [19].

3 Preprocessing

3.1 Construct Hierarchical Structure

Tight-octree is firstly proposed by Luebke and Erikson [15]. In a tight-octree, each node of the octree is tightened to the smallest axis-aligned bounding cube that enclosed the relevant vertices before subdividing further, as shown in Fig.2 (a).

We start our algorithm by defining the tight-octree node type. Each node stores a representative vertex, the number of vertices in this node, the bounding box width and height, and the pointers to its eight sub-nodes. We calculate the normal of each vertex by adding up the normals of its adjacent triangles.

For all the points in one node, we use a MLS (Mean Least Square) to find a point that is nearest to the average point of all the vertices in this node and set it as the representative vertex of this octant. To get the bounding box of each node, we find the maximum and minimum coordinates of x, y, z-axis. Therefore, the bounding box is axis-aligned. We record the length, width, and height of bounding box in each level in memory when constructing the tree.

We use a recursive method to generate the tight-octree in depth first method. Firstly, we find the bounding box for the whole model. Then we divide the bounding box into eight octants. By examining the coordinate of each vertex, we divide all the vertices into each octant. Then for each octant we recursively do the same step as the top level, until only one vertex in each octant. The final hierarchy is shown in Fig.2 (b).

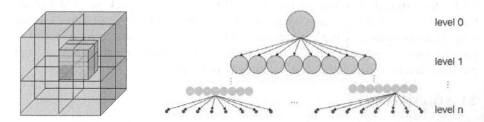

Fig. 2. (a) Tight bounding box (b) Hierarchical structure with different bounding box size

3.2 Store Hierarchical Structure

We use BFS to traverse the tree and make a list to store the representative vertex and the bounding box information of each node in the hierarchical structure.

When constructing the tight-octree, we record the bounding box information, the length, width, and height for each node. However, in LOD selection process, not all these information is needed. In order to guarantee all the projected size of bounding boxes in optimal level are smaller than or equal to the pixel size. We can only use the bounding box that has the biggest projected size. Because of rotation, translation, scaling or changing of eye position, the projected area of bounding box is changing, but it always relates to the edge length of the biggest bounding box in this level, as shown in Fig.3. Therefore, we only record the biggest bounding box length in each axis.

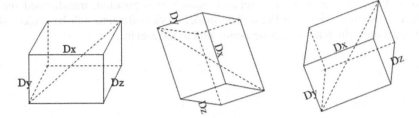

Fig. 3. No matter how we transfer the model or change the eye position, All the bounding box projected size will be always less than body diagonal of the big bounding box in this level. When scale the model, we only need to scale the body diagonal correspondingly.

The file is written in level sequence. The head information of each level includes the level number, the representative vertices index in this level, and the biggest bounding box length in each axis. Since we only add the level information to the original file. This process can be done in real-time. All the points in the upper level are contributed to the current level, which means we only have to add the lower levels data to zoom in or remove upper levels data to zoom out. We render all the vertices from top level to the optimal level according to the interactive information. How to choose the optimal level is given in section 4.

4   LOD Selection

A new LOD selection method is proposed in this paper. It depends on the distance from observer to the object and switches between levels by a constraint that: All the projected bounding box size in one level should equal to the pixel size, if not, it should be less than the pixel size. With this constraint, the algorithm can guarantee the there are no holes on the final image.

The constraint of our algorithm can be changed into: The biggest bounding box projected size in this level is equal to or less than the pixel size. We firstly define that viewport size is same as the window size, suppose both the resolution is window_resolution_width x window_reslolution_height in unit of pixel. Then we define the view frustum in world space. After transformation and projection, the 3D model in view frustum will be projected to the viewport.

We will explain our method to get the pixel size in the following section.

4.1   Pixel Size in Perspective Projection

Let's review the fundamental transformation of 3D model. Supposing the transfer matrix is Model_matrix, and the current vertex coordinates is (x, y, z), the transferred coordinates will be:

$$(transf\_x, transf\_y, transf\_z) = Model\_matrix * (x, y, z). \qquad (1)$$

Supposing the view frustum is (left, right, top, bottom, zNear, zFar) and the eye position is eye (eyeX, eyeY, eyeZ). Since changing the eyes position equals to transforming the model and keeping the eye position, we denote the vertex coordinates as (transf_x, transf_y, transf_z). The relation among eyes position, transformed model and view frustum is shown in Fig.4. The model in view frustum will be projected to the image plane which at –zNear perpendicular to the z-axis.

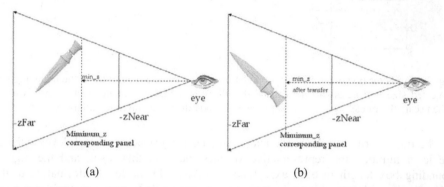

(a)   (b)

Fig. 4. Calculating the width and height of min_z corresponding plane. The min_z corresponding plane will be projected to the image plane which at position –zNear on z axis.

We calculate the current corresponding plane size according to Fig.4 as:

$$\frac{min\_z\_corresponding\_plane\_width}{right - left} = \frac{|min\_z|}{|eyeZ - zNear|}$$

$$\frac{min\_z\_corresponding\_plane\_height}{top - bottom} = \frac{|min\_z|}{|eyeZ - zNear|} \quad (2)$$

Since the current corresponding plane will project to the viewport, we get the current pixel size as:

$$pixel\_width = \frac{|eyeZ - zNear|*(right - left)}{|min\_z|*window\_resolution\_width}$$

$$pixel\_height = \frac{|eyeZ - zNear|*(top - bottom)}{|min\_z|*window\_resolution\_height} \quad (3)$$

As Fig.5 shows, even the same length line will not have same projected length. That is to say, the pixels' sizes will not be the same in perspective projection. In order to simplify the problem, we still use formulation (3) to calculate the pixel size. Even though there is an error, the experiment result can satisfy the requirement.

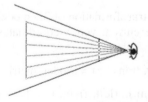

Fig. 5. Pixels' sizes are different in perspective projection

4.2 LOD Level Selection

After getting the pixel size, we check the bounding box size (BB_width x BB_height) in each level from the top in tight-octree hierarchy. The level is the optimal level for the current situation which bounding box satisfies: BB_width ≤ Pixel_with && BB_height ≤ Pixel_height.

The pixel size is always changing according to the distance that between the plane in the view frustum and the viewer changing. If the viewer changes the view position, the pixel size will change too. We calculate the pixel size by examining the model position in the view frustum; once the model transformed or the eye position changed, find the optimal level again. If the new optimal level is smaller than the previous optimal level, that means, the object moves further from the viewer, we need to remove vertices.

In Fig.6 (a), we suppose the former optimal level is level n, and the new optimal level is level k. We know the vertices number in each level, so we delete the data from list directly, as Fig.6 (c). If the new optimal level is larger than the old optimal level, as Fig.6 (b), that means the object gets closer to the viewer, we need to read the vertices from level k+1 to level n from the file and add them to the list. All the operation we mentioned above is based on the fact that our hierarchical data structure satisfies that the upper levels data are all included in the lower levels, as explained in section3.

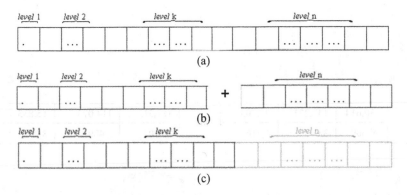

Fig. 6. The rendering vertex list

The translation, rotation of model and the change of eye position will affect the distance between viewer and model, which will affect the pixel size. The algorithm keeps on finding the optimal level and switching from one level to another corresponding to the interactive information. When the optimal level is the last level of the tree, and the viewer comes nearer, even we render all the vertices, holes will come out. In that situation, we will read the triangle information from original ply file, and with all the vertex information in rendering list, render the mesh model instead of PBR.

5   Experiment Data

The experiment results show in Table1 and Fig.7. The experiment data file size ranges form 13,574k to 86,306k, vertex number ranges from 249,284 to 1,098,617. There is no hole on each LOD level model, and LOD level selection is user interactively.

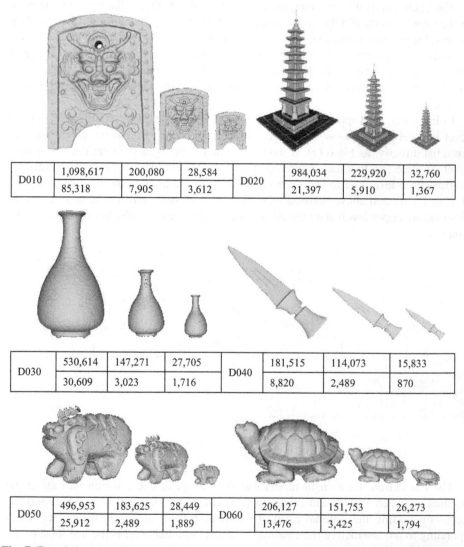

D010	1,098,617	200,080	28,584	D020	984,034	229,920	32,760
	85,318	7,905	3,612		21,397	5,910	1,367

D030	530,614	147,271	27,705	D040	181,515	114,073	15,833
	30,609	3,023	1,716		8,820	2,489	870

D050	496,953	183,625	28,449	D060	206,127	151,753	26,273
	25,912	2,489	1,889		13,476	3,425	1,794

Fig. 7. Experiment data: The data in upper row are the vertices numbers, the lower rows are the number of pixels the image occupied on 800x600-resolution window

In loading process, we read the all the original data form ply file, normalize the vertex coordinates, and compute the face normal for each triangle. Then we make a hierarchical tight-octree and write the levels information into files. LOD level selection process includes getting the optimal level according to the distance, and switching between levels. Each process experiment times show in Table1.

Table 1. Experiment Data on Our System

Model	No. of vertex	Load File & NAN (ms)	MHT (ms)	LOD Level Selection	
				Come near (ms)	Go further (ms)
D010	1,098,617	13,687	31,610	94+2,013	94+35
D020	984,034	12,656	28,063	94+1,656	94+3
D030	530,614	6,485	14,703	94+984	94+16
D040	181,515	2,234	4,859	94+313	94+15
D050	496,953	6,828	14,281	94+828	94+16
D060	206,127	2,532	5,344	94+344	94+15

MHT: Make Hierarchical Tight-octree.
NAN: Normalize vertices coordinates and get normal of each vertex.
Note: The values in Come near column are the time read data from lowermost level to uppermost level, and the values in Go further column are the times delete data from uppermost level to lowermost level. 94 ms is the time to select the optimal level.

Compared to the progressive mesh simplification (PMesh), in Table2, our preprocess time is less than PMesh pre-process., including loading files, calculating the normals of vertices, making tight-octree, and writing back files. PMesh uses too much time when deal with huge data that we only compare D030 and D040 small models. Loading and building edge list including the time that writes the hierarchical information back to files. In LOD level selection, 94ms is the time to get the optimal level index. The latter part data is the maximum time to read data or erase data from rendering vertex list. Although our method takes time in LOD levels switching when adding or removing data, it is in real time.

Table 2. Compare with PMesh

PMesh	No. of Vertex	Loading and Building edge list	LOD Level Selection	
D040	249,284	11,890ms	16ms (add or remove 40 triangles)	
D030	530,614	1,145,297ms		
Our Method	No. of Vertex	Loading, Making and writing back tight-octree	LOD Level Selection	
D040	249,284	11,890ms	come near	94+313ms
			go further	94+15ms
D030	530,614	41,751ms	come near	94+984ms
			go further	94+16ms

6 Conclusion and Future Work

We have constructed a hierarchical data structure using tight-octree, the representative vertices in each node in the same level will compose one level of detail of the model. Since the tremendous data will occupy too much memory, we write the level information back. When the user transforms the object, or changes the viewer position, the model will move nearer or further. By recalculating the pixel size, and comparing with the bounding box information in each level, we can decide to add the lower levels vertices to the rendering vertex list or remove the upper levels vertices form the rendering vertex list.

Acknowledgement

This research was supported by the Ministry of Education, Seoul, Korea, under the BK21 project. The contact author of this paper is Taeg-Keun Whangbo (tkwhangbo@kyungwon.ac.kr).

References

1. Pfister, H., Zwicker, M., van Baar, J. and Gross, M., 2000. Surfels: Surface elements as rendering primitives. Computer Graphics, ACM Press / ACM SIGGRAPH / Addison Wesley Longman, K. Akeley (ed.), Siggraph (2000), 335-342.
2. Marc Levoy,   Turner Whitted , The Use of Points as a Display Primitive Technical Report 85-022, Computer Science Department, University of North Carolina at Chapel Hill(1985).
3. Hugues Hoppe, Derose T., Duchamp T., Mcdonald J., Stuetzie W.: Surface Reconstruction from Unorganized Points, PhD Thesis, Depart-ment of Computer Science and Engineering, University of Washington. In Proc. ACM SIGGRAPH (1992), 71-78.
4. Grossman, J.P., and William J. Dally, "Point Sample Rendering", 9th Eurographics Workshop on Rendering, August (1998), 181-192.
5. Szymon Rusinkiewicz and Marc Levoy, "QSplat: A Multiresolution Point Rendering System for Large Meshes", to appear in Proc. SIGGRAPH 2000, July (2000), 343-351.
6. BOTSCH M., KOBBELT L.: High-quality point-based rendering on modern GPUs. In Proceedings of Pacific Graphics 2003 (2003), 335-343.
7. David Luebke, Beniamin Watson, Level of Detail for 3D Graphics. Elsevier Science & Technology Books(2002). ISBN 1-55860-838-9.
8. Garland, M., and Heckbert, P. Surface simplification using quadric error metrics. Computer Graphics (SIGGRAPH '97 Proceedings) (1997), 209-216.
9. Hoppe, H. Progressive Meshes. Computer Graphics (SIGGRAPH '96 Proceedings) (1996), 99-108.
10. Rossignac, J and P Borrel. Multi-Resolution 3D Approximation for Rendering Complex Scenes. Technical Report RC 17687-77951. IBM Research Division. T J Watson Research Center, Yorktown Heights, NY (1992).
11. Turk,G Re-tiling Polygonal Surfaces. Computer Graphics (SIGGRAPH '92 Proceedings) (1992), 55-64.

12. Pajarola, DeCoro,C. Eficient implementation of real-time view-dependent multiresolution meshing, Visualization and Computer Graphics, IEEE Transactions. (2004), 353-368.
13. J.Krivanek, Representing and Rendering Surfaces with Points, Postgraduate Study Report DC-PSR(2003)
14. A.Kalaiah and A.Varshney. Modeling and rendering points with local geometry. IEEE Transactions on Visualization and Computer Graphics(2003), 30-42.
15. D. Luebke and C. Erikson, "View-dependent simplification of arbitrary polygonal environments," in Proceedings of SIGGRAPH '97 (Los Angeles, CA). ACM SIGGRAPH, Computer Graphics Proceedings, Annual Conference Series (1997), 198–208.
16. Tan Kim Heok; Daman, D.; A review on level of detail Computer Graphics, Imaging and Visualization, 2004. CGIV 2004. Proceedings. International Conference on 26-29 July (2004), 70-75.
17. Fang Meng; Hongbin Zha; An easy viewer for out-of-core visualization of huge point-sampled models 3D Data Processing, Visualization and Transmission. 3DPVT 2004. Proceedings. 2nd International Symposium on 6-9 Sept. (2004), 207-214.
18. Callahan, S.P.; Comba, J.L.D.; Shirley, P.; Silva, C.T.; Interactive rendering of large unstructured grids using dynamic level-of-detail Visualization, 2005. VIS 05. IEEE 23-28 Oct. (2005), 199-206.
19. Danovaro, E.; De Floriani, L.; Magillo, P.; Puppo, E.; Sobrero, D.; Sokolovsky, N.; The half-edge tree: a compact data structure for level-of-detail tetrahedral meshes Shape Modeling and Applications, 2005 International Conference 13-17 June (2005), 332-337.

Fast Ray-Triangle Intersection Computation Using Reconfigurable Hardware

Sung-Soo Kim, Seung-Woo Nam, and In-Ho Lee

Digital Content Research Division,
Electronics and Telecommunications Research Institute,
305-700, 161 Gajeong-dong, Yuseong-gu, Daejeon, South Korea

Abstract. We present a novel FPGA-accelerated architecture for fast collision detection among rigid bodies. This paper describes the design of the hardware architecture for several primitive intersection testing components implemented on a multi-FPGA Xilinx Virtex-II prototyping system. We focus on the acceleration of ray-triangle intersection operation which is the one of the most important operations in various applications such as collision detection and ray tracing.

Our implementation result is a hardware-accelerated ray-triangle intersection engine that is capable of out-performing a 2.8 GHz Xeon processor, running a well-known high performance software ray-triangle intersection algorithm, by up to a factor of seventy. In addition, we demonstrate that the proposed approach could prove to be faster than current GPU-based algorithms as well as CPU based algorithms for ray-triangle intersection.

Keywords: Collision Detection, Graphics Hardware, Intersection Testing, Ray Tracing.

1   Introduction

The problem of fast and reliable collision detection has been extensively studied [4]. Despite the vast literature, real-time collision detection remains one of the major bottlenecks for interactive physically-based simulation and ray tracing [1][12]. One of the challenges in the area is to develop the *custom hardware* for collision detection and ray tracing. However, one major difficulty for implementing hardware is the multitude of collision detection and ray tracing algorithms. Dozens of algorithms and data structures exist for hierarchical scene traversal and intersection computation. Though the performance of these algorithms seems to be similar to software implementations, their applicability to hardware implementation has not yet been thoroughly investigated.

Since collision detection is such a fundamental task, it is highly desirable to have hardware acceleration available just like 3D graphics accelerators. Using specialized hardware, the system's CPU can be freed from computing collisions.

Main Results: We present a novel FPGA-accelerated architecture for fast collision detection among rigid bodies. Our proposed custom hardware for collision detection supports 13 intersection types among rigid bodies. In order to evaluate the proposed hardware architecture, we have performed the VHDL implementation for various intersection computations among collision primitives.

A. Gagalowicz and W. Philips (Eds.): MIRAGE 2007, LNCS 4418, pp. 70–81, 2007.

We demonstrate the effectiveness of our hardware architecture for collision queries in three scenarios: (a) ray-triangle intersection computation with 260 thousands of static triangles, (b) the same computation with dynamic triangles and (c) dynamic sphere-sphere intersection tesing. The performance of our FPGA-based hardware varies between 30 and 60 msec, depending on the complexity of the scene and the types of collision primitives. In order to evaluate our hardware performance for large triangle meshes, we also present our hardware to different benchmark models. For our comparative study we also analyze three popular *ray-triangle intersection algorithms* to estimate on the size of hardware resource. More details are given in Section 4. As compared to prior methods, our hardware-accelerated system offers the following advantages:

- Direct applicability to collision objects with dynamically changing topologies since geometric transformation can be done in our proposed hardware;
- Sufficient memory in our board to buffer the ray-intersection input and output data and significant reduction in the number of data transmission;
- Up to an order of magnitude faster runtime performance over prior techniques for ray-triangle intersection testing;
- Interactive collision query computation on massively large triangulated models.

The rest of the paper is organized as follows. We briefly survey previous work on collision detection in Section 2. Section 3 describes the proposed hardware architecture for accelerating collision detection. We present our hardware implementation of ray-triangle intersection in Section 4. Finally, we analyze our implementation and compare its performance with prior methods in Section 5.

2 Related Work

The problems of collision detection and distance computation are well studied in the literature. We refer the readers to recent surveys [4]. In this section, we give a brief overview of related work on the collision detection, programmable GPU-based approaches, and the custom hardware for fast collision detection.

Collision Detection: Collision detection is one of the most studied problems in computer graphics. *Bounding volume hierarchies* (BVHs) are commonly used for collision detection and separation distance computation. Most collision detection schemes involve updates to bounding volumes, pairwise bounding volume tests, and pairwise feature tests between possibly-intersecting objects. Complex models or scenes are often organized into BVHs such as sphere trees [7], OBB-trees [5], AABB-trees, and k-DOP-trees [8]. Projection of bounding boxes extents on the coordinate axes is the basis of the sweep-and-prune technique [4]. However, these methods incur overhead for each time interval tested, spent *updating* bounding volumes and collision pruning data structures, regardless of the occurrence or frequency of collisions during the time interval.

Programmable GPU: With the new programmable GPU, tasks which are different from the traditional polygon rendering can explore their parallel programmability. The GPU can now be used as a general purpose SIMD processor, and, following this idea, a lot of existing algorithms have been recently migrated to the GPU to solve problems as global illumination, linear algebra, image processing, and multigrid solvers in a fast way. Recently, GPU-based ray tracing approaches have been introduced [11]. Ray tracing was also mapped to rasterization hardware using programmable pipelines [11]. However, according to [12] it seems that an implementation on the GPU cannot gain a significant speed-up over a pure CPU-based implementation. This is probably because the GPU is a *streaming architecture*. Another disadvantage which they share with GPUs is the *limited memory*. Out-of-core solutions are in general not an alternative due to the high bandwidth needed.

Custom Hardware: The need for custom graphics hardware arise with the demand for interactive physically simulations and real-time rendering systems. The AR350 processor is a commercial product developed by Advanced Rendering Technologies for accelerating ray tracing [3]. Schmittler et al. proposed hardware architecture (SaarCOR) for real time ray tracing and implemented using an FPGA [14]. The performance of the SaarCOR depends on a number of scene-space-subdivisions.

The first publications of work on dedicated hardware for collision detection was presented in [15]. They focused on a space-efficient implementation of the algorithms, while we aim at maximum performance for various types of collision queries in this paper. In addition, they presented only a functional simulation, while we present a full VHDL implementation on an FPGA chip.

3 Hardware Architecture

In this section, we give an overview of hardware architecture for accelerating the collision detection. Our hardware architecture is based on a modular pipeline of collision detection. The proposed architecture includes three key parts such as *input registers*, the *collision detection engine*, and the *update engine* in the Fig. 1.

3.1 Input Registers and Transformer

Our proposed hardware has three inputs which are *counter register*, *primary data register file*, and *secondary data register file*. The *transformer* provides the geometric transformation functions for secondary objects to improve the performance. The counter register contains the number of primary objects and the number of secondary objects. The geometries of the primary objects are stored in the primary data register file. The secondary data register file also holds geometries of the secondary objects for collision queries. In our research, we suppose that the primary objects $\mathcal{P}$ change for each time. On the other hand, the secondary objects $\mathcal{S}$ does not change their geometries in local coordinate system. Therefore, the $\mathcal{S}$ just can be applied the geometric transformations such as translation and rotation. For instance, the triangulated models are $\mathcal{S}$ and rays are $\mathcal{P}$ to perform the intersection computations in ray tracing applications. More specifically, $\mathcal{S}$ denotes as $\mathcal{S} = \{(\mathcal{T}_1, ..., \mathcal{T}_n)| \ n \geq 1\}$, where $\mathcal{T}$ is a triangle defined by three vertices $V_j \in \mathbf{R}^3, j \in \{0, 1, 2\}$. The $\mathcal{P}$ is the set of rays which contain their origins O and directions D. When testing the intersection between the primary objects and secondary objects, we perform the following processing steps. First, we upload the

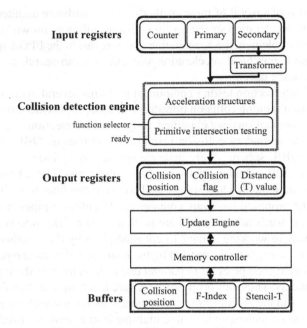

Fig. 1. The proposed hardware architecture

secondary objects to on-board memory at once through direct memory access (DMA) controller. Second, we transfer the primary objects to on-chip memory in the *collision detection engine* (CDE). To do this step, we use the register files which are packet data of the primary object to reduce the feeding time for the CDE. Finally, we invoke the ray-triangle intersection module in the CDE to compute the intersection between primary objects and secondary objects.

One of the primary benefits of the *transformer* in our architecture is to reduce the number of re-transmission for the secondary objects from main memory to on-board memory. If certain objects from the geometry buffer have to be reused, they can be transformed at the transformer without re-transmission from main memory. Therefore, we can reduce the bus bottleneck since we reduce the number of re-transmission. The bus width from *secondary register file* to CDE is 288 ($= 9 \times 32$) bits. We can transfer 288 bits to the collision detection engine in every clock. The ultimate goal of our work is applying our results to physically-based simulation. So, we use single precision for representing a floating point to provide more accurate results.

3.2 Collision Detection Engine

The collision detection engine (CDE) is a modular hardware component for performing the collision computations between $\mathcal{P}$ and $\mathcal{S}$. The CDE consists of the acceleration structures and primitive intersection testing components. As already discussed earlier in Section 2, a wide variety of acceleration schemes have been proposed for collision detection over the last two decades. For example, there are octrees, general BSP-trees, axis-aligned BSP-trees (kd-trees), uniform, non-uniform and hierarchical grids, BVHs, and several hybrids of several of these methods. In our hardware architecture, we can adapt hierarchical acceleration structures for collision culling as shown in Fig. 1. However, we could not implement the acceleration structure due to the FPGA resource limit. But if we use the hierarchical acceleration structure, we can search the index or the smallest T-value much faster.

The primitive intersection testing component performs several operations for intersection computations among collision primitives. In order to provide various operations for intersection computations, we classified 13 types of intersection queries according to the primary and secondary collision primitives: ray-triangle, OBB-OBB, triangle-AABB, triangle-OBB, sphere-sphere, triangle-sphere, ray-cylinder, triangle-cylinder, cylinder-cylinder, OBB-cylinder, OBB-plane, ray-sphere, and sphere-OBB intersection testing. We have implemented hardware-based collision pipelines to verify these intersection types. The proposed hardware contains the 13 collision pipes, and more pipes can be available if hardware resources are sufficient. The CDE selects one collision pipe which is ready to working among 13 collision pipes by the *function selector* signal. Each pipe can be triggered in parallel by the *ready signal* of each pipe. However, it is difficult to execute each pipeline in parallel due to limitation of the input *bus width* and *routing* problems. Thus, our proposed hardware reads input packet from on-board memory and stores in the *register file* which contains two or more elements.

We use a *pipelined technique* in which multiple instructions are overlapped in execution. This technique is used for real hardware implementation in order to improve performance by *increasing instruction throughput*, as opposed to decreasing the execution time of an individual instruction. There are four outputs which are *collision flag* (F-value), *collision position* (CP), *index*, and *separation distance* or *penetration depth* (T-value). In order to get these outputs, the CDE performs the intersection testing between $\mathcal{P}$ and $\mathcal{S}$. If a collision occurs, CDE will store output values for CP, index, T-value and F-value. The CP denotes a collision position of the object pair and index is the triangle ($\mathcal{T}$) index of the triangulated mesh. The T-value denotes the penetration depth between two objects and F-value is set true. Otherwise, CP and index have invalid value, T-value is the separation distance between two objects and F-value is set false.

3.3   Update Engine

We can simplify routing data lines and make memory controller efficient by coupling buffers such as F-index buffer and two stencil-T buffers as shown in Fig. 1. We compare old T-value from stencil-T buffer0 (or 1) with new T-value from CDE and update smaller T-value from stencil-T buffer1 (or 0) of the two values within one clock. We do not transfer T-values from the stencil-T buffer to CPU in order to find the smallest or the largest T, which makes it possible to reduce transmission time. Stencil value in the stencil-T buffer is used for masking some regions of the F-index buffer to save searching time for the index of the collision object.

We use single precision floating point of IEEE standard 754 for representing each element of the vertex or vector and T-value in order to compare with the speed of the CPU arithmetic. One of the main reasons that we use single precision floating point is to provide more accurate results in physically-based simulation systems. So, we create many floating point arithmetic logics with CoreGen library supported by Xilinx tool

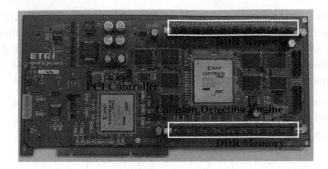

Fig. 2. The acceleration board with 64bits/66MHz PCI interface. On the board, there are Xilinx V2P20 for PCI controller, Xilinx V2P70 for memory and the collision detection logic. This board also includes two 1 GB DDR memories with 288 bit input bus, seven 2 MB SRAMs with 224 bit output bus.

ISE. We use two types of memories on the board. One is uploading-purpose memory which is consists of two DDR SDRAMs. The other is storing-purpose memory which is consist of six SRAMs to store output results (see Fig. 2). Block RAMs on the FPGA is used for buffering the $\mathcal{P}$. Primary register file matches the block RAM on the FPGA.

In our ray-triangle intersection computation, the primary object data $\mathcal{P}$ contains an origin point O and a direction vector D of a ray. Total 256 rays can be transferred from main memory to block RAMs on the FPGA at a time. Each secondary object data in S is a triangle $\mathcal{T}$ which contains three vertices. When the number of the rays is more than 256, the rays are divided by a packet which contains 256 rays and packets are transferred one by one at each step. We define this step as processing collision detection between a packet of primary object and all secondary objects. The bigger size of the block RAMs is, the better performance of the CDE is. While FPGAs usually have several small memories, the advantage of using such a memory is that the several memory blocks can be accessed in parallel. Each triangle of the secondary object is represented using 288 (9×32)-bit data. Nearly 55 million triangles can be transferred from main memory to two DDR SDRAMs on the board through the DMA controller. So, we designed the large bus width of the secondary object data to eliminate input bottleneck of the CDE. Therefore, we are able to read one triangle data from the queue of the DDR SDRAM in each hardware clock.

4   Analysis of Ray-Triangle Intersection Algorithms

In this section we present the analysis results for ray-triangle intersection algorithms in terms of hardware resources. We have investigated three major ray-triangle intersection algorithms, the first one is Badouel's algorithm [2], the second one is Möller and Trumbore's algorithm [9], and the last one is the algorithm using Plücker coordinates [10]. We review Möller and Trumbore's algorithm since this algorithm requires smaller hardware resources in terms of hardware implementation than others. We will skip Badouel's algorithm and the algorithm using Plücker coordinates and refer to the original publications instead [2][10].

Möller-Trumbore's Algorithm: The algorithm proposed by Möller and Trumbore does not test for intersection with the triangle's embedding plane and therefore does not require the plane equation parameters [9]. This is a big advantage mainly in terms of memory consumption – especially on the GPU and the custom hardware – and execution performance. The algorithm goes as follows:

1. In a series of transformations the triangle is first translated into the origin and then transformed to a right-angled unit triangle in the $y - z$ plane, with the ray direction aligned with x. This can be expressed by a linear equation

$$\begin{pmatrix} t \\ u \\ v \end{pmatrix} = \frac{1}{P \cdot E_1} \begin{pmatrix} Q \cdot E_2 \\ P \cdot T \\ Q \cdot D \end{pmatrix} \tag{1}$$

where $E_1 = V_1 - V_0$, $E_2 = V_2 - V_0$, $T = O - V_0$, $P = D \times E_2$ and $Q = T \times E_1$.
2. This linear equation can now be solved to find the barycentric coordinates of the intersection point (u, v) and its distance t from the ray origin.

We compared these algorithms in terms of the latency, the number of I/O and hardware resources as shown in Table 1 and 2. We could not use Plücker test which contains too many multipliers and inputs relative to Möller's algorithm and Badouel's algorithm. Preprocessing of Plücker reduces the number of inputs and the latency of the hardware pipeline. However, it still needs more storage than others. Möller's algorithm is similar to Badouel's one in terms of the latency of the hardware pipeline, the number of I/O, and hardware resources as shown in Table 1 and 2. Möller's algorithm has been more efficient than Badouel's algorithm in view of the processing speed and usage of storage [9]. Therefore, we choose the Möller's algorithm for VHDL implementation for real circuit on the FPGA.

Table 1. Comparison of ray-triangle intersection algorithms in terms of the number of inputs, the number of outputs and latency for hardware implementation

Algorithms	The number of inputs	The number of outputs	Latency
Badouel's	9	6	16
Möller's	9	6	10
Plücker's	15	6	17

Table 2. Analysis of the hardware resources for ray-triangle intersection algorithms

Hardware Components	Badouel's	Möller's	Plücker's
Multiplier	27	27	54
Divider	2	1	1
Adder	13	12	31
Subtractor	23	15	17
Comparator	6	8	3
AND	3	2	2

5   Implementation and Analysis

In this section we describe the implementation of our collision detection hardware and highlight its application to perform ray-triangle intersection testing for massive triangulated meshes.

5.1   Implementation

We have implemented ray-triangle collision detection engine with VHDL and simulated it with ModelSim by Mentor Graphics. The ray-triangle intersection algorithm which we used is Möller's algorithm. In order to evaluate our hardware architecture, we created this algorithm as circuits on an FPGA. In our experiments, the primary input is a dynamic ray and triangulated terrain which contains 259,572 triangles for secondary objects in Fig. 3(a). The origin of the ray moves on the flight path shown as a red curve and direction of the ray changes randomly in every frame in Fig. 3(b). We have evaluated our hardware on a PC running Windows XP operating system with an Intel Xeon 2.8GHz CPU, 2GB memory and an NVIDIA GeoForce 7800GT GPU. We used OpenGL as graphics API and Cg language for implementing the fragment programs [13]. We can classify three configurations of collision detections according to the properties of collision primitives. A *static object* is the object which the topology is not changed in the scene. On the other hand, a *dynamic object* is an object which the topology is changed in the scene for each frame.

Static Objects vs. Static Objects: In this scenario, the performance depends on the number of primary objects due to limitation of the block RAMs on an FPGA. Thus, we choose the objects which have small number of objects in our architecture. If the number of the objects is larger than the size of the block RAM, then data transmission from main memory to block RAM occurs in two or more times.

Static Objects vs. Dynamic Objects: We choose dynamic objects as the secondary object. Since the transformation is performed in our hardware, we do not need to

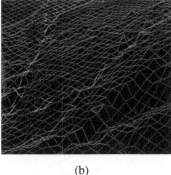

(a)   (b)

Fig. 3. Our test terrain model: (a) terrain: 259,572 triangles (b) a ray (blue line) is shot on the triangulated terrain in arbitrary direction for each frame

retransfer data of dynamic objects except that objects are disappeared or generated newly. Position and orientation of the dynamic objects can be transformed by transformer in Fig. 3. We expect the performance is comparable to above case.

Dynamic Objects vs. Dynamic Objects: Our hardware architecture only supports transformation function for secondary objects. In this scenario, transmission time is defined by the number of the primary objects which are transformed in the CPU. Thus, the performance depends on the number of the primary objects and the CPU processing speed. We will evaluate performance of our proposed architecture in each case comparing with that of CPU and GPU. The proposed hardware checks 259,572 ray-triangle collision tests per frame, which takes 31 milliseconds including the ray data transmission time, while it takes 2,100 milliseconds for CPU based software implementation as shown in Fig. 4(a). Our hardware was about 70 times faster than CPU-based ray-triangle implementation. To compare with GPU-based approach, we have implemented the efficient ray-triangle intersection tests on the GPU using the Nvidia Cg shading language [6][13]. The proposed hardware is four times faster than the GPU-based ray-triangle intersection approach. For dynamically moving vertices of the triangles on the terrain, the proposed hardware was 30 times faster than the CPU-based approach as shown in Fig. 4(b).

We also performed another experiment for dynamic sphere-sphere collision detection. In this scenario, one thousand of sphere move dynamically in every frame. The input data contains a center point and a radius of the sphere which is represented four 32-bit floating points. In collision detection among dynamically moving spheres, our hardware is 1.4 times faster than CPU based implementation since sphere-sphere intersection algorithm consists very simple operations. In order to evaluate our hardware performance for large triangle meshes, we also have applied our hardware to different benchmarks as shown in Table 3. We measured the average computation time of ray-triangle intersection for each benchmark model. Our approach provides significant performance improvement for huge triangle meshes.

Fig. 6 shows snapshots of intersection trajectories for our benchmark models.

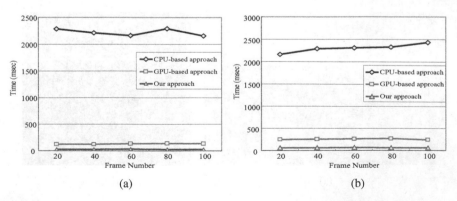

(a)   (b)

Fig. 4. The comparison result of the ray-triangle intersection testing: (a) static vs. static, (b) static vs. dynamic

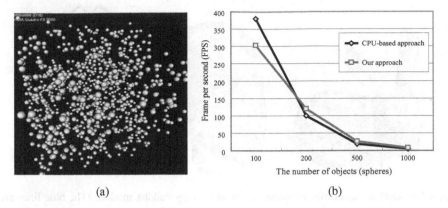

| (a) | (b) |

Fig. 5. Dynamic sphere-sphere collision testing: (a) snapshot of collision testing, (b) the comparison result according to the number of objects

Table 3. Performance comparison for ray-triangle intersection

Model	Vertices	Triangles	CPU-based (msec)	Ours (msec)
Bunny	35,947	69,451	488	4
Venus	50,002	100,002	695	5
Rabbit	67,039	134,073	925	8
Dragon	437,645	871,414	5.887	47
Happy buddha	543,644	1,085,634	7,290	53
Blade	882,954	1,765,388	11,220	65

5.2 Analysis and Limitations

Our hardware provides good performance of collision detection for large triangulated meshes. The overall benefit of our approach is due to two reasons:

- **Data reusability:** We exploit the *transformer* in the proposed hardware to avoid the transmission bottleneck due to the transformation in the CPU. As a result, we have observed 30 - 70 times improvement in ray-triangle intersection computation over prior methods based on CPU and GPU.
- **Runtime performance:** We use the high-speed processing power of the proposed hardware. We also utilize *instruction pipelining* to improve the throughput of the collision detection engine. Moreover, our current hardware implementation involves no hierarchy computation or update.

Based on these two reasons, we obtain considerable speedups over prior methods. Moreover, we are able to perform various collision queries at almost interactive frame rates.

Limitations: plusOur approach has a few limitations. Our hardware architecture includes the component of *acceleration structures*, such as kd-tree, grids and BVHs in Fig. 3. However, we could not implement this component due to the hardware resource

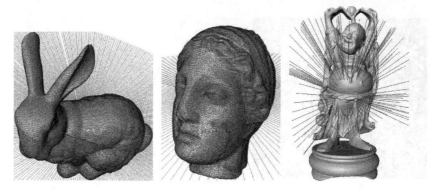

Fig. 6. Intersection trajectories of bunny, venus and happy buddha models. (The blue lines are random rays and the red triangles are intersected triangles with rays.)

limit. So, our current implementation does not support hierarchical collision detection. However, if traversal of acceleration structures is performed in CPU, we can solve this problem easily.

6   Conclusion

We present the dedicated hardware architecture to perform collision queries. We evaluate the hardware architecture for ray-triangle and sphere-sphere collision detection under the three configurations.

We have used our hardware to perform different collision queries (ray-triangle intersection, sphere-sphere intersection) in complex and dynamically moving models. The result is a hardware-accelerated ray-triangle intersection engine that is capable of outperforming a 2.8 GHz Xeon processor, running a well-known high performance software ray-triangle intersection algorithm, by up to a factor of seventy. In addition, we demonstrate that the proposed approach could prove to be faster than current GPU-based algorithms as well as CPU based algorithms for ray-triangle intersection.

References

1. N. Atay, J. W. Lockwood, and B. Bayazit, A Collision Detection Chip on Reconfigurable Hardware, In *Proceedings of Pacific Conference on Computer Graphics and Applications (Pacific Graphics)*, Oct. 2005.
2. D. Badouel, *An Efficient Ray-Polygon Intersection*, Graphics Gems I, pp. 390-394, 1990.
3. C. Cassagnabere, F. Rousselle, and C Renaud, Path Tracing Using AR350 Processor, In *Proceedings of the 2nd International Conference on Computer Graphics and Interactive Techniques in Australasia and South East Asia*, pp. 23-29, 2004.
4. C. Ericson, *Real-Time Collision Detection*, Morgan Kaufmann, 2004
5. S. Gottschalk, M. C. Lin, D. Manocha, OBB tree: A Hierarchical Structure for Rapid Interference Detection, In *Proceedings of ACM SIGGRAPH*, pp. 171-180, 1996.
6. Alexander Greß, Michael Guthe, and Reinhard Klein, GPU-based Collision Detection for Deformable Parameterized Surfaces, *Computer Graphics Forums (Eurographics 2006)*, Vol. 25, Num. 3, 2006.

7. P. M. Hubbard, Collision Detection for Interactive Graphics Applications, *IEEE Transactions on Visualization and Computer Graphics*, pp. 218-230, 1995
8. J. T. Klosowski, M. Held, J. S. B. Mitchell, H. Sowizral and K. Zikan, Efficient Collision Detection Using Bounding Volume Hierarchies of k-DOPs, *IEEE Transactions on Visualization and Computer Graphics*, 4(1), pp. 21-36, 1998.
9. T. Möller and B. Trumbore, Fast, Minimum Storage Ray-Triangle Intersection *Journal of Graphics Tools*, pp.21-28, 1997.
10. J. Plücker, On A New Geometry Of Space, *Phil. Trans. Royal Soc. London*, 155:725-791, 1865.
11. T. J. Purcell, I. Buck, W. R. Mark, P. Hanrahan, Ray Tracing on Programmable Graphics Hardware, *ACM Transactions on Graphics*, 21(3), pp. 703-712, 2002.
12. A. Raabe, B. Bartyzel, J. K. Anlauf, and G. Zachmann, Hardware Accelerated Collision Detection-An Architecture and Simulation Result, In *Proceedings of IEEE Design Automation and Test in Europe Conference*, vol. 3, pp. 130-135, 2005.
13. Philippe C.D. Robert and Daniel Schweri, GPU-Based Ray-Triangle Intersection Testing, *Technical Report*, University of Bern, 2004.
14. Jörg Schmittler, Ingo Wald, and Philipp Slusallek, SaarCOR-A Hardware Architecture for Ray Tracing, In *Proceedings of SIGGRAPH/Eurographics Workshop on Graphics Hardware*, pp. 27-36, 2002.
15. G. Zachmann and G. Knittel, An architecture for hierarchical collision detection, In *Journal of WSCG'2003*, pp. 149-156, 2003.

An Applicable Hierarchical Clustering Algorithm for Content-Based Image Retrieval

Hongli Xu, De Xu, and Enai Lin

School of Computer & Information Technology, Beijing Jiaotong University,
3 Shangyuancun Xizhimenwai 100044, Beijing, China
{hlxu, dxu, 04120411}@bjtu.edu.cn

Abstract. Nowadays large volumes of data with high dimensionality are being generated in many fields. ClusterTree is a new indexing approach representing clusters generated by any existing clustering approach. It supports effective and efficient image retrieval. Lots of clustering algorithms have been developed, and in most of them some parameters should be determined by hand. The authors propose a new ClusterTree structure, which based on the improved CLIQUE and avoids any parameters defined by user. Using multi-resolution property of wavelet transforms, the proposed approach can cluster at different resolution and remain the relation between these clusters to construct hierarchical index. The results of the application confirm that the ClusterTree is very applicable and efficient.

1 Introduction

Recently large volumes of data with high dimensionality are being generated in many fields. Many approaches have been proposed to index high-dimensional datasets for efficient querying. Existing multidimensional tree-like indexing approaches can be classified into categories: space partitioning and data partitioning. A data partitioning approach partitions a dataset and builds a hierarchy consisting of bounding regions. Popular index structures include R-Tree, R*-tree, SS-Tree, SS*-Tree and SR-Tree. In R-tree, all nodes have minimum bounding rectangles; SS-Tree uses hyper-spheres as region units; SR-Tree is an index structure which combines the bounding spheres and rectangles for the shapes of node regions to reduce the blank area. One disadvantage of partitioning approach is that the bounding boxes (rectangles or hyper-sphere) associated with different nodes may overlap. Space partitioning approaches recursively divide a data space into disjoint subspaces. K-D-B tree and Pyramid-Tree are this type. The K-D-B Tree partitions a d-dimensional data space into disjoint subspace by (d-1)-dimensional hyper-planes, it has the advantage that the search path for querying a data point is unique. The Pyramid-Tree is to divide the data space first 2d pyramids; each pyramid is then sliced into slices parallel to the base of the pyramid. One disadvantage of the Pyramid-Tree can not ensure that the data points in one data page are always neighbors.

Among those approaches, the ClusterTree is the first work towards building efficient index structures from clustering for high-dimensional datasets. The ClusterTree

A. Gagalowicz and W. Philips (Eds.): MIRAGE 2007, LNCS 4418, pp. 82–92, 2007.

has the advantage of supporting efficient data query for high-dimensional datasets. A ClusterTree is a hierarchical representation of the clusters of a dataset. It organizes the data based on their cluster information from coarse level to fine, providing an efficient index structure on the data according to clustering. Nowadays existing clustering approaches need predefine some parameters, such as the number of clusters, density threshold, the grid granularity, agglomerative and divisive threshold, etc. In this paper, we propose an applied hierarchical clustering approach. The method has not any parameters decided by user. We apply wavelet transform to deal with the density curves. Due to the multi-resolution characteristic of wavelet transformation, we can construct the hierarchical clustering structure from coarse level to fine.

The remainder of the paper is organized as follows. In section 2, some related works are introduced. We describe the multi-resolution clustering for high dimensional data in detail in section 3. This is followed by a brief analysis on its performance in section 4. In section 5, we present the experimental results. Section 6 draws conclusions and points out future work.

2   Related Work

There are many kinds of clustering method at present time, which can be categorized into partitioning method, hierarchical method, density-based method, grid-based method, model-based method, and subspace clustering method. Partitioning algorithms construct a partition of a database of N objects into a set of K clusters, they firstly make sure the number K of clusters. Hierarchical algorithms (BIRCH[1], CURE [2]) are to decompose data set hierarchically. The disadvantage is that the termination condition has to be specified and it is order-sensitive. Density based algorithms (DBSCAN[3], DENCLUE [4], CURD[5], CODU[6]) rely on a density-based notion of clusters, which control the cluster increasing according to the density threshold. Grid-based algorithms (STING[7], WaveCluster[8]) quantize the space into a finite number of cells and then do all operations on the quantized space. They depend only on the number of cells in each dimension in the quantized space.

For real high dimension data set, it is very difficult to specify the parameters of the number of clusters, agglomerative and divisive threshold, density threshold, and the grid granularity by prior knowledge. The common use of the Euclidean distance for computing a similarity measure appears unjustified. In high dimension, the more scattering data distribution is, the poorer the performance of clustering is. So, it is realistic to consider subspace clustering. CLIQUE[9] is a subspace clustering method that integrate density-based and grid-based methods. It is very effective for high dimension data in large database. CLIQUE extracts clustering units in every subspace from top to bottom. For extracting the clusters in d-dimension, the clusters in all (d-1)-dimension must first be obtain, this is going to make the spatial and time efficiency become very low. Meanwhile, user must preset two parameters before clustering, namely, inter-cluster distance and density threshold. These parameters are sensitive to sample data distribution. And it is difficult for user to set these parameters. But CLIQUE method is insensitive for data order. In SIAM international conference on data mining, Karin et al [10] and Carlotta et al [11] proposed the clustering methods in high dimension respectively to improve the subspace clustering method. Karin introduced SUBCLU(density-connected subspace clustering), which is able to detect arbitrarily shaped and positioned clusters in the subspaces, and the process of generating all clusters is in a bottom up way. The method of Carlotta is to discover clusters in subspaces spanned by different combinations of dimensions via local weightings of features.

Our proposed algorithm integrates the characteristic of hierarchical, grid-based, and subspace-clustering methods. First, the feature space is quantized and the density curve of every dimension is calculated. Secondly, we apply wavelet transform to deal with these density curves, and point out the "peak" and "valley" by hill climbing. The objects between two valleys belong to one cluster. According to the multi-resolution characteristic of wavelet transformation, we can construct the hierarchical structure.

3   ClusterTree* and Its Construction

3.1   Construction of ClusterTree*

The ClusterTree* is a hierarchical representation of the clusters of a dataset. Its construction is similar to the construction of ClusterTree. It has two kinds of nodes: internal and leaf nodes. The internal nodes are defined as:

$$Node : Node\_id, CL_{id}, CH_{id}, CC_{id}, \gamma, (CP_1, CP_2, ..., CP_\gamma)$$

Where $Node\_id$ is the node identifier, γ is the number of the child nodes in the node. A child node is created for each sub_cluster of the cluster. CP_i is a pointer to the next level child node, CL_{id} and CH_{id} is the low and high coordinates of the $Node\_id$, CC_{id} is the center of the cluster. The child nodes of the same parent are ordered as CC_{id}. The leaf nodes are defined as:

$$Leaf : Leaf\_id, \kappa, (ADR_1, ADR_2, ..., ADR_\kappa)$$

Where κ is the number of data points contained in the leaf node. ADR_i is the address of the data point.

3.2   ClusterTree* Algorithm

Let $S = A_1 \times A_2 \times ... \times A_d$ be a d-dimensional numerical space. We refer to $A_1, A_2, ..., A_d$ as the dimensions (features) of S. Given a set of image data $\{O_i, 1 \le i \le N\}$ where $O_i = (f_{i1}, f_{i2}, ..., f_{id})$. f_{ij} is the projection of O_i on A_j. We partition the every dimension into ξ intervals. The goal of the algorithm is to detect clusters and assign labels to the images based on the cluster that they belong to. The main idea in our algorithm is to count image data distributing curve in each dimension and smooth these curve by applying wavelet transform. It yields sets of clusters at different resolutions and scales through finding the peaks and valleys of the distributing curve. At the same time, it records the relation between clusters of different resolution, which can be use to construct the hierarchical index. The main steps are shown as follows:

Algorithm 1 ClusterTree* algorithm
Input: Image data $\{O_i, 1 \le i \le N\}$, $O_i = (f_{i1}, f_{i2}, \ldots, f_{id})$
Output: Hierarchical clustering tree

1. Computation of ξ at each dimension.
2. The distributing curve of each dimension.
3. Applying wavelet transform on these distributing curves, Record the scales λ.
4. Identification of clusters at every scale.
    4.1 Finding the range between valleys automatically on the every dimension using hill-climbing.
    4.2 Implementing subspace clustering from top to bottom.
    4.3 Recording the valleys about these clusters.
5. Repeat the step 3, 4 until the scale is λ.
6. Output the hierarchical clustering.

In the experiment of constructing the ClusterTree*, we use RGB histogram feature, and save the identification of clusters at every scale to the preprocessing file. Its construction is shown as follows:

(Image file Name, RGB-Hist, Level0Id, Level1Id, Level2Id, Level3Id,......)

According to the preprocessing file, the index file is shown as follows:

(ClusterId, LevelId, ParentId, CL_i, CH_i, CenterOfCluser)

3.3 Partitioning the Dimension

How to confirm the number ξ of interval in each dimension?

MAFIA[12] proposes an adaptive interval size to partition the dimension depending on the distribution of data in the dimension. First, the algorithm sets the maximum value of the histogram in a dimension within a small window. Adjacent windows are merged to form larger windows within a certain threshold. The algorithm then combines adjacent cells of similar density to form larger cells. In this manner, the dimension is partitioned based on the data distribution and the resulting boundaries of the cells capture the cluster perimeter more accurately than fixed sized grid cells.

In addition to requiring a density threshold parameter, MAFIA also requires the user to specify threshold for merging adjacent windows. Windows are essentially subset of bins in a histogram that is plotted for each dimension. Adjacent windows within the specified threshold are merged to form larger windows. The formation of the adaptive grid is dependent on these windows. Also, to assist the adaptive grid algorithm, MAFIA takes a default grid size as input for dimensions where the data is uniformly distributed. In such dimensions, the data is divided into a small, fixed number of partitions. Despite the adaptive nature of the grids, the algorithm is rather sensitive to these parameters. In MAFIA, the window size is 5, the threshold of 20% is used to merge adjacent windows.

The computation cost of MAFIA will increase with the window size and emerging parameter. In our experiment, we assume the window size is 5 and 10, the threshold for merging is 20% and 10%, respectively. When the window size is 10 and the emerging threshold is 10%, the result is acceptant. For reducing the computational cost, we used the fixed number ξ of partitions. The reasoning is following.

If there are N objects in the data space, averagely k objects in each interval, for the sake of distinguishing objects effectively and insuring the convergence at clustering along with N increasing, k must abide by three conditions:

$$\lim_{N\to\infty} k = \infty \tag{1}$$

$$\lim_{N\to\infty} N^{-1}k = 0 \tag{2}$$

$$\lim_{N\to\infty} (\log N)^{-1} k = \infty \tag{3}$$

$k\infty\sqrt{N}$ is a especial result according to above conditions, we assume $k = \sqrt{N}$, the number of equally partitioning is $\xi = N / k = \sqrt{N}$.

The size of the interval in our algorithm is an important issue that affects the performance of clustering. The size of the interval is selected according to the number of objects. If the number of objects is fewer and the size of the interval is bigger, the distributing curve cannot reveal the distributing character of objects in the feature space. Our algorithm is better when the number of image is larger.

3.4   Wavelet Transform of the Distributing Curves

Applying wavelet transform on a signal decomposes it into different frequency sub-bands. If we regard the distributing curve in the original space as a 1-dimensional signal, we can use discrete wavelet transform on it and get multi-resolution representation of each dimensional distributing curve. The high frequency components in the transformed space correspond to the biggish change of the distributing curve in the original space; we can say a high frequency component partitions two clusters. The low frequency components in the transformed space correspond to these regions where objects are convergent in the original space. They are just these clusters. A coarser approximation of the one-dimensional distributing curve in the transformed space is to smooth the distributing curve in the original space, and wipe off some smaller clusters or possible noise. The coarser approximation at different scale is got rid of the effect of noises and outliers at different grade. The bigger the scale is, the coarser the clustering is.

In the third step of ClusterTree* algorithm, 1D wavelet transform is applied on every distributing curve. Wavelet transforming at a time correspond to once smoothing for the distributing curve in original space. It means that many small clusters are combined. Then, our algorithm is to find the valleys on the smoothed curve in each dimension, the objects between two valleys belong to one cluster. We apply the method to every scale and obtain the partitions from coarse to fine.

The largest scale λ is computed by comparing the distributing curve change. If there are not any changes about the valleys after wavelet transforming, it is to stop transforming. But the computation cost is very bigger. In our experiment, when the scale is more than 3, the distributing curve is little change.

3.5 Identification of Clusters at Every Scale

The first step of ClusterTree* is to quantize the feature space, where each dimension in the d-dimensional feature space will be equally divided into ξ intervals. Let $O_i = (f_{i1}, f_{i2}, \ldots, f_{id})$ be the feature vector of the object O_i in the original feature space. Let $D_j = (v_{j1}, v_{j2}, \ldots, v_{j\xi})$ denote ξ intervals of the j-th dimension in the original feature space where v_{jk}, $1 \le k \le \xi$, $1 \le j \le d$, is the location of the interval on the j-th dimension of the feature space. Let $g(v_{jk})$ be the number of $\{O_i, 1 \le i \le N\}$ projecting in the k-th interval on the jth dimension, the distributing curve of the j-th dimension is defined as $y_j = \{g(v_{jk}), 1 \le k \le \xi\}$.

To find the partitioning point of clusters, we use the hill-climbing method at every scale. The hill-climbing algorithm is shown as follows:

```
1. Compare g(v_jk) with g(v_jk+1) on the j-th dimension.
     If g(v_jk) is less than g(v_jk+1), this is climbing up;
     If g(v_jk) is more than g(v_jk+1), this is down.
2. Memorize the valley as i,
   if g(v_jk) < g(v_jk-1), g(v_jk) > g(v_jk+1), 1 ≤ j ≤ d, 1 ≤ k ≤ ξ.
3. These objects between two valleys correspond to a
   cluster.
4. Implement the hill-climbing method in every
   dimension
```

When completing MRCA on the j-th dimension, given C_{j-1} clusters in the subspace of the $(j-1)$ dimensions, use above the hill-climbing method for these objects in the C_{j-1} clusters to find the valleys and get sub-clusters on the j-th dimension. If there is only one peak at the projection of the j-th dimension corresponding to the objects in a cluster of the $(j-1)$ dimensions, the cluster is not dealt at the j-th dimension.

Several questions must be considered in our method. The first is the beginning point locates at peak. How to make sure the first valley of the peak? Secondly, when the method is still climbing up at end, if the last interval is regarded as the valley, how to ascertain the second valley of the last peak? The third is the computational cost.

For the questions, we can assume that the first and last hills are symmetrical, and then point out another valley. For the first question, if the second valley of the first peak is at m, the first valley is at $-m$. For the second question, if the first valley of the last peak is at m, the end valley is at $\xi + (\xi - m)$. Because our clustering method is the partition of objects, the range of the first and last hill will not affect the clustering result. So above hypothesis is feasible. Because we carry out subspace clustering at first scale, and at next scale we only search the labels of covered clusters, not all objects. The complexity of ClusterTree* is $O(md)$.

4   Properties of the ClusterTree* Approach

There some typical request about clustering, such as the handling of noises and outliers, order insensitive with respect to input data, the least special knowledge to decide the parameters, and arbitrary shape cluster et al. We briefly evaluate the performance of our method.

Effective Handing of Noises: There are two ways to reduce the affect of noises in our method. One is to identify the effective peak and valley. Another is to use the coarser information of the wavelet transforming to get the smoothing curves.

Order insensitive of input data: Because the distributing curves are to count the projecting of all objects on very dimension, they are not affected by input data.

The least special knowledge: There are not the parameters specified by users in our method, and it does not depend on the special knowledge.

Complexity: The complexity of ClusterTree* is $O(md)$, m is the number of input data, d is the number of feature space.

Retractility: ClusterTree* is good at clustering for big data set. Because finding the peaks is after input data projecting, storage space and cost calculation are only relevant with the distributing curves, and the number of input data does not affect the retractility of ClusterTree*. Along with increasing the number of input data, the distributing characteristic is more distinct, and the clustering effect is better.

5   Experimental Results

In this section, we present experimental results on the performance of the hierarchical clustering algorithm in an image dataset. These images consist of 5000 pictures, including flower, racing car, sunrise and sundown, animal, butterfly, and texture picture as follows Fig.1. The images are from Corel Photo Gallery. The experimental environment is Intel (R) 4 PC, 256M memory, Windows 2000, Microsoft Access 2000, VC++6.0.

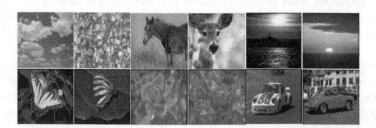

Fig. 1. Sample pictures in the experiment

5.1   Clustering at Different Scale

Firstly, we select 1006 pictures from our image dataset, consisting of flower, butterfly, and texture. Table 1 lists different clustering results for different resolution wavelet transforming. The image features include RGB histogram, Coarse wavelet and Co-occurrence. Coarse wavelet is the low frequency components of image wavelet transform. On the table 1 we can know the higher the scale of the wavelet transforming the distributing curve is, the less the clustering number is as well as the coarser the clustering result is.

Table 1. Clustering image data at different scale and features using Haar wavelet transform

The number of clustering	The scale of Haar wavelet transform			
Image features	0	1	2	3
RGB	many	7	5	3
Coarse wavelet	9	6	4	1
Co-occurrence	12	9	6	2

Secondly, we perform the method on the similar image dataset, which is composed of 100 flower pictures, 100 butterfly pictures, and 100 texture pictures. COLOR Cumulative Histogram is selected to represent the images and the number of dimensions is 192. Fig.2 shows the hierarchical relation between clusters at different scale. There are five clusters at scale 1. The cluster2 includes two sub-clusters at scale 2. At scale 3, the cluster2, butterfly1 and butterfly2 are merged. Finally, we obtain the hierarchical clustering structure of five clusters at different scale. The texture pictures and flower pictures respectively are congregated very well. There are 3 butterfly clusters summing 38 pictures, and at the same time 62 butterfly pictures are not partitioned. The reason is that these butterflies are quite similar to flowers, and another is that we do not use the shape feature.

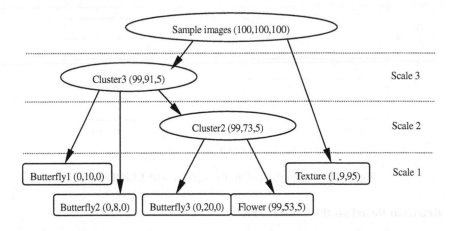

Fig. 2. An example of the Cluster Tree* structure. The image data set includes flower, butterfly, and texture images, and every class has 100 images. The order of sample images is flower, butterfly, and texture.

Table 2. The number of clustering at different scale for different size dataset

dataset size	0-level	1-level	2-level	3-level
1000	78	5	3	1
2000	82	5	3	1
3000	86	4	3	1
4000	128	7	2	1
5000	151	4	2	1

Thirdly, we perform the method on the whole dataset, Table 2 lists the number of clustering at different scale for different size dataset. The results demonstrate the effectiveness of the ClusterTree*.

5.2   The Complexity of ClusterTree*

In Fig.3, we can see the clustering time for the 5 different cluster sizes we chose. The x-axis shows the size of each cluster. The ClusterTree* clustering time is faster than CLQUE, because the complexity of ClusterTree* is $O(md)$ and CLQUE is $O(C^d + md)$.

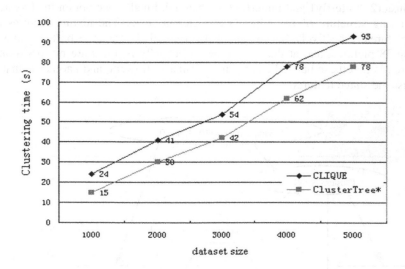

Fig. 3. The Comparison of the ClusterTree with CLIQUE

5.3   Retrieval Based on the ClusterTree*

We further performed timing experiments based on 5000 images from Corel Photo Gallery. Figure 4 presents some of the retrieval results that can be obtained by the ClusterTree*, R-tree and KNN algorithm. The based ClusterTree* retrieval time is smaller than R-Tree and KNN. In the hierarchical clustering, neighboring points may fall into different clusters. So its recall may not higher than them. But the efficiency is more important for the retrieval of great capacity database.

The retrieval based on the ClusterTree* algorithm is shown as follows:

```
1. Input the querying image
   and compute the image feature qif ;
2. For high_level to low_level;
3. 1f  CL_id ≤ qif ≤ CH_id  Then goto the next level node
   Else the next node of the same level;
4. Return the retrieval results.
```

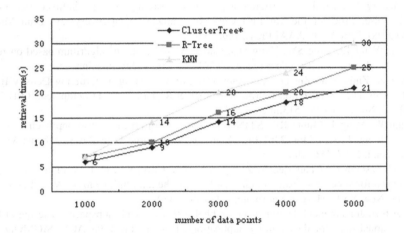

Fig. 4. The Comparison of the ClusterTree* retrieval time with R-Tree and KNN

6 Conclusion

High dimensional data is increasingly common in many fields, especially in image retrieval application. Many extensive researches need predefine some parameters. Our proposed algorithm integrates the characteristic of hierarchical, grid-based, and subspace-clustering methods, and there is not the parameters input by users. It can identify some smaller clusters. The experimental results show its effectiveness.

Many issues need be researched about the ClusterTree*. Besides Haar wavelet, we will use another wavelet to smooth the distributing curves. For the effectiveness, most distinguishing feature should be selected. We also can use parallelization to boost efficiency just like MAFIA. Meanwhile, we will compare farther the proposed approach with other algorithms.

Acknowledgements

This work was supported by the Beijing Jiaotong University Research Project under Grant No. 2004SM013.

References

1. Tian Zhang, Raghu Ramakrishnan, and Miron Livny. BIRCH: An Efficient Data Clustering Method for Very Large Databases. In Proceedings of the 1996 ACM SIGMOD International Conference on Management of Data, pages 103-114, Montreal, Canada, 1996.
2. Guha S, Rastogi R, Shim K. CURE: an efficient clustering algorithm for large databases. Proc. of the ACM SIGMOD Int'l Conf. on Management of Data. Seattle: ACM Press, 1998. 73~84.
3. Ester M, Kriegel H, Sander J, Xu XW. A density-based algorithm for discovering clusters in large spatial databases with noise. Proc. of the 2nd Int'l Conf. on Knowledge Discovery and Data Mining (KDD'96). Portland: AAAI Press, 1996. 226~231.
4. Hinneburg A, Keim D. An efficient approach to clustering in large multimedia databases with noise. Proc. of the 4th Int'l Conf. on Knowledge Discovery and Data Mining (KDD'98). New York: AAAI Press, 1998. 58~65.
5. Ma S, Wang TJ, Tang SW, Yang DQ, Gao J. A fast clustering algorithm based on reference and density. Journal of Software, 2003,14(6):1089~1095. in china.
6. Liu Kan, Zhou Xiao Zheng , and Zhou DongRu. Clustering by Ordering Density-Based Subspaces and Visualization Journal of Computer Research and Development, Oct1 2003 Vol. 40, No. 10, 1509~1513,in china.
7. Wang W, Yang J, Muntz RR. STING: A statistical information grid approach to spatial data mining. Proc. of the 23rd Int'l Conf. on Very Large Data Bases. Athens: Morgan Kaufmann, 1997. 186~195.
8. Sheikholeslami G, Chatterjee S, Zhang AD. WaveCluster: A multi-resolution clustering approach for very large spatial databases. Proc. of the 24th Int'l Conf. on Very Large Data Bases. New York: Morgan Kaufmann, 1998. 428~439.
9. Rakesh A, Johanners G, Dimitrios G, Prabhakar R. Automatic subspace clustering of high dimensional data for data mining applications. Proc. of the 1998 ACM SIGMOD Int'l Conf. on Management of Data. Minneapolis: ACM Press, 1998. 94~105.
10. Karin Kailing, Hans-Peter Kriegel, Peer Kroger. Density-Connected Subspace Clustering for High-Dimensional Data. In Proc. 4th SIAM Int. Conf. on Data Mining, pp.246-257, Lake Buena Vista,FL,2004
11. Carlotta Domeniconi, D. Papadopoulos, D. Gunopulos, Sheng Ma. Subspace Clustering of High Dimensional Data, SIAM International Conference on Data Mining (SDM), Apr. 2004, http://www.cs.ucr.edu/~dimitris/publications.html
12. Sanjay Goil, H. Nagesh, A. Choudhary. MAFIA: Efficient and Scalable Subspace Clustering Clustering for Very Large Data Sets. Technical Report CPDC-TR-9906-010, Northwestern University, 2145 Sheridan Road, Evanston IL 60208, June 1999.

MADE: A Composite Visual-Based 3D Shape Descriptor

Biao Leng, Liqun Li, and Zheng Qin

Department of Computer Science & Technology, Tsinghua University,
100084, Beijing, China
School of Software, Tsinghua University, 100084, Beijing, China
{lengb04,lilq05}@mails.tsinghua.edu.cn, qingzh@tsinghua.edu.cn

Abstract. Due to the widely application of 3D models, the techniques of content-based 3D shape retrieval become necessary. In this paper, a modified Principal Component Analysis (PCA) method for model normalization is introduced at first, and each model is projected in 6 different viewpoints. Secondly, a new adjacent angle distance Fouriers (AADF) descriptor is presented, which captures more precise contour feature of black-white images. Finally, based on modified PCA method, a novel composite 3D shape descriptor MADE is proposed by concatenating AADF, Tchebichef and D-buffer descriptors. Experimental results on the criterion of 3D model database PSB show that the proposed descriptor MADE has gained the best retrieval effectiveness compared with three single descriptors and two composite descriptors LFD and DESIRE.

1 Introduction

Nowadays, text-based information retrieval systems are ubiquitous, for instance the Google system. On the contrary, there are few of multimedia retrieval systems for 3D models, because it lacks of an efficient, meaningful and computable approach for the representation of models [11]. A lot of approaches are proposed to address the issue. They are generally classified into geometry-based and shape-based approaches. Geometry-based approach matches 3D models according to geometry information and distribution. Osada [15] proposed a method called shape distribution for computing shape signatures of 3D models. Funkhouser [17] utilized spherical harmonics to compute discriminating similarity measures. Kazhdan [9] presented a novel method for matching 3D models that factors the shape matching equation as the disjoint outer product of anisotropy and geometric comparisons. Shape-based approach matches 3D models according to the similarity of projected images. Chen [6] proposed a visual similarity-based 3D model retrieval system based on the main idea that if two 3D models are similar, they also look similar from all viewing angles. Ohbuchi [14] introduced an appearance-based shape-similarity comparison algorithm for 3D shapes defined as polygon soup. Pu [8] presented a method to retrieve desired 3D models by measuring the similarity between user's sketches and 2D orthogonal views.

A. Gagalowicz and W. Philips (Eds.): MIRAGE 2007, LNCS 4418, pp. 93–104, 2007.

For state-of-the-art reviews in content-based 3D shape retrieval, please refer to [11,16,1].

Content-based 3D shape retrieval mainly focuses on exploring various 3D shape descriptors, hoping to find the "best" one to represent 3D models. Shilane [12] compared 12 different shape descriptors on the criterion of 3D model database Princeton Shape Benchmark (PSB), and Light Filed Descriptor (LFD) [6] was declared as the best one. Vranic [5] proposed a composite 3D shape descriptor called DESIRE, and the experimental results showed that the proposed hybrid descriptor performed better than LFD. Thus DESIRE is regarded as the best shape descriptor representing 3D models.

In this paper, we investigate a new algorithm for 3D shape retrieval based on orthogonal projections, and regard it as a composite visual-based 3D shape descriptors called MADE. At first, in order to reduce the number of projected images and acquire image feature with more characteristic, a modified Principal Component Analysis (PCA) method for model normalization is presented, and each model is projected in 6 different viewpoints. Secondly, a original adjacent angle distance Fouriers (AADF) is proposed, which is more appropriate to contour feature extraction for projected images. Finally, based on the modified PCA method, a novel composite 3D shape descriptor MADE is presented by concatenating contour-based descriptor AADF, region-based descriptor Tchebichef and the standard 2D discrete Fourier transform D-buffer descriptor. Compared with several single shape descriptors and two composite descriptors LFD and DESIRE, the experimental results on the 3D model repositories PSB show that the proposed descriptor MADE has achieved the best retrieval effectiveness, as it has a little better retrieval performance than that of DESIRE with different measures.

The rest of the paper is organized as follows. The model normalization modified PCA method is introduced in Section 2. Section 3 presents the contour-based AADF descriptor at first, secondly describes two basic descriptors, and finally proposes a novel composite 3D shape descriptor MADE. Experimental results compared with several shape descriptors and some discussions are given in Section 4. Finally, the conclusion and future work are showed in Section 5.

2   Modified PCA

Because the scale, rotation and orientation of original models are quite different, the procedure of model normalization is a must for shape-based 3D model retrieval.

In [8] Pu proposed Maximum Normal Distribution (MND) method. It is just for CAD models since CAD models are constitutive of several hundred meshes, while multimedia models consist of thousands meshes and its structure is unpredictable. To find the canonical coordinate system of models, the most prominent method to address the issue is basic PCA method [4]. The purpose of this method is to estimate the pose of a 3D mesh model, and produce an affine transformation.

3D models are composed of thousands of meshes, and any two of them are different with each other. Only the vertex spatial positions are taken into account, basic PCA method is not effective to solve the model normalization problem. Because vertex spatial position is just one of the essential elements of 3D model, and there are some other factors which also affect the model normalization, such as linear length between two vertices, and triangular area associated with adjacent three vertices. They also have relationship with vertex spatial positions. Considering the different area of triangles and length of lines for corresponding vertices, we apply weighing factors proportional to triangular area and linear length.

3D model is given by a set of vertices v_i in 3D space. V stands for vertex set, and n is total number of vertices. Let m_v be mean of V.

The weighing factor wa_i is proportional to triangle area based on vertex v_i.

$$wa_i = \frac{nA_i'}{3A} \text{ and obviously, } \sum_{i=1}^{n} wa_i = n \qquad (1)$$

where A_i' is sum of triangular area associated with vertex v_i, and A is sum of all triangular area in 3D model.

The weighing factor wl_i is proportional to linear length based on vertex v_i.

$$wl_i = \frac{nL_i'}{2L} \text{ and obviously, } \sum_{i=1}^{n} wl_i = n \qquad (2)$$

where L_i' is sum of linear length associated with vertex v_i, and L is sum of all linear length in 3D model.

The most important covariance matrix $C_{cov} \in C^{3 \times 3}$ is defined below:

$$C_{cov} = \frac{1}{n} \sum_{i=1}^{n} wa_i \times wl_i \times (v_i - m_v)(v_i - m_v)^T \qquad (3)$$

The rest procedure of modified PCA method is the same with basic PCA method. Based on eigenvalues of C_{cov}, the transformation matrix C_{tra} is determined. Then the original vertice v_i is transformed to the new one v_i':

$$v_i' = C_{tra}(v_i - m_v) \qquad (4)$$

After the modified PCA method, 3D models originally with an arbitrary rotation and orientation are invariant to translation and rotation in the canonical coordinate system. Figure 1 shows some examples obtained by MND method and modified PCA method respectively. It is obviously that the arbitrary mesh models transformed in the canonical coordinate system obtained by modified PCA method are more intuitive than those obtained by MND method.

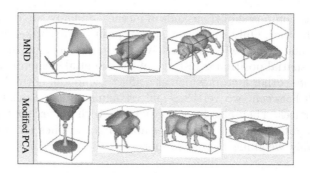

Fig. 1. Model normalization using MND and modified PCA methods

3 "MADE" Descriptor

Based on modified PCA method, each 3D model is rendered using parallel projection with six grey-scale depth images, each two for one of the principle axes. For the details of projection, please refer to [4]. The dimensions of images are $N \times N$, and in our experiments N is 256. After rendering, the feature of these images should be extracted. The six grey-scale depth images are transformed by D-buffer descriptor, while for the AADF and Tchebichef only three black-white images with each principle axe are used.

3.1 Adjacent Angle Distance Fourier Descriptor

In content-based image retrieval (CBIR) research, Zhang studies different Fourier descriptors, and shows that centroid distance is the best shape signature, detailed analysis and explanation are presented in [3]. The feature extraction of projected images in 3D shape retrieval is quite different from CBIR, because it processes 2D images to retrieval 3D models while CBIR just deals with 2D images. Even for two models in the same class, their projected images with the same viewpoint are different because of some aspects, such as model normalization, model geometric distribution, etc. Therefore, the centroid distance Fouriers is not suitable for feature extraction. Nevertheless, the concept and processing of centroid distance Fouriers are very useful, and can be utilized for feature extraction in 3D shape retrieval.

Based on similarity translation invariance of Fouriers, the center of regional content is translated and regional content is scaled for image preprocessing. Then shape contour are captured and the longest contour is regarded as contour of regional content. All contour vertices are taken into a cyclic sequence L and the total number is N. The center point of contour L is O, and each vertex is described as:

$$L_i = (X_i, Y_i) = O + \rho_i(\cos \theta_i, \sin \theta_i),\ 0 \leq i \leq N - 1 \tag{5}$$

where i stands for sequence number in contour L. ρ_i expresses the distance between vertex v_i and O. θ_i is the angle between vertex v_i and O in polar coordinates.

Based on L, contour vertices are sampled with adjacent angle, exactly every two angles one vertex. To avoid vacancy, the contour is extended as introduced before. The adjacent angle sequence S with 180 vertices is defined below:

$$S_j = L_i \ if \ \rho_i = \max P_j, \ P_j = \{\rho_i | \frac{2j\pi}{180} \le \theta_i < \frac{2(j+1)\pi}{180}\} \tag{6}$$

where $0 \le j < 180$. The sequence S may lose some contour information seriously if many sequential vertices are not sampled from L to S. Thus, to avoid severe contour information failure, and allow a little slight contour feature loss, some vertices, which are not sampled by S, will be add into sequence S. For every two sequential vertices v_u and v_{u+1} in S, if there are more than two vertices are not sampled between v_u and v_{u+1} in L, adjacent distance vertices will be inserted into S. Then, the adjacent angle distance sequence T is formed, described as:

$$T = \begin{cases} T \cup S_j, \ \tau(S_{j+1}) - \tau(S_j) \le 2 \\ T \cup \psi_j, \ \tau(S_{j+1}) - \tau(S_j) > 2 \\ with \ \psi_j = \{L_i | i = \tau(S_j) + 2n, \tau(S_j) \le i < \tau(S_{j+1})\} \end{cases} \tag{7}$$

where $\tau(S_j)$ is sequence number of vertex S_j in L. The next step is centroid distance Fourier transformation based on contour sequence T, and the novel algorithm is called adjacent angle distance Fouriers. Figure 2 displays an ant with three different contours. For feature extraction of projected images, the first 30 coefficients of AADF are exploited.

Fig. 2. An ant with different contours . (left is basic contour, middle is adjacent angle contour, and right is adjacent angle distance contour).

3.2   Tchebichef Descriptor

Shape feature descriptors are generally classified into two primarily categories: region-based and contour-based descriptors. The AADF just extracts the information of contour shape, and fails to emphasize shape interior content. On the contrary, in region-based approaches, all vertices within shape region are taken into account to obtain shape representation. Mukundan [13] proposed the Tchebichef (a.k.a. Chebyshev) moments that can be effectively used as pattern features in the analysis of two-dimensional images. The experiments showed that Tchebichef moments were superior to the conventional orthogonal moments.

In [13] Mukundan introduced Tchebichef moments based on the discrete orthogonal Tchebichef polynomial. The scaled orthogonal Tchebichef polynomials for an image of size $N \times N$ are defined according to the following recursive relation:

$$
\begin{aligned}
t_0(x) &= 1 \\
t_1(x) &= (2x - N + 1)/N \\
t_p(x) &= \frac{(2p-1)t_1(x)t_{p-1}(x) - (p-1)\{1 - \frac{(p-1)^2}{N^2}\}t_{p-2}(x)}{p}, \quad p > 1
\end{aligned}
\tag{8}
$$

and the squared-norm $\rho(p, N)$ is given by

$$
p(p, N) = \frac{N(1 - \frac{1}{N^2})(1 - \frac{2^2}{N^2}) \ldots (1 - \frac{p^2}{N^2})}{2p + 1}, \quad p = 0, 1, \ldots, N - 1
\tag{9}
$$

The radial Tchebichef moment of order p and repetition q is defined as:

$$
S_{pq} = \frac{1}{2\pi\rho(p, m)} \sum_{r=0}^{m-1} \sum_{\theta=0}^{2\pi} t_p(r)e^{-jq\theta} f(r, \theta)
\tag{10}
$$

where m denotes $(N/2) + 1$.

In the above equation, both r and θ take integer values. The mapping between (r, θ) and image coordinates (x, y) is given by:

$$
x = \frac{rN}{2(m-1)} \cos(\theta) + \frac{N}{2}, \quad y = \frac{rN}{2(m-1)} \sin(\theta) + \frac{N}{2}
\tag{11}
$$

Tchebichef moments consists of several different $|S_{pq}|$, for the details, please refer to [13,10]. In this paper, only 10 Tchebichef moments coefficients with $q = 0$ and $0 \le p \le 9$ to describe the region shape.

3.3   D-Buffer Descriptor

Both AADF and Tchebichef descriptors extract shape feature of projected black-white images from one side, while D-buffer [4] descriptor acquires characteristics of grey-scale depth images including contour and region aspects.

In [4], the two-dimensional discrete Fourier transform (2D-DFT) of depth-buffers are used to represent the feature in the spectral domain. Because of the computational complexity and separability, the DFT is reduce from a 2-dimensional operation to two 1-dimensional operations.

$$
\hat{f}_{pq} = \frac{1}{\sqrt{M}} \sum_{a=0}^{M-1} (\frac{1}{\sqrt{N}} \sum_{b=0}^{N-1} f_{ab}e^{-j2\pi qb/N})e^{-j2\pi pa/M}
\tag{12}
$$

where $M = N$, j is the imaginary unit, $p = 0, \ldots, M - 1$, $q = 0, \ldots, N - 1$, and f_{ab} is the gray-scale value of pixel (a, b).

In this paper, 73 components of D-buffer descriptor is obtained to represent gray-scale images. For the details of D-buffer descriptor, please refer to [4].

3.4   Composite Descriptor

Finally, we present a composite shape descriptor, based on the modified PCA (M) model normalization method, obtained from the **AADF** (A) descriptor, the **D**-buffer (D) descriptor, and the Tchebichef (E) descriptor. Thus, we call the composite descriptor "MADE".

Feature vector of AADF descriptor is $\mathbf{a}=(a_1,\ldots,a_A)$, Tchebichef descriptor is $\mathbf{t}=(t_1,\ldots,t_T)$, and $\mathbf{d}=(d_1,\ldots,d_D)$ is for D-buffer descriptor. The feature vector of composite MADE descriptor $\mathbf{m}$ is formed by concatenating the basic feature vectors, $\mathbf{m}=(\mathbf{a}|\ \mathbf{t}|\ \mathbf{d})$, whence the dimension of the MADE descriptor is $M = A + T + D$. As discussed above that, $A = 30 \times 3 = 90$, $T = 10 \times 3 = 30$, and $D = 73 \times 6 = 438$, therefore, $M = 558$.

4   Experiments

In this section, we first introduce the 3D model repositories, and several standard measures, such as precision vs. recall figures, nearest neighbor, first-tier, etc. Then experimental results compared with several descriptors and some discussions are presented.

4.1   Retrieval Evaluation

Our experiments are based on the criterion of 3D model repositories PSB [12], containing 1814 3D objects of general categories, like plane, human, building, vehicle, and so on, yielding the ground truth. In our experiment, each classified model was used as a query object, and the models belonging to the same class were taken as relevant objects.

To evaluate the effectiveness of 3D shape retrieval, the *precision vs. recall figures* [2], a standard evaluation technique for retrieval systems, is applied. Precision indicates that the ability to retrieve the relevant models based on the retrieved models. Recall indicates that the ability to retrieve the relevant models based on the whole relevant models. In addition to the precision at different recall levels, several widely used measures *nearest neighbor, first-tier, second-tier, and Discounted Cumulative Gain (DCG)*[12] are also employed. Nearest neighbor is defined as the percentage of the closest match that belongs to the same class as query model. First-tier and second-tier are associated with the percentage of models in the query model class that appear within the top G matches. Specially, for the query model class with $|C|$ members (excluding the query model), when $G = |C|$ for the first-tier, and $G = 2 * |C|$ for the second-tier. DCG is a statistic that weights correct results near the front of the list more than correct results later in the ranked list under the assumption that a user is less likely to consider elements near the end of the list. With the choice of similarity measure, we employ the l_1 (Manhattan) distance, as the experiments show that l_1 acquires the best retrieval results compared with other Minkowski distances.

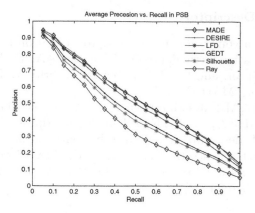

Fig. 3. Average precision vs. recall figures for MADE and other several shape descriptors

4.2 Effectiveness Comparison

In the experiments, the proposed descriptor MADE is compared with several single descriptors and two composite descriptors using the ground truth. Figure 3 shows the average precision versus recall figures for MADE and other descriptors. It is obvious that the composite descriptors MADE, DESIRE and LFD have better retrieval effectiveness than single descriptors GEDT, Silhouette and Ray. Among the composite descriptors, LFD is the worst one. The precision at different recall levels of MADE is almost the same with that of DESIRE, as there are only slight difference between them, even can be negligible.

To evaluate the detailed retrieval performance of MADE, it is compared with other descriptors in several model classes. Figure 4 shows the average retrieval performance for the human_arms_out model class. It indicates that the performance ordering for this model class is the same with that of performance on

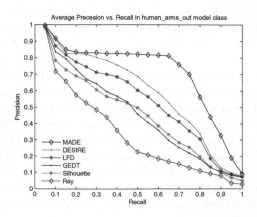

Fig. 4. Average precision vs. recall figures for the human_arms_out model class

Table 1. The comparison of 6 shape descriptors in PSB

shape descriptor	dimension	nearest neighbor	first-tier	second-tier	DCG
MADE	558	69.81%	41.57%	53.43%	67.80%
DESIRE	472	65.82%	40.45%	51.33%	66.31%
LFD	4700	61.77%	33.01%	46.54%	65.52%
GEDT	544	57.55%	32.29%	43.24%	59.62%
Silhouette	300	54.69%	30.51%	40.56%	57.96%
Ray	136	51.49%	25.56%	34.58%	53.68%

average. The descriptor MADE outperforms other five descriptors, while Ray does the worst. The difference of precision at different recall levels between MADE and DESIRE is distinct.

Table 1 shows the comparison of 6 shape descriptors with feature vector dimension and several measures, e.g., nearest neighbor, first-tier, second-tier and DCG. For the dimension column, LFD has as much as 4700, which needs more storage space and execution time, while the dimension of other five descriptors is about several hundreds. From the table, it is evident that the retrieval effectiveness of MADE with four different measure is better than that of other descriptors. For each measure column, the statistic of MADE is a little better than that of DESIRE, therefore, the MADE descriptor is more suitable for most categories than DESIRE.

Figure 5 shows the average nearest neighbor and first-tier retrieval statistics. It is apparent that MADE does the best. Compared with DESIRE, one can observe effectiveness improvement of 6.06% in terms of nearest neighbor using MADE. For the first-tier, the MADE descriptor provides a retrieval performance 2.77% better than DESIRE.

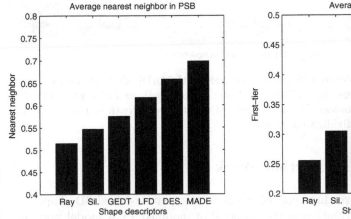
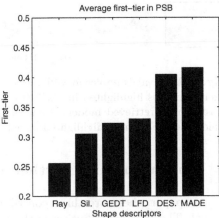

Fig. 5. Average nearest neighbor and first-tier retrieval statistics

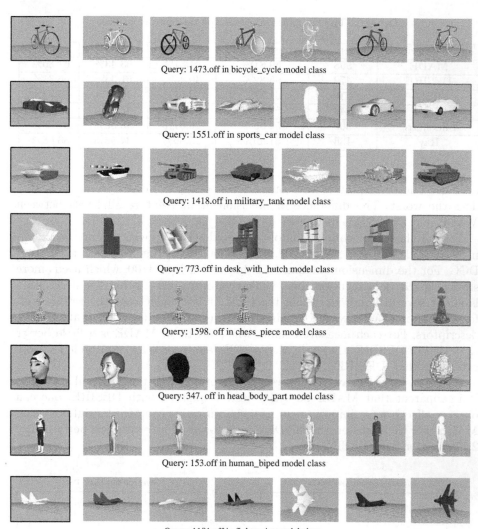

Query: 1473.off in bicycle_cycle model class

Query: 1551.off in sports_car model class

Query: 1418.off in military_tank model class

Query: 773.off in desk_with_hutch model class

Query: 1598. off in chess_piece model class

Query: 347. off in head_body_part model class

Query: 153.off in human_biped model class

Query: 1181.off in fighter_jet model class

Fig. 6. Retrieval examples for different class models with MADE shape descriptor. The query model is highlighted in black (the left one in each row), and it displays the six most similar retrieved models (from the second one to the seventh in each row), in which the irrelevant is highlighted in red.

5   Conclusion and Further Work

In this paper, there are three contributions to the content-based 3D shape retrieval. The first contribution is the proposal of modified PCA model normalization method, which reduces the number of projected images, acquires image feature with more characteristics, and converts the 3D models originally with an arbitrary rotation and orientation into invariant to translation and rotation in the canonical coordinate system. Secondly, a new adjacent angle distance Fouriers descriptor is presented, which is based on the concept of centroid distance Fouriers. The AADF can capture more precise contour feature of black-white images, and is more appropriate to the contour feature extraction in 3D shape retrieval. Finally, based on the modified PCA method, a novel composite 3D shape descriptor MADE is proposed by concatenating contour-based descriptor AADF, region-based descriptor Tchebichef and the standard 2D discrete Fourier transform D-buffer descriptor. The experimental results on the criterion of 3D model database PSB show that the proposed descriptor MADE has gained the best retrieval effectiveness compared with three single descriptors and two composite descriptors LFD and DESIRE, with several measures, such as nearest neighbor, first-tier, and so on.

Results from section 4 suggest that the MADE descriptor is more effective than LFD and DESIRE. However, the effectiveness is one marked advantages of MADE. Compared with LFD, the advantage of feature vector dimensions is obvious, as feature vector components of MADE are only 11.87% of that in LFD. The composite descriptor DESIRE is composed of D-buffer, Silhouette and Ray descriptors. The D-buffer and Silhouette descriptors belongs to the shape-based approach, while the Ray descriptor is a member of the geometry-based approach, therefore, the process of feature extraction in DESIRE is more complex than that in MADE. In a summary, the proposed composite MADE descriptor is a significantly better technique.

For further study, we plan to study the interactive learning mechanism as well as the relevance feedback technique [7] hoping that the retrieval performance can be improved by dynamically assigning different weights or by training through the classified 3D models.

Acknowledgement

This work is supported by the National Grand Fundamental Research 973 Program of China (No. 2004CB719401), the National Research Foundation for the Doctoral Program of Higher Education of China (No. 20060003060), and the National Natural Science Foundation of China (No. 60542004).

References

1. Bustos B., Keim D.A., Saupe D., Schreck T., and Vranic D.V. Feature-based similarity search in 3d object databases. *ACM Computing Surveys*, 37(4):345–387, 2005.
2. Ricardo B.Y. and Berthier R.N. *Modern Information Retrieval*. Addison-Wesley, Cambridge, 1999.
3. Zhang D. and Lu G. Generic fourier descriptor for shape-based image retrieval. In *Proceedings of IEEE International Conference on Multimedia and Expo (ICME)*, pages 425–428, Lausanne, Switzerland, Auguest 2002.
4. Vranic D.V. *3D Model Retrieval*. PhD thesis, University of Lcipzig, Leipzig, Germany, 2004.

5. Vranic D.V. Desire: a composite 3d-shape descriptor. In *Proceedings of IEEE International Conference on Multimedia and Expo (ICME)*, pages 962–965, Amsterdam, Holand, July 2005.
6. Chen D.Y., Tian X.P., Shen Y.T., and Ouhyoung M. On visual similarity based 3d model retrieval. *Computer Graphics Forum*, 22(3):223–232, 2003.
7. Leifman G., Meir R., and Tal A. Semantic-oriented 3d shape retrieval using relevance feedback. *The Visual Computer*, 21(8-10):865–875, 2005.
8. Pu J.T. and Ramani K. On visual similarity based 2d drawing retrieval. *Computer-Aided Design*, 38(3):249–259, 2006.
9. Kazhdan M., Funkhouser T., and Rusinkiewicz S. Shape matching and anisotropy. *ACM Transactions on Graphics*, 23(3):623–629, 2004.
10. Celebi M.E. and Aslandogan Y.A. A comparative study of three moment-based shape descriptors. In *Proceedings of IEEE International Conference on Information Technology: Coding and Computing (ITCC05)*, pages 788–793, Las Vegas, Nevada, USA, April 2005.
11. Iyer N., Jayanti S., Lou K.Y., Kalyanaraman Y., and Ramani K. Three-dimensional shape searching: state-of-the-art review and future trends. *Computer-Aided Design*, 37(5):509–530, 2005.
12. Shilane P., Min P., Kazhdan M., and Funkhouser T. The princeton shape benchmark. In *Proceedings of Shape Modeling and Applications (SMI)*, pages 167–178, Palazzo Ducale, Genova, Italy, June 2004.
13. Mukundan R., Ong S.H., and Lee P.A. Image analysis by tchebichef moments. *IEEE Transaction on Image Processing*, 10(9):1357–1364, 2001.
14. Ohbuchi R., Nakazawa M., and Takei T. Retrieving 3d shapes based on their appearance. In *Proceedings of the 5th ACM SIGMM international workshop on Multimedia information retrieval*, pages 39–45, Berkeley, California, USA, November 2003.
15. Osada R., Funkhouser T., Chazelle B., and Dobkin D. Shape distributions. *ACM Transactions on Grgphics*, 21(4):807–832, 2002.
16. Funkhouser T., Kazhdan M., Min P., and Shilane P. Shape-based retrieval and analysis of 3d models. *Communications of the ACM*, 48(6):58–64, 2005.
17. Funkhouser T., Min P., Kazhdan M., and Chen J. A search engine for 3d models. *ACM Transactions on Grgphics*, 22(1):83–105, 2003.

Research of 3D Chinese Calligraphic Handwriting Recur System and Its Key Algorithm

Ying-fei Wu, Yue-ting Zhuang, Yun-he Pan, Jiang-qin Wu, and Fei Wu

College of Computer Science, Zhejiang University, Hangzhou, China, 310027
hardwyf@hotmail.com, {yzhuang, panyh, wujq, wufei}@zju.edu.cn

Abstract. Chinese calligraphy is a precious Chinese art. It is pictographic and each calligraphist has his own writing style. Even people whose native language is Chinese will have difficulties in writing a demanded beautiful calligraphy style, not to say people who know little about Chinese calligraphy. In order to help people enjoy the art of calligraphy writing and find out the process how it was written, we implement a new approach to animate its writing process by 3D visualization method. In the paper two novel algorithms are also presented to extract the intrinsic feature which is needed to rebuild the writing process: 1) extract strokes order from an offline Chinese calligraphic handwriting; 2) estimate varied stroke's thickness. Finally, experiment result is given to demonstrate the application.

1 Introduction

Ancient Chinese began to use brush made of hair of weasel or goat to record events thousands of years ago. Gradually, a typical form of art called Chinese calligraphy came into being. Chinese calligraphy is an important cultural fortune of the whole world. However, some calligraphic works were written thousands of years ago. Modern people can not see how they were written at that time. The key issue in learning to write such calligraphy is to figure out its writing process. Our research aim is to extract the intrinsic features, such as strokes order and stroke's thickness and animate the writing process using a 3D visualization method.

Some previous research focused on strokes order extraction, e.g. estimating drawing order of single-strokes handwritten image [1] and retrieving temporal information of single-strokes skeleton image with solving a traveling salesman problem [2]. These researches are based on the assumption that handwriting is written with the minimization of curvature that human writer tends to minimize the curvature during writing. One advantage of these algorithms is that they omitted the variation of stroke's thickness of Chinese calligraphic handwriting which is also an important feature that can affect the strokes order.

Another task is stroke's thickness extraction. Wong et al. defined a virtual brush, a model-based approach to realistically synthesize the Chinese calligraphic handwriting. In the scheme different ellipses are used to simulate a stroke segment [3]. One disadvantage is that after extracting skeleton and contour from Chinese calligraphic

A. Gagalowicz and W. Philips (Eds.): MIRAGE 2007, LNCS 4418, pp. 105–116, 2007.

handwriting, each pixel is discrete so it is difficult to use ellipse to describe stroke's thickness.

In this paper we introduce the architecture of 3D Chinese Calligraphic Handwriting Recur System and its key algorithms. The system can help people enjoy the writing beauty of calligraphy handwriting and set good writing examples for user to follow. The system adopts new methods to extract strokes order from a Chinese calligraphic handwriting. Strokes order is extracted by character structure analysis and CONDESATION tracking. Method to extract stroke's thickness from a skeleton image and its contour is also introduced.

2 System Architecture

3D Chinese Calligraphic Handwriting Recur System has two main modules as shown in Fig. 1, the Calligraphic Image Pre-processing Module and the Client Module.

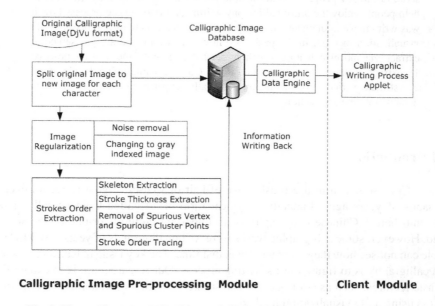

Calligraphic Image Pre-processing Module   **Client Module**

Fig. 1. The architecture of 3D Chinese Calligraphic Handwriting Recur System

The Calligraphic Image Pre-processing Module is responsible for extracting strokes order, stroke's thickness and storing them into the database. The Calligraphic Image Pre-processing Module includes three main steps.

The first step is to split the whole image into small images according to the border of character.

The second step is to regularize character image: 1) Reducing noise of character image; a noisy hole in image will result in an imperfect skeleton; 2) Convert color image into gray image.

The third step is to extract stroke's thickness and strokes order: 1) Skeleton extraction: the thinning algorithm is used to obtain the skeleton of image; 2) Stroke's thickness extraction: Stroke's thickness is an important feature of a character and it is also used to remove spurious cluster pixels; 3) Removal of spurious vertex and spurious cluster pixels: Before extracting strokes order, spurious vertex and spurious cluster pixels should be removed else it returns wrong result of strokes order extraction; 4) Strokes order tracing: This function is realized by character structure analysis and tracing all the substrokes using the CONDENSATION Tracking based on CCM. The following section will mainly introduce the key algorithms of stroke' thickness and strokes order recovery.

The Client Module is responsible for animating the writing process by communicating with the Calligraphic Data Engine to retrieve strokes order and stroke's thickness information from database. This module is an applet coded in Java with Java 3D API. Users can view the animation of calligraphic handwriting process by their browsers.

3 Stroke's Thickness and Strokes Order

The thinning algorithm is applied to a calligraphic character image to extract skeleton. Skeleton keeps the main stroke structure of a calligraphy character. The degree ρ of a skeletal pixel is the number of pixels existed in its 8-neighborhood. Skeletal pixels can be categorized into three types according to ρ :

1) If $\rho = 1$, then it is defined as a vertex pixel;

2) If $\rho = 2$, then it is defined as a line pixel;

3) If $\rho > 2$, then it is defined as a branch pixel;

Vertex pixel is the start point or end point of a stroke so it can be further categorized into two categories: start vertex and end vertex. Hidden start/end vertex is a special type of branch pixel which is served as start or end vertex in some circumstance.

Line segment starts from a start vertex or a hidden start/end vertex and ends at an end vertex or a hidden start/end vertex. Line segment can be denoted as a 2-tuple (v_s, v_e), where v_s can be start vertex or hidden start/end vertex, and v_e can be end vertex or hidden start/end vertex. All the other pixels of line segment (v_s, v_e) except v_s and v_e are line pixel.

Cluster is a group of branch pixels which have path connected with each other without passing any line pixel. The member of a cluster is denoted as cluster pixel.

3.1 Stroke's Thickness

Stroke's thickness is an important feature to rebuild writing process. Wong et al. describes a method using ellipse to obtain stroke's thickness [3]. After we get the skeleton of a Chinese calligraphic character, every pixel is discrete so it is difficult to use ellipse to describe stroke's thickness.

Here we use a Maximum Surrounding Degree (MSD) algorithm to estimate thickness w of a skeletal pixel:

$$w = d + \frac{T_b}{T_d} \tag{1}$$

where d represents the horizontal or vertical distance from the destination skeletal pixel to the ring of which all the pixels are black, and T_b is the total number of black pixels of the gray ring, and T_{d+1} is the total number of pixels of the gray ring, as shown in Fig. 2. T_{d+1} can be calculated from:

$$T_{d+1} = (2(d+1)-1)^2 - (2d-1)^2 = 8d \tag{2}$$

We can get the thickness w from (1) and (2):

$$w = d + \frac{T_b}{8d}$$

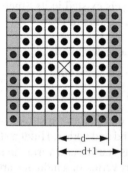

Fig. 2. The square marked with "X" is a skeletal pixel. (d+1) is the distance from the skeletal pixel to the first ring of which not all the contour pixels are black.

3.2 Strokes Order Tracing

3.2.1 Character Structure Analysis

When people learn how to write a Chinese calligraphic character in the right way, writing rules are very important [4]. The general principle of these rules is writing from left to right, from top to bottom, from outside to inside. Chinese characters have many structure types, such as left-right structure, top-bottom structure, surrounding structure, semi-surrounding structure and so on. For example, if a character has left – right structure, it should trace over all the substrokes in the left part and then the substrokes of right part. To use these rules, character structure should be analyzed first.

We propose a new character structure analysis algorithm by calculating the orientation relationship between substrokes of skeleton. All the strokes can be represented by the skeleton $G = \{g_1, ... g_i, ., g_n\}$, where g_i represents a substroke/radical consisting of line segments which have path connected with each other. There is no path between any two different elements of G .

To extract the character structure, we need to calculate the orientation relationship between each pair of substrokes/radicals of G . Let g_k and g_l be two substrokes/radicals, where g_k consists of a line segments $\{s_1, s_2, ..., s_a\}$ and g_l consists of b line segments $\{s'_1, s'_2, ..., s'_b\}$. The orientation relationship can be represented by a 2-tuple $R = (R_h, R_v)$, where R_h represents the horizontal orientation relationship, and R_v represents the vertical orientation relationship. Table 1 shows the probable orientation relationship between two substrokes/radicals. The orientation relationship has four types: left side, right side, up side, down side.

$$R_h = T(h_l, h_r), \text{ where } T = \begin{cases} 1, if\,(h_l > h_r) \\ 0, if\,(h_l = h_r) \\ -1, if\,(h_l < h_r) \end{cases}$$, and h_l is the probability of g_k at

the left side of g_l , and h_r is the probability of g_k at the right side of g_l , R_v is defined in the same way as R_h .

Formula (3) is the definition of h to calculate h_l, h_r, h_u or h_d according to the orientation relationship needed to be compared between g_k and g_l :

$$h = \frac{\sum_{i=1, j=1}^{i=a, j=b} p(f_1(s_i), f_2(s_j))}{a * b}, s_i \in g_k, s_j \in g_l \tag{3}$$

where $p = \begin{cases} 0, if\,(f_1(s_i) \geq f_2(s_j)) \\ 1, if\,(f_1(s_i) < f_2(s_j)) \end{cases}$. f_1 and f_2 have different definitions

according to different orientation relationship to be compared. Table 2 shows the definitions of f_1 and f_2 . With this method we can get the orientation relationship of any two substrokes/radicals and can use distance measurement of centroid to classify them to get the whole character structure.

3.2.2 CONDENSATION Tracking on CCM

After character structure analysis, we get the tracing sequence of sub-graphs and can start to extract strokes order from each substrokes/radicals. Previous researches made the same assumption that writer will write with the minimization of curvature to extract strokes order [1], [2]. This assumption is only applicable to western handwriting and can not meet needs of Chinese calligraphic handwriting. The main cause of the difference between western and Chinese calligraphic handwriting is the writing tool. Chinese calligraphic handwriting is written with a soft brush which will cause variation of stroke's thickness. Table 3 shows two different samples with almost the same skeleton after the thinning. The main difference between these two samples is the stroke's thickness relation at the cross as shown in Fig. 3. The extraction result of strokes order of Sample A is correct with the assumption of the minimization of curvature. For Sample B the extraction result of strokes order is wrong if the assumption is still used.

Table 1. Orientation relationship between two sub-graphs corresponding to R_h and R_v

	Orientation Relationship
$R_h = 1$	g_k is at the left side of g_l
$R_h = 0$	g_k is neither at the left side nor at the right side of g_l
$R_h = -1$	g_k is at the right side of g_l
$R_v = 1$	g_k is at the up side of g_l
$R_v = 0$	g_k is neither at the up side nor at the down side of g_l
$R_v = -1$	g_k is at the down side of g_l

Table 2. Function f_1 and f_2 corresponding to orientation relationship. v_s and v_e is the start vertex and the end vertex of a stroke of g_k. v_s' and v_e' is the start vertex and the end vertex of a stroke of g_l. Although at this time we can not distinguish which vertex is start vertex and which vertex is end vertex but it will not return a wrong result.

Orientation Relationship	f_1	f_2
h_l	$Max(v_s.x, v_e.x)$	$Min(v_s'.x, v_e'.x)$
h_r	$Min(v_s.x, v_e.x)$	$Max(v_s'.x, v_e'.x)$
h_u	$Max(v_s.y, v_e.y)$	$Min(v_s'.y, v_e'.y)$
h_d	$Min(v_s.y, v_e.y)$	$Max(v_s'.y, v_e'.y)$

3.2.2.1 CCM Definition. In the system we use a CONDESATION tracking algorithm based on Chinese Calligraphic Model (CCM) to extract strokes order from Chinese Calligraphic handwriting. Chinese Calligraphic Model (CCM) includes the stroke's thickness feature extracted from contour and other features extracted from the skeleton of a calligraphic image after thinning. CCM can be denoted as a 4-tuple:

$M = \{r, k, w, o\}$, where r means the relationship between line segments of a substroke/radical, k, w and o represent curvature, stroke's thickness and direction of skeletal pixel respectively. An instance of CCM model can identify a Chinese calligraphic character.

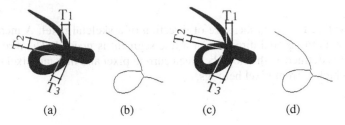

Fig. 3. Sample A and B has the similar skeleton (a) Stroke's thickness relation of Sample A is $T_1<T_3<T_2$ (b) Skeleton of Sample A (c) Stroke's thickness of Sample B relation is $T_1<T_2<T_3$ (d) Skeleton of Sample B

Table 3. Comparison of strokes order recovered with previous method with assumption of minimization of curvature and the real strokes order

Sample	Source image	Previous method result	Real strokes order
A			
B			

a) Line Segment Relation

The relationship between line segments can be represented by means of Attributed Relational Graph (ARG). In an ARG, the nodes denote the primitives and the arcs denote the relationship between nodes [5]. Fig. 4 (a) is ARG of Sample B.

b) Discrete Curvature

The skeleton of a Chinese calligraphic character can be considered as a discrete curve if the strokes order is already known. Curvature of discrete curve can be calculated by K-slope method. The K-slope at a pixel is defined as the slope of a line connecting that pixel with its Kth right neighbor. The K-curvature at a pixel is defined as the difference between the K-slope at that pixel and the K-slope of its Kth left neighbor. K-curvature can be calculated:

$$k(\theta) = \left\{ \tan^{-1}\left(\frac{y_{i+k} - y_i}{x_{i+k} - x_i} \right) - \tan^{-1}\left(\frac{y_i - y_{i-k}}{x_i - x_{i-k}} \right) \right\} \bmod 2\pi$$

c) Direction

Discrete curvature is a local measure of direction of a skeletal pixel. A measurement which represents the global direction of a line segment is needed. The direction of a skeletal pixel is defined as the slope between current pixel and the start pixel of the line segment to which current pixel belongs.

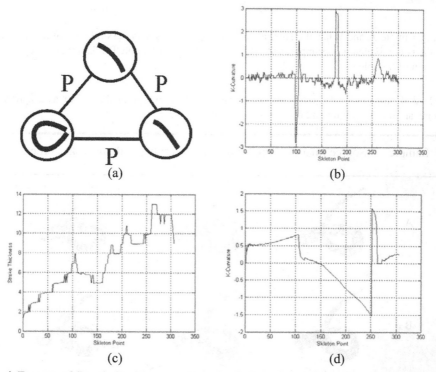

(a)   (b)

(c)   (d)

Fig. 4. Features of Sample B with assumption of anti-clockwise strokes order at cross point (a) ARG representation, the relation codes "P" stand for end-to-end adjacency (b) K-curvature variation over time (c) Stroke's thickness variation over time (d) Direction variation over time

3.2.2.2 Tracking Process. The aim of tracking process is to search the best matching model in the model database with the input pattern based on CCM thus we can get the strokes order of the input pattern. According the definition of CCM we can find that the tracking process is a hybrid statistical- structural method which includes two steps: coarse selection and fine selection. Corse selection belongs to relational matching and the fine selection belongs to probabilistic matching.

a) Coarse Selection

The purpose of coarse selection is to select a small subset of candidate models for fine selection. Coarse selection can be accomplished by relational matching. Relational matching is the search for a correspondence between the input pattern and the models in the model database with Attributed Relational Graph (ARG) which is one of the features of CCM. A well-known heuristic search algorithm, the A* search has been used for ARG matching in the system.

b) Fine Selection

The aim of fine selection is to find the best matching models from the subset selected by coarse selection. The fine selection is based on CCM with CONDENSATION Tracking.

The CONDENSATION algorithm belongs to the general class of Monte Carlo filters and it provides a framework for dynamic state estimation. The algorithm uses a set of random samples or particles to represent the propagation of arbitrary probability densities over time. The advantage of the algorithm is that it is able to propagate the probability densities of many states in the search space and it is particularly useful for multiple-tracking problems. The algorithm can be used to find the most likely state, which is best match with input or observation data [6].

Strokes order is a kind of time sequence information so that the CONDENSATION tracking can be performed to CCM. The goal is to take a set of M models trajectories $\{m^{(\mu)}, \mu = 1,...,M\}$, where $m^{(\mu)} = (m_1^{(\mu)},...,m_K^{(\mu)})$, and match them against an input pattern according CCM. The whole tracking process on CCM includes four main steps: initializing, prediction, updating, and selection.

Initializing

The search space is firstly initialized by initializing S model states according the result of coarse selection. This produces a states set $\{s_t^{(n)}, n = 1,..., S\}$, where $s_t = (\mu, k, w, o)$ represents a state at time t.

Prediction

Let $Z_t = (z_t, z_{t-1},...)$ be the observation data, the skeletal pixels sequence with certain strokes order. The observation vector for a particular trajectory i is $Z_{t,i} = (z_{t,i}, z_{(t-1),i}, z_{(t-2),i},....)$ according the definition of CCM. To find likelihood for each state, dynamic time warping is performed. This is calculated as the probability of the observation z_t given the state s_t is given by:

$$p(z_t \mid s_t) = \prod_{i=0}^{K} p(Z_{t,i} \mid s_t)$$

where

$$p(Z_{t,i}) = \frac{1}{\sqrt{2\pi\sigma_i}} \exp \frac{-\sum_{j=0}^{l-1}\left((z_{(t-j),i} - m_{(t-j),i}^{(\mu)})\right)}{2\sigma_i(l-1)},$$

where l is the size of the temporal window over which matching from t backwards to $t-l-1$ occurs, σ_i is an estimate of the standard deviation for the trajectory i for the whole sequence. With definition of $p(z_t \mid s_t)$, the probability distribution of the whole search space at one time instant can be created. The weighting is calculated as follows:

$$\pi_t^{(n)} = \frac{p(z_t \mid s_t^{(n)})}{\sum_{i=1}^{S} p(z_t \mid s_t^{(i)})}$$

Updating

This step is responsible for update the status of state according the new weighting value $\pi_t^{(n)}$.

Selection

Selection is responsible for select a state from time $t-1$ according to the probability distribution at time $t-1$. Current probability distribution over states is used to choose likely states to predict into the future. This is done by constructing a cumulative probability distribution with $\pi_{t-1}^{(n)}$. Cumulative probability is defined as:

$$c_{t-1}^{(0)} = 0$$

$$c_{t-1}^{(0)} = c_{t-1}^{(n-1)} + \pi_{t-1}^{(n)}$$

States with high cumulative probability may have more opportunity to be chosen, while others with low weight may not be chosen at all.

4   Experiment Result

Sample B is tested as an input pattern and first step is to resize to standard size: 150×200 pixels. Fig. 4(a) is the ARG of Sample B and Table 4 shows the results of coarse selection. Sample B has two possible strokes orders choice at loop part that one is clockwise, denoted as S_1, and the other is anti-clockwise, denoted as S_2. S_1 and S_2 are applied CONDENSATION Tracking respectively. The values of σ_* is chosen to be 0.06 for k, 0.09 for w and o. l is chosen to be 8. Table 5 shows the probability distribution of 8 models matched with S1 and S2 at time instant 300. We can find that Model 6 has the maximum probability and it is the best matching model of Sample B when it is anti-clockwise at the loop. So the strokes order of S_1 is the real strokes order of Sample B.

Table 4. Models selected after coarse selection

Model 1	Model 2	Model 3	Model 4
Model 5	Model 6	Model 7	Model 8

Table 5. Probability distribution of CONDENSATION Tracking of two strokes order choice of Sample B, time instant equals 300

Mo del	1	2	3	4	5	6	7	8
S_1	0.13	0.21	0.16	0.06	0.06	0.82	0.12	0.12
S_2	0.18	0.19	0.15	0.06	0.09	0.12	0.13	0.08

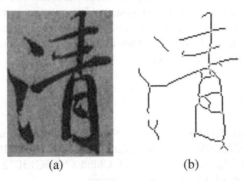

(a)   (b)

Fig. 5. (a) Original calligraphy character and (b) its skeleton

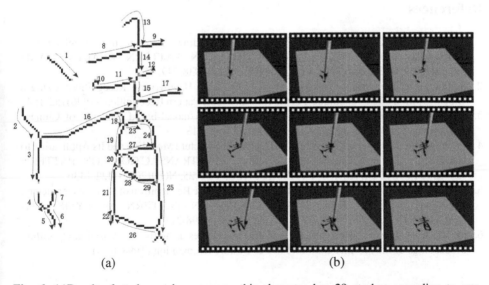

(a)   (b)

Fig. 6. (a)Result of strokes order recovery: this character has 29 strokes according to our proposed stroke extraction rule (b) Screen shots of the writing process: one shot every 3 seconds

To widely test CONDENSATION Tracking on CCM, we build the samples of 40 frequently used radicals with different styles from *Chinese Calligraphy Collected Edition* published by Rong Bao Zhai. Strokes order of these samples is manually set. We use another 1000 handwriting also selected from the other volume of *Chinese Calligraphy Collected Edition* as input sample. The final result of tracking process achieves 94 percent accuracy. The inaccuracy is mostly caused by poor image quality as most of them are rubbed from stone inscriptions.

Fig. 5(a) is part of works written by WANG Xi-zhi, a famous Chinese calligraphist who lived about 1600 years ago and Fig. 5(b) is the skeleton after applied the thinning algorithm. Fig. 6(a) is the result of strokes order extraction. Fig. 6(b) demonstrates some screen shots of the writing process captured from the Client Module.

In this paper we discuss methods to extract stroke's thickness and strokes order from Chinese calligraphic handwriting. Basing on these methods, we implemented a 3D Chinese Calligraphic Handwriting Recur system. This system can help people enjoy the writing beauty of calligraphy character and set good writing examples for user to follow. Now this system is put into use (www.cadal.zju.edu.cn) and has about 2000 samples for animating the writing process.

Acknowledgement

This project supported by the National Natural Science Foundation of China (No.60533090, No.60525108), 973 Program (No.2002CB312101), Science and Technology Project of Zhejiang Province of China (2005C13032, 2005C11001-05) and China-US Million Book Digital Library Project.

References

1. Yoshiharu Kato, Makoto Yasuhara: Recovery of drawing order from single-strokes handwriting images", IEEE TRANSACTIONS ON PATTERN ANALYSIS AND MACHINE INTELLIGENCE, VOL.22, NO.9, (2000) 938-949,
2. Stefan Jäger: Recovering Writing Traces in Off-Line Handwriting Recognition: Using a Global Optimization Technique", Proc. 13th Int'l conf. Pattern Recognition, (1996)152-154,
3. Helena T.F. Wong, Horace H.S. Ip.: Virtual brush: a model-based synthesis of Chinese calligraphy, Computers & Graphics, Vol. 24(2000)99-113
4. In-Jung Kim, Jin-Hyung Kim: Statistical Character Structure Modeling and Its Application to Handwritten Chinese Character Recognition, IEEE TRANSACTIONS ON PATTERN ANALYSIS AND MACHINE INTELLIGENCE, VOL.25, NO.9(2003)1422-1436
5. Cheng-Lin Liu, Stefan Jaeger, Masaki Nakagawa: Online Recognition of Chinese Characters: The State-of-the-Art, IEEE TRANSACTIONS ON PATTERN ANALYSIS AND MACHINE INTELLIGENCE, VOL. 26, NO. 2(2004)198-213
6. M. Black, A. Jepson. : Recognizing temporal trajectories using the condensation algorithm, Proceedings of the 3rd Int'l Conf on Face & Gesture Recognition (1998)16-21

Clouds and Atmospheric Phenomena Simulation in Real-Time 3D Graphics

Jakub Grudziński and Adrian Dębowski

The Silesian University of Technology,
Institute of Computer Science,
ul. Akademicka 16, 44-100 Gliwice, Poland
{jakub.grudzinski, adrian.debowski}@polsl.pl
http://www.polsl.pl

Abstract. The paper introduces a new, computationally inexpensive, real-time method of simulation of clouds for dynamic particle-based cloud rendering. The method covers such phenomena as atmospheric fronts, stable and unstable balance, thunderstorms, simplified simulation of middle and high clouds, correlation between wind and clouds and even tornadoes. The simulation is based on several simple numeric global parameters, like average temperature and average amount of clouds, which determine the local weather. It is also capable of generating multiple forms of clouds (from *stratus* through *cumulonimbus*), which may fluently change during the simulation.

1 Introduction

Generation of dynamic, realistic clouds for 3D graphics engines is a task consisting of two main stages: simulation and rendering. During the past years many cloud simulation and rendering systems have been introduced. In some cases emphasis was put on both of the stages; the simulation was based on the *Navier-Stokes* equations for incompressible flow [1], *Lattice Boltzmann* Model [2] or cellular automaton [3]. In other cases the first stage was omitted [4] and emphasis was put only on realistic cloud rendering. It is obvious that the last method is computationally least expensive as the simulation itself puts heavy load on a processor. However, it is also least flexible, as it requires cloud models created by artists. The cloud dynamics is therefore limited to simple formation and dissipation only.

The new method presented in this paper introduces a simplified simulation, which may not be as precise as methods based on the *Navier-Stokes* equations or *Lattice Boltzmann* Model, but is computationally far less expensive. The emphasis is also put on flexibility; the two stages mentioned above are separated, so any rendering-only system may be used to render the generated clouds. Additionally, the simulation may be easily controlled by any superior program (i.e. a computer game, flight simulator, simple presentation program etc.), so that any type of weather may be generated and transitions between different types of weather are always fluent.

A. Gagalowicz and W. Philips (Eds.): MIRAGE 2007, LNCS 4418, pp. 117–127, 2007.

2 Simplified Probabilistic Weather Model

Main idea of the discussed weather simulation system is random generation of particles (in the simulation a single particle represents a certain volume of condensed vapor, therefore being an elementary part of a cloud). Therefore the term "probabilistic weather model" is used. In contrast with models based on the *Navier-Stokes* equations, *Lattice Boltzmann* Model or cellular automatons, the space is continuous and is **not** represented as a 3D grid. The particles are dynamic objects with many parameters, such as position, velocity, trajectory, life span etc., like in a classic particle systems [5]. Without the 3D grid the system needs only to update a certain percentage of particles in a single simulation frame (making the percentage a parameter makes it possible to balance the accuracy of the simulation and the load it puts on the processor), without the necessity of calculating each cell's state. This makes the system far more efficient than any grid-based systems.

2.1 Cloud Generation Function

The particles are generated in random positions and random number. A distribution function is therefore used to control the number of generated particles. The function is a 2D matrix function covering the whole simulation area. It is called *cloud generation function* and is a generalization of a probability density function. In each simulation frame, a number of particles is generated with distribution determined by the function. Therefore, if the value of the function is high in a certain area, it is highly probable that a cloud is forming there. On the other hand, the sky remains clear above the areas where the values are low.

If a particle is generated, its exact starting position (in horizontal plane) is determined by a uniform distribution in the corresponding function cell. This ensures that the positions of the particles are real values, not limited to the resolution determined by the cloud generation function.

2.2 Generation of Particles

The cloud generation function determines where particles are generated and therefore determines the types of clouds forming and dissipating in the sky. If the function is flat, the whole sky is covered with clouds (*stratus* clouds), because the distribution is close to uniform. On the contrary, the more its values differ, the higher and more clear *cumulus* clouds form in the sky (refer to chapter 2.3 for more details). However, the function is only a technical solution of the issue of generating particles. The real processes that take place during the formation of clouds must be taken into consideration for the simulation to give realistic results.

The forming and dissipating clouds influence physical quantities like temperature, pressure and wind. For example, a forming *cumulus* cloud sucks the air from the area around the cloud (therefore making wind grow stronger) because under and inside the cloud an updraft appears. If the current is strong enough and general weather conditions are favorable, the *positive feedback* causes the cloud to grow into a *cumulonimbus* cloud followed by a thunderstorm (refer to [6] and [7] for more details). With the cloud generation function, simulation of the feedback is trivial: the value of the function where a particle comes into being is increased, therefore causing the cloud to grow by generating more particles.

Along with the positive feedback in the cloud generation function, the values of physical quantities (wind, temperature, pressure and humidity) are also changed in the neighborhood of the point where a particle is generated. The quantities are represented by 2D scalar and vector fields, which represent their values close to the ground level. Each generated particle represents an elementary part of a forming cloud and therefore increases the updraft under the cloud. Pressure is therefore decreased by a certain number for each generated particle (updrafts cause the pressure to decrease while downdrafts increase it). Temperature is also decreased for the lack of sunshine and cooling effect of precipitation. However, the local variations in the values of these fields do not influence the shapes of forming clouds – they are rather an additional output of the model than integral part. The average values of the fields are important though (compare with chapter 2.3), because they influence the cloud generation function. Low temperature flattens the function by a percentage depending on the temperature's value once for a certain number of simulation frames, therefore causing it to generate *stratus* clouds. On the contrary, if the temperature is high, the function is amplified, therefore increasing the probability of a thunderstorm being generated.

Wind simulation is more complex, because the local wind variations influence the clouds. Its main idea has been described in chapter 2.5. Refer to [8] for more details about the wind simulation and to [6] for more information about other fields.

2.3 Global Parameters

In chapter 2.2 general weather conditions were mentioned. It is obvious that the positive feedback which makes *cumulus* clouds grow not always leads to a formation of *cumulonimbus*. If humidity or temperature are too low and the simulation area is not under influence of an atmospheric front, *cumulus* clouds grow to a certain extent and then dissipate. General weather conditions which determine the weather in the whole simulation area are therefore introduced, such as global temperature or global pressure. Local atmospheric phenomena like formation of clouds influence the local variations of physical quantities, while their average values are given as simulation parameters. If a parameter's value is changed, the values of the corresponding field are fluently scaled to the given value, therefore causing the weather to change fluently. This also prevents positive feedback in cloud generation function from making the function's values grow constantly.

Apart from average values of fields, *balance type* [21] is one of the most important parameters. In case of a warm atmospheric front a *stable balance* occurs, causing *stratus* clouds to grow, while in case of a cold atmospheric front an *unstable balance* causes variable and strong wind and forming of *cumulonimbus* clouds. If the balance type is a numeric parameter, it can easily control the cloud generation function by flattening or amplifying it (in a way similar to temperature; see chapter 2.2), depending on the value of the parameter. For low values (stable balance) the function is more flat and therefore generates *stratus* clouds through generating particles with distribution close to uniform. Because of the correlation between clouds and physical quantities, like wind, every aspect of the weather is typical of a warm front in this case. On the other hand, for high parameter values (unstable balance), *cumulus* and *cumulonimbus* clouds are generated with strong and unstable wind.

Atmospheric fronts are also strongly connected with special types of clouds appearing before the front passes through the simulation area [21]. These are clouds forming in middle and upper layers (middle and high clouds), like *cirrus, cirrocumulus, cirrostratus, altocumulus* or *altostratus* [21]. These clouds are simulated as separate objects, without the use of particles (the problem of atmospheric fronts is very complex – please, refer to [6] and [7] for more details).

2.4 Realistic, Three-Dimensional Clouds

Generation of particles based on a 2D probability density function is not enough for realistic 3D clouds, because it does not cover the height of the clouds. As it was stated in chapter 2, like in classic particle systems [5], particles have many parameters, like life span and velocity. However, the most important of all are trajectory parameters. Air inside the cloud together with condensed water vapor constantly move, changing the shape and size of the cloud. It is therefore crucial to determine the trajectories of particles.

In most cases clouds form through convection [21]. Hot air moves upwards and expands and therefore becomes cooler, while water vapor condenses forming a cloud. Then cooled air floats aside (in cases of strong convection cells forming a characteristic anvil-shaped *cumulonimbus* clouds) and down[1]. This movement trajectory can be estimated by exponent[2]:

$$z = h(1 - \exp(-x'/X)),\qquad(1)$$

where z is the current particle's ceiling, h is its maximum ceiling, x' is a distance between current particle's position and the point where it was generated (in horizontal plane only) and X is a constant value.

The parameters of a certain particle are determined by the value of the cloud generation function (with the exception of X' axis which is random in horizontal plane) in the point where the particle was generated. The velocity, maximum ceiling and life span are in direct proportion to the cloud generation function – therefore in case of high function value the particle floats aside when it is close to reaching its maximum ceiling. This leads to a formation of anvil-shaped *cumulonimbus* clouds. In case of lower function value, the particle's life span is much shorter, so that it disappears before reaching ceiling high enough to float aside. This leads to a formation of *cumulus* and *stratocumulus* clouds. If the function is flat, trajectories of particles are similar, so that *stratus* clouds form (*vide* fig. 1).

Clouds dissipate fluently as soon as the values of the cloud generation function lower, because less particles are generated and their parameters' reduce in values.

---

[1] Such phenomena occur mostly in case of unstable balance.

[2] The exponent estimates only the first part of the trajectory (an updraft and then floating aside). However, during the last stage (downdraft) vapor does not condense and therefore no clouds appear.

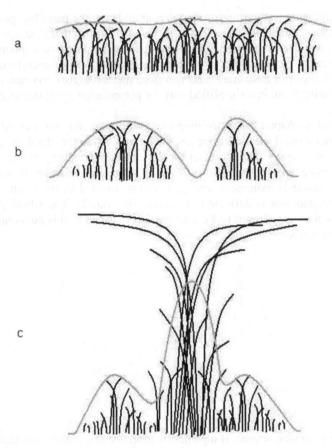

Fig. 1. Relationship between cloud generation function and particles' trajectories (vertical section of clouds). *Grey lines* represent cloud generation function and *black lines* represent trajectories of particles; *a – stratus, b – cumulus, c – cumulonimbus.*

Stratus clouds form mainly due to *advection* [21]. The velocities of particles are therefore low. In each simulation frame all particles' positions are updated[3] according to the velocity parameter and wind. If the parameter's value is low, the particle moves horizontally because the component resulting from wind (and wind is represented as a 2D vector field) is much higher. Therefore *stratus* clouds look realistic although the corresponding particles' trajectories are vertical (see fig. 1: in the picture the wind velocity component is not covered).

2.5 Other Atmospheric Phenomena

Apart from clouds and physical quantities, many other atmospheric phenomena are simulated. These include tornadoes, rotation of supercells, precipitation and atmospheric discharges, which are discussed in the following subchapters.

---

[3] In fact, a certain percentage of particles is updated, as was stated in the beginning of chapter 2.

Tornadoes. Giving consideration to wind during updating the particles' positions not only makes stratus clouds look more realistic, but also ensures that clouds move in the sky. However, wind may also be useful for the simulation of such phenomena as tornadoes. In reality tornadoes occur seldom, but make havoc of everything on their paths and often result in casualties, and therefore meteorologists pay much attention to them. Simulating them in a simplified way for presentation programs might be very useful then.

As was stated in chapter 2.2, a forming *cumulus* or *cumulonimbus* cloud sucks the air from the area around the cloud because under and inside the cloud an updraft appears. In case of a heavy thunderstorm the current may be strong enough to create a tornado. For extremely high values of the cloud generation function the wind generated under the cloud is extremely strong. It is not directed to the point, where the particle is generated, but is deflected sideways (*vide* fig. 2). The whole problem is mathematically too complicated to be thoroughly described in this publication. Refer to [8] for more details.

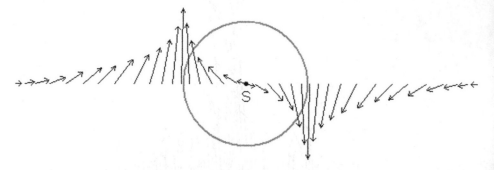

Fig. 2. Tornado generation scheme. If a particle is generated at a certain point (here point *S*), several *wind vectors* in random positions are added to the wind vector field, with directions and values depending on the value of the cloud generation function in point *S* and distance between point *S* and the point where a vector is calculated. During the simulation many particles are generated and therefore many vectors are added, which may result in a tornado being generated (*grey circle*).

Generating rotation in wind vector field is not enough for a tornado to appear. A number of particles must be generated right above the face of the earth. The initial ceiling of particles depends on the value of the cloud generation function, pressure and wind – if the wind velocity at the point where a particle is generated is extremely high, the initial ceiling is very low. Therefore, as the air starts to rotate – and wind gets stronger – the *wall cloud* and then *funnel cloud* appear. If the critical wind value is reached, the tornado hits the face of the earth. Notice that particles forming the tornado automatically "behave" the way they should: they move upwards very fast due to high value of the cloud generation function and rotate with velocity determined by the wind. Tornadoes are therefore an inseparable part of the whole simulation, with all their aspects covered.

Rotating Supercells. Rotation is a common phenomenon in atmosphere. Apart from tornadoes which rotate in micro scale, in macro scale *cyclones* and *anticyclones* [21] rotate due to Coriolis force. These are gigantic pressure systems which cannot be simulated in real time for the cloud visualization. However, the rotation sometimes occurs in a smaller scale in case of heavy thunderstorms, called *supercells* [21]. Such rotation can be easily simulated by twisting the trajectories of the particles into spirals. This can be achieved by rotating the X' axis for each trajectory (see fig. 1) by a small angle in every simulation frame. Because each trajectory in its beginning is almost vertical, the rotation is imperceptible. Therefore, it can be seen only in case of large *cumulonimbus* clouds.

Precipitation. Precipitation is simulated as an additional scalar field. A matrix is used to "store" the number of particles (and therefore density of a cloud layer) which are currently over each 2D cell. Precipitation is proportional to the thickness and density of a cloud layer. However, in reality not always heavy cloud layer results in precipitation. This is caused mainly by strong updrafts in case of thunderstorms. Therefore high cloud generation function value decreases precipitation in the corresponding area (notice that high values of the function always result in strong updrafts).

Atmospheric Discharges. Atmospheric discharges are generated randomly in areas where the cloud generation function reaches very high values. However, in real world the discharges occur only in case of *cumulonimbus* clouds. Balance type (see chapter 2.3) is therefore taken into consideration; the probability of a discharge is in direct proportion to the numeric value of the balance type global parameter. This ensures that no thunders follow *stratus* or *nimbostratus* clouds, while some occur if the balance is unstable and *cumulonimbus* clouds can be seen.

3 Rendering Issues

The discussed model generates data for visualization as a set of particles. Many different rendering techniques may be used then. The simplest way is to render every particle in each simulation frame with proper texture and proper level of transparency (maximum level of transparency after "birth" and before "death" and minimum level during "adult age"). Such method is computationally expensive though, as particles appear in great numbers in case of heavy clouds. Rendering distant clouds to impostors may be used then to greatly increase the performance [4, 9].

Shading and lighting are also important issues. For real-time cloud rendering on a large area a simple method may be used; shading depends only on density of cloud layer and ceiling of each particle. Cloud base is therefore dark, while upper parts are light. Such method does not include the position of the sun – it gives moderate results though, with good performance[4].

More advanced rendering techniques may be used. These have been introduced in [1], [3] and [9-15]. Rain and snow rendering methods have been presented in [16] and [17]. Refer to the listed references for more details.

---

[4] This method is used in current implementation in the *Flexible Reality Simulation* 3D graphics rendering engine [7, 17-19]. Refer to chapter 4 to view the results.

4 Conclusions and Results

Current implementation of the presented method works in *Flexible Reality Simulation* real-time 3D graphics engine [7, 17-19]. With the simulation area covering a 15 * 15 km square, deep profiling of the whole engine showed that the *weather simulation itself takes only about 2% of the whole load the engine puts on a processor and graphics adapter* (the engine includes terrain, animated 3D models, particle effects, rendering, sound, scripting etc. – refer to [7, 17-19] for more details) while the simulation is running in real time with about 30 frames per second. Such a result is more than satisfactory. However, cloud rendering is still computationally expensive and takes much more time than the simulation itself. Many optimization schemes may be implemented though, like rendering distant clouds to impostors [4]. With such schemes implemented, real-time (i.e. at least about 20-30 frames per second) weather simulation and cloud rendering may be performed on an area far larger than in case of other simulation methods presented in the referenced publications. However, as the discussed method is much more simplified than the *Navier-Stokes* or *Lattice-Boltzmann*-based mathematical models, it is not as accurate and might not be useful for presentation of a detailed formation of a single cloud.

In the figures 3 through 6, several types of clouds and a tornado are presented[5].

Fig. 3. *Cumulus humilis* clouds

---

[5] The presented clouds look far better in color. This paper in color is available for download from www.artifexmundi.com.

Fig. 4. *Cumulus mediocris* clouds

Fig. 5. *Nimbostratus* clouds

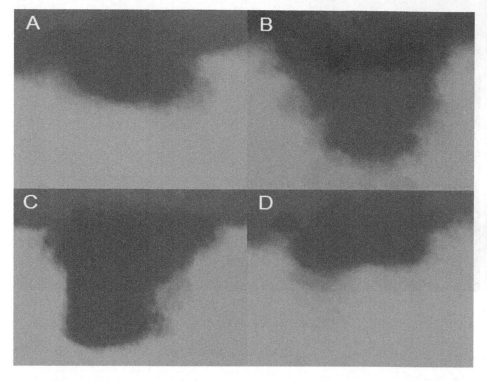

Fig. 6. Tornado evolution: A – *wall cloud*, B – *funnel cloud*, C – mature stage, D – dissipating

References

1. Harris, M. J.: Real-Time Cloud Simulation and Rendering. Technical Report, Department of Computer Science, University of North Carolina 2003
2. Wei, X., Li, W., Mueller, K., Kaufman, A. E.: The Lattice-Boltzmann Method for Simulating Gaseous Phenomena. IEEE Transactions on Visualization and Computer Graphics, vol. 10, no. 2, pp. 164-176, March/April, 2004
3. Dobashi, Y., Keneda, K., Yamashita, H., Okita, T., Nishita, T.: A Simple, Efficient Method for Realistic Animation of Clouds. SIGGRAPH 2000
4. Wang, N.: Realistic and Fast Cloud Rendering in Computer Games. SIGGRAPH 2003
5. Błaż, J.: Particle Systems and their Use in Computer Graphics for Modeling Selected Physical Phenomena, M.Sc. Thesis, The Silesian University of Technology, Gliwice 2004
6. Grudziński, J.: Realt-Time Atmospheric Phenomena Simulation Algorithms. M.Sc. Thesis, The Silesian University of Technology, Gliwice 2005
7. Grudziński, J., Dębowski, A.: Real-Time Weather Simulation in FRS Engine. Studia Informatica, vol. 27 no. 1 (66), The Silesian University of Technology, Gliwice 2006
8. Grudziński, J., Dębowski, A., Grudziński, T.: The Use of Particle Systems in Real-Time Atmospheric Phenomena Simulation and Rendering in FRS Engine. Studia Informatica, The Silesian University of Technology, Gliwice 2007 (in preparation)
9. Harris, M. J.: Real-Time Cloud Rendering for Games. Proceedings of Game Developers Conference 2002. March 2002

10. Harris, M., Lastra, A.: Real-Time Cloud Rendering. Computer Graphics Forum, Blackwell Publishers, vol. 20, pp. 76-84, 09.2001
11. Elbert, D.: Procedural Volumetric Modeling and Animation of Clouds and Other Gaseous Phenomena, SIGGRAPH 2002
12. Schpock, J., Simons, J., Ebert, D. S., Hansen, C.: A Real-Time Cloud Modeling, Rendering, and Animation System. SIGGRAPH 2003
13. Erez, E.: Interactive 3D Lighting in Sprites Rendering. Gamasutra 2005
14. Heinzlreiter, P., Kurka, G., Volkert, J.: Real-Time Visualization of Clouds. V. Skala, editor, Journal of WSCG 2002, volume 10(3), 2002
15. Trembilski, A., Broßler, A.: Surface-Based Efficient Cloud Visualisation for Animation Applications. V. Skala, editor, Journal of WSCG, volume 10, 2002
16. Wang, N., Wade, B.: Rendering Falling Rain and Snow. SIGGRAPH 2004
17. Dębowski, A., Grudziński, J.: The Issues and Methods of The Real-Time Atmospheric Phenomena Rendering in FRS Engine. Studia Informatica, The Silesian University of Technology, Gliwice 2007 (in preparation)
18. Grudzinski, T., Myslek, T., Ross, J.: The Issues of Three-Dimensional Collision Detection in FRS Engine. Studia Informatica, vol. 26 no. 4 (65), The Silesian University of Technology, Gliwice 2006
19. Grudzinski, T., Myslek, T., Ross, J.: The Advanced Techniques of Three-Dimensional Skeleton Models Animation in FRS Engine. Studia Informatica, vol. 27 no. 1 (66), The Silesian University of Technology, Gliwice 2006
20. Finnigan, J.: Mathematics in Environmental Science. Mathematical Sciences Symposium at the University of NSW, 23.02.1996, CSIRO Centre for Environmental Mechanics
21. Environmental Science Published for Everybody Round the Earth, http://www. espere.net/

Feature Points Detection Using Combined Character Along Principal Orientation

Sicong Yue, Qing Wang, and Rongchun Zhao

School of Computer Science and Engineering,
Northwestern Polytechnical University, Xi'an 710072, P.R. China
typhoonadam@gmail.com, qwang@nwpu.edu.cn

Abstract. Most existing methods for determining localization of the image feature point are still inefficient in terms of the precision. In the paper, we propose a new algorithm for feature point detection based on the combined intensity variation status along the adaptive principal direction of the corner. Firstly, we detect principal orientation of each pixel, instead of calculating the gradients along the horizontal and vertical axes. And then we observe the intensity variations of the pixel along the adaptive principal axes and its tangent one respectively. When the combined variation status is classified into several specific types, it can be used to determine whether a pixel is a corner point or not. In addition to corner detection, it is also possible to use our proposed algorithm to detect the edges, isolated point and plain regions of a natural image. Experimental results on synthetic and natural scene images have shown that the proposed algorithm can successfully detect any kind of the feature points with good accuracy of localization.

Keywords: feature point detection; principal orientation; intensity variation.

1 Introduction

Basically, 2D feature points are key points in the image, which have significant local variations in two directions, including not only the traditional corners, for example, L-, T-, Y- and X- junctions, but also the line terminals and respective features with significant 2D structure. As the feature point contains much information in image, it is the most economical way to describe an object using 2D feature points. As a result, feature point detection plays an important role in many applications such as image registration, scene analysis, stereo matching, 3D scene reconstruction and some other typical applications of computer vision.

In last decades, a great number of approaches for feature point detection have been proposed in the literatures [1-13], most of which are based on gray scale level. In order to emphasize the essence of feature point detection, we reviewed and compared them extensively in the following and divided them into four groups, which are contour-based feature point detection [1-3], gray scale level based methods [4-9], parametric model based feature point detection [10,11] and local energy model based approaches [12,13].

A. Gagalowicz and W. Philips (Eds.): MIRAGE 2007, LNCS 4418, pp. 128–138, 2007.

First of all, contour-based corner detection methods regarded the corner points as the junction of two or more edge lines. The typical procedure is to extract edges and transform them into chain codes first, and then to search the corner points by maximal curvature, or to search for the lines intersections by performing a polygonal approximation on the chains, or to extract the convex points from the edge points. The two main drawbacks of contour-based corner detectors are: on the one hand, for those edge detectors dependent on Gaussian filters, the detected corners are not well localized near the corners due to the rounding effect; on the other hand, the non-maximal suppression that is usually applied in edge detection will make the straight line curved, which is of course adverse to the corner detection.

Gray scale level based corner detection computes some measures indicating the presence of a corner directly from gray level of images. The main issues of those detectors are: firstly, there is no universal threshold due to the sensitivity to gray scale level, and thus a disadvantage to the corner detection on image sequences; secondly, Gaussian smoothing filter, which is usually used to reduce the noise, will undoubtedly decrease the accuracy of the localization; and finally, only limited types of feature points can be detected since some kinds of assumptions on the geometric structure for the feature point are used in these methods.

Parametric model based corner detection involved finding corners by fitting image signals with parametric models. The problem of this kind of detectors is that it is impossible to design suitable models with any directions and angles. As a result, incorrect results of corners detection often occur due to the complicated structures.

Local energy model based corner detector inspects corners in the frequency domain and thus gets rid of the limitation on the shape of the corners. This model postulates that feature points are perceived at points in an image where the Fourier components are maximally congruent in the phase domain. Since phase congruency is directly proportional to the local energy, it is possible to alternate corners detection to local energy inspection. The advantage of these methods is that they can be used to detect different kinds of interest points with good accuracy of localization. However, there still existed some issues, first of which is quite computationally expensive and another one is that there is no universal threshold for feature points.

According to Schmid's report in the literature [14], in all cases the results of Harris corner detector are better or equivalent to those of other existed detectors. However the accuracy of the localization by Harris detector is poor and Harris method cannot detect any type of corner in nature scene image. Our proposed method is to solve the problem on accuracy of the localization at corner and limitation of types of feature points. On the base of principal orientation detected, the representative intensity feature of corner points is obtained by observing the variations along the positive and negative directions respectively, which is consistent with human vision system.

The main contributions of the paper are:

1. The accuracy of localization of feature points can be achieved comparing with traditional methods as it dispenses with smoothing to reduce the noise disturbance and use the information of the adaptive principal axes at corner.
2. The intensity variations along the principal and tangent axes are much representative for recognizing the corner since each corner has much more distinct characteristics on its intrinsic principal direction than other directions.

3. Different kinds of feature points can be detected since it does not make any assumption on the geometric structure of feature points.

The paper is organized as follows: The foundation and advantages of intensity variation along the adaptive principal orientation and tangent axes are introduced in Section 2. In Subsection 2.1-2.4 the method of the computation of principal orientation and combined variation status is discussed and it is then shown how a pixel can be classified into the practical types from status-type tables. The procedure of feature point detection is proposed in Section 3. Finally, experimental results and conclusion are presented in Section 4 and 5 respectively.

2 Foundation and Advantages of Combined Status Along the Adaptive Principal Orientation Axes

The foundation of the proposed method can be found and illustrated in the Figure 1 and 2. Suppose an image $I(x, y)$ have a corner at (x_0, y_0), there must exist an axes $\mathbf{e_1}$, which is termed as the principal orientation axis, such that

(1) If $I(x, y)$ slice along the line $L_1 = [x_0, y_0] + \lambda \mathbf{e_1}$ ($\lambda \in R$), a step-like cross section can be obtained;

(2) If $I(x, y)$ slice along the line $L_2 = [x_0, y_0] + \lambda \mathbf{e_2}$ ($\lambda \in R$), where $\mathbf{e_2} \perp \mathbf{e_1}$, a ridge-like cross section can be obtained.

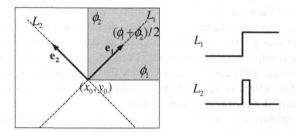

Fig. 1. The illustration of variations along the two perpendicular axes at the corner and cross section

In contrast, if (x_0, y_0) is on an edge as shown in Figure 2, after slicing, step-like functions are obtained for both line L_1 and L_2 (or a step-like function along L_1 and a constant-like function along L_2). If (x_0, y_0) is on a plain, after slicing, constant-like functions are obtained for both the two directions. Thus using the variations along the adaptive principal orientation axes is a good way to recognize whether a pixel is a corner.

The proposed method seems similar to the algorithms based on gradient measurement of gray scale level. However, there are several key differences, which are the advantages of the proposed algorithm.

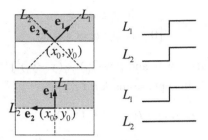

Fig. 2. The illustration of variations along the two perpendicular axes at the edge and cross section

(1) We observe the intensity variations along the specific line $L_1 = [x_0, y_0] + \lambda \mathbf{e}_1$ ($\lambda \in R$) and $L_2 = [x_0, y_0] + \lambda \mathbf{e}_2$ ($\lambda \in R$), which vary with the localized character of the image, instead of measuring intensity character along horizontal and vertical axes. Using adaptive principal orientation axes can improve the accuracy of corner detection, since in an image there are usually many corners whose orientations are far from 0 (the direction of horizontal axis) and $\pi/2$ (the direction of vertical axis). And, at the same time, we can obtain the exact angle of each corner with accurate estimation.

(2) We measure the sum of variations along the directions of $\mathbf{e}_1$, $-\mathbf{e}_1$, $\mathbf{e}_2$ and $-\mathbf{e}_2$, respectively (see equation (6)), which is more resistant to noise, instead of doing the first order differentiation. If we do the first order differentiation of $\partial/\mathbf{e}_i$ ($i = 1, 2$), which cannot separate the variations along $+\mathbf{e}_i$ and $-\mathbf{e}_i$, we can only observe three types of variations: (1) rising(+1), (2) falling(-1), and (3) remaining as a constant(0). Consequently, the information is too less to well recognize whether a pixel is a corner. However, to well distinguish between a corner and an edge, we suggest that the variations along $+\mathbf{e}_i$ and $-\mathbf{e}_i$ should be observed separately. If we observe the variations along $+\mathbf{e}_i$ and $-\mathbf{e}_i$ respectively, then along the line $L_i = [m, n] + l\mathbf{e}_i$ there are 9 types of variation status can be observed: (1) (-1,-1), (2) (-1,0), (3) (-1,+1), (4) (0,+1), (5) (0,0), (6) (+1,+1), (7) (0,-1), (8) (+1,-1) and (9) (+1,0). We illustrated them in detail in subsection 2.2. Since more types of variation can be observed, the more precision of corner detection can be obtained. Using them together with the status-type tables (see Table 1-4), we can distinguish a corner well from a complicated nature image.

(3) In addition to corner detection, with a little modification we can also use our algorithm to do edge detection, isolated dot detection, and plain region detection for an image. If we classify the pixel types into more subdivision, the proposed algorithm can extend to more detection applications.

2.1 Computing the Principal Orientation Angle of the Corner

Suppose that (x_0, y_0) is an ideal corner in the image $I(x, y)$, and surrounding the ideal corner, $I(x, y)$ can be expressed as:

$$I(x, y) = \begin{cases} k & \text{if } \phi_1 \le \phi \le \phi_2 \\ 0 & \text{if } \phi < \phi_1 \text{ or } \phi > \phi_2 \end{cases} \qquad (1)$$

where $\phi = \arg[(x-x_0)+j(y-y_0)]$ and $[(x-x_0)^2+(y-y_0)^2]^{1/2} \le R$.

If we convolve $I(x, y)$ with a phase-mask $P_m(x, y)$,

$$I_1(x, y) = I(x, y) * P_m(x, y) \qquad (2)$$

where $P_m(x, y) = -r\exp(j\varphi)$, if $r \le R$; otherwise $P_m(x, y) = 0$, $\varphi = \arg(x+jy)$, $r = (x^2+y^2)^{1/2}$.

We can prove that

$$\begin{aligned} I_1(x_0, y_0) &= \iint_{x^2+y^2 \le R} I(x_0+x, y_0+y)P_m(-x,-y)dxdy \\ &= \int_0^R \int_{\phi_1}^{\phi_2} kr\exp(j\varphi)d\varphi dr \\ &= -j\pi kR^2(e^{j\phi_2} - e^{j\phi_1}) \\ &= \pi kR^2 \sin\left((\phi_2-\phi_1)/2\right)e^{j(\phi_1+\phi_2)/2} \end{aligned} \qquad (3)$$

Notice that $(\phi_1+\phi_2)/2$ (that is $\arg[I_1(x_0, y_0)] = (\phi_1+\phi_2)/2$) is just the principal orientation of the corner. Thus, if we convolve an image with the phase-mask in (2) and take the phase part, at the corner pixel, we can explicitly obtain the principal orientation of the corner. Thus, in our algorithm, we treat $\arg[I_1(x, y)]$ as the principal orientation axis $\mathbf{e}_1$ and set the tangent axis $\mathbf{e}_2$ to satisfy $\mathbf{e}_1 \perp \mathbf{e}_2$.

In the form of digital implementation, the process of phase-mask convolution can be rewritten as:

$$I_1[m, n] = I[m, n] * P_m[m, n] \qquad (4)$$

where $I[m, n]$ is input image, $P_m[m, n] = -(m+jn)/(m^2+n^2)^{1/2}$, $m, n \in (-R, R)$. R is a small integer constant. For a 256×256 natural image, it is proper to choose R=3~10. After $I_1[m, n]$ is computed, we can define $\mathbf{e}_1$ and $\mathbf{e}_2$ as:

$$\begin{aligned} \mathbf{e}_1 &= (\cos\theta_1, \sin\theta_1) \\ \mathbf{e}_2 &= (\sin\theta_1, -\cos\theta_1) \end{aligned} \qquad \text{where } \theta_1[m, n] = \arg(I_1[m, n]) \qquad (5)$$

2.2 Measure the Combined Status of Intensity Variations

After $\mathbf{e}_1$ and $\mathbf{e}_2$ are determined in Section 2.1, we define the combined status of intensity variations along the four directions: $\mathbf{e}_1, \mathbf{e}_{-1}, \mathbf{e}_2$ and $\mathbf{e}_{-2}$ ($\mathbf{e}_{-1} = -\mathbf{e}_1$ and $\mathbf{e}_{-2} = -\mathbf{e}_2$). For each of the directions $\mathbf{e}_i$ ($i = \pm 1, \pm 2$), L pixels away from the center pixel will be considered. Assuming that pixel [m, n] as the center pixel in process, we use $[x_{li}[m, n], y_{li}[m, n]]$ ($i = \pm 1, \pm 2$, $l = 1 \sim L$) to denote the coordinate of the pixel on the direction of e_i with distance of l from $[m, n]$. Then, we measure the variations $V_i[m,n]$ along e_i ($i = \pm 1, \pm 2$):

$$V_i[m,n] = \sum_{l=1}^{L} M \left(I \left[x_{l_i}[m,n], y_{l_i}[m,n] \right] - I[m,n] \right) \tag{6}$$

where $M(\ )$ is some non-decreasing mapping function satisfying $M(a) = -M(-a)$. Then we choose some threshold T ($T > 0$) and classify the status of variations into three types:

Type 1: $V_i[m,n] \geq T$ (denoted by +1). It means the gray-level grows larger along the direction of e_i ;

Type 2: $-T < V_i[m,n] < T$ (denoted by 0). It means the gray-level changes less along the direction of e_i ;

Type 3: $V_i[m,n] \leq -T$ (denoted by -1). It means the gray-level grows smaller along the direction of e_i .

Thus, for each of the directions, there are 3 types of variations. We can combine the variations along e_i and e_{-i} ($i = 1, 2$), then along the line $L_i = [m,n] + le_i$ ($i = 1, 2$) there are 9 types of variation: (1) (-1,-1), (2) (-1,0), (3) (-1,+1), (4) (0,+1), (5) (0,0), (6) (+1,+1), (7) (0,-1), (8) (+1,-1) and (9) (+1,0). Note that case (7) (0,-1), case (8) (+1,-1) and case (9) (+1,0) are in fact the same as case (2) (-1,0), case (3) (-1,+1) and case (4) (0,+1) respectively, since e_i and e_{-i} are the direction-opposite vector on the same line L_i . The meaning of (-1,-1), for example, is that the cross section along L_i is a ridge-like function. Moreover, for (-1,+1) or (0,+1), we can conclude that the cross section along L_i is a step-like function.

2.3 Status-Type Tables

We can use the combined status of intensity variation obtained in subsection 2.2 to recognize whether a pixel is at a corner, on an edge, or on a plain. For example, from Figure 1, we can see that, if at the pixel $[m, n]$, the combined status of variation is: along L_1 (0,-1) and along L_2 (-1,-1), then $[m, n]$ is a corner. In addition, from Figure 2, if the status of variation is L_1 :(-1,+1) and L_2 :(-1,+1), the pixel is on an edge. If the status of variation is L_1 :(0,0) and L_2 :(0,0), the pixel is on a plain. In subsection 2.2, we have illustrated that along the principal orientation or tangent line L_i ($i = 1, 2$), there are 9 kinds of variation. Thus there are totally 81 kinds of combined status of variation. Apart from multi representation forms of one status, only 36 kinds of status are irrelevant and independent with each other. Accordingly we can classify the 36 kinds of combined status into several types of image feature so as to conclude a set of status-type tables. In Table 1-4, we show the all combined status for each type of image feature. With them and the combined status of intensity variations, we can recognize whether a pixel is at a corner, on an edge, or on a plain.

Table 1. The combined status at a corner

Type	Corner									
L_1	(1)	(1)	(2)	(2)	(3)	(3)	(4)	(4)	(6)	(6)
L_2	(2)	(3)	(1)	(4)	(1)	(6)	(2)	(6)	(3)	(4)

Table 2. The combined status on an edge

Type	Edge								
L_1	(2)	(2)	(3)	(3)	(3)	(3)	(4)	(4)	(5)
L_2	(2)	(3)	(2)	(3)	(4)	(5)	(3)	(4)	(3)

Table 3. The combined status on a plain region

Type	Plain				
L_1	(2)	(4)	(5)	(5)	(5)
L_2	(5)	(5)	(2)	(4)	(5)

Table 4. The combined status at other pixel (such as ridge, valley or isolated dot)

Type	Other											
L_1	(1)	(1)	(1)	(1)	(2)	(4)	(5)	(5)	(6)	(6)	(6)	(6)
L_2	(1)	(4)	(5)	(6)	(6)	(1)	(1)	(6)	(1)	(2)	(5)	(6)

2.4 Non-maximum Suppression

After looking for the status-type tables, some pixels are recognized as the corners. This is not the final result, since in the region surrounding a corner there is usually more than one pixel recognized as a corner. We should use some criterion to choose the corner among the corner candidates. In this paper criterion is defined as:

$$c[m,n] = \sum_{i=\pm1,\pm2} |V_i[m,n]| \tag{7}$$

Then use non-maximum suppression to find the local peaks of neighborhood and choose them as corners.

3 Computation Procedure of the Proposed Algorithm

From Sections 2, we can conclude the computation process of feature point detection using combined characteristic of principal orientation as follows:

1) Use the phase mask to determine the principal orientation axis e_1 for each pixel.
2) Then measure the intensity variations along the directions of e_1, $-e_1$, e_2 and $-e_2$ to obtain the combined status.

3) Use the status-type tables to recognize whether the pixel can be treated as a candidate for corner.

4) Among the corner candidates, select the ones whose scores are larger than the neighboring corner candidates using non-maximum suppression.

4   Experimental Results and Discussion

In Fig. 3 and 4, some contrast experiments are implemented on the synthetic and natural scene images by our algorithm and Harris' algorithm. Red crosses are used to show the localization of detected corners. In experiments, the threshold is manually tuned to produce the best result. Finally, a non-maximal suppression with window size of 5×5 is made on the both detectors.

Fig. 3. The illustrations of the detection results on a synthetic image with two detectors. (a) a synthetic test image containing a variety of 2D image features. (b) and (c) are the results of 2D features points detected by the proposed method based on combined character along principal orientation and Harris detector, respectively.

Fig. 4. The illustration of the feature point detection results with the different detectors on a natural scene and a portrait image. (a) and (b) are the original image of Arenberg castle and Lena respectively, which contain different kinds of 2D features. (c) and (d) show the feature points detected by our proposed algorithm. By contrast, (e) and (f) show the results detected by the Harris detector respectively.

Firstly, we investigate the behavior of the proposed approach. Figure 3(a) is the original synthetic image and the feature points map based on our approach using combined character along principal orientation axes are shown in (b). All the feature points are detected successfully and localized accurately. However, some of markings are made due to the aliasing effects of step on the edges of the slope.

The feature points detected by Harris detector are shown in Figure 3(c). The Harris corner detector performs not as good as the former detector. Apart from one T-junctions on the up-left dark region undetected, all the interest points are extracted, but the localization is relatively poor. At the same time, two feature points are detected at three Y-junctions of different intensity regions intersection in the middle of the image while there is only one cross point at each intersection region. Another problem is just like the case that occurred in our proposed method, which is that some of feature points were detected on the edges of slope. This is because slope edges are not so smooth that the positive corner occurs at each step on slope.

Experiment results by the different corner detectors on a natural scene image (Arenberg castle) and Lena image are also shown in Figure 4. Figure 4(a) is the original image of the Arenberg castle image, which contains different kinds of 2D feature points. Figure 4(c) and (e) show the feature points detected by our proposed method and the Harris detector respectively. We can see that almost all feature points in Arenberg castle image are detected by the two detectors successfully, so both detectors perform pretty much the same thing and are both satisfying.

Figure 4(b) is the original image of Lena image, which is very complicated, and the detection results based on two detectors are shown in Figure4 (d) and (f). Harris method misses some feature points at eyes and nose of the face, while our algorithm does well. On the other hand, many edge pixels are recognized as corner by Harris detector. It is shown that our proposed algorithm can reduce the probability of misunderstanding the pixels in the regions of edges.

5 Conclusions

The intensity variation, along the adaptive principal orientation at all kinds of 2D features in an image, including gray-level corners, line terminations and different kinds of junction point, corresponds to the maximum in all direction of pixel, which is effective for 2D image feature detection. In the paper, we proposed a novel method for feature point detection based on combined variations of brightness along the principal orientation axes. The main points of our work can be concluded as: firstly, the accuracy of localization of feature points can be achieved comparing with traditional methods as it determines the practical principal orientation at each pixel; secondly, intensity variation along the practical principal orientation axes is the most representative character of each corner; and finally, different kinds of feature points can be detected since it does not make any assumption on the geometric structure of feature points. Experimental results on synthetic and natural scene images have shown that the proposed method can successfully detect almost all the feature points with good accuracy of localization. In addition, with some modification, the proposed method can be used for edge detection. However, the main shortcoming of the proposed method is that it is quite time consuming due to the many times convolution of image with filters for determining the principal orientation.

Acknowledgments. The work in this paper was supported by Aerospace Support Fund and National Natural Science Fund (60403008), P. R. China.

References

1. Mokhtarian, F., Suomela, R.: Robust Image Corner Detection through Curvature Scale Space. IEEE Transactions on Pattern Analysis and Machine Intelligence. 20(1998) 1376-1381.
2. Pikaz, A., Dinstein, I.: Using Simple Decomposition for Smoothing and Feature Point Detection of Noisy Digital Curves. IEEE Transactions on Pattern Analysis and Machine Intelligence. 16(1994) 808-813.
3. Minakshi, B., Kundu, M.K., Mitra, P.: Corner Detection using Support Vector Machines. Proceedings of the International Conference on Pattern Recognition. Cambridge, U.K. (2004) 819-822.
4. Harris, C., Stephens, M.: A Combined Corner and Edge Detector. Proceedings of the 4th Alvey Vision Conference. Manchester, U.K. (1988) 147-151.
5. Trajkovicm, H.M.: Fast Corner Detection. Image and Vision Computing. 16(1998) 75-87.
6. Smith, S.M., Brady, J.M.: SUSAN - A New Approach to Low Level Image Processing. International Journal of Computer Vision. 23(1997) 45-78.
7. Deriche, R., Giraudon, G.: A Computational Approach for Corner and Vertex Detection. International Journal of Computer Vision.10(1993) 101-124.
8. Zhiqiang, Z., Han, H., Eam, K.T.: Analysis of Gray Level Corner Detection. Pattern Recognition Letters. 20(1999) 149-162.
9. Kenney, C.S., Zuliani, M., Manjunath, B.S.: An Axiomatic Approach to Corner Detection. Proceedings of the International Conference on Computer Vision and Pattern Recognition. San Diego, USA. (2005) 191-197.
10. Baker, S., Nayar, S.K., Murase, H.: Parametric Feature Detection. International Journal of Computer Vision, 27(1998) 27-50.
11. Parida, L., Geiger, D., Hummel, R.: Junctions: Detection, Classification, and Reconstruction. IEEE Transactions on Pattern Analysis and Machine Intelligence. 20(1998) 687-698.
12. Benjamin, J.R.: The Detection of 2D Image Feature using Local Energy. Perth: Department of Computer Science, The University of Western Australia. 1996
13. Peter, K.: Image Features from Phase Congruency. Videre: Journal of Computer Vision Research, MIT, 1(1999) 1-26.
14. Schimid, C., Mohr, R., Bauckhage, C.: Evaluation of Interest Point Detectors. International Journal of Computer Vision. 37(2000) 151-172.

Fast Virtual Cloth Energy Minimization

Tung Le Thanh and André Gagalowicz

INRIA Rocquencourt, Rocquencourt 78153, France
Tung.Lethanh@inria.fr

Abstract. In this paper we present a method for fast energy minimization of virtual garments. Our method is based upon the idea of multi-
resolution particle system. When garments are approximately positioned
around a virtual character, their spring energy may be high, which will
cause instability or at least long execution time of the simulation. An energy minimization algorithm is needed; if a fixed resolution is used, it will
require many iterations to reduce its energy. Even though the complexity
of each iteration is O(n), with a high resolution mass-spring system, this
minimization process can take a whole day. The hierarchical method presented in this paper is used to reduce significantly the execution time of
the minimization process. The garments are firstly discretized in several
resolutions. Once the lowest resolution particles system is minimized (in
a short time), a higher resolution model is derived, then minimized. The
procedure is iterated up to the highest resolution. But at this stage, the
energy to minimize is already much lower so that minimization takes a
reasonable time.

1 Introduction

With advances in computer graphics over the last few decades, virtual garment
simulation became popular in many applications, from movie industry to fashion
and textile. Many papers in the area of virtual clothing have been published,
from simplified cloth models [17], [11], to more accurate ones [1] [2] [7] [9], some
surveys and comparisons of recent researches are available in [19], [14]. A virtual
garment is normally represented by its two-dimensional patterns. These patterns
can be used to produce real garments in the textile industry (CAD systems), or
produced by a fashion designer. More information is needed to be added to the
2D patterns in order to produce garments. The automatic pre-positioning of a
garment around a digital body is a difficult and challenging problem as we have
to sew the different pieces correctly. Some approaches for dressmaking have been
proposed. Some have been introduced in the literature [2], [13]. In this approach,
2D patterns are positioned by hand around the body and then, sewing is performed automatically. We developed an automatic virtual dressing system [21]
which can be used easily by a normal user who wants to try garments virtually.
This technique proposes a 2D manipulation method which will be coupled to a
3D mapping technique allowing to reach the final positioning. Even though this
method gives a fully automatic pre-positioning, the springs used in the particle

A. Gagalowicz and W. Philips (Eds.): MIRAGE 2007, LNCS 4418, pp. 139–149, 2007.

system are usually very deformed, which implies a very hight energy that the system has to dissipate; this requires a very small time step in the simulator leading to a long simulation time, so that an energy minimization algorithm for the particle system is needed. In this paper we introduce an efficient method for the energy minimization using hierarchical decomposition. The garment is firstly discretized in various resolutions (from lowest to highest). Then the lowest resolution particles system is minimized using a local minimization algorithm, since the complexity of this algorithm is O(n), it requires a short time to perform the minimization. Next, a higher resolution of the garment is reconstructed from the previous minimization result and the spring deformation are further reduced. This procedure is iterated until the highest resolution garment is minimized.

1.1 Related Work

Hierarchy decomposition methods. have been proposed to accelerate simulation for deformable objects using finite element methods [30], subdivision frameworks [5], skeleton driven deformations [6], physically based subdivisions [8], multi-resolution collision handlings [16], etc. Multi-level optimization algorithms have also been proposed in [15] to accelerate the performance of a nonlinear optimizer. Li and Volkov in [22] also introduce an adaptive method to refine and simplify the cloth meshes locally.

Energy minimization. for mass/spring systems is used to avoid an expensive computation. As physically-based methods require a large computation time to compute equation 1 at each time step (See [1]):

$$(M - h\frac{\partial f}{\partial v} - h^2\frac{\partial f}{\partial x})\Delta v = h(f_0 + h\frac{\partial f}{\partial x}v_0) \tag{1}$$

the simulation of a complex nonlinear and hysteretical garment can require a whole day to a week (in an early work of Breen). To avoid the use of the simulator to minimize the energy of the mass/spring system, we propose a fast geometrical minimization algorithm. Adopting the idea of multi-resolution, we introduce an efficient method to decompose the garment in several resolutions; each resolution can be reconstructed easily from another one. Once the energy of the lowest resolution has been minimized, we then reconstruct the next one from this one and its minimization is applied. This process loops until the highest resolution has been minimized.

The remainder of this paper is organized as follows: Section 2 describes input data used in our algorithm. Section 3 details the principle of energy minimization for mass/spring systems. We present our multi-resolution technique for virtual garment simulation in Section 4, by explaining the decomposition of garments keeping their boundaries untouched. Section 5 briefly presents the method used for collision detection in our system. We finally give some results validating our approach in Section 6, before concluding in Section 7.

2   Input Data

The shape of the virtual garment is reconstructed from a set of 2D patterns; these patterns come from a CAD system or are created by a designer. In general, a mass/spring system is used to model the mechanical behavior of cloth. Any virtual cloth modeled by a mass/spring system can be applied to our method. The input to the technique presented in this paper is simply the output of the technique presented in [21]. Such an input is visualized on the left and middle part of figure 1. The garment is already positioned around the body but its energy is very high (the garment is highly deformed compared to the final result - See the right of figure 1). Therefore a long computation time is required to obtain an acceptable result (stable position of the garment).

The discrete resolution of the cloth used in our work varies from 50mm to 5mm. These resolutions are nowadays used in most physically-based simulation systems. The higher the resolution, the better the garment is modeled, but the computing times grows exponentially.

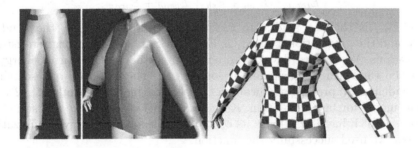

Fig. 1. Input garment shape (left, middle) and output result using simulator (right)

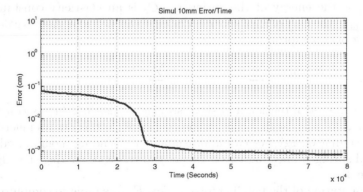

Fig. 2. Simulation time (average spring error in cm) convergence after 80,000 seconds, spatial resolution 10mm

3   Energy Minimization

Garment models are modeled as triangular or rectangular grids, with points of finite mass at the intersections of the grids and the mass points are joined by springs having no mass but modeling various mechanical behaviors of cloth (tension, shear, bending ....). The energy of the garment is estimated by the average elongation of all the springs of the system. We will calculate the energy of the whole garment from a set of equations and determine the shape of the garment by moving the points to achieve a minimum energy state. The reconstruction from 2D patterns to 3D shape can be denoted as a function:

$$F : R^2 \rightarrow R^3 \text{ or } (u, v) \rightarrow (x, y, z)$$

where each particle P_i of the garment has its 2D coordinates (u_i, v_i) and 3D coordinates (x_i, y_i, z_i). We denote by r_{ij} the spring connecting P_i and P_j. The equilibrium length of r_{ij} is its length in 2D coordinates denoted by L_{ij}, its current length is its length in 3D coordinates denoted by l_{ij}. The energy equation of the garment shape can be represented as follows :

$$E_{total} = E_{ten} + E_{sh} + E_{bend} + E_{grav} \tag{2}$$

Where E_{ten} is the energy due to tension, E_{sh} to shear, E_{bend}, the bending energy, and the gravitational energy is E_{grav}. In fact, springs strongly resist the deformations. We aim to develop an equation so that the elasticity energy is high when the spring is stretched or compressed. There is a lot of research in cloth modeling, [4] propose a Kawabata model, some models of cloth ([1], [2]) use a linear model for fast simulation. Kawabata model gives a more realistic cloth simulation but it has a drawback: its computation time. For energy minimization purposes, we used successfully the function:

$$Er_{ij} = C_s k_{ij} (\frac{l_{ij}}{L_{ij}} - 1)^2 \tag{3}$$

where Er_{ij} is the energy of the spring r_{ij}. C_s is an elasticity constant. The function E_{elast}, the part of E_{total} corresponding to tension and shear is calculated by summing over all springs:

$$E_{elast} = \sum_{r_{ij} \in M_e} Er_{ij} = C_s \sum_{r_{ij} \in M_e} k_{ij} (\frac{l_{ij}}{L_{ij}} - 1)^2 \tag{4}$$

where M_e is the set of tension and shear springs, k_{ij} is the stiffness constant of the spring r_{ij}. Observing that the tension energy of cloth is always much higher than the bending energy, we can approximate the bending along an edge AB by a virtual spring connecting two points of two triangles sharing the edge AB. (See Figure 3).

This presentation of the bending force makes E_{bend} simple to compute. E_{bend} is simplified as:

$$E_{bend} = \sum_{r_{ij} \in M_b} Er_{ij} = C_b \sum_{r_{ij} \in M_b} k_{ij} (\frac{l_{ij}}{L_{ij}} - 1)^2 \tag{5}$$

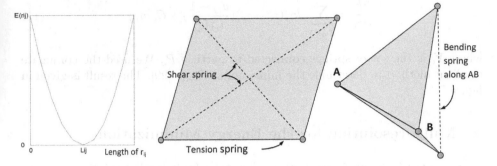

Fig. 3. Springs structure and energy function

where M_b is the set of bending springs. The particle's energy due to gravity is simply defined as:

$$E_{grav} = C_g \sum_{i=0}^{N} m_i g h_i = C_g \sum_{i=0}^{N} m_i g(z_i - Z_0) \tag{6}$$

where N is the number of particles, m_i is the weight of particle P_i. C_g, Z_0 are a density constant and the reference altitude of the system respectively. The energy of the cloth shape can be represented as:

$$\begin{aligned} E_{total} = C_s \sum_{r_{ij} \in M_e} k_{ij} (\frac{l_{ij}}{L_{ij}} - 1)^2 \\ + C_b \sum_{r_{ij} \in M_b} k_{ij} (\frac{l_{ij}}{L_{ij}} - 1)^2 \\ + C_g \sum_{i=0}^{N} m_i g(z_i - Z_0) \end{aligned} \tag{7}$$

In fact, we store these springs in only one array $M = M_e \cup M_b$, each spring has its own stiffness constant, E_{total} is calculated as:

$$E_{total} = \frac{1}{2} \sum_{r_{ij} \in M} k_{ij} (\frac{l_{ij}}{L_{ij}} - 1)^2 + C_g \sum_{i=0}^{N} m_i g(z_i - Z_0) \tag{8}$$

Note that E_{total} is defined as a continuous function, if we let $a_{ij} = \frac{l_{ij}}{L_{ij}}$ and call E as E_{total}, the partial differential equation of the total energy can be easily calculated:

$$\frac{\partial E}{\partial x_i} = \sum_{r_{ij} \in V_i} k_{ij} (x_i - x_j)(\frac{a_{ij} - 1}{a_{ij} L_{ij}^2}) \tag{9}$$

$$\frac{\partial E}{\partial y_i} = \sum_{r_{ij} \in V_i} k_{ij} (y_i - y_j)(\frac{a_{ij} - 1}{a_{ij} L_{ij}^2}) \tag{10}$$

$$\frac{\partial E}{\partial z_i} = \sum_{r_{ij} \in V_i} k_{ij}(z_i - z_j)(\frac{a_{ij} - 1}{a_{ij} L_{ij}^2}) + C_g m_i g \qquad (11)$$

where V_i is the set of springs connected to particle P_i. We used the conjugate gradient method to determine the minimum of E_{total} [29]. The result is given in figure 5.

4   Multi-resolution for the Energy Minimization

As presented in figure 5, the computation time for a small resolution garment is much faster than for a high one, but the error reached remains much higher. The problem we want to solve is to decrease substantially the computing time to reach the same minimum as that one of the highest resolution.

Multi-resolution methods are presented in many papers as [22], [15], but they are restricted to the case of simple triangular meshes to model cloth. The triangular mesh can be easily decomposed in several child triangles to obtain a new unified mesh. However, these methods cannot be applied in the case of our model [21,26], where the connectivity of springs is more complex.

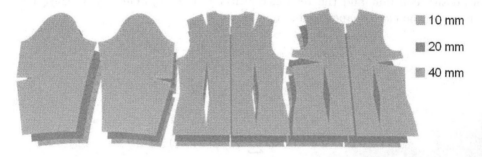

Fig. 4. Multi-resolution of a shirt garments

We developed a new decomposition method that can work independently of the cloth structure. The main idea is to predefine the 2D garments in several resolutions beforehand. We then determine the correspondences of each particle in a given resolution with other particles in other resolutions. Given a 3D cloth particle at a certain resolution, we can calculate its location in another resolution without difficulty.

Each garment is discretized in N resolutions. Its shape S at level n with $n = \overline{1..N}$ is denoted by S_n. The shape is defined by a set of particles $\{P_n\}$, springs $\{R_n\}$ and triangles mesh $\{T_n\} : S_n(P_n, R_n, T_n)$. For each particle $p \in P_n$, we find a triangle $t_i \in T_{n-1}$ so that the *distance* from p to t_i is minimum:

$$distance(p, t_i) = \begin{cases} 0 & \text{if } t_i \quad \text{contains} \quad p \\ |po_i| & \text{if } t_i \text{ does not contain } p \end{cases}$$

where o_i is the gravity center of t_i. The correspondence between p and t_i is computed by employing a positional constraint method. We call p_0, p_1 and p_2 the particles of triangle t_i, the barycentric coordinates of p on t_i are (w_0, w_1, w_2). The particle is reconstructed so that its barycentric coordinates on the triangle t_i does not change. When the cloth shape S_{n-1} is minimized, the new position of particle p is calculated as follows :

$$p = w_0 p_0 + w_1 p_1 + w_2 p_2 \qquad (12)$$

In order to reconstruct S_n from S_{n-1}, we have to know the correspondences of all particles of S_n on the triangles of S_{n-1}. The most time consuming task is to compute the distance from each particle of S_n to the triangles of S_{n-1}. A naive approach is to compute the distance from each particle to all triangles. Since the task has complexity $O(K^2)$ with K is the number of particles, the computation time is small at low resolution. However, with a higher one (for example about 30.000 particles), the computing time can take a whole day. It is unacceptable even if the computation will be performed only one time before the minimization process starts.

We propose an efficient method to compute the correspondences. This method uses bounding boxes ([31]) for the set of triangles for each level. Each node of the bounding box contains a linked list of triangles. For each particle, we find the node corresponding to its bounding box. Distances from the particle to all triangles contained by the node are computed in order to find the minimum one.

Since the bounding box method has the complexity $O(n)$, we can compute the correspondences for very high resolution with a reasonable time.

5   Collision Detection

The geometrically based minimization has to handle self collisions and collisions between the human body and the cloth. Several methods have been proposed in the last few years [2],[25],[3]. We have decided to solve the problem approximately by not testing particles against triangles and edges against each other; we consider only particles. Clearly, we now have to hold the particles a little bit away from the human body or away from each other to avoid artifacts of not detected intersecting triangles. But this approach saves a lot of computation.

We have used a hierarchy of bounding boxes for the garment. The hierarchy is built once at the beginning and the bounding boxes are updated after each step. For collision detection between the garment and the human body we hold the particles away from the body surface at a predefined distance δ. Now we are able to determine the closest distance between the particles and the triangles. From the surface normal at the closest distance we can determine if the particle is inside the body or just close to it. In any case the collision response moves the particle so that it is away from the body by δ.

6   Results

Figure 5 gives some computing times for our energy minimization algorithm on a workstation INTEL 2.4 GHz. Compared to the results available from our previous work [21] (See figure 1) we designed a new optimization technique which allows to reduce the simulation time drastically. For example, in the case of figure 1, the garment simulation lasted roughly 50,000 seconds to reach convergence. With the new technique, the same simulation result (compare right of figure 1 with right of figure 7) is obtained after roughly 5,000 seconds only. In the average, computing time was reduced by a factor of 10.

This is due to the fact that the garment prepositioning is now from a very different nature. Before automatic prepositioning designed the garment around the body with very high deformations (compare figure 1 middle and right) that our simulation took time to dissipate. Now, the automatic prepositioning brings the garment with almost no deformations (compare left and right of figure 7) only geometrically and the simulation is only used for fine tuning, to bring the garment in contact with the mannequin.

The multi-resolution algorithm gives better results for minimization. For these experiences we used a human model with approx. 15,000 vertices. Our algorithm is implemented in C++ and OpenGL.

Our system controls Kawabata characteristics for tension, shear and bending. This is required to model the mechanical behavior of garment faithfully.

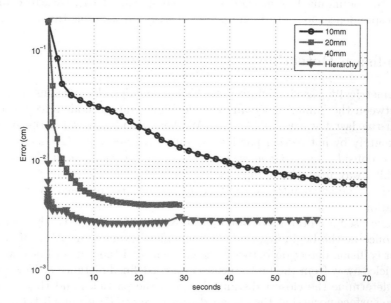

Fig. 5. Comparison of various prepositionings using the minimization with the different spatial samplings of the garment and with the multi-resolution approach

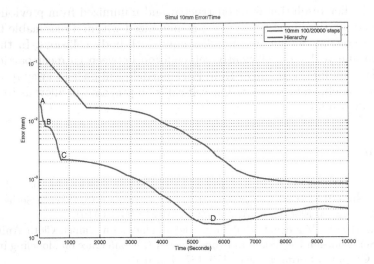

Fig. 6. Comparison of complete simulations for a unique (highest) resolution and for the hierarchical approach. The multi-resolution starts at: A 50mm, B 25mm, C 10mm. The simulation can stop at D.

Fig. 7. Result of the prepositioning (left) and after the complete simulation (right)

7   Conclusion and Future Work

We have presented a new and efficient method for garment simulation. The main feature of this new simulation technique relies in the design of a powerful automatic prepositioning of a garment around a mannequin. This is obtained by starting from an automatic prepositioning designed previously [21], but we incorporated an optimization algorithm with allows to obtain a prepositioning result (performed only geometrically) which corresponds almost to the final result, thus reducing drastically the computing time. We studied various optimization techniques and the hierarchical approach proved to be the most efficient.

The garment is firstly discretized in various resolutions (from lowest to highest). Once the lowest resolution particles system is minimized in a very short time, the higher resolution is reconstructed and minimized from previous resolutions. Finally, the highest resolution is minimized within a reasonable time.

At this moment our method handles only cloth-body collisions. In the near future, we aim to handle efficiently self-collision between garment particles by improving bounding boxes algorithm. Each particle will be kept away from each other at a predefined distance β. The self-collision process will allow us to obtain much better results.

References

1. David Baraff, Andrew Witkin. Large Steps in cloth simulation. In Micheal Cohen, editor, SIGGRAPH 98 Conference Proceedings, Annual Conference Series, pages 43–54, Orlando, Florida, USA, July 1998. ACM SIGGRAPH.
2. Lafleur Benoit, Magnenat Thalmann Nadia, Thalmann Daniel. Cloth Animation with Self Collision Detection. In Proceedings IFIP Conference on Modeling in Computer Graphics. Springer, pages 179–187, Tokyo 1991.
3. Robert Bridson, Ronald Fedkiw, and John Anderson. Robust treatment of collisions, contact and friction 106 for cloth animation. In ACM Transactions on Graphics, SIGGRAPH 2002, Vol 21, 2002.
4. David E.Breen, Donald H.House, Michael J.Wozny. Predicting the drape of woven cloth using interacting particles. SIGGRAPH '94, Pages 365–372, 1994.
5. Steve Capell, Seth Green, Brian Curless, Tom Duchamp, Zoran Popoviéc. A Multiresolution Framework for Dynamic Deformations. ACM SIGGRAPH 2002.
6. Steve Capell, Seth Green, Brian Curless, Tom Duchamp, Zoran Popoviéc. Interactive Skeleton-Driven Dynamic Deformations. ACM SIGGRAPH 2002.
7. Kwang-Jin Choi and Hyeong-Seok Ko. Stable but responsive cloth. In ACM Transactions on Graphics, SIGGRAPH 2002, Vol 21, 2002.
8. Patrick Chouraqui and Gershon Elber. Physically Based Adaptive Triangulation of Freeform Surfaces. CGI'96, Page 144. Los Alamitos, CA, USA, 1996.
9. Philippe Decaudin, Dan Julius, Jamie Wither, Laurence Boissieux, Alla Sheffer, Marie-Paule Cani. Virtual Garments: A Fully Geometric Approach for Clothing Design. In EUROGRAPHICS 2006, Vol 25, No 3. 2006.
10. Bernhard Eberhardt, Olaf Etzmu, and Michael Hauth. Implicit-explicit schemes for fast animation with particle systems. In Eurographics Computer Animation and Simulation Workshop 2000, 2000.
11. C.Feynman. Modeling the Appearance of Cloth. Master's thesis, Dept. of EECS, Massachusetts Inst. of Technology, Cambridge, Mass., 1986.
12. Arnulph Fuhrmann, Clemens Gross, and Volker Luckas. Interactive animation of cloth including self collision detection. Journal of WSCG, Vol 11, No 1 pages 141–148, February 2003.
13. Clemens Gross, Arnulph Fuhrmann, Volker Luckas. Automatic pre-positioning of virtual clothing. In Preceedings of the 19th spring conference on Computer Graphics, pages 99–108. Budmerice, Slovakia 2003.
14. Donald H. House and David E. Breen, editors. Cloth Modeling and Animation. A. K. Peters, 2000.
15. Dave Hutchinson, Martin Preston, Terry Hewitt. Adaptive Refinement for Mass/Spring Simulations. Computer Animation and Simulation96, Pages 31–45 1996.

16. Nitin Jain, Ilknur Kabul, Naga K. Govindaraju, Dinesh Manocha, Ming Lin. Multi-resolution collision handling for cloth-like simulations. Computer Animation and Virtual Worlds. Volume 16, Issue 3–4, Pages 141–151. John Wiley & Sons, Ltd, 2005.
17. Weil Jerry. The Synthesis of Cloth Objects. In Proceeding SIGGRAPH'86. Vol 20, No 4, pages 49–54. Computer Graphics 1986.
18. X. Ju, N. Werghi, and P. Siebert. Automatic segmentation of 3d human body scans. In IASTED International Conference on Computer Graphics and Imaging, CGIM 2000, pages 239-244, 2000.
19. Hing N.Ng, Richard L.Grimsdale. Computer techniques for modeling cloth. Computer Graphics and Applications, Vol. 16 No.5, pp.28-41, 1996.
20. Young-Min Kang and Hwan-Gue Cho. Bilayered approximate integration for rapid and plausible animation of virtual cloth with realistic wrinkles. In Computer Animation 2002, page 203, Geneva, Switzerland, 2002.
21. T. Le Thanh, A. Gagalowicz. Virtual cloth pre-positioning. Proceedings of Mirage 2005, March 2005
22. Ling Li and Vasily Volkov. Cloth animation with adaptively refined meshes. ACSC '05: Proceedings of the Twenty-eighth Australasian conference on Computer Science. 2005.
23. Johannes Metzger, Stefan Kimmerle, and Olaf Etzmu. Hierarchical techniques in collision detection for cloth animation. Journal of WSCG, Vol 11, No 2, pages 322-329, February 2003.
24. Mark Meyer, Gilles Debunne, Mathieu Desbrun, and Alan H. Barr. Interactive animation of cloth-like objects for virtual reality. The Journal of Visualization and Computer Animation, Vol 12 pages 1-12, May 2001.
25. Dongliang Zhang and Matthew M.F. Yuen. Collision detection for clothed human animation. In Proceedings of the 8th Pacific Graphics Conference on Computer Graphics and Application, pages 328-337, 2000.
26. Xavier Provot. Deformation Constraints in a Mass-Spring Model to Describe Rigid Cloth Behavior, In Proc. Graphics Interface '95, pages 147–154. 1995.
27. Xavier Provot. Collision and self-collision handling in cloth model dedicated to design garments. In Graphics Interface 97, pages 177-189, 1997.
28. Luca Chittaro and Demis Corvaglia. 3D Virtual Clothing : from Garment Design to Web3D Visualization and Simulation. In Web3D'03 : Proceeding of the 8th international conference on 3D Web technology, page 73. Saint Malo, France, 2003.
29. William H. Press, William T. Vetterling, Saul A. Teukolsky, Brian P. Flannery. Numerical Recipes. In C : The art of scientific Computing. Cambridge University press, 1992.
30. Demetri Terzopoulos, John Platt, Alan Barr, and Kurt Fleischer. Elastically Deformable Models. Computer Graphics, Pages 205–214, July 1987.
31. Gino van den Bergen. Efficient collision detection of complex deformable models using AABB trees. In Journal of Graphics Tools. Vol 2. Jan 1998.

Model-Based Feature Extraction for Gait Analysis and Recognition

Imed Bouchrika and Mark S. Nixon

ISIS, Department of Electronics and Computer Science
University of Southampton, SO17 1BJ, UK
{ib04r,msn}@ecs.soton.ac.uk

Abstract. Human motion analysis has received a great attention from researchers in the last decade due to its potential use in different applications. We propose a new approach to extract human joints (vertex positions) using a model-based method. Motion templates describing the motion of the joints as derived by gait analysis, are parametrized using the elliptic Fourier descriptors. The heel strike data is exploited to reduce the dimensionality of the parametric models. People walk normal to the viewing plane, as major gait information is available in a sagittal view. The ankle, knee and hip joints are successfully extracted with high accuracy for indoor and outdoor data. In this way, we have established a baseline analysis which can be deployed in recognition, marker-less analysis and other areas. The experimental results confirmed the robustness of the proposed method to recognize walking subjects with a correct classification rate of %92.

Keywords: Model-based feature extraction, motion analysis, gait, gait analysis.

1 Introduction

Much research in computer vision is directed into the analysis of articulated objects and more specifically, the analysis of human motion. This research is fuelled by the wide range of applications where human motion analysis can be deployed such as virtual reality, smart surveillance, human computer interfaces and athletic performance. A vision-based system for human motion analysis consists of three main phases: detection, tracking and perception. In the last phase, a high-level description is produced based on the features extracted during the previous phases from the temporal video stream. In fact, it has been revealed by psychological studies that the motion of human joints contains enough information to perceive the human motion.

Currently, the majority of systems used for motion analysis are marker-based and they are commercially available. Marker-based solutions rely primarily on markers or sensors attached at key locations of the human body. However, most applications such as visual surveillance require the deployment of an automated markerless vision system to extract the joints' trajectories. On the other hand,

A. Gagalowicz and W. Philips (Eds.): MIRAGE 2007, LNCS 4418, pp. 150–160, 2007.

automated extraction of the joints' positions is an extremely difficult task as non-rigid human motion encompasses a wide range of possible motion transformations due to its highly flexible structure and to self occlusion. Clothing type, segmentation errors and different viewpoints pose a significant challenge for accurate joint localization.

Since human motion analysis is one of the most active and challenging research topics in computer vision, many research studies have aimed to develop a system capable of overcoming the difficulties imposed by the extraction and tracking of human motion features. Various methods are surveyed by [1] and [2].Two approaches are being used for human motion anaylsis: model-based and non-model based methods. For the the first one, a priori shape model is established to match real images to this predefined model, and thereby extracting the corresponding features once the best match is obtained. Stick models and volumetric models [3] are the most commonly used methods. Akita [4] proposed a model consisting of six segments comprising of two arms, two legs, the torso and the head. Guo *et al* [5] represented the human body structure in the silhouette by a stick figure model which had ten sticks articulated with six joints. Rohr [6] proposed a volumetric model for the analysis of human motion, using 14 elliptical cylinders to model the human body. Recently, Karaulova *et al.* [7] have used the stick figure model to build a novel hierarchical model of human dynamics represented using hidden Markov models. The model-based approach is the most popular method being used for human motion analysis due to its advantages [8]. It can extract detailed and accurate motion data, as well as having the capability to cope well with occlusion and self-occlusion.

For the non-model based method, feature correspondence between successive frames is based upon prediction, velocity, shape, texture and colour. Shio *et al.* [9] proposed a method to describe the human body using moving blobs or 2D ribbons. The blobs are grouped based on the magnitude and the direction of the pixel velocity. Kurakake and Nevatia [10] worked on the extraction of joint locations by establishing correspondence between extracted blobs. Small motion between consecutive frames is the main assumption, whereby feature correspondence is conducted using various geometric constraints.

As there have been many vision approaches aimed to extract limbs, and a dearth of approaches specifically aimed to determine vertices, we propose a new method to extract human joints with better accuracy then blobs via incorporating priori knowledge to refine accuracy. Our new approach uses a model-based method for modelling human gait motion using elliptic Fourier descriptors, whereby the gait pattern is incorporated to establish a model used for tracking and feature correspondence. The proposed solution has capability to extract moving joints of human body with high accuracy for indoor data as well as outdoor data filmed in an unconstrained environments. Further, we assess the recognition capability using gait to demonstrate the potency of the approach described.

This paper is structured as follows: in the next section, we describe the method used for parameterizing arbitrary moving shapes using the elliptic Fourier descriptors. Section 3 is devoted to the discussion of the approach adopted for the localization of human joints. Finally, the experimental results on a set of processed videos from the SOTON databases are drawn in section 4.

2 Arbitrary Shape Parametrization Using Fourier Descriptors

A new model-based approach is proposed to extract the joints' trajectories of walking people. Although, the Fourier series is the most accurate way for modelling gait motion, most previous methods adopted simple models [11] to extract gait angular motion via evidence gathering using a few parameters. This is mainly due to complexity and computational cost. Grant *et al* [12] presented a new temporal evidence gathering method to extract arbitrary moving shapes. Fourier descriptors are used to parametrize the templates of moving shapes in a continuous form.

The Fourier theory has been used for the analysis of curves and boundaries of shapes for several years. The Fourier analysis provides a means for extracting features or descriptors from images which are useful characteristics for image understanding. These descriptors are defined by expanding the parametric representation of a curve in Fourier series. Let f be the function for the boundary of a given shape, the function f is represented using elliptic Fourier Descriptors [13,14], where the Fourier series is based on a curve expressed by a complex parametric form as shown in equation (1):

$$f(t) = x(t) + iy(t) \tag{1}$$

where $t \in [0, 2\pi]$. $x(t)$ and $y(t)$ are approximated via the Fourier summation by n terms as shown in equation (2)

$$\begin{bmatrix} x(t) \\ y(t) \end{bmatrix} = \begin{bmatrix} a_0 \\ b_0 \end{bmatrix} + \begin{bmatrix} X(t) \\ Y(t) \end{bmatrix} \tag{2}$$

such that a_0 and b_0 define the position of the shape's centre, and $X(t)$ and $Y(t)$ are computed as defined in equation (3) :

$$X(t) = \sum_{k=1}^{n} a_{x_k} cos(kt) + b_{x_k} sin(kt)$$
$$Y(t) = \sum_{k=1}^{n} a_{y_k} cos(kt) + b_{y_k} sin(kt) \tag{3}$$

where a_{x_k},a_{y_k}, b_{x_k} and b_{y_k} are the set of the elliptic phasors which can be computed by a Riemann summation [14]. For a representation invariant to rotation and scaling, we need to represent f in a parametrized form to cover all the possible graphs or shapes which can be derived by applying appearance transformation to the function f including rotation and scaling. Henceforth, the function f can be rewritten in the parametric form shown in equation (4):

$$\begin{bmatrix} x(t) \\ y(t) \end{bmatrix} = \begin{bmatrix} a_0 \\ b_0 \end{bmatrix} + \begin{bmatrix} cos(\alpha) & -sin(\alpha) \\ sin(\alpha) & cos(\alpha) \end{bmatrix} \begin{bmatrix} X(t) * s_x \\ Y(t) * s_y \end{bmatrix} \tag{4}$$

where α is the rotation angle, s_x and s_y are the scaling factors across the horizontal and vertical axes respectively. The last equation (4) can be written concisely in its complex form as defined in equation (5):

$$\begin{cases} f = T + R_\alpha \left(s_x X(t) + s_y Y(t)i \right) \\ T = a_0 + b_0 i \\ R_\alpha = \cos(\alpha) + \sin(\alpha)i \end{cases} \quad (5)$$

Based on the final parametric format of f shown in equation (5), any shape can be represented using five parameters which are: a_0, b_0, α, s_x and s_y. $X(t)$ and $Y(t)$ are pre-computed using equation (3) from the original shape. In fact, the number of free parameters needed for the Hough Transform is totally independent of the complexity of shape which is defined using the elliptic Fourier Descriptors, as the defined parameters are related to the appearance transformations which define all the shapes that can be derived form the original shape.

To use the Hough transform with these templates represented via the parametric form described in equation (5), a five-dimensional space is required. Thus, the algorithm would be computationally intensive and infeasible to implement. In spite of the fact that some methods were proposed to reduce the computational requirements of the Hough Transform [15,16], the computational load of these methods does not meet the requirements of most applications [16]. Alternatively, the heel strike data could be incorporated to reduce the complexity of the parameter space and therefore, dramatically reduce the computational cost as done here.

3   Extraction of the Anatomical Landmarks

3.1   Heel Strike Extraction

The detection of the human gait period can provide important information to determine the positions of the human joints. Cutler *et al* [17] proposed a real time method for measuring periodicity for periodic motion based on self-similarity. Instead, the heel strikes of the subject can provide an accurate measure for gait periodicity as well as the gait stride and step length. Moreover, the extraction of heel strikes can be used as a strong cue to distinguish walking people from other moving objects in the scene [18].

During the strike phase, the foot of the striking leg stays at the same position for half a gait cycle, whilst the rest of the human body moves forward. Therefore, if we use a low-level feature extraction method (edges or corners), then a dense region will be accumulated at the heel strike regions. Since the primary aim of this research is the perception of human motion, we have chosen to use corners instead of edges, as they maintain enough information to perceive the human motion, in contrast to edges which may cause ambiguity in the extraction process due to the excess data they may contain. Furthermore, a robust vision system based on corner detection can work for low-resolution applications. We have applied the Harris corner detector on every frame t from the video sequence and then accumulated all the corners into one image using equation (6):

$$C_i = \sum_{t=1}^{N} H(I_t) \tag{6}$$

where H is the output of the Harris corner detector, I_t is original image at frame t. Because the striking foot is stabilized for half a gait cycle, as result, a dense area of corners is detected in the region where the leg strikes the ground. In order to locate these areas, we have estimated a measure for density of proximity. The value of proximity at point p is dependent on the number of corners within the region R_p and their corresponding distances from p. R_p is assumed to be a square area with centre p, and radius of r that is determined as the ratio of total image points to the total of corners in C_i which is about 10. We have first computed proximity value d_p of corners for all regions R_p in C_i using equation (7). This is an iterative process starting from a radius r. The process then iterates to accumulate proximity values of corners for point p.

$$\begin{cases} d_p^r = \frac{N_r}{r} \\ d_p^i = d_p^{i+1} + \frac{N_i}{i} \end{cases} \tag{7}$$

where d_p^i is the proximity value for rings of radius i away from the centre p, and N_i is the number of corners which are of distance i from the centre, rings are single pixel wide. Afterwards, we accumulate all the densities for the subregions R_p for all points p into one image to produce the corners proximity image using (8).

$$D = \sum_{x=0}^{X} \sum_{y=0}^{Y} shift(d_p) \tag{8}$$

where X and Y are the width and height of the image respectively. d_p is the corners proximity value for region R_p. The $shift$ function places the proximity value d_p on a blank image of size $X \times Y$ at the position p. An output of the corner proximity for an example image is shown in Figure (1). The input image contains points spread all over the image with a number dense regions. The resulting image has darker areas which correspond to the crowded regions in the input image.

Figure (2) shows the corner proximity images for two walking subjects being captured in different environments. The first subject is walking in the sagittal plane near the camera, whilst the second subject is recorded in an oblique view walking away from the camera. A similar algorithm to [19] is used to derive the positions of the peaks as local maxima.

3.2   Moving Joints Extraction

In order to recognize people by their gait, the model-based method is used for the localization of the joints for walking people. The evidence gathering process is the most common method used for the extraction of articulated objects. It is

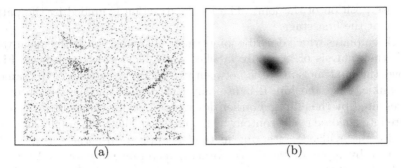

Fig. 1. Example Results for the Corner Proximity Measure: (a) Input Image, (b) Corner Proximity Image

Fig. 2. Heel Strike Extraction using the Proximity Measure: (a) Sagittal Indoor View, (b) Oblique Outdoor View

usually used in conjunction with the Hough Transform consisting of two phases: i) global pattern extraction, and ii) local feature extraction. The objective of the global extraction is to find the best motion pattern based on the predefined model i.e. prior knowledge from the whole video sequence. The motion model is defined in a parametric form using the elliptic Fourier Descriptors. The Hough Transform is used to determine the optimum parameters through the matching process of feature points (corners) across the whole sequence to the parametric function, and increase votes in the accumulator space accordingly. The second stage of the evidence gathering is a frame-by-frame search aimed to extract the precise position of the joint. The local extraction is guided by the pattern extracted at the first stage.

Model templates which describe joints' motion are derived as the mean values through the analysis of manually labelled data of 30 video sequences. Figure (3) shows the joint motion paths between two successive strikes of the same leg for the ankle, knee and hip. Because only closed and continuous contours can be represented by the elliptic Fourier descriptors, we have converted the model template into a closed cyclic contour by looping back along the graph. The voting process for the evidence gathering method is applied on corners images which are obtained by appliying the Harris corner detector on every frame. Anatomical knowledge [20] of the body segments properties is used to limit the search area.

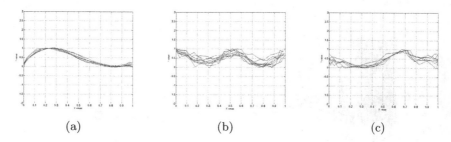

(a)   (b)   (c)

Fig. 3. Motion Analysis of the Joints: (a) Ankle, (b) Hip , (c)Knee

For the extraction of the ankle motion path, the five-dimensional parametric equation (5) is rewritten in terms of only one parameter s_y as described in equation (9). Because the heel strike points are known and lie on the motion graph of the ankle as both ends of the graph, henceforth, this knowledge is used to deduce the two parameters s_x and α as the distance and angle between the two strikes respectively.

$$s_y = \frac{(y - y_{s_n}) - (X(t) - x_e)s_x \sin(\alpha)}{(Y(t) - y_e)\cos(\alpha)} \tag{9}$$

where (x, y), (x_e, y_e) and (x_{s_n}, y_{s_n}) are the coordinates of the locus point, left end point of the model template and the nth strike respectively. The translation parameters are then computed after determining the best value of s_y using the following equation (10):

$$T = s_n - (\cos(\alpha) + i\sin(\alpha))(x_e s_x + y_e s_y i) \tag{10}$$

where i is the complex number. In the same way, the dimensionality of the parametric equation is reduced to three parameters for the global search of the hip and knee joints.

After obtaining the global motion pattern for the joints between the strikes s_n and s_{n+2}, a local search is performed within every frame to find the precise position of the joints. By gait analysis, people more or less have the same horizontal velocity pattern for the ankle, hip and knee displacement when walking. Therefore, a velocity model is produced and used to estimate the spread of x values through the temporal data. Let N the number of frames between the two strikes s_n and s_{n+2}. The x values for the joints trajectories can be estimated as expressed by the following equation:

$$x_f = s_x \times V\left(\frac{f}{N}\right) + x_{si} \tag{11}$$

where f is the frame number, x_s is the x coordinate of the heel strike s_n and V is the horizontal velocity model function for the joint (ankle, hip or knee). After getting the x_f values, then we use the motion graph derived from the global search to obtain the y coordinates of the joints.

4   Experimental Results

To demonstrate the efficacy of this approach, we have run the algorithm on a set of 120 different subjects from the SOTON database [21]. 100 subjects of the test database were filmed in an indoor environment with controlled conditions. The remaining 10 subjects were filmed in outdoor environment. Subjects walked from left to right normal to the viewing plane.

For the detection of the heel strike points, the proposed method extracted successfully %99.2 of the strikes from a total of 514 strikes. The mean error

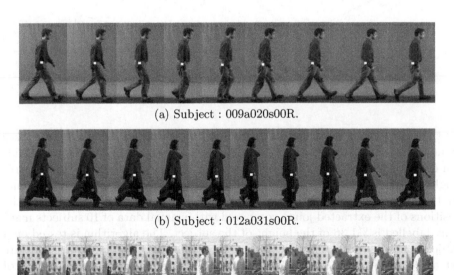

(a) Subject : 009a020s00R.

(b) Subject : 012a031s00R.

(c) Subject : 012a031s00R.

Fig. 4. Joints Extraction for Indoor Data

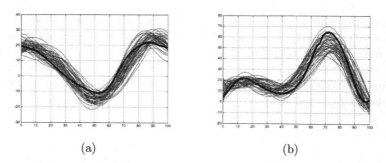

Fig. 5. Gait Angular Motion during one Gait Cycle: (a) Hip, (b) Knee

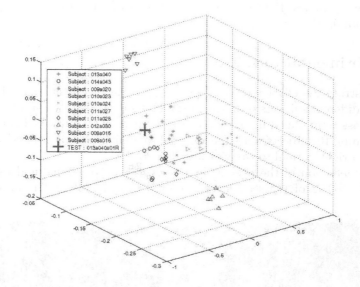

Fig. 6. Canonical Space Projection

for the positions of 65 strikes extracted by the algorithm compared to strikes manually labelled is %0.52 of the person height. The error is measured by Euclidean distance between the two strikes normalized to a percentage of the person's height as this is the normal basis for normalization. We have extracted the joints for the ankles, knees and hip as shown in Figure (4). The mean error for the positions of the extracted joints compared with manual data of 10 subjects manually labelled is %1.36 of the height of the subject. The algorithm is tested on a subject wearing Indian clothes which covered the legs. The joints positions are extracted successfully as shown in Figure 4(b) which reveals the potentials of this approach to handle occlusion. Figure (5) shows the relative angle for both the hip and knee computed from the extracted joints of 10 subjects. The graphs show the results obtained via this approach are consistent with biomechanical data by Winter [22] shown in bold in Figure (5).

To evaluate the recognition performance of our algorithm, we have fused both dynamic and static gait features to yield a feature vector consisting of 48 features. Static features include the body height, stride and heights of different body parts whilst dynamic features are mainly the phase-weighted magnitudes of the Fourier frequencies for the hip and knee angular motions. The gait signature is derived using the adaptive forward floating search algorithm via selecting the features with higher discriminability values. The gait signatures for every sequence are projected into the canonical space whereby the k-nearest neighbor rule is used for classification. The system achieved a correct classification rate of %92 using the leave-one-out validation rule. This is shown in Figure (6) with only 10 of the 20 subjects being projected.

5   Conclusions and Future Work

We propose a model-based method to extract moving joints via evidence gathering technique. Spatial model templates for human motion are derived from the analysis of gait data collected from manual labelling. Model templates are represented in a parametric form based on elliptic Fourier descriptors. Gait knowledge is exploited via heel strike extraction to reduce the the parameter space dimensionality and therefore reduce the computational load of the Hough Transform being used in the extraction process. The described method is proved to to work for both indoor and outdoor environments with potential to localize joint positions with better accuracy. Furthermore, the recognition potency is evaluated using the data extracted via the described model-based method. The proposed solution has achieved a classification rate of %92 for people recognition. The model-based is suited to more generalized deplyment and this will be the focus for future work.

References

1. Wang, L.A., Hu, W.M., Tan, T.N.: Recent developments in human motion analysis. Pattern Recognition **36**(3) (2003) pp. 585–601
2. Aggarwal, J.K., Cai, Q., Liao, W., Sabata, B.: Nonrigid motion analysis: Articulated and elastic motion. CVIU **70**(2) (1998) 142–156
3. Yoo, J.H., Nixon, M.S., Harris, C.J.: Extraction and description of moving human body by periodic motion analysis. Proc. ISCA 17th International Conference on Computers and Their Applications (2002) pp. 110–113
4. Akita, K.: Image sequence analysis of real world human motion. Pattern Recognition **17**(1) (1984) pp. 73–83
5. Guo, Y., Xu, G., Tsuji, S.: Understanding human motion patterns. In: Proc. the 12th IAPR International Conference on Pattern Recognition. Volume 2. (1994) pp. 325–329
6. Rohr, K.: Towards model-based recognition of human movements in image sequences. CVGIP: IU **74**(1) (1994) pp. 94–115
7. Karaulova, I.A., Hall, P.M., Marshall, A.D.: A hierarchical model of dynamics for tracking people with a single video camera. In: Proc of the 11th BMVC. (2000) 262–352

8. Huazhong, N., Tan, T., Wang, L., Hu, W.: People tracking based on motion model and motion constraints with automatic initialization. Pattern Recognition **37**(7) (2004) 1423–1440

9. Shio, A., Sklansky, J.: Segmentation of people in motion. In: IEEE Workshop on Visual Motion. Volume 2. (1991) 325–332

10. Kurakake, S., Nevatia, R.: Description and tracking of moving articulated objects. In: Proc. 11th IAPR ICPR. Volume 1. (1992) 491–495

11. Cunado, D., Nixon, M., Carter, J.: Automatic Extraction and Description of Human Gait Models for Recognition Purposes. Computer Vision and Image Understanding **90**(1) (2003) 1–41

12. Grant, M.G., Nixon, M.S., Lewis, P.H.: Extracting moving shapes by evidence gathering. Pattern Recognition **35**(5) (2002) 1099–1114

13. Granlund, G.H.: Fourier preprocessing for hand print character recognition. IEEE T-Comp **21** (1972) pp. 195–201

14. Aguado, A.S., Nixon, M.S., Montiel, M.E.: Parameterising arbitrary shapes via fourier descriptors for evidence-gathering extraction. CVGIP: IU **2** (1998) 547–51

15. Leavers, V.F.: Which Hough transform? CVGIP: Image Understanding **58**(2) (1993) 250–264

16. Aguado, A., Nixon, M., Montiel, M.: Parameterizing Arbitrary Shapes via Fourier Descriptors for Evidence-Gathering Extraction. CVIU **69**(2) (1998) 202–221

17. Cutler, R., Davis, L.S.: Robust real-time periodic motion detection, analysis, and applications. IEEE Transactions on Pattern Analysis and Machine Intelligence **22**(8) (2003) pp. 781–796

18. Bouchrika, I., Nixon, M.S.: People Detection and Recognition using Gait for Automated Visual Surveillance. IEE International Symposium on Imaging for Crime Detection and Prevention (2006)

19. Fujiyoshi, H., Lipton, A.J., Kanade, T.: Real-time human motion analysis by image skeletonization. IEICE Trans on Information and System (2004) 113–120

20. Pheasant, S.T.: Body sapce: Anthropometry, Ergonomics and Design. Taylor & Francis (1988)

21. Shutler, J.D., Grant, M.G., Nixon, M.S., Carter, J.N.: On a large sequence-based human gait database. In: Proceedings of Recent Advances in Soft Computing, Nottingham, UK (2002) pp. 66–71

22. Winter, D.A.: The Biomechanics and Motor Control of Human Movement. second edn. John Wiley & Sons (1990)

Interactive System for Efficient Video Cartooning

Sung-Soo Hong°, Jong-Chul Yoon[†], In-Kwon Lee[‡], and Siwoo Byun[*]

°,[†],[‡]Dept. of Computer Science, Yonsei University, Korea
[*]Dept. of Digital Media, Anyang University, Korea
maeno@cs.yonsei.ac.kr°, media19@cs.yonsei.ac.kr[†], iklee@yonsei.ac.kr[‡],
swbyun@anyang.ac.kr[*]

Abstract. Non-Photorealistic Rendering (NPR) can offer increased concentration and familiarity to the watcher. For this reason, many media such as movies, games, and commercials currently use the NPR method to deliver information. In this paper, we suggest an interactive system for video cartooning based on the mean-shift segmentation of image and video. In order to solve the problems of time complexity and memory allocation, the conventional problems of video mean-shift segmentation, this paper proposes several techniques such as foreground object based segmentation and sequential segmentation. We also propose the interactive correction technique to get enhanced results. For more cartoonic representation, we used spline curve approximation of segment boundaries in the final rendering results. With our method, we can easily create cartoon rendering output using the video streams such like home video, which can be obtained easily in our daily life.

1 Introduction

Non-Photorealistic Rendering (NPR) has many advantages. It can offer ease and familiarity to the watcher, and deliver information efficiently by expressing its main object in detail while simplifying the others. For this reason, the NPR technique is popularly used in many media such as movies, games and commercials nowadays. As a branch of NPR, cartoon rendering focuses on representing the object with cartoonic feeling.

Conventional cartoon rendering involved shading technique which was based on 3D geometric information [1]. The central problem with cartooning using shading technique is that the procedure of modeling and animation is drastically labor intensive and time consuming. In order to perform these procedures, producers may have to use many skillful experts, and the production time can be enormous. Currently, many approaches to cartooning and abstracting images and video have been researched, which can easily seek to retrieve input data in our life.

Generally, cartoon can be presented as cell and stroke. Here, cell is the homogeneous region that can be expressed by one color. And stroke can be drawn between cell and cell. For video cartooning, we must detect coherent cell region through the whole video, and must draw the line as well. Our work aims to convert video into cell-cartoon using noise reduction and mean-shift segmentation

A. Gagalowicz and W. Philips (Eds.): MIRAGE 2007, LNCS 4418, pp. 161–172, 2007.

technique. Because the mean-shift segmentation algorithm is a non-parametric inference method to segment image and video [2], this shall be effective in representing the object's distinguishable features. In addition, the mean-shift segmentation algorithm can not only control the detail of the result by verifying bandwidth, but it can also expand the dimension in order to apply segmentation, as in image to video [3,4].

When using mean-shift segmentation for video, however, there are also some clear limitations just like below. First, as mean-shift segmentation algorithm solves global optimization problem, every pixels in video must be referenced. To address this problem, we propose a method that can minimize the data set of mean-shift segmentation. And we propose the sequential segmentation technique, in order to get time-coherent segmented result also. The second limitation is that, although mean-shift segmentation can control the degree of details by verifying the bandwidth, it is hard to get the satisfactory result by choosing the appropriate bandwidth. If we use a small bandwidth, input may be segmented too much. If we use large one, we may not capture the important features of the object. To address this problem, we propose the noise reduction, segment annexation, and layering techniques.

The contributions of our research can be summarized as follows:

- We propose to stabilize segmentation by performing two steps: the noise reduction and the segment annexation.
- We introduce the methodology to accelerate the speed of 3D mean-shift segmentation which can be applied to high-resolution video.

2   Related Work

In their work, Santella and Decarlo [5] have proposed a method of abstracting photographs. They achieved automatic abstraction of photographic images with the assumption that the abstraction of the image may be a more effective method of translating the image's characteristics to the watcher. This system used perception-based method, but couldn't express the detail part for using gaussian filtering.

For video stylization, Agarwala et al. [6] proposed tracking based video stylization. This work adopted geometric information based curve to track moving objects. Compensating with tracking technique without geometric consideration, this method could enhance quality of tracking with less error. Wang et al. [7] proposed another video stylization in their work. They suggested stylizing video using the anisotropic kernel mean-shift technique [8]. Wang proposed the procedure of user-interaction process to obtain the cartoonized video. Although this approach can obtain excellent results, mean-shift based segmentation must be performed with the entire video data set. For mean-shift based video segmentation, overnight timing and enormous memory capacity is required. Recently, Holger et al. [9] proposed video abstraction in real time. For them, however, purpose of work is not cartooning video, but rather abstracting. For abstracting video, they adopt a filter-based method. Bilateral filtering [10] was used to enhance the input image or video.

In other side, research to improve user interaction has also been conducted. Kang et al. [11] offered great user interaction to get result at their work. In this work, the user can detect objects with intelligent scissors. The detected contour can be manipulated by the user to reconstruct the multi-resolution B-spline curve. With this approach, the user can detect objects, control the degree of detail, and choose the style of result with less interaction and fewer parameters.

3 System Overview

Figure 1 shows the procedure for our video cartooning system. We perform noise reduction as a pre-processing step. After pre-processing, we calculate the background image in order to divide video into fore and background sequences. The region that is identified as a foreground is used for making the video volume which can minimize the 3D mean-shift segmentation's production time. Using minimized video volume, we perform a sequential segmentation process in order to segment the video volume. After this step, unnecessary segments are eliminated by both system and user interaction. The properly segmented video volume is synthesized with the background image. Finally, by using segmented video, we can achieve the result by using Bezier-curve approximation.

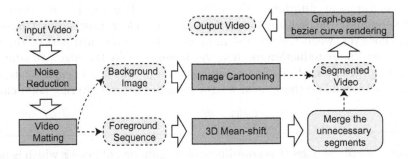

Fig. 1. Procedure of video cartooning

For fast production time, we restrict the input video in two aspects. First, the input video must be filmed in a fixed angle. And second, there is no sudden changing of camera exposure align to the time axis.

4 Stabilizing Segmentation

For the representation of a satisfactory cartoon-like segment, we must perform segmentation to coincide with human perception. This is necessary to prevent similar cells from being segmented individually or dissimilar cells be presented as one segment. Because mean-shift segmentation uses Euclidian distance of color space, if the degree of color difference that a human perceives does not match with the two color vectors in Euclidian distance, the wrong segmentation may result. We discuss the method to relieve this artifact in this section.

4.1   Input Stabilization

Noise plays an important role in the discordance between Euclidian color distances and human perception. For our research targets not only professional film production, but also home video, proper noise reduction step is required. By stabilizing the input data, we can prevent unnecessary segments from being

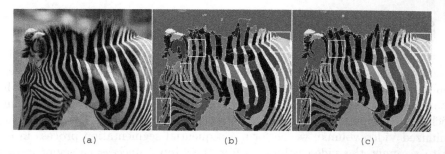

(a)   (b)   (c)

Fig. 2. Result of noise reduction: (a)Zebra (b)Segmented result (c)Segmented result using noise-reduced input

created as a result of noise in the input while mean-shift segmentation is being performed. Gaussian filtering is the well-known method which can reduce the input to eliminate the high-frequency data. There is clear drawback in Gaussian filtering, however, when the process must describe the detailed part of the image. We need a noise reduction method which can preserve the edge. We adapted spatio-temporal bilateral filtering to address the problem. To demonstrate our approach, we formulate the spatial weight term of bilateral filtering [12] below:

$$s(x,\hat{x}) = e^{-\frac{1}{2}\left(\frac{\|x-\hat{x}\|}{\sigma_d}\right)^2 - (\|x_f - \hat{x_f}\|^2)^{\sigma_f}}. \tag{1}$$

x is coordinate of the pixel. $\hat{x}$ is coordinate of neighboring of pixel x which is used to calculate the result. σ_d represents the spatial parameter, where σ_f controls the weight of frame distance.

In our experiment, we found that spatio-temporal bilateral filtering prominently reduced the unnecessary segments when we applied the same bandwidth to input video(or image) and noise-reduced video. Furthermore, even when we are applying different bandwidths to images to create the same number of segments, the feature and contour of the object is much clearer when we apply noise-reduction. Figure 2 shows the segmentation result using noise reduction. We can see that Figure 2(c) represents the contour of the zebra clearly while a wiggle contour created in Figure 2(b). Also, the stripe of the zebra is much clearer in Figure 2(c).

4.2   Segment Annexation and Layering

Generally, the user wants to describe the important object in detail while the others be described simply. That is, the user wants different degrees of abstraction in the representation of objects. When we perform mean-shift with a small

Fig. 3. Degree of detail: (a)Large bandwidth: simplified (b) Small bandwidth: more detailed but contains many segments (c) Optimal segmentation

bandwidth, the object may be divided into many small segments. Or if we apply large bandwidth, segments may neglect the features of the object.

Figure 3(a) represents each object simply, but we cannot capture the man's facial features because the figure is too simplified. By contrast, we can detect almost every feature of the objects in Figure 3(b), but the image contains too many unnecessary segments. The desirable result may be seen in Figure 3(c). In Figure 3(c), the human's face is properly segmented while the background is adequately simplified. To achieve this result, we use layering method and segment annexation to control the degree of detail. Especially for images, the user can control the degree of detail by layering with ease. After segmentation, the system performs the annexation task automatically.

For segmentation result may contain lots of unnecessary segments, we can remove these segments by segment annexation process, which perform merging adjacent two segments by some condition. If the segment's area is too small or the color distance is too close to the neighbor segment, that segment may be annexed with their neighbor. We calculate score between target segment and every neighbor segment using below formulation:

$$w_e \frac{A_d}{A_n} + w_d \frac{N}{\|C_n - C_t\|},\tag{2}$$

where A_d and A_n represent the area of target segment and neighbor segment respectively. C_n and C_t are the color vectors of target and its neighbor segment. w_e and w_d represent the weight factor and N is the normalizing factor. In addition to the system's annexation of segments, we also offer the user an interaction interface which is used to annex the unnecessary segment.

5   Fast Mean-Shift Video Segmentation

As mentioned in the previous section, mean-shift segmentation must refer every pixels in every frame of the video. Many previous approach performed mean-shift segmentation for all of the video data set as pre-processing, this causes the system to take enormous time and memory. We discuss how to accelerate the mean-shift segmentation algorithm which can be applied to high-resolution video in this section for the fast production time.

5.1 Foreground Extraction

Because the static region (background region) of the video can be separately processed as a single image from the dynamic region (foreground part), we first extract the foreground dynamic region(s) from the whole video. As we specified above, our video source has been filmed with fixed angle camera with no sudden exposure exchange, thus, we can simply extract the background image just by taking the median value of every spatial pixel which is aligned to the time axis (see Figure 4). Let $V_t(x, y)$, $1 \leq t \leq T$, be a pixel value in the tth frame image at the pixel coordinate (x, y). Then, the background pixel $B(x, y)$ is computed by:

$$B(x, y) = \text{Med}_{t=1}^{T} V_t(x, y), \tag{3}$$

where the median function "Med" returns the value in the middle of the sorted list of the pixel values $V_t(x, y)$, $1 \leq t \leq T$.

(a)   (b)

Fig. 4. Background extraction: (a) Original video (b)Background image extracted by median function

Some problems may occur when moving objects stay in the same position for a long time. To address this problem, our system supports a user interactions to correct the error. By using an acquired background image, we can create a foreground object mask by using below predicate:

$$G(x, y, \sigma) = \begin{cases} \text{true} & \text{if } (V_t(x, y) - B(x, y))^2 > \sigma \\ \text{false} & \text{if } (V_t(x, y) - B(x, y))^2 \leq \sigma \end{cases} . \tag{4}$$

This approach is quite simple, but the result may contain some noise. We can reduce the noise by using conventional noise reduction techniques such as the morphological filtering technique [13,14] (see Figure 5).

5.2 Foreground Data Reduction

Now the background image can be separately processed (from the dynamic foreground region) to the cartoon background image using the method described in Section 4 using image mean-shift segmentation technique [4].

(a)   (b)

Fig. 5. Noise reduction in foreground extraction: (a) Foreground mask before noise reduction, (b) Foreground mask after noise reduction

As for the foreground sequence, we perform the 3D mean-shift segmentation. Before the segmentation, we reduce the video volume using the following two methods:

- Separating the multiple objects in a foreground and perform segmentation individually, and
- Creating video volume with shifted coordinates.

The object separation can be easily accomplished by taking the bounding box of each connected component in the foreground mask images. For example, the original foreground region of size 179×115 in Figure 6(a) is separated into two foreground object regions (in Figure 6(b)) of size 50×113 and 33×102,

(a)   (b)

(c)   (d)

Fig. 6. Reducing foreground video volume: (a) Original foreground region having two objects, (b) Two regions after object separation, (c) Foreground region without coordinate shifting, (d) Foreground video volume after coordinate shifting

respectively. We can also reduce the size of data by shifting each frame's coordinates to obtain reduced foreground volume. The idea of coordinate shifting is to lump together the consecutive frames of image objects to construct a narrow video volume (see the coordinate shifting example from Figure 6(c) into Figure 6(d)). Let $V_t(x,y)$ and $V_{t+1}(x,y)$ be the pixel values at the image coordinates (x,y) in two consecutive frame t and $t+1$ in the same foreground video object. Then, the shifting offsets for $(t+1)$th image – (dx, dy) – can be computed by solving the following optimization problem:

$$\text{Minimize} \sum [V_t(x,y) - V_{t+1}(x+dx, y+dy)]^2 . \qquad (5)$$

For simplicity, we initially set the center of bounding box of $(t+1)$th image to be coincide with the center of bounding box of tth image, and try to check several dx and dy from the initial position to compute the optimal offset values. Using this technique, the size of the foreground region can be, for example, reduced from 145×122 (Figure 6(c)) into 58×122 (Figure 6(d)).

Before shifting the coordinates, we must ensure that the target object does not vary suddenly between consecutive frames. If the object suddenly changes shape or color, shifting the coordinates may destroy the time coherency and spatial information. For successful shifting, the system must verify the proportions of the object's width and height as well as area and color changing.

5.3   Sequential Mean-Shift Segmentation

For mean-shift video segmentation uses an enormous amount of memory, the whole video stream cannot be segmented at once. We perform segmentation by dividing the whole video stream into several fractions. In this process, the time coherency between the consecutive fractions should be preserved. Our idea to solve this problem is using the last part of ith fraction's result as the input of $(i+1)$th fraction (see Figure 7). By concatenating the cartoonized result of the previous fraction with the new video input in the current fraction, we could accomplish satisfactory result.

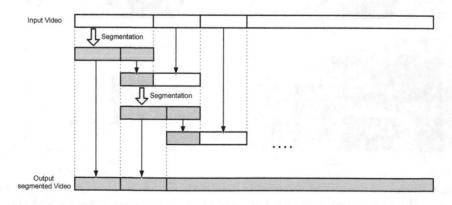

Fig. 7. Sequential segmentation

6   Rendering

The boundary of each segment in the segmented video is now approximated with a set of Bezier curves [15]. This is for maintaining the final output as a series of vector images, which is robust in arbitrary scaling. The size of the vector image output is also much smaller than the bitmap image output. And by performing this process, we can also detect the line structure to express the stroke of the cartoon to make result with cartoon-like stylization. Stroke of the cartoon is generally exist between segment and segment. Important thing that we consider in rendering process is the thickness of the boundary curve in the output image. In our system, a boundary curve between two segments having large color difference is more thicker than the boundary curve between two segments having similar colors. Thus, the segments having similar colors in a single object, for example, the segments representing the two tone colors generated by the the lighting effect in the same solid colored cloth, are separated with thinner boundary curves. While, the boundary curve between two segments included in two totally different objects (e.g., a human and background) possibly is more thicker than other boundary curves. Let H_p, I_p, and C_p represent the hue, intensity, and color values of the currently considered segment p, and H_q, I_q and C_q are the corresponding values of a neighboring segment q of p. The thickness of the boundary curve between two segments p and q are computed by the following simple rule:

$$\text{if } e^{\frac{\|H_p - H_q\|}{N_h}} > \sigma_H \text{ and } e^{\frac{\|I_p - I_q\|}{N_i}} > \sigma_I, \tag{6}$$

$$\text{Thickness} = \frac{\|C_p - C_q\|}{N_c} * W,$$

where σ_H and σ_I are tolerance values for hue and intensity, W is the thickness weight, and N_h, N_i, and N_c are the normalization factors to scale the difference values to be in the range [0..1].

7   Experimental Result

Figure 8 shows the final result of this paper. Figure 8(b) is the result of image cartooning from the original photo 8(a). We performed layering and annexation tasks for this example. By using segment annexation, the number of segments is reduced from 673 to 272. In experiments, we observed that the number of segments reduced between 25% and 50% after the annexation for almost all examples. The figure illustrates that the detailed features of the human face can be easily distinguished while the background is enough simplified.

Figure 8(c),(d) (example Video 1), and Figure 8(e),(f) (example Video 2) show the results of the video cartooning. The data reduction and corresponding processing time reduction are shown in the Table 1. In both examples, the foreground extraction and the data reduction techniques make the number of pixels for video segmentation and the processing time to be dramatically decreased

Table 1. Reduced data and time for video cartooning

	Original resolution	# of frames	Total # of pixels	# of pixels after data reduction	Original Processing time	Reduced Processing time
Video 1	400 × 224	200	17920000	744720	175 min	9 min
Video 2	640 × 352	100	21120000	367200	398 min	6 min

Fig. 8. Some experimental results: (a)(b) image cartooning, (c)(d) video 1 cartooning, and (e)(f) video 2 cartooning

than the naive full video processing. Although the original data size of Video 2 is larger than the Video 1 example, we can observe that the number of pixels after data reduction for Video 2 example is smaller than that of Video 1. This is because Video 2 example has less dynamic region than Video 1 example.

8   Conclusion and Future Work

We proposed a technique for cartooning video within fast production time. We have discussed how to stabilize the input by using spatio-temporal bilateral filtering, and annex the segment to enhance the segmentation result by using the score based on the sizes and colors of the neighboring segments. By layering, we were also able to control the degree of details. Finally, we have discussed a method of segmenting the video with acceleration by using sequential mean-shift segmentation with a minimized video data set.

Although the system segments and cartoonizes input images and video properly, there are some obvious limitations in our work.

First, though mean-shift is a robust algorithm to perform the segmentation, it is not appropriate for interactive use. Second, because our system performance is inversely proportional to the foreground object's area, it does not work well when the foreground mask is large. To overcome these knotty points, we must consider more effective algorithm for the video segmentation, or enhance the mean-shift algorithm itself. Third, our system only works at a fixed camera angle, and this restriction reduces the applicability a lot. We can address this by using better matting method, or potentially stabilizing the video angle automatically. We believe that spatio-temporal alignment through comparing the feature vector may also be useful to solve this problem.

Acknowledgement

This work was supported by the Ministry of Information & Communications, Korea, under the Electronics and Telecommunicatins Research Institute(ETRI) Support Program.

References

1. Gooch, B., Gooch, A.: Non-Photorealistic Rendering. AK Peters, Ltd (2001)
2. Fukunaga, K., L.D.Hostetler: The estimation of the gradient of a density function, with applications in pattern recognition. IEEE Transaction on Information Theory **21** (1975) 32–40
3. Comaniciu, D., Meer, P.: Robust analysis of featuer spaces:color image segmentation. In: Proceedings of 1997 IEEE CVPR. (1997) 750–104
4. Comaniciu, D., Meer, P.: Mean shift: A robust approach toward feature space analysis. IEEE Transaction on Pattern Analysis and Machine Intelligence **24** (2002) 603–619

5. Decarlo, D., Santella, A.: Stylization and abstraction of photographs. In: Proceedings of ACM Siggraph. (2002) 769–776
6. Assem Agarwala, Aaron Hertzmann, D.H.S., Seitz, S.M.: Keyframe-based tracking for rotoscoping and animation. ACM Transaction on Graphics **23** (2004) 584–591
7. Jue Wang, Yingqung Xu, H.Y.S., Cohen, M.F.: Video tooning. ACM Transaction on Graphics **23** (2004) 574–583
8. Jue Wang, Bo Thiesson, Y.X.M.C.: Image and video segmentation by anisotropic kernel mean shift. In: Computer Vision - ECCV 2004. (2004) 238–249
9. Holger Winnem, S.C.O., Gooch, B.: Real-time video abstraction. ACM Transaction on Graphics **25** (2006) 1221–1226
10. Tomasi, C., Manduchi, R.: Bilateral filtering for gray and color images. In: IEEE International Conference on Computer Vision. (1998)
11. H. Kang, C.C., Charkraborty, U.: Interactive sketch generation. The Visual Computer **21** (2005) 821–830
12. weiss, B.: Fast median and bilateral filtering. ACM Transaction on Graphics **25** (2006) 519–526
13. Gonzalez, R.C., Woods, R.E.: Digital Image Processing second eddition. Prentice Hall (2002)
14. Gose, E., Johnsonbaugh, R.: Pattern Recognition and Image Analysis second eddition. Prentice Hall PTR (1996)
15. Elaine Cohen, R.F.R., Elber, G.: Geometric Modeling with Splines. A K Peters (2001)

Virtual Reality Technology Used to Develop Didactic Models

Alcínia Zita Sampaio and Pedro Gamerio Henriques

Technical University of Lisbon, IST/ICIST, Department of Civil Engineering and Architecture,
Av. Rovisco Pais, 1049-001 Lisbon, Portugal
{zita,pgameiro}@civil.ist.utl.pt

Abstract. Virtual Reality techniques were used to develop educational didactic models in the area of Civil Engineering. The visualization of the distinct physical steps of a construction is shown in the virtual applications here presented. The developed models bring new perspectives in the teaching activity as a support to expose new curricular programmes or complex sequence construction. In order to obtain models, which would be able to visually simulate the geometric evolution of the construction activity, techniques of geometric modelling and virtual reality were used. The models make it possible to view the physical evolution of the work, to follow the planned construction sequence and to visualize details of the form of every component of the works. They also support the study of the type and method of operation of the equipment necessary for these construction procedures. These models have been used to distinct advantage as educational aids in first-degree courses in Civil Engineering.

1 Introduction

Three-dimensional geometric models are usually created to present final works in architectural and engineering activities. Those models not allow the observation of physical evolution needed during the construction. The sequence of the construction processes in not visualized and some error or incompatibilities in that activity could occur. That kind of models couldn't alert for that fact and some mistakes are not avoided. The visual simulation of the construction process needs to be able to produce changes to the geometry of the project dynamically. It is then important to extend the usefulness of design information to the construction planning and construction phases. The integration of geometrical representations of the building together with scheduling data is the basis of 4D (3D + time) models in construction domain. 4D models combine 3D models with the project timeline [1]. 4D-CAD models are being used more and more frequently to visualize the transformation of space over time. To date, these models are mostly purely visual models. On a construction project, a 4D-CAD environment enabled the team, involved in the project, to visualize the relationships between time (construction activities) and space (3D model of the project) [2].

In the present study, two engineering construction work models were created, from which it was possible to obtain three-dimensional models corresponding to different states of their form, simulating distinct stages in their construction. The use of techniques of virtual reality in the development of these educational applications brings

A. Gagalowicz and W. Philips (Eds.): MIRAGE 2007, LNCS 4418, pp. 173–179, 2007.

new perspectives to the teaching of subjects in the area of Civil Engineering. The work described here makes up part of two on-going research projects at ICIST: *Automatically generating model of the graphic representation of bridges* [3] A. Zita Sampaio (main research) and *Virtual reality in optimisation of construction project planning* [4], Pedro G. Henriques (coordinator).

In order to create models, which could visually simulate the construction process, the authors turned to techniques of geometric modelling and virtual reality (VR). The applications developed for this purpose refer to the construction of a masonry cavity wall and a bridge. These models make it possible to show the physical evolution of the work, the monitoring of the planned construction sequence, and the visualization of details of the form of every component of each construction. They also assist the study of the type and method of operation of the equipment necessary for these construction procedures. The virtual model can be manipulated interactively allowing the user to monitor the physical evolution of the work and the construction activities inherent in its progression.

One of the applications developed corresponds to the model of a masonry cavity wall, one of the basic components of a standard construction. To enable the visual simulation of the construction of the wall, the geometric model generated is composed of a set of elements, each representing one component of the construction. Using a system of virtual reality technologies, specific properties appropriate to the virtual environment are applied to the model of the wall. Through direct interaction with the model, it is possible both to monitor the progress of the construction process of the wall and to access information relating to each element, namely, its composition and the phase of execution or assembly of the actual work, and compare it with the planned schedule. This model had been used to distinct advantage as an educational aid in Civil Engineering degree course modules.

The second model created allows the visual simulation of the construction of a bridge using the cantilever method. The geometric model of the bridge deck was created through a bridge deck modelling system. A system of virtual reality was used to program the visual simulation of the bridge construction activities. Students are able to interact with the model dictating the rhythm of the process, which allows them to observe details of the advanced equipment and of the elements of the bridge. The sequence is defined according to the norms of planning in this type of work. The aim of the practical application of the virtual model of bridge construction is to provide support in those disciplines relating to bridges and construction process both in classroom-based education and in distance learning based on e-learning technology.

2   Virtual Model of the Construction of a Wall

Described here are the processes both of the modelling of an exterior wall of a standard building and of the association of virtual properties with the created model, the intended outcome being the interactive exhibition of its construction [5]. The model of the masonry cavity wall, including the structure of the surrounding reinforced concrete and the elements in the hollow area (bay elements), was created using a three dimensional graphic modelling system in widespread use in planning offices, namely,

AutoCAD. The virtual environment was applied to the model through the computer system *EON Studio* [6].

2.1 Modelling the Construction Elements of the Wall

The representation of this model of an exterior wall of a conventional building comprises the structural elements (foundations, columns and beams), the vertical filler panels and two bay elements (door and window). The structural elements of the model were created with parallelepipeds and were connected according to their usual placement in building works. Because this is an educational model, the steel reinforcements were also defined. In the model, the rods of each reinforcement are shown as tubular components with circular cross-section (Fig. 1).

The type of masonry selected corresponds to an external wall formed by a double panel of breezeblocks, *11 cm*, wide with an air cavity, *6 cm,* wide (Fig. 1).

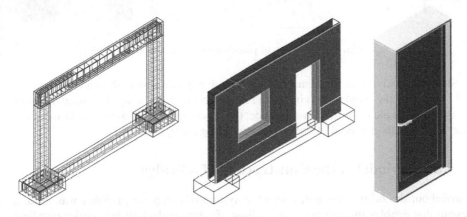

Fig. 1. Phases in modelling the masonry wall

Complementary to this, the vertical panels were modelled, these comprising: the thermal isolation plate placed between the brick panels, the plaster applied to the external surface of the wall, the stucco applied on the internal surface, two coats of paint both inside and out and the stone slabs placed on the exterior surface. Finally, two usual bay elements (Fig. 1), a door and a window, were modelled. The completed model was then transferred to the virtual reality system *EON* (as a *3ds* drawing file).

2.2 Definition of the Virtual Environment in the Evolution of a Construction

In the EON system [6], the visual simulation of the building process of the wall, following a particular plan, was programmed. For this effect, 23 phases of construction were considered. The order in which components are consecutively exhibited and incorporated into the virtual model, translates into the method of the physical evolution of the wall under construction (Fig. 2). During the animation, the student can control the length of time that any phase is exhibited and observe the model using the most suitable camera and zoom positions for a correct perception of the details of construction elements. It is possible to highlight the component incorporated at each new phase and to examine it in detail (Fig. 2).

Included, under the window in which the virtual scene is exhibited, is a bar, which shows the progress of the construction. Throughout the animation, the bar is filled, progressively, with small rectangles symbolizing the percentage built at the time of the viewing of that particular phase, in relation to the completed wall construction (Fig. 2).

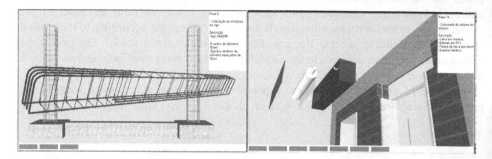

Fig. 2. Exhibition of phases in building evolution

Simultaneously, with the visualization of each phase, a text is shown (in the upper right corner of the window) giving data relating to the stage being shown, namely, its position within the construction sequence, the description of the activity and the characterization of the material of the component being incorporated.

3 Virtual Model of the Construction of a Bridge

Throughout the bridge research project, a system of computer graphics was used, a system that enables the geometric modelling of a bridge deck of box girder typology [3]. This system was used to generate, three-dimensional (3D) models of deck segments necessary for the visual simulation of the construction of the bridge [7]. In addition to the three-dimensional models of each segment, models of the pillars, form travellers, abutments and false work were made. The attribution of virtual properties to the model of the bridge was implemented by using the *EON Studio*.

The North Viaduct of the Quinta Bridge [8] in Madeira, Portugal, was the case selected for representation in the virtual environment. In cross-section, the deck of the viaduct shows a box girder solution and its height varies parabolically along its three spans. The most common construction technique for this typology is the cantilever method of deck construction. The construction of the deck starts by applying concrete to a first segment on each pillar and then proceeds with the symmetrical positioning of the segments starting from each pillar.

3.1 Modelling the Elements of the Construction Scenario

The deck segments were created through the use of the representational system for bridges mentioned above. To complete the model of the bridge, the pillars and abutments were modelled using the *AutoCAD* system. The advanced equipment is composed of the form traveller, the formwork adaptable to the size of each segment, the work platforms for each formwork and the rails along which the carriages run (Fig. 3). As, along with the abutments, the deck is concreted with the false work on the ground, the scaffolding for placement at each end of the deck (Fig. 3) was also modelled. Terrain suitable for the simulation of the positioning of the bridge on its foundations was also modelled.

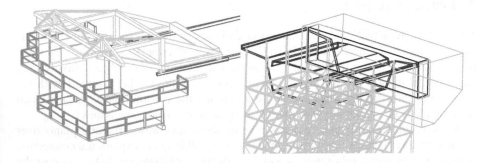

Fig. 3. 3D models of the elements of the construction scenario

3.2 Programming the Virtual Construction Animation

Once all the 3D models of the construction scenario had been generated, they were transposed, in *3ds* extension data file format, to the virtual reality system. The definition of the construction sequence is based on a counter, which determines the next action when a mouse button is clicked. The first action consists of the insertion of the pillars in the first scenario, which is composed solely of the landscape. The next step is to place one of the segments on top of each of the pillars. After this, a form traveller is placed on each segment. The construction of the deck is defined symmetrically in relation to each pillar and simultaneously (Fig. 4). In each phase, two pairs of segments are defined. For each new segment the following steps are established: raising the form traveller; moving the rails in the same direction as the construction (relocating them on the latest segment to have been concreted); moving the form traveller on the rails, positioning it in the zone of the next segment to be made; concrete the segment. Finally, the zone of the deck near the supports is constructed, the false work resting on the ground.

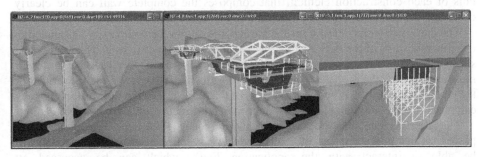

Fig. 4. Simulation of the construction process

Moving the camera closer to the model of the bridge and applying to it routes around the zone of interest, it is possible to visualize the details of the form of the components involved in the construction process. In this way, the student can interact with the virtual model, following the sequence specifications and observing the details of the configurations of the elements involved.

4 Learning Aspects

The models are actually used in face-to-face classes of disciplines of Civil Engineering curriculum: Technical Drawing (1st year), Construction Process (4th year) and Bridges (5th year). The traditional way to present the curricular subjects involved in those virtual models are 2D layouts or pictures. Now, the teacher interacts with the 3D models showing the sequence construction and the constitution of the modelled building element. Essentially, the models are used to introduce new issues.

As in Technical Drawing, students have to define and draw structural plants over the architectural layouts, the virtual model of the wall helps to explain the connection between the architectural drawings and the structural solutions needed to support the house configuration. Some indication must be assumed when choosing a structural solution in order to minimize the unpleasant visual appearance in the interior of a house when structural elements (beans, columns, ...) are included in it. The students are 1st year degree, so they have some difficulty to understand the spatial localization of the structural elements and how they must be built and located almost inside the walls. The relations between the architectural configurations and the structural elements in a building are well explained following the virtual exhibition of the wall's construction.

In the discipline of Construction Process, in order to prepare students to visit real work places, the teacher shows the construction animation and explains some aspects of the construction process of the wall. Namely, the way the net of irons is defined inside a bean or a column and specially the complexity of the connexion between the distinct types of irons near the zone where the structural elements connect each other. In order to clearly explain this issue related to the structural elements, the iron nets were created as 3D models with distinct colours, and they appear on the virtual scenario following a specific planned schedule. The type, sequence and thickness of each vertical panels that composes a cavity wall is well presented in the virtual model showing step by step the relative position between each other. The configuration details of each construction element that composes the complete wall can be clearly observed manipulating the virtual scenario of the wall's construction.

The construction model of a bridge particularly shows the complexity associated to the concrete work of the deck bridge that is done in a symmetric way. The model also shows the way of displacement of the advanced equipment. In class, the professor must explain way the process must follow that sequence of steps and the movement of the equipment devices. When the students, of the 5th year, goes to the work place they can observe the complexity and the sequence of construction previously explained.

The students can also interact with those models. For that, the models were posted on the Internet pages of undergraduate Civil Engineering. The student will be able to interact with the application *EonX,* which can be accessed at: http://download.eonreality.com.

5 Conclusions

It has been demonstrated, through the examples presented here, how the technology of virtual reality can be used in the elaboration of teaching material of educational interest in the area of construction processes.

The models generated represent building in two standard situations. The student can interact with the virtual model in such a way that he can set in motion the construction sequence demanded by actual construction work, observe the methodology applied, analyse in detail every component of the work and the equipment needed to support the construction process and observe how the different pieces of a construction element mesh with each other and become incorporated into the model.

These models are used in disciplines involving construction in courses in Civil Engineering and Architecture administered by the Higher Technical Institute of the University of Lisbon. They can be used in classroom-based education and in distance learning supported by e-learning technology.

Acknowledgements

Foundation of Science and Technology (FCT) financially supports the research projects involved in this work.

References

1. Leinonen, J., Kähkönen, K., Retik, A.: New construction management practice based on the virtual reality technology, in book 4D CAD and Visualization in Construction: Developments and Applications, editors Raja R.A. Issa, Ian Flood William J. O'Brien. Ed. A.A. Balkema Publishers (2003), 75-100.
2. Liston, K., Fischer, M., Winograd, T.: Focused sharing of information for multi-disciplinary decision making by project teams, ITcon Vol. 6 (2001), 69-82.
3. Sampaio, A., Reis, A., Braz, H., Silva, L.: Project program report: Automatically generating model of the graphic representation of bridges, POCTI/1999/ECM/ 36328, ICIST/FCT, Lisbon, Portugal (1999).
4. Henriques, P., Sampaio, A., Bento, J., Braz, H.: Project program report: Virtual reality in optimization of construction project planning, POCTI/1999/ECM/ 36300, ICIST/FCT, Lisbon, Portugal (1999).
5. Sampaio, A., Henriques, P., Studer, P.: A virtual environment tool applied to visualize construction processes, in Proceeding of TP.CG.04 – Theory and Practice of Computer Graphics 2004 Conference, Bournemouth, U.K., (2004)78-85.
6. Introduction to working in EON Studio, EON Reality, Inc. 2003.
7. Sampaio, A.: Definition of a bridge deck geometrical modelling process to automate design graphical representations, in Proceeding of IKM 16th International Conference on the Applications of Computer Science and Mathematics in Architecture and Civil Engineering, Weimar, Germany (2003), abstract pp. 62 - CDROM 6 pgs.
8. Graphical documentation of the design of North Viaduct of the Quinta Bridge - 1st phase, GRID Planning office, Lisbon, 1995.

Copying Behaviour of Expressive Motion

Maurizio Mancini[1], Ginevra Castellano[2],
Elisabetta Bevacqua[1], and Christopher Peters[1]

[1] IUT de Montreuil
University of Paris8
[2] InfoMus Lab, DIST
University of Genova

Abstract. In this paper we present an agent that can analyse certain human full-body movements in order to respond in an expressive manner with copying behaviour. Our work focuses on the analysis of human full-body movement for animating a virtual agent, called Greta, able to perceive and interpret users' expressivity and to respond properly. Our system takes in input video data related to a dancer moving in the space. Analysis of video data and automatic extraction of motion cues is done in EyesWeb. We consider the amplitude and speed of movement. Then, to generate the animation for our agent, we need to map the motion cues on the corresponding expressivity parameters of the agent. We also present a behaviour markup language for virtual agents to define the values of expressivity parameters on gestures.

1 Introduction

A critical part of human-computer interaction is the ability for systems to respond affectively to users [Pic97]. That means that systems must be able to detect the user's emotional state and to plan how to give an appropriate feedback.

Virtual agent systems represent a powerful human-computer interface, as they can embody characteristics that a human may identify with and may therefore interact with the user in a more empathic manner [RN96].

In our work we focus on the analysis of human full-body movement and the synthesis of a virtual expressive agent, since our general goal is to create a system capable of affective responses. The automatic extraction of movement characteristics is done by EyesWeb [CMV04], while the synthesis is done by the virtual agent called Greta [PB03].

We present a preliminary approach to the creation such a system: an agent that exhibits copying behaviour. For each gesture performed by the human, the agent will respond with a gesture that exhibits the same quality. We do not aim at copying the user's gesture shape but only the quality: that is, some of the physical characteristics of movement. In fact, we are interested in studying the importance of the quality of motion independently by its shape, in order to understand what kind of information it can convey. So, the novelty of our work is that the agent's animation is not a straight copy of the original: only the global characteristics of the input motion are retained. For example, if a user moves his/her hand far out to the side fast, the agent may move its hand upward fast. In the near future we also want to extend the set of motion cues by introducing for example the fluidity and continuity of movement.

A. Gagalowicz and W. Philips (Eds.): MIRAGE 2007, LNCS 4418, pp. 180–191, 2007.

A possible application of the actual system may be to conduct tests in which subjects are asked to evaluate the emotion perceived in the agent's copying behaviour. Then learning algorithms could be implemented to map user's quality of movement to his emotional state. The system will use such information to influence the response and the behavior of the virtual agent.

The presented work is divided into two main parts. The first part focuses on sensing and analysis of data coming from a real environment. The second part describes how this information is used to generate copying behaviour with a virtual agent.

2   Previous Work

In the human-computer interaction field, there is an increasing attention on automated video analysis aiming to extract and describe information related the emotional state of individuals. Several studies focus on the relationships between emotion and movement qualities, and investigate expressive body movements ([SW85],[WS86], [DeM89], [Wal98], [BC98], [Pol04]). Nevertheless, modelling emotional behaviour starting from automatic analysis of visual stimuli is a still poorly explored field. Camurri and colleagues ([CLV03], [Cas06], [CCRV06]) classified expressive gesture in human full-body movement (music and dance performances) and in motor responses of subjects exposed to music stimuli: they identified cues deemed important for emotion recognition and showed how these cues could be tracked by automated recognition techniques. Other studies show that expressive gesture analysis and classification can be obtained by means of automatic image processing ([BRI+05], [DBI+03].

Several systems have been proposed in which virtual agents provide visual feedback/response by analysing some characteristics of the user behaviour. In such systems the input data can be obtained from dedicated hardware (joysticks, hand gloves, etc), audio, movement capture, video source. SenToy [PCP+03] is a doll with sensors in its arms, legs and body. According to how the user manipulates the doll in a virtual game, the system is able to understand the emotional state of the user. Taylor et al. [TTB] developed a system in which the reaction of a virtual character is driven by the way the user plays a music instrument. The user has to try to vary her execution to make virtual character reacts in some desired way. Wachsmuth's group [KSW03] described a virtual agent capable of imitating natural gestures performed by a human using captured data. Imitation is conducted on two levels: when mimicking, the agent extracts and reproduces the essential form features of the stroke which is the most important gesture phase; the second level is a meaning-based imitation level that extracts the semantic content of gestures in order to re-express them with different movements

In two previous works the Greta virtual agent has been used to respond to the user input. The first one, presented by Mancini et al. [MBP05], is a system obtained by connecting emotion recognition in musical execution with Greta. That is, the facial expression and head movements of the agent were automatically changed by the audio in input in real-time. The second work by Bevacqua et al. [BRP+06] aimed at animating the same virtual agent off-line by providing data coming both from video recognition of the user expression/behaviour and from scripted actions.

In addition, preliminary research [CP06] has been presented regarding the calculation of global full-body humanoid motion metrics, in particular quantity and expansiveness of motion, using the EyesWeb expressive gesture processing library [CMV04]. Input can be linked to either a video camera, for sensing a real dancer in the real environment, or a synthetic vision system [Pet05] for sensing a virtual dancer in a virtual environment. Higher level processes, such as behaviour planning, are invariant with respect to the source of the input data, allowing for comparison of behavioural algorithms designed for virtual environments with their real world counterparts.

3   Overview

We present a scenario where an agent senses, interprets and copies a range of full-body movements from a person in the real world. In that scenario, we refer to a system able to acquire input from a video camera, process information related to the expressivity of human movement and generate copying behaviour. Our work focused on full-body motion analysis of a dancer. In our system, the agent responds with copying behaviour accordingly to expressive human motion descriptors like the quantity of motion and the contraction/expansion of movement.

Figure 1 shows an overview of our architecture, based on a *TCP/IP* network connection. The *EyesWeb* block performs the automatic extraction of movement characteristics that are described in the next section. The *Copying* block computes the expressivity parameters (see 6) from the movements cues. Finally the *Animation Computation* and *Visualization* are performed using the virtual agent system Greta.

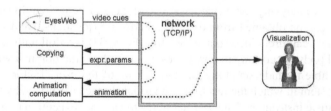

Fig. 1. Overview of the system architecture

4   Analysis of Input Data

Our system takes in input video data related to a dancer moving in the space. Video analysis started with the extraction of the silhouette of the dancer from the background. We then automatically extracted motion cues from the full-body movement of the dancer. Analysis of video data and automatic extraction of motion cues were done in EyesWeb [CCM+04], and particularly by using the EyesWeb Expressive Gesture Processing Library [CMV04]. We analysed global indicators of the movement of the dancer, related to the amount of movement he makes and his use of the space. More specifically, we extracted the following motion cues.

1. **QoM** - *Quantity of motion*

Quantity of Motion is an approximation of the amount of detected movement, based on Silhouette Motion Images (see Figure 1). A Silhouette Motion Image (SMI) is an image carrying information about variations of the silhouette shape and position in the last few frames.

$$SMI[t] = \{\sum_{i=0}^{n} Silhouette[t-i]\} - Silhouette[t] \tag{1}$$

The SMI at frame t is generated by adding together the silhouettes extracted in the previous n frames and then subtracting the silhouette at frame t. The resulting image contains just the variations happened in the previous frames.

Fig. 2. A measure of QoM using SMIs (the shadow along the dancer's body)

QoM is computed as the area (i.e., number of pixels) of a SMI, normalised in order to obtain a value usually ranging from 0 to 1. That can be considered as an overall measure of the amount of detected motion, involving velocity and force.

$$QoM = Area(SMI[t, n])/Area(Silhouette[t]) \tag{2}$$

2. **CI** - *Contraction Index*

Contraction Index is a measure, ranging from 0 to 1, of how the dancers body uses the space surrounding it. That can be calculated using a technique related to the bounding region (see Figure 2), i.e., the minimum rectangle surrounding the dancers body: the algorithm compares the area covered by this rectangle with the area currently covered by the silhouette.

Automatic extraction allows to obtain temporal series of the selected motion cues over time, depending on the video frame rate. As explained in the following sections, the agent motor behaviour generation requires the definition of a specific mapping between the human motion cues and the expressivity parameters of the agent. We segmented the video of the dancer in five main phases, according to the main gestures performed by him. For each phase, we computed the mean of the QoM and the CI of the dancer. These values were mapped onto the expressivity parameters of the agent.

Fig. 3. A measure of CI using the bounding region

5   Virtual Agent Expressivity Parameters

Several researchers (Wallbott and Scherer [WS86], Gallaher [Gal92], Ball and Breese [BB00], Pollick [Pol04]) have investigated human motion characteristics and encoded them into dimensional categories. Some authors refer to body motion using dual categories such as slow vs fast, small vs expansive, weak vs energetic, small vs large, unpleasant vs pleasant. In particular Wallbott and Sherer have conducted perceptual studies that show that human beings are able to perceive and recognise a set of these dimensions [WS86]. We define *expressivity of behaviour* as the "How" the information is communicated through the execution of some physical behaviour. There are many systems available for synthesising expressive emotional animation of a virtual agent. Badler's research group developed EMOTE (Expressive MOTion Engine [CCZB00]), a parameterised model that procedurally modifies the affective quality of 3D character's gestures and postures motion. From EMOTE the same research group derived FacEMOTE [BB02], a method for facial animation synthesis that altered pre-existing expressions by setting a small set of high level parameters.

The Greta's animation engine is an expressive engine. Starting from the results reported in [WS86], we have defined and implemented expressivity [HMP05] as a set of parameters that affect the gesture (performed by arms or head) quality of execution speed of arms / head, spatial volume taken by the arms / head, energy and fluidity of arms / head movement, number of repetitions of the same gesture. Thus, the same gestures or facial expressions are performed by our agent in a qualitatively different way depending on these parameters, something with great promise for generating variable character behaviours.

In the present work we will focus on the parameters affecting the spatiality and speed of arm movement, respectively *Spatial extent* and *Temporal extent*:

1. **SPC** - *Spatial extent*
   This parameter basically affects the amplitude of arm movements. The space in front of the agent that is used for gesturing is represented as a set of sectors following McNeill's diagram [McN92]. We expand or condense the size of each sector through scaling. Wrist positions in our gesture language are defined in terms of

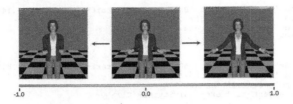

Fig. 4. Spatial Extent - execution of the same gesture can be small or large

these sectors (see Figure 4). To find the location of articulation for a gesture, we calculate joint angles needed to reach a some points in the resized sectors.

2. **TMP** - *Temporal extent*

    This parameters represents the speed of execution of gestures. We start from a constraint on the position of the end of the gesture stroke because we want to ensure the synchronicity of the gesture end of stroke for example with stressed syllables of speech (in the presented work there is no speech anyway). Then, depending on the temporal parameter we place the preceding and proceeding gesture phases (preparation, stroke start, retraction) in time. Figure 5 illustrates the variation of the stroke start position relative to the stroke end depending on the temporal parameter.

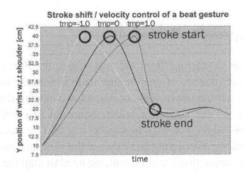

Fig. 5. Temporal Extent - execution of stroke is faster or slower

5.1 Expressivity Specification

In the Greta system we specify expressivity parameters values either on a sequence of consecutive gestures (that is all the gestures have the same) or on single gestures. In Greta, gestures are stored in a pre-defined gesture library. At runtime they are instantiated following the given timing and expressivity. This information can be passed to Greta by writing a text file in a *ad-hoc* behaviour markup language.

Figure 5.1(a) shows an example of such file. In the example we want Greta to produce two gestures (*gesture1* and *gesture2*) and we added the information about the expressivity of each gesture (see tags *expressivityspc* and *expressivitytmp*). The content of the file can be seen as the temporal diagram in Figure 5.1(b).

```
<gesture id='gesture1' type='BEAT=UPRIGHT' start='0.32' end='1.14'/>
<gesture id='gesture1' stroke='0.500'/>
<gesture id='gesture1' expressivityspc='0'/>
<gesture id='gesture1' expressivitytmp='1.0'/>

<gesture id='gesture2' type='ADJECT=LARGE' start='2.06' end='4.86'/>
<gesture id='gesture2' stroke='0.5'/>
<gesture id='gesture2' expressivityspc='1.0'/>
<gesture id='gesture2' expressivitytmp='0'/>
```

(a)

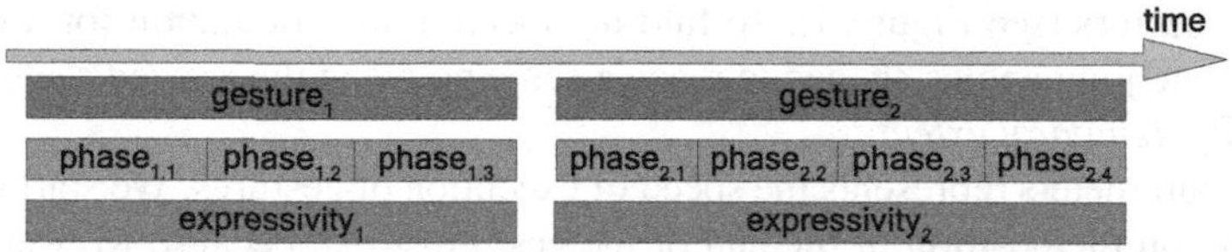

(b)

Fig. 6. Expressivity parameters values are specified separately for each gesture: the behaviour specified in the example (a) can be seen as a temporal diagram of gestures with different expressivity values (b)

6   Copying of Expressive Behaviour

As explained in section 4, starting from the real video, the dancer's performance is manually divided in 5 sequences of movements with almost the same shape. In fact, since the dancer moves continuously, without pauses, we have to find a way to identify gestures whose quality we can copy. We select sequences of similar movements as a single gesture with repetitions. For each gesture performed by the dancer the analysis system computes its quality calculating the value of the motion cues CI and QoM.

Then, to generate the animation for our agent, we need to map the motion cues on the corresponding expressivity parameters. In this work we take into account Spatial Extent and Temporal Extent. In fact, the Contraction Index can be mapped to the Spatial Extent since, as we have seen before, the first one describes how the dancer's body uses the space surrounding it and the second one describes the amplitude of movements. Instead, the Quantity of Motion can be mapped to the Temporal Extent since both of them are linked to the velocity of movements.

The analysis system calculates the motion cues for each frame of the video, while the synthesis system needs a single value for each expressivity parameters to define the quality of a whole gesture. For such a reason the analysis system must calculate the mean value of QoM and CI for every gesture performed by the dancer, in this way we obtain a single value that we can map to the corresponding expressivity parameter.

Now, since the motion cues and the expressivity parameters varies in different ranges, a scaling procedure is needed. Regarding the CI, we reversed the sign of Spatial Extent. In fact, if a gesture has a high value of CI, it means that during its performance the arms remain near the body (as explained in 4). So, a high value of CI corresponds a low value of SPC. First of all we define the boundaries mapping the minimum and the maximum values of CI computed during the whole dancer's performance respectively to the maximum and the minimum values of the spatial parameter. Then we can map the CI of each gesture to a meaningful value of SPC using the formula:

$$SPC = (((QoM_{ges} - QoM_{min})/(QoM_{max} - QoM_{min})) * 2) - 1;[1] \quad (3)$$

Instead, for the QoM, we simply map its minimum and the maximum values computed during the whole dancer's performance to the minimum and the maximum values of the Temporal Extent to determine the boundaries of the interval. Then we can map the QoM of each gesture to a meaningful value of TMP. Figure 7 shows an example of the mapping between QoM and TMP.

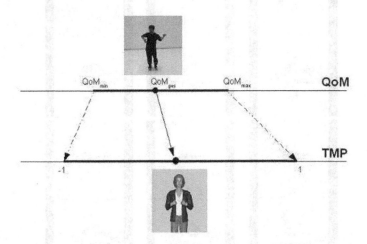

Fig. 7. Example of caling from QoM to Temporal Extent

In Figure 8 three sequences of copying behaviour are shown. The corresponding video can be seen at:
http://www.iut.univ-paris8.fr/greta/clips/copying.avi

7   Future Work

We are working towards the creation of a real-time system that recognises emotions of users from human movement and an expressive agent that shows empathy to them. In the near future we want to extend the set of motion cues by introducing for example the fluidity and continuity of movement. Next steps of our work will be to map movement expressivity of the user to his emotional state, so that the agent can plan affective response accordingly to that. In fact, if the agent can understand the user's emotional

---

[1] The SPC paramater can vary in the interval [-1,1]; the value of 2 represents the amplitude of such interval.

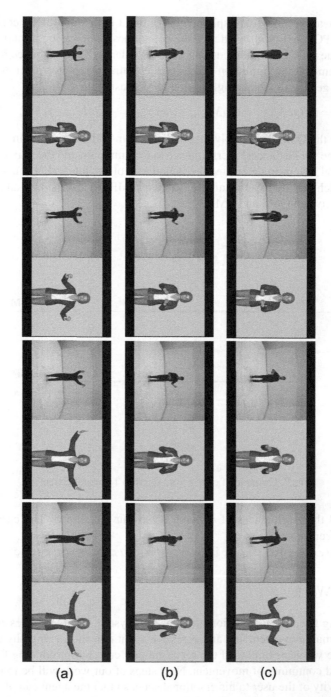

Fig. 8. Three sequences showing copying behaviour with different level of CI: (a) large, (b) small, (c) medium

state analysing the quality of his gesture, it can decide which facial expression to show. We are particularly interested in responding to threat and showing empathy with expressions of happiness or sadness. Here are some examples about how motion cues can be perceived by the agent and how it could respond to them:

- high QoM, low CI and low fluidity (that is large, fast and rigid movement) could be perceived as a threat: in this case Greta could show fear.
- high QoM, low CI and high fluidity (large, fast and fluid movement) could be seen as happiness or enthusiasm: Greta could show happiness.
- low QoM and medium CI (slow and small movements) can be associated to sadness: Greta could respond with sadness.

In the last two examples we want to link the motion cues to empathy.

Further, the definition of a mapping between movement and emotions can contribute to validate algorithms for movement expressivity analysis and synthesis. Perceptive tests with users aimed to associate emotional labels to affective - real and virtual - videos are planned.

Acknowledgements

This work has been partially funded by the Network of Excellence Humaine (Human-Machine Interaction Network on Emotion) IST-2002-2.3.1.6 / Contract no. 507422 (http://emotion-research.net/).

References

[BB00]   Gene Ball and Jack Breese, *Emotion and personality in a conversational agent*, Embodied conversational agents, MIT Press, Cambridge, MA, USA, 2000, pp. 189–219.

[BB02]   Meeran Byun and Norman Badler, *Facemote: Qualitative parametric modifiers for facial animations*, Symposium on Computer Animation (San Antonio, TX), July 2002.

[BC98]   R. Thomas Boone and Joseph G. Cunningham, *Childrens decoding of emotion in expressive body movement: the development of cue attunement*, Developmental Psychology **34** (1998), 10071016.

[BRI+05]   Themis Balomenos, Amaryllis Raouzaiou, Spiros Ioannou, Athanasios Drosopoulos, Kostas Karpouzis, and Stefanos Kollias, *Emotion analysis in man-machine interaction systems*, Machine Learning for Multimodal Interaction (Hervé Bourlard Samy Bengio, ed.), Lecture Notes in Computer Science, vol. 3361, Springer Verlag, 2005, pp. 318–328.

[BRP+06]   Elisabetta Bevacqua, Amaryllis Raouzaiou, Christopher Peters, Georges Caridakis, Kostas Karpouzis, Catherine Pelachaud, and Maurizio Mancini, *Multimodal sensing, interpretation and copying of movements by a virtual agent*, PIT06:Perception and Interactive Technologies (Germany), June 19-20 2006.

[Cas06]   Ginevra Castellano, *Human full-body movement and gesture analysis for emotion recognition: a dynamic approach*, Paper presented at HUMAINE Crosscurrents meeting, Athens, June 2006.

[CCM⁺04]   Antonio Camurri, Paolo Coletta, Alberto Massari, Barbara Mazzarino, Massimil-
iano Peri, Matteo Ricchetti, Andrea Ricci, and Gualtiero Volpe, *Toward real-time
multimodal processing: Eyesweb 4.0*, in Proc. AISB 2004 Convention: Motion,
Emotion and Cognition, 2004.

[CCRV06]   Antonio Camurri, Ginevra Castellano, Matteo Ricchetti, and Gualtiero Volpe, *Subject interfaces: measuring bodily activation during an emotional experience of music*, Gesture in Human-Computer Interaction and Simulation (J.F. Kamp S. Gibet,
N. Courty, ed.), vol. 3881, Springer Verlag, 2006, pp. 268–279.

[CCZB00]   Diane Chi, Monica Costa, Liwei Zhao, and Norman Badler, *The emote model for
effort and shape*, ACM SIGGRAPH '00 (New Orleans, LA), July 2000, pp. 173–
182.

[CLV03]   Antonio Camurri, Ingrid Lagerlöf, and Gualtiero Volpe, *Recognizing emotion from
dance movement: Comparison of spectator recognition and automated techniques*,
International Journal of Human-Computer Studies, Elsevier Science **59** (2003),
213–225.

[CMV04]   Antonio Camurri, Barbara Mazzarino, and Gualtiero Volpe, *Analysis of expressive gesture: The eyesweb expressive gesture processing library*, Gesture-based
Communication in Human-Computer Interaction (G.Volpe A. Camurri, ed.), LNAI
2915, Springer Verlag, 2004.

[CP06]   Ginevra Castellano and Christopher Peters, *Full-body analysis of real and virtual
human motion for animating expressive agents*, Paper presented at the HUMAINE
Crosscurrents Meeting, Athens, June 2006.

[DBI⁺03]   Athanasios Drosopoulos, Themis Balomenos, Spiros Ioannou, Kostas Karpouzis,
and Stefanos Kollias, *Emotionally-rich man-machine interaction based on gesture
analysis*, Human-Computer Interaction International, vol. 4, june 2003, p. 1372
1376.

[DeM89]   Marco DeMeijer, *The contribution of general features of body movement to the
attribution of emotions*, Journal of Nonverbal Behavior **28** (1989), 247 – 268.

[Gal92]   Peggy E. Gallaher, *Individual differences in nonverbal behavior: Dimensions of
style*, Journal of Personality and Social Psychology **63** (1992), no. 1, 133–145.

[HMP05]   Bjoern Hartmann, Maurizio Mancini, and Catherine Pelachaud, *Towards affective
agent action: Modelling expressive ECA gestures*, Proceedings of the IUI Workshop on Affective Interaction (San Diego, CA), January 2005.

[KSW03]   Stefan Kopp, Timo Sowa, and Ipke Wachsmuth, *Imitation games with an artificial
agent: From mimicking to understanding shape-related iconic gestures*, Gesture
Workshop, 2003, pp. 436–447.

[MBP05]   Maurizio Mancini, Roberto Bresin, and Catherine Pelachaud, *From acoustic cues
to an expressive agent*, Gesture Workshop, 2005, pp. 280–291.

[McN92]   David McNeill, *Hand and mind - what gestures reveal about thought*, The University of Chicago Press, Chicago, IL, 1992.

[PB03]   Catherine Pelachaud and Massimo Bilvi, *Computational model of believable conversational agents*, Communication in Multiagent Systems (Marc-Philippe Huget,
ed.), Lecture Notes in Computer Science, vol. 2650, Springer-Verlag, 2003,
pp. 300–317.

[PCP⁺03]   Ana Paiva, Ricardo Chaves, Moisés Piedade, Adrian Bullock, Gerd Andersson, and Kristina Höök, *Sentoy: a tangible interface to control the
emotions of a synthetic character*, AAMAS '03: Proceedings of the second international joint conference on Autonomous agents and multiagent systems (New
York, NY, USA), ACM Press, 2003, pp. 1088–1089.

[Pet05]   Christopher Peters, *Direction of attention perception for conversation initiation in virtual environments*, International Working Conference on Intelligent Virtual Agents (Kos, Greece), September 2005, pp. 215–228.

[Pic97]   Rosalind Picard, *Affective computing*, Boston, MA: MIT Press, 1997.

[Pol04]   Franck E. Pollick, *The features people use to recognize human movement style*, Gesture-based Communication in Human- Computer Interaction (G. Volpe A. Camurri, ed.), LNAI 2915, Springer Verlag, 2004, pp. 20–39.

[RN96]   Byron Reeves and Clifford Nass, *The media equation: How people treat computers, television and new media like real people and places*, CSLI Publications, Stanford, CA, 1996.

[SW85]   Klaus R. Scherer and Harald G. Wallbott, *Analysis of nonverbal behavior*, HANDBOOK OF DISCOURSE: ANALYSIS, vol. 2, Academic Press London, 1985.

[TTB]   Robyn Taylor, Daniel Torres, and Pierre Boulanger, *Using music to interact with a virtual character*, The 2005 International Conference on New Interfaces for Musical Expression.

[Wal98]   Harald G. Wallbott, *Bodily expression of emotion*, European Journal of Social Psychology **13** (1998), 879–896.

[WS86]   Harald G. Wallbott and Klaus R. Scherer, *Cues and channels in emotion recognition*, Journal of Personality and Social Psychology **51** (1986), no. 4, 690–699.

Illumination Compensation Algorithm Using Eigenspaces Transformation for Facial Images

Junyeong Yang and Hyeran Byun

Dept. of Computer Science, Yonsei University, Seoul, Korea, 120-749
gundid,hrbyun@cs.yonsei.ac.kr

Abstract. This paper presents a new low-dimensional face representation using the proposed eigenspaces transformation. The proposed algorithm is based on face images which is acquired with c illumination conditions. We define face images as a non-illumination class and illumination classes from light source conditions and derive the linear transformation function in a low-dimensional eigenspace between a non-illumination class and illumination classes. The proposed illumination compensation algorithm is composed of two steps. In the optimal projection space which is obtained from the DirectLDA algorithm, we first select the illumination class for a given image and then we generate a non-illuminated image by using eigenspace transformation of the illuminated class. We provide experimental results to demonstrate the performance of the proposed algorithm with varying parameters of proposed algorithm.

Keywords: illumination compensation, face modeling, illumination modeling.

1 Introduction

In many vision recognition system, it is an important problem to solve the variation of illumination[7]. The appearance of object is dramatically varied from specific direction and intensity of light source. To handle the effect of illumination is an important in face recognition system also. Many approaches which has been studied by many researchers can be categorized by illumination invariant feature approaches[2][5][11], illumination compensation approaches[7][8][10] based on illumination model, and face representation[1][3][4][6][12] in low dimensional space. Illumination invariant feature approaches focus on extracting illumination invariant features such as edges and contour. However such features are sensitive to structure such as glasses and discard useful information for recognition. Illumination compensation approaches model an illumination model from images which were acquired from various illumination conditions. They then compensate the effect of illumination by using the constructed model. Low dimensional face representation approaches move a vector space of training images into a low dimensional vector space in a least-squares sense such as eigenface and fisherfaces. Those methods based on appearance have both the ease of implementation and high performance. In this paper, we propose a novel low-dimensional representation of face in various illumination conditions. The proposed method is based on images which are obtained

A. Gagalowicz and W. Philips (Eds.): MIRAGE 2007, LNCS 4418, pp. 192–199, 2007.
© Springer-Verlag Berlin Heidelberg 2007

by various illumination conditions. We divide a training database into c illumination classes by illumination conditions and then derive the linear transformation function between illumination classes in a low-dimensional eigenspace. From the linear transformation function, we propose the reconstruction equation between a non-illumination class and illumination classes. However the proposed reconstruction algorithm can be used when we know the illumination class corresponding to a given image. To classify the illumination class, we used DirectLDA[12] algorithm to find optimal projection to classification. For a given image, we select the illumination class which has the minimum Euclidean distance between a test pattern and centroids of c illumination classes in optimal projection. Section 2 describes proposed reconstruction equation between a non-illumination class and illumination classes. Section 3 presents a illumination compensation algorithm based on proposed reconstruction equation.

2   The Reconstruction Between Illumination Classes in Low Dimensional Eigenspaces

In this Section, we propose a linear transformation function between non-illuminated images and images illuminated by a specific light source. First, images which are obtained from c light conditions in fixed pose are labeled as one of c illumination classes. Each vector space of c illumination classes are transformed into each low dimensional eigenspace. Then, we derive a linear transformation function between a non-illumination class and c illumination classes. We propose the reconstruction equation between a non-illumination class and other illumination classes by using the proposed linear transformation function.

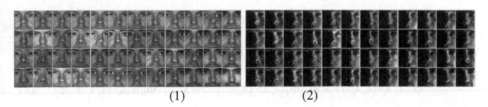

(1)   (2)

Fig. 1. (1) Some images of the non-illumination class X_0 (2) Some images of illumination class X_i

2.1   The Definition of a Non-illumination Class and Illumination Classes

The proposed algorithm is based on the images which are acquired from c light conditions in fixed pose. We selected Yale Database B[6] for an experiment. Images of Yale Database B were captured by 65 illumination conditions in each particular pose. Illumination conditions of Yale Database B is varied with the azimuth and elevation of the single light source direction. Let $I(i, j) \in \Re^{m \times n}$ represents an images in Yale Database B. We make each image as each column vector $x \in \Re^{N = (mn)}$ formed by concatenating the rows of $I(x, y)$. We define a target illumination class from the images that were captured by the light source direction which is at 0 degrees azimuth and 0 degrees elevation as a non-illumination class $X_0 \in \Re^{N \times K}$. Images with other illumination conditions are defined as one of the illumination class $X_i \in \Re^{N \times K}$, $i = 1,\dots,c$. Fig 1 shows some examples of X_0 and X_i.

2.2   The Derivation of a Linear Transformation Function Between a Non-Illumination Class and Illumination Classes

When a illumination class $X_i \in \Re^{N \times K}$ is applied to PCA, a pattern $x_i \in X_i$ is represented by follow PCA reconstruction.

$$x_i \approx \overline{X}_i + \Phi_i \left(\Phi_i^T \left(x_i - \overline{X}_i \right) \right) \tag{1}$$

where $\overline{X}_i$ and $\Phi_i \in \Re^{N \times M}$, $M \le K$ are the mean and eigenvectors of X_i. We define the linear function between a non-illumination class X_0 and a illumination class X_i as :

$$\overline{X}_0 + \Phi_0 A_0 \approx M_{i0} \left(\overline{X}_i + \Phi_i A_i \right) + \varepsilon_{i0} \tag{2}$$

where $A_0 = \Phi_0^T \left(X_0 - \overline{X}_0 \right) \in \Re^{M \times M}$ and $A_i = \Phi_i^T \left(X_i - \overline{X}_i \right) \in \Re^{M \times M}$ are the coefficient of X_0 and X_i. $M_{i0} \in \Re^{N \times N}$ and ε_{i0} are the matrix for linear transformation from X_i to X_0 and the linear approximation error. If we use $\overline{X}_0 \approx M_{i0} \overline{X}_i + \varepsilon_{i0}$ after expansion of (2), we can get the follow equation.

$$\overline{X}_0 + \Phi_0 A_0 \approx M_{i0} \left(\overline{X}_i + \Phi_i A_i \right) + \varepsilon_{i0} \Rightarrow \Phi_0 A_0 \approx M_{i0} \Phi_i A_i \tag{3}$$

We multiply a pseudo inverse matrix $\left(A_i A_i^T \right) \left(A_i A_i^T \right)^{-1}$ and $\Phi_i^T = \Phi_i^{-1}$ both sides.

$$\Phi_0 A_0 A_i^T \left(A_i A_i^T \right)^{-1} \approx M_{i0} \Phi_i \left(A_i A_i^T \right) \left(A_i A_i^T \right)^{-1} \Rightarrow M_{i0} \approx \Phi_0 A_0 A_i^T \left(A_i A_i^T \right)^{-1} \Phi_i^T \tag{4}$$

it follows from (3) and (4) that

$$A_0 \approx M_{i0} A_i, \ M_{i0} = A_0 A_i^T \left(A_i A_i^T \right)^{-1} \in \Re^{M \times M} \tag{5}$$

2.3   The Reconstruction Between a Non-illumination Image and a Illumination Image

The reconstruction equation of a non-illumination image $x_0 \in X_0$ from a illumination image $x_i \in X_i$ can be simply derived from (5). If $\hat{x}_0$ is a non-illumination image which is reconstructed from x_i, it follows that

$$\Phi_0^T \left(\hat{x}_0 - \overline{X}_0 \right) = M_{i0} A_i \tag{6}$$

If we use $\Phi_0^T = \Phi_0^{-1}$ for (6), we have

$$\hat{x}_0 = \overline{X}_0 + \Phi_0 M_{i0} A_i \qquad (7)$$

In same manner, the reconstruction equation mapping a non-illumination image $x_0 \in X_0$ into a illumination image $\hat{x}_i$ can be derived by follow equation.

$$\hat{x}_i = \overline{X}_i + \Phi_i M_{i0}^{-1} A_0 \qquad (8)$$

3   Illumination Compensation Based on Reconstruction

A reconstruction equation between illumination classes proposed in Section 2.3 can be used when we know the illumination class corresponding to a given image. We use DirectLDA algorithm to find optimal projection to classify the illumination class. Because the main variation of training database is represented by leading components of eigenvectors and is illumination in this paper, we use a concatenation of first n eigenvectors of c illumination classes as a feature extraction matrix $B = \left\{\phi_1^{(1)}, \cdots, \phi_n^{(1)}, \phi_2^{(c)}, \cdots, \phi_n^{(c)}\right\} \in \Re^{N \times (n \times c)}$, $\phi_j^{(i)} \in \Phi_i, 1 \le j \le M$. Then we apply DirectLDA to $Y_i = B^T X_i \in \Re^{(n \times c) \times K}$, $i = 0, \ldots, c$. The between-class scatter matrix S_B is defined as

$$S_B = \sum_{i=0}^{c} K (m_i - m)(m_i - m)^T \qquad (9)$$

and the within-class scatter matrix S_W is defined as

$$S_W = \sum_{i=1}^{c} \sum_{y_j \in Y_i} (y_j - m_i)(y_j - m_i)^T \qquad (10)$$

where $m \in \Re^{(n \times c)}$, $m_i \in \Re^{(n \times c)}$, and K are the mean of all patterns, the mean of Y_i, and the number of patterns of a class. DirectLDA finds the projection W to maximize the follow objective function.

$$\arg \max_{W} \frac{\left| W S_B W^T \right|}{\left| W S_W W^T \right|} \qquad (11)$$

First, we compute the projection Z which diagonalizes the numerator of (11) and then the projection U which diagonalizes $Z^T S_W Z$. The optimal projection $U \in \Re^{(n \times c) \times m}$, $m < c - 1$ is eigenvectors corresponding to the smallest eigenvalues. The classification equation is the follow equation about a test image $x \in \Re^N$.

$$X^* = \arg\min_{i \in 0,\dots,c} \left\| \hat{m}_i - U^T B^T x \right\|^2, \ where \ \hat{m}_i = U^T m_i \tag{12}$$

where X^* is the index of illumination classes.

4 Experimental Result

We chose 3330 images which satisfy one-to-one mapping in Yale Database and then grouped 3330 images into 45 illumination classes which contains 74 images. Each image is annotated with 62 landmarks and warped into the mean shape which is about 6000 pixels wide by using the piece-wise affine warping algorithm. Therefore, the dimension of each illumination class $X_i, i = 0,\dots,44$ is $\mathfrak{R}^{6000 \times 74}$. We defined images labeled with '+000E+00' as non-illumination class X_0 and computed the linear transform $M_{i0}, i = 1,\dots,44$ from (5). We used the follow equation to estimate the quality of reconstruction.

$$\gamma_{i0} = \frac{1}{74} \sum_{x_k \in X_i} \left\| x_0 - \hat{x}_0 \right\|^2, \ where \ x_0 \in X_0, \ \hat{x}_0 = \overline{X}_0 + \Phi_0 M_{i0}\left(\Phi_i^T \left(x_k - \overline{X}_i\right)\right) \tag{13}$$

We computed the mean of Euclidean distance between ground truth x_0 and $\hat{x}_0$ reconstructed from x_k by using (7). All of the reconstruction error $\gamma_{i0}, i = 1,\dots,44$ was 0 in experimental result. When we know the index of a illumination class corresponding to a test image x_k, the reconstruction error which is obtained by proposed linear transformation M_{i0} is very close to zero. Next, we did an experiment to find the optimal parameter. We computed the index of images of each illumination class X_i by using (12) and estimated the error from the mean of the number of patterns which satisfy $X^* \neq i$. We did an experiment to find the optimal number n for a matrix B. Fig 2 shows the experimental result for first n eigenvectors. When n is 2, the performance is optimal. We defined a matrix to extract feature for DirectLDA as $B \in \mathfrak{R}^{6000 \times (2 \times 45) = 6000 \times 90}$ from an experiment and did an experiment to find the optimal rank of Z and U which are projection matrix of DirectLDA. Fig 3 and Fig 4 show an experimental result on the rank of Z of U. We determined that the rank of Z and U was 44 and 6 from an experimental result. By using leaving-one-out technique, we did an additional experiment with parameters determined by an experiment on samples which were not trained. We chose images about one person for testing and the linear transformation matrix $M_{i0}, i = 1,\dots,44$ is computed from the remaining nine person. This procedure was repeated 10 times. Fig 5 shows the experimental result of the leaving-one-out technique. It shows that the performance does not depend on a specific training set. Note that this result is not the

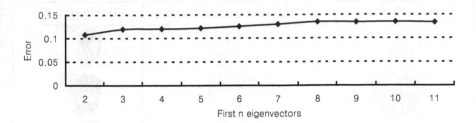

Fig. 2. The error rate by first n eigenvectors

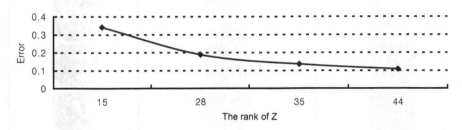

Fig. 3. The error rate by the rank of Z

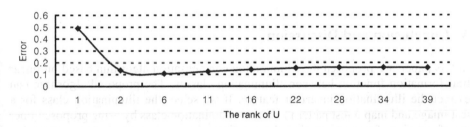

Fig. 4. The error rate by the rank of U when the rank of Z is 44

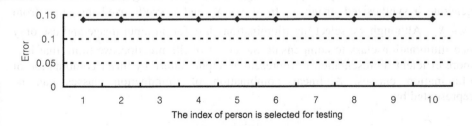

Fig. 5. The error rate by the leaving-one-out technique

reconstruction error but the classification error. Fig 6 shows the reconstruction images for test patterns which were classified wrongly. Reconstruction image $\hat{x}_0$ and ground truth image x_0 is very similar in spite of wrong classification.

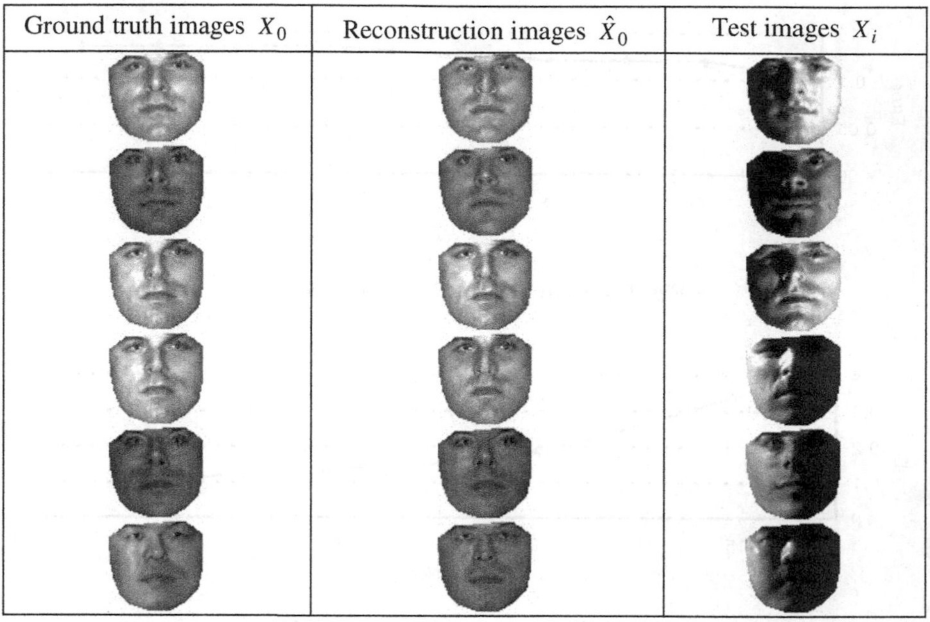

Ground truth images X_0	Reconstruction images $\hat{X}_0$	Test images X_i

Fig. 6. Examples of images which are reconstructed from test image X_i that satisfies $X^* \neq i$

5   Conclusion and Discussion

In this paper, we proposed the illumination compensation algorithm based on linear transformation function between illumination classes. The proposed algorithm can extract the illumination invariant feature. If we select the illumination class for a test image and map a test pattern into non-illumination class by using proposed liner transformation function of the illumination class, we can always extract the coefficient of the eigenspace of X_0 for input images. Also, it can generate images which are illuminated by a specific light source. By using (7) and (8), we can generate a synthesized image $\hat{x}_0$ from $x_i \in X_i$ and a synthesized image $\hat{x}_i$ from $x_0 \in X_0$. Although we select the illumination class for an input image and use only one illumination class to compensate the effect of illumination, we think that it is more efficient representation to represent an input pattern by linear combination of illumination classes. A linear combination of illumination classes can be represented by

$$x_0 = \overline{X}_0 + \Phi_0 \left[\sum_{i=1}^{c} w_i M_{i0} A_i \right] \tag{13}$$

Here $W = \{w_1, \ldots, w_c\}, w_i \in \Re$ is similar to a permutation matrix. In the proposed method, only one element of W is 1, and other elements are 0. Because images acquired from various illumination conditions are the elements of the subset of the continuous manifold in the high-dimensional vector space, a pattern can lie close to more than one illumination subspaces. Because of this reasons, Fig 6 shows that reconstruction image $\hat{x}_0$ and ground truth image x_0 is very similar in spite of wrong classification. We will study this problem in future work and apply the proposed algorithm to the face recognition system.

Acknowledgement

This research was supported by the Ministry of Information and Communication, Korea under the Information Technology Research Center support program supervised by the Institute of Information Technology Assessment, IITA-2005-(C1090-0501-0019).

References

1. M. Turk and A. Pentland.: Eigenfaces for Recognition, Journal of Cognitive Neuroscience, Vol. 3, 1991, pp. 71-96
2. R. Brunelli and T. Poggio.: Face Recognition: Features vs. Templates, IEEE Transaction. Pattern Analysis and Machine Intelligence, Vol. 3, 1991, pp. 71-96
3. B. Moghaddam and A. Pentland.: Probabilistic Visual Learning for Object Representation, IEEE Transaction. Pattern Analysis and Machine Intelligence, Vol. 19, 1997, pp. 696-710
4. H. Murase and S. Nayar.: Visual Learning and Recognition of 3D objects from appearance, International Journal of Computer Vision, Vol. 14, 1995, pp. 5-24
5. L. Wiskott, J. Fellous, N. Kruger, and C. von der Malsburg.: Face Recognition by Elastic Bunch Graph Matching, IEEE Transaction. Pattern Analysis and Machine Intelligence, Vol. 19, 1997, pp. 775-779
6. P. N. Belhumeur, J. P. Hespanha, and D. J. Kriegman.: Eigenfaces vs. Fisherfaces: Recognition Using Class Specific Linear Projection, IEEE Transaction. Pattern Analysis and Machine Intelligence, Vol. 19, 1997, pp. 711-720
7. Athinodoros S. Georghiades, David J. Kriegman, and Peter N. Belhumeur.: Illumination Cones for Recognition Under Variable Lighting: Faces, IEEE Conference on Computer Vision and Pattern Recognition, 1998, pp. 52-58
8. Michael J. Tarr, Daniel Kersten, Heinrich H. Bulthoff.: Why the visual recognition system might encode the effects of illumination, Pattern Recognition, 1998
9. P. N. Belhumeur and D. J. Kriegman.: What is the set of images of an object under all possible lighting conditions?, International Journal of Computer Vision, Vol. 28, 1998, pp. 245-260
10. A. S. Georghiades, P. Belhumeur, and D. Kriegman.: "From Few to Many", Generative Models for Recognition under Variable Pose and Illumination, Proceedings of IEEE International Conference on Automatic Face and Gesture Recognition, 2000, pp. 277-284
11. A. Shashua, T. R. Raviv.: The quotient image: Class based re-rendering and recognition with varying illuminations, IEEE Transaction. Pattern Analysis and Machine Intelligence, Vol. 23, 2001, pp. 129-139
12. H. Yu and J. Yang.: A direct LDA algorithm for high-dimensional data with application to face recognition, Pattern Recognition, Vol. 34, 2001, pp. 2067-2070

Reverse Engineering Garments

Nils Hasler, Bodo Rosenhahn, and Hans-Peter Seidel

Max-Planck-Institut für Informatik, 66123 Saarbrücken, Germany
hasler@mpi-inf.mpg.de

Abstract. Segmenting garments from humanoid meshes or point clouds is a challenging problem with applications in the textile industry and in model based motion capturing. In this work we present a physically based template-matching technique for the automatic extraction of garment dimensions from 3D meshes or point clouds of dressed humans. The successfull identification of garment dimensions also allows the semantic segmentation of the mesh into naked and dressed parts.

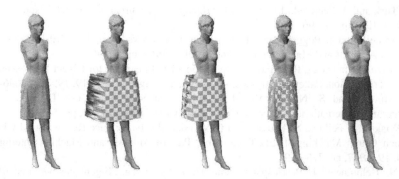

Fig. 1. The laser scan of a dressed person is segmented into dressed and naked parts by fitting the parameterised template of a garment to the mesh

1 Introduction

Segmenting point clouds or meshes of dressed humans into covered and naked parts is a problem with applications e. g. in the textile and movie industry. A number of general mesh segmentation algorithms have been published [1] but they cannot be applied to the given problem because they provide a segmentation but are unable to supply labels for the segmented parts. So a different approach is suggested here. Like Jojic and Huang [2] we fit a simulated cloth to the 3D data to recreate the observed configuration. Segmenting the mesh or point cloud is then straightforward.

Another application of the approach is to provide initialisation informations for a model-based motion capture algorithm of loosely dressed humans such as [3]. For this approach it is essential that a good model of both the tracked person and of the loose garments worn during the motion capture session is available. Since the model of the tracked person can easily be acquired using a full-body laser scanner, we here deal

A. Gagalowicz and W. Philips (Eds.): MIRAGE 2007, LNCS 4418, pp. 200–211, 2007.
© Springer-Verlag Berlin Heidelberg 2007

with the more challenging problem of extracting the dimensions of the attire from the 3D scan of a person. Additionally, extracting the dimensions of the clothing allows the semantic segmentation of the 3D data into covered and unclad parts.

The approach proposed here is a template based analysis-by-synthesis technique [4]. That is we assume a priori knowledge of the general type of garments worn but not their exact dimensions. These dimensions of the parameterised garments are chosen by a simulated annealing algorithm [5] and the resulting attire is draped over the mesh or point cloud. The evaluation function of the procedure is based on the distance from the simulated cloth to the measured 3D data, the stretch of the springs, and the silhouettes of model and simulated garment.

The remainder of this work is structured as follows: Section 2 introduces publications related to the present work. Section 3 presents details about the employed draping procedure. Results are presented in Section 4 and a summary is given in Section 5.

2 Previous Work

Even though the algorithm presented here is aimed at segmenting a mesh into parts describing the garments the scanned human is wearing and those that belong to the person itself, the approach cannot readily be compared with general mesh segmentation algorithms such as [1]. These approaches are after all only aimed at segmenting arbitrary shapes into smaller parts that do not necessarily have any intuitive semantics attached to them. Even if they do these cannot be assigned automatically to the segments which defeats their applicability to the given problem.

Other approaches were specially adapted to segmenting human shapes. Nurre [6] or Xiao et al. [7] are able to reliably segment a human body scan into torso and limbs and can label the parts automatically. However, the approaches were not designed to work with dressed humans.

Allen et al. [8] introduced a different class of algorithms that can be used to segment the scan of a human. They proposed to fit a generic human model to the observed mesh by deforming it locally. That is an affine transformation is applied to every point of the mesh. Local smoothness of the transformations, the distance between the two models, and the distance of manually selected landmarks are used to evaluate a configuration. They also show that reasonable results can be obtained if no landmarks or even if landmarks but no further surface information is available. Since the template model may contain arbitrary additional information, segmentation or animation of the model becomes trivial.

Seo and Magnenat-Thalmann [9] presented a similar approach, which operates in two phases. They first roughly find the pose and scale of a skeleton based template model and then iteratively fit the surface of the template model to the measured 3D data. Unfortunately, their rough fitting stage requires the manual localisation of landmarks. A recent survey of these and related human model generation and animation techniques was presented by Magnenat-Thalmann et al. [10].

Unfortunately, all of the above techniques work well only for tightly or scantily dressed models. Going the other way, Oh et al. [11] propose a technique for creating animatable models of dressed humans that rely on simulating the garments only during model generation. They proceed by first draping the garments over the undressed model. Then they remove hidden surfaces and transfer skinning weights from the underlying model to the cloth surface. During animation the model can then be deformed based on simple skinning weights attached to a skeleton.

With a completely different goal in mind but arguably the work most closely related to our own Jojic and Huang [2] presented an approach for estimating the static parameters of a square piece of fabric from range data. Their algorithm follows a two-phased pattern. In the first phase a simulated piece of cloth is attracted to the triangulated range data of an object which is covered by a square textile. They do this to ensure that the simulation converges to the same minimum energy configuration as the real-world fabric did when it was draped over the real object. In the second phase the attraction forces are turned off and the simulation is again run until it comes to rest. The mean distance between the simulated cloth and the range data is used to tune the static cloth properties of their simulation.

Since the approach that is proposed here involves the simulation of a piece of fabric, a brief overview of the particle based cloth simulation literature is given in the following. Physically based cloth simulation was pioneered by Terzopoulos et al. [12]. In their work a number of techniques that are still common today such as semi-implicit integration, hierarchical bounding boxes, and adaptive time-step control were proposed. Until Baraff and Witkin reintroduced semi-implicit integration [13], decreasing the computational cost of cloth simulation significantly, explicit integration techniques were common.

In the last few years two major strands of development can be made out in the cloth simulation community. One, aiming for real-time simulation, focusses on computation speed alone, sacrificing expressiveness and accuracy of the employed model if necessary. Desbrun et al. simplified the equation system that needs to be solved every step by precomputing parts of it [14]. Kang and Choi used a coarse mass-spring discretisation and added wrinkles in a post-processing step by interpolating with a cubic spline [15].

The other strand attempts to simulate cloth as realistically as possible. The use of nonlinear and hysteretic cloth properties has been introduced by Eberhardt et al. [16]. Simplified nonlinearities have since been integrated into a number of systems such as [17,18]. Impressive results have been presented by Volino and Magnenat-Thalmann [19].

3   Algorithm

In this section the template deformation approach for estimating garment dimensions is detailed. We first give a rough overview of the approach and then provide details for the different components of the system.

The method for segmenting a 3D scan into dressed and naked parts proposed here can be seen as a physically based template deformation approach. That is we assume a priori knowledge of the type of garment the scanned person is wearing but not the exact measurements of the attire. The garments are also manually prepositioned roughly on the scan. A physically based cloth simulation system is used to drape the garment template over the captured mesh. The resulting resting position of the garment is evaluated using the distance to the captured mesh, the stretch of the springs employed in the cloth simulation, and the silhouettes of 3D scan and simulated clothing. A simulated annealing algorithm then modifies the dimensions of the garments and updates the drape until convergence is reached.

3.1 Garment Templates

Two generic garment templates are shown in Figure 2. The skirt pattern has four degrees of freedom one vertical measurement (the length of the skirt) and three horizontal ones: One at the waistline which in this case actually sits on the upper hip, one at the hem and an additional measurement at the lower hip. Similarly the T-shirt template has a length, a width which is normally the same at all places for a simple T-shirt, sleeve length, and sleeve circumferences at the seam and at the hem. Unfortunately, we found that the T-shirt frequently rests so closely on the skin that it is impossible to extract the neckline from range data alone. So parameters defining the shape of the neckline were omitted from the optimisation procedure. As the parameters chosen by the optimisation procedure define the complete circumference of the garment the lengths have to be distributed to the different parts the garment is made of. The distribution of the parameters to the different parts of the pattern is also marked in Figure 2.

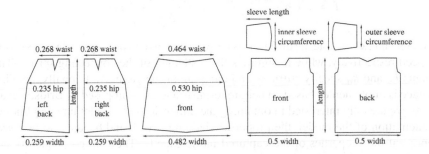

Fig. 2. Generic patterns of a skirt and a T-shirt

During optimisation the garment dimensions are modified in a way similar to the technique described by Volino et al. [20]. Only the restlengths of affected springs, the areas of deformed triangles and masses of involved particles are modified. Their 3D coordinates are left unchanged. That way invalid configurations, such as parts of the cloth extending into the body, are avoided and abrupt parameter changes are handled smoothly. The general procedure for applying dimension changes is shown in Figure 3. The length of a T-shirt, for example, is changed by modifying the two-dimensional coordinates of affected points of the unrefined Delaunay triangulation. Particle positions

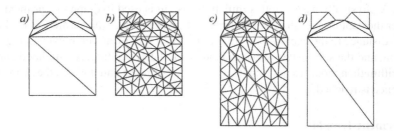

Fig. 3. When modifying the length of a T-shirt first the original underlying Delaunay triangulation gets changed (a, d). The coordinates of the refined triangles are then derived from their barycentric coordinates within this triangulation (b, c).

of the refined triangulation are derived from their barycentric coordinates within this original triangulation.

3.2   Cloth Simulation

The cloth simulation employed at the heart of the optimisation procedure is in essence a damped mass-spring system as used in most cloth simulations. The force $\mathbf{f}$ on two connected mass-points is given by

$$\mathbf{f} = \pm \left(k_s \frac{|\Delta \mathbf{x}| - l_0}{|\Delta \mathbf{x}|} + k_d \frac{\Delta \mathbf{x} \cdot \Delta \mathbf{v}}{|\Delta \mathbf{x}|^2} \right) \Delta \mathbf{x}$$

where $\Delta \mathbf{x}$ and $\Delta \mathbf{v}$ denote the differences between the two involved particles in position and speed respectively, while l_0 signifies the restlength of the connecting spring. The constants k_s and k_d specify stiffness and damping of the cloth. Additionally, bending resistance is implemented based on neighbouring triangles as proposed by Bridson et al. [21]. As we are only interested in obtaining the dimensions of the clothing and finding a segmentation of the model, the properties defining stretch and bending do not have to represent the properties of the captured fabric exactly. They are consequently not included in the optimisation.

One of the greatest problems encountered when employing physically based cloth simulations to real-world modelling such as tracking or in this case draping of garments is that cloth simulations are inherently instable [17]. That is slight deviations of the initial configuration or the simulation physics can cause significantly different outcomes. The only solution to the problem is to introduce attraction forces between the simulation and the observed configuration. So additional linear forces $\mathbf{f_a}$ act on all particles of the simulation.

$$\mathbf{f_a} = k_a \cdot d(\mathbf{p}, \mathbf{M})$$

Here k_a is the stiffness of the attraction force and $d(\mathbf{p}, \mathbf{M})$ is a function returning a vector pointing from particle $\mathbf{p}$ to the closest point of the model $\mathbf{M}$. If the model is a point cloud d always returns a vector pointing to one of $\mathbf{M}$'s points. If it is, however, a mesh any point on the surface of the mesh may be its target.

To speed up the computation of the closest point the k-DOP bounding box hierarchy, also used for collision detection, was engaged. Collisions are, however, completely disabled in our experiments because the attraction forces antagonise the collision resolution forces slowing the simulation significantly. In addition it was found that garment dimensions tended to get overestimated if collisions were enabled.

3.3 Optimisation

The optimisation procedure we use is a simulated annealing variant of the downhill simplex method as described by Press et al. [5]. The error $E(\mathbf{x})$ is a function of the parameter set $\mathbf{x}$.

$$E(\mathbf{x}) = \alpha \cdot E_{dist}(\mathbf{x}) + \beta \cdot \sqrt{|1 - E_{stretch}(\mathbf{x})|} + \gamma \cdot E_{sil}(\mathbf{x}) \tag{1}$$

It is a weighted sum of three evaluation functions. The first, $E_{dist}(\mathbf{x})$, describes the average distance of garment particles to the model.

$$E_{dist}(\mathbf{x}) = \frac{1}{N_p} \sum_{i=1}^{N_p} |d(\mathbf{p_i}, \mathbf{M})|$$

Here N_p is the number of particles of the garment template and $\mathbf{p_i}$ stands for the position of a particle in space. $E_{stretch}(\mathbf{x})$ computes the average stretch of the springs employed in the simulation.

$$E_{stretch}(\mathbf{x}) = \frac{1}{N_s} \sum_{i=1}^{N_p} \sum_{j=1}^{N_p} \frac{|\mathbf{P_i} - \mathbf{P_j}|}{l_0(i,j)} \cdot c(i,j), \quad i \neq j$$

with

$$c(i,j) = \begin{cases} 1 & \text{if } \mathbf{p_i} \text{ and } \mathbf{p_j} \text{ are connected} \\ 0 & \text{otherwise} \end{cases}$$

and N_s representing the number of springs in the cloth. In Equation (1) $|1 - \ldots|$ is employed because the average deviation from the restlength (stretch or compression) of all springs is the property we are really interested in. The square root of the whole term emphasises the valleys in the otherwise fairly shallow error surface. The last component of Equation (1), $E_{sil}(\mathbf{x})$, is a measure for the difference in the silhouettes. It is computed as follows

$$E_{sil}(\mathbf{x}) = \sum_{i=1}^{4} \frac{\sum |\mathbf{S_m}(i) - \mathbf{S_g}(i)|}{\sum \mathbf{S_g}(i)},$$

where $\mathbf{S_m}(i)$ denotes the silhouette of the model from side i and $\mathbf{S_g}(i)$ the silhouette of the garment. The $\sum$ operator applied to one of these matrices computes the sum of all elements.

The factor α is always set to 1 while β, and γ are chosen such that the three terms of Equation (1) range in the same order of magnitude. The exact value of these parameters, however, was found to be of low importance.

3.4 Mesh

If a mesh is used instead of a point cloud additional information is available. Namely, the orientation of the triangles conveys the notion of inside and outside. Assuming that the garment's triangles are oriented in the same way it then becomes possible to define more selective attraction forces. By attracting cloth particles only to faces that have similar normals the convergence of the procedure can be improved significantly. This is visualised in Figure 4. On the left the initial position of the garment is shown. In the middle cloth particles were attracted to the closest point on the surface of the model. The sleeve crumples on the upper surface of the arm. On the right the sleeve's lower half gets attracted by the arm's lower side because only their normals are sufficiently similar. The sleeve expands as expected.

Fig. 4. On the left the initial configuration of a T-shirt template is shown. In the middle cloth particles are attracted to the closest point on the surface. On the right attraction forces are restricted to faces with similar normals.

Another advantage of using meshes instead of point clouds is that attraction forces are not limited to discrete particle positions but can be defined to arbitrary points on the mesh's triangular surfaces. As a consequence the cloth slides more easily over the surface of the mesh.

A significant disadvantage of using meshes, however, results from the fact that a closed surface is normally generated from a point cloud. Consider for example the lower edge of the skirt shown in Figure 5. The triangulation algorithm adds an additional surface at the bottom connecting the skirt to the legs. If a skirt that is slightly too long or was initially placed slightly too low is draped on this model, its hem will simply be attracted by this lower surface folding towards the legs. This behaviour is first of all unnatural and secondly defeats our silhouette based evaluation function. If the surface is missing, the hem of the simulated skirt will be attracted by the hem of the model pushing the whole skirt up.

3.5 Segmentation

After the dimensions of the garments have been found and the draped configuration of the garments on the scan has been calculated it is trivial to segment the mesh into parts belonging to the clothing and those that are unclad or tightly dressed. The shortest

Fig. 5. On the left a closed model was used to drape the skirt on. The cloth clearly folds at the bottom instead of pushing the fabric up. On the right the plane connecting legs and the hem of the skirt was manually cut out. The skirt hangs straight as would be expected of a real skirt.

distance from a point of the scan to the garment can simply be used to classify the point as belonging to the garment or not employing a simple, hard threshold.

3.6 Layered Garments

In order to segment persons wearing layered garments an iterative approach is used. That is the dimensions of only one garment are estimated at a time, starting at the outermost layer working towards the inside. The first iteration is identical to the above procedure when only the outermost article of clothing is considered. After the point cloud has been labelled the outermost garment is removed from the simulation and the next piece of clothing is inspected. For the second and all following garments the procedure is slightly altered. If a point of the simulated cloth is attracted to a mesh point that has previously been labelled as belonging to another garment the attraction force is attenuated. This prevents inner garments from being deformed more than necessary by points not actually belonging to the garment. The attraction forces cannot, however, be omitted completely because the hidden particles would be unsupported causing the garment to crumple inside the body, dragging neighbouring particles along.

4   Results

In this section we present results using on the one hand, manual measurements of the employed garments and renderings of finished segmentations on the other. For all estimation experiments the optimisation was run three times and the run with the smallest error was selected for presentation.

In Table 1 three different scans of the same skirt are used to estimate its dimensions. While the first scan works almost perfectly the other two overestimate the length of the skirt. This happens because it is almost impossible to distinguish the upper edge of the skirt in the scan data alone. The only cue a human can perceive is that the belly button is visible. So the skirt must end below it.

Table 2 shows the same evaluation for two different T-shirts. The T-shirts' dimensions were estimated using the same template and the same optimiser settings.

Table 3 and Figure 6 show a very another advantage of the algorithm. Even in the presence of severe data corruption it is possible to estimate the dimensions of the skirt

Table 1. Top: Comparison between ground truth (GT) and estimated (est.) measurements in cm. The rows show length, width, waist, and hip measurements. Bottom: Segmentation results.

experiment 1		experiment 2		experiment 3	
GT	est.	GT	est.	GT	est.
54	56	54	59	54	62
110	107	110	109	110	114
78	79	78	76	78	74
94	94	94	93	94	90

Table 2. Top: Comparison between ground truth (GT) and estimated (est.) measurements in cm. The rows show length, width, sleeve length, and sleeve circumference at the opening and at the seam. Bottom: Segmentation results.

experiment 1		experiment 2		experiment 3		experiment 4	
GT	est.	GT	est.	GT	est.	GT	est.
62	62	62	63	76	77	76	78
112	117	112	109	125	127	125	178
17	6.2	17	13	17	-46	17	35
40	43	40	38	42	46	42	37
44	70	44	68	50	47	50	41

well and by substituting the missing points with the simulated cloth the holes can be filled nicely.

Layered garments are estimated one at a time. While estimation of the outermost garment is equivalent to estimating just one garment. Inner garments are harder to

Table 3. Tables: Comparison between ground truth (GT) and estimated (est.) measurements in cm. The rows show length, width, waist, and hip measurements. Images: Segmentation results in the presence of severe data corruption.

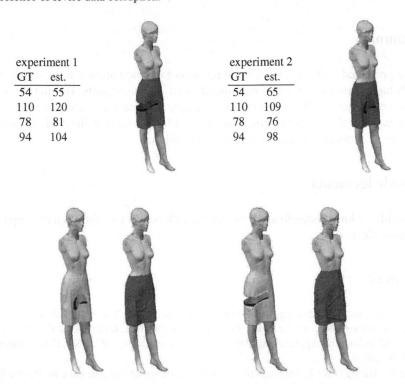

experiment 1			experiment 2	
GT	est.		GT	est.
54	55		54	65
110	120		110	109
78	81		78	76
94	104		94	98

Fig. 6. Even in the presence of severe data corruption garment fitting allows the reasonable filling of holes

Table 4. Tables: Comparison between ground truth (GT) and estimated (est.) measurements in cm. The rows show length, width, waist, and hip measurements. Images: Segmentation results of a skirt which is partially covered by a T-shirt.

experiment 1			experiment 2	
GT	est.		GT	est.
54	63		54	91
110	111		110	161
78	92		78	67
94	119		94	101

estimate. Some dimensions such as the length of the skirt or the waist circumference are impossible to estimate if the upper half of the skirt is covered by a T-shirt. The results for these measurements presented in Table 4 consequentially deviate more severely.

5   Summary

We have presented a physically based template-deformation approach for segmenting full body laser scans of dressed humans into dressed and naked parts. The method at the same time estimates the dimensions of the garments the scanned person is wearing providing a model of the garments which can be used for example by the cloth simulation at the heart of a model based motion capture algorithm.

Acknowledgements

We gratefully acknowledge funding by the Max-Planck Center for Visual Computing and Communication.

References

1. Attene, M., Katz, S., Mortara, M., Patane, G., Spagnuolo, M., Tal, A.: Mesh segmentation - a comparative study. In: SMI '06: Proceedings of the IEEE International Conference on Shape Modeling and Applications 2006 (SMI'06), Washington, DC, USA, IEEE Computer Society (2006)
2. Jojic, N., Huang, T.S.: Estimating cloth draping parameters from range data. In: Proceedings of the International Workshop on Synthetic-Natural Hybrid Coding and Three Dimensional Imaging, Rhodes, Greece (1997) 73–76
3. Rosenhahn, B., Kersting, U., Powell, K., Seidel, H.P.: Cloth x-ray: Mocap of people wearing textiles. In: Pattern Recognition (DAGM). (2006) 495–504
4. Bhat, K., Twigg, C., Hodgins, J., Khosla, P., Popović, Z., Seitz, S.: Estimating cloth simulation parameters from video. In: Proceedings of ACM SIGGRAPH/Eurographics Symposium on Computer Animation (SCA 2003), ACM Press (2003) 37–51
5. Press, W., Vetterling, W., Teukolsky, S., Flannery, B.: Numerical Recipes in C++: the art of scientific computing. 2nd edn. Cambridge University Press (2002)
6. Nurre, J.H.: Locating landmarks on human body scan data. In: NRC '97: Proceedings of the International Conference on Recent Advances in 3-D Digital Imaging and Modeling, Washington, DC, USA, IEEE Computer Society (1997) 289
7. Xiao, Y., Siebert, P., Werghi, N.: A discrete reeb graph approach for the segmentation of human body scans. In: The 4th International Conference on 3-D Digital Imaging and Modeling, Banff, Alberta, Canada, IEEE Computer Society (2003)
8. Allen, B., Curless, B., Popović, Z.: Articulated body deformation from range scan data. In: SIGGRAPH '02: Proceedings of the 29th annual conference on Computer graphics and interactive techniques, New York, NY, USA, ACM Press (2002) 612–619
9. Seo, H., Magnenat-Thalmann, N.: An automatic modeling of human bodies from sizing parameters. In: SI3D '03: Proceedings of the 2003 symposium on Interactive 3D graphics, New York, NY, USA, ACM Press (2003) 19–26

10. Magnenat-Thalmann, N., Seo, H., Cordier, F.: Automatic modeling of animatable virtual humans - a survey. In: 4th International Conference on 3D Digital Imaging and Modeling (3DIM 2003). (2003) 2–11
11. Oh, S., Kim, H., Magnenat-Thalmann, N., Wohn, K.: Generating unified model for dressed virtual humans. The Visual Computer 21 (2005) 522–531
12. Terzopoulos, D., Platt, J., Barr, A., Fleischer, K.: Elastically deformable models. In: Computer Graphics (Proceedings of ACM SIGGRAPH 87), ACM Press (1987) 205–214
13. Baraff, D., Witkin, A.: Large steps in cloth simulation. In: Proceedings of ACM SIGGRAPH 98, ACM Press (1998) 43–54
14. Desbrun, M., Schröder, P., Barr, A.: Interactive animation of structured deformable objects. In: Proceedings of Graphics Interface (GI 1999), Canadian Computer-Human Communications Society (1999) 1–8
15. Kang, Y.M., Cho, H.G.: Bilayered approximate integration for rapid and plausible animation of virtual cloth with realistic wrinkles. In: Proceedings of Computer Animation, IEEE Computer Society (2002) 203–214
16. Eberhardt, B., Weber, A., Straßer, W.: A fast, flexible, particle-system model for cloth draping. IEEE Computer Graphics and Applications 16 (1996) 52–59
17. Choi, K.J., Ko, H.S.: Stable but responsive cloth. ACM Transactions on Graphics (ACM SIGGRAPH 2002) 21 (2002) 604–611
18. Bridson, R.: Computational aspects of dynamic surfaces. PhD thesis, Stanford University (2003)
19. Volino, P., Magnenat-Thalmann, N.: Accurate garment prototyping and simulation. Computer-Aided Design Applications 2 (2005) 645–654
20. Volino, P., Cordier, F., Magnenat-Thalmann, N.: From early virtual garment simulation to interactive fashion design. Computer-Aided Design 37 (2005) 593–608
21. Bridson, R., Marino, S., Fedkiw, R.: Simulation of clothing with folds and wrinkles. In: Proceedings of ACM SIGGRAPH/Eurographics Symposium on Computer Animation (SCA 2003), ACM Press (2003) 28–36

3D Reconstruction of a Human Face from Images Using Morphological Adaptation

Daria Kalinkina[1], André Gagalowicz[1], and Richard Roussel[2]

[1] INRIA-Rocquencourt, Domaine de Voluceau BP105 78153 Le Chesnay, France
`{darya.kalinkina, andre.gagalowicz}@inria.fr`
[2] XID Technologies Pte Ltd, 15 Queen Street, Singapore 188537
`richardroussel@xidtech.com`

Abstract. This paper presents a method for 3D face modeling from a set of 2D images. This method is based on deformation of a pre-defined generic polygonal face mesh to the specific face of the person, presented on several images taken from different views. This deformation is based upon matching points and silhouette curves. To provide high accuracy we have chosen an interactive way of getting information from the image. Firstly the user defines several feature points on the images. Then the algorithm adapts the generic model to the real face presented on the image by matching the projections of the generic characteristic points to those of the images. Finally, the reconstruction is improved by matching the silhouettes of the deformed model to those of the images.

1 Introduction

Realistic human face modeling is a research domain of Computer Graphics which is developing very rapidly. This task is a part of many applications such as special effects generation, games, virtual reality, teleconferencing, sculpture and many others. This paper presents an algorithm for accurate 3D human face reconstruction from a small set of images. This method produces very realistic and accurate models, which can be further used, for example, for model-based human face tracking in video, face-to-face retargeting. However, the method doesn't work in real-time and requires a bit of interaction from a user. A first version of the algorithm was first presented in [1]. We brought many improvements described in this paper while keeping the same general idea.

1.1 State of the Art

In this Section, we will review the various techniques that exist in 3D face reconstruction domain. One general approach is to use some sophisticated equipment for capturing 3D information form the real world. For instance, 3D information of the face surface can be acquired by a laser capture device as it was done in [2]. Possible holes in the scanned data were eliminated by fitting in a generic model. Another type

A. Gagalowicz and W. Philips (Eds.): MIRAGE 2007, LNCS 4418, pp. 212–224, 2007.

of device projects a luminous grid on the face that gives, according to the deformation of this luminous grid, the geometry of the face [3]. In [4], markers are tracked on faces to accurately compute the face deformation of a model acquired by a range scanner. Other techniques are often based on the deformations of 3D generic meshes by deformation of the feature points [5-7], but such techniques generally lack precision, because of an insufficient number of points for exact adaptation. In [8], 3D face creation is performed on a prototype shape, according to statistics obtained by anthropological face measurements. Most existing methods either require much manual labor by a skilled artist, expensive active light 3D scanners [9], or the availability of high quality texture images as a substitute for exact face geometry [10]. More recent efforts have focused on the availability of an underlying model for human faces. [11-14]. Shape from silhouettes techniques have also been used to reconstruct 3D shapes from multiple silhouettes of an object [15-19]. Such techniques do not produce correct 3D reconstructions in the case of non convex shapes like faces. In [20], authors propose to add 3D face models to improve the silhouette based technique. They use a 3D face database. The four techniques that are closest to ours are [21, 11, 12, 20 and 14]. In [21], the authors use a 3D scan of the face as an initialization of the 3D reconstruction. As this data is noisy and partial, they introduce a generic face model (as we do) that they also deform in order to match it to the 3D scanned data as well as possible. In [11], an important data base consisting of hundreds of 3D scans and a PCA technique, associated to an analysis by synthesis procedure, produces very good results as well. In [12], the techniques use only characteristic points, but the authors utilize many more points than we do (up to 100), and matching the image and the model points is therefore difficult. In [20], a large 3D face database is required. In [14], the input is a complete image sequence, but the 3D model is computed with a minimal user interaction. In our case, we need only a few images but more user interactions. The main difference is the use of silhouettes to deform a generic model which produces a more accurate 3D face model.

1.2 Organization of the Paper

The goal of the proposed algorithm is to reconstruct the 3D model of the face of a particular person, being given a limited set of images of this person's face with a more or less neutral expression taken from different viewpoints. Accuracy of the modeling increases with the number of images used, but experiments showed that five images are enough to get a quite good result (1% precision). All the deformations are applied to some initial generic face model. The first part of the algorithm consists of the creation and positioning of a set of cameras for all the images and of the initial deformation of the generic mesh. Both operations are performed through the correspondence between several characteristic 3D points on the mesh and their 2D positions on each image, which are defined manually by the user. The whole process of cameras calibration and mesh reconstruction is described in section 2. The second part of the algorithm uses user-defined silhouette contours on the image face to adapt the 3D model more accurately. Contour adaptation is described in details in section 3. And the last section presents the results and future research directions.

2 Calibration and Deformation Based Upon Characteristic Points

On order to be able to get 3D information from images for the deformation of the generic model we need to calibrate the camera(s) used to obtain the images; in other words, we need to define camera parameters for the model according to each image. Calibration is performed by POSIT algorithm [22], which estimates and minimizes the error between the projection of some known 3D positions on each image and their known 2D positions in the image. Since in the very beginning the generic mesh doesn't not correspond at all to the real face, POSIT won't be able to find correct camera parameters, so we start the algorithm with manual calibration. When all the cameras are positioned, the 3D reconstruction of the characteristic points is done based on the information from the images. After the reconstruction the projections of the new 3D positions of vertices of the generic model are better correlated with the user-defined points, so now we can apply POSIT to get a better camera calibration. Having refined camera positions we can again perform 3D reconstruction to get better points match, and so on. This calibration/reconstruction loop can be repeated several times until all the 3D vertices that correspond to the characteristic points project exactly where they should. The following subsections will describe all these procedures step-by-step.

2.1 Characteristic Points Selection

The very first step of the algorithm consists of selecting the vertices on the generic model which will further serve as "characteristic" points. The main idea is to choose only those vertices that can be easily matched both on the images and the generic model. For example, they can be the corners of the eyes, mouth etc. Example of such choice and the positions of the chosen points on the generic model are illustrated in Fig. 1. Points like the one on the forehead and on the chin are usually not very well defined on human faces, but they are still necessary to get the global orientation of the camera (bending of the face). In fact, the more characteristic points we have the better the calibration by POSIT will work (in case of exact matching between the 2D points of the images and the associated 3D points). We propose to use the 38 characteristic points, shown in Fig. 1, but we leave it up to the user to add or modify points in order to adapt them to the specific features of the face being modeled and to the available images of the person.

2.2 Interactive Calibration / Reconstruction

The technique that is used for calibration of the cameras is based on POSIT [22]. The principle of POSIT is as follows: the algorithm iteratively tries to minimize the difference between estimated projections of some 3D points of the object and their 2D locations in the image until the error (which is the maximum difference of pixel locations), falls below a threshold. POSIT allows to calculate only the extrinsic parameters of the camera, which are the translation vector between the model and the reference frame of the camera and the rotation matrix between the face coordinates system and the camera coordinates system. In other words it gives the relative position and attitude of the camera with respect to the face. As for the intrinsic

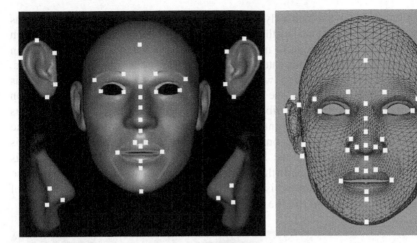

Fig. 1. Presentation of the proposed characteristic points for camera calibration (in red) are shown on the left image and possible choice by the user of their 3D location (in green) on the generic model

parameters (focal distance, aspect ratio), they are assumed to be known. There was made an effort to detect intrinsic parameters as well by performing several calibrations and based on their results trying to find the real intrinsic parameters. But experiments showed that minimum calibration error doesn't always correspond to the real camera characteristics as focal length and depth of the object with respect to the camera are correlated.

The generic model doesn't correspond at all to the face in the image, so using POSIT in the beginning may result in a very bad camera position. So we advise the user to perform an initial manual calibration. It is not necessary to do it very precisely, but globally the position of the model should resemble the one on the image as shown in Fig. 2.

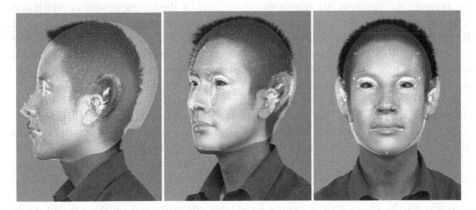

Fig. 2. Manual calibration results

After the model has been manually positioned in front of each image, the user has to click on the equivalent points of those characteristic points that are visible in each image. This process doesn't require much time and is illustrated in Fig. 3. The main idea is that each point should be located exactly in the same position in all the images, otherwise final POSIT calibration won't be perfect. For example, if point "2" is located at the level of the eyes in one image, it should be located at the same location in all other images, where it is visible. If one doubts, where to place a point, it is better to omit it. However some points (as "1" and "4") define global rotation of the face in POSIT, so they can't be omitted, even if their position on the images is questionable (when they are hidden behind the beard or hair, for example). In this case if the calibration result is bad (the output error of POSIT), the user may analyse calibration error for each characteristic point, change accordingly 2D positions of some characteristic points and run the algorithm again.

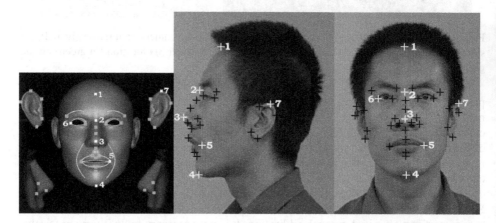

Fig. 3. Positions of the 2D characteristic points defined by user

After all the positions of the characteristic points have been defined by user for all the images, we perform 3D stereo reconstruction of the characteristic points based upon the manual cameras calibration. In other words for each point we build a set of 3D rays, starting from the optical center of the camera and going to the corresponding projection of this point in each image, calculate the middle point of the segment defining the minimum distance between each couple of rays and take the gravity center of all these middle points as a new 3D position of the characteristic point.

If some point *pt* is seen only from one image, we use the symmetry of the face to reconstruct it. So, if the symmetric point has been successfully reconstructed, the point closest to it, which lies on the ray of light for the projection of *pt* will be taken as a new position of *pt*. Otherwise we do not reconstruct this point.

Our algorithm adapts also to the case when only one image of a person is available, performing simple orthogonal reconstruction (based upon the generic model geometry) for all the characteristic points.

When all the characteristic points have been reconstructed in 3D, we can apply POSIT to correct the positions of the cameras and then again perform 3D reconstruction. Repeating this loop several times we can achieve a very precise

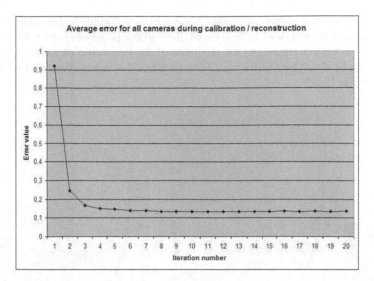

Fig. 4. Average decrease of the error during the calibration/reconstruction process. Error values are given in centimeters.

camera calibration along with 3D points which project exactly where they should. Usually 3-4 iterations are enough to achieve a good result. The dynamics of the error decrease during 20 iterations is presented in Fig. 4.

Until this moment we haven't been changing anything but the characteristic vertices of the model. Now we need to apply the deformation to the rest of the vertices. Having resulting deformation vectors for our characteristic points we obtain deformation vectors for other vertices of the generic model by using RBF (radial basis functions) technique. In other words, deformation of each vertex is proportional to some radial based function of the distance between this vertex and each characteristic point. We choose this distance itself as a value of the function, because it provides a smooth interpolation. More details about RBF technique can be found in [1, 23].

2.3 Problems

The problems that haven't been solved in the first version [1] of the technique are the following. During the reconstruction we may encounter serious problems when images correspond to anti-parallel positions of the cameras. The 3D rays emitted from the cameras related to these views are almost parallel so that the computation of their intersection is highly ill-conditioned. As a result some characteristic points are pulled in the wrong direction and cause visible distortions on the mesh. A typical case occurs when we have the left and right side view of a face and when we have to determine the characteristic points of the symmetry plane of the face (see points 1, 2, 3 and 4 of Fig. 3, for example). The first solution proposed consists in computing the angle between the two rays and in skipping the intersection computation if the angle is below some threshold. However the value of this threshold is not so evident since it has to be big enough to discover possible errors and small enough not to reject good reconstruction. Taking into account the fact that error of this kind mostly occurs to the central characteristic points, we added a special technique constraining the 3D reconstruction of these points to be located close to the plane of symmetry. The plane of symmetry is built according to the positions of the symmetric characteristing points on the whole model. The illustration of the problem described above and its solution can be found in Fig. 5.

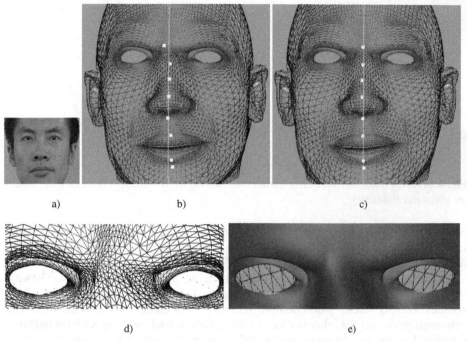

a)   b)   c)

d)   e)

Fig. 5. a) Front view image; b) Result of calibration/reconstruction without special treatment of parallel views, some cenral characteristic points are ill-positioned; c) Result of calibration/reconstruction using the constraint of the symmetry plane; d),e) Enlarged region between the eyes where distortion of the mesh (in b) is most visible

3   Silhouette Contour Adaptation

After the deformation of the generic model based on characteristic points we obtain only an approximate geometry of the face. There still remain local areas where our 3D face differs from the real one due to the limited number of characteristic points. An example of such mismatch is shown in Fig. 6. In order to correct this defect, the adaptation of silhouette contours of the 3D model to the limbs of each image is performed. In other words, for each image we compute the external 3D silhouette contour on the mesh (which is seen from the camera corresponding to this image), project it on the image and deform the model so that this silhouette maps exactly the limbs of the face on each image.

How de we realize the operation? The idea consists in creating a 2D RBF deformation function which will deform each projected 3D model limb towards the available 2D image limb first. This is performed by automatically determining matches between a set of points of these two curves. Then the 2D deformation vectors are reconstructed in 3D and are applied to the corresponding vertices of the model. If necessary, several iterations are performed.

The real contour of the face should be preferably extracted manually from the images to provide best accuracy of the method and avoid recognition problems in the case of cluttered background. We propose a special interface for drawing contours based on Bezier curves, so this manual part of work is not time consuming. Also is it not necessary to specify the complete contour curves for each image, it is sufficient to draw them in the areas where the two sets of silhouettes (3D model and image ones) do not match as it is pointed out in Fig.6.

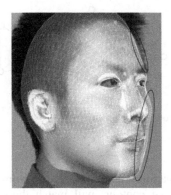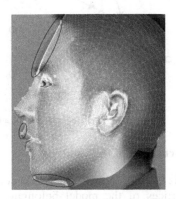

Fig. 6. Generic model after calibration/reconstruction and RBF interpolation. Regions where adaptation is not good are outlined with black.

3.1 Automatic Extracting of the Silhouette Contours from the 3D Mesh

The construction of the 3D silhouette contour on the mesh implies an ordered list of vertices which form the closed external contour of the mesh observed from a specific camera. To obtain this list we developed a new robust technique, which has been significantly improved compared to its first version described in [1]. The computing time of this algorithm has been reduced drastically; it is essential as the algorithm has to be iterated many times during the 3D reconstruction.

The general idea is the same in [1]. First, we search a vertex, which is undoubtedly included in the contour (for example, it can be a vertex with a maximum y-coordinate value in 2D projection), and then among all the edges related to it we search an edge, which projection forms the smallest angle (counter-clockwise) with the projection of the previous one. If we take the first vertex as mentioned above, we assume as a "previous" edge the unit vector in Y-axis direction.

After such edge has been found, we apply the same algorithm to the second vertex, attached to it and proceed in this way until the next vertex we get is equal to the initial one. The first two steps of this process are shown in Fig. 7.

To solve the problem of intersection of the edges in 2D projection, we don't calculate all the intersections in 2D as in [1], but check each edge that we include in the contour. If this edge has intersection with any other edge, we replace these two edges by four and iterate the process of edge selection until the edge we got doesn't have any intersections. So the number of intersection's calculation has been significantly reduced.

Also it has been noticed that only the edges located between a visible and an invisible facet (in the current camera system) can form the 3D contour, so the initial set of edges, to which we apply the algorithm described above, can be reduced significantly by verifying the facets visibility.

All these improvements reduced calculation time related to the extraction of the 3D contour from 60 to 1.2 seconds on our standard PC.

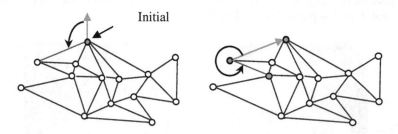

Fig. 7. Building a contour on the mesh

3.2   Deformation of the Contour

Our goal is to build for each image 3D deformation vectors which, after being applied to the vertices of the model belonging to the contour, will match the projected silhouette of the model to the user-drawn Bezier curves on the image.

Getting 2D Deformation of the Projected Contour. We start by getting 2D deformation vectors for the projected 3D contour. To do this, we need first to define which parts of the contour have to be adapted, in other words, which parts of the silhouette correspond to the manually drawn curves. For each Bezier curve B we detect a related section of the projected contour C by finding the closest points on the C to the beginning, ending and middle points of B as shown in Fig. 8. Since the contour is closed, we simply take all the points of the contour that are located between the boundary points and include the middle point.

Then for each point of the contour that we got we search the closest one on the Bezier curve in consequent order (to avoid crossing problems) and form a corresponding 2D deformation vector. In order to reduce computation time we do not take into consideration all the deformation vectors we obtained, but the longest ones. In order to select these vectors we build a histogram for each Bezier curve, which shows distances to the Bezier curve for all the points of the contour, affected by this curve, and then simply choose all the local maxima on this histogram as deformation vectors.

The process, described above is performed for all Bezier curves and all the images.

Experimentally we found that almost the same adaptation speed can be achieved if we take around 15-20 longest deformation vectors from all the Bezier curves and all the views. This allows to reduce the size of the RBF matrix and therefore to reduce significantly the computation time and memory usage in comparison with the first version of the algorithm described in [1].

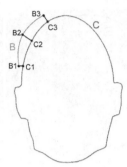

Fig. 8. Correspondence between a user-drawn Bezier curve and the projected contour

Splitting the Contour into Continuous Parts. As it has been said before, the projected silhouette edges of the model may intersect, so the sequence of the vertices in the contour doesn't always consist of neighboring vertices. Thus it may happen that the 3D contour located on the mesh and the 2D curves drawn by the user do not correspond to the same parts of the face. Such an example is presented in Fig. 9: since the contour hasn't been yet adapted the cheeks of the generic model have less volume than they should and let the tip of the nose to appear on the contour. So if we directly apply contour adaptation the nose will be deformed together with the cheeks (as shown on d) in Fig. 9). To avoid this we perform 3D contour segmentation in the new version of the algorithm, so that each segment includes only neighboring vertices. This being done, we consider only "long" segments (consisting of more than three elements) for adaptation, so that the parts of the face which have been accidentally included in the contour were not taken into account.

Reconstruction of the Deformation Vectors in 3D. After the 2D deformations have been obtained, they are reconstructed in 3D and applied to the vertices of the contour, to which they correspond. Reconstruction is done in the following way (see Fig. 10): for each 2D vector PR (where P is a projection of the vertex P_0 of the contour on the image plane and R is a point of a Bezier curve) two 3D rays are emitted from the optical center of the camera, one passing through points P and P_0 and the other passing by R and the new position R_0 of the vertex P_0 is taken as the intersection of the second ray with the normal vector to the first ray in the point P_0. So the vector P_0R_0 represents the required 3D deformation vector.

After obtaining all the deformations vectors from the curves, we apply them to the corresponding vertices and interpolate the deformation for the whole model using radial based functions, keeping zero deformation for the characteristic points.

Iterative Adaptation. Usually one has to perform several iterations to adapt all the contours. Each iteration completely repeats the sequence described above: the mesh is projected on all the images, contours are extracted, 3D deformation vectors are obtained and RBF is incremented by keeping all the deformations, performed in the previous iterations and adding the new ones coming from the 2D silhouette vectors chosen.

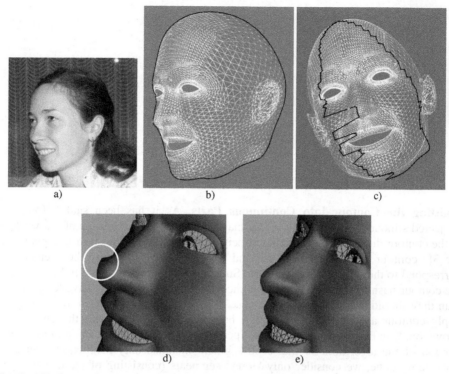

Fig. 9. a) Reference image, clearly the nose doesn't belong to the contour; b) Projection of the 3D contour of the model; c) 3D contour on the mesh, part of it is located on the nose; d) Result of the contour adaptation without contour splitting; e) Result of the contour adaptation with contour splitting

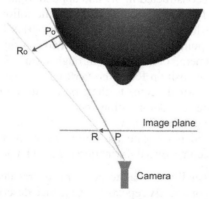

Fig. 10. An example of the reconstruction of the 2D deformation vector in 3D (view from the top)

If some point is selected twice as a point with maximum deformation vector that means that for some reasons the calibration was not perfect and some part of the model can't be adapted finely in all the views at one time. In other words, an effort to adapt the contour in one view may cause significant errors in the other. New version of the algorithm handles such cases and smoothes this inconsistency by taking the average deformation.

3.3 Refining the Calibration Using Adaptation of the Contour

Contour adaptation can be applied only in case, when the calibration of all the cameras is rather exact. Sometimes calibration based only on characteristic points is not enough because the positions of some characteristic points on the image are too bad. For example, ears can be covered with hair, chin – with a beard and some points can be hidden due to the camera perspective. As it has been said before, it is better (if possible) to "guess" where these points are and point them out, even if it is not very precise, to provide global view calibration.

Anyhow, unsatisfactory calibration results can be much improved by creating a calibration/reconstruction loop during silhouette adaptation. After each iteration of the curves matching we get both 3D positions of the points that we want to adapt and their exact 2D projections, extracted from the Bezier curves. It is sufficient to send this set of points as an input to the calibration/reconstruction iterative process along with characteristic points in order to get much better calibration, controlled this time by the whole curves and not only the characteristic points. This stabilizes the calibration considerably.

4 Conclusion

This paper proposes a new technique for modeling a 3D face of a particular person based on several input images. This technique doesn't use markers, but requires minimum interaction with the user. In future we are planning to add hair, eyes and teeth to the model to make it look more real and to use the results for human face tracking and, further on, realistic dubbing in the movies. Compared to the first version of the technique [1], this one is much more reliable and precise after the improvements described in sections 2.3 and 3 and computing time has been reduced drastically.

References

1. Roussel, R., Gagalowicz, A.: Morphological Adaptation of a 3D Model of Face from Images. MIRAGES 2004.
2. LEE, Y., Terzopoulos, D., Waters, K.: Realistic Modeling for Facial Animation in Computer Graphics. Proc. SIGGRAPH 95, 449–456.
3. Proesmans, M., Gool, L. V.: Reading Between the Lines a Method for Extracting Dynamic 3D with Texture. ACM Symposium on Virtual Reality Software and Technology, VRST 97, 95–102.
4. Guenter, B., Grimm, C., Wolf, D., Malvar, H., Pighin, F.: Making Faces. ACM SIGGRAPH 98, Addison Wesley Longman, Los Angeles, 55–66.
5. Akimoto, T., Suenaga, Y., Wallace, R.: Automatic Creation of 3D Facial Models. IEEE Computer Graphics and Applications, 1993, Vol. 13, 16–22.

6. Ip, H., Yin, L.: Constructing a 3D Individual Head Model from Two Orthogonal Views. The Visual Computer 12, 254–266, 1996.
7. Kurihara, T., And Arai, K.: A Transformation Method for Modeling and Animation the Human Face from Photographs. Springer-Verlag Tokyo, 45–58, 1991.
8. Decarlo, D., Metaxas, D., Stone, M.: An Anthropometric Face Model Using Variational Techniques. SIGGRAPH 98 Proceedings, 67–74.
9. Terzopoulos, D., Waters, K.: Physically-Based Facial Modelling, Analysis, and Animation. The Journal of Visualization, Analysis, and Animation 1, 2 (Dec.), 73–80, 1990.
10. M. Tarini, H. Yamauchi, J. H., Seidel, H.-P.: Texturing Faces. Graphics Interface 2002 Proceedings, 89– 98.
11. Blanz, V., Vetter, T.: A Morphable Model for the Synthesis of 3D Faces. ACM SIGGRAPH 99, 187–194.
12. F. Pighin, J. Hecker, D. L. R. S., Salesin, D.: Synthesizing Realistic Facial Expressions from Photographs. SIGGRAPH 98 Proceedings.
13. J.J. Atick, P. G., Redlich, N.: Statistical Approach to Shape from Shading: Reconstruction of 3D Face Surfaces from Single 2D Images. 1321–1340, 1996.
14. Y. Shan, Z. L., Zhang, Z.: Model-Based Bundle Adjustment with Application to Face Modeling. Proceedings of ICCV'01, 644–651.
15. S. Lazebnik, E. B., Ponce, J.: On Computing Exact Visual Hull of Solids Bounded by Smooth Surfaces. 156–161, 2001.
16. W. Matusik, C. Buehler, R. R. L. M., Gortler, S.: Image-Based Visual Hull. SIGGRAPH 2000 Proceedings.
17. Potmesnil., M.: Generating Octree Models of 3D Objects from Their Silhouettes in a Sequence of Images. CVGIP 40, 1–29, 1987.
18. Szeliski, R.: Rapid Octree Construction from Image Sequences. 23–32, 1993.
19. Zheng, J.: Acquiring 3D Models from Sequences of Contours. 1994.
20. J. Lee, B.Moghaddam, H. P. R. M.: Silhouette-Based 3D Face Shape Recovery. Graphics Interface, 2003.
21. Kohler, K., Haber, J., Yamauchi, H., Seidel, H.-P.: Head Shop: Generating Animated Head Models with Anatomical Structure. Proceedings of the 2002 ACM SIGGRAPH Symposium on Computer Animation, 55–64.
22. Dementhon, D., L.S.Davis.: Model-based Object Pose in 25 Lines of Code. International Journal of Computer Vision, Vol. 15, 123–141, 1995.
23. Martin D. Buhmann: Radial Basis Functions: Theory and Implementations. Justus-Liebig-Universität Giessen, Germany.

Robust Automatic Data Decomposition Using a Modified Sparse NMF

Oksana Samko, Paul L. Rosin, and A. Dave Marshall

School of Computer Science, Cardiff University, UK
{O.Samko, Paul.Rosin, Dave.Marshall}@cs.cf.ac.uk

Abstract. In this paper, we address the problem of automating the partial representation from real world data with an unknown a priori structure. Such representation could be very useful for the further construction of an automatic hierarchical data model. We propose a three stage process using data normalisation and the data intrinsic dimensionality estimation as the first step. The second stage uses a modified sparse Non-negative matrix factorization (sparse NMF) algorithm to perform the initial segmentation. At the final stage region growing algorithm is applied to construct a mask of the original data. Our algorithm has a very broad range of a potential applications, we illustrate this versatility by applying the algorithm to several dissimilar data sets.

1 Introduction

The objective of this paper is to present a novel automatic method for learning a meaningful sub-part representation from real world data with an unknown a priori structure.

Modelling the data sub-parts individually has great advantages. The underlying representation has proven to be accurate in representing the specificity of the data and capturing small but important variation in the data that are otherwise lost in standard approaches. For example in tracking human motion the hierarchy is naturally the key joints of the human skeleton suitably decomposed into the whole body, torso, arms legs upper arms etc. Adopting such a hierarchy and projecting down through the subspaces led to greater tracking accuracy in the model. In the talking head application, the hierarchy uses both visual and speech features. The hierarchy developed here may utilise sets of features in a variety of combinations. The top level of the hierarchy seeks to capture the main modes of variation of the complete data. However, other levels may be used to model specific relationships between certain features, for example the complete visual head data (modelled as hierarchical appearance model where nodes represent shape and texture of facial features) or the speech data or specific interactions of speech with facial features (e.g. lower face, lips, eyebrows). Again such a model has proven to be robust in tracking facial features and also resynthesising video-realistic new faces.

The principal difficulty in creating such models is in determining which parts should be used, and identifying examples of these parts in the training data.

A. Gagalowicz and W. Philips (Eds.): MIRAGE 2007, LNCS 4418, pp. 225–234, 2007.

The task of finding patterns embedded in the data is a popular research field in computer science [2], [13], [18].

Nonnegative matrix factorization (NMF) [16] is a promising tool in learning the parts of objects and images. NMF imposes non-negativity constraints in its bases and coefficients. These constraints lead to a parts based representation because they allow only additive, not subtractive, combinations. Later in [14] Hoyer presented Sparse non-negative matrix factorisation (sparse NMF) with an adjustable sparseness parameter. This allows it to discover parts-based representations that are qualitatively better than those given by the basic NMF. Because of its parts-based representation property, NMF and its variations have been used to image classification [3], [8], [9], [11], face expression recognition [4], face detection [5], face and object recognition [19], [20], [21].

In all of those papers the number of data parts was quite large and was chosen manually. In this paper, we propose intrinsic dimensionality estimation to find correct number of the parts.

The novelty of this paper is that we use NMF for an automatic data mask construction. We consider the construction of our model in Section 2 and demonstrate the effectiveness of our algorithm applying it to the different data types: talking head data, emotional head data and articulated human motion data in Section 3. Finally, the conclusion is given in Section 4.

2   Partial Data Representation

2.1   Data Format and Preprocessing

Initial data for our algorithm can be represented by a parameterised model or by images. The output generated is a mask identifing different data parts.

This algorithm works best with well aligned data, i.e. the data obtained from a sequence of observations. But it is not really suitable for separation of images of highly articulated objects or objects viewed from significantly different viewpoints into parts.

A normalisation step is needed to make the patterns of interest more evident. Data normalisation is provided as a preprocessing step before NMF, in the same manner as in Li et al. [18].

At the first step of our algorithm we set the number of the data parts. We choose this number to be the same as the intrinsic dimension of the data manifold. We use the k-NN method described in [7] to estimate the intrinsic dimensionality. In this method the dimension is estimated from the length of the minimal spanning tree on the geodesic NN (nearest neighbour) distances computed by the Isomap algorithm [23]. To automate the k-NN method we choose the number of nearest neighbours using the algorithm described in [22].

2.2   Sparse NMF Modification and Initialisation

Classical NMF is a method to obtain a representation of data using non-negativity constraints. These constraints lead to a part-based representation because they only allow additive, not subtractive, combinations of the original data [16]. Given initial data expressed by an $n \times m$ matrix X, where each column is an n-dimensional non-negative vector of the original data (m vectors), it is possible to find two new matrices (W and H) in order to approximate the original matrix:

$$X_{ij} \approx (WH)_{ij} = \Sigma_{l=1}^{r} W_{il} H_{lj} \tag{1}$$

The dimensions of the factorised matrices W and H are $n \times r$ and $r \times m$ respectively. Each column of W contains a basis vector while each column of H contains the weight needed to approximate the corresponding column in X using the bases from W.

Given a data matrix X, the optimal choice of matrices W and H is defined to be those nonnegative matrices that minimise the reconstruction error between X and WH. Various error functions have been proposed [17], the most widely used one is the squared error (Euclidean distance) function

$$E(W, H) = \|X - WH\|^2 = \Sigma_{ij}(X_{ij} - (WH)_{ij})^2 \tag{2}$$

However, the additive parts learned by NMF are not necessarily localised, as was pointed out by Li et al. in [18]. To obtain meaningful partial representation we want to restrict energy of each NMF basis to the most significant components only. Therefore we use sparse NMF [14] which proved to be more appropriate in part-based object decomposition than original NMF.

In sparse NMF the objective (2) is minimised under the constraints that all columns of W and rows of H have common sparseness σ_W and σ_H respectively. The sparseness $\sigma(x)$ is defined by the relation between the Euclidean norm $\|.\|_2$ and 1-norm $\|x\|_1 := \Sigma_i \mid x_i \mid$ as follows

$$\sigma(x) := \frac{\sqrt{n} - \frac{\|x\|_1}{\|x\|_2}}{\sqrt{n} - 1} \tag{3}$$

if $x \in R^n \setminus 0$. Since $\frac{1}{n}\|x\|_1 \leq \|x\|_2 \leq \|x\|_1$ equation (3) is bounded $0 \leq \sigma(x) \leq 1$. In particular, $\sigma(x) = 0$ for minimal sparse vectors with equal non-zero components, and $\sigma(x) = 1$ for maximally sparse vectors with all but one vanishing components.

Sparse NMF Modification: Random Acol Initialisation. It is well known that good initialisation can improve the speed and the accuracy of the solutions of many NMF algorithms [24]. Langville et al. proposed in [15] random Acol initialisation as an inexpensive and effective initialisation technique. Random Acol forms an initialisation of each column of the basis matrix W by averaging p random columns of X. We use the random Acol technique for our modified sparse NMF instead of a random initialisation.

So far, we have three unspecified parameters in our method: initialisation parameter p and sparseness parameters σ_W and σ_H. To automate the algorithm we put p to $[\frac{m}{r}]$ value. We learn useful features from basis W and leave the sparseness of H unconstrained. For all our experiments we set σ_W to 0.78 for simplicity. For more accurate estimation of the sparseness one can use the method described at [12].

Sparse NMF Modification: Earth Mover's Distance. Figure 1 shows the example of sparse NMF basis from the Hoyer paper [14]. It is can be seen that there are significant similarities among the learned bases. Guillamet and Vitria proposed that the Earth mover's distance (EMD) is better suited to this problem because one can explicitly define a distance which will depend on the basis correlation [10].

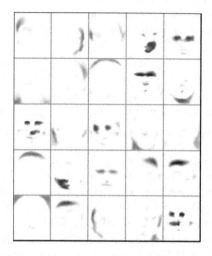

Fig. 1. Features learned from the ORL database using sparse NMF

EMD can be stated as follows: let I be a set of suppliers, J a set of consumers and d_{ij} the cost to ship a unit of supply from $i \in I$ to $j \in J$. We define d_{ij} as the Euclidean distance. We want to find a set of f_{ij} that minimises the overall cost:

$$dist(x, y) = \min \Sigma_{i \in I} \Sigma_{j \in J} d_{ij} f_{ij} \qquad (4)$$

subject the following constraints:

$$f_{ij} \geq 0, x_i \geq 0, y_j \geq 0, i \in I, j \in J$$

$$\sum_{i \in I} f_{ij} \leq y_j, j \in J$$

$$\sum_{j \in J} f_{ij} \leq x_i, i \in I$$

$$\Sigma_{i \in I} \Sigma_{j \in J} d_{ij} f_{ij} = min(\Sigma_{i \in I} x_i, \Sigma_{j \in J} y_j)$$

where x_i is the total supply of supplier i and y_j is the total capacity of consumer j.

We used EMD as the distance metric instead the Euclidean distance as in our experiments we obtain better partitioning with this metric.

2.3   Data Postprocessing: Mask Construction

After getting the modified sparse NMF basis we need to analyse the result. At this step we produce a mask of the data by construction of the boundaries between the basis vectors.

We consider the mask construction for the images as it demonstrates the result most clearly. However, our algorithm can be used on a wide range of data. In the next section we describe postprocessing example for 3D human motion data.

Examples of the modified sparse NMF basis are shown in Figures 3 and 6. Each of the basis vectors represents a part of the original image. There is substantial noise in each vector, and some vectors contain several separated parts.

First we consider each vector of the basis separately to reduce the noise. We define a vector element as noise if a 7×7 pixel square centered at this element has any other pixels with zero values. After deleting such components we label each nonzero basis vector component according to its vector number and merge the vectors.

Next we use region growing technique which is a basic yet effective method. Region growing [1] is a technique which begins with a seed location and attempts to merge neighboring pixels until no more pixels can be added to it. Because of basis sparseness, we have considerable amount of pixels that were not assigned a label and now needs one to be allocated. These errors have to be removed in a second postprocessing step. The most dominant regions, i.e. the regions with largest component values, are selected as seed regions for a region growing process. Region growing is implemented as a morphological operation. A 3×3 square is moved over the merged basis. When a neighbor to the point of interest (the center of the square) has a label assigned, the point of interest is checked for compatibility to that region. In case it is found to be compatible (i.e. all point neighbors belongs to the same basis label), it is assigned the label of the corresponding region. If there are conflicting regions, i.e. there are different regions adjacent to the point of interest, the largest region is preferred. This is also the case if the center pixel is already labeled.

When this process is completed, every pixel is assigned one of the possible basis labels, this completes our data partitioning algorithm.

3   Experimental Results

In this section we evaluate how the proposed algorithm processes several real world data sets with different characteristics. The first data considered in Section 3.1 is the talking head. On this example we show how our algorithm works with large images where data variation concentrated mainly on a small region (mouth). Next we consider facial emotional head data. Here we have data variation across the whole image. Section 3.3 describes the model visualisation ability with 3D coordinates of a walking person.

3.1 Talking Head Data

The algorithm described in the previous section was tested on the data from [6]. Initially, it was the video of a speaker reading a text, recorded at 25fps. The subject was recorded front-on with as little out of plane head movement as possible.

We extracted the texture from each frame of the video as described in [6]. Figure 2 shows examples of the texture. We perform the data normalisation [18] to improve algorithm convergence and to make the patterns of interest more evident. Intrinsic dimensionality of the data chosen by the automated k-NN method is eight. Setting the number of basis vectors to 8, we perform the second step of our algorithm. The result of this step is shown at Figure 3. One can see parts of the face there: eyes, cheeks, chin.

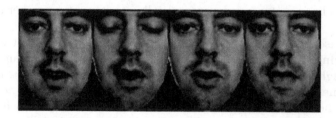

Fig. 2. Talking head data: examples

We use the postprocessing algorithm described in Section 2.3 to automatic basis analysis. Figure 4 shows the mask generated by our algorithm, data mask, which looks appropriate. It can be seen that the automatically constructed partitioning extracts the most important features of the face. We have eyes region, three mouth regions (upper lip, lower lip, inside part of the mouth), cheeks, chin, cheek bones and eyebrow regions. Such partitioning could be very useful for the further data analysis offering us a trade-off between keeping fine detail in the data and the large data dimensionality.

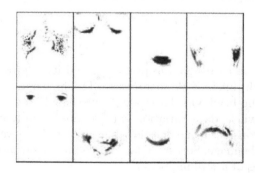

Fig. 3. Talking head data: modified NMF basis

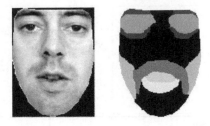

Fig. 4. Talking head data: mask

3.2 Emotion Head Data

For our next experiment we used data sets from two different people. Each person performed a different facial expressions: happiness, sadness and disgust, see Figure 5 for the examples.

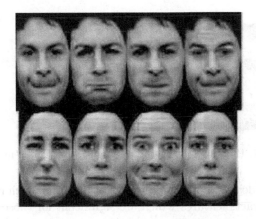

Fig. 5. Emotional head data one (top) and two (bottom)

Unlike the talking head data, the emotional head data has lots of variation across the whole face. In order to see how our algorithm can deal with emotions, we apply it to each data set. As expected, both sets have the same estimated intrinsic dimensionality, equal to 6. Thus we got 6 modified sparse NMF basis vectors which are shown at Figure 6. The basis vectors for the emotion head data look similar to the vectors from the previous example. Because the mouth variation is not significant for this example, a vector representing this variation is missed here, while we have 3 mouth variation vectors for the talking head. Instead we got more vectors to represent other face parts which displayed greater variation in these data sets.

To analyse the modified sparse NMF basis we perform data postprocessing, as described in Section 2.3. The results are shown in Figure 7. Again, the results are natural and similar to the talking head mask, but with more attention paid

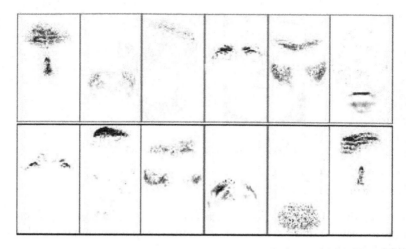

Fig. 6. Emotional data one (top) and two (bottom): modified NMF bases

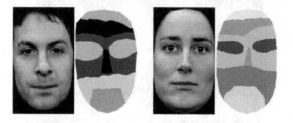

Fig. 7. Emotional data one (left) and two (right): masks

to the general face details. For example, we got a vector which represents a nose. Our algorithm extracts features which are significant for those particular data.

3.3   Motion Data

We tested our algorithm with two motion data sets. The first set represents the motion of a walking person, consisting of two steps, right turn and one step. The second set represents a two step motion without turn. The initial feature parameters represent the coordinates of human (arms, legs, torso) in the 3D space. Each pose is characterised by 17 points.

Following the preprocessing step of our algorithm, we choose the intrinsic dimensionality [7], which is 2 for each set. After running modified NMF we get a sparse basis sets for analysis.

We cannot apply the postprocessing step from Section 2.3 because of the data type. Therefore we perform postprocessing in a different way.

We define that a 3D pose junction point belongs to the basis in which this point has maximum summed basis coefficients. Figure 8 illustrates the bases for both sets. On the left hand side of Figure 8 one can see data partitioning for the walking with turn. The first basis vector here is represented by the torso and forearms, and the second one is represented by legs and shoulders. On the right hand side of Figure 8 we show data partitioning for the straight walking. Here we have a different partitioning, which consists of two pieces too. The first basis vector represents a motion of the right arm and the left leg, while the second basis vector represents the left arm, the torso and the right leg. Such partitioning isolates variation in subregions from the rest of the body and provides a high degree of control over different body parts. For example, it is straight forward to find out which part is responsible for moving the legs (the first case), or describes relationships between legs and arms movements (the second case).

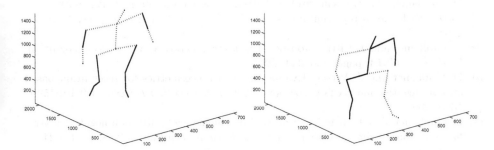

Fig. 8. 3D motion data partitioning - different bases are represented by different line drawing styles

4 Conclusions

We have described a new algorithm for automatic data decomposition using a modified sparse NMF basis analysis, in which the number of basis vectors is selected to be the same as the estimated intrinsic dimensionality of the data. Segmentation is then performed by applying region growing to the set of basis vectors.

We demonstrate the algorithm's ability to produce good partitioning of real data sets. In these examples we show that our algorithm extracts the most important features for the particular data set. Such partitioning provides a powerful tool for automating construction of parts based data models.

In future work we hope to extend our algorithm for more complex cases, such as highly articulated objects. We also plan to improve the postprocessing step by performing more advanced segmentation.

References

1. R. Adams and L. Bischof. Seeded region growing. In *Proc. of IEEE Transactions on Pattern Analysis and Machine Intelligence*, volume 16, pages 641–647, 1994.
2. M. Brand. Structure learning in conditional probability models via an entropic prior and parameter extinction. *Neural Computation*, 11(5):1155–1182, 1999.
3. G. Buchsbaum and O. Bloch. Color categories revealed by non-negative matrix factorization of munsell color spectra. *Vision Research*, 42:559–563, 2002.

4. I. Buciu and I. Pitas. Application of non-negative and local non-negative matrix factorization to facial expression recognition. In *Proc. of ICPR*, volume 1, pages 288–291, 2004.
5. X. Chen, L. Gu, S.Z. Li, and H.J. Zhang. Learning representative local features for face detection. In *Proc. of ICPR*, volume 1, pages 1126–1131, 2001.
6. D.P. Cosker, A.D. Marshall, P.L. Rosin, and Y. Hicks. Speech driven facial animation using a hierarchical model. In *Proc. of IEE Vision, Image and Signal Processing*, volume 151, pages 314–321, 2004.
7. J. Costa and A. O. Hero. Geodesic entropic graphs for dimension and entropy estimation in manifold learning. In *Proc. of IEEE Trans. on Signal Processing*, volume 52, pages 2210–2221, 2004.
8. D. Guillamet, M. Bressan, and J. Vitrià. A weighted non-negative matrix factorization for local representations. In *Proc. of CVPR*, volume 1, pages 942–947, 2001.
9. D. Guillamet and J. Vitrià. Non-negative matrix factorization for face recognition. In *Proc. of CCIA*, pages 336–344, 2002.
10. D. Guillamet and J. Vitrià. Evaluation of distance metrics for recognition based on non-negative matrix factorization. *Pattern Rocognition Letters*, 24(9-10):1599–1605, 2003.
11. D. Guillamet, J. Vitriá, and B. Schiele. Introducing a weighted non-negative matrix factorization for image classification. *Pattern Recognition Letters*, 24(14):2447–2454, 2003.
12. M. Heiler and C. Schnorr. Learning sparse representations by non-negative matrix factorization and sequential cone programming. *JMLR*, (7):1385–1407, 2006.
13. G. Hinton, Z. Ghahramani, and Y. Teh. Learning to parse images. In *Proc. of NIPS*, pages 463–469, 1999.
14. P. O. Hoyer. Non-negative matrix factorization with sparseness constraints. *Journal of Machine Learning Research*, 5:1457–1469, 2004.
15. A. N. Langville, C. D. Meyer, R. Albright, J. Cox, and D. Duling. Initializations for the nonnegative matrix factorization. In *Proc. of the 12 ACM SIGKDD International Conference on Knowledge Discovery and Data Mining*, 2006.
16. D. D. Lee and H. S. Seung. Learning the parts of objects by non-negative matrix factorization. *Nature*, 401(6755):788–791, 1999.
17. D.D. Lee and H. S. Seung. Algorithms for non-negative matrix factorization. In *Proc. of NIPS*, pages 556–562, 2000.
18. S. Li, X. Hou, and H. Zhang. Learning spatially localized, parts-based representation. In *Proc. of IEEE CVPR*, volume 1, pages 207–212, 2001.
19. W. Liu and N. Zheng. Learning sparse features for classification by mixture models. *Pattern Recognition Letters*, 25(2):155–161, 2004.
20. W. Liu and N. Zheng. Non-negative matrix factorization based methods for object recogni-tion. *Pattern Recognition Letters*, 25:893–897, 2004.
21. M. Rajapakse, J. Tan, and J. Rajapakse. Color channel encoding with nmf for face recognition. In *Proc. of ICIP*, volume 3, pages 2007–2010, 2004.
22. O. Samko, A.D. Marshall, and P.L. Rosin. Selection of the optimal parameter value for the isomap algorithm. *Pattern Rocognition Letters*, 27:968–979, 2006.
23. J. B. Tenenbaum, V. de Silva, and J. C. Langford. A global geometric framework for nonlinear dimensionality reduction. *Science*, 290:2319–2323, December 2000.
24. S. Wild. Seeding non-negative matrix factorizations with the spherical k-means clustering. *Master's Thesis, University of Colorado*, 2003.

A Brain MRI/SPECT Registration System Using an Adaptive Similarity Metric: Application on the Evaluation of Parkinson's Disease

Jiann-Der Lee [1], Chung-Hsien Huang [1], Cheng-Wei Chen [1],
Yi-Hsin Weng [2], Kun-Ju Lin [3], and Chin-Tu Chen [4]

[1] Department of Electrical Engineering, Chang Gung University, Tao-Yuan, Taiwan
jdlee@mail.cgu.edu.tw, {d8921004,m9421001}@stmail.cgu.edu.tw
[2] Movement Disorder Session, Department of Neurology, Chang Gung Memorial Hospital
and University, Taipei, Taiwan
yhweng@adm.cgmh.org.tw
[3] Molecular Image Center and Nuclear Medicine Department, Chang Gung Memorial
Hospital, Linko, Taiwan
lin4857@adm.cgmh.org.tw
[4] Department of Radiology and Committee on Medical Physics, The University of Chicago,
Chicago, Illinois, USA
cchen3@uchicago.edu

Abstract. Single photon emission computed tomography (SPECT) of dopamine transporters with ^{99m}Tc-TRODAT-1 has recently been proposed to provide valuable information of assessing the dopaminergic system. In order to measure the binding ratio of the nuclear medicine, registering magnetic resonance imaging (MRI) and SPECT image is a significant process. Therefore, an automated MRI/SPECT image registration algorithm of using an adaptive similarity metric is proposed. This similarity metric combines anatomic features characterized by specific binding (SB), the mean counts per voxel within the specific tissues, of nuclear medicine and distribution of image intensity characterized by the Normalized Mutual Information (NMI). In addition, we have also built a computer-aid clinical diagnosis system which automates all the processes of MRI/SPECT registration for further evaluation of Parkinson's disease. Clinical MRI/SPECT data from eighteen healthy subjects and thirteen patients are involved to validate the performance of the proposed system. Comparing with the conventional NMI-based registration algorithm, our system reduces the target of registration error (TRE) from >7 mm to approximate 4 mm. From the view point of clinical evaluation, the error of binding ratio, the ratio of specific-to-non-specific ^{99m}Tc-TRODAT-1 binding, is 0.20 in the healthy group and 0.13 in the patient group via the proposed system.

Keywords: Registration, MRI, SPECT, Medical Imaging, Similarity Metric.

1 Introduction

Medical images obtained from various modalities usually provide valuable information for diagnosis and are categorized into two characteristic groups as

A. Gagalowicz and W. Philips (Eds.): MIRAGE 2007, LNCS 4418, pp. 235–246, 2007.

functional imaging and anatomical imaging. Functional imaging provides metabolic or neuro-chemical changes, and anatomical imaging offers structural properties. Therefore, multi-modality image registration, bringing images from different modality into spatial correspondence, is becoming an increasingly important clinical tool in many clinical applications [1, 2].

According to intrinsic features of images, registration algorithms for medical images can be grouped into two general categories as feature-based approaches and similarity-based approaches. Feature-based approaches utilize anatomical knowledge to extract some corresponding features or landmarks which could be points, edges, contours or surfaces. Since only relying on a relatively small number of feature points, feature-based approaches can be faster. However, the performance of feature-based approaches usually depends on the success of the strategy of feature extraction. On the other hand, similarity-based approaches estimate the spatial transformation by using entire intensity information of images. They are performed by iteratively updating the transformation via optimizing a similarity metric. Similarity-based approaches can be fully automatic and avoid the difficulties of a feature extraction stage. Unfortunately, they cause a heavily computational burden.

Parkinson's disease (PD) is a progressively neuro-degenerative disorder characterized by symptoms, including akinesia, rigidity and tremors. In the clinical application of PD, functional imaging techniques such as positron emission tomography (PET) or single photon emission computed tomography (SPECT) provide the useful information for detecting in vivo metabolic and neuro-chemical changes characteristic of PD pathology. Recent research has shown that

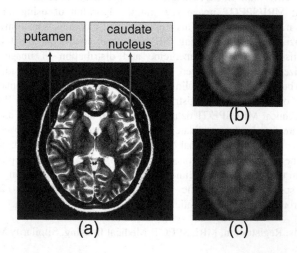

Fig. 1. Examples of T2-Weighted MRI and ^{99m}TC- TRODAT-1 SPECT (a) MRI image, (b) SPECT image from a healthy subject, and (c) SPECT images from different PD's patients

^{99m} Tc-TRODAT-1 is useful in the diagnosis of PD [3] because TRODAT-1 can bind to the dopamine transporter sites at pre-synaptic neuron membrane and can easily be labeled with ^{99m}Tc.

Two brain tissues named putamens and caudate nuclei are involved in the clinical evaluation of PD. A T2-weighted MRI of a healthy subject and its corresponding ^{99m}TC-TRODAT-1 SPECT are shown in Fig. 1(a) and (b), respectively, while a patient's SPECT is shown in Fig. 1(c). From Fig. 1, the region of interest (ROI), or the uptake region, in the SPECT of healthy subject is of stronger intensity than in the SPECT of patient. The intensity of ROI standing for the uptake of nuclear medicine not only distinguishes healthy subjects from patients but also is an important index indicating the degenerative degree of PD. It can be quantified by calculating the so-called specific-to-nonspecific binding ratio of ^{99m}TC-TRODAT-1 SPECT.

The clinical routine for calculating the binding ratio is summarized as follows [3]. SPECT image is first registered on its corresponding MR image and then fine adjusted manually with a visual inspection of the overlaid images. The slice with the highest activity is selected for measuring the ^{99m}TC-TRODAT-1 binding ratio. Then, the ROIs, putamens, caudate nucleus, and occipital cortex, are contoured manually from the MR image. Finally, the ROIs are overlaid directly to the registered SPECT image, calculating the binding ratio by Eq. 1.

$$BR = (CP - OCC) / OCC \tag{1}$$

where CP and OCC represent the mean counts per voxel within the caudate nuclei and the putamens and within the occipital cortex, respectively.

However, we have noticed that there are some steps of the current routine can be improved by the aid of computer. First, manually labeling the ROIs on MRI is really a heavy and complicated task especially for tons of patient's images. Second, only one SPECT slice with the highest activity is concerned in computing binding index because it's difficult to accomplish the labeling of the whole MRI image set. Third, an accurate and reliable MRI/SPECT registration is also necessary. As a result, we have built an automatic MRI/SPECT registration system. It embraces two main functions, labeling ROIs on MRI and registering MRI and SPECT. It also automates all the procedures.

This paper is organized as in the follows. The details of the proposed registration system are presented in Section 2. The experiment results are shown in Section 3. Finally, we conclude in Section 4.

2   Material and Methods

2.1   Clinical MRI and SPECT Data

This study included 31 subjects, 18 healthy subjects and 13 PD patients, listed in Table 1. Each individual has one MRI data set and its corresponding SPECT data sets.

Table 1. Summary demographic data for each group

Characteristic	Healthy subject (n = 18)	PD patient (n = 13)
Gender		
Male	7 (39%)	9 (69%)
Female	11 (61%)	4 (31%)
Age (y)	45 ± 17	63 ± 11

High-resolution T2-weighted MRI was acquired from a VISION VB33D 1.5-T instrument (SIEMENS Medical Systems) with a repetition time 4000 ms, an echo time 90 ms, and a slice thickness 3 mm. The data series was obtained from axial view and contained approximately 36 images. Each image was in 256×256 matrices with pixel size 0.78×0.78 mm.

Before scanning SPECT of PD patients, all anti-parkinsonian drugs and neuroleptic medications had been discontinued at least 12 hours. A dose of 925 MBq ^{99m}TC-TRODAT-1 was injected intravenously. After 4 hours, SPECT images were obtained using a Siemens MULTISPECT triple-head γ-camera, with fanbeam collimators and 120 equally spaced projections over 360°, taking 20 seconds per step. Individual images were reconstructed with back-projection using a ramp-Butterworth filter, with a cutoff of 0.3 cm^{-1} and an order of 10. The format of SPECT images is 128×128×64 voxels, and each voxel is a 2.9 mm cubic. The reconstructed data of SPECT was provided by Chang Gung Memorial Hospital, Lin-Kou, Taiwan, using their standard injection and reconstruction protocol.

2.2   The Proposed MRI/SPECT Registration System

The problem definition of rigid image registration can be described as follows. Given a fixed image A and a moving image B, after performing a spatial transformation, both images have some overlapping voxels V in common where $A, B, V \in R^d$, with d = 2 for the 2-D image registration and d = 3 for the 3-D image registration. In this study, we will mostly be concerned with 3-D image registration. More precisely, $V = \{v_i \mid i = 1...n , v_i \in A \cap T(B)\}$ where n is the number of voxels in V, and T means the transformation transforming the moving image onto the fixed image. The overlapping voxels of the fixed image and the moving image transformed are denoted as A_V and B_V where $A_V \subset A$ and $B_V \subset T(B)$, respectively. The intensity of the corresponding voxel v_i in A_V and B_V is referred to as $f_a (v_i)$ and $f_b (v_i)$. Registering A and B is equivalent to estimating the transformation T by optimizing a similarity measure, SM, as the following equation:

$$\underset{T}{opt}\, SM\,(A_V, B_V) \qquad (2)$$

Previous reviews of MRI/SPECT registration [4-7] so far are all intensity-based approaches based on the registration framework proposed by Maes [8]. Zhu et al. [7] compared different implementation strategies of MRI/SPECT registration by the mutual information (MI) with a predefined standard implementation as one that uses tri-linear interpolation, 64×64 bins, Powell's optimization and multi-resolution strategy. MI is an entropy-based similarity metric based on information theory, and previous studies have demonstrated that MI is useful for multi-modality image registration [9]. However, in a 3D multi-modality medical registration, misalignment can be so large with respect to the imaged field of view that statistics invariance is an important consideration. Therefore, Studholme et al. [10] proposed a new entropy-based similarity metric called normalized mutual information (NMI) which is insensitive to the overlapped region of the two images.

We follow the registration framework in [8] but propose an adaptive similarity metric which increases the performance of the MRI/SPECT registration. The flowchart is illustrated in Fig. 2. MRI - the fixed image A - and SPECT - the moving image B - scanned from the same individual are imported. MRI is then labeled by registering elastically with a labeled MRI template. Giving B an initial transformation T, then the similarity at the overlap of two images is computed by an adaptive similarity measure named *ANMISB* (for short of Adaptive similarity metric combining Normalized Mutual Information and Specific Binding). The transformation T keeps updating until the similarity indicates reaching a maximum via Powell's method [14], an optimization algorithm.

The proposed similarity metric, *ANMISB*, takes anatomic feature and image intensity into account in the rigid registration framework and is described by the following equation:

$$ANMISB = w_1 \times NMI + w_2 \times SB \tag{3}$$

$$SB = \frac{1}{m} \sum_{j=1}^{m} f_b(v_j), v_j \in V_{ROI} \tag{4}$$

where NMI represents the normalized mutual information of A_V and B_V, and SB represents the specific binding measured by the mean of voxel intensity within the ROIs. The w_1 and w_2 are weighting parameters of NMI and SB, respectively, and m is the number of voxels belonging to V_{ROI}.

The weighting parameters w_1 and w_2 are the trade-off between *NMI* and *SB*. Denote k as the k-th iteration. Start the iterative algorithm with w_1=0.5 and w_2=0.5, then update them adaptively by the following rules:

$$if\,((NMI_{k+1} < NMI_k)\,\&\,(SB_{k+1} \geq SB_k))$$

$$w_1 = w_1 \cdot \frac{NMI_k}{NMI_{k+1}}$$

$$elseif\,((NMI_{k+1} \geq NMI_k)\,\&\,(SB_{k+1} < SB_k))$$

$$w_2 = w_2 \cdot \frac{SB_k}{SB_{k+1}}$$

$$else$$

$$w_1 = w_1$$

$$w_2 = w_2$$

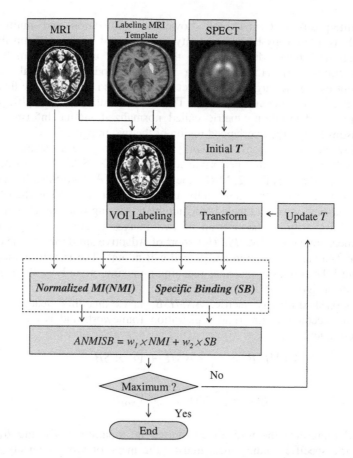

Fig. 2. The flowchart of the proposed MRI/SPECT registration system

In this research, we formulate the MRI labeling problem as registering a labeled MRI template on an individual MRI. First, a series of T2-weighted MRI regarded as atemplate was downloaded from BrainWeb (http://www.bic.mni.mcgill.ca/brainweb). The ROIs including caudate nuclei and putamens are labeled manually in the template MRI, and then a individual MRI can be labeled via registering the labeled template on it. Figure 3 illustrates an example of MRI labeling. Given an MRI image and a labeled MRI template, the template and its labels are deformed by elastically registering them on the MRI image. Finally, the MRI image is labeled by laying the labels of the deformed template.

In this study, we used the elastic registration model proposed by Periaswamy [11]. This method models the transformation between images as locally affine but globally smooth. It also explicitly accounts for local and global variations in image intensity. The formulation can be divided into two parts as local affine model and global smoothness.

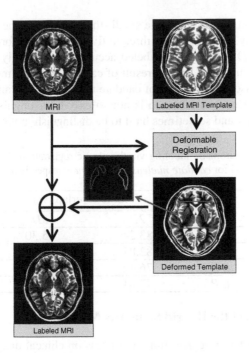

Fig. 3. An illustration of ROI labeling by deformable registration

3 Results and Discussion

3.1 The Validity of MRI Labeling Via Elastic Registration

In order to validate the MRI labeling by using the elastic registration algorithm, we compare the automatic labeling results with those of manually labeling the real MRI images from eighteen normal subjects and thirteen patients. The results of the manual labeling were accomplished by an experienced user and are regarded as a ground true. Each of these labeled results was then compared to every other using a criterion called percent volume overlap for quantifying reliability [12]. Given two different labeled structures, denoted by S_1 and S_2, and a function $V(S)$ returns the volume of S. Therefore, the percent volume overlap is given by the following equation:

$$O(S_1, S_2) = \frac{V(S_1 \cap S_2)}{(V(S_1) + V(S_2)/2)} \times 100\% \tag{5}$$

Table 2 shows the results of labeling ROIs via the elastic registration. There are two different approaches to label ROIs. The first approach denoted as *2D* in Table 2 is registering elastically only one slice which contains the largest cross-sections of caudate nucleus and putamens. The second approach denoted as *3D* is registering elastically the whole 3D volume of individual MRI and template. Obviously, registering the whole 3D volume which results 48-66 % volume overlap is quite worse than only deforming a signal slice, 76-83 % volume overlap.

The reason is that the ROIs are quite small -the caudate is generally smaller than a peanut. The ROIs may only be seen in three to five slices. Therefore, due to the partial volume effect, the ROIs can not be labeled accurately, especially in top and bottom slices. On the other hand, the labeling result of caudate nuclei is more accurate than it of putamens. The reason is the shape of caudate nucleus is clear and distinct from the background, but the shape of putamen is not so easy-to-distinguish, especially at its tail part. It is quite blur and sometimes hard to be distinguish in visual.

Table 2. The results of automatic labeling via the elastic registration. *R* and *L* stand for *right* and *left*, and *C* and *P* stand for *caudate nucleus* and *putamen*, respectively.

	Volume Overlap (%)	
	2D	3D
R C	83.24	65.30
L C	82.81	66.16
R P	76.42	48.76
L P	77.41	52.78

3.2 The Evaluation of the Hybrid Similarity Measure

The difficulty of validating registration algorithms on clinical data is that the ground truth is not known. Thurfjell et al. [6] evaluated MRI/SPECT registration involving three scans (one MRI scan and two SPECT scans on different occasions), which are to be registered sequentially. This sequential chain is also called a registration circuit. Grova et al. [4] and Yokoi et al. [5] used simulated SPECT data from segmented MRI as a gold standard to evaluate registration algorithms. On the other hand, Pfluger et al [13] showed that an interactive registration performed by experienced observers, who are trained radiologists with a suitable graphical user interface (GUI) had the lowest registration error of MRI/SPECT registration. As a result, we preferred choosing the registration results obtained by interactive registration as a gold standard.

The GUI for interactive registration was coded in C++ and is shown in Fig. 4. Sagittal, coronal and transverse views are displayed simultaneously on a split screen. The level and width of view window can be adjusted to get a suitable contrast and brightness. Color-coded SPECT images are overlaid with gray-scale MRI images in each view. For image registration, the SPECT image can be moved freely with three translations and three rotations by the arrow buttons.

To implement the multimodality registration based on the registration scheme proposed by Maes [8], some different implementation strategies, such as interpolation methods, histogram bin strategies, optimization algorithms, multiresolution or subsampling schemes, and similarity measures, have been discussed in [5-7]. According to their results, we therefore adopted trilinear interpolation, using the Powell's optimization as an optimizer, exploiting a sub-sampling scheme andmeasuring similarity by NMI. The Powell's optimization, a direction-set method

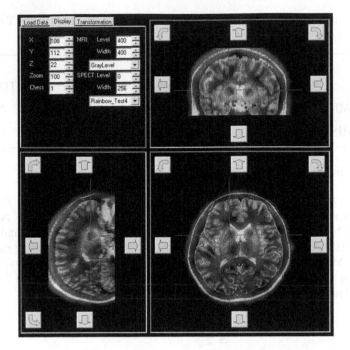

Fig. 4. The GUI designed for manual MRI/SPECT registration

in multi-dimensions, loops on a set of directions and finds the minima along each direction [14]. However, the optimization method cannot guarantee that a global optimal result will be found. To avoid trapping into a local minimum and to increase the speed of convergence, an approach using sub-sampling proved to be helpful. A three-level sub-sampling scheme was utilized in this study. The sampling rate was 4:4:2 (x:y:z) at the first level, 2:2:1 at the second level and 1:1:1 at the third level. The number of bins was 64 at the first level, 128 at the second and 256 at the third. MRI and SPECT were rescaled to the same number of bins at each level.

The target registration error (*TRE*) are utilized to assess the spatial error of the transformations between registration algorithm T and interactive registration T_{IR}. The registration error calculates the mean of spatial distance of 5000 voxels between two image positions. The following equation shows the *TRE*:

$$TRE = \frac{1}{5000}\sum_{i=1}^{5000}\left\|T(p_i)-T_{IR}(p_i)\right\|$$ (6)

where T can be either T_{NMI} or T_{ANMISB}, p_i means the points selected randomly in the brain, and $\|\cdot\|$ stands for Euclidean distance.

Results of eighteen healthy subjects and thirteen PD patients are shown in Table 3. If the mean is close to zero, the result is regarded as accurate. If the standard deviation (STD) is small, the result is regarded as precise.

Table 3. The mean and STD TRE of NMI-based and ANMISB-based MRI/SEPCT registration among healthy subjects and PD patients

	Healthy Subject		Patient	
	Mean (mm)	STD (mm)	Mean (mm)	STD (mm)
NMI	7.71	2.59	7.50	2.19
ANMISB	4.24	2.33	4.47	1.39

3.3 The Clinical Evaluation

The binding ratio (Eq. 1) calculating the intensity ratio of specific to nonspecific region is an important indicator in distinguishing healthy subjects from patients. In general, the binding ratio of a healthy subject is between 1.5 and 2.5, and that of a patient is less than 1.5 [3]. Table 4 shows that the mean error of binding ratio (*EBR*, Eq. 7) of N MRI/SPECT registration couples ($N = 18$ at healthy group and $N = 13$ at patient group) where R and L stand for *right* and *left*, and C and P stand for *caudate nucleus* and *putamen* correspondingly.

$$EBR = \frac{1}{N} \sum_{n=1}^{N} |BRIR_n - BR_n| \qquad (7)$$

where *BRIR* and *BR* denote for the binding ratio at the specific region obtained by interactive registration and by ANMISB-based registration algorithm, respectively. Since the mean of EBR is 0.20 in 2D and 0.18 in 3D in the healthy group. It is 0.13 in both 2D and 3D in patient group.

Table 4. The mean of error of binding ratio at specific regions

	Healthy Subjects		Patients	
	2D	*3D*	*2D*	*3D*
R C	0.24	0.25	0.12	0.14
L C	0.20	0.20	0.19	0.20
R P	0.20	0.13	0.12	0.10
L P	0.17	0.14	0.09	0.08
mean	0.20	0.18	0.13	0.13

4 Conclusion

In this study, we have built a computer-aided diagnosis system for evaluating ^{99m}Tc-TRODAT-1 SPECT. Two main functions are included in this system: one is an automatic ROI labeling via an elastic registration, and the other is an automatic MRI/SPECT registration based on an adaptive similarity metric.

The system was coded by C++ language. The labeling step takes approximately one and half hours in *3D* case and approximately 10 minutes in *2D* case and the registration step takes approximately 2 minutes on a compatible PC (1.4 GHz CPU, 512M RAM, and Windows XP).

Accuracy and performance of the proposed system was validated by using both healthy subjects' and patients' data. Comparing to the conventional NMI-based registration algorithm, the proposed ANMISB-based registration algorithm decreases the TRE from 7.71 mm to 4.24 mm among healthy subjects and form 7.50 mm to 4.47 mm among PD patients. Physicians can use the result of registration as an initial position and then adjust manually for a high precise registration. From the view point of clinical evaluation of Parkinson's disease, the error of binding ratio is 0.20 in healthy group and 0.13 in patient group via this fully automatic computer-aid system. It is due to the error of MRI/SPECT registration and ROI labeling. As a result, in the future, we will focus on more reliable algorithms, especially for MRI labeling.

Acknowledgement

This work was supported by National Science Council, R.O.C. with Grant No. NSC95-2221-E-182-033-MY3 and NSC 94-2614-E-182-002.

References

1. Pohjonen, H.K., Savolainen, S.E., Nikkinen, P.H., Poutanen, V.P., Korppi-Tommola, E.T., Liewendahl, B.K.: Abdominal SPECT/MRI fusion applied to the study of splenic and hepatic uptake of radiolabeled thrombocytes and colloids. Ann Nucl Med 10 (1996) 409-417.
2. Forster, G.J., Laumann, C., Nickel, O., Kann, P., Rieker, O., Bartenstein, P.: SPET/CT image co-registration in the abdomen with a simple and cost-effective tool. Eur J Nucl Med Mol Imaging 30 (2003) 32-39.
3. Weng, Y.H., Yen, T.C., Chen, M.C., Kao, P.F., Tzen, K.Y., Chen, R.S.: Sensitivity and specificity of ^{99m}Tc-TRODAT-1 SPECT imaging in differentiating patients with idiopathic Parkinson's disease from healthy subjects. J Nucl Med 45 (2004) 393-401.
4. Grova, C., Biraben, A., Scarabin, J.M., Jannin, P., Buvat, I., Benali, H.: A methodology to validate MRI/SPECT registration methods using realistic simulated SPECT data. Lecture Notes in Computer Science 2208. Springer, Netherlands (2001) 275-282.
5. Yokoi, T., Soma, T., Shinohara, H., Matsuda, H.: Accuracy and reproducibility of co-registration techniques based on mutual information and normalized mutual information for MRI and SPECT brain images. Ann Nucl Med 18 (2004) 659-667.
6. Thurfjell, L., Lau, Y.H., Andersson, J.L.R., Hutton, B.F.: Improved efficiency for MR-SPET registration based on mutual information. Eur J Nucl Med 27 (2000) 847-856.
7. Zhu, Y.M., Cochoff, S.M.: Influence of implementation parameters on registration of MR and SPECT brain images by maximization of mutual information. J Nucl Med 43 (2002) 160-166.
8. Maes, F., Collignon, A., Vandermeulen, D., Marchal, G., Suetens, P.: Multimodality image registration by maximization of mutual information. IEEE Trans Med Imaging 16 (1997) 187–198.

9. Pluim J. P. W., Maintz J. B. A., and Viergever M.A.: Mutual-information-based registration of medical images: a survey. IEEE Trans Med Imaging 22 (2003) 986-1004.

10. Studholme C., Hill D. L. G., and Hawkes D. J.: An overlap invariant entropy measure of 3D medical image alignment. Pattern Recognition 32 (1999) 71-86.

11. Periaswamy S., and Farid H.: Elastic registration in the presence of intensity variations. IEEE Trans Med Imaging 22 (2003) 865-874.

12. Collins D.L., Dai W., Peter T., and Evans A.: Automatic 3D model-based neuroanatomical segmentation," Hum Brain Mapp 3 (1995) 190-208.

13. Pfluger T., Vollmar C., Wismuller A., Dresel S., Berger F., Suntheim P., et al.: Quantitative comparison of automatic and interactive methods for MRI-SPECT image registration of the brain based on 3-Dimensional calculation of error. J Nucl Med 41 (2000) 1823-1829.

14. Press W. H., Flannery B. P., Teukolsky S. A., and Vetterling W. T.: Numerical Recipes in C, 2nd edition. Cambridge University Press.

Hand Gesture Recognition with a Novel IR Time-of-Flight Range Camera–A Pilot Study

Pia Breuer[1], Christian Eckes[2], and Stefan Müller[3]

[1] Universität Siegen
pbreuer@informatik.uni-siegen.de
[2] Fraunhofer Institute Intelligente Analysis- and Informationsystems IAIS
christian.eckes@iais.fraunhofer.de
[3] Universität Koblenz-Landau
stefanm@uni-koblenz.de

Abstract. We present a gesture recognition system for recognizing hand movements in near realtime. The system uses a infra-red time-of-flight range camera with up to 30 Hz framerate to measure 3d-surface points captured from the hand of the user. The measured data is transformed into a cloud of 3d-points after depth keying and suppression of camera noise by median filtering. Principle component analysis (PCA) is used to obtain a first crude estimate on the location and orientation of the hand. An articulated hand model is fitted to the data to refine the first estimate. The unoptimized system is able to estimate the first 7 Degrees of Freedom of the hand within 200 ms. The reconstructed hand is visualized in AVANGO/Performer and can be utilized to implement a natural man-machine interface. The work reviews relevant publications, underlines the advantages and shortcomings of the approach and provides an outlook on future improvements.

Keywords: gesture recognition, range camera, PCA, segmentation, human computer interaction, AVANGO, SGI Performer, computer graphics, computer vision, model based matching.

1 Introduction

Human computer interaction (HCI) plays a important role in many applications today. It exists the desire to realize more natural forms of interaction between humans and machines. One of these forms is the interaction via gestures, e.g. by recognizing natural hand- or full-body movements. Many researchers have focused on measuring the articulation of the whole body neglecting the hand posture since full-body posture is in itself already a complex task, even when problems due to clothing, self-occlusion and non-rigid tissue can be avoided. On the other hand, the human hand has more that 24 degrees-of-freedom in finger/thumb articulation and forms a very difficult problem on its own. Solutions to both problems have been developed but they violate an important aspect in HCI, which is called "come as you are". This paradigm is one of the most influential goals in HCI but also the most difficult one to achieve: The intentions of the human user must be recognized effortlessly and non-invasive, e.g. without

A. Gagalowicz and W. Philips (Eds.): MIRAGE 2007, LNCS 4418, pp. 247–260, 2007.

attaching any special hardware to the human body. Data gloves, suits, inertial tracking devices and optical markers attached to the hand, face or body of the human user must be avoided.

Hence, we present in this paper an approach for non-invasive gesture recognition in real time. We focus on making the hand and its movements useful for human computer interaction. We regard hand gesture recognition as a composition of two separate problems, namely reconstruction and recognition. Reconstruction deals with the problem of inferring the various degrees-of-freedom of the hand from sensor data, e.g. by matching and aligning domain knowledge in form of an articulated 3d-model with sensed data. The second step, recognition, classifies the gesture as belonging to an instance stemming from a predefined set of relevant gestures. There exist many well-known methods for classifying time-dependent data stemming from the reconstruction, for instance methods based on hidden Markov models (HMM) are the most common ones. We consider the problem of recognition as solved (or at least, as easier) and focus in our study on the problem of reconstruction, instead.

We decided to investigate the usefulness of the new Swissranger SR2 miniature time-of-flight range camera for gesture recognition, as this new hardware exhibits significant advantages over more traditional type of camera sensors: It is able to deliver range data in real time, namely with a framerate of 30 Hz without the need to solve the correspondence problem, as it is mandatory in depth estimation by means of stereo triangulation. Furthermore no special background or skin color model is required for the segmentation of the hand, so it can be used at many different places. The camera is based on active IR illumination and is therefore more robust against illumination changes than an optical hand localization based on skin color would be. However, despite these advantages it remains to be investigated in this study how useful the Swissranger SR2 really is for gesture recognition, where its weaknesses and limits are and how these problems might be investigated by further studies.

After reviewing some relevant previous work (Sect. 2) this paper presents the working principle of the range camera (Sect. 3.1). This is followed by explaining in detail how the camera is calibrated (Sect. 3.1). The following sections present our approach to reduce sensor noise (Sect. 3.1), how the hand can be segmented from the background (Sect. 3.1) and we show how a first estimation of the hand pose can be obtained from a PCA (Sect. 3.2). The next sections deal with the model based fine-matching (Sect. 3.2), present the results (Sect. 4) and conclude this paper with a final discussion. Let us now start with Sect. 2 by looking at some related work.

2   Previous Work

A common method for real-time range-scanning is the use of structured-light. Hall-Holt and Rusinkiewicz [1] use a standard video camera and a DLP projector to produce range images at 60 Hz. Infra-red structured light pattern together with stereo reconstruction are used by Ypsilos et al. [2].

One of the first who worked with range data for hand gesture recognition were Malassiotis et al. [3]: 3D information was acquired following a structured light approach with a frame rate of twelve image pairs per second. But they did not use range data exclusively, since the hand is segmented from the background by means of skin color segmentation. Bray et al. [4] applied a similar method by using also structured light to generate depth maps in combination with a skin color model to eliminate the background. Perrin et al. [5] worked with a target-oriented laser beam and two mirrors to perform 3D tracking. The authors determine distance measurements by using the absolute value of the reflected light but the system cannot be used in real time.

Using IR range data from a time-of-flight camera in gesture recognition is relatively new. One of the few authors following this approach are Liu and Fujimura [6]. Their system works in real-time, but it uses the range data only for segmentation to cut out the region nearest to the camera. The model parameters are estimated by doing shape comparisons on basis of 2D images.

Our work is also motivated by the project "Virtual Cyberglove" of the Computer Graphics Group of the University of Bonn (cp. [7] and [8]). This project aims at estimating global position and all degrees of freedom of a hand (e.g. of the back of the hand) by using multiple video cameras.

A careful selection of the hand model is also relevant for efficient hand gesture recognition. We use the model developed by [9] which aims at achieving an anatomically correct reconstruction and animation of human hand.

3 Gesture Recognition with the Swissranger SR2

3.1 The Swissranger ToF Camera

Hardware, ToF Principle. The infra-red time-of-flight range camera Swissranger SR2 was developed by CSEM ([10] and [11]). It does not only measure local brightness, but a complete distance map. Both range images and grey scale images are delivered via USB 2.0 interface to the host PC.

The emitter sends out a radio-frequency modulated light field, which is reflected by the scene and sensed by the camera. The distances between the camera

resolution	max. 124x160*
depth resolution	up to 5mm
wavelength	870nm
luminance	800mW (optical)
max. distance	7,5m
frame rate	up to 30fps**
lense	f = 8mm, F/# = 1.4, M 12x0.5
proportions	135(w)x45(h)x32(d)
weight	0.2kg

* depending on ROI
** depending on camera settings

Fig. 1. Swissranger SR2 and its technical specification (taken from [12])

and the scene objects are computed by using the time-of-flight principle, e.g. by measuring the time the light needs for reaching the objects and becoming reflected back to the sensor of the camera.

$$TOF = \frac{2D}{c} \quad \text{with speed of light } c = 3 \cdot 10^8 m/s$$

Instead of emitting impulses, the SR2 sends out continuously modulated light waves with a modulation frequency of 20 MHz. Demodulation is done by sampling. The incoming signal gets sampled four times per period (each sample shifted by 90°), whereby the signal can be clearly reconstructed. Every sampling corresponds to an integration of the photo generated electrons over the relevant part of the period. To reduce the signal-to-noise rate the integration values are summed up over many periods. So not the time is measured but the phase shifting between emitted and detected wave. The ambiguity distance is $7.5m$, before a phase shift of 2π is reached.

Hence, the distance is computed according to

$$D = L \cdot \frac{\varphi}{2 \cdot \pi} \quad with \quad L = \frac{c}{2 \cdot f_m}$$

$\varphi = \arctan\left(\frac{c(\tau_3)-c(\tau_1)}{c(\tau_0)-c(\tau_2)}\right)$ phase shift
L: unambiguous distance range
c: speed of light
f_m: (radiofrequency) RF modulation frequency

This algorithm is called four buckets or four steps method because of sampling four times each period. More detailed information about the camera can be found in [13] and [14].

Calibation. A comprehensive calibration turned out to be very difficult (cp. [15] and [16]). Gut [17] even talks about the necessity of multiple calibration. We decided to do it as follows: To analyze the output of the camera, we made a experimental setup composed of a container with fixed wheels and two books placed at different distances. We established a z value of 8000 from the camera corresponding to a range of 1000mm.

To convert the pixel values (u,v) to a position in the real world depending on the range, we use the following formula:

$$\boldsymbol{x} \equiv \begin{pmatrix} x \\ y \\ z \end{pmatrix} = \begin{pmatrix} u \\ v \\ 0 \end{pmatrix} + \begin{pmatrix} -u \\ -v \\ f \end{pmatrix} \cdot \frac{d}{\sqrt{u^2 + v^2 + f^2}} \tag{1}$$

$(x\ y\ z)^T$: 3D coordinates
$(u\ v)^T$: camera coordinates
f: focal length
d: measured range

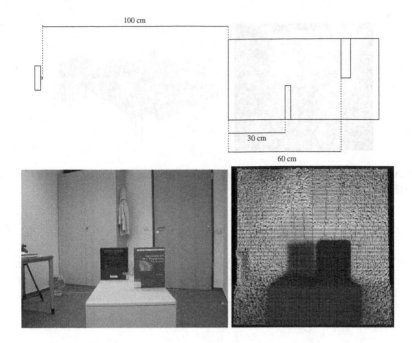

Fig. 2. Experimental setup (here at a range of 1.0m)

It can be derived from Fig. 4 (taken from [15]) via the theorem on intersecting lines.

For efficiency reasons the values of the square-root are computed only once and stored in a look up image with the size of the sensor. It depends only on the (u,v) positions and the focal length, which do not change over the time.

Noise Suppression. There is a significant amount of noise present in the sensor data, as Fig. 3 reveals. We are able to reduce speckle noise significantly by applying a median filter to the range image. This method, however, cannot suppress the most annoying reason for incorrect measurements, which give rise to the so called "tail of a comet": The surface near the object border seem to meld with the background, precise measurements near object borders become impossible. One reason for this systematic errors lies in the limited resolution of the sensor chip: Each pixel has to average over background and object at the borders because both photons from the background and photons from the object are collected by the same pixel. Moreover, the incident angle reaches $\pi/2$ near the object borders and results in a significant reduction of the number of reflected photons.

Depth Segmentation. Arm and hand are segregated from the background by simple depth keying, e.g. we define a region of interest (ROI) in depth and discard any measurements which do not fall within the predefined range of depth. The depth range defines also a working point for our recognition system as it marks the optimal trade off between two conflicting properties: The hand

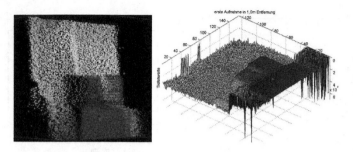

Fig. 3. Visualization of the measured data (here at a range of 1.0m): representation with SR2-Tool (left) with MatLab (right)

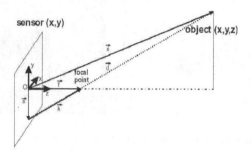

Fig. 4. Model to determine the coordinates [15]

should cover as much area of the camera sensor as possible, but any overexposure must be avoided. Overexposure results in serious errors as it impairs the depth measurements of the complete scene significantly. The last image in Fig. 5 shows the effect: The background in the lower area seems to be nearer to the camera compared to the initial state (image at the upper middle), but has in fact not moved at all. Due to this effect, there exist an optimal distance between hand and camera for which the depth measurements works best. For these purposes we scrutinized the correlation between distance, sensor coverage and overexposure and analyzed measurements of a hand at different distances. Fig. 5 shows a selection of the results.

Overexposure can also be reduced by decreasing the integration time. We use a depth range between 0.5m and 1.0m, which correspond to z-values of the camera between 4000 and 8000. We solve the segmentation problem by performing connected component analysis and selecting the largest remaining connected sub-segment as input to the reconstruction methods.

3.2 Measuring Hand Geometry

Coarse Analysis. A first crude estimation of the hand is obtained by fitting an ellipsoid into the data points which form a point cloud after the segmentation. We perform a principal component analysis to compute the position and the principal axes of the ellipsoid: We calculate the average/mean of the point cloud

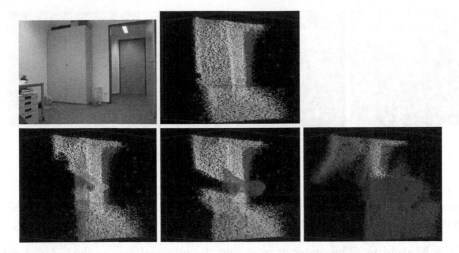

Fig. 5. Selection of the results visualized with the SR2-Tool: The first row shows the initial state (middle: visualization of the data as points; left: photo of the scene for comparison). The second row shows the data when the hand is located at distances of 2.0m, 1.0m and 0.5m, respectively. The left image shows the hand at a very large distance. The right image shows the hand at a very short distance where overexposure cannot be avoided. The image at the middle shows the optimal trade-off which is used as the working point of the system.

and compute the covariance matrix. Eigenvectors and eigenvalues of this matrix form the principal axes with their corresponding dimensions.

From [18]: Given a sequence $x = x_1, \ldots, x_n \in R^m$ of m-dimensional data points the $m \times m$ matrix

$$\text{CovMat}(x) = \frac{1}{n} \sum_{i=1}^{n} (x_i - \bar{x}) \cdot (x_i - \bar{x})^T$$

denotes the *covariance matrix* of x. The vector $\bar{x} = \frac{1}{n} \sum_{i=1}^{n} x_i$ is the mean vector of the different components of $x_1, \ldots, x_n$.

Because of working in the 3D space, every vector x consists of three values, the pixel position (x,y) in the image and the measured distance. Thus the covariance matrix looks like this:

$$\text{CovMat} = \begin{pmatrix} \text{Cov}_{x,x} & \text{Cov}_{x,y} & \text{Cov}_{x,z} \\ \text{Cov}_{y,x} & \text{Cov}_{y,y} & \text{Cov}_{y,z} \\ \text{Cov}_{z,x} & \text{Cov}_{z,y} & \text{Cov}_{z,z} \end{pmatrix}$$

in which $\text{Cov}_{a,b} = \frac{1}{n} \sum_{i=1}^{n} (a_i - \bar{a}) \cdot (b_i - \bar{b})^T$ the covariances are.

Figure 6 shows the point cloud with its principal axes visualized in AVANGO/Performer. The processing performed so far can already be used for a simple and crude gesture interface: By tracking the center of mass of the human hand cloud, the user might control a pointer or an object on the screen in which the principal

Fig. 6. Point cloud with principal axes

axes can also provide the direction. Think about playing darts: The center of mass should mark the position to drop and the largest of the principles axis marks the direction the dart is thrown away.

Fine Matching. The center of mass and the principal axes of the point cloud provide a good estimate for fitting an articulated hand model to the point cloud, as the visualization of the results have revealed. The aim of this first fine matching is to determine translation, rotation and scaling of the model accordingly. A skeleton of three dimensional hand model should be placed into the point cloud so that the distance of the surface points to the measured data is minimized. For these purposes we used a three dimensional hand model. It consists of 1,515 vertices and 3,000 triangles and corresponds to a human hand with anatomical structure. It was build for real time animation using a physically based muscle simulation and elastic skin attributes. Mrs. Irene Albrecht [9] made it available to us for this work. In our work we do not use the muscle model, we use only the triangle mesh and the vertices respectively.

The next step in our gesture recognition systems is the fitting process which aims at minimizing the distance between model and point cloud based on the sum of point-to-point distances. In this case, the Hausdorff distance may be used as a metric. On the other hand, metrics based on pure pairwise distances between point clouds do not take benefit from the more explicit surface properties of the hand model since it "only" tries to position the point clouds together as near as possible (similar to ICP registration). Alternatively, one might compare the surfaces/visual hulls between model and reconstructed surface patches by minimizing the volumne between surface patches directly since the model also consist of a triangle mesh.

More formally, the model must be placed at a good starting position inside of the point cloud to provide an adequate starting point for registration. Thus we look at the solution of the correspondence problem, e.g. matching the model data to the sensor data. The correspondences are needed to be able to compute the absolute distances between model points and point cloud the algorithm tries to minimize. We define the following cost function for the sum of minimal square distances, in which we first aim at parameterization of the first 7 DoFs:

$$K(\boldsymbol{\alpha}, t) := \sum_{<i,j>} \left[\left[\boldsymbol{x}_i^{(P)}(t) - \boldsymbol{x}_j^{(M)}(\boldsymbol{\alpha}) \right]^2 M_{ij} \right]$$

$\boldsymbol{\alpha} = (t_x, t_y, t_z, \phi_x, \phi_y, \phi_z, s)$: vector including the possible DoFs (three for translation, three for rotation and one for scaling).

$\boldsymbol{x}_i^{(P)}(t)$: ith point of the point cloud at time t

$\boldsymbol{x}_j^{(M)}(\boldsymbol{\alpha})$: jth model point after executing all of the transformations in $\boldsymbol{\alpha}$ $M_{ij} \in \{0, 1\}$: this matrix represents the correspondences between 3D point i and model vertex j; is there found a 3D point i being nearest to the considered model point j, the matrix gets the value 1 at the position ij; the pairs with the smallest distances are defined by these correspondences.

The system aims at finding a minimum of this cost function depending on the parameters $\boldsymbol{\alpha}$. However, one problem complicates the minimization procedure, the self-occlusion of the model: not all points of the model are visible for the camera: A point of a model is regarded as visible if it is not placed outside the field of view and the normal of the corresponding triangle does not point away from the camera. Hence, the articulation must discard (self)-occluded surface points automatically. The PCA delivers the rough position of the point cloud, which correspond as the rough position of the skeleton. First the skeleton is moved to the measured center of mass (global translation) and rotated to become aligned to the second principal axis. By calculating the "length" of the object within the field of view (expansion of the point cloud along the second principal axis) using the bounding box, the model can be moved along this axis (the forearm) accordingly, so that the finger tips are at the border of the point cloud. Finally the model has to be scaled because of the perspective distortion and distance from the camera sensor.

So we pursued an iterative approach during optimization: With every iteration the scaling factor of the model gets heightened or lowered by 0.1 until no more scaling causes decreasing of the point distances, i.e. the cost function gets minimized. Visibility of each point is classified using the above mentioned criteria at each iteration step – only visible model points contribute to the cost function. On the other hand, the less vertices are visible, the less are used in the cost function and may cause a lower sum of square distances. To make the cost function invariant to the total number of vertices, we normalize all distances by dividing the cost by the number of visible point pairs. However, as the estimation of the DoF must be statistically significant, we use an some additional constrains: If less than one third of the model points are visible the reconstruction is stopped, as we must avoid situations in which an incorrectly upscaled hand model with minimal visible points still fits a part of the point cloud, since only a part of the hand model matches with the sensor data.

4 Results

Figs. 8 and 9 document a felicitous recognition. The hand model is well fitted into the point cloud and follows it as the frontal and side view demonstrate. Fig. 10 shows an more problematic recognition: the algorithm has difficulty in detecting the hand moving into the scene. The entry orientation has been detected wrong in image 1. Image 2 shows how the algorithm tries to fit the model into the small point cloud. The usage of the median distance had not the intended effect, as

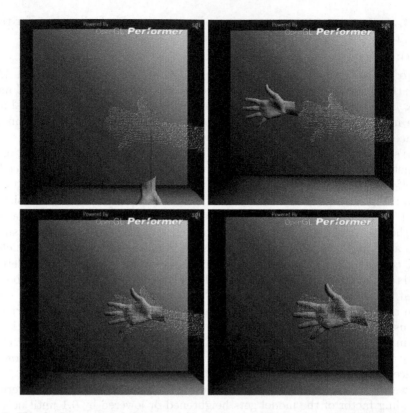

Fig. 7. Work flow upper left: moved to the center of mass; upper right: rotated on the second principal axis; lower left: moved into the point cloud; lower right: scaled

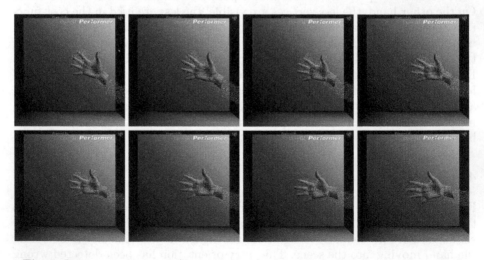

Fig. 8. Image sequence 1 (frontal view): shows a small movement downward

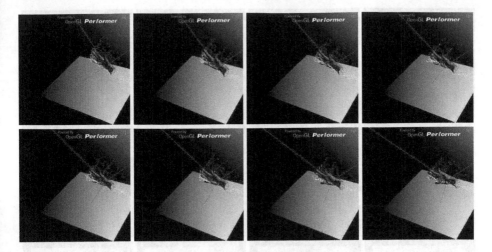

Fig. 9. Image sequence 1 (side view): shows the same movement as Fig. 8 from another perspective

also image 9 and 11 reveal. Moreover, the scaling is also incorrect. The remaining images show how the model is fitted into the point cloud correctly.

We achieved a recognition of seven DoFs within a frame rate of 2-3fps, using a 3.00GHz Intel Pentium 4 with 2GByte RAM. However, the algorithms not being optimized for speed and efficiency. One of the main objectives of this paper was to investigate gesture recognition with the new special hardware, the Swissranger SR2, and to summarize the advantages and disadvantages of such an approach.

The primary advantage of the special hardware is to be able to receive images with the depth information of the scene with considerable high frame rates. Furthermore there is no special background necessary. Worst-case problems in video-based segmentation, e.g. "blue pullover in front of a blue wall" or "a hand in front of a skin colored background" loose their horror. On the other hand, if there is a lot of sun/light the range camera gets interfered. One can observe two fundamental effects: On the one hand the intensive background light generates a lot of additional electrons which causes higher photon shot noise. Thereby it influences the preciseness of the measurement negatively. And on the other hand the electrons generated by the background light over-saturate the pixel sensor and thereby completely overload their capacity.

Despite these rather technical advantages and shortcomings due the special hards, the correspondences search remains a considerable difficult problem for which efficient and robust methods are rare. Two problems have also be kept in mind:

1. *visibility and occlusion:* The problem of self-occlusion has to be considered, since the range camera delivers $2\frac{1}{2}$D data (by sampling surface points from the cameras point of view) but the model and the objects are an real 3-dimensional objects. Moreover, the objects may only be partly visible due to the limited frustrum volume and the depth segmentation. On this account these points become extraneous to the "marriage" of the model with the

Fig. 10. Image sequence 2: shows the incoming of the hand into the field of view and the following movement downwards

point cloud because the camera also does only see the front of the scene (quasi $2\frac{1}{2}$D). Only a correct classification as invisible points may help which can only be performed after correct registration – an classical "chicken and egg problem", which we have tried to solve by using iterations.

2. *tail of a comet:* The "tail of a comet" produces many problematic 3D-points which cannot be matched correctly with any model. We have circumvented the problem by using some ad-hoc constraints - first principal axis points to the depth, second axis specifies the direction of the forearm and the third axis determines the "thickness" of the arm - to minimize its influence on the recognition. However, it is our believe that a more careful analysis will replace our constrains in the future.

Last but not least, it is important to use a good model. The model currently used is qualified because of its anatomical structure and its real time capability. It can be animated and fitted into the point cloud.

5   Conclusion and Outlook

5.1   Conclusion

We have described a pilot study of doing hand gesture recognition with a novel IR time-of-flight range camera. After calibration and noise reduction to get useful measured data we defined a region of interest and interpreted the remaining data as a point cloud. This approach gave us the opportunity to do a principal component analysis on it, which returned the principal axes of the point cloud being a clue for the precise positioning of the model. Visualization of the intermediate results showed how good PCA works on the measured data, i.e. how good the clue is. After showing some already possible ways for human-computer interaction we continued with the fine matching. A realistic 3D hand model was fitted into the point cloud. The correspondence problem and classification of visibility have been analyzed and were solved in an iterated algorithm aiming at minimizing a cost function based on point-to-point distances. Finally we identified global translation, rotation and scaling to fit the model into the data at the best possible rate. The system was able to recognize 7DoFs of a human hand with 2-3 Hz framerate. This is a promising result and defines a road map for further research in the future.

5.2 Outlook

Current work aims at improving the robustness of the system against out-liners by registering the model to the sensor point clouds with more robust algorithms, such as Random Sample Consensus (RANSAC). The introduction of a tracking mode, e.g. by adding a particle filter to the system might significantly decrease the processing time. The fast tracking mode might refine the hand model in a highly reduced search space and should support significant higher framerate. Another promising field of research lies in exploiting the currently discarded IR intensity measurements. Moreover, data stemming from additional calibrated high-resolution video cameras may further increase the precision of the reconstructed hand parameters. Image processing algorithms and sensor fusion methods may combine the depth, IR and sensor data from the visible acquisition hardware in a consistent manner.

Last but not least, the new model of the 3D-camera, the Swissranger 3000, has recently been made available by CSEM. The new hardware supports to set the integration time for each pixel individually. Hence, smaller distances between camera and the human hand without over-saturation of the photo integrators become feasible and may result in an increased sample density. Thereby, more detail of the hand becomes visible and might also increase the number of recognizable DoF significantly.

Acknowledgement

This work was funded by the German research project "Virtual Human" under the grand 01IMB01.

References

1. Hall-Holt, O., Rusinkiewicz, S.: Stripe boundary codes for real-time structured-light range scanning of moving objects. In: Eighth International Conference on Computer Vision (ICCV). (2001)

2. Ypsilos, I.A., Hilton, A., Rowe, S.: Video-rate capture of dynamic face shape and appearance. fgr (2004) 117
3. Malassiotis, S., Tsalakanidou, F., Mavridis, N., Giagourta, V., Grammalidis, N., Strintzis, M.G.: A face and gesture recognition system based on an active stereo sensor. In: Proceedings 2001 ICIP, Thessaloniki, Greece, 7-10 Oct. 2001, vol.3. (2001) 955–8
4. Bray, M., Koller-Meier, E., van Gool, L.: Smart particle filtering for 3d hand tracking. In: Proceedings. FGR2004, Seoul, South Korea, 17-19 May 2004. (2004) 675–80
5. Perrin, S., Cassinelli, A., Ishikawa, M.: Gesture recognition using laser-based tracking system. In: Proceedings. FGR2004, Seoul, South Korea, 17-19 May 2004, IEEE Comput. Soc (2004) 541–6
6. Liu, X., Fujimura, K.: Hand gesture recognition using depth data. In: Proceedings. FGR2004, Seoul, South Korea, 17-19 May 2004, IEEE Comput. Soc (2004) 529–34
7. : computer graphik, universität bonn. http://cg.cs.uni-bonn.de/ (2005)
8. Bendels, G.H., Kahlesz, F., Klein, R.: Towards the next generation of 3d content creation. In: Proceedings. AVI '04. (2004) 283–89
9. Albrecht, I., Haber, J., Seidel, H.P.: Construction and animation of anatomically based human hand models. In: SCA '03: Proceedings of the 2003 ACM SIG-GRAPH/Eurographics Symposium on Computer animation. (2003) 98–109
10. : Swiss center for electronics and microtechnology. www.csem.ch/ (2005)
11. : Swissranger sr-2 miniature time of flight camera. www.swissranger.ch/ (2005)
12. CSEM: Swiss ranger sr-2 datasheet. www.swissranger.ch/ pdf/SR-2_DataSheet.pdf (2005)
13. Oggier, T., Michael Lehmann, Rolf Kaufmann, M.S., Richter, M., Metzler, P., Lang, G., Lustenberger, F., Blanc, N.: An all-solid-state optical range camera for 3d real-time imaging with sub-centimeter depth resolution (swissranger). In: SPIE, conference on optical system design, St. Etienne, September 2003. (2003)
14. Oggier, T., Büttgen, B., Lustenberger, F., Becker, G., Rüegg, B., Hodac, A.: Swissranger sr3000 and first experiences based on miniaturized 3d-tof cameras. In: Proceedings, 1st Range Imaging Research Day, September 8/9, 2005 at ETH Zurich Switzerland. (2005) 97–108
15. Kahlmann, T., Ingensand, H.: Calibration and improvements of the high-resolution range-imaging camera swissranger. In: Proceedings of SPIE Vol. 5665; Videometrics VIII; 16-20 January 2005, San Jose, California, USA. (2005)
16. Kahlmann, T., Ingensand, H.: Range imaging sensor properties and calibration. In: Proceedings, 1st Range Imaging Research Day, September 8/9, 2005 at ETH Zurich Switzerland. (2005) 71–80
17. Gut, O.: Untersuchungen des 3d-sensors swissranger. Master's thesis, ETH Zürich (2004)
18. Dreiseitl, S.: Skriptum zu mat3 ws2004/05 (2005)

3D Reconstruction of Human Faces from Occluding Contours

Michael Keller, Reinhard Knothe, and Thomas Vetter

University of Basel, Computer Science Department, Basel, Switzerland
{michael.keller,reinhard.knothe,thomas.vetter}@unibas.ch

Abstract. In this paper we take a fresh look at the problem of extracting shape from contours of human faces. We focus on two key questions: how can we robustly fit a 3D face model to a given input contour; and, how much information about shape does a single contour image convey.

Our system matches silhouettes and inner contours of a PCA based Morphable Model to an input contour image. We discuss different types of contours in terms of their effect on the continuity and differentiability of related error functions and justify our choices of error function (modified Euclidean Distance Transform) and optimization algorithm (Downhill Simplex).

In a synthetic test setting we explore the limits of accuracy when recovering shape and pose from a single correct input contour and find that pose is much better captured by contours than is shape. In a semi-synthetic test setting – the input images are edges extracted from photorealistic renderings of the PCA model – we investigate the robustness of our method and argue that not all discrepancies between edges and contours can be solved by the fitting process alone.

1 Introduction

Automatic face recognition from a given image is one of the most challenging research topics in computer vision and it has been demonstrated that variations in pose and light are the major problems [Zha00]. Since 2D view based methods are limited in their representation, most face recognition systems show good results only for faces under frontal or near frontal pose. Methods that are based on the fitting of deformable, parametrized 3D models of human heads have been proposed to overcome this issue [Bla03].

Our work investigates the problem of recovering the 3D shape of human faces from a single contour image. Previous work shows that shape recovery methods based on pixel intensities or color are inappropriate for matching edges accurately, while multi-feature approaches such as [Rom05], where contour features are used among other features, achieve higher accuracies at the edges. To further understand the benefits and limits of the contour feature, here, we take a step back to look at this feature in isolation. Our first interest lies in building a system to robustly find a solution with a small contour reconstruction error. Our second interest lies in determining the degree to which such a solution and therefore the 3D shape of the face is constrained by the input contour.

A. Gagalowicz and W. Philips (Eds.): MIRAGE 2007, LNCS 4418, pp. 261–273, 2007.

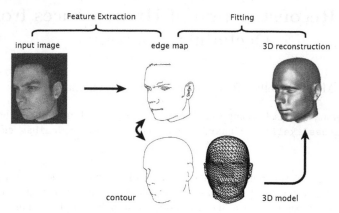

Fig. 1. Schematic view of the problem (see Section 1.1)

1.1 The Problem

Adapting a model to contours in an image can be decomposed into two subproblems: feature extraction and fitting (see Fig. 1). In a naive approach, feature extraction is performed by applying a general-purpose edge detection algorithm, such as [Can86]. Face model and camera parameters are then optimized by minimizing a distance between the model contours and the edge image.

There is an important discrepancy where the two processes interface: edge extraction computes edges and not contours. Even though most contours are found among the edges, they are incomplete and noisy. There are several ways to deal with this problem, **(a)** using a robust distance function which ignores both unmatched edges and unmatched contours, **(b)** using the model to identify which edges correspond to contours, **(c)** using a more specific form of contour detection in the first place.

In this paper we present and discuss a system based on the first approach: can we robustly fit model contours against edges by using an appropriate image distance measure. Additionally we investigate the ultimately more interesting question: assuming contour extraction was ideally solved, how well could we fit our model to a correct and complete input contour (synthesized from the model) and how good is the reconstruction of shape and pose.

1.2 Related Work

Moghaddam *et al.* [Mog03] built a system similar to our own and applied it both to video sequences and to photos acquired with a multi-camera rig – single images are not discussed. Only silhouettes are used, detected using background subtraction. Another difference lies in the error function used in their system.

Roy-Chowdhury *et al.* [Roy05] also model faces from video sequences, but as opposed to this work a locally deformable model is used. In the second part of their paper silhouettes and control points of the model are matched against edges extracted from the video frames. Model and optimization technique are very different from ours, except that an Euclidean Distance Transform is used for image comparison.

Ilic *et al.* [Ili05] adapt an implicit surface representation of a morphable PCA model to silhouette contours by solving a system of differential equations. Very interesting is their integrated approach of detecting the contour based on the location and direction of the model contour.

Both [Mog03] and [Roy05] use multiple images to achieve higher accuracy. While this is legitimate, our basic question of the constraint imposed by a single contour cannot be answered. None of the cited papers provide quantitative results describing reconstruction performance ([Roy05] do, but only for their SfM experiment, which is not based on contours).

In the remainder of the paper we first discuss types of contours and their properties, to develop exact terminology. We then explain in detail the design and implementation of our fitting system. Finally we motivate and describe our experiments, and discuss results.

2   Contours

Different authors often mean different things when using the term "contour". Sometimes, contours are "image contours" (f.i. in the context of Active Contour Models) a synonym of what we call "edges". In the context of shapes, contour is often used interchangeably with "silhouette". Other definitions of contours are implied by terms such as "inner contours", "texture contours", or "shadow contours".

2.1   Types of Contours

We define contours as the collection of those edges whose *image locations are invariant to lighting*. Contours fall then into two classes: those originating in the geometry of the solid ("occlusion contours"), and those originating in material properties ("texture contours"). Please note that a line drawing of a face would characteristically consist of just these edges.

Occluding Contours. Assuming a smooth solid shape [Koe90], occluding contours can be formally defined as the projection of those points P of the surface whose surface normal n is perpendicular to the direction e from the eye to P, i.e. $\langle n, e \rangle = 0$. This definition encompasses both "outer" contours (silhouettes) and "inner" contours (self-occluding contours), where the latter only appear on non-convex solids.

Texture Contours. Texture Contours are salient edges on texture maps. For faces, such contours are found at the lips, the eyes, the eyebrows, as well as at hair boundaries and within hair.

2.2   Continuity and Differentiability

We will now investigate how different types of contours behave differently under parameter changes in terms of continuity and differentiability of related error functions. These characteristics are very important when choosing an optimization algorithm.

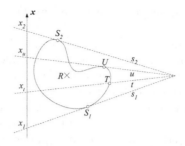

Fig. 2. 2D analogy of contour projection (see 2.2)

For simplicity's sake we describe the problem in a 2D analogy (Fig. 2). We observe the projections of silhouette (S_1, S_2), inner contour (U) and texture contour (T) with respect to a rotation ρ around R.

Only T is fixed with respect to the rotating body. Without knowledge of the shape of the body its projection x_t and its speed $\frac{dx_t}{d\rho}$ can be analytically determined, as long as T is not occluded.

Let now s_1, s_2 be defined as the two tangent rays with the maximum angle between them, and u the third tangent ray in the figure. When rotating the body clockwise, u will disappear. When rotating it counter-clockwise, u will coincide with s_2 to form a bitangent, then disappear.

Therefore the projection x_u is not defined for all ρ. Whether absence of the contour is penalized or not, x_u will contribute a discontinuity to a compound error measure. The projections x_1, x_2 are always present and unique, but where s_2 becomes a bitangent the derivative $\frac{dx_2}{d\rho}$ is undefined.

In 3D the situation is analogous: the movement of texture contour points with respect to parameters is analytically differentiable [Rom05], silhouette movement is piecewise differentiable (albeit generally not analytically), and inner contour movement is discontinuous (with 3D solids, contours appear, disappear, split and merge under parameter changes [Koe90]).

2.3   Contour Matching

Which contour features are accessible for matching depends of course on the application context. If indeed one was reconstructing faces from a shadow play, then only silhouettes would be available. Much more common is a scenario where the input is an ill-lit photograph and all types of contours are in principle accessible. While it is our goal to use all types of contours, we concentrate for now on silhouettes and inner contours, where the latter are arguably the hardest feature to work with.[1] Because the error function is neither differentiable nor even continuous, our chosen optimization algorithm is Downhill Simplex [Nel65], which uses only function evaluations and deals well with ill-behaved functions.

---

[1] Please note that in most related works only the silhouette feature is used, which does not suffer from discontinuities.

3 Implementation

Our face model is computed from a database of $m = 200$ laser scanned faces. Each face is defined by $n = 23888$ 3D vertices which are in correspondence across the database [Bla03]. Let $\boldsymbol{x}_i \in \mathbb{R}^{3n}, 1 \leq i \leq m$ be vector representation of these faces, then our $(m\text{-}1)$-dimensional face space is the affine subspace $\{\sum_{i=1}^{m} \alpha_i \boldsymbol{x}_i | \sum_{i=1}^{m} \alpha_i = 1\}$, or $\{\bar{\boldsymbol{x}} + \boldsymbol{v} | \boldsymbol{v} \in V\}$ with $\bar{\boldsymbol{x}}$ the mean face and V the vector subspace spanned by the mean-free vectors $(\boldsymbol{x}_1 - \bar{\boldsymbol{x}}, ..., \boldsymbol{x}_m - \bar{\boldsymbol{x}})$.

We estimate the probability of faces by fitting a multi-variate Gaussian distribution to the mean-free data, yielding the pdf $p(\mathbf{p}) = c \exp\left(-\frac{1}{2}\mathbf{p}^{\mathbf{T}}\boldsymbol{\Sigma}^{-1}\mathbf{p}\right)$ for coefficient vectors $\mathbf{p} \in \mathbb{R}^m$, where $\boldsymbol{\Sigma} = \frac{1}{m}\mathbf{X}\mathbf{X}^{\mathbf{T}}$ and c a normalization constant. This assumption allows us to judge plausibility of results and to randomly sample test cases.

In practise we work with an orthonormal basis $\mathbf{U} = (\boldsymbol{u}_1, ..., \boldsymbol{u}_m)$, where $\mathbf{U}$ is such that $\mathbf{U}^{\mathbf{T}}\boldsymbol{\Sigma}\mathbf{U} = \boldsymbol{\Lambda}$, with $\boldsymbol{\Lambda}$ the diagonal matrix of eigenvalues of $\boldsymbol{\Sigma}$ (in descending order). This transformation is called Principal Component Analysis, and allows us to make a feature reduction which incurs a minimal L^2 error. Specifically if $\hat{\boldsymbol{p}} \in \mathbb{R}^k$ is a projection of $\boldsymbol{p} \in \mathbb{R}^m$ onto the k-dimensional subspace $\text{span}(\boldsymbol{u}_1, ..., \boldsymbol{u}_k)$, then $E[||\mathbf{U}\mathbf{p} - \mathbf{U}\hat{\mathbf{p}}||^2] = \sum_{i=k+1}^{m} \lambda_i$. In our case the sum of the first 30 eigenvalues comprise 96% of the sum of all 200 eigenvalues, therefore fitting in a 30-dimensional subspace is mostly sufficient for good results.

Hair. While the hair line for an individual person may remain steady for years, hair length and hair style do not. Additionally hair often covers more innate and salient features such as ears and chin. In our opinion, hair is a destructive factor when creating a PCA-based model, leading to many false correspondences.

For this reason our head model is completely without hair. When registering heads we then need robust procedures which simply ignore portions of the input picture covered by hair. Future work may attempt to use such portions of input pictures constructively, but for the time being our model has no concept of hair.

Shape Error. Although we understand that the L^2 error is not optimal to describe shape similarity as perceived by humans, it is sufficient in our context. We quote the L^2 error as root-mean-squared error, with unit mm. This error is easy to visualize as average distance of the reconstructed surface from the true surface (although this is of course only correct if the error is relatively uniform). With the definitions for m, n, λ_i from above the L^2 distance between two faces described by shape vectors $\boldsymbol{p}, \boldsymbol{q}$ is calculated as:

$$L^2(\boldsymbol{p}, \boldsymbol{q}) = \sqrt{\frac{1}{n}\sum_{i=1}^{m} \lambda_i (p_i - q_i)^2}. \tag{1}$$

3.1 Error Function

Let $\boldsymbol{p}' \in \mathbb{R}^k, k = m + 7$ be a shape vector extended by the seven camera parameters of the pinhole camera model. Then the error function to be minimized must map such parameter vectors p' to scalar values. Since the binary contour image $I \in \{0,1\}^{w \cdot h}$ is in the 2D domain, it is reasonable to compose the error function E as $E(p) = D(I, R(p))$ with $R : \mathbb{R}^k \to \{0,1\}^{w \cdot h}$ a rendering function and $D : \{0,1\}^{w \cdot h} \times \{0,1\}^{w \cdot h} \to \mathbb{R}$ an image comparison function ("distance"). As opposed to previous work, we do not add a prior probability term to our error function, as overfitting has not been an issue in our experiments.

Rendering Function. The contour is found and rendered by determining front and back facing polygons on the mesh parametrized by p. Edges between a back and a front facing polygon are contour candidates. Hidden contours are eliminated through z buffering. Finally the remaining edges are projected onto an image.

Distance Function. Choosing a good distance function is much more difficult. Edge comparison is a research topic in its own right with many interesting approaches, such as elastic matching, Fourier Descriptors, or Shock Graphs [Sid98], to name a few. All of them are computationally expensive and require relatively noise-free input. As long as we are dealing with unreliable input from the Canny edge detector, we choose the more primitive yet robust approach of distance transforms, which solves correspondence implicitly (albeit not necessarily well).

The Euclidean Distance Transform [Fel04] of an input contour image is a scalar field $d : \mathbb{R}^2 \to \mathbb{R}$ where $d(x,y)$ is the Euclidean Distance of the pixel at (x,y) to the nearest contour pixel. With $S = \{(x,y)|R(p)(x,y) = 1\}$ the set of "on" pixels in the synthetic contour image, we calculate the distance term as

$$D(I, R(p)) = \frac{1}{|S|} \sum_{(x,y) \in S} d(x,y). \tag{2}$$

Such a distance term is fairly robust against unmatched edges, although such edges can create an undesirable potential. On the other hand, contours not present in the input image will create large error terms and optimization will drive them toward completely unrelated edges. To prevent this, the gradient far away from input edges should be small or zero.

We experimented with three modifications of the EDT, of the form $g(x,y) = f(d(x,y))$: **(a)** "Linear with plateau" $f(d) = d$ for $d < c$, $f(d) = c$ for $d \geq c$, **(b)** "Quadratic with plateau" $f(d) = d^2$ for $d < c$, $f(d) = c^2$ for $d \geq c$, **(c)** "Exponential" $f(d) = \exp(-d/c) + 1$ for some $c > 0$. **(a)** and **(b)** result in distance transforms with a gradient of zero at pixels that are further than c pixels away from any input contour point, while **(c)** produces a monotonically decreasing gradient. Note that the latter is qualitatively most similar to the boundary-weighted XOR function of [Mog03].[2]

3.2 Minimizing Algorithm

For fitting against occluding contours, where the error function is not well behaved and analytical gradients are not available (see above), we chose an op-

---

[2] Moghaddam *et al.* integrate their error over the entire area between input and synthetic silhouette, with penalties of $1/d$ per pixel.

timization algorithm based on function evaluations only, the Downhill Simplex algorithm due to Nelder and Mead [Nel65] in an implementation from [Pre99].

Much effort went into the setup of the initial simplex, and an appropriate restarting behavior. Our initial simplex is based on the *estimated standard deviation* of $p_G - p_T$ (the difference of initial guess to ground truth). Therefore, if σ is the vector of the estimated standard deviations of the k parameters to be adjusted, our initial simplex is made up of the $k + 1$ points $p_i = p_0 + \sigma_i$ for $1 \leq i \leq k$ and $p_0 = p_G - \frac{1}{k}\sigma$, the initial guess.[3]

After convergence of the algorithm, the algorithm was restarted with an initial simplex constructed in the same way as above, but with the point of convergence in place of the initial guess. The algorithm was started no more than ten times for a given test case, and aborted if three consecutive runs did not produce a new minimum. This resulted in an average of around 6000 error function evaluations per test case.

3.3 Camera Model and Initial Pose Estimate

Our camera model is the pinhole camera model which has seven degrees of freedom: three rotations (azimuth α, declination δ, rotation ρ around viewing axis), and four translations (left x, up y, distance from object to focal point f, distance from focal point to photographic plate d). Only α, δ, f have influence on occluding contour formation, while the other parameters describe a 2D similarity transform. When randomizing test cases the contour-defining parameters were sampled uniformly: $\alpha \in [-90°, 90°], \delta \in [-30°, 30°], 1/f \in [0m^{-1}, 2m^{-1}]$.

From the rotations we derived our pose error measure, the *aspect error*. The aspect error is the angle of the compound rotation required to align the coordinate frame of the ground truth with the coordinate frame of the estimate. For small angles and frontal views this is approximately the sum $\alpha + \delta + \rho$.

Like in previous work we always assume that an initial guess for $\alpha, \delta, \rho, x, y$ and the scale f/d has been provided by either a manual procedure or another program. When randomizing test cases we simulate this condition by randomly scattering the parameters in question. Examples of the low accuracy of the initial guess can be seen in Fig. 4 and 5.

4 Experiments

4.1 Test Settings

We differentiate between three types of test settings: realistic, synthetic and semi-synthetic. The realistic test setting is an application of the system to real photos; while being the most difficult test setting, reconstruction accuracy cannot be quantified, unless the test subject is laser scanned.

In the synthetic test setting, geometrically correct contours are generated from random configurations of the model (Fig. 3 (a)). This simulates the condition

---

[3] When using an uncentered simplex with $p_0 = p_G$ we observed a bias of the error of the reconstructed parameters toward positive values.

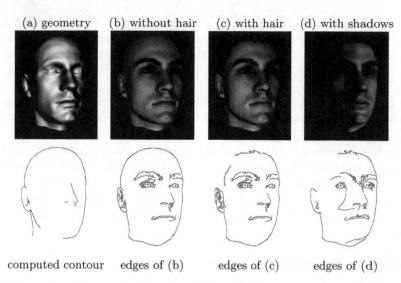

(a) geometry   (b) without hair   (c) with hair   (d) with shadows

computed contour   edges of (b)   edges of (c)   edges of (d)

Fig. 3. Hierarchy of the used test settings: (a) synthetic: contour computed from geometry. (b)-(d) semi-synthetic: edges extracted from renderings with increasingly many features.

where feature extraction has been optimally solved (Fig. 1) and an exact match is possible.

In the semi-synthetic test setting, random configurations of the model are rendered photorealistically and edges extracted [Can86]. This mimics the realistic case, except that reconstruction accuracy can be easily measured since the ground truth is known. Additionally, the difficulty of the problem can be controlled and specific aspects of contour fitting can be investigated by f.i. enabling or disabling hair texture and hard shadows (see Fig. 3 (b)-(d)).

4.2   Synthetic Experiments

The purpose of this experiment is to answer our second key question, how much information about shape does a single contour image convey *in the best imaginable case*.

We achieved best results matching 30 principal components and an unmodified Euclidean Distance Transform (the modifications in 3.1 are designed for the semi-synthetic case). On a large test set with 500 test cases the distance term was under 0.5px for 90% of the results (Fig. 4).

The aspect error of the fits are on average very small: 92% with aspect error $e_a < 3°$. Please note, that in a first approximation $e_a \approx e_\alpha + e_\delta + e_\rho$. Therefore the pose is indeed very well estimated.

In terms of shape error the fits are not significantly nearer to the ground truth than the mean is. It is worth mentioning that this by no means signifies that the recovered head is "practically random". Let p, q be independent random heads, where all components p_i, q_i are taken from a normal distribution with $\mu = 0$ and $\sigma = 1$. With $E[(p_i - q_i)^2] = 2$ and (1) it can easily be shown

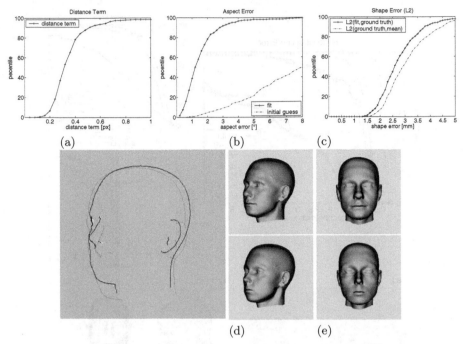

Fig. 4. Synthetic Case: (a) Matched contour (black), input contour (white, mostly covered by matched contour), contour of initial guess (gray). (b),(c) ground truth (actual camera parameters, frontal view). (d),(e) reconstruction (estimated camera parameters, frontal view). Comparing 3D reconstruction to ground truth demonstrates that even near-perfect fitting of contour may result in very dissimilar 3D shape. Distance error and aspect error were near the median ($e_{\mathrm{dist}} = 0.29$px, $e_{\mathrm{asp}} = 1.47°, e_{L2} = 3.61$mm).

that $E[L^2(p, q)^2] = 2E[L^2(p, 0)^2]$. Therefore L^2(fit, ground truth) would be on average $\sqrt{2}$ times larger than L^2(ground truth, mean) if the reconstructed heads were indeed random.

Nevertheless, the fact that the mean is almost as similar in L^2 terms as the reconstructed heads is very interesting. Obviously reconstructed heads can be very different from the ground truth, while displaying virtually the same contours (Fig. 4). This supports the view that contour does not constrain shape tightly, even with a holistic head model.

More evidence is provided by a look at correlations: while aspect error correlates strongly with contour distance (correlation coefficient $c = 0.62$), L^2 error correlates less ($c = 0.44$).[4]

4.3   Semi-synthetic Experiments

The purpose of this experiment is to see whether we can formulate the distance function in such a way, that comparing an edge map to model contours automatically leads to correct correspondence between contours and edges.

---

[4] To determine correlation, results with a distance term > 1px (1.6% of results) were excluded.

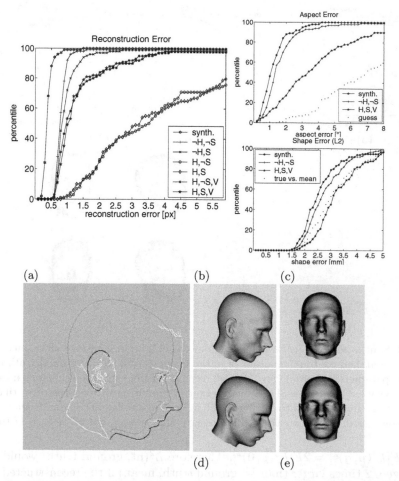

(a)   (b)   (c)

(d)   (e)

Fig. 5. Semi-Synthetic Case (H, S): Characteristic test result with vertex selection; reconstruction, aspect and L^2 error near the median ($e_{\mathrm{rec}} = 0.97\mathrm{px}, e_{\mathrm{asp}} = 3.99°, e_{L^2} = 3.18\mathrm{mm}$). (a) Matched contour (black), input contour (white), contour of initial guess (gray). (b),(c) ground truth (actual camera parameters, frontal view). (d),(e) reconstruction (estimated camera parameters, frontal view).

We used the same test set as in the previous paragraph, and generated edge maps for the four "unwanted feature" combinations, test persons with/without hair (predicate H), hard shadows enabled/disabled (predicate S). For brevity we notate *e.g.* the case "with hair, shadows disabled" as $H, \neg S$.

Image Errors. Since the input is now an edge map, which is generally quite different from the synthetic contour $R(\boldsymbol{p_T})$ (in the notation of 3.1 with $\boldsymbol{p_T}$ the parameters of the ground truth), we are now faced with a *residual error* $e_{\mathrm{res}} = D(I, R(\boldsymbol{p_T})), e_{\mathrm{res}} \geq 0$. This residual error is highly dependent on the nature of each test case as well as edge extraction parameters. Therefore it would be a mistake to quote the distance error $e_d = D(I, R(\boldsymbol{p_R}))$ of a result vector $\boldsymbol{p_R}$, as its value does not describe reconstruction quality.

Instead we quote the *reconstruction error* $e_{\text{rec}} = D(R(\boldsymbol{p_T}), R(\boldsymbol{p_R}))$, the difference between the resulting contour and the synthetic input contour. This error measures the performance of the algorithm to match the model to the unknown true contour.

However, we must be aware that the algorithm can only minimize e_d and never e_{rec} (for which the ground truth must be known). If there is a solution with $e_d < e_{\text{res}}$ the system will prefer it, even if it means e_{rec} becomes larger.

Reconstruction. Our foremost goal is to reduce the above *reconstruction error*, e_{rec}. In a comparison of the three variants of the distance transform described above, "linear with plateau" was best in every respect. Especially the non-zero gradient of the exponential variant proved troublesome with incomplete input. The plateau constant c was chosen depending on the amount of noise in the input ($c = 25$ for $\neg H, \neg S$, until $c = 5$ for H, S).

Results were best if only 20 principal components were matched. Be aware though that if $\boldsymbol{p}$ is a random shape vector, $E[L^2(\boldsymbol{p}, \boldsymbol{0})] = 3.26$mm, while for $\boldsymbol{q}, q_i = p_i (1 \leq i \leq 20), q_i = 0$ (else) $E[L^2(\boldsymbol{q}, \boldsymbol{0})] = 3.14$mm. So on average the first 20 components carry 96% of the L^2-"content".

An interesting result in itself is that the presence of hard shadows made virtually no difference on reconstruction accuracy (Fig. 5) – when looking again at Fig. 3 (c) and (d), this makes a strong case for contour matching, considering how different the lighting is between these two pictures.

On the other hand, hair had a very destructive influence on reconstruction quality, mainly because our model is an entire head and in many test cases the silhouette of the head was matched against the hair line of the input image. For this reason we include results where the model was artificially restricted to the face area ("vertex selection", predicate V).

Results for both aspect and shape error (Fig. 5) are in line with expectations from reconstruction errors. The results are by no means bad in absolute terms (Fig. 5), but compared to the synthetic case much accuracy is lost.

5   Conclusions

We have shown that it is possible to compute a shape and a pose of a human face explaining a given input contour with consistently very high accuracy. While the original pose is recovered very well, the recovered shape often differs greatly from the ground truth. This predestines contour matching as part of a system combining several features, as it can ensure contour consistency while not imposing tight constraints on the shape.

More difficult is the case where the input contour is replaced by an edge map from a picture, because of the different nature of edges and model contours. While it is possible to design a distance function to solve correspondence implicitly, there are limits to robustness where an unwanted edge is too close to a missed contour. We showed that restricting fitting to areas where such misunderstandings are least likely to occur does alleviate the problem, but would like to point out that this solution suffers from the problem that the scope of the restriction is arbitrary and has to be appropriate for all test cases simultaneously.

In our problem description we have listed three basic options how to overcome the edge-contour correspondence problem: **(a)** using a robust distance function, **(b)** using the model to establish correspondence, **(c)** using a more elaborate feature detection process. In this paper we thoroughly explored the first option, showing on one hand that despite the simplicity of the method, good results can be achieved most of the time. On the other hand certain kinds of false correspondences are difficult to avoid without exploring the other options, which will be our focus in future work.

Furthermore we have laid out that different types of contours require different optimization techniques; we believe that combining subsystems for different types of contours may prove to be a powerful concept.

Acknowledgements

This work was supported by a grant from the Swiss National Science Foundation 200021-103814.

References

[Nel65] J. A. Nelder, R. A. Mead, "A Simplex Method for Function Minimization," *Comput. J.* 7, 308-313, 1965.

[Can86] J. Canny, "A computational approach to edge detection," *IEEE Trans. on Pattern Analysis and Machine Intelligence*, 8:679-698, November 1986.

[Mog03] B. Moghaddam, J. Lee, H. Pfister, and R. Machiraju, "Model-based 3-D face capture with shape-from-silhouettes," *IEEE International Workshop on Analysis and Modeling of Faces and Gestures, Nice, France*, pages 2027, October 2003.

[Bla99] V. Blanz, Th. Vetter, "A morphable model for the synthesis of 3d faces," *SIGGRAPH '99*, pages 187–194, New York, NY, USA, 1999. ACM Press/Addison-Wesley Publishing Co.

[Bla03] V. Blanz, Th. Vetter, "Face Recognition Based on Fitting a 3D Morphable Model," *IEEE Transactions on Pattern Analysis and Machine Intelligence 2003*, 25(9).

[Fel04] P. Felzenszwalb, D. Huttenlocher, "Distance transforms of sampled functions," *Cornell Computing and Information Science Technical Report* TR2004-1963, September 2004.

[Koe90] J. J. Koenderink, "Solid Shape," *The MIT Press, 1990.*

[Pre99] W. H. Press, S. A. Teukolsky, W. T. Vetterling, B. P. Flannery, "Numerical Recipes in C / the Art of Scientific Computing," *Cambridge University Press, 1999.*

[Rom05] S, Romdhani, Th. Vetter, "Estimating 3D shape and texture using pixel intensity, edges, specular highlights, texture constraints and a prior, " *CVPR'05, San Diego*, 2:986–993, 2005.

[Roy05] A. Roy-Chowdhury, R. Chellappa, H. Gupta, "3D Face Modeling From Monocular Video Sequences," *Face Processing: Advanced Modeling and Methods (Eds. R.Chellappa and W.Zhao)*, Academic Press, 2005.

[Ili05] S. Ilic, M. Salzmann, P. Fua, "Implicit surfaces make for better silhouettes," *CVPR'05, San Diego*, 1:1135–1141, 2005.
[Zha00] W. Zhao, R. Chellappa, A. Rosenfeld, P. Phillips, "Face recognition: A literature survey," *UMD CfAR Technical Report CAR-TR-948*, 2000.
[Sid98] K. Siddiqi, A. Shokoufandeh, S. J. Dickinson, S. W. Zucker, "Shock Graphs and Shape Matching," *Computer Vision*, pages 222–229, 1998.

The Multiresolution Analysis of Triangle Surface Meshes with Lifting Scheme

Agnieszka Szczęsna

Silesian University of Technology, Institute of Computer Science, ul. Akademicka 16,
44-100 Gliwice, Poland
Agnieszka.Szczesna@polsl.pl

Abstract. Nowadays, there are many applications that take advantage of the availability of three-dimensional (3D) data sets. These objects are represented as complex polygonal surfaces formed by hundreds of thousands of polygons, which causes a significant increase in the cost of storage, transmission and visualisation. Multiresolution modeling, which allows an object to be represented by set of approximations, each with a different number of polygons, has been successfully presented as a solution for the efficient manipulation of this type of objects. The main contribution of this work is the use of the complete lifting scheme for the multiresolution analysis of irregular meshes with proposition of new prediction block.

1 Introduction

3D objects have applications in computer graphics, medicine, games, simulators, scientific visualisation, CAD systems, GIS and virtual reality systems, etc. Better and more popular 3D geometry acquisition systems result in million-polygons models. Complex three-dimension objects must be processed, stored, transferred, animated and analysed which is very expensive. Multiresolution models (Fig. 1) arise a lot of interest because they make it possible to represent and process geometric data in different levels of detail (LOD) depending on application needs [7], [11].

Multiresolution analysis and wavelets have been very popular lately, after processing signals, sounds, images and video, wavelets have been applied for digital geometry processing. This new class of application needs a processing toolbox of fundamental algorithms such as denoising, compression, transmission, enhancement, detection, analysis and editing with suitable mathematical and computational representations. The basic framework for these tools is the multiresolution analysis that decomposes an initial data set into a sequence of approximations and details.

This paper presents a new wavelet-based multiresolution framework for decomposition and reconstruction of irregular, triangular meshes. The generalisation from the first generation of wavelets to the second one gives an opportunity to construct wavelets on irregular meshes. This solution is based on lifting scheme as a wavelet construction tool.

A. Gagalowicz and W. Philips (Eds.): MIRAGE 2007, LNCS 4418, pp. 274–282, 2007.

Fig. 1. Level of detail of model

2   Wavelet-Based Multiresolution Analysis of Surface Meshes

The triangle mesh is a pair $M = (P, T)$ where P is a set of n points $p_i = (x_i, y_i, z_i)$ with $1 \leq i \leq n$ and T is a simplicial complex which contains information about topology of a mesh. The complex is a set of three types subsets called simplices: vertices $v = \{i\}\epsilon V$, edges $e = \{i, j\}\epsilon E$, faces $v = \{i, j, k\}\epsilon F$. Two vertices $\{a\}$ and $\{b\}$ are neighbours if $\{a, b\}\epsilon E$. The 1-ring neighbourhood of vertex $\{a\}$ is the set $N(a) = \{b | \{a, b\}\epsilon E\}$. The valence of a vertex is the number of edges meeting at this vertex. There are three types of triangular meshes: regular (every vertex has valence equals 6), semi-regular (the most vertices have valence 6, few isolated vertices have any valence), irregular (vertices can have any valence).

The first connection between wavelets and subdivision (semi-uniform Loop subdivision) allows to define multiresolution surface representation for semi-regular mesh with subdivision connectivity, was presented in [10], [12]. In this case input mesh first must be rebuild with remeshing algorithms [12], [13]. The BLaC-wavelets [14], [15] define local decomposition which is generalisation of Haar wavelets for non-nested spaces. The connection of hierarchical Delaunay triangulation allows to build multiresolution model of planar or spherical, irregular surface mesh. The next proposition in literature is wavelet-based multiresolution analysis of irregular meshes using a new irregular subdivision scheme [16], [17]. This is expansion of the solution presented in [10], [12].

Another direction in research is the use of non-uniform subdivision schemes to build wavelet analysis. In [9], [8] the central ingredient of multiresolution analysis is a non-uniform relaxation operator which minimises divided differences. This operator together with the mesh simplification method (progressive mesh [20]) and pyramid algorithm (Burt-Adelson pyramid) allows to define signal processing tools for irregular connected triangle meshes. In [18] progressive meshes and a semi-uniform discrete Laplacian smoothing operator were used to perform multiresolution editing tool for irregular meshes. Lifting scheme is used for multiresolution analysis in [19] where a prediction block is non-uniform relaxation operator based on surface curvature minimisation. This transformation is not a complete lifting scheme because it does not have update block.

3   Second Generation Wavelets

The second generation wavelets [1], [3], [4] are generalisation of biorthogonal classic wavelets (called first generation wavelets) [5], [6]. The second generation wavelets are not necessarily translated and dilated of one function (mother function) so they cannot be constructed by Fourier transformation. The second generation wavelets may use many basic functions, but must be possible to define nested spaces necessary for describing multiresolution analysis.

The lifting scheme [1], [2], [3], [4] is a simple but powerful tool to construct the second generation wavelets. The main advantage of this solution is the possibility of building wavelet analysis on non-standard structures of data (irregular samples, bounded domains, curves, surfaces, manifolds) while keeping all powerful properties of the first generation wavelets such as speed and good ability of approximation. A general lifting scheme (Fig. 2) consists of three types of operation:

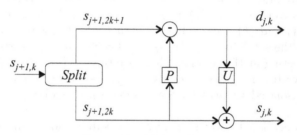

Fig. 2. The lifting scheme

- **Split**: splits input dataset into two disjoint sets of even and odd indexed samples (1). The definition of lifting scheme [2] doesn't impose any restriction on how the data should be split nor on the relative size of each subsets.

$$(s_{j+1,2k+1}, s_{j+1,2k}) = S(s_{j+1,k}) \tag{1}$$

- **Predict**: predicts odd indexed sample based on even samples. Next the odd indexed input value is replaced by the offset (difference) between the odd value and its prediction (2).

$$d_{j,k} = s_{j+1,2k+1} - P(s_{j+1,2k}) \tag{2}$$

- **Update**: updates the output, so that coarse-scale coefficients have the same average value as the input samples (3). This step is necessary for stable wavelet transform [3].

$$s_{j,k} = s_{j+1,2k} + U(d_{j,k}) \tag{3}$$

This calculations can be performed in-place. In all stages input samples can be overwritten by output of that step. Inverse transform (Fig. 3) is easy to find by reversing the order of operations and flipping the signs.

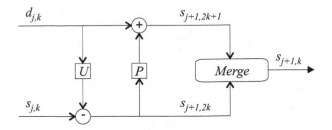

Fig. 3. The reverse lifting scheme

4   Analysis of Surface Mesh by Second Generation Wavelets

The most important advantage of the lifting scheme is generality which allows to construct the second generation wavelets on data with non-standard structures. This section presents proposition of transform based on the lifting scheme for multiresolution analysis of irregular, triangle closed mesh (2-manifold). Main operations can be singled out:

- Select from input mesh M^k (where k is the resolution level) the even and odd vertices (split block). The odd vertex will be removed from mesh. One step of lifting scheme removes only one vertex. It is possible to pick more odd vertices with disjoint neighbourhood and processes them in a parallel way.
- Predict odd vertex based on even ones.
- Compute detail vector as difference between predicted and original vertex.
- Remove the odd vertex from the mesh by an edge collapse [20]. The inverse operation is a vertex split.
- Update even vertices. The output is the coarser mesh M^{k-1} that is the approximation of initial mesh.

4.1   Split

The main task of this block is selecting vertex to remove (odd vertex) from input mesh. Different methods can be used to choose which vertex should be removed first. The criterion may be applied from mesh simplification methods [21], [22], [7], for example: quadric error metric [23], distance to local average plane [24], edge length.

The new suggested criterion is vertex distance to regression plane defined by 1-ring neighbourhood of this vertex (see Sect. 4.2).

4.2   Predict

The prediction operator estimates the odd vertex using even vertices. In this block relaxation operators from non-uniform subdivision schemes can be used,

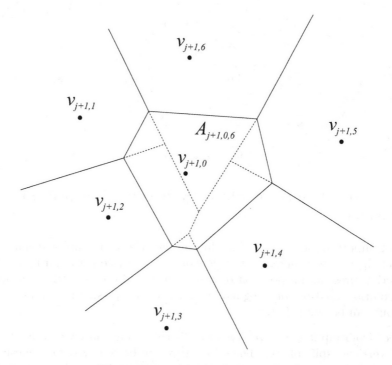

Fig. 4. Natural interpolation method

for example: surface curvature minimisation [19], minimisation of divided differences [9], [8], discrete Laplacian operator [18]. These prediction operators are based on the local surface geometry and allows to define the position of odd vertex as a combination of even vertices with suitable weight coefficients.

The new proposition of prediction block takes advantage of natural interpolation method [25]. The unsigned areas of the Voronoi cells of odd vertex (with index 0) and its 1-ring neighbours before and after removal (Fig. 4) are used for calculation in two dimensions. The prediction coefficients $\beta_{j,k}$ (where j is the resolution level, k is the index of neighbour of odd vertex) are simply the proportions of central cells areas, taken by neighbours (4).

$$\beta_{j,k} = \frac{A_{j+1,0,k}}{A_{j+1,0}} \qquad (4)$$

In (4) $A_{j+1,0}$ is the area of central cell of odd vertex with index 0 and $A_{j+1,0,k}$ is the part of central cell area assigned to neighbour (even vertex) with index k. The prediction coefficients are positive and sum up to one, so the scheme has at least one vanishing moment and guarantee stable transform [3]. The value of prediction of odd vertex $P(v_{j+1,0})$ is linear combination of neighbouring values and its coefficients (5).

$$P(v_{j+1,0}) = \sum_{k \in N(v_{j+1,0})} \beta_{j,k} v_{j+1,k} \qquad (5)$$

Before calculating coefficients the local parameterization of odd vertex and its 1-ring neighbour should be determined. The searched parametric plane is total least squares plane [28]. This is the best-fitting plane to a given set of vertices in 1-ring neighbour by minimizing the sum of the squares of the perpendicular distances of the points from the plane. The best solution utilizes the Singular Value Decomposition (SVD) [27] which allows to find the point of plane (centroid of data) and normal vector. This is used as local parametric plane and after projection vertices on this plane, the parameter value (t, u) associated with odd and 1-ring neighbour could be computed (Fig. 5). After that we can treat three coordinates (x_i, y_i, z_i) as value of function in two dimension parameter space (t_i, u_i). This parameterization is needed for using natural interpolation.

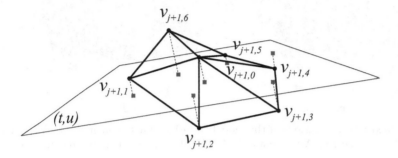

Fig. 5. Local parameterization on total least squares plane

4.3   Update

The suggested update block is a simple assurance that the values of the input and output (in coarser resolution) vertices have the same average. If this step is missing, the even indexed values proceed unchanged to the next level.

4.4   Results

The presented results concern the application of the lifting scheme into multiresolution analysis of irregular surface mesh. Initial mesh (Fig. 6.a) contains 2903 vertices and 5804 faces. In one step of transform one vertex is removed and the detail vector, which is the difference between the odd vertex and its prediction, is calculated. In this solution splitting block uses vertex distance to regression plane defined by its 1-ring neighbourhood criterion (see Sect. 4.1). Predict uses local parameterization on this plane. Coefficients are calculated by natural interpolation (see Sect. 4.2). Last step is update block (see Sect. 4.3). Fig. 6.b - 6.d show next approximations obtained from described transform. The average length of detail vector is 0.297280 and this value is between 0.088417 and 0.432680. One step of the lifting scheme transformation is presented on Fig.7.

The main advantage of proposed solution is that it has features of methods for irregular meshes [8], [9], [19], [20], [23], [24] such as progressive transmission, hierarchical representation and mesh approximation. Additionally the detail encode

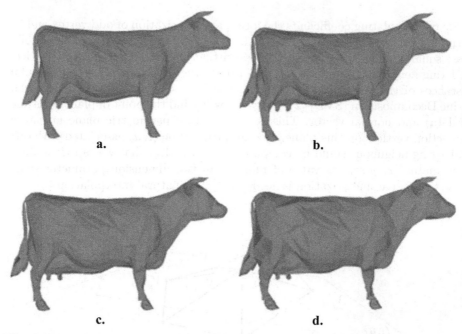

Fig. 6. Next approximations of the model. a. Original irregular mesh. b. After removal of 25% of vertices. c. After removal of 50% of vertices. d. After removal of 75% of vertices.

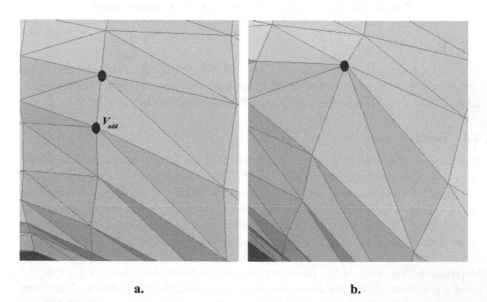

Fig. 7. The lifting scheme transformation for triangle mesh. a. The chosen odd vertex. b. The result mesh after the application of predict and update operation and removal of the odd vertex by the shortest edge collapse.

the data lost by the next approximations and can be seen as frequency spectrum. This make possible to build many applications such as filtering, smoothing, enhancement and denoising surface mesh. In hierarchical, multiresolution structure based on this scheme is no need to remember any additional coefficients only the value of detail vector. This method can be also used for processing vertex attributes.

5 Summary

This paper presents new proposal of connection criterions from mesh simplification methods, non-uniform subdivision and the lifting scheme. This solution allows to define the second generation wavelet transformation for multiresolution analysis of irregular, triangle, surface meshes. The paper also presents new prediction block which is built by taking advantage of natural interpolation. Further research will be focused on widening transform by processing different vertex attributes (such as color, temperature, texture coordinates) and examining properties of the proposed transform. The next step will be to build the multiresolution model with the support of level of detail (LOD) questions and variable resolution level of detail (region of interest, ROI) visualizations [7], [11], [26].

References

1. Sweldens W.: The lifting scheme: A construction of second generation wavelets. SIAM J. Math. Anal. (1997)
2. Sweldens W.: The Lifting Scheme: A new philosophy in biorthogonal wavelet constructions. Wavelet Applications in Signal and Image Processing III, (1995)
3. Jansen M., Oonincx P.: Second Generation Wavelets and Applications. Springer, (2005)
4. Stollnitz E. J., DeRose T., Salesin D. H.: Wavelets for Computer Graphics: Theory and Applications. Morgan Kaufmann, (1996)
5. Stang G., Nguyen T.: Wavelets and Filter Bank. Wellesley-Cambridge Press, (1996)
6. Bialasiewicz J.: Falki i aproksymacje. Wydawnictwo Naukowo-Techniczne, Warszawa, (2000)
7. Puppo E., Scopigno R.: Simplification, LOD and Multiresolution - Principles and Applications. EUROGRAPHICS (1997)
8. Daubechies I., Guskov I., Schröder P., Sweldens W.: Wavelets on Irregular Point Sets. Royal Society, (1999)
9. Guskov I., Sweldens W., Schröder P.: Multiresolution Signal Processing for Meshes. Computer Graphics Proceedings, (1999)
10. Lounsbery J.M.: Multiresolution analysis for surfaces of arbitrary topological type. Ph.D. thesis. Department of Mathematics, University of Washington, (1994)
11. Floriani L. De, Magillo P.: Multiresolution Mesh Representation: Models and Data Structures. In Multiresolution in Geometric Modelling. Floater M., Iske A., Quak E. (editors), Springer-Verlag, (2002)
12. Eck M., DeRose T., Duchamp T., Hoppe H., Lounsbery M., Stuetzle W.: Multiresolution Analysis of Arbitrary Meshes, SIGGRAPH, (1995)

13. Lee F., Sweldens W., Schröder P., Cowsar L., Dobkin D.: MAPS: Multiresolution Adaptive Parameterization of Surfaces. Computer Graphics Proceedings, (1998)
14. Bonneau G.-P.: Multiresolution analysis on irregular surface meshes. IEEE Transactions on Visualization and Computer Graphics 4, (1998)
15. Bonneau G.-P., Gerussi A.: Hierarchical decomposition of datasets on irregular surface meshes. Proceedings CGI'98, (1998)
16. Valette S., Kim Y.S., Jung H.J., Magnin I., Prost R.: A multiresolution wavelet scheme for irregularly subdivided 3D triangular mesh. IEEE Int. Conf. on Image Processing ICIP99, Japan, (1999)
17. Valette S., Prost R.: Wavelet Based Multiresolution Analysis Of Irregular Surface Meshes. IEEE Transactions on Visualization and Computer Graphics, (2004)
18. Kobbelt L., Campagna S., Vorsatz J., Seidel H.-P.: Interactive Multi-Resolution Modeling on Arbitrary Meshes. ACM SIGGRAPH '98 proceedings, (1998)
19. Roy M., Foufou S., Truchetet F.: Multiresolution analysis for irregular meshes with appearance attributes. In Proceedings of International Conference on Computer Vision and Graphics, (2004)
20. Hoppe H.: Progressive meshes. In Proceedings of ACM SIGGRAPH, (1996)
21. Heckbert P., Garland M.: Survey of Polygonal Surface Simplification Algorithms. Siggraph 97 Course Notes (1997)
22. Luebke D.: A Developer's Survey of Polygonal Simplification Algorithms. IEEE Computer Graphics and Applications, (2001)
23. Garland M., Heckbert P.: Surface Simplification Using Quadric Error Metrics. In Proceedings of SIGGRAPH, (1997)
24. Schröder W.J., Zarge J.A., Lorensen W.E.: Decimation of triangle meshes. Computer Graphics (1992)
25. Sibson R.: A brief description of natural neighbour interpolation. In V.Barnet, editor, Interpolating Multivariate Data, Lecture Notes in Statistics (1981)
26. Floriani L.De, Kobbelt L., Puppo E.: A Survey on Data Structures for Level-Of-Detail Models. In: Advances in Multiresolution for Geometric Modelling, Series in Mathematics and Visualization, Dodgson N., Floater M., Sabin M. (editors), Springer Verlag, (2004)
27. Golub G. H., Loan C. F. V.: Matrix Computations. The John Hopkins University Press, (1996)
28. Van Huffel S., Vandewalle J.: The Total Least Squares Problem. Computational Aspects and Analysis, Philadelphia: SIAM, (1991)

A Note on the Discrete Binary Mumford-Shah Model

Jérôme Darbon*

Department of Mathematics, University of California (UCLA)
Los Angeles, CA Box 90095, USA
jerome@math.ucla.edu

Abstract. This paper is concerned itself with the analysis of the two-phase Mumford-Shah model also known as the *active contour without edges* model introduced by Chan and Vese. It consists of approximating an observed image by a piecewise constant image which can take only two values. First we show that this model with the L^1-norm as data fidelity yields a contrast invariant filter which is a well known property of morphological filters. Then we consider a discrete version of the original problem. We show that an inclusion property holds for the minimizers. The latter is used to design an efficient graph-cut based algorithm which computes an exact minimizer. Some preliminary results are presented.

1 Introduction

The Mumford-Shah functional is a well-known model for image segmentation but its minimization is also a difficult task [2,26]. Many models based on this functional have been proposed [12,31]. Most of them consist of assuming that the segmented image is piecewise constant [26]. In particular the active contour without edges (ACWE) model, described by Chan and Vese in [12], consists of approximating an image with another image which can take only two values with an additional smoothness constraint. The latter is still difficult to optimize exactly. In this paper we shed new light on the analysis of the two-phase Mumford-Shah model (or ACWE) along with a new algorithm which computes an exact global minimizer.

Assume v is an observed image defined on Ω, a subset of $\mathbb{R}^2$ which takes values in $\mathbb{R}$. We intend to approximate v with an image which can take only two values μ_0 or μ_1. Let us denote by Ω_1 the set of the pixels of the image u that

* Part of this work has been done while the author was with EPITA Research and Development Laboratory (LRDE), 14-16 rue Voltaire, F-9427 Le Kremlin-Bictre France. This work was also supported by grants from the ONR under contracts ONR N00014-06-1-0345, the NIH from the grant NIH U54-RR021813 and the NSF from grant NSF DMS-0610079.

A. Gagalowicz and W. Philips (Eds.): MIRAGE 2007, LNCS 4418, pp. 283–294, 2007.
© Springer-Verlag Berlin Heidelberg 2007

takes the value μ_1, i.e., $\Omega_1 = \{x \in \Omega \mid u(x) = \mu_1\}$. The energy E associated to the two-phase Mumford-Shah segmentation model is defined as follows :

$$E(\Omega_1, \mu_0, \mu_1 | v) = \beta \, Per \, (\Omega_1)$$
$$+ \int_{\Omega \setminus \Omega_1} f(\mu_0, v(x)) dx \tag{1}$$
$$+ \int_{\Omega_1} f(\mu_1, v(x)) dx \ ,$$

where $Per(A)$ stands for the perimeter of the set A and where β is a weighted positive coefficient. The perimeter acts as a regularization term. Generally we have that $f(\mu_1, v(x)) = f(\mu_1 - v(x))$ and f is a *convex* function. For instance, f may be a power of a norm, i.e, $f(\cdot) = \| \cdot \|^p$ with $p \geq 1$.

Most of the available algorithms which minimize energy (1) either solve a system of coupled partial differential equations or perform alternate minimizations first for Ω_1, then for (μ_0, μ_1), and iterate until convergence to a local minimizer. The second optimization for (μ_1, μ_2) is not an issue [12]. However, the first one is difficult since it is a non-convex minimization problem [11]. For this one, the most popular methods rely on a level set formulation [12,27,31]. We refer the reader to [30] and the recent work of [23] for efficient level set based optimization. Nonetheless if one assume that the two values μ_0 and μ_1 are fixed, then one can compute a global minimizer by following the work of [11]. It consists in mapping the original non-convex problem into a convex one via the use of the Total Variation. Thus the problem reduces to perform an energy minimization with the Total Variation as the smoothness term. Many algorithms have been devoted to perform this minimization. Such an approach has also been applied in [7] to solve the active contour model.

If the support Ω is discretized then minimization over Ω_1 can be performed efficiently and exactly using graph-cut techniques [6,20,25] (See section 4). However, a straightforward application of these approaches to optimize over (Ω_1, μ_0) (or equivalently over (Ω_1, μ_1)) fails. This is one of the goals of this paper.

The main contributions of this paper are the following: first we show that if the data fidelity is modelled via the L^1 norm, i.e, $f(\cdot) = | \cdot |$, then minimization of the energy (1) defines a filter invariant by a change of contrast. The latter is a well known property of morphological filter [22,29] Then, we consider a discrete version of the two-phase Mumford-Shah model. We show an inclusion property of the minimizers of this discrete energy. The latter is used to propose an efficient algorithm which computes an exact minimizer. To our knowledge these results are new. The structure of this paper is as follows. In Section 2 we show the morphological behavior of the model using a L^1 data fidelity term. In Section 3 we describe some optimality results. The latter are used to design our new minimization algorithm that is presented in Section 4 along with some preliminary numerical results. Finally, we draw some conclusions in Section 5.

2   A Morphological Property

In this Section, we assume that data fidelity f is the L^1 norm, i.e, $f(\cdot) = |\cdot|$. Besides we suppose that images take values in $I = [0, L]$, with $L < \infty$ rather than $\mathbb{R}$. We show that under these assumptions the ACWE model yields a contrast invariant filter. The approach followed here is similar to the one proposed in [15] to show that the Total Variation minimization with the L^1 data fidelity term yields a morphological filter. We first introduce the notion of change of contrast before proving the morphological property.

First we define the lower level set u^λ, of an image u with level $\lambda \in I$, as follows $u^\lambda(x) = \mathbb{1}_{u(x) \le \lambda} \ \forall x \in \Omega$. We follow the work of Guichard and Morel [22] and call any continuous non-decreasing function. a continuous change of contrast. We now introduce a lemma proved in [21].

Lemma 1. *Assume that g is a continuous change of contrast and u is a real function defined on Ω. The following holds for almost all λ:*

$$\exists \mu, \ (g(u))^\lambda = u^\mu \ .$$

In other words, after a change of contrast the structure of the level lines remains the same, only their associated gray levels change. In the sequel, equalities are given for almost all λ. We now reformulate the energy on the level sets of the two variables μ_0 and μ_1. First note that for any $(a, b) \in \mathbb{R}^2$ we have $|a - b| = \int_{\mathbb{R}} |a^\lambda - b^\lambda| d\lambda$. Using the latter equality we get:

$$E(\Omega_1, \mu_0, \mu_1 | v) = \beta Per(\Omega_1)$$
$$+ \int_{\Omega \setminus \Omega_1} \left\{ \int_I |\mu_0^\lambda - v_s^\lambda| d\lambda \right\} \tag{2}$$
$$+ \int_{\Omega_1} \left\{ \int_I |\mu_1^\lambda - v_s^\lambda| d\lambda \right\} \ .$$

By interchanging the integral we have:

$$E(\Omega_1, \mu_0, \mu_1 | v) =$$
$$\int_I \underbrace{\left\{ \frac{\beta}{L} P(\Omega_1) + \int_{\Omega \setminus \Omega_1} |\mu_0^\lambda - v(x)^\lambda| dx + \int_{\Omega_1} |\mu_1^\lambda - v(x)^\lambda| dx \right\}}_{E^\lambda(u, \mu_0^\lambda, \mu_1^\lambda | v^\lambda)} d\lambda. \tag{3}$$

Finally, we have the reformulation of the whole energy as an integral over gray level values of binary energies associated to each level set:

$$E(u, \mu_0, \mu_1 | v) = \int_I E^\lambda(u, \mu_0^\lambda, \mu_1^\lambda | v^\lambda) d\lambda \ . \tag{4}$$

The next proposition states the contrast invariant property of the ACWE-model with L^1 data fidelity.

Theorem 1. *Let* v *be an observed image and* g *be a continuous change of contrast. Besides assume* $(\hat{u}, \hat{\mu}_0, \hat{\mu}_1)$ *is a global minimizer of* $E(\cdot, \cdot, \cdot | v)$.
Then $(\hat{u}, g(\hat{\mu}_0), g(\hat{\mu}_1))$ *is a global minimizer of* $E(\cdot, \cdot, \cdot | g(v))$.

Proof: Due to the decomposition of the energy on the level sets given by Eq. 4, it is enough to show that for any level $\lambda \in I$, a minimizer for $E(\cdot, \cdot, \cdot | g(v)^\lambda)$ is $(\hat{u}, g(\hat{\mu}_0)^\lambda, g(\hat{\mu}_1)^\lambda)$. Lemma 1 yields the existence of μ such that $v^\mu = g(v)^\lambda$. A minimizer for $E^\mu(\cdot, \cdot, \cdot | v^\mu)$ is $(\hat{u}, \hat{\mu}_0{}^\mu, \hat{\mu}_1{}^\mu)$. Since we have $\hat{\mu}_i = g(\hat{\mu}_i)^\lambda$, for $i \in \{1, 2\}$ we can state that $(\hat{u}, g(\hat{\mu}_0)^\lambda, g(\hat{\mu}_1)^\mu)$ is a minimizer for $E^\mu(\cdot, \cdot, \cdot | g(v)^\lambda)$. This concludes the proof. □

In other words, the ACWE model with L^1 data fidelity seen as a filter, commutes with any change of contrast. A direct consequence of the latter proposition is that optimal values of μ_0 and μ_1 necessarily belong the set of gray level values which are present in the observed image. To our knowledge this theoretical result is new.

3   An Inclusion Property

In this section, we first discretize the energy defined by Eq. (1). Then we present our main result which describe the behavior of the set Ω_1 of minimizers with respect to the gray levels variables μ_0 and μ_1.

3.1   Discretization and Reformulation

For the rest of this paper we assume the following. An image u is defined on a discrete lattice S endowed with a neighborhood system $\mathcal{N}$. We consider a neighborhood defined by the C-connectivity ($C \in \{4, 8\}$). Two neighboring sites s and t are referred to as $s \sim t$. We denote by u_s the value of the pixel at site $s \in S$. Moreover we assume that pixels take value in the discrete set $\{0, \delta, \ldots, L - \delta, L\}$ where $\delta > 0$ is a positive quantization step. Now the set Ω_1 is a subset of the discrete lattice S. We define the binary image u as the *characteristic function* of the set $\Omega \setminus \Omega_1$, i.e., we have:

$$\forall s \in S \ u_s = (\chi_{\Omega \setminus \Omega_1})_s = \begin{cases} 0 & \text{if } s \notin \Omega \setminus \Omega_1 \\ 1 & \text{if } s \in \Omega \setminus \Omega_1 \ . \end{cases}$$

We approximate locally the perimeter of a set as justified by Boykov *et al.* in [4]. Only pairwise interaction are considered:

$$Per(\Omega_1) = Per(\Omega \setminus \Omega_1) = \sum_{(s,t)} w_{st} |u_s - u_t| \ ,$$

where the coefficients w_{st} are positive constants. Since data fidelity f is separable, its discretization is a summation over all sites of the lattice S. A discrete form of the energy given by Eq. (1) is thus:

$$E(u, \mu_0, \mu_1) = \beta \sum_{(s,t)} w_{st} |u_s - u_t|$$
$$+ \sum_{s \in S} (1 - u_s) \{ f(\mu_1, v_s) - f(\mu_0, v_s) \} \tag{5}$$
$$+ \sum_{s \in S} f(\mu_0, v_s) \ .$$

Now we introduce the new variable K which measures the difference between the two labels μ_0 and μ_1, i.e:

$$\mu_1 = \mu_0 + K \ . \tag{6}$$

Without loss of generality we can assume that $\mu_1 \geq \mu_0$ and thus $K \geq 0$. Instead of considering the energy $E(u, \mu_0, \mu_1)$, we work on the energy $E(u, \mu_0, K)$ defined as follows:

$$E(u, \mu_0, K) = \beta \sum_{(s,t)} w_{st} |u_s - u_t|$$
$$+ \sum_{s \in S} u_s \{ f(\mu_0, v_s) - f(\mu_0 + K, v_s) \} \tag{7}$$
$$+ \sum_{s \in S} f(\mu_0 + K, v_s) \ .$$

Now assume that K is fixed to some value and define the restricted energy $E^k(u, \mu_0)$ as $E^k(u, \mu_0) = E(u, \mu_0, K)$. In the next Subsection, we give an inclusion property for the energy $\underset{u}{\operatorname{argmin}} E^k(u, \cdot)$.

3.2   An Inclusion Lemma

We first introduce the notion of convexity for a function along with a useful equivalence.

Definition 1. *Let f be a one-dimensional function $f : \mathbb{R} \mapsto \mathbb{R}$. This function is said* convex *if it satisfies one of the two equivalent propositions:*

a) $\forall x \forall y \ \forall \theta \in [0,1] \ f(\theta x + (1 - \theta)y) \leq \theta f(x) + (1 - \theta)f(y)$
b) $\forall x \ \forall y \geq x \ \forall d \geq 0 \ d \leq (y - x) \quad f(x) + f(y) \geq f(x + d) + f(y - d) \ .$

The proof of the latter equivalence is given in [14]. We endow the space of binary images with the following partial order:

$$a \preceq b \text{ iff } a_s \leq b_s \ \forall s \in S \ .$$

We are now ready to formulate our inclusion property.

Theorem 2. *Assume $\widehat{\mu_0} \leq \widetilde{\mu_0}$. Let us defined the binary images $\widehat{u}$ and $\widetilde{u}$ as minimizers of $E^K(\cdot, \widehat{\mu_0})$ and $E^K(\cdot, \widetilde{\mu_0})$ respectively, i.e:*

$$\widehat{u} \in \min\{u | E^K(u, \widehat{\mu_0})\} \ ,$$

$$\widetilde{u} \in \min\{u | E^K(u, \widetilde{\mu_0})\} \ .$$

Then we have the following inclusion:

$$\widehat{u} \preceq \widetilde{u} \ . \tag{8}$$

Proof: The proof is an adaptation of the one proposed in [16]. First note that if a and b are two binary variables then we have the following equality $|a - b| = a + b - 2ab$. So starting from the energy defined by Eq. (7), the local posterior energy of $E^K(u_s, \mu_0 | v_s, u_t, t \sim s)$ at the site s rewrites as:

$$E^K(u_s, \mu_0 | v_s, u_t, t \sim s) = \phi_s(\mu_0)\, u_s + \psi_s(\mu_0),$$

where

$$\phi_s(\mu_0) = \beta \sum_{t \sim s} w_{st}(1 - 2u_t) + f(\mu_0, v_s) - f(\mu_0 + K, v_s) \ , \tag{9}$$

and

$$\psi_s(\mu_0) = \beta \sum_{t \sim s} w_{st} u_t + f(\mu_0 + K, v_s) \ .$$

Thus the Gibbs local conditional posterior probability [32] is

$$P(u_s = 1 | N_s, \mu_0) = \frac{\exp -\phi_s(\mu_0)}{1 + \exp -\phi_s(\mu_0)} = \frac{1}{1 + \exp \phi_s(\mu_0)} \ .$$

The rest of the proof relies on coupled Markov chains [28,18]. One can create two Gibbsian samplers of the two posterior distributions for the two level $\widehat{\mu_0}$ and $\widetilde{\mu_0}$. It is shown in [16] that if $\phi_s(\mu_0)$ is a *non-increasing* function with respect to μ_0 and if $\phi_s(\mu_0)$ does not depend on u_s, then one can devise a coupled Markov chain [28,18] such that the two distributions are sampled while the inclusion property given by the inequality (8) is preserved. The same result holds using a simulated annealing procedure [19], and thus we get two global minimizers for the two posterior distribtion with the desired inclusion property.

Let us prove that the above assumptions are satisfied. It is easily seen that $\psi_s(\mu_0)$ does not depend on u_s. Thus, it remains to show that $\phi_s(\cdot)$ is a *non-increasing* function. The part $\beta \sum_{t \sim s} w_{st}(1 - 2u_t)$ in Eq. (9) satisfies the *non-increasing* assumption since it does not depend on μ_0. Thus, it only remains to show that for all $\mu_0, \bar{\mu}_0$ such that $\mu_0 \geq \bar{\mu}_0$, we have

$$f(\mu_0) - f(\mu_0 + K) \geq f(\bar{\mu}_0) - f(\bar{\mu}_0 + K) \ .$$

This is equivalent to

$$f(\mu_0) + f(\bar{\mu}_0 + K) \geq f(\bar{\mu}_0) + f(\mu_0 + K) \ .$$

And the latter corresponds to the convexity of the function f as described in Definition 1-b) with $K \geq 0$ as defined by Eq. (6). This concludes the proof. $\square$

A similar inclusion property has been shown for models involving the Total Variation with convex data fidelity [9,16,24,33]. Proofs in these papers can also be adapted to show Theorem 2. To our knowledge, this inclusion for the discrete binary Mumford-Shah is an original contribution. In the next Section we show how to use this inclusion property to compute a global minimizer.

4   Exact Optimization and Result

This section is devoted to the design of a fast and exact global minimizer of the ACWE-model. It takes benefit from the inclusion property of Lemma 2.

A direct minimization fo the energy $E(u, \mu_0, \mu_1)$ defined by Eq. (5) is a difficult problem. Here we propose an algorithm which computes a global optimizer by solving a family of simpler problems. Assume the two values μ_0 and K are set to some fixed values and we desire to find $\min\{u | E^K(u, \mu_0)\}$. Although this problem is still a non-convex one however it can be solved exactly in variational framework following the work of Chan et al. in [10].

Another approach consists of noticing that finding a global minimizer of $E(\cdot, \mu_0, K)$ corresponds to computing a Maximum a posteriori estimator of an Ising model [32]. This combinatorial problem can be efficiently computed via tools borrowed from graph theory as originally proposed by Greig et al. in [20]. This approach consists of building a graph such that its minimum cost cut (or equivalently its maximum flow [1]) yields an optimal binary configuration which minimizes the energy. Since this seminal work, many graph construction has been devised along with some efficient algorithm to perform the minimum cut. In this paper, we use the graph construction of [25] and the minimum cut algorithm described in [5]. It is shown in [5] that using this latter approach yields a quasi-linear algorithm with respect to the number of pixels, although the worst case complexity of the maximum flow algorithm of [5] is exponential. We refer the reader to [1,13] for polynomial maximum-flow algorithms.

A direct algorithm using this minimum cut approach consist of minimizing the energy for all possible values of the couple (μ_0, K) and to keep the couple which gives the lowest energy. We now present two improvements to get better performance.

When K is fixed to some value, we can apply lemma 2 in order to reduce the size of the problem (and thus the size of the graph to build). Indeed, assume that $\hat{u}$ and $\bar{u}$ are two global minimizers associated to the two levels $\hat{\mu}_0$ and $\bar{\mu}_0$ such that $\hat{\mu}_0 \leq \bar{\mu}_0$. Then due to Lemma 2 we have $\forall s\ \hat{u}_s = 1 \Rightarrow \bar{u}_s = 1$. Consequently, at the level $\bar{\mu}_0$ it is useless to put into the graph construction a pixel whose value is 1 at the level $\hat{\mu}_0$ (since we already know its value.) Thus we perform a traversal on the discrete set $\{0, \delta, \ldots, L - \delta, L\}$ from the lowest to the highest level, and we keep track of pixels which are already set to 1. This procedure allows for building smaller graphs.

However a much better improvement can be achieved. Instead of keeping track of pixels which can change their values, we keep track of the *connected components* of the pixels which can change their value (i.e., pixels whose value is 0). Due to the pairwise Markovian nature of the interaction in the energy (7), optimization of this energy restricted over two disjoint connected components can be performed *independently* as shown in [16]. The latter procedure yields much smaller graph constructions in practice. Both the tracking of pixels and the connected components updates can be efficiently implemented using Tarjan's Union-Find algorithm [13]. The pseudo-code of the algorithm is described on Figure 1.

$\forall s \in S \ \hat{u}_s \leftarrow 0$
   for $(K = 0; K < L; ++K)$
      Reset connected component map
      for $(\mu_0 = 0; (\mu_0 + K) < L; ++\mu_0)$
         $u' \leftarrow \underset{u}{\operatorname{argmin}} \ E^K(u, \mu_0)$

         if $(E^K(u', \mu_0) < E^K(\hat{u}, \mu_0))$
            $\hat{u} \leftarrow u'$
         update connected component map
   return $\hat{u}$

Fig. 1. Inclusion-based minimization algorithm

For the experiments, we have used 4-connectivity, set $w_{st} = 1$ for all interactions, and set the parameters $L = 255$ and $\delta = 1$. The data fidelity is modelled by the L^1-norm.

Figure 2 depicts the original image *cameraman* and *squirrel* along with the optimal results for $\beta = 10$ and a L^1 data fidelity. Using these parameters the optimal values are $\mu_0 = 14$ and $\mu_1 = 159$

Figure 3 depicts the original image *squirrel* with the optimal results for different values of the perimeter regularization coefficient $\beta = 10, 20, 30$. For $\beta = 10$, we obtain $\mu_0 = 64$ and $\mu_1 = 129$ while we get $\mu_0 = 67$ and $\mu_1 = 130$ for both $\beta = 20$ and $\beta = 30$. As expected, the higher β is the more the border of the segmented regions are smooth. Small regions that are observed for low β disappear as the regularization becomes stronger. Note that the result for $\beta = 30$ depicted in Figure 3 presents some blocky region. This behavior is due to the fact that 4-connectivity is used. It can be easily corrected by using better perimeter numerical schemes for perimeter approximation such as those presented in [3,17].

The complexity of the direct algorithm is $\Theta(L^2 \cdot T(n, m))$ where $T(n, m)$ is the time required to compute a minimum-cut on a graph of n nodes and m edges. Recall that we are using the algorithm proposed by Boykov and Kolmogorov [5] that have a quasi-linear time complexity in practice. For our experiments n is the number of pixels and $m = O(4n)$ since we are using 4-connectivity. The worst case complexity for the inclusion-based algorithm is the one of the direct

(a)   (b)

Fig. 2. Original image of *cameraman* is depicted in (a) while the optimal minimizer for the ACWE model with L^1-norm as data fidelity and with $\beta = 10$ is shown in (b)

Table 1. Time results in seconds (on a 3GHz Pentium IV) of the direct (inside parentheses) and inclusion-based algorithms for different weight coefficient β and different size of the image *cameraman*

Size	$\beta = 5$	$\beta = 10$	$\beta = 15$
32^2	4.16 (13.1)	4.4 (13.8)	4.8 (14.6)
64^2	17.1 (54.3)	17.8 (57.5)	18.5 (60.7)
128^2	72.57(243.3)	77.2 (254.6)	81.1 (268.4)
256^2	364.8 (1813.4)	382.2 (1851.7)	414.3 (2081.6)

algorithm. Indeed, the worst case for the inclusion based algorithm happens when no inclusion are present during the optimization process. For instance, a worst case happens when the optimal result is a constant image whose all pixels take the value $(L-1)$. However, for natural images this scenario is highly improbable. Time results (on a 3GHz Pentium IV) of the two minimization algorithms for the ACWE model with L^1 data fidelity, on different size of the image *cameraman*, and with different weighted coefficient β, are presented in Table 1. As one can see, both algorithms have a small dependence with the weighted coefficient β. In practice, both of them have a quasi-linear behavior with respect to the number of pixels. The same kind of results were obtained for the *squirrel* image. The gain we obtain using the inclusion-based algorithm compared to the direct approach varies from about 3 (for 32^2 size image) to about 4 (for 256^2 size images). Further studies need to be done to understand this behavior.

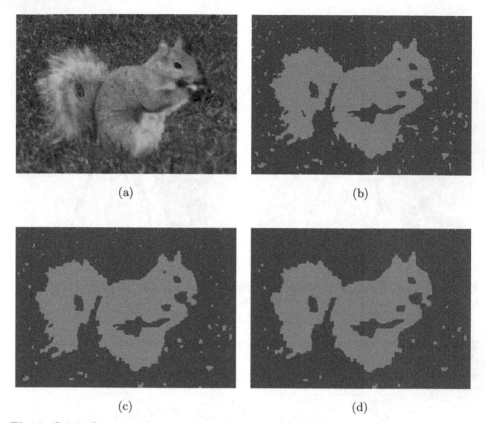

(a)   (b)

(c)   (d)

Fig. 3. Original image of *squirrel* is depicted in (a) while the optimal minimizer for the ACWE model with L^1-norm as data fidelity for $\beta = 10, 25$ and 30 are respectively shown in (b), (c) and (d)

5   Conclusion

We have presented new results on the analysis of the binary Mumford-Shah model. In particular we have shown that it yields a contrast invariant filter if L^1 data fidelity is used. Besides, we have shown an inclusion of the minimizers. The latter has been used to propose an efficient algorithm which computes an exact minimizer.

Comparisons with non optimal schemes such as the ones described in [7,8,12] remain to be done. Comparison with other segmentation methods such the one of Boykov and Jolly with [3] has also to be done. This will be presented in a forthcoming paper along with another algorithm which also takes benefit from the inclusion property of the minimizers.

Acknowledgements

The author thanks Marc Sigelle form Ecole Nationale des Télćommunications (ENST) and Antonin Chambolle from CMAP Ecole Polytechnique for fruitfull discussions. The author also thanks Ali Haddad and Guy Gilboa from UCLA for nice suggestions and careful last minute proofreading. Any remaining errors are of course my own.

References

1. R.K Ahuja, T.L. Magnanti, and J.B. Orlin. *Network Flows: Theory, Algorithms and Applications*. Prentice Hall, 1993.
2. G. Aubert and P. Kornprobst. *Mathematical Problems in Image Processing*. Springer-Verlag, 2002.
3. Y. Boykov and M.-P Jolly. Interactive graph cuts for optimal boundary and region segmentation of objects in n-d images. In *Proceedings of International Conference on Computer Vision*, pages 105–112, 2001.
4. Y. Boykov and V. Kolmogorov. Computing geodesic and minimal surfaces via graph cuts. In *International Conference on Computer Vision*, volume 1, pages 26–33, 2003.
5. Y. Boykov and V. Kolmogorov. An experimental comparison of min-cut/max-flow algorithms for energy minimization in vision. *IEEE Transactions on Pattern Analysis and Machine Intelligence*, 26(9):1124–1137, 2004.
6. Y. Boykov, O. Veksler, and R. Zabih. Fast approximate energy minimization via graph cuts. *IEEE Transactions on Pattern Analysis and Machine Intelligence*, 23(11):1222–1239, 2001.
7. X. Bresson, S. Esedoglu, P. Vandergheynst, J.P. Thiran, and S. Osher. Global minimizers of the active contour/snake model. Technical Report 05-04, UCLA CAM Report, 2005.
8. V. Caselles and A. Chambolle. Anistropic curvature-driven flow of convex sets. Technical Report 528, CMAP Ecole Polytechnique, 2004.
9. A. Chambolle. Total variation minimization and a class of binary mrf models. In *Energy Minimization Methods in Computer Vision and Pattern Recognition*, volume LNCS 3757, pages 136 – 152, St. Augustine, Florida, USA, 2005.
10. T. F. Chan, S. Esedoglu, and M. Nikolova. Finding the global minimum for binary image restoration. In *Proceedings of the ICIP 2005*, pages 121–124, Genova, Italy, 2005.
11. T.F. Chan, S. Esedoglu, and M. Nikolova. Algorithms for Finding Global Minimizers of Image Segmentation and Denoising Models. Technical Report 54, UCLA, 2004.
12. T.F. Chan and L. Vese. Active contours without edges. *IEEE Transactions on Image Processing*, 10(2):266–277, 2002.
13. T.H. Cormen, C.E. Leiserson, R.L. Rivest, and C. Stein. *Introduction to Algorithms*. The MIT Press, 2001.
14. J. Darbon. *Composants Logiciels et Algorithmes de minimisation exacte d'énergies dédiś au traitement des images*. PhD thesis, Ecole Nationale Supérieure des Télécommunications, October 2005.
15. J. Darbon. Total Variation minimization with L^1 data fidelity as a contrast invariant filter. In *Proceedings of the 4th IEEE International Symposium on Image and Signal Processing and Analysis (ISPA 2005)*, Zagreb, Croatia, September 2005.
16. J. Darbon and M. Sigelle. A fast and exact algorithm for Total Variation minimization. In *Proceedings of the 2nd Iberian Conference on Pattern Recognition and Image Analysis (IbPRIA)*, volume 3522, pages 351–359, Estoril, Portugal, June 2005. Springer-Verlag.

17. J. Darbon and M. Sigelle. Image restoration with discrete constrained Total Variation part I: Fast and exact optimization. *Journal of Mathematical Imaging and Vision, Online First*, 2005.
18. P.M. Djurić, Y. Huang, and T. Ghirmai. Perfect sampling : A review and applications to signal processing. *IEEE Signal Processing*, 50(2):345–256, 2002.
19. S. Geman and D. Geman. Stochastic relaxation, Gibbs distributions, and the bayesian restoration of images. *IEEE Transactions on Pattern Analysis and Machine Intelligence*, 6(6):721–741, 1984.
20. D. Greig, B. Porteous, and A. Seheult. Exact maximum a posteriori estimation for binary images. *Journal of the Royal Statistics Society*, 51(2):271–279, 1989.
21. F. Guichard and J.-M. Morel. *Image Iterative Smoothing and PDE's*. please write email to fguichard@poseidon-tech.com, 2000.
22. F. Guichard and J.M. Morel. Mathematical morphology "almost everywhere". In *the Proceedings of Internationnal Symposium on Mathematical Morpholy*, pages 293–303. CSIRO Publishing, April 2002.
23. L. He and S. Osher. Solving the chan-vese model by a multuphase level set algorithm based on the topological derivative. Technical Report CAM 06-56, University of California, Los Angeles (UCLA), October 2006.
24. D. S. Hochbaum. An efficient algorithm for image segmentation, markov random fields and related problems. *Journal of the ACM*, 48(2):686–701, 2001.
25. V. Kolmogorov and R. Zabih. What energy can be minimized via graph cuts? *IEEE Transactions on Pattern Analysis and Machine Intelligence*, 26(2):147–159, 2004.
26. D. Mumford and J. Shah. Optimal approximation by piecewise smooth functions and associated variational problems. *Comm. on Pure and Applied Mathematics*, 42:577–685, 1989.
27. S. Osher and N. Paragios, editors. *Geometric Level Set Methods*. Springer, 2003.
28. J. G. Propp and D. B. Wilson. Exact sampling with coupled Markov chains and statistical mechanics. *Random Structures and Algorithms*, 9(1):223–252, 1996.
29. J. Serra. *Image Analysis and Mathematical Morphology*. Academic Press, 1988.
30. B. Song and T.F. Chan. A fast algorithm for level set based optimization. Technical Report CAM 02-68, University of California, Los Angeles (UCLA), December 2002.
31. L. Vese and T.F. Chan. A mutiphase level set framework for image segmentation using the Mumford-Shah model. *International Journal of Computer Vision*, 50(3):266–277, 2002.
32. G. Winkler. *Image Analysis, Random Fields and Dynamic Monte Carlo Methods*. Applications of mathematics. Springer-Verlag, 2nd edition, 2003.
33. B.A. Zalesky. Network Flow Optimization for Restoration of Images. *Journal of Applied Mathematics*, 2:4:199–218, 2002.

Model-Based Plane-Segmentation Using Optical Flow and Dominant Plane

Naoya Ohnishi[1] and Atsushi Imiya[2]

[1] School of Science and Technology, Chiba University, Japan
Yayoicho 1-33, Inage-ku, Chiba, 263-8522, Japan
ohnishi@graduate.chiba-u.jp
[2] Institute of Media and Information Technology, Chiba University, Japan
Yayoicho 1-33, Inage-ku, Chiba, 263-8522, Japan
imiya@faculty.chiba-u.jp

Abstract. In this paper, we propose an algorithm for plane segmentation using an optical flow field computed from successive images captured by an uncalibrated moving camera. The proposing method does not require any restrictions on the camera motion and the camera-configuration geometry. Our segmentation algorithm is based on the algorithm of dominant-plane detection. The dominant plane is a planar area in the world, and it corresponds to the largest part of an image. By iterative processing dominant-plane detection, our algorithm detects multiple planes in an image. We present experimental results using image sequences observed with a moving camera in a synthesized environment and a real environment.

Keywords: Plane segmentation, Optical flow, Dominant plane.

1 Introduction

In this paper, we propose an algorithm for plane segmentation using an optical flow field computed from successive images captured by an uncalibrated moving camera. Our segmentation algorithm is based on dominant-plane detection strategy for robot navigation [19]. The dominant plane is a planar area in the world, and it corresponds to the largest part of an image.

Plane segmentation in an image [13] is a long studied problem, since planes in an image are fundamental features for modeling and 3D reconstruction of the scene. Furthermore, planes in an image are used for the camera calibration [22] and mobile robot navigation [18,21]. There are many methods for detecting planar areas using vision systems [9]. For example, the edge detection of images observed by omni and monocular camera systems [12], and the observation of pre-defined landmarks [8] are the classical ones. However, since these methods are dependent on the environment around a robot, it is not easy to use these methods in general environments. Dominant-plane detection is used as the main part of robot navigation [18]. In this paper, we show that our

A. Gagalowicz and W. Philips (Eds.): MIRAGE 2007, LNCS 4418, pp. 295–306, 2007.

dominant-plane detection strategy allows us to segment planar areas in an image by applying dominant-plane detection successively to the image. Therefore, using dominant-plane detection algorithm as the main part of visual controlling of autonomous mobile robot, the robot can navigate in general environments and understand three-dimensional configurations of the robot workspace. On the other hand, optical flow [1,11,14], which is the apparent motion of the scene, is a fundamental feature for the construction of environment information in the context of biological data processing [23]. Therefore, the use of the optical flow field is an appropriate method for image understanding for autonomous mobile robots.

The planar-area detection and segmentation methods using optical flow are also proposed [5,16,20,28]. Enkelmann [5] proposed the plane-detection method using the model vectors from motion parameters. Santos-Victor and Sandini [20] also proposed a plane-detection algorithm for a mobile robot using the inverse projection of optical flow to a ground floor, assuming that the motion of the camera system mounted on a robot is pure translation with a uniform velocity. However, even if a camera is mounted on a wheel-driven robot, the vision system does not move with a uniform velocity due to mechanical errors of the robot and unevenness of the floor.

The model based methods for image segmentation are also proposed. Homography based methods [4,27] use the plane-to-plane homography for detecting a plane. The motion segmentation with layers is proposed in [24,25,26]. Brox et. al. proposed an algorithm for image segmentation by the level set method [3]. We use the dominant-plane model for segmenting multiple planar areas. Since the dominant plane is a planar area in the world and it corresponds to the largest part of an image, our algorithm does not require any restrictions for the camera motion and geometric configurations between the camera and objects.

In Section 2, we describe our algorithm for detecting the dominant plane using an optical flow field [19]. In Section 3, we propose the algorithm for multiple plane segmentation using the dominant plane detection. Section 4 presents experimental results using a synthesized image sequence and a real image sequence captured by an uncalibrated moving camera. After detecting planar areas, it is possible to reconstruct three-dimensional configurations of planar areas in the space. In this paper, we only deal with the segmentation algorithm in an image.

2   Dominant Plane Detection from Optical Flow

In this section, we briefly describe the algorithm for dominant plane detection using an optical flow field observed through an uncalibrated moving camera. The details of our algorithm are described in [19]. First, we describe the computation of optical flow. Next, we define the dominant plane in an image, and we describe the relationships between optical flow and the dominant plane. Finally, we present the algorithm for detecting the dominant plane.

2.1   Optical Flow and Homography

Setting $I(x, y, t)$ and $(\dot{x}, \dot{y})^\top$ to be the time-varying gray-scale-valued image at time t and optical flow, optical flow $(\dot{x}, \dot{y})^\top$ at each point $(x, y)^\top$ satisfies

$$\frac{\partial I}{\partial x}\dot{x} + \frac{\partial I}{\partial y}\dot{y} + \frac{\partial I}{\partial t} = 0. \tag{1}$$

The computation of $(\dot{x}, \dot{y})^\top$ from $I(x, y, t)$ is an ill-posed problem, Therefore, additional constraints are required to compute $(\dot{x}, \dot{y})^\top$. The most commonly used constraints are those indicated by Horn and Schunck [11], Lucas and Kanade [14], and Nagel and Enkelmann [17].

We use the Lucas-Kanade method with pyramids [2]. Therefore, Eq. (1) can be solved by assuming that the optical flow vector of pixels is constant in the neighborhood of each pixel. We set the window size to be 5×5. The Eq. (1) is expressed as a system of linear equations,

$$I_{\alpha x}\dot{x} + I_{\beta y}\dot{y} + I_t = 0, \quad |\alpha| \leq 2, |\beta| \leq 2 \tag{2}$$
$$I_{\alpha\beta}(x, y, t) = I(x + \alpha, y + \beta, t + 1), \tag{3}$$

where $I_{\alpha\beta}(x, y)$ is spatial neighborhood of the pixel. Optical flow $(\dot{x}, \dot{y})^\top$ is solved by Lucas-Kanade method [14]. Setting this phase is estimation of optical flow at level 0 of the pyramid representation of the image, we estimate optical flow at the levels $0 \ldots 4$.

Setting $I^0(x, y, t) = I(x, y, t)$ is the original image and $I^i(x, y, t)$ is the pyramid transformation of the image $I(x, y, t)$ at level i, the pyramid representation is expressed as

$$I^{i+1}(x, y, t) = \sum_{\alpha,\beta \in N_i} a_{\alpha\beta} I^i(x - \alpha, y - \beta, t), \tag{4}$$

where N_i is the neighborhood of the point $(x, y)^\top$ at level i and $a_{\alpha\beta}$ are weight parameters of the neighborhood pixels. We set N_i is the 3×3 neighborhood and

$$a_{\alpha\beta} = \begin{cases} \frac{1}{4}, & (\alpha = 0, \beta = 0) \\ \frac{1}{8}, & (\alpha = \pm 1, \beta = 0), (\alpha = 0, \beta = \pm 1) \\ \frac{1}{16}, & (\alpha = \pm 1, \beta = \pm 1) \end{cases} \tag{5}$$

Finally, this optical flow is obtained by integration of optical flows of each level of the pyramid representation. The procedure is illustrated in Fig. 1, which is referred to Bouguet [2]. We call $\boldsymbol{u}(x, y, t)$, which is a set of optical flow $(\dot{x}, \dot{y})$ computed for all pixels in an image, the optical flow field at time t.

Using pyramid transform, the optical-flow field is computed by the next algorithm, where u and w stand for the optical-flow computational algorithm in each pyramid revel and the warping operation described as

$$w(I, \boldsymbol{u}) = I(\boldsymbol{x} + \boldsymbol{u}).$$

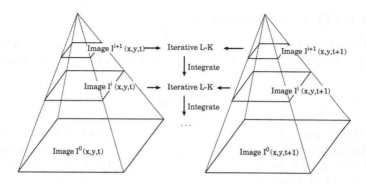

Fig. 1. Procedure for computing optical flow in L-K method with pyramids. Optical flow is obtained by integration of optical flows of each level of the pyramid representation.

In this algorithm, I_t^l stands for the pyramidal representation at level l of an image $I(x, y, t)$ at time t.

```
Input I_t^L ··· I_t^0, I_{t+1}^L ··· I_{t+1}^0
l := L
while l ≠ 0 do
begin
d_t^l := u(I_t^l, I_{t+1}^l)
I_{t+1}^{l-1} := w(I_{t+1}^{l-1}, d_t^l)
l := l - 1
end
```

2.2   Definition of the Dominant Plane

We define the dominant plane as a planar area in the world corresponding to the largest part in an image. Assuming that the dominant plane in an image corresponds to the ground plane on which the robot moves, the detection of the dominant plane enables the robot to detect the feasible region for navigation in its workspace.

An example of the dominant plane is shown in Fig. 2. In Fig. 2, an obstacle is placed in front of the robot and the camera moves toward the obstacle. In the captured image, the white region is the dominant plane, which corresponds to the ground plane in the robot workspace.

2.3   Optical Flow on the Dominant Plane

In this section, we present geometrical properties of optical flow on the dominant plane.

Setting $\boldsymbol{H}$ to be a 3×3 matrix [10], the homography between the two images of a planar surface can be expressed as

$$(x', y', 1)^\top = \boldsymbol{H}(x, y, 1)^\top, \tag{6}$$

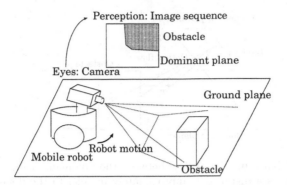

Fig. 2. Perception and cognition of motion and obstacles in workspace by an autonomous mobile robot. The mobile robot has a camera, which corresponds to eyes. The robot perceives an optical flow field from ego-motion [18].

where $(x, y, 1)^\top$ and $(x', y', 1)^\top$ are homogeneous coordinates of corresponding points in two successive images. Assuming that the camera displacement is small, matrix H is approximated by affine transformations. These geometrical and mathematical assumptions are valid when the camera is mounted on a mobile robot moving on the dominant plane. Therefore, the corresponding points $p = (x, y)^\top$ and $p' = (x', y')^\top$ on the dominant plane are expressed as

$$p' = Ap + b, \tag{7}$$

where A and b are a 2×2 affine-coefficient matrix and a 2-dimensional vector, which are approximations of H.

We can estimate the affine coefficients using the RANSAC-based algorithm [6,10,19]. Using estimated affine coefficients, we can estimate optical flow on the dominant plane $(\hat{x}, \hat{y})^\top$,

$$(\hat{x}, \hat{y})^\top = A(x, y)^\top + b - (x, y)^\top, \tag{8}$$

for all points $(x, y)^\top$ in the image. We call $(\hat{x}, \hat{y})^\top$ *planar flow*, and $\hat{u}(x, y, t)$ *planar flow field* at time t, which is a set of planar flow $(\hat{x}, \hat{y})$ computed for all pixels in an image.

2.4 Dominant Plane Detection

If an obstacle exists in front of the robot, the planar flow on the image plane differs from the optical flow on the image plane, as shown in Fig. 3. Since the planar flow vector $(\hat{x}, \hat{y})^\top$ is equal to the optical flow vector $(\dot{x}, \dot{y})^\top$ on the dominant plane, we use the difference between these two flows to detect the dominant plane. We set ε to be the tolerance of the difference between the optical flow vector and the planar flow vector. Therefore, if the inequality

$$\left| (\dot{x}, \dot{y})^\top - (\hat{x}, \hat{y})^\top \right| < \varepsilon \tag{9}$$

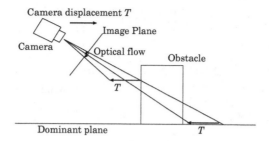

Fig. 3. The difference in optical flow between the dominant plane and an obstacle. If the camera moves a distance T approximately parallel to the dominant plane, the optical flow vector in the obstacle area in the image plane shows that the obstacle moves the distance T, or the optical flow vector at the dominant-plane area in the image plane shows that the dominant plane moves the distance T. Therefore, the camera observes the difference in the optical flow vectors between the dominant plane and an obstacle.

is satisfied, we accept the point $(x, y)^\top$ as a point on the dominant plane. Then, the image is represented as a binary image by the dominant plane region and the obstacle region. Therefore, we set $d(x, y, t)$ to be the dominant plane, as

$$d(x, y, t) = \begin{cases} 255, & \text{if } (x, y)^\top \text{ is on the dominant plane} \\ 0, & \text{if } (x, y)^\top \text{ is on the obstacle area} \end{cases}.$$

We call $d(x, y, t)$ the dominant plane map.

Our algorithm is summarized as follows:

1. Compute optical flow field $u(x, y, t)$ from two successive images.
2. Compute affine coefficients in Eq.(7) by selecting randomly three points.
3. Estimate planar flow field $\hat{u}(x, y, t)$ from affine coefficients.
4. Match the computed optical flow field $u(x, y, t)$ and estimated planar flow field $\hat{u}(x, y, t)$ using Eq.(9).
5. Assign the points $\left|(\dot{x}, \dot{y})^\top - (\hat{x}, \hat{y})^\top\right| < \varepsilon$ as the dominant plane. If the dominant plane occupies less than the half of the image region, then return to step(2).
6. Output the dominant plane $d(x, y, t)$ as a binary image.

Figure 4 (Top) shows examples of the captured image $I(x, y, t)$ and the detected dominant plane $d(x, y, t)$. Figure 4 (Bottom) shows the optical flow field $u(x, y, t)$ and the planar flow field $\hat{u}(x, y, t)$.

3   Iterative Plane Segmentation

Using the dominant-plane-detection algorithm iteratively, we develop an algorithm for multiple-plane segmentation in an image.

Our basic algorithm detects the dominant plane in an image. After removing the region corresponding to the dominant plane from an image, we can extract

Fig. 4. Examples of dominant plane and optical flow fields. (Top left) Captured image $I(x,y,t)$. (Top right) Detected dominant plane $d(x,y,t)$. The white area is the dominant plane, and the black area is an obstacle. (Bottom left) Optical flow $u(x,y,t)$. (Bottom right) Planar flow $\hat{u}(x,y,t)$.

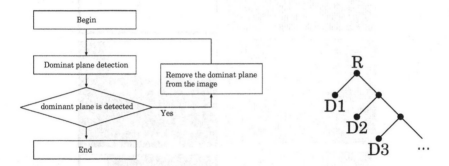

Fig. 5. Iterative plane segmentation algorithm using dominant plane detection. The left figure is the procedure for our algorithm. The right figure is the binary tree, which expresses the hierarchical structure of planar areas. R is the root of the tree and D_k are planes on an image.

the second dominant planar region from the image. Since the first dominant plane is the ground plane from the assamption, the second dominant plane corresponds to obstacle area. Then it is possible to extract the the third dominant plane by removing the second dominant planar area. This process is expressed as

$$D_k = \begin{cases} \mathbf{A}(R \setminus D_{k-1}), & k \geq 2, \\ \mathbf{A}(R), & k = 1, \end{cases} \tag{10}$$

where $\mathbf{A}$, R and D_k stand for the dominant-plane-extraction algorithm, the region of interest observed by a camera, and the k-th dominant planar area, respectively. The algorithm is stopped after iterated to a pre-determined iteration time or the size of k-th dominant plane is smaller th pre-determined size. The procedure of the algorithm is shown in Fig. 5(left).

Fig. 6. Captured image and computed optical flow. There are three orthogonal planes in front of the camera, and the camera moves forward.

Fig. 7. Estimated planar flows and detected dominant planes at each step. First, second, and third rows are the first, second, and third steps for the detection, respectively. The white area is the dominant plane.

Setting R to be the root of the tree, this process derives a binary tree such that

$$R\langle D_1, R \setminus D_1 \langle D_2, R_2 \setminus D_2 \langle \cdots, \rangle \rangle. \tag{11}$$

Assuming that D_1 is the ground plane on which the robot moves, D_k for $k \geq 2$ is the planar areas on the obstacles. Therefore, this tree expresses the hierarchical structure of planar areas on the obstacles. We call this tree the binary tree of planes. The binary tree is illustrated in Fig. 5(right). Using this tree constructed

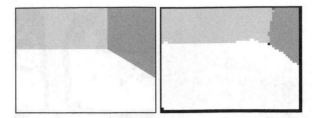

Fig. 8. Ground truth and result. The white area is the first dominant plane. The light-gray and dark-gray areas are second and third dominant plane.

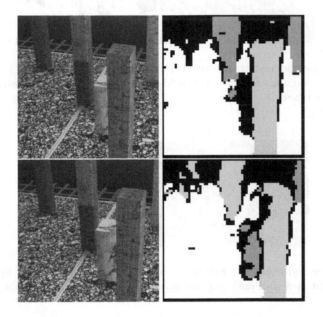

Fig. 9. Image and results estimated from Marbled-Block image sequence[15]. The white area is the first dominant plane. The light-gray and dark-gray areas are second and third dominant plane.

by the dominant-plane detection algorithm, we obtain geometrical properties of planes in a scene. For example, even if an object exists in a scene and it lies on D_k $k \geq 2$, the robot can navigate ignoring this object, using the tree of planes.

4   Experimental Results

First, we use the image sequence captured from a synthetic environment. The first frame of the image sequence is shown in Fig. 6(left). There are three orthogonal planes in front of the camera, and the camera moves forward. Therefore, the computed optical flow is Fig. 6(right). For the computation of optical flow,

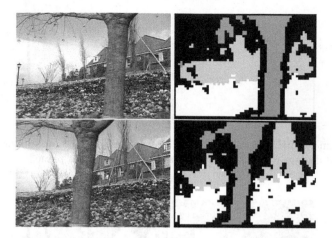

Fig. 10. Images and results estimated from Flower Garden sequence [7]. The white area is the first dominant plane. The light-gray and dark-gray areas are second and third dominant plane.

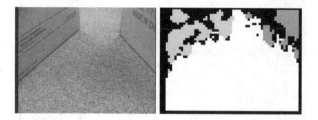

Fig. 11. Image and result in a real environment. The white area is the first dominant plane. The light-gray and dark-gray areas are second and third dominant plane.

we use the Lucas-Kanade method with pyramids [2]. In the experiments, the width of images is 320 pixel. The tolerance for the matching of flow vectors in Eq.(9) is set to be $\varepsilon = 0.2$, which is fixed experimentally.

The top row in Fig. 7 is the estimated planar flow and the detected dominant plane at the first step. In the image of the detected dominant plane, the white and black areas represent the dominant plane and the other area, respectively. In Fig. 7, the middle and bottom rows are the results at the second and third step, respectively. Figure 8 shows the ground truth of the image and the result of the detection. In this figure, the white, light-gray, and dark-gray area are the first, second, and third dominant planes. These results show that our algorithm accurately detects multiple planes in a scene.

Other experimental results are shown in Figs. 9, 10, and 11. The sequences in Figs. 9 and 10 are Marbled-Block image sequence [15] and Flower Garden sequence [7], respectively. The image in Fig. 11 is captured by a camera mounted on a mobile robot in a real environment. The robot moves forward and two obstacles are placed in front of the robot. These results also show that our algorithm accurately detects multiple planes and layers for real image sequences. However, the results obtained from the real image sequence are noisy compared to the synthetic image. These noise are caused by the error of the optical flow computation.

5   Conclusion

Based on our navigation algorithm, which was proposed in reference [18], for an autonomous mobile robot, we introduced a procedure for the decomposition and detection of multiple planar areas in an image. Therefore, our algorithm is capable to use both for navigation in a space and perception of a space for the autonomous mobile robot. This property of the algorithm is the advantage of our method, since an optical flow field is sufficient for the input to the visual-robot-control robot for navigation and perception.

Psychologically, it is known that the optical flow field is a basic cue for the understanding of the motion. Our results also suggest that the optical flow field is a cue for understanding of the obstacle configuration in a workspace.

The application of the binary tree of planes extructed by our algorithm for the spatial recognition is a future problem.

References

1. Barron, J.L., Fleet, D.J., and Beauchemin, S.S.: Performance of optical flow techniques. International Journal of Computer Vision, **12** (1994) 43–77
2. Bouguet, J.-Y.: Pyramidal implementation of the Lucas Kanade feature tracker description of the algorithm. Intel Corporation, Microprocessor Research Labs, OpenCV Documents, (1999)
3. Brox, T., Bruhn, A., and Weickert, J.: Variational motion segmentation with level sets. ECCV'06, (2006) 471–483
4. Chum, O., Werner, T., and Matas, J.: Two-view geometry estimation unaffected by a dominant plane. CVPR'05, **1** (2005) 772–779
5. Enkelmann, W.: Obstacle detection by evaluation of optical flow fields from image sequences. Image and Vision Computing, **9** (1991) 160–168
6. Fischler, M.A. and Bolles, R.C.: Random sample consensus: A paradigm for model fitting with applications to image analysis and automated cartography. Comm. of the ACM, **24** (1981) 381–395
7. Flower Garden sequence, Signal Analysis and Machine Perception Laboratory, Ohio State University,
   available at http://sampl.ece.ohio-state.edu/data/motion/sflowg/index.htm
8. Fraundorfer, F.: A map for mobile robots consisting of a 3D model with augmented salient image features. 26th Workshop of the Austrian Association for Pattern Recognition, (2002) 249–256
9. Guilherme, N. D. and Avinash, C. K.: Vision for mobile robot navigation: A survey. IEEE Trans. on PAMI, **24** (2002) 237–267
10. Hartley, R., and Zisserman, A.: *Multiple View Geometry in Computer Vision*. Cambridge University Press, (2000)

11. Horn, B.K.P. and Schunck, B.G.: Determining optical flow. Artificial Intelligence, **17** (1981) 185–203

12. Kang, S. B. and Szeliski, R.: 3D environment modeling from multiple cylindrical panoramic images. Panoramic Vision: Sensors, Theory, Applications, (2001) 329–358

13. Kaufhold, J., Collins, R., Hoogs, A., and Rondot, P.: Recognition and segmentation of scene content using region-based classification. ICPR'06, (2006) 755–760

14. Lucas, B. and Kanade, T.: An iterative image registration technique with an application to stereo vision. Int. Joint Conf. on Artificial Intelligence, (1981) 674–679

15. Marbled-Block sequence, recorded and first evaluated by Otte and Nagel, KOGS/IAKS, University of Karlsruhe, available at http://i21www.ira.uka.de/image_sequences/

16. Mémin, E. and Pérez, P.: Dense estimation and object-based segmentation of the optical flow with robust techniques. IEEE Trans. on Image Processing, **7** (1998) 703–719

17. Nagel, H.-H. and Enkelmann, W.: An investigation of smoothness constraint for the estimation of displacement vector fields from image sequences. IEEE Trans. on PAMI, **8** (1986) 565–593

18. Ohnishi, N. and Imiya, A.: Featureless robot navigation using optical flow. Connection Science, **17** (2005) 23–46

19. Ohnishi, N. and Imiya, A.: Dominant plane detection from optical flow for robot navigation. Pattern Recognition Letters, **27** (2006) 1009–1021

20. Santos-Victor, J. and Sandini, G.: Uncalibrated obstacle detection using normal flow. Machine Vision and Applications, **9** (1996) 130–137

21. Pears, N. and Liang, B.: Ground plane segmentation for mobile robot visual navigation. IROS'01, (2001) 1513–1518

22. Sturm, P.F. and Maybank, S.J.: On plane-based camera calibration: A general algorithm, singularities, applications. CVPR'99, (1999) 432–437

23. Vaina, L.M., Beardsley, S.A., and Rushton, S.K.: *Optic flow and beyond*. Kluwer Academic Publishers, (2004)

24. Weiss, Y.: Smoothness in layers: Motion segmentation using nonparametric mixture estimation. CVPR, (1997) 520–527

25. Wang, J.Y.A. and Adelson, E.H.: Representing moving images with layers. IEEE Trans. on Image Processing Special Issue: Image Sequence Compression, **3**, (1994) 625–638

26. Xiao, J. and Shah, M.: Accurate motion layer segmentation and matting. CVPR'05, **2** (2005) 698–703

27. Yang, A.Y., Rao, S., Wagner, A., and Ma, Y.: Segmentation of a piece-wise planar scene from perspective images. CVPR'05, **1** (2005) 154–161

28. Zucchelli, M., Santos-Victor, J., and Christensen, H.I.: Multiple plane segmentation using optical flow. BMVC'02, (2002)

A Study on Eye Gaze Estimation Method Based on Cornea Model of Human Eye

Eui Chul Lee[1] and Kang Ryoung Park[2]

[1] Dept. of Computer Science, Sangmyung University,
7 Hongji-dong, Jongro-Ku, Seoul, Republic of Korea
Biometrics Engineering Research Center (BERC)
oryong@smu.ac.kr
[2] Division of Digital Media Technology, Sangmyung University,
7 Hongji-dong, Jongro-Ku, Seoul, Republic of Korea
Biometrics Engineering Research Center (BERC)
parkgr@smu.ac.kr

Abstract. In this paper, we propose a new gaze estimation method by analyzing the cornea surface model which is estimated through three dimensional analysis of human eye in HMD (Head Mounted Display) environments. This paper has four advantages over previous works. First, in order to obtain accurate gaze position, we use a cornea sphere model based on Gullstrand eye scheme. Second, we calculate the 3D position of the cornea sphere and a gaze vector by using a camera, three collimated IR-LEDs and one illuminated IR-LED. Third, three coordinates such as camera, monitor and eye coordinates are unified, which can simplify the complex 3D converting calculation and allow for calculation of the 3D eye position and gaze position on a HMD monitor. Fourth, a simple user dependent calibration method is proposed by gazing at one position of HMD monitor based on Kappa compensation. Experimental results showed that the average gaze estimation error of the proposed method was 0.89 degrees.

1 Introduction

Gaze estimation is the procedure of detecting the position on a monitor plane that a user is looking at. Gaze estimation for desktop monitor environments has been widely researched. However, comparatively little has been done about gaze estimation for HMD (Head Mounted Display) environment. We propose a new vision-based gaze detecting method by using a small camera, an illuminated IR-LED (Infra-Red Light Emitting Diode) and three collimated IR-LEDs in HMD.

Researches about gaze estimation can be classified into two categories: the two-dimensional (2D) and the three-dimensional (3D) approaches. The 2D approach does not consider the 3D motion or the 3D structure of the eyes. This approach transforms the coordinates of the eye features or eye intensity values in a 2D image frame into the coordinates of the gaze point in the 2D monitor plane by using "mapping functions" [1][17]. Recently, several 3D approaches have been reported, which utilize a high resolution eye image captured by a zoom-in camera [2][3]. Since the camera

A. Gagalowicz and W. Philips (Eds.): MIRAGE 2007, LNCS 4418, pp. 307–317, 2007.

captures only one eye, it produces enough resolution to analyze 3D movements. The advantages of the above 3D approach are more accurate with simple user-dependent calibration compared to those of 2D approach. All the 2D and 3D techniques mentioned above were developed in desktop monitor and they are difficult to be used in HMD monitor due to the weight limitation of camera system [15]. In desktop monitor environments, there is no physical limitation to the camera systems. So, focus and zoom control cameras, multiple lenses, pan/tilt equipment and sometimes stereo cameras can be used [2][3]. However, in HMD environments, the camera system attached on HMD must be as light as possible because users wear it. It is impractical to employ complicated camera systems like stereo cameras or multiple lenses.

To overcome such problems, we propose a new gaze estimation method based on 3D approach by using a small USB (Universal Serial Bus) camera, an illuminated IR-LED and three collimated IR-LED illuminators in HMD environment.

2   The Proposed Method

Fig.1 shows our gaze detection system in HMD environment based on following policies. First, we use a monocular camera with a single lens. Second, we Model a cornea sphere for calculating the equation of human eyeball. Third, we use a 3D approach to eye gaze estimation based on user-dependent calibration by gazing at only one position of HMD monitor.

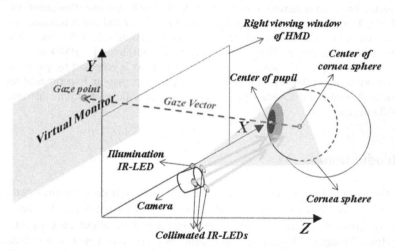

Fig. 1. Overview of proposed gaze detection system in an HMD environment

We used a monocular camera without complex lenses to ensure that the system was lightweight. Also, our system did not require the complicated user dependent calibration. For that, we used a cornea sphere model to calculate the equation of human eyeball. And, we used three collimated IR-LEDs to measure the accurate 3D positions of cornea sphere and final gaze point on a virtual monitor plane of HMD.

2.1 Proposed Gaze Detection System

As shown in Fig.1, our gaze detection system is a vision-based one which consists of a HMD system [4], a small sized USB camera [5], one illumination IR-LED (850nm) and three collimated IR-LEDs (880nm) [6].

Our HMD system has the display resolution of 800(horizontal) pixels by 600(vertical) pixels and the field of view of 26 degrees diagonal. Also, virtual image size is same to the size of when user sees the 70*inch* at 3937*mm* away from right viewing window of Fig. 1.

In our system, we use infrared LEDs of two types. One of them is the collimated IR-LEDs. Their illumination angle is so narrow(2.9°) that we could generate small bright spots on cornea surface in order to estimate the cornea sphere equation. In section 2.4, we will describe the method of estimating cornea equation by using these collimated IR-LEDs. Another infrared LED is the illumination IR-LED. Because the illumination angle of this IR-LED is so wide(36°), we could capture the appropriate eye images having a clear edge between pupil and iris through illuminating the entire eye region.

In used camera, by attaching an IR-pass filter in front of the camera lens and using IR illuminators, our system is robust to environmental lighting conditions. In addition, since we used invisible IR lights, we were able to reduce the 'dazzling' effect on the user's eye. Also, since we used a USB camera, a frame grabber board was not required. This helped to keep the weight of the system be a minimum. For eye image capturing, we used the spatial resolution of 640×480 pixels with a frame rate of 15 frames per second.

2.2 Human Eye and Cornea Sphere Model

First, we analyze the 3D structure of the human eye. Based on the Gullstrand human eye scheme which represents the structure of the human eye very accurately [9], we can apply this scheme to our gaze estimation method. Based on that eye scheme,

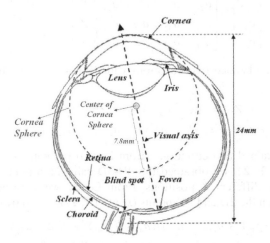

Fig. 2. Human eye and cornea sphere model [10]

he reported that the anterior cornea was a sphere whose radius was 7.8mm. Since this anterior cornea is the exterior prominent part of human eye, we can observe it by using the camera attached on HMD as shown in Fig. 1. Also, since the anterior cornea surface is a sphere with the radius of 7.8mm, we can estimate the equation of cornea sphere by using three collimated IR-LEDs as shown in Eq.(6) (see section 2.4).

2.3 Camera Calibration

In our system, we defined three coordinate: monitor, camera and eye. Because the camera was attached below the monitor plane (in HMD environment), it was necessary to consider the panning and tilting angle of the camera coordinates in relation to the monitor coordinates. Also, there are the translational vector between the monitor coordinate and the gimbals of the camera and that between the gimbals and the CCD center.

That is because users gaze at a point on the monitor, and then the eye feature point is projected to the camera coordinate. So, in order to obtain the 2D perspective point (c_h) of w_h of the camera coordinate, we first aligned the camera and monitor coordinates as shown in Eq.(1) [7][18].

$$c_h = PCRGw_h \tag{1}$$

Here, P is the perspective transform matrix, and C is the translation matrix between the gimbal center and the CCD center. R is the rotation matrix caused by panning and tilting angle of the camera coordinate in relation to the monitor coordinate. G is the translation matrix between the monitor coordinate and the gimbal center of the camera.

To determine (calibrate) the internal and external camera parameters, we defined Eq. (1) as $c_h = Aw_h$ (here, $A = PCRG$) by homogeneous representation as shown in Eq. (2) [7] [18].

$$\begin{bmatrix} c_{h1} \\ c_{h2} \\ c_{h3} \\ c_{h4} \end{bmatrix} = \begin{bmatrix} a_{11} & a_{12} & a_{13} & a_{14} \\ a_{21} & a_{22} & a_{23} & a_{24} \\ a_{31} & a_{32} & a_{33} & a_{34} \\ a_{41} & a_{42} & a_{43} & a_{44} \end{bmatrix} \begin{bmatrix} X \\ Y \\ Z \\ 1 \end{bmatrix} \tag{2}$$

From Eq.(2), we obtained two equations with 12 unknown coefficients, as shown in Eq.(3).

$$a_{11}X + a_{12}Y + a_{13}Z - a_{41}xX - a_{42}xY - a_{43}xZ - a_{44}x + a_{14} = 0$$
$$a_{21}X + a_{22}Y + a_{23}Z - a_{41}yX - a_{42}yY - a_{43}yZ - a_{44}y + a_{24} = 0 \tag{3}$$

Because we obtained two equations (from Eq.(3)) per pair of 2D-3D calibration points (x, y) - (X, Y, Z), we obtained the 2D-3D calibration points by a calibration panel according to different Z positions. From Eq.(3), we were able to obtain the relationship between the 2D and 3D points (x, y) - (X, Y, Z), as shown in Eq.(4).

$$x = (a_{11}X + a_{12}Y + a_{13}Z - a_{14})/(a_{41}X + a_{42}Y + a_{43}Z + a_{44})$$
$$y = (a_{21}X + a_{22}Y + a_{23}Z - a_{24})/(a_{41}X + a_{42}Y + a_{43}Z + a_{44}) \tag{4}$$

With the calculated $a_{11} \sim a_{44}$ and Eq.(2), we were able to obtain the 2D position (c_h) of the camera coordinate from the 3D points (w_h) of the monitor coordinate. In addition, with the $a_{11} \sim a_{44}$, Eq.(2) and the known Z distance, we were able to obtain the 3D points (w_h) in the monitor coordinate from the 2D position (c_h) in the camera coordinate.

2.4 Calculating Cornea Sphere Equation by Three Points on the Cornea Surface

In this paper, we use a Z-distance measuring method that uses only one gaze detection camera and a collimated IR-LED. This method is shown in Fig. 3 [8][18].

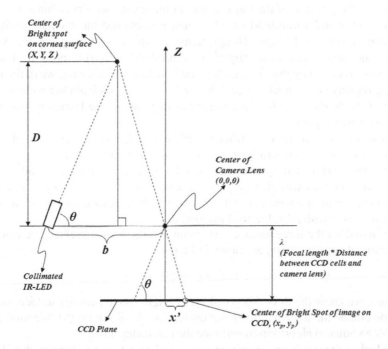

Fig. 3. Measuring Z-distance between camera and eye by a camera and a collimated IR-LED[8]

In Fig. 3, **b** is the distance between the collimated IR-LED and the center of the camera lens, θ is the angle between the lens plane and the direction of the collimated IR-LED, **x'** is the distance between the center of the bright spot in the image and the center of the image. Here, **b** and θ did not change after the initial setup of camera and the collimated IR-LED. So, we obtained the values by initial camera calibration and used them as constant values. (x_p, y_p) is the image coordinate point of the bright spot center which is shaped by the collimated IR-LED. From that, the Z distance (D) of the bright spot was calculated as follows [8]:

$$D = \frac{b \cdot \lambda}{\lambda \cdot \cot \theta + x'} \tag{5}$$

So, by using three bright spots made by three collimated IR-LEDs, we could obtain accurate equation of the cornea sphere based on the measured three Z-distance(D)s and Eq.(6).

In captured eye images, there were three bright spots in the input image, which were generated by the three collimated IR-LEDs, respectively. The collimated IR-LEDs (880 nm) have narrow illumination angles and are used for measuring the Z distance between the eye and the camera. On the other hand, the Illuminated IR-LED (850 nm) has a wide illumination angle and is used for illuminating the entire eye region. In addition, the pupil center is used for calculating the user's gaze vector. So, we detected the pupil region by using the illumination IR-LED and we detected the bright spots by using three collimated IR-LEDs.

To detect the position of the pupil center in the image, we firstly binarized the input image (by using a threshold of 30). Then, we obtained the accurate position by component labeling and ellipse Hough transform in the searching region. We then binarized the input image again (by using a threshold of 200) in order to detect the bright spots produced by the three collimated IR-LEDs. In this case, we defined three searching regions in the input image. Then, we were able to obtain the accurate center position of the bright spots by component labeling and ellipse Hough transform [14] in each searching region.

Because we used an IR-Pass filter (which passes IR light over a wavelength of 750nm) in front of the camera lens with an IR-LED illuminator, the variance of the image brightness (affected by environmental lighting) was not great. In addition, the HMD monitor (which was closely positioned in front of the user's eye) was able to block some amount of environmental light. Due to those reasons, we were easily able to determine the threshold value for binarization.

Then, based on the three obtained 3D points on the cornea surface, we calculated the equation of cornea sphere, as shown in Eq.(6).

$$(x - x_c)^2 + (y - y_c)^2 + (z - z_c)^2 = 7.8^2 \tag{6}$$

Because we knew the three 3D positions of bright spot on cornea surface, we were able to determine the three unknown parameters (X_c, Y_c, Z_c) in Eq.(6). We used a LMS (Least Mean Square) algorithm to estimate the parameters [16].

To calculate the user's gaze position on a HMD monitor, we obtained the 3D position of the pupil center. For that, we detected the pupil center in the 2D and obtained the 3D line which passes through the pupil center and the center of the camera lens based on Eq.(1). Then, we obtained the 3D position of the pupil center which is the intersected point of the 3D line and the calculated cornea sphere equation. Based on the detected 3D positions of the pupil center and the center of cornea sphere, we were able to obtain the gaze direction in the HMD monitor coordinate.

2.5 Compensating Angle Kappa

However, we should compensate for the discrepancy between the pupillary and the visual axis in order to obtain a more accurate gaze position. We define the "papillary axis" as the line passing through the center of the pupil perpendicularly to the pupil plane [10].

When a human gazes at an object, the eye rotates to make light rays fall on the fovea. The fovea is a small area in the retina where most cones are located. The line passing through the pupil center and the fovea is called the line of sight or "visual axis", which represents a true gaze vector. Generally, the "visual axis" does not coincide with the "pupillary axis". There exists an angular discrepancy usually known as angle Kappa between the two axes. However, the "visual axis" is more difficult to measure because the fovea is invisible [12].

The Kappa variance is so great [13] and it can increase final gaze error much. To overcome such problem in our system, when each person uses our gaze system, he or she is requested to gaze at the one point of monitor plane at initial user-dependent calibration stage [18]. From that, the angle Kappa is measured based on offset between the position of pupillary arrival point and the one point of monitor. Through user dependent calibration like this, we could compensate the discrepancy having individual variation caused by angle Kappa.

2.6   Calculating Gaze Position on a Virtual Monitor Screen of HMD

Conventional HMD systems use a convex lens in front of a physical monitor screen and the user can see the magnified virtual monitor screen. From the HMD specifications [4], we know the size of the virtual monitor screen and the distance between the physical and virtual monitor screen. In addition, the size of the virtual monitor screen corresponds to the monitor resolution of our HMD virtual screen (800 × 600 pixels).

Based on the HMD spec. [4], we obtained the 3D position of the virtual monitor screen as $Z = -3,937$ from the right viewing window plane of Fig. 1. We then calculated the gaze position on the virtual monitor screen from the intersection point between the gaze vector and $Z = -3,937$. In this case, as mentioned in section 2.5, the directional angle of gaze vector is previously compensated by the measured angle Kappa, horizontally and vertically.

3   Experimental Results

Our gaze detection algorithm was tested with a Pentium-IV 2.4 GHz CPU. To measure accuracy, we performed a following test. A total of 50 users were asked to gaze at 12 specific points, as shown in Fig. 4. The test was iterated 20 times. Experimental results showed that the average gaze detection error was about 0.89°.

In the first experiment, we compared the accuracy of our method to that of a conventional 3D method [2]. In this experiment of measuring the accuracy of the conventional 3D approach (which was applied to our HMD environment), we compensate the angle Kappa by using our method as shown section 2.5. Fig. 4 (b) shows an example of the conventional gaze point estimation result. Experimental results show that the gaze error of the conventional 3D method was 1.1 degrees, which was greater than ours. That is because conventional 3D methods [2] are optimized for gaze estimation

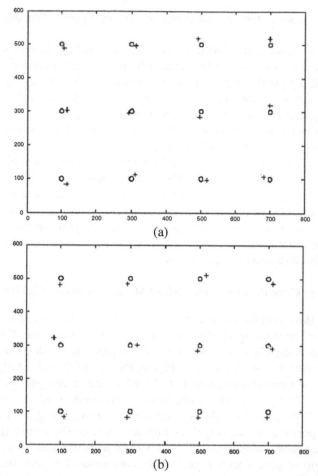

Fig. 4. Examples of gaze detection results when using the proposed method compared to those when using a conventional 3D approach [2]. (a) Example of gaze results when using the proposed method. (b) Example of gaze results when using a conventional 3D approach [2] (Reference points are marked with "○" and estimated gaze points are marked with "+").

in desktop environments. The advantage of our proposed method is that since it can automatically compute the 3D position of the cornea surface by using three collimated IR-LEDs and a calibration matrix, the estimated 3D position of the eyeball and the final gaze position are very accurate having the gaze error of 0.89 degrees. Also, our method requires user to gaze at only one point for user-dependent calibration.

In the next experiment, we compared the accuracy of our method to that of the 2D method. The 2D method uses functions which map 2D eye feature points into the gaze position in the virtual screen of a HMD monitor without calculating the 3D position or the direction of the eyeball and the monitor [1][11].

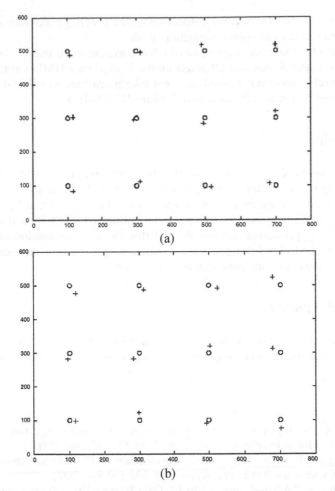

Fig. 5. Examples of gaze detection results using linear interpolation and the geometric transform method. (a) Example of the gaze result using linear interpolation (b) Example of the gaze result using the geometric transform method.

The 2D method uses two kinds of mapping functions, which are the linear interpolation mapping function [1] and the geometric transform mapping function [10][11]. The linear interpolation method requires that the user minimally gazes at two positions on a monitor (such as the upper-right corner and the lower-left corner positions of the virtual screen). Based on the two-gaze position information, other gaze positions can be calculated by linear interpolation. To increase gaze detection accuracy, four positions (such as the upper-right, lower-right, upper-left and lower-left positions of the virtual screen) may be used in the user calibration stage [1]. However, since the virtual screen is rectangle, they use the geometric transform method for mapping points between the distorted quadrangle and rectangle [10][11]. Experimental results showed that the RMS errors of gaze detection by linear interpolation and geometric transform were 1.8 and 1.2 degrees, respectively, which were greater than ours. Fig. 5 shows examples of the gaze point estimation results.

In experimental result, the gaze error of 0.89° corresponds to that of about 34 pixels (27 pixels on the X axis and 20 pixels on the Y axis) on a HMD virtual screen of 800 × 600 pixels. Also, our method does not take much time to calculate the user's gaze position on a monitor (26 ms with a Pentium-IV 2.4GHz).

4 Conclusion

In this paper, we present a new method for estimating gaze points with requiring user to gaze at only one point for user-dependent calibration. In order to estimate the 3D direction of an eyeball, we used a cornea sphere model and calculated the 3D position of the cornea eyeball by using a camera, three collimated IR-LEDs and one illuminated IR-LED. Experimental results showed that the gaze estimation error of our proposed method was 0.89 degree. In future work, we plan to measure gaze detection accuracy in various environments with more field tests.

Acknowledgements

This work was supported by the Korea Science and Engineering Foundation (KOSEF) through the Biometrics Engineering Research Center (BERC) at Yonsei University.

References

1. J. Kim et al., "Intelligent process control via gaze detection technology," Engineering Appl ications of Artificial Intelligence, vol. 13, no. 5, pp. 577-587, Aug. 2000.
2. J. G. Wang and E. Sung, "Study on eye gaze estimation," IEEE Transactions on Systems, Man and Cybernetics, Part B, vol. 32, no. 3, pp. 332-350, June 2002.
3. S. W. Shih et al., "A Novel Approach to 3-D Gaze Tracking Using Stereo Cameras," IEEE Trans. on SMC, Part B, vol. 34, no. 1, pp. 234-245, Feb. 2004.
4. http://www.i-glassesstore.com, (accessed on October 20th, 2005)
5. http://www.logitech.com, (accessed on October 20th, 2005)
6. http://www.acroname.com, (accessed on September 20th, 2005)
7. Mubarak Shah, "Fundamentals of Computer Vision", pp. 9-14, 1992.
8. Ramesh Jain, Rangachar Kasturi, Brian G.Schunck, "Machine Vision", McGraw-Hill Inte rnational Editions, pp. 301-302, 1995.
9. Gullstrand A, "Helmholz's physiological optics", Optical Society of America, pp. 350-358, 1924.
10. Rafael C. Gonzalez, Richard E. Woods, "Digital Image Processing", Prentice-Hall, Inc., Se cond Edition, 2002
11. Jeong Jun Lee et al., "Gaze detection system under HMD environments for user interface", the Joint Conference of ICANN/ICONIP, Istanbul, Turkey, June 26-29, 2003.
12. Eskridge JB et al., "The Hirschberg test: a double-masked clinical evaluation", American j ournal of optometry and physiological optics, September, 1988.
13. F. Schaeffel, "Kappa and Hirschberg Ratio Measured with an Automated Video Gaze Trac ker", Optometry & Vision Science. Vol. 79(5), pp.329-334, May 2002

14. Rafael C. Gonzalez, Richard E. Woods, "Digital Image Processing", Prentice-Hall, Inc., Se cond Edition, pp 587-591, 2002
15. Jeong Jun Lee, "Three Dimensional Eye Gaze Estimation in Wearable Monitor Environme nt", Ph.D Thesis, Yonsei University, 2005
16. Steven C. Chapra *et al.*, "Numerical Methods for Engineers", McGraw-Hill, 1989
17. K.R. Park et al., "Gaze Position Detection by Computing the 3-Dimensional Facial Positio ns and Motions", Pattern Recognition, Vol. 35, No.11, pp.2559~2569, 2002
18. Eui Chul Lee, "A Study on Gaze Tracking Method based on Three Dimensional Analysis o f Human Eye", Samsung Human-Tech Paper Award, submitted.

Generation of Expression Space for Realtime Facial Expression Control of 3D Avatar

Sung-Ho Kim

School of Computer, Information and Communication Engineering, Sangji Univ.
660 Usan-dong, Wonju, Gangwon-do 220-702, Korea
kimsh1204@sangji.ac.kr

Abstract. This paper describes expression space generation technology that enables animators to control the expressions of 3-dimensional avatars in real-time by selecting a series of expressions from facial expression space. In this system, approximately 2400 facial expression frames are used to generate facial expression space. In this paper, distance matrixes that present distances between facial characteristic points are used to show the state of an expression. The set of these distance matrixes is defined as facial expression space. However, this facial expression space is not space that can be transferred to one space or another in a straight line, when one expression changes to another. In this technology, the route for moving from one expression to another is approximately inferred from captured facial expression data. First, it is assumed that two expressions are close to each other when the distance between distance matrixes that show facial expression states is below a certain value. When two random facial expression states are connected with the set of a series of adjacent expressions, it is assumed that there is a route between the two expressions. It is further assumed that the shortest path between two facial expressions is the path when one expression moves to the other expression. Dynamic programming is used to find the shortest path between two facial expressions. The facial expression space, which is the set of these distance matrixes, is multidimensional space. The facial expression control of 3-dimensional avatars is carried out in real-time when animators navigate through facial expression space. In order to assist this task, multidimensional scaling is used for visualization in 2-dimensional space, and animators are told to control facial expressions when using this system. This paper evaluates the results of the experiment.

1 Introduction

Humans express feelings better using facial expressions than language. This is why there has been much research[1],[2],[3],[4], [13], [14], [15], [17] on how to show facial expressions using 3-dimensional computer graphics. Recently, as character animation[16] that uses motion capture has become popular in computer animation, the facial motion of actors have been captured to be used in 3-dimensional character animation. Generally, there are two ways to use captured data. One is motion retargeting, to apply the motion data of an actor to a new model[4],

A. Gagalowicz and W. Philips (Eds.): MIRAGE 2007, LNCS 4418, pp. 318–329, 2007.
© Springer-Verlag Berlin Heidelberg 2007

[12]. Motion retargeting, was developed for body motion[12] and then developed for facial expressions[4]. But, this paper doesn't deal with motion retargeting. The other way is to generate new actions by selecting and connecting a certain pose stored in the database, built by capturing an many actor's actions as possible. This method was developed first for body motion [5] and then developed for facial expressions[18]. But, [18] proposed data-driven animation system for expressive facial animation synthesis and editing. However, no method has been developed for facial expression control yet. Therefore, this paper describes the way to generate facial expression space for real-time facial expression control, by distributing facial motion capture data into intuitive space and allowing animators to select their own facial expressions.

First, facial expressions are captured with the help of a face actor, by using an optical motion capture system. One hundred reflection markers are placed on the actors major facial muscles. Then, ten different facial expressions are made, to be captured at 60 frames per second. Every facial motion begins from an expressionless state to a specific expression, and then it changes back to the initial expressionless state. As one marker has three coordinate values, one facial expression is 300-dimensional data. In order to generate facial expression space by deciding the shortest path between two arbitrary facial expressions, and check the space with eyes, Multidimensional Scaling(MDS)[8],[9] is used to project it on 2-dimensional space. In order to control the facial expression in real-time, animators are told to navigate projected 2-dimensional space, and a 3-dimensional face model of actor, which is created by points of a navigation route is displayed in real-time.

Chapter 2 deals with facial motion data captured by the optical motion capture system. Chapter 3 suggests a facial expression state expression method to express facial states based on facial motion data. Also, it calculates the distance between facial expression states using the facial expression state expression method, and describes how to generate facial expression space. With MDS, chapter 4 reduces multidimensional facial expression space in 2-dimensional space, and projects it to the 2-dimensional plane. Chapter 5 uses the user interface developed in this paper to analyze test results for controlling 3-dimensional avatar facial expressions created by navigating facial expression space projected on the 2-dimensional plane. Finally, chapter 6 presents research results and concludes this paper.

2   Facial Motion Capture

In order to control 3-dimensional avatar facial expressions with facial motion data, the following pre-steps should be done. First, the optical motion capture system captures actor's facial expressions. The system used in this paper is an optical motion capture system by Motion Analysis, which uses eight Falcon cameras specifically developed for facial expression capture. In facial expression capture, one hundred reflection markers are attached to an actor's major facial muscles. Then, the actor makes ten different expressions to be captured at 60 frames per second. Each facial motion begins from an expressionless state to a certain facial state, then returns to the initial expressionless state. This process takes on average three to five seconds. One marker has 3-dimensional coordinate values, meaning one facial status contains 300-dimensional data. The front photo of the actor is used for 3-dimensional face modeling. In addition, by connecting one hundred markers with each 3-dimensional avatar's facial part (the position of a marker), it is possible to generate facial expressions. In order to achieve this, we use 3D Studio MAX R5.1 and Bones Pro V3.0, which are plug-ins for 3D Studio Max.

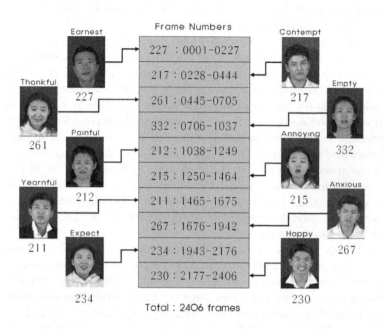

Fig. 1. Consolidation of ten motion data captured by actor. Ten facial expression images used to motion capture by actor. (Numbers under figures are the number of frames of each motion).

As facial motion data are gathered by capturing the responses of the actor, and the number of frames for each facial expression is different, as shown in Fig. 1. Motion data captured by the motion capture system is composed of various file information(DataRate, CameraRate, NumFrames, NumMarkers, Units, OrigDataRate, OrigDataStartFrame, OrigNumFrames) and the frame number, time, and marker's 3-dimensional position data of each frame. In this paper, as only each marker's 3-dimensional position data are needed, other data are deleted. Also, ten motion data composed only by marker's position data are put together as shown in Fig. 1, to generate one continuous motion file with a total of 2406 frames. In Fig. 1, the numbers under each picture are the number of frames of motion data, and the numbers accumulated in the middle are the added numbers of frame data according to order of motion data.

3   Generation of Facial Expression Space

3.1   Representation of Facial Expression State

In order to generate facial expression space, each facial expression state should be presented in numbers. A facial expression state is decided by the positions of each marker on the face. The expression of a facial expression state should well describe the relative distance between facial expressions. The simplest way to describe facial expression states is to use state vectors composed of markers' positions. In this paper, as one hundred markers are used and each has three coordinate values, facial expression state vectors are 300-dimensional. Let's call this method "position vector". When facial expression states are described in this paper, position vectors are not used. Instead, "distance matrixes", which describe the distance between two arbitrary markers are used. This is because distance matrixes can hold more information on markers' distribution states than position vectors; therefore, they can describe more accurately the distance between two facial expressions. When two position vectors are compared, the distance between the two expressions is calculated. In this case, the distance between the facial expressions of each marker are calculated regardless of other markers. Compared to this, if distance matrixes describe facial expression states, the correlations between facial expressions are naturally taken into consideration. Of course, the distance matrixes of facial expressions can be acquired from the position vectors of facial expressions; however, as information of position vectors are not used to calculate the distance between states, the fact that position vectors have useful information is not helpful. Therefore, distance matrixes that describe information clearly are a better way to describe states.

The distance matrix method, which is based on sets of distance between markers is as follows. The distance between markers is calculated from one frame, and position vectors are coordinated with 4950, to express facial expression states. We removed global rotation and translation in advance from the first frame of the first motion as it uses only relative measurements. This could also be achieved in the original space by removing global offsets. The set of points of 4950-dimensional space,X can be calculated as shown in formula 1

$$X = \{m_f \times (m_f - 1)/2\}, f = 1, ..., 2406 \tag{1}$$

Here, m is constant 100, which is the number of reflection markers. f is the number of facial expression states. In this chapter, 2406 facial expression states composed of 4950-dimensional data are gathered.

3.2   Generation of Facial Expression Space

When facial expression states are described with distance matrixes, the straight distance between facial expressions is expressed in the straight distance between the two distance matrixes. A facial expression state is decided by deciding the distance between two arbitrary distance matrixes. In this paper, a distance matrix is considered as a vector. And the straight distance between these vectors are used as straight distance between distance matrixes. This means, two facial expressions, which have similar distance between two arbitrary markers, are considered to be adjacent expressions. Facial expression space is not vector space that can express distance between two facial expressions as straight distance between two arbitrary facial expressions. This is because various limits of a face make the process from one expression to another expression move through complex routes. Facial expression space is manifold space similar to a sphere. Distance in the manifold space is defined as the distance of the shortest route between two points that are not out of space[7]. In this paper, this manifold space approximated. In order to do this, when the distance between two distance matrixes is under a certain value, it is considered that the straight distance is close to the shortest path between the two expressions. These two expressions that satisfy this condition are called an "Adjacent facial expression," and facial expressions close to arbitrary expressions are decided as shown in Fig. 2.

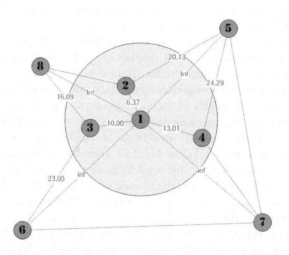

Fig. 2. Graph creation method for Floyd algorithm: The adjacent facial expression state vector is the facial state vector belonging to a virtual circle, with specification distance value to radius for each other frame. Given eight states, state 2, 3, and 4 are adjacent to state 1. The states 5, 6, 7 and 8 are not adjacent. Distance between adjacent facial expressions is given by a certain value. The distance between non adjacent facial expressions is infinitive. This means that one state cannot move to another state directly. A radius shows the adjacent distance limit.

When an adjacent facial expression is given, it is considered that one expression can move to the other expression. It is assumed that when two expressions are not close to each other, they can move to each other only via the facial expressions between them. However, it is not easy to decide the limit distance for adjacent facial expressions. Therefore, the optimal distance should be decided by conducting many tests. However, the adjacent distance threshold should be set to have enough adjacent facial expressions that are needed for one arbitrary facial expression to move to the adjacent facial expression. When adjacent facial expressions are decided, the distance between two facial expressions which are adjacent to each other is decided by adding the distance of adjacent facial expression between them. In order to achieve this, Floyd algorithm(Dynamic Programming)[6] is used. When the shortest path between two arbitrary facial expressions is decided, the corresponding manifold space is decided. In this paper, over 2400 facial expressions are used to form manifold space.

4   Multidimensional Scaling(MDS)

The manifold space of facial expression created in the previous stage is 4950-dimensional space. However, in this space, an animator cannot choose a facial expression that he wants. Therefore, 2-dimensional or 3-dimensional facial expression space that describes approximately the original facial expression space is first acquired, and then the space is navigated. In this paper 2-dimensional space is generated. To do this, MDS is used. MDS is a method to get the sets of coordinate values that represent the distribution of these values, when the distance between multidimensional data is given. In this case, the dimensions of coordinates should be decided in advance. In this paper, since coordinate values are presented visually, 2-dimensional coordinates are used.

Let's say n points, with facial expression state in multi-dimensional manifold space, are $x_1, ..., x_n$ in X, and manifold distance between arbitrary facial expression state x_i and x_j in X are $d_{ij}, i, j = 1, ..., n$. The distance matrix composed of d_{ij} is $\{d_{ij}\}$. Matrix, $D = \{d_{ij}\}$ is a symmetric matrix, with diagonal elements all 0. This is usually called non-similar symmetric matrix in MDS theory. Let's say points in p dimensional space that describe approximately multidimensional facial expression space are $y_i, ..., y_n$. Each y_i is called a configuration vector. The configuration vectors are mostly used to be visualized, p is usually 2 or 3. Let's say the distance between point y_i and y_j of p-dimensional space is δ_{ij}. Generally, when MDS is applied, we can find the set of points of p-dimensional space, $Y = \{y_i\}$, which can have $\{\delta_{ij}\}$, have the most approximate distribution to D, the set of the distance of multidimensional manifold. Set Y can be described as $n \times p$ and is called the configuration matrix. MDS relys on optimization strategies.

There are three different optimizing functions. The first is to minimum the square function of distance, $STRESS(y_1, ..., y_n) = \sum_{i,j=1}^{n}(d_{ij} - \delta_{ij})^2$. The second is to minimum square function of distance square, $SSTRESS(y_1, ..., y_n) = \sum_{i,j=1}^{n}(d_{ij}^2 - \delta_{ij}^2)^2$. Here, $STRESS$ comes from "Standard Residual Sum of Squares." This kind of optimization problem involves the initial coordinates of variable $\{y_i\}$. Basically, variable $\{y_i\}$'s initial coordinates are decided randomly or by $PCA(Principal\ Component\ Analysis)$. When optimization is carried out, variable $\{y_i\}$ is updated until the optimizing function has a minimum value. The third optimizing function, which is used in this paper, is not about obtaining the closest distance matrix $\{\delta_{ij}\}$ to D, but about obtaining $Y = \{y_i\}$, the set of points of p-dimensional plane after acquiring matrix $B = \{b_{ij}\}$, the closest matrix to matrix $\{(\tau\delta_{ij}^2)\}$ is transformed from D. In this case, the optimizing function is described as formula 2, and called STRAIN function[9], [10]. STRAIN is the "Standardized Residual sum of squares between the quantities And the Inner products."

$$STRAIN(B) = \sum_{i,j=1}^{n} (b_{ij} - \tau(d_{ij}^2))^2 \tag{2}$$

Here, $B = \{b_{ij}\}$ is a positive semidefinite matrix with a rank under p. $\{\tau(d_{ij}^2)\} = -\frac{1}{2}H\{d_{ij}^2\}H$. $H = I - \frac{J}{n}$. Here, I_n is n's identity matrix, J is a $n \times n$ square matrix of all elements of which are 1. The method to find matrix B, which minimizes formula 2 and is acquired $Y = \{y_i\}$, is based on well-developed theories. This method is developed by Torgerson[9] and Mardia[10]. The first part is to obtain matrix, B which minimizes formula 2. The second part is to obtain set, $\{y_i\}$ from matrix B. Let's assume a matrix that minimizes formula 2 is B^*. The optimizing matrix, B^* is acquired with the eigenvalue and eigenvector of $B^0 = \{\tau(d_{ij}^2)\}$. Let's assume B^0's eigenvalues are $\lambda_1 \geq ... \geq \lambda_n > 0$. ($B^0$ is positive semidefinite, and all eigenvalues are bigger than 0). Let's say the eigenvectors for them are $v_1, ..., v_n$. When $\lambda_i^+ = max(\lambda_i, 0), i = 1, ..., p$, and $\lambda_i^+ = 0, i = p+1, ..., n$, formula 2's global minimizer can be described as formula 3.

$$B^* = \sum_{i=1}^{n} \lambda_i^+ v_i v_i' = \sum_{i=1}^{p} \lambda_i^+ v_i v_i' \tag{3}$$

The set $\{y_i\}$ is acquired by using matrix B^* from formula 3 which is the optimizing matrix of formula 2. The matrix B^* can be described as formula 4. In this case, Y is the set of points, $\{y_1, ... y_n\}$.

$$B^* = YY' \tag{4}$$

The matrix B^* can be expressed as formula 5 by factorizing.

$$B^* = \Gamma \Lambda \Gamma^T \tag{5}$$

Here, $\Lambda = diag(\Lambda_1^+, ..., \Lambda_p^+)$. It is a diagonal matrix of matrix B^*'s eigenvalues. $\Gamma = (v_1, ..., v_p)$, which is the matrix of eigenvectors matching eigenvalues. Therefore, the set of p-dimensional points, Y can be calculated as shown in formula 6.

$$Y = \Gamma \Lambda^{\frac{1}{2}} = \{v_i \sqrt{\lambda_i^+}\}, i = 1, ..., p \tag{6}$$

The set of points on 2-dimensional plane, $\{y_i\}$ is acquired from formula 6 by setting $v = 2$.

5   Verification and Experiment Results

5.1   Verification

In the experiment, with facial expression states described as distance matrixes, adjacent distance thresholds, which decide adjacent facial expressions, should be optimized by experiments. In this paper, the following two standards are applied to set thresholds. First, according to adjacent distance thresholds, the correlations of distribution of facial expressions' shortest path between 4950-dimensional manifold space and 2-dimensional space are changed. In this case, it is better to use adjacent distance thresholds that have higher correlations between two distributions. Since 2-dimensional space approximately represents multidimensional space, it is better to have higher correlations between distributions. Second, it is better to choose stable thresholds among thresholds with high correlations. In this paper, "thresholds are stable" meaning that when thresholds are used, 2-dimensional shortest path distribution is not much different from when adjacent thresholds are used. 2-dimensional short path distribution can be checked by the users. A little change in adjacent distance threshold makes a large difference in the distribution of 2-dimensional shortest paths. This means the distribution of corresponding multidimensional shortest paths changes considerably. This is because we consider only thresholds that make higher correlations between two spaces. It is difficult to believe that adjacent thresholds represent actual adjacent distance if they are not stable. This because actual adjacent distance is expected to have the stability defined in this paper. In order to apply the first standard, the Pearson's coefficient, r[11] is used for correlations between the distribution of multidimensional shortest paths and the distribution

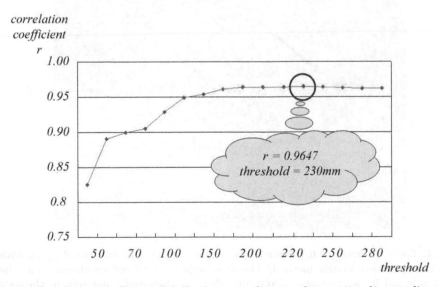

Fig. 3. Correlation coefficient distribution according to changes in adjacent distance threshold

of 2-dimensional shortest paths. Let's express distance between arbitrary facial expression state x_i and x_j in manifold space with one vector. Let's say this is V_d. Let's express distance between point y_i and y_j projected on 2-dimensional plane with one vector. Let's say it is V_y. The coefficient r will be $-1 \leq r \leq 1$. The following formula 7 is created by vectors V_d and V_y.

$$r = \frac{\sum_{i=1}^{n}(v_{di} - \bar{V}_d)(v_{yi} - \bar{V}_y)}{\sqrt{\sum_{i=1}^{n}(v_{di} - \bar{V}_d)^2 \cdot \sum_{i=1}^{n}(v_{yi} - \bar{V}_y)}} \tag{7}$$

Here, $v_{di} \in V_d$, $v_{yi} \in V_y$, $\bar{V}_d$ is V_d average, and $\bar{V}_y$ is V_y's average. Generally when coefficient, $r \geq 0.90$, it indicates high correlation. When $r = 1.0$, two spaces are identical. In this paper, thresholds with the highest correlation are calculated using test numbers. According to the test results, the highest relation is acquired when $r = 0.9647$, as shown in Fig. 3, and the adjacent distance threshold is $230mm$.

Fig. 4 is the distribution of 2-dimensional shortest paths acquired with this threshold.

In order to apply the second standard, by slowly moving the threshold to be $230mm$, the threshold with the highest correlation ($220mm \sim 240mm$) and the

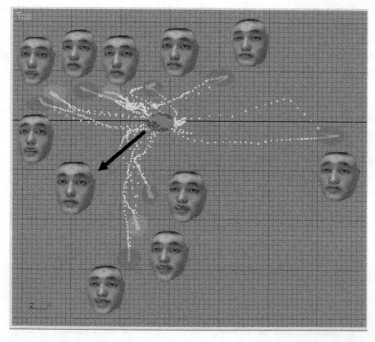

Fig. 4. Facial expression distribution chart that is ranged to intuitional space with results by distance matrix method. The most outstanding faces are shown along the route selected by an animator. (Actually, they are displayed separately in the user interface, but are placed into this chart for the convenience).

distribution of 2-dimensional shortest paths are generated. According to their resulting order, distance distributions are displayed and checked. As a result, when the threshold increases from $220mm$ to $230mm$, the distance between adjacent facial expressions in the distribution of the shortest paths is lowered. In addition, when the threshold increases from $230mm$ to $240mm$, the distance between adjacent facial expressions is close, but is still somewhat different. This means that the 2-dimensional distance distribution doesn't change much around threshold of $230mm$. Therefore, the threshold of $230mm$ that makes the correlation between two spaces highest is chosen in this paper. On the other hand, when thresholds ($220mm \sim 240mm$) that make the correlation between two spaces very high, are used, there is no case for path between two facial expressions. However, when used is a threshold (under $63mm$) of a correlation coefficient (under $r = 0.9040$), the correlation between spaces becomes low, and there are many facial expressions that have no path between them. This takes place since there is no shortest path between two facial expressions when a low threshold is chosen for the shortest path. In this paper, as shown in Fig. 4, facial expression space is generated with 2-dimensional distance distribution created with threshold $230mm$. It is not clearly commented in this paper, but when potion vectors are used to describe facial expression states, the above-mentioned results don't appear. In other words, when a threshold that makes the correlation between two spaces highest is used, there are some cases that have no shortest path between two facial expressions. In addition, because of this reason, it is meaningless to find a stable adjacent threshold.

5.2   Experiment Results

In this test, MDS results are distributed in intuitive space by relating them with facial expression frames, then an animator is told to navigate in real-time. As shown in Fig. 5, a user interface is built that can check facial expressions by applying in real-time each facial expression frame to a 3-dimensional face model.

With the user interface developed for this paper, it is confirmed that ten different facial expressions are radiated from the center of an expressionless face. From the expressionless face, the distance between each facial expression is the same or very similar. However, as facial expressions become increasingly different, the distance between each facial expression becomes greater. In addition, the 3-dimensional avatar face model shows that ten different facial expressions are developed naturally from the expressionless face, just as face motion data. In order to verify this, the information(frame number) about face states on a 2-dimensional plane is checked. As a result, with enough space, facial expressions are shown in the same order as the frame number of face motion data used in the test. Currently, this facial expression space consists of the distribution of the ten motion data. But with the user interface, animator can control facial expressions of 3D avatar in realtime, by generating various rough to smooth facial motions more than ten facial motions.

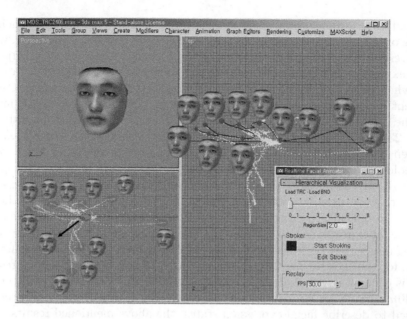

Fig. 5. User interface: The left top is a 3-dimensional avatar face model for visual checkup. The right is facial expression space on a 2-dimensional plane. The bottom left shows the most significant facial expressions so that an animator can easily make a decision.

6   Conclusion

We have discussed how to generated facial expression space in order to control 3-dimensional avatar's face in real-time. The user interface is developed to test and verify real-time facial expression control of facial expression space. To achieve this task, face motion data is position data captured by the optical motion capture system at 60 frames per second. In order to generate facial expression space composed of face motion capture data, we have to calculate the distance between facial expressions. To achieve this, it should be decided first how to describe facial expressions. In this paper distance matrixes are used to describe facial expression states. In addition, by selecting the optimal distance threshold between facial expressions, adjacent facial expressions are decided. The Floyd algorithm is used to find the distance between facial expressions. However, since the distance between facial expressions is distance in manifold space, it is impossible for an animator to navigate multidimensional space. Therefore, manifold space is reduced to be 2-dimensional, and facial expression space is distributed onto a 2-dimensional plane. In this paper, the user interface is developed to check whether facial expression space distributed on 2-dimensional plane is well generated. It is possible to check how well facial expression space is generated in this paper, by allowing an animator to navigate facial expression space on a 2-dimensional plane and control 3-dimensional avatar facial expression in real-time.

References

1. Demetri Terzopoulos, Barbara Mones-Hattal, Beth Hofer, Frederic Parke, Doug Sweetland, Keith Waters.: Facial animation : Past, present and future. Panel, Siggraph97
2. Frederic I. Parke, Keith Waters.: Computer facial animation. A K Peters, 1996
3. Won-Sook Lee, Nadia Magnenat-Thalmann.: Fast head modeling for animation. Journal Image and Vision Computing, Volume 18, Number 4, pp.355-364, Elsevier, 1 March, 2000
4. Cyriaque Kouadio, Pierre Poulin, and Pierre Lachapelle.: Real-time facial animation based upon a bank of 3D facial expressions. Proc. Computer Animation 98, June 1998
5. Jehee Lee, Jinxiang Chai, Paul Reitsma, Jessica Hodgins, and Nancy Pollard.: Interactive Control of Avatars Animated with Human Motion Data. ACM Transactions on Graphics (Siggraph 2002), volume 21, number 3, 491-500, July 2002
6. R. W. Floyd.: Algorithm 97 : Shortest Path. CACM Vol.5, pp. 345, 1962
7. J. Tenenbaum.: Mapping a manifold of perceptual observations. In Advances in Neural Information Processing Systems, volume 10, pages 682–688. MIT Press, 1998
8. T. Cox and M. Cox.: Multidimensional Scaling. Chapman & Hall, London, 1994
9. W. S. Torgerson.: Multidimensional scaling: I. theory and method. Psychometrica., 17:401-419, 1952
10. K. V. Mardia.: Some properties of classical multi-dimensional scaling. Communications in Statistics-Theory and Methods, A7:1233-1241, 1978
11. Uprendra Shardanand.: Social information filtering for music recommendation. Master's thesis, MIT, 1994
12. Michael Gleicher.: Retargetting motion to new characters. Proceedings of SIGGRAPH 98. In Computer Graphics Annual Conference Series, 1998
13. Vlasic, D., Brand, M., Pfister, H., Popovic, J. : Face Transfer with Multilinear Models. ACM Transactions on Graphics (TOG), Vol. 24, pp.426-433, 2005
14. Zhigang Deng, Pei-Ying Chiang, Pamela Fox, Ulrich Neumann. : Animating blendshape faces by cross-mapping motion capture data. pp. 43-48, Proceedings of the 2006 symposium on Interactive 3D graphics and games 2006, March 14-17, 2006
15. Douglas Fidaleo, Ulrich Neumann.: Analysis of co-articulation regions for performance-driven facial animation. Journal of Visualization and Computer Animation, Volume: 15, pp. 15-26, 2004
16. Lee, J., J. Chai, P. S. A. Reitsma, J. K. Hodgins, and N. S. Pollard.:Interactive Control of Avatars Animated with Human Motion Data. ACM Transactions on Graphics (SIGGRAPH 2002), vol 21, num 3, pp. 491-500, 2002
17. Jun-Yong Noh and Ulrich Neumann.:Expression cloning. In Proceedings of SIGGRAPH 2001, pp. 21-28, 2001
18. Z. Deng and U. Neumann.:eFASE: Expressive Facial Animation Synthesis and Editing with Phoneme-Isomap Controls. Proc. of ACM SIGGRAPH/EG Symposium on Computer Animation (SCA) 2006, pp. 251-259, 2006

Improving Efficiency of Density-Based Shape Descriptors for 3D Object Retrieval

Ceyhun Burak Akgül[1,2], Bülent Sankur[1], Yücel Yemez[3], and Francis Schmitt[2]

[1] Department of Electrical and Electronics Engineering, Boğaziçi University,
Istanbul, Turkey
[2] GET - Télécom Paris - CNRS UMR 5141, Paris, France
[3] Department of Computer Engineering, Koç University, Istanbul, Turkey

Abstract. We consider 3D shape description as a probability modeling problem. The local surface properties are first measured via various features, and then the probability density function (pdf) of the multidimensional feature vector becomes the shape descriptor. Our prior work has shown that, for 3D object retrieval, pdf-based schemes can provide descriptors that are computationally efficient and performance-wise on a par with or better than the state-of-the-art methods. In this paper, we specifically focus on discretization problems in the multidimensional feature space, selection of density evaluation points and dimensionality reduction techniques to further improve the performance of our density-based descriptors.

1 Introduction

A 3D shape descriptor can be viewed as a mapping from the space of 3D objects to some finite-dimensional vector space. The design objective of 3D shape descriptors is to maximize the shape discrimination ability with a low-dimensional and sparse feature set. Thus, while descriptors should enable effective retrieval, they should also satisfy practical requirements of computation and storage efficiency [1].

Density-based shape description is an analytical framework to extract 3D shape descriptors from local surface features characterizing the object geometry [2]. Processing the feature information with the kernel methodology for density estimation (KDE) [3], the probability density function (pdf) of the local feature is estimated at chosen target points. The shape descriptor vector is then simply a sampled version of this pdf. This density-based approach provides a mechanism to convert local shape evidences, using KDE, into a global shape description. Our recent work on density-based shape descriptors [2,4,5] for 3D object retrieval has proven that this scheme is both computationally rapid and performance-wise on a par with or better than the state-of-the art methods [1,6,7,8].

In the present work, we depart from the pdf-based shape description scheme and investigate variations to improve its efficiency and effectiveness. In particular, we address the following issues: (i) the effect of the descriptor size;

A. Gagalowicz and W. Philips (Eds.): MIRAGE 2007, LNCS 4418, pp. 330–340, 2007.

(ii) the choice of the dissimilarity measure associated with the descriptor; (iii) the descriptor dimensionality reduction techniques.

The paper is organized as follows. In Sect. 2, we define the local features used in density-based shape description and present the methods to determine the feature range for target selection. In Sect. 3, we discuss issues related to 3D object retrieval and introduce dimensionality reduction techniques specifically for density-based descriptors: marginalization and probability density pruning. Experimental results are presented in Sect. 4 and conclusions drawn in Sect. 5.

2 Density-Based Shape Description: Target Selection Problem

A density-based descriptor of a 3D shape is defined as the sampled pdf of some surface feature, such as radial distance or direction. The feature is local to the surface patch and treated as a random variable. At each surface point, e.g., at each mesh vertex and/or triangle, one has a realization of this random variable. To fix the notation, let S be a random variable taking values within a subspace $\mathcal{R}_S$ of $\mathbb{R}^d$ and let $f(s|O_t)$ be the pdf of S evaluated on the surface of the object O_t. In the sequel, random variables appear as uppercase letters while their specific instances as lowercase. Suppose furthermore that we have specified a finite set of points $\overline{\mathcal{R}}_S = \{s_n \in \mathcal{R}_S : n = 1, \ldots, N\}$, called *the target set*, within $\mathcal{R}_S$. The density-based descriptor $\mathbf{f}_{S|O_t}$ for the object O_t (with respect to the feature S) is then simply an N-dimensional vector whose entries consist of the pdf samples at the target set, that is, $\mathbf{f}_{S|O_t} = [f(s_1|O_t), \ldots, f(s_N|O_t)]$.

Density-based shape description consists of three stages. First, we should choose a good local feature that accumulates to a global shape descriptor. We refer to this as the design problem. Second, we need an efficient computational scheme to estimate $f(s|O_t)$ at arbitrary points in the range $\mathcal{R}_S$. This issue is the generic computational problem that can be tackled in different ways [3]. In [2,4,5], we have used the kernel approach in conjunction with a fast algorithm, the fast Gauss transform [9]. Finally, in the target selection stage, we determine the sampling locations (set $\overline{\mathcal{R}}_S$) within $\mathcal{R}_S$, the final output being the object descriptor $\mathbf{f}_{S|O_t}$.

2.1 Local Surface Features

We briefly present two of the local features as a reminder to facilitate the subsequent discussions. These features were already analyzed in [2,4]. In this work, 3D shapes are represented by triangular meshes and their centers of mass coincide with the origin. Let $\mathbf{Q} = (X, Y, Z)$ stand for a point Q, lying on some 3D surface, $\hat{\mathbf{N}} = (\hat{N}_x, \hat{N}_y, \hat{N}_z)$ for the unit surface normal vector at Q, and $\langle \cdot, \cdot \rangle$ for the usual dot product. A local geometric feature is a mapping S from the points of the surface into a d-dimensional space, usually constrained into a finite subspace $\mathcal{R}_S$ of $\mathbb{R}^d$. Each dimension of this space corresponds to a specific geometric measure, characterizing the shape locally. We now consider two of these local geometric features.

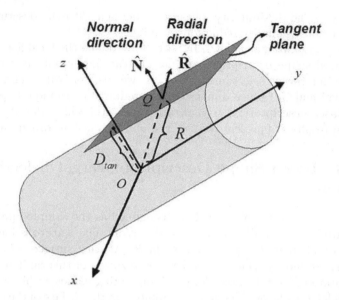

Fig. 1. The components of radial and tangent plane based features at a surface point Q

The radial feature S_{rad} at the point Q is a 4-tuple defined as

$$S_{rad}(Q) \triangleq (R, \hat{R}_x, \hat{R}_y, \hat{R}_z) \triangleq (R, \hat{\mathbf{R}}) \text{ with } R \triangleq \left\| \hat{\mathbf{Q}} \right\| \text{ and } \hat{\mathbf{R}} \triangleq \mathbf{Q} / \left\| \hat{\mathbf{Q}} \right\|.$$

The *magnitude* component R measures the radial distance from the origin. The *direction* component $\hat{\mathbf{R}}$, pointing to the location of the surface point, is a 3-vector with unit-norm and lies on the unit 2-sphere $\mathcal{S}^2$. Since the magnitude component is spread between zero and some r_{max} depending on the scale of the surface, S_{rad} takes values within the Cartesian product of $\mathcal{I}_R = (0, r_{max}) \subset \mathbb{R}$ and $\mathcal{S}^2$, thus $\mathcal{R}_{S_{rad}} = \mathcal{I}_R \times \mathcal{S}^2$.

The tangent plane-based feature S_{tan} at the point Q is a 4-tuple defined as

$$S_{tan}(Q) \triangleq (D_{tan}, \hat{N}_x, \hat{N}_y, \hat{N}_z) \triangleq (D_{tan}, \hat{\mathbf{N}}) \text{ with } D_{tan} \triangleq \left| \left\langle \mathbf{Q}, \hat{\mathbf{N}} \right\rangle \right|.$$

Similar to the S_{rad}-feature, S_{tan} has a *magnitude* component D_{tan} taking values within $\mathcal{I}_{D_{tan}} = (0, d_{tan,max}) \subset \mathbb{R}$, which is the distance of the tangent plane to the origin, and a *direction* component $\hat{\mathbf{N}}$. The normal $\hat{\mathbf{N}}$ is a unit-norm vector by definition and lies on the unit 2-sphere $\mathcal{S}^2$. Consequently, the range of S_{tan} is $\mathcal{R}_{S_{tan}} = \mathcal{I}_{D_{tan}} \times \mathcal{S}^2$. Fig. 1 illustrates these two local features. Note that the above features are neither scale- nor rotation-invariant. Accordingly, any method making use of them must assume prior scale and pose normalization of the mesh.

2.2   Target Selection

The target selection problem was defined as sampling the range of the feature at which the pdf is evaluated. The ranges $\mathcal{R}_{S_{rad}}$ and $\mathcal{R}_{S_{tan}}$ of our local features

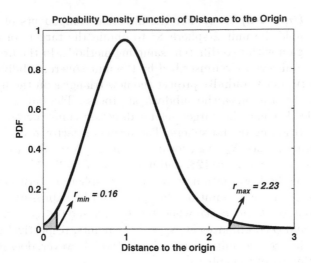

Fig. 2. Probability density function of R displayed with the lower and upper 1% intervals clipped

S_{rad} and S_{tan} both consist of the Cartesian product of an interval $\mathcal{I}$ on the real line with the unit 2-sphere $\mathcal{S}^2$. This decoupling allows us to sample $\mathcal{I}$ and $\mathcal{S}^2$ independently into N_m and N_d points respectively, and to take the Cartesian product of the two resulting sets to yield the target set $\overline{\mathcal{R}}_S$ of size $N = N_m \times N_d$. In the following, we discuss the sampling of $\mathcal{I}$ and $\mathcal{S}^2$ separately, providing two different methods for each.

Sampling the Magnitude Interval: For features that are not scale-invariant, 3D objects must be normalized. In [2,4,5], we rescaled all objects to unit mean radial distance. Vranic [7] has experimentally shown that this constitutes a good choice for retrieval. Other scale normalizers in the literature use scale measures ranging from the radius of the enclosing sphere to the mean coordinate variance [7,8]. The support of the mean-normalized radial distance, $\mathcal{I} = (r_{min}, r_{max})$, is determined by the 98-percentile of the distribution of R. Thus, we set the limits to satisfy $Pr\{R < r_{max}\} = \int_0^{r_{max}} f(r)dr = 0.99$ and $Pr\{r_{min} < R\} = 0.99$, where $f(r)$ is the pdf of R, calculated over all objects. More specifically, one has

$$f(r) = \sum_{t=1}^{T} f(r, O_t) = \sum_{t=1}^{T} f(r|O_t)Pr\{O_t\} = \frac{1}{T}\sum_{t=1}^{T} f(r|O_t), \qquad (1)$$

assuming that all objects are equiprobable. In Fig. 2, we display the pdf of R and the clipping points delimiting the 98-percentile for the Princeton Shape Benchmark (PSB) [6]. The same method also applies for the tangent feature interval $\mathcal{I}_{D_{tan}}$.

Once the domain of the pdf is set, the N_m targets points remain to be determined. The two methods we consider are to either partition the interval into N_m equally spaced (uniform) regions and take the midpoints, or to partition the interval into N_m equal probability regions.

Sampling the Unit 2-Sphere: For the direction components of both S_{rad} and S_{tan}, we sample the unit 2-sphere $\mathcal{S}^2$ to obtain the targets of their pdfs. We experiment again with two different sampling methods. In the first one [10], we consider an octahedron circumscribed by the unit sphere, subdivide in four each of its eight triangles, radially project the new triangles on the unit sphere, and iterate a factor of a times the subdivision process. The barycenters of the resulting triangles become the target set for direction components. This leads to a uniform partitioning of the sphere. The recursion factor a determines the number of resulting points N_d; e.g., for $a = 1$, we get $N_d = 8 \times 4 = 32$ points; for $a = 2$, we get $N_d = 8 \times 16 = 128$, and in general $N_d = 2^{2a+3}$.

In the second method, we parameterize the unit sphere in terms of spherical coordinates. Recall that any point on the sphere can be expressed as a 3-tuple given by $(sin\theta sin\phi, cos\theta sin\phi, cos\phi)$ where $0 \leq \theta < 2\pi$ and $0 \leq \phi < \pi$. Uniformly sampling the θ- and ϕ-coordinates at N_θ and N_ϕ points, respectively, results in $N_d = N_\theta \times N_\phi$ points on the unit-sphere. This method, however, does not provide a uniform partitioning of the sphere.

3   3D Object Retrieval: Improving Efficiency

3.1   Dissimilarity Measures

The classical dissimilarity measures between two pdfs, which are also our shape descriptors, are Minkowski metrics ($L^p, p = 1, 2, \infty$), symmetric Kullback-Leibler distance, Chi-Square distance and Bhattacharya distance [7,8]. For $\mathbf{f}_{S|O_t}$ and $\mathbf{f}_{S|O_u}$ representing discretized pdfs of some feature S on objects O_t and O_u, the continuous metric δ can be approximated as

$$\bar{\delta}(\mathbf{f}_{S|O_t}, \mathbf{f}_{S|O_u}) = \sum_{s_n \in \mathcal{R}_S} \eta\left(f\left(s_n|O_t\right), f\left(s_n|O_u\right)\right) \Delta s_n, \qquad (2)$$

where η is a point-wise dissimilarity function, e.g., for L^1, $\eta(\cdot, \cdot) = |\cdot - \cdot|$ and where Δs_n is the discretization step size. For uniform partitioning of $\mathcal{R}_S$, Δs_n is constant and can be dropped.

3.2   Dimensionality Reduction

We consider schemes to reduce the dimension of the descriptor vectors for computation and memory advantages, without sacrificing the retrieval performance. This is important because the descriptors may be quite high dimensional, in the order of thousands.

Marginalization: Features can be selectively removed from the multidimensional descriptor by marginalization, that is, by integrating out feature variables. To remove the component S_k from some d-dimensional feature $S = (S_1, S_2, \ldots, S_d)$, we use

$$f_{S_{\not k}|O_t} \triangleq f\left(s_1, \ldots, s_{k-1}, s_{k+1}, \ldots, s_d|O_t\right) = \int_{S_k} f\left(s_1, \ldots, s_k, \ldots, s_d|O_t\right) ds_k. \qquad (3)$$

This gives the pdf of a "reduced" feature vector $S_{\not k} \triangleq (S_1, \ldots, S_{k-1}, S_{k+1}, \ldots, S_d)$. Reducing the descriptor $f_{S|O_t}$ to $f_{S_{\not k}|O_t}$ saves us one dimension at the cost of any information brought by the component S_k. For instance, marginalizing the magnitude component R from the pdf of S_{rad}-feature vector, the size of the descriptor $\mathbf{f}_{S_{rad}, \not R|O_t}$ is N_m times smaller than that of $\mathbf{f}_{S_{rad}|O_t}$ since the target set for S_{rad} contains $N_m \times N_d$ points. We hope then to identify features that can be marginalized without compromising descriptor's discrimination ability. An obvious instance is the case of a redundant component in the directional parts $\hat{\mathbf{R}}$ and $\hat{\mathbf{N}}$, respectively, of the local features S_{rad} and S_{tan}. For example, $\hat{\mathbf{R}}$ is unit norm with $\hat{R}_x^2 + \hat{R}_y^2 + \hat{R}_z^2 = 1$, hence given any two components, say $\hat{R}_x$ and $\hat{R}_y$, the third one $\hat{R}_z$ is completely determined up to the sign. Thus, we conjecture that $\hat{R}_z$ can be marginalized out without deteriorating performance. We show this experimentally in Sect. 4.

Probability Density Pruning: The second approach to reduce a descriptor's dimensionality involves pruning the unconditional pdf of features S, as defined in Eq. 1. The idea of pruning signifies removing negligible unconditional pdf bins from the descriptor. Thus, for a selected threshold λ, the new target set $\overline{\mathcal{R}}_S^\lambda$ is defined as $\overline{\mathcal{R}}_S^\lambda = \{s_n \in \overline{\mathcal{R}}_S : f(s_n) > \lambda\}$. The reduced descriptor for some object O_t becomes then $\mathbf{f}_{S|O_t}^\lambda = [f(s_n|O_t)]_{s_n \in \overline{\mathcal{R}}_S^\lambda}$. Notice that feature selection methods are not practical when the feature vector size is in the order of thousands. Pruning by suppressing small pdf values, albeit not tantamount to feature selection, still serves the goal by reducing the descriptor size.

4   Experiments

We have tested our descriptors in a retrieval scenario on the training set of the Princeton Shape Benchmark (PSB) [6], which consists of 3D objects described as triangular meshes. PSB training set contains 907 models, categorized into 90 classes. The meshes contain 7460 triangles and 4220 vertices on the average. We have validated our results using the test set of PSB and on another database, Sculpteur (SCUdb) [2,8], which is fundamentally different from PSB in terms of both classification semantics and mesh quality. The performance figures are given in terms of discounted cumulative gain (DCG) and nearest neighbor (NN) scores [6]. Recall that NN is the percentage of the closest matches that belong to the query class and DCG is a statistic between 0 (worst) and 1 (best), weighting correct results, i.e., models of the same class as the query model, near the front of the list more than correct results later in the ranked list. Our descriptors have size $N_m \times N_d = 1024$. Specifically, the magnitude set for targets is chosen by uniform sampling ($N_m = 8$) and the direction set by octahedron subdivision (recursion factor $a = 2$, $N_d = 128$). We also note that all descriptors have been normalized prior to distance calculation.

Table 1. Percent DCG For Standard Dissimilarity Measures, $N_m = 8$ and $N_d = 128$

Feature	L^1	L^2	L^∞	KL	χ^2	B
S_{rad}	56.7	54.7	44.4	54.4	57.0	56.7
S_{tan}	59.9	55.3	47.1	58.2	61.1	59.4

Table 2. Percent DCG Values on PSB Test Set and SCUdb using Various Metrics

Database	Feature	$L^{0.6}$	L^1	L^2	L^∞	KL	χ^2	B
PSB Test	S_{rad}	55.0	54.4	52.0	43.6	53.4	54.7	54.9
	S_{tan}	58.9	58.0	54.5	47.0	55.8	58.9	58.6
SCUdb	S_{rad}	70.9	71.1	70.7	62.8	70.1	71.3	71.0
	S_{tan}	72.8	72.0	69.5	63.1	70.1	71.6	71.3

4.1 Effect of the Dissimilarity Measure

We test the impact of the chosen distance metric on the retrieval performance, namely, those of L^p, Kullback-Leibler (KL), Chi-Square (χ^2), and Bhattacharya (B) distances. For L^p, $p = 1, 2, \infty$, descriptors are rescaled to have unit L_p-norm. For KL, χ^2, and B, on the other hand, we have rescaled the descriptors to unit L^1-norm because these measures are designed for histograms and/or pdfs. We have observed that for all metrics, appropriate normalization invariably improves discrimination. In Table 1, we provide DCG scores using these metrics. For both the radial feature S_{rad} and the tangent plane-based feature S_{tan}, the measures L^1, χ^2, and B yield the best results while L^∞ has the poorest performance. Intrigued by the lower performance of L^2 with respect to L^1, we explored the variability of DCG as a function of the p parameter of the L^p-metric within the interval $p \in]0, 2]$. As illustrated in Fig. 3, the performance degrades significantly for $p > 1$, and for $0 < p \leq 1$, DCG peaks around $p = 0.6$, even outperforming χ^2 and B, the best measures of the previous experiment (see Table 1). This $L^{0.6}$ peak is however minor with respect to L^1, hence we preferred the computationally cheaper L^1-metric in the following results. We remark also that the performance order of the considered metrics remain the same for PSB test set and SCUdb [2,8] as can be seen in Table 2.

4.2 Effect of the Sampling Scheme and the Target Set Size

In Table 3, we provide the DCG and NN scores corresponding to all combinations of the sampling schemes presented in Sect. 2.2. We would like to point a few subtleties in target selection. For uniform sampling of the pdf, the step size factor Δs_n becomes constant and then irrelevant. When sampling the magnitude with equal probability intervals (same area under the pdf curve) and/or when sampling the unit sphere with equal spherical coordinate steps, neglecting the Δs_n-factor causes significant performance loss. When Δs_n-factor is included in Eq. 2, then the performances of equal area sampling and uniform (equal distance) sampling of the magnitude become virtually equal (within 1%). The same

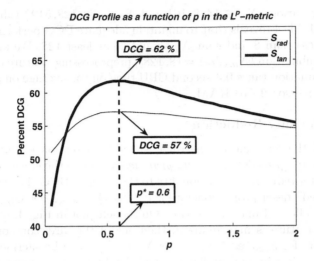

Fig. 3. DCG Performance vs the p parameter in the L^p-metric, N_m and $N_d = 128$

Table 3. DCG and NN Performances Using Different Sampling Schemes For Target Selection, N_m and $N_d = 128$, **1**: magnitude set: *uniform*, direction set: *by subdivision*, **2**: magnitude set: *uniform*, direction set: *by spherical coordinates*, **3**: magnitude set: *equal probability*, direction set: *by subdivision*, **4**: magnitude set: *equal probability*, direction set: *by spherical coordinates*

	S_{rad}				S_{tan}			
	1	**2**	**3**	**4**	**1**	**2**	**3**	**4**
%DCG	56.7	56.8	56.0	56.3	59.9	60.5	59.5	60.1
%NN	57.3	55.9	55.7	55.1	58.7	60.8	59.8	60.5

Table 4. Percent DCG For Various Target Set Sizes

	S_{rad}			S_{tan}		
	$N_d = 512$	$N_d = 128$	$N_d = 32$	$N_d = 512$	$N_d = 128$	$N_d = 32$
$N_m = 16$	57.2	56.6	52.2	60.7	60.6	58.3
$N_m = 8$	57.0	56.7	52.0	60.5	59.9	58.1
$N_m = 4$	55.8	55.4	49.9	57.3	57.1	53.4

observation also holds for sampling the unit sphere by octahedron subdivision and by spherical coordinates. Table 3 shows that all sampling schemes result in equivalent performances. We have also investigated the effect of changing the clipping level to determine the magnitude level. Our experiments with clipping levels 0.5%, 1%, 2%, and 5% yielded comparable results.

We have also analyzed the effect of changing the descriptor size N between 128 and 8192 under uniform sampling (i.e., uniform magnitude set and octahedron subdivision for direction set) using the L^1-metric. We have tested the combinations of various $N_m \in \{4, 8, 16\}$ and $N_d \in \{32, 128, 512\}$ values for the target set size. Table 4 reveals that to maintain adequate DCG performance, N_m should not be less than 8 and that N_d should be at least 128. We also remark that, for the combination $(N_m, N_d) = (8, 128)$, preprocessing, feature calculation and density estimation takes 0.4 second CPU time on the average on a Pentium M 1.86 GHz processor, 1 GB RAM.

4.3   Dimensionality Reduction

We now report the outcome of the dimensionality reduction experiments via *marginalization* and *probability density pruning*. We define the efficiency ϵ as the ratio of DCG after reducing dimensionality to the baseline DCG (i.e., the DCG of the "non-reduced" descriptor), concretely, $\epsilon = \mathrm{DCG}_{S,reduced}/\mathrm{DCG}_{S,full}$. Fig. 4 summarizes the effect of marginalization. On the left plot in Fig. 4, we see that, when only one feature is marginalized, then one of the direction components, i.e., $\hat{R}_x, \hat{R}_y$ or $\hat{R}_z$ for S_{rad}, and $\hat{N}_x, \hat{N}_y$ or $\hat{N}_z$ for S_{tan}, can be sacrificed. We do not incur into any loss in marginalizing one of the direction components and the descriptor size is halved. This should not be a surprise since the redundancy of a directional component given the other two was already pointed out in Sect. 3.2. Even more impressive economies can be attained by marginalizing two components, as shown on the right of Fig. 4. As long as we retain the magnitude component and keep only one of the direction components, we can still achieve DCG efficiency at around 95% with 83% reduction in descriptor size (i.e., the size is reduced by a factor of 6). It is also worth noting that, with these results at our disposal, we can directly estimate the pdf of the most informative components and reduce the computational overhead beforehand. Although, due to space restrictions, we cannot provide our validation results on the effect of marginalization using PSB test set and SCUdb, we note that the above observations hold invariably for other databases.

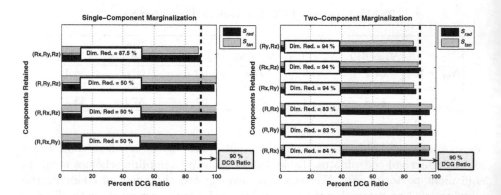

Fig. 4. Effect of dimensionality reduction by marginalization on DCG performance: horizontal axis stands for percent ratio of DCG after marginalization to the original DCG obtained using the full descriptor of size $N = 8 \times 128 = 1024$

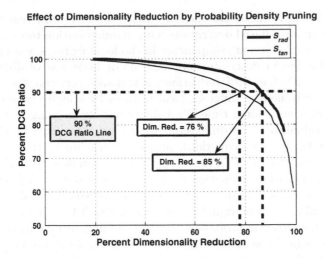

Fig. 5. Effect of reducing dimensionality by probability density pruning on DCG performance

Finally, we experiment with the probability density pruning technique by varying the threshold parameter λ (Sect. 3.2). In Fig. 5, we display the DCG efficiency as a function of percent reduction in descriptor size. We observe that DCG efficiency profile remains nearly flat at around 100% up to 40% reduction in descriptor size and starts to degrade afterwards. Comparing Figs. 4 and 5, at the 90% DCG efficiency level, descriptor simplification with pruning is slightly less effective (85%) than with marginalization (94%). We want to point out that for density pruning, unlike marginalization, the reduction in size is controllable as a function of the performance loss incurred. Furthermore, insignificant targets can be eliminated off from density estimation stage, reducing the computational overhead beforehand.

5   Conclusion

In this work, we have investigated density-based 3D shape descriptors [1, 2, 3] from the perspective of retrieval efficiency and effectiveness. While standard dissimilarity measures for histogram and/or pdf matching, such as L^1, χ^2, and B, provide similar and satisfactory retrieval performances, the best metric has proven to be the non-classical $L^{0.6}$. More generally, the DCG performance profile of the L^p-metric as a function of p, strictly increases from $p = \infty$ to $p = 0.6$, and then decreases. Nevertheless, we advise the use of the L^1-metric as it provides adequate discrimination with the least computational effort. The experiments on target selection demonstrate that, as long as discretization step size is taken into account in dissimilarity computation, all sampling schemes are equally effective on retrieval performance. We did not gain much by increasing the descriptor size after $N = 1024$ and the best (N_m, N_d)-configuration has been (8,128).

We have also introduced two flexible dimensionality reduction techniques specifically for density-based descriptors. Our marginalization tool exploits possible redundancy of different components in the local features and can provide significant reduction in descriptor size with no or little loss of discrimination ability ($\epsilon_{marg} = 100\%$ at 50% reduction). Marginalization can also be used to explore the effectiveness of different local features by selectively removing one or multiple components at a time. Probability density pruning, maybe not as efficient as marginalization in dimensionality reduction for fixed DCG efficiency ($\epsilon_{pruning} = 100\%$ at 40% reduction), provides a machinery that controls the amount of performance loss as a function of reduction in descriptor size and vice versa. In marginalization, reduction in descriptor size occurs in discrete steps; in density pruning, the parameter λ enables us to reduce the descriptor size arbitrarily. Finally, while marginalization tells us which feature *components* are more effective for retrieval; probability density pruning, although not to the full extent, guides us in choosing more informative feature *locations*, i.e., targets.

Our future work will concentrate on enlarging the repository of local features for use in the density-based shape description framework. Furthermore, we will consider joining the radial and tangent plane-based features and perform density estimation on this "augmented" space in order to exploit the full surface information probed by these features.

References

1. Bustos, B., Keim, D.A., Saupe, D., Schreck, T., Vranic, D.V.: Feature-based similarity search in 3D object databases. ACM Comput. Surv. **37** (2005) 345–387
2. Akgül, C.B., Sankur, B., Yemez, Y., Schmitt, F.: Density-based 3d shape descriptors. EURASIP Journal on Advances in Signal Processing **2007** (2007) Article ID 32503, 16 pages doi:10.1155/2007/32503.
3. Härdle, W., Müller, M., Sperlich, S., Werwatz, A.: Nonparametric and Semiparametric Models. Springer Series in Statistics. Springer (2004)
4. Akgül, C.B., Sankur, B., Schmitt, F., Yemez, Y.: Density-based shape descriptors for 3D object retrieval. In: International Workshop on Multimedia Content Reresentation, Classification and Security (MRCS '06), Istanbul, Turkey (2006)
5. Akgül, C.B., Sankur, B., Yemez, Y., Schmitt, F.: A framework for histogram-induced 3D descriptors. In: European Signal Processing Conference (EUSIPCO '06), Florence, Italy (2006)
6. Shilane, P., Min, P., Kazhdan, M., Funkhouser, T.: The Princeton shape benchmark. In: Proc. of the Shape Modeling International 2004 (SMI '04), Genoa, Italy (2004) 167–178
7. Vranić, D.V.: 3D Model Retrieval. PhD thesis, University of Leipzig (2004)
8. Tung, T.: Indexation 3D de bases de données d'objets par graphes de Reeb améliorés. PhD thesis, Ecole Nationale Supérieure des Télécommunications (ENST), Paris, France (2005)
9. Yang, C., Duraiswami, R., Gumerov, N.A., Davis, L.: Improved fast Gauss transform and efficient kernel density estimation. ICCV **1** (2003) 464
10. Zaharia, T., Prêteux, F.: Shape-based retrieval of 3D mesh models. In: Proc. of the IEEE International Conference on Multimedia and Expo (ICME'2002), Lausanne, Switzerland (2002)

Segmentation of Soft Shadows Based on a Daylight- and Penumbra Model

Michael Nielsen and Claus B Madsen

Aalborg University, Computer Vision and Media Technology Laboratory, Niels Jernes
Vej 14, DK-9220 Aalborg, Denmark
{mnielsen,cbm}@cvmt.dk

Abstract. This paper introduces a new concept within shadow segmentation for usage in shadow removal and augmentation through construction of an alpha overlay shadow model. Previously, an image was
considered to consist of shadow and non-shadow regions. We construct a
model that accounts for sunlit, umbra and penumbra regions. The model
is based on theories about color constancy, daylight, and the geometry
that causes penumbra. The behavior of the model is analyzed and a
graph cut energy minimization is applied to estimate the alpha parameter. The approach is demonstrated on natural complex image situations.
The results are convincing, but the alpha gradient in penumbra must be
improved.

1 Introduction

There are many applications that benefit from shadow detection. For example
segmentation of foreground objects without obstruction from shadows, classification of e.g. faces with shadows that could make it difficult to find the best
match, and extraction of illumination such as light source direction and color.
We want to find a model that can be used for shadow segmentation as well as
shadow synthesis.

Our aim is to make a purely pixel driven method which works on single images
in un-augmented scenes with no geometric knowledge about the scene.

1.1 State of the Art

Salvador [1,2] distinguished between cast shadows (onto the ground plane) and
self shadow. The detection relied on the edge image of a linearized chromaticity
image. They considered dark pixels a-priori to be shadows and corrected this
belief using heuristics concerning the edges of the real image and edges of the
chromaticity image. This worked well in images with controlled simple geometry.
It was tested with still images (of fruit) and video (moving people and cars).

Madsen [3] described shadows as an RGB alpha overlay. It is not just a black
layer with an alpha channel, because the shadows are not only darker versions
of the illuminated areas, but there is a change of hue, caused by the difference
in hue between direct and ambient light. There is a fixed alpha for any given

A. Gagalowicz and W. Philips (Eds.): MIRAGE 2007, LNCS 4418, pp. 341–352, 2007.

region. α can be described as the degree of shadow and the overlay color relates to the the tonal and intensity change of the shadow. Furthermore, shadows are characterized as full shadow, *umbra*, and half shadow *penumbra*, assuming only one light source. Multiple light sources would generate more complex grades of shadow regions.

Finlayson [4][5] takes advantage of planckian light and retinex theory. Assuming a single direct light source and another ambient light (different hue) computes a 1-d invariant image from the known path (illuminant direction) the shadow imposes on a 2-d log-ratio chromaticity plot. Note that ambient occlusion and surface normal direction is not taken into account in this model. The known path/offset is to be pre-calibrated. The edge maps of this invariant image can be used just like in [1] or to set a threshold in a retinex path [5]. The results were images that looked flat and unsaturated with attenuated shadows and blur around the boundaries. The detected boundaries were high quality.

Cheng Lu [6] continued Finlayson's work using graph cuts for optimizing the shadow mask. Their method finds a binary shadow mask and use the illumination invariant chromaticity transform [4] as a static clue for computation of the capacities of the capacities in the graph model. They do not use any data term but considered the brightness changes in the means of windows around the supposed shadow edges as well as the chromaticity "shift" caused by the illumination color. It is not tested for difficult scenes and it does require knowledge of log illumination direction.

Previous work segmented shadows as a binary mask and used the edges as clues. They tested their algorithms in simplistic setups and had strict requirements to their cameras. We will construct an α-overlay shadow model based on Finlayson's color theory. It must be invertible so it can be used to generate shadows and to remove shadows. The degree of shadow should be adjustable through the α-parameter. The color theory does not explain what happens in the penumbra region. In the following the main theory is presented and the penumbra region is investigated. Followed by a graph cut algorithm for estimation of the α-channel for a series of natural images.

1.2   Outdoor Color Theory

Equation 1 shows that in log chromaticity space the perception of color on a surface changes by altering the color temperature T (refer to [4] for further description of the factors).

$$\acute{r}_k = log(r_k) = log(s_k/s_p) + (e_k - e_p)/T, \quad p = 1...3, k \neq p \qquad (1)$$

where $\acute{r}_k$ is a log chromaticity for the color k in relation to the color p. $s_k = Ic_1\lambda_k^{-5}S(\lambda_k)q_k$ and $e_k = -c_2/\lambda_k$. $(e_k - e_p)$ is called the illuminant direction, which should not be confused with the geometric direction but in a 2-d plot of two chromaticities (e.g. red and blue) varying T forms a straight line with the direction $(e_k - e_p)$. The model contains some major assumptions that might not hold for any given camera: Narrow-band (delta-function) sensitivity. Spectral sharpening can be used to approximate narrow band sensitivity, but this may be insignificant [7]. Linearity or simple gamma correction which does not change the log illumination direction. The log illumination direction $e_k - e_p$ must be known (through calibration). Variation of the angle of surface and the visibility of hemisphere (ambient occlusion) is not taken into account.

It follows from this generalization (because $log(a * b) = log(a) + log(b)$) that the color of a surface in full shadow is assumed to be a product of its color in sunlight and a fixed shading factor [5]:

$$\begin{bmatrix} R_{shad} \\ G_{shad} \\ B_{shad} \end{bmatrix} = \begin{bmatrix} \alpha R_{sun} \\ \beta G_{sun} \\ \gamma B_{sun} \end{bmatrix} \tag{2}$$

This relation holds for all pixels in the image. However, it will be necessary to be able to weight the shading effect by an *alpha* in the penumbra areas. See figure 1. The left side shows the illumination direction in log chromaticity space shows the direction that a surface color moves in the 2-d plot from the color temperature changes from full sun to full shadow. It follows a straight line. Surface 1 (S^1) is plotted in sun and shadow (umbra). This relates to the alpha model as full α. We extend the model to account for varying degrees of shadow. Surface 2 (S^2) is plotted in sun, half shadow, and full shadow. However, tonal changes from $\epsilon \rightarrow 0$ and inter-reflections do not map into the straight line. $\epsilon \rightarrow 0$ maps towards $[0, 0]$, while inter-reflections maps toward the colors of the reflecting surfaces.

The right side (in fig. figure 1) shows how umbra and penumbra regions can occur and how α should respond to those regions (in a photo taken directly from above). In the corner at the first box is a situation where the shadow becomes darker because the hemisphere is less accessible from those locations. This is not accounted for in the model.

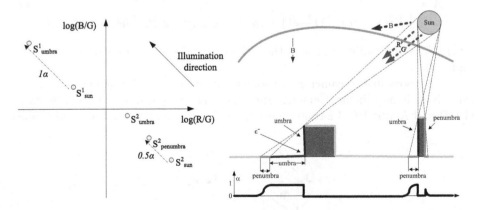

Fig. 1. [Left] 2-d log chromaticity space and illumination direction. [Right] Geometry causing penumbra and umbra.

1.3 Limitations

Consider the physics based model of camera response ρ in channel k to wavelengths λ in equation 3. The surface albedo $S(\lambda)$ is illuminated by the weighted irradiance E from the sky E_{sky} and the sun E_{sun}. Note that the E_{sky} is the integration of light from the entire hemisphere except where the sun is and ϵ accounts for occlusion of the hemisphere (ambient occlusion). This means that it is not valid in the case of a sunset, where the hemisphere can be bright and orange in the western half, and dark blue in the eastern half. In order to make the angular ($cos\theta$) dependence of the sun explicit $\hat{E}_{sun}$ is a specific irradiance of the sun onto a perpendicular surface.

The camera sensors have certain sensitivities Q to the wavelengths λ. Then the camera applies a white balance correction W and a nonlinear dynamic range compression γ, e.g. a gamma 2.2 correction.

$$\rho_k = \gamma \left(w_k \int Q_k(\lambda)S(\lambda)(\epsilon E_{sky}(\lambda) + cos\theta \hat{E}_{sun}(\lambda))d\lambda \right), \quad k = R, G, B \quad (3)$$

It relates to an α-layer model very well, where $alpha$ is a simplification of ϵ and $cos\theta$ and maps to the degree of shadow, and the overlay color maps to the tonal change that occurs because of the hemisphere-to-sun color difference. Three factors that are not taken into account are $cos\theta$, $\epsilon \to 0$ and inter-reflections between surfaces.

It also follows from the nature of the penumbra that edge detection can fail as the gradient may be too low for an edge detection.

The penumbra region is not a linear gradient in the radiance/image domain. It follows an s-curve that can be computed geometrically from the area of the circular segment of the sun that becomes gradually visible from the penumbra region. Equation 4 shows the area (A) from 0 to half of the total area of the circle.

$$A = \begin{bmatrix} R^2 cos^{-1}\left(\frac{R-h}{R}\right) - (R-h)\sqrt{2Rh - h^2}, \text{ where } h \in [0..R] \\ R^2(\pi - cos^{-1})\left(\frac{h-R}{R}\right) - (h-R)\sqrt{4R^2 - 2Rh - h^2}, h \in]R..2R] \end{bmatrix} \quad (4)$$

where R is the radius and h is the height of the visible circular segment (see figure 2).

The sensors in the cameras are somewhat linear, but the human perception sensitivity is non linear. Cameras apply post processing to the linear raw data. sRGB and Adobe RGB formats have applied a gamma 2.2 function (which does

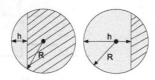

Fig. 2. Area of circular segment. Left: $h \leq R$ Right: $h > R$.

not affect the direction of the log chromaticity space). However, cameras normally compress the dynamic range in an even more complicated manner, using e.g. an S-curve. In practice, there are some non-linearities in the darkest shadows and brightest highlights.

2   Shadow Model

The shadow model is two main tasks: Shadow Augmentation for which the shadow region as a function of the sunlit region is needed. Shadow Removal for which the sunlit region as a function of the shadow region is needed. The following model takes advantage of the relation described in equation 2. It is adapted to control the degree of shadow with α in equation 5 (for each pixel i).

$$\rho_k^{shad} = (1 - \alpha O_k)\rho_k^{sun}, \quad k = R, G, B \tag{5}$$

The shadowless image can be calculated from the original image and an estimated α.

$$\rho_k^{sun} = (1 - \alpha O_k)^{-1}\rho_k^{shad} \tag{6}$$

The optimal overlay color is easy to express. The notation of the following investigation of optimal overlay color ($O = \{o_r, o_g, o_b\}$) will be simplified. The surface color (albedo) will be denoted S. The irradiance from the sky will be E_{sky} and the irradiance from the sun will be E_{sun}. We consider a sunlit pixel to be $S(E_{sky} + E_{sun})$ and an umbra pixel to be SE_{sky}. Furthermore, ambient occlusion and sunlight direction is assumed to be fixed at zero.

$$SE_{sky} = (1 - \alpha_{max}O)S(E_{sky} + E_{sun}) \tag{7}$$

$$O = \frac{(1 - \frac{SE_{sky}}{S(E_{sky}+E_{sun})})}{\alpha_{max}} = \frac{(1 - \frac{E_{sky}}{E_{sky}+E_{sun}})}{\alpha_{max}}$$

α_{max} can be selected arbitrarily. The simplest would be to use $\alpha_{max} = 1$. Note that the evidence needed to compute O is an umbra pixel divided by its corresponding sunlit pixel. Consider $\alpha = 0$, then the sunlit pixel is weighted by 1, i.e. no change. Consider $\alpha = 0.5 * \alpha_{max}$, then the color moves gradually toward umbra. Consider $\alpha = \alpha_{max}$ then the sunlit pixel is weighted by the exact intended ratio between sunlit pixels and umbra pixels.

Figure 3(a, x) shows how the model reacts to $\alpha = \{0, 0.1, 0.2, .., 1\}$ to a given albedo and a given overlay color. The model moves the 2-d log chromaticity plot along an approximate straight line. The points are not evenly distributed, so $\alpha = 0.5$ is not halfway toward umbra.

The profile in the image domain would be a straight line, if the alpha domain is a straight line. This makes it complicated to generate a true s-curve in a penumbra region. It would be easier to generate shadows with a linear alpha-channel, and it may be easier for an estimation algorithm to optimize a linear gradient in the alpha channel as well. The s-curve can be incorporated into the

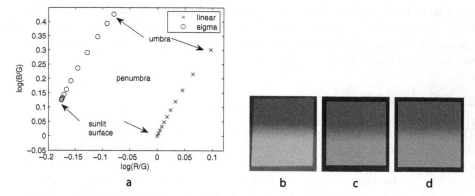

Fig. 3. [a] The effect of different alphas on the log chromaticity plot on two albedos with linear (x) and sigmoid (o) models. The model approximates Finlaysons's model of shadows as a straight line. [b] Photo macbeth square with soft shadow. [c] Linear synthetic. [d] Sigma synthetic.

model by replacing α in equations 5 and 6 with a sigmoid function. Equation 8 is a standard sigmoid function.

$$s(t) = \frac{1}{1 + e^{-t*K}} \tag{8}$$

where $K = 1/3$ and controls the steepness of the S curve. $S(t) \in]0,1[$ within $t \in [-10, 10]$ α has to be scaled such that: $t = (\alpha - 0.5)*20$. Thus in the interval $\alpha \in [0..1]$ then $S(t) \in [0.0344, 0.9656]$ which must be scaled to $S(t) \in [0..1]$.

In the end we have:

$$S(\alpha) = (\frac{1}{(1 + e^{-(\alpha-0.5)*6.\bar{6}})} - 0.0344)*1.074 \tag{9}$$

$S(\alpha) = 0$, when $\alpha = 0$ and $S(\alpha) = 1$, when $\alpha = 1$. $S(\alpha)$ replaces α in equations 5 and 6. This is referred to as the sigmoid model. Figure 3(a, o) shows a plot using the sigmoid model. Note that it is more evenly distributed. Figure 3 (b-d) shows an photo of a single square of the macbeth color checker with a soft shadow covering the upper half, a similar synthesized image where the shadow is generated by the linear shadow model and the sigmoid model.

Figure 4 shows the profiles of the real and synthesized images scaled by different factors to match the same albedo (outgoing/observed light = albedo reflectance times incoming light).

The presented models are based on two basic rules in color and illumination theory for diffuse surfaces: (1) A change in the ratio of sun light and sky light is a color temperature change, and (2) the observed wavelengths from a surface are based on its albedo proportional to the light that illuminates it. This gives the model a simple construction and a simple initialization. If the ratio between a sunlit surface and its corresponding shadow can be found, it is easy to find the overlay color.

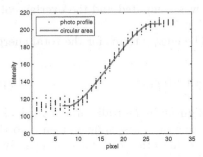 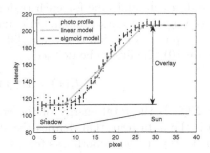

Fig. 4. The dots are pixels from a profile of fig. 3(b). It clearly shows the S curve shape. [Left] A fit of the area function A in eq. 4. [Right] Overlapping profiles from the penumbra regions in fig. 3(c-d). The height between the high and low depends on the overlay color. A simple sketch of the profile of the α channel is imposed in the bottom of the plot.

Two versions of the model are given; a linear penumbra model and a sigmoid penumbra model. The linear model is more simple to compute, but it is more difficult to use it for making natural looking penumbras. The sigmoid model is a better model for the natural penumbra, because all you have to o is to decide the width of the penumbra and make a linear slope from 0 to 1 in the α-channel. For detection of shadows it is hard to predict which model is more useful. However, it may be easier for an algorithm to optimize a linear slope in the α-channel than a sigmoid curve.

2.1   Estimation of α Via Graph Cuts

Even though the aim is unsupervised segmentation we used a simple kind of user interaction such as [8]. They used a few strokes from the user to train gaussian mixture models in order to segment complex foreground objects with alpha channels such as hair and spider webs using graph cuts. Our user interaction consisted of pointing out a square of a surface in sun light and the same surface in shadow. The mean R,G and B intensities of these squares were used to calculate the overlay color (eq. 7).

We treated the α estimation as a piecewise smooth labeling problem. An energy function would be minimized using graph cuts. If an energy function can be described as binary variables with regular energy terms with robust metrics, it is fast to find a strong local minimum [9]. The energy function should relate to the question "what is the probability that this relatively dark segment is the result of a partially translucent overlay upon the real image?".

The problem formulation was defined as a graph cut minimization of α_i in equation 5, because the the overlay is in fact constant for the whole image. The α channel of the overlay was estimated through α-expansions (thus reducing the problem to binary labels). The color of the overlay was given by manual initialization by handpicking a sunlit surface and its shadow counterpart. The mean red, green, and blue for each region was computed and the overlay color was given by $1 - \mu_{shadow}/\mu_{sun}$ as in equation 7.

The graph construction is given in [9]. The energy terms for the total energy (equation 10) remains to be defined.

$$E(f) = D^i(f) + V^{i,j}(f) \tag{10}$$

where $E(f)$ is the total energy of the configuration f of all variables (pixels). $D^i(f)$ is the data term that defines the static cost of assigning a given α to the pixel i. $V^{i,j}(f)$ is the smoothness term that defines the cost of assigning a given set of neighboring α's to the pixels i, j.

There were a number of ideas how to use the data term and the simplest method is to use a constant, because there is no way to tell if a given pixel is shadow. A sunlit black matte surface is darker than most bright surfaces in shadow.

The segmentation relied on the smoothness constraint. Common hypotheses are that the shadow changes gradually and is piecewise smooth. Common examples of discontinuity preserving energy terms are Potts term and the truncated linear difference term. In addition some heuristics about chromaticity edges could be used. We used the illumination direction vector as to label edges as albedo edge or shadow edge. For all edges we found the direction and angle between the illumination direction vector and the chromaticity edge using cross- and dot products. If an edge was over a certain threshold and the angle was under a certain threshold then it was considered a shadow edge, else it was an albedo edge.

Pott's energy term (eq. 11) was used when there was no edge or the edge was an albedo edge.

$$V_{i,j \in N}(f(i), f(j)) = \begin{cases} 0 & , \text{if} f(i) = f(j) \\ \lambda & , \text{if} f(i) \neq f(j) \end{cases} \tag{11}$$

If an edge was a shadow edge and its gradient was consistent with the gradient in the α-channel (consistent when they are opposite each other), then the energy was given by the absolute difference between the neighboring pixels in the estimated shadow free image (eq. 12) without the use of windows. In addition there was a second smoothness term that imposes a gradient on the α-channel. If the gradients were inconsistent the energy would be very large (λ_2).

$$V(p,q) = V_1(p,q) + V_2(p,q) \tag{12}$$
$$V_1(p,q) = |sf(p) - sf(q)| * w_{sf} \tag{13}$$
$$V_2(p,q) = |\alpha(p) - \alpha(q)| * w_\alpha \tag{14}$$

where w_{sf} and w_α controls importance between smoothness in the shadow free image and the α channel.

This smoothness term is not a regular metric at the shadow edges, so it is made regular through truncation. When building the graph, regularity is tested $(V(1,0) + V(0,1) \geq V(0,0) + V(1,1))$. When it is not regular, the energies are

Fig. 5. Results trying to remove the shadow from figure 3(right)(sigma). [Left] Image (top) and detected shadow edges (bottom). [Middle] Estimation of α using linear model. [Right] using sigmoid model. [Top] estimated shadow free image. [Bottom] estimated alpha channel. Black is $\alpha = 0$ and white is $\alpha = 1$.

manipulated in such a way that the information given by the shadow edge is still maintained while $V(1,0) + V(0,1) = V(0,0) + V(1,1)$.

To avoid problems with soft edges a neighborhood system that resembles pyramid scale space jumps was used. It was based on a 4-connected neighborhood (having two neighborhood relations; $x-1$ and $y-1$) and was extended to 4-layers by adding neighborhood relations at -2, -4, and -8.

An aggressive edge-preserving graph cut image restoration algorithm was applied to remove disturbing high frequency noise and texture in for example concrete and grass texture.

3   Experimental Results

The algorithm was applied with the sigmoid model to real life situations.

First we tested the approach in perfect conditions: A synthetic macbeth color checker image with 3 color squares surrounded with an almost black border so that the algorithm cannot rely on intensities. See figure 5. Five different α levels were estimated. It is not a perfect reconstruction of the penumbra area. The entire penumbra region was not accurately labeled as shadow edges. This causes an uneven gradient in the α channel. In real images we can expect even more inaccurate edge labels.

For generality we chose a two examples with a professional linear camera in RAW format (see figure 6) and two examples with a nonlinear consumer camera in JPEG format (see figure 7). Three different α levels were estimated for all images except the first photo of the camera man shadow, where there were five levels.

Figure 6(left) shows a typical situation where the shadow of the camera man is in the image. The penumbra areas are very wide here. The shadow free image shows that some parts of penumbra are overestimated and others are underestimated. The pavement in the upper right corner is falsely segmented as shadow. This is probably due to ambient occlusion from the building next to it.

Fig. 6. Results with a linear professional camera (Canon eos-1 mark II). RAW format. [Top left] Original image. [Top right] estimated shadow free image. [Bottom left] Shadow edges based on 4-connected neighborhood. [Bottom right] estimated alpha channel.

Fig. 7. Results with a nonlinear consumer camera (Minolta Dimage 414). JPEG format.

Figure 6(right) shows a large connected shadow from a larger building onto a smaller building. despite of many false shadow edges, the general region of shadow is found. However, a wet darker spot on the parking lot causes the shadow region to "bleed" into this spot, too. The penumbra areas are not well represented here and it shows at the shadow borders in the shadow free image.

Figure 7(left) A building in Berlin. Some of the windows are falsely segmented as shadows. Otherwise the result is very accurate. The penumbra areas are not well represented here either.

Figure 7(right) 4 people on a street in Berlin. The round tower is very encouraging because the penumbra is present and makes for a smooth transition. The faces of the buildings in the background that faces away from the sun are accurately segmented as shadow. The people's faces are also divided into left part in sun and right part on shadow and it shows in the shadow mask (3 out 4 faces are correctly segmented). Their shirts are also rather accurate. The penumbra areas are missing at the shadow on the ground from the people. The road to the left of the people are falsely segmented as shadow because the shadow free estimation just happened to match the pavement.

3.1 Discussion

The sigmoid shadow model made it easy to augment a natural soft shadow. The model work both ways; it can compute the shadowed areas from sunlit areas and compute sunlit areas from shadowed areas. This has been used to control a graph cut segmentation of shadows and removal of shadows on real images. The model need initialization of the overlay color, which is related to Finlayson's calibration of "illumination direction".

The results demonstrated that it is possible to make useful estimates of the α parameter in the model for real images. The quality of such estimation was to a degree where it may be possible to extract information about the sun position given some rough information about geometry. Surprisingly it was possible to use the algorithm on JPEG images from a consumer camera with automatic settings.

The exact width of the soft shadows were difficult to estimate. The lesser the number of α levels that were possible, the better the segmentation was. This might be solved by introducing a second pass in between each iteration that optimizes the gradient at the shadow edges. Without a data term a connected shadow region is most likely to be detected if the major part of its boundary it covered inside the image and by shadow edges.

The model need initialization of the overlay color, which is related to Finlayson's [4] calibration of "illumination direction". In every day situations it is not feasible to assume fixed camera parameters, so an image based initialization is required.

Future work involves automatic initialization through gaussian mixture color cluster based classification that may also be used as a data term, and alpha gradient optimization possibly as a second step in a 2-pass algorithm. The effect of ambient occlusion and to some degree surface normals and inter-reflections would be interesting aspects to consider if they can be approximated by the models as well.

4   Conclusions

Our contribution is two novel models of shadows such that natural shadows can be segmented and augmented virtual objects can cast exact soft shadows. The new feature in these models is the ability to represent natural penumbra (soft shadows). A graph cut based solution was presented using irregular energy terms which was truncated to enforce regularity. A neighborhood scheme that emulated pyramid sampling was introduced. It was demonstrated that this solution could make convincing but not perfect estimates of the α parameter in the model for real images.

Acknowledgments

This research is funded by the CoSPE project (26-04-0171) under the Danish Research Agency. This support is gratefully acknowledged.

References

1. Salvador, E., Cavallaro, A., Ebrahimi, T.: Shadow identification and classification using invariant color models. In: Proc. of IEEE Signal Processing Society International Conference on Acoustics, Speech, and Signal Processing (ICASSP-2001) Salt Lake City (Utah, USA), 7-11 May. (2001) 1545–1548
2. Salvador, E., Cavallaro, A., Ebrahimi, T.: Cast shadow segmentation using invariant color features. Comput. Vis. Image Underst. **95** (2004) 238–259
3. Madsen, C.B.: Using real shadows to create virtual ones. In Bigün, J., Gustavsson, T., eds.: SCIA. Volume 2749 of Lecture Notes in Computer Science., Springer (2003) 820–827
4. Finlayson, G.D., Hordley, S.D., Drew, M.S.: Removing shadows from images. In Heyden, A., Sparr, G., Nielsen, M., Johansen, P., eds.: ECCV (4). Volume 2353 of Lecture Notes in Computer Science., Springer (2002) 823–836
5. Finlayson, G.D., Hordley, S.D., Drew, M.S.: Removing shadows from images using retinex. In: Color Imaging Conference, IS&T - The Society for Imaging Science and Technology (2002) 73–79
6. Lu, C., Drew, M.S.: Shadow segmentation and shadow-free chromaticity via markov random fields. In: IS&T/SID 13th Color Imaging Conference. (2005)
7. Barnard, K., Funt, B.: Experiments in sensor sharpening for color constancy. In: IS&T/SID Sixth Color Imaging Conference: Color Science, Systems and Applications Scottsdale, Arizona,November 1998. (1998) 43–46
8. Wang, J., Cohen, M.F.: An iterative optimization approach for unified image segmentation and matting. In: ICCV, IEEE Computer Society (2005) 936–943
9. Kolmogorov, V., Zabih, R.: What energy functions can be minimized via graph cuts? IEEE Trans. Pattern Anal. Mach. Intell. **26** (2004) 147–159

Sub-pixel Edge Fitting Using B-Spline

Frédéric Bouchara[1], Marc Bertrand[1], Sofiane Ramdani[2],
and Mahmoud Haydar[1]

[1] Université du Sud Toulon-Var,UMR CNRS 6168 LSIS,
B.P. 20132, 83957 La Garde Cedex, France
{bouchara,bertrand}@univ-tln.fr
[2] Université de Montpellier I, EA 2991 EDM, France
sofiane.ramdani@univ-montp1.fr

Abstract. In this paper we propose an algorithm for the sub-pixel edge detection using a B-spline model. In contrast to the usual methods which are generally sensitive to local perturbations, our approach is based on a global computation of the edge using a Maximum Likelihood rule. In the proposed algorithm the likelihood of the observations is explicitly computed, it ensures the filtering of the noisiest data. Experiments are given and show the adequacy and effectiveness of this algorithm.

1 Introduction

Extracting object boundaries accurately is one of the most important and challenging problems in image processing. An important approach of edge extraction is concerned with improving the detection accuracy and different sub-pixel edge detectors can be found in the literature.

A popular approach used to compute the subpixel location of the edge is based on the moments of the image. Among the methods belonging to this category one can find algorithms using the gray level moments [1], the spatial moments [2,3,4,5] or the Zernike moments [6,7].

The interpolation of the image is another method used to compute the subpixel coordinates of the edge. In [8], Nomura *et al.* propose a method in which the first derivative perpendicular to the orientation of the edge is approximated by a normal function. The location of the edge is estimated to subpixel accuracy by computing the maximum of this function. Other studies are based on linear [9], quadratic interpolation [10], B-spline [11] or other kind of non-linear functions [12].

Others have extended the sub-pixel localization technique to corners and vertex [13,14] or circular edges [15].

However, in all of these approaches, the estimation is local and does not include a model of the noise. Hence, in these processes, the local perturbations strongly disturb the final result. An usual filtering approach consists in introducing an *a priori* information in the estimation process. In edge detection, this can be achieved by using a deformable model such as the snake model proposed by Kass *et al.* [16]. In more recent works, the deformable contour is modelled

A. Gagalowicz and W. Philips (Eds.): MIRAGE 2007, LNCS 4418, pp. 353–364, 2007.
© Springer-Verlag Berlin Heidelberg 2007

using piecewise polynomial functions (B-spline snakes) [17,18]. Such a formulation of an active contour allows local control, compact representation, and it is mainly characterized by few parameters.

In this paper, we propose an algorithm for the estimation of the sub-pixel edges using a global approach based on a B-spline model. Our approach is similar to the model proposed in [19]. However, in our method the statistical properties of the observations are computed and used in a Maximum Likelihood estimation which insures an efficient filtering of the noisy data.

This paper is organized as follows. In section 2, we briefly recall the classical formulation of the B-spline model. In section 3 we present the proposed extension to the sub-pixel case. Finally section 4 is devoted to the experimental results of this algorithm.

2   B-Spline Model

In this section, we present a brief theoretical review of B-spline contour formulation (for more details see [20]).

Let $\{t_0, t_1, \ldots, t_{k-1}\}$ be the set of so-called knots. By definition, spline functions are polynomial inside each interval $[t_{i-1}, t_i]$ and exhibit a certain degree of continuity at the knots. The set $\{B_{i,n(t)}, i = 0, \ldots, k - n - 1\}$ of the so called B-splines, constitutes a basis for the linear space of all the splines on $[t_n, t_{k-n}]$. Thus, a spline curve $f(t)$ of degree n is given by :

$$f(t) = \sum_{i=0}^{k-n-1} p_i B_{i,n}(t) \tag{1}$$

where p_i are the weights applied to the respective basis functions $B_{i,n}$. The B-Spline functions are defined by the Cox-deBoor recursion formulas:

$$B_{i,0}(t) = \begin{cases} 1 & \text{if} \quad t_i \leq t \leq t_{i+1} \\ 0 & \text{else} \end{cases} \tag{2}$$

and

$$B_{i,n}(t) = \frac{t - t_i}{t_{i+n} - t_i} B_{i,n-1}(t) + \frac{t_{i+n+1} - t}{t_{i+n+1} - t_{i+1}} B_{i+1,n-1}(t) \tag{3}$$

The $B_{i,n}(t)$ are nonnegative, $B_{i,n}(t) \geq 0$ and verify the partition of unity property : $\sum_i B_{i,n}(t) = 1$ for all t.

In the sequel of the paper, cubic B-spline will be used and without lost of generality we will drop the index n. Relation (1) can be expressed compactly in matrix notation as:

$$f(t) = B^T(t).\theta \tag{4}$$

$B(t)$ is the vector of B-spline functions: $B(t) = (B_0(t), B_2(t), \ldots B_{N-1}(t))$ and θ is the vector of weights: $\theta = (p_0, ., p_{N-1})^T$

The $\mathcal{R}^2$ version of (1) describes an open parametric snake on the plane: $v(t) = \left(x(t), y(t) \right)$. The $p_i = (p_{xi}, p_{yi})$ are now 2D vectors and are called the control points.

To describe a closed curve, which is the case of interest for boundary representation, a periodic extension of the basis functions and of the knot sequence is generally used.

3   Subpixel B-Spline Fitting

3.1   Observational Model

In this sub-section we shall derive the expression of the likelihood of the observation. In order to get tractable computations, we have developed our model in the case of a white additive Gaussian noise b. We denote σ_b its standard deviation.

Let $v_e = \left\{ v_e(i.h) = \left(x_e(i.h), y_e(i.h) \right), i \in \{1, ..., M\} \right\}$ be a set of edge pixels with integer coordinates computed by a classical algorithm (as the classical active contour algorithm). For the sake of simplicity, we will denote in the following v_{ei} the element $v_e(i.h)$, this rule will be applied for all the variables relative to the pixel i.

For each pixel of this set we suppose available the observation vector $O_i = (X_i, H_i)$. The vector $H_i = (H_{xi}, H_{yi})$ is the local gradient of the image and X_i corresponds to an estimation of the sub-pixel position of the edge along H_i. The value X_i is estimated in the local coordinate system of the pixel thanks to a quadratic interpolation (see [21] and the appendix for more explanations). These variables are supposed to be the observation version of the "true" variables (Y_i, G_i). The cartesian coordinates of the observation O_i will be noted (x_{oi}, y_{oi}) in the sequel.

Let now $v_s(t) = (x_s(t) = B(t).\theta_x, y_s(t) = B(t).\theta_y)$ be the B-spline model of the edge, where $\theta = (\theta_x, \theta_y)$ is the vector of k control points (with $M >> k$).

The likelihood $P(O_i/\theta)$ can be expressed as the product of two elementary probability density function (pdf):

$$P(O_i/\theta) = P(X_i/H_i, \theta) P(H_i/\theta) \tag{5}$$

In order to derive the first factor of this expression, we make the assumption that X_i only depends on $v_s(t(i)) = \left(x_s(t(i)) = x_{si}, y_s(t(i)) = y_{si} \right)$, the corresponding edge point in the direction H_i of which the polar coordinates are (Y_i, H_i). In first approximation we have modelled the pdf $P(X_i/H_i, Y_i)$ with a Gaussian law. According to our tests, this approximation remains accurate even for significant noise levels. Then we get:

$$P(X_i/H_i, \theta) = P(X_i/H_i, Y_i) \tag{6}$$

$$= \frac{1}{\sqrt{2\pi}\sigma_{Xi}} \exp\left(-\frac{(X_i - Y_i)^2}{2.\sigma_{Xi}^2} \right)$$

$$= \frac{1}{\sqrt{2\pi}\sigma_{Xi}} \exp\left(-\frac{(x_{oi} - x_{si})^2 + (y_{oi} - y_{si})^2}{2.\sigma_{Xi}^2} \right)$$

The computation of σ_{Xi}, based on a modified version of the method proposed in [22], is described in the appendix.

Let us now compute the expression of $P(H_i/\theta)$. The components of H_i are classically computed by convoluting the original image with derivative kernels noted K_x and K_y. Using the assumption of a Gaussian additive noise, it is straightforward to show that $P(H_i/G_i)$ is also Gaussian. The cross-correlation and auto-correlation functions of the vertical and horizontal components of H are given by the following well known relation:

$$C_{xy}(x_i - x_j, y_i - y_j) = E[H_{xi}.H_{yj}] - E[H_{xi}]E[H_{yj}] \qquad (7)$$
$$= \sigma_b^2 \delta(x_i - x_j, y_i - y_j) \otimes K_x(x,y) \otimes K_y^*(-x,-y)$$

Where K_x^* and K_y^* are the complex conjugate of the matrices K_x and K_y.

Using this relation it is easy to show that:

$$E[H_{xi}.H_{yi}/G_{xi}G_{yi}] - E[H_{xi}/G_{xi}G_{yi}]E[H_{yi}/G_{xi}G_{yi}] = 0 \qquad (8)$$

and

$$E[H_{xi}.H_{xi}/G_{xi}] - E[H_{xi}/G_{xi}]E[H_{xi}/G_{xi}] = \sigma_b^2 \cdot \sum_{i,j} K_x(i,j))^2 \qquad (9)$$

$$= \sigma_b^2 \cdot \sum_{i,j} K_y(i,j)^2 = \sigma_H^2 \qquad (10)$$

where $E[w/z]$ represents the conditional expected value of w assuming z.

Let J_i be the vector defined by $J_i = (G_{yi}, -G_{xi})$ and let R_i be the unit vector collinear to v_s in v_{si}. H_i and J_i are clearly related by a normal distribution.

To express the law $P(H_i/\theta)$ we use the well known property of the edge to be orthogonal to the local gradient. Then, we get:

$$P(H_i/\theta) = P(H_i/R_i(\theta)) = \int \frac{P(H_i/J_i)P(J_i)}{P(R_i(\theta))} \qquad (11)$$

where the integration is achieved for all the values of J_i collinear to R_i that is for $J_i = a.R_i$. Equation (11) can be expressed by:

$$P(H_i/\theta) = \frac{\left(2\pi\sigma_H^2\right)^{-1}}{P(R_i)} \int_{-\infty}^{+\infty} \exp\left(-\frac{(H_{yi} - a.R_{xi})^2}{2.\sigma_H^2}\right) \times$$
$$\exp\left(-\frac{(H_{xi} + a.R_{yi})^2}{2.\sigma_H^2}\right) P(J_i) da \qquad (12)$$

In the previous equation, $P(J_i)$ is the *a priori* probability of J_i. The gradient has not a privileged direction and the uniform regions are supposed to be more frequent than the regions with a high gradient magnitude. Thus, $P(J_i)$ is modelled with the following centered normal law:

$$P(J_i) = \frac{1}{\sqrt{\pi}\Sigma} \exp\left(-\frac{\|J_i\|^2}{\Sigma^2}\right) = \frac{1}{\sqrt{\pi}\Sigma} \exp\left(-\frac{a^2}{\Sigma^2}\right) \qquad (13)$$

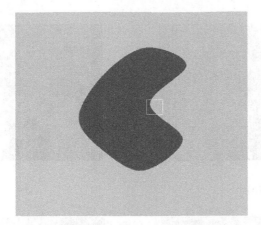

Fig. 1. Test image

Using this assumption we can compute the equation (12):

$$P(H_i/\theta) = K.\exp\left(-\frac{H_{yi}^2 + H_{xi}^2}{2\sigma_H^2 + \Sigma^2}\right)\exp\left(-\frac{(H_{xi}R_{xi} + H_{yi}R_{yi})^2\Sigma^2}{2\sigma_H^2(2\sigma_H^2 + \Sigma^2)}\right) \quad (14)$$

with K a normalization constant involving $P(R_i)$, Σ and σ_H.

We assume Σ large compared to σ_H and we write:

$$P(H_i/\theta) \approx K.\exp\left(-\frac{H_{yi}^2 + H_{xi}^2}{\Sigma^2}\right)\exp\left(-\frac{(H_{xi}R_{xi} + H_{yi}R_{yi})^2}{2\sigma_H^2}\right) \quad (15)$$

In the above, vector R_i is given by:

$$R_i = \frac{T_i}{\|T_i\|} \qquad \text{where} \qquad T_i = \left(\frac{\partial x_s(t(i))}{\partial t}, \frac{\partial y_s(t(i))}{\partial t}\right)^T$$

$T = \|T_i\|$ is assumed to be constant along the edge.

The components of vector T_i are also B-spline functions of which the spline basis functions have the following expression:

$$\frac{\partial B_{n,i}(t)}{\partial t} = \frac{n}{t_{i+n} - t_i}B_{i,n-1}(t) - \frac{n}{t_{i+n+1} - t_{i+1}}B_{i+1,n-1}(t) \quad (16)$$

The global likelihood is simply estimated by assuming that the O_i's are conditionally independent. Hence, the global likelihood is factorized as: $P(O/v_s) = \prod_i P(O_i/v_s)$.

3.2 Numerical Implementation

To compute θ we simply apply the Maximum Likelihood rule, that is:

$$\hat{\theta} = \arg.\max_\theta \prod_i P(X_i/H_i, \theta)P(H_i/\theta) \quad (17)$$

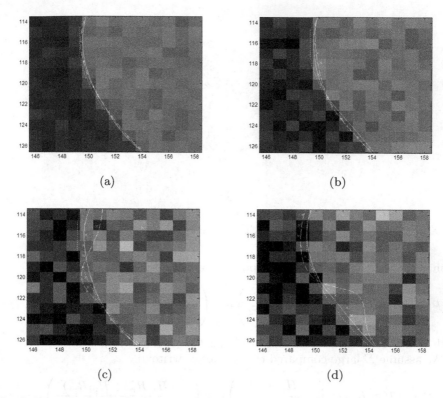

(a)   (b)

(c)   (d)

Fig. 2. Comparative results between the proposed algorithm (solid), the true edge (dotted) and the classical spline interpolation (dashed). The measured subpixel coordinates are noted with white crosses (x). (a) 10 percent of noise, (b) 20 percent of noise, (c) 40 percent of noise and (d) 50 percent of noise.

This relation classically yields to the minimization of an energy function which, in our case, is the following quadratic function:

$$E(\theta) = (\mathbf{d} - \mathcal{B}\theta)^T W (\mathbf{d} - \mathcal{B}\theta)$$ (18)

In the above, $\mathbf{d}$ is a $(3M \times 1)$ vector defined by:

$$\mathbf{d} = (x_{o1}, \ldots, x_{oM}, y_{o1}, \ldots, y_{oM}, 0, \ldots, 0)^T,$$

W is a $(3M \times 3M)$ diagonal matrix with $W_{i,i} = W_{i+M,i+M} = \frac{1}{\sigma_{Xi}^2}$ and $W_{i+2M,i+2M} = \frac{1}{T^2\sigma_H^2}$,

$\mathcal{B}$ is a $(3M \times 2N)$ matrix: $\mathcal{B} = \begin{pmatrix} \mathbf{B} & 0 \\ 0 & \mathbf{B} \\ \mathbf{B_x} & \mathbf{B_y} \end{pmatrix}$

The components of matrix $\mathbf{B}$ are obtained from the $B_i(t)$ functions: $\mathbf{B}_{ij} = B_j(t(i))$. In the current implementation of the algorithm we have simply used a uniform distribution of the $i's$ points, that is, $t(i) = i/M$.

The components of $\mathbf{B_x}$ and $\mathbf{B_y}$ are computed from (15) and (16): $\mathbf{B_{x}}_{ij} = NH_{xi}\left(B_{i,2}(i/M) - B_{i+1,2}(i/M)\right)$ and $\mathbf{B_{y}}_{ij} = NH_{yi}\left(B_{j,2}(i/M) - B_{j+1,2}(i/M)\right)$

As classically, the solution $\hat{\theta} = \arg\min_\theta E(\theta)$ is given by the weighted least square relation: $\hat{\theta} = (\mathcal{B}^T W \mathcal{B})^{-1}\mathcal{B}^T W \mathbf{d}$.

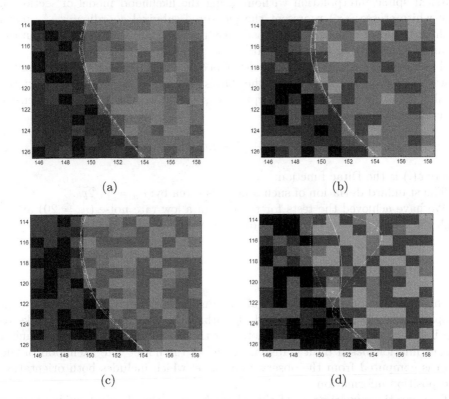

(a)   (b)

(c)   (d)

Fig. 3. Comparative results between the proposed algorithm (solid), the true edge (dotted) and the classical spline interpolation (dashed). The measured subpixel coordinates are noted with white crosses (x). (a) $p_0 = 0.2\ \gamma = 0.3$, (b) $p_0 = 0.2\ \gamma = 0.6$, (c) $p_0 = 0.4\ \gamma = 0.3$ and (d) $p_0 = 0.4\ \gamma = 0.6$.

4   Experimental Results

In order to validate the proposed algorithm, we have achieved several tests on the synthetic 256×256 image, normalized between 0 and 1, shown on figure 1. We have numerically simulated the optical integration of the intensity over the pixels in low-pass filtering and sub-sampling a 2048×2048 version of this image. The reference 'true' edge can be hence easily computed. For all the tests achieved in this section we have computed the gradient by using the derivative of a Gaussian kernel with a standard deviation equal to 1. The number of knots N is set to $M/4$.

We present the results for a small area localized by a small square in figure 1.

First, we have tested this algorithm for a white additive Gaussian noise with standard deviations equal to 0.1, 0.2, 0.4 and 0.5 which represent respectively 10, 20, 40 and 50 percent of the maximum amplitude. In figure 2, we compare the results obtained with this algorithm with the reference 'true' edge and the classical spline interpolation without using the likelihood model of section 3. The white crosses ($\times$) represent the measured subpixel coordinates. As usual with this kind of approach, the most noisy measures are weakly involved in the estimation process en hence filtered.

The proposed model has been developed in the case of a Gaussian noise. However, it remains efficient for other kinds of noise. In figure 3 we present the results obtained with a salt & pepper noise of which the probability density function is defined by:

$$P(x) = p_0\delta(x - \gamma) + (1 - 2.p_0)\delta(x) + p_0\delta(x + \gamma)$$

where $\delta(.)$ is the Dirac function.

The standard deviation of such a noise is given by: $\sigma_n = \gamma\sqrt{2p_0}$.

We have achieved the tests for the case of a low rate noise ($p_0 = 20$) and a high rate noise ($p_0 = 40$) with two different values of the amplitude γ.

5   Conclusion

In this paper we have presented an algorithm for the estimation of the edge with subpixel accuracy. In the proposed algorithm, the edge is modelled thanks to the B-spline approach. The parameters of the model are computed by using a ML estimation based on a Gaussian model of the noise. The likelihood of the data is computed from the observation model which includes both orientation and position information.

Comparative experiments of this algorithm and the classical spline interpolation have been carried out for two different kinds of noise: a Gaussian noise and a Salt & Pepper noise. These numerical experiments have shown that our algorithm outperforms the classical approach for these two kinds of noise.

References

1. A. J. Tabatabai, R. Mitchell, Edge localisation to sub-pixel values in digital imagery, IEEE Trans. Patt. Anal. Mach. Intell. **6**, pp 188-201 (1984)
2. E.P. Lyvers, O. R. Mitchell, Precision edge contrast and orientation estimation, IEEE Trans. Patt. Anal. Mach. Intell. **10**, pp 927–937 (1988)
3. E.P. Lyvers, O. R. Mitchell, M. L. Akey, A. P. Reeves, Sub-pixel measurements using a moment based edge operator, IEEE Trans. Patt. Anal. Mach. Intell. **11**, pp 1293–1309 (1989)
4. Y. Shan, G. W. Boon, Sub-pixel localisation of edges with non-uniform blurring: a finite closed-form approach, Image and Vision computing **18**, pp 1015–1023 (2000)

5. Shyi-Chyi Cheng, Tian-LuuWu, Subpixel edge detection of color images by principal axis analysis and moment-preserving principle, Patt. Recog. **38**, pp 527–537 (2005)
6. S. Ghosal, R. Mehrotra, Orthogonal moment operators for sub-pixel edge detection, Patt. Recog. **26**, pp 295–306 (1993)
7. Q. Ying-Donga, C. Cheng-Songa, C. San-Benb, L. Jin-Quan, A fast subpixel edge detection method using SobelZernike moments operator, Image and Vision Computing, **23**, pp 11–17 (2005)
8. Y. Nomura, M. Sagara, H. Naruse, A. Ide, "Edge location to sub-pixel precision and analysis," System Comput. in Japan, **22**, pp 70–80 (1991)
9. Stephan Hussmann, Thian H. Ho, A high-speed subpixel edge detector implementation inside a FPGA, Real-Time Imaging **9**, pp 361–368,(2003)
10. M. Baba,K. Ohtani, A novel subpixel edge detection system for dimension measurement and object localization using an analogue-based approach, IOP Publishing Journal of Optics A: Pure & Applied Optics, **3**, pp 276–83, (2001)
11. F. Truchetet, F. Nicolier, O. Laligant, "Subpixel edge detection for dimensional controle by artificial vision," J. Electronic Imaging **10**, pp 234–239 (2001)
12. K. Jensen, D. Anastassiou, "Subpixel edge localization and the interpolation of still images," IEEE Trans. Image Processing **4**, pp 285–295 (1995)
13. R. Deriche, G. Giruadon, "A computational approach for corner and vertex detection," Int. J. Comp. Vision **10**, pp 101–124 (1993)
14. H. Wang, M. Brady, "Real-time corner detection algorithm for motion estimation," Image and Vision Computing **13**, pp 695–703, (1995).
15. Fei-Long Chen, Shiaur-Wehn Lin, "Subpixel estimation of circle parameters using orthogonal circular detector," Computer Vision & Image Underst. bf 78, pp 206–221 (2000)
16. M. Kass, A. Witkin, and D. Terzopoulos, "Snakes: Active contour models," Int. J. Comp. Vision **1**, pp 321–331, (1988)
17. P. Brigger, J. Hoeg , and M. Unser, B-splines snakes: A flexible tool for parametric contour detection, IEEE Trans. Image processing **9**, pp. 1484–1087, (2000).
18. Ravinda G.N. Meegama and Jagath C. Rajapakse, NURBS, Image and Vision Computing **21** , pp. 551–562, (2003).
19. S. Venkatesh, M. Kisworo, G. A. West, "Detection of curved edges at sub-pixel accuracy using deformable models," In *Proceedings of IEEE conf. Vis. Image Signal Process.*, pp 304–312, (1995).
20. C. deBoor. A Practical Guide to Splines. Springer Verlag, N. York, (1978).
21. F. Devernay, "A Non-Maxima Suppression Method for Edge Detection with Sub-Pixel Accuracy," INRIA Sophia Antipolis Research Report Nb. 2724, (1995).
22. F. Bouchara, "Efficient algorithm for computation of the second-order moment of the subpixel-edge position," Applied Optics **43**, pp 4550–4558, (2004).
23. R. Deriche, Using Canny's criteria to derive a recursively implemented optimal edge detector, Int. J. Comp. Vision **1**, pp 167–187, (1987).

A   Computation of σ_X

The method used to interpolate the subpixel coordinate is basically an improvement of a well-known edge detection method sometimes called NMS (Non-Maxima Suppression). The NMS method consists of the suppression of the local non-maxima of the magnitude of the gradient of image intensity in the direction of this gradient [23]. The sub-pixel approximation proposed in [21] adds a new step to the NMS process: when the point (x, y) is a local maximum then the position of the edge point in the direction of the gradient is given by the maximum of a quadratic interpolation on the values of the squared gradient norms at (x, y) and the neighboring points (figure 4).

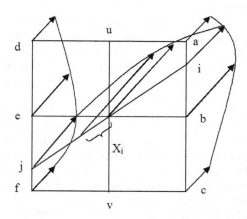

Fig. 4. Estimation of the subpixel location X_i by using quadratic interpolation of the square gradient norm

Let i be an edge pixel and let a, b, c, d, e, f, u and v be its vicinity. Let N_a, N_b ... and N_i be the corresponding squared gradient norms.

Let (H_{xs}, H_{ys}) be the two coordinates of the gradient vector at S and let:

$$\alpha = \frac{H_{ys}}{H_{xs}} \tag{19}$$

We consider here the case $\alpha < 1$. In the direction defined by α the squared gradient norms N_k and N_l in k and l are interpolated using two quadratic functions involving respectively N_a, N_b, N_c and N_d, N_e, N_f. The subpixel coordinate X_s of the edge is obtained by computing the maximum of a third quadratic curve defined by the points k, l and i. After some computations we obtain:

$$X_s = \frac{(N_e - N_b) + \frac{1}{2}(N_a - N_c + N_d - N_f)\alpha + \ldots}{2(N_b + N_e - 2N_i) + (N_c - N_a + N_d - N_f)\alpha + \ldots} \frac{\ldots - \frac{1}{2}(2N_b - N_a - N_c + N_d - 2N_e + N_f)\alpha^2}{\ldots (N_a - 2N_b + N_c + N_d - 2N_e + N_f)\alpha^2} \tag{20}$$

Which can be written:

$$X_s = \frac{(M_1 \otimes N)_{(0,0)}}{(M_2 \otimes N)_{(0,0)}} = \frac{A}{B} \tag{21}$$

Where $\otimes$ represents the convolution operator. Matrices M_1 and M_2 have the following expressions:

$$M_1 = \begin{pmatrix} -\alpha - \alpha^2 & 0 & -\alpha + \alpha^2 \\ -2 + 2\alpha^2 & 0 & 2 - 2\alpha^2 \\ \alpha - \alpha^2 & 0 & \alpha + \alpha^2 \end{pmatrix} \quad M_2 = \begin{pmatrix} 2\alpha + \alpha^2 & 0 & -2\alpha + \alpha^2 \\ 4 - 4\alpha^2 & -4 & 4 - 4\alpha^2 \\ -2\alpha + 2\alpha^2 & 0 & 2\alpha + 2\alpha^2 \end{pmatrix}$$

To compute the standard deviation of $X_s = \frac{A}{B}$ we first define this ratio of two random variables as follows:

$$\frac{A}{B} = \frac{A_c + E[A]}{B_c + E[B]} \tag{22}$$

In the above, A_c and B_c are the centered parts of A and B. We then apply a second order power series approximation on the denominator variable around $E[B]$. After some computations we get:

$$E\left[\frac{A}{B}\right] \approx \frac{E[A]}{E[B]} - \frac{C_{AB}}{E[B]^2} + \frac{E[A]\sigma_B^2}{E[B]^3} \tag{23}$$

$$E\left[\left(\frac{A}{B}\right)^2\right] \approx \frac{E[A]^2}{E[B]^2} + \frac{\sigma_A^2}{E[B]^2} + 3\frac{E[A]^2\sigma_B^2}{E[B]^4} - 4\frac{E[A]C_{AB}}{E[B]^3}$$
$$+ 3\frac{\sigma_A^2\sigma_B^2 + 2C_{AB}^2}{E[B]^4} \tag{24}$$

Where $\sigma_A^2 = E[A_c^2]$, $\sigma_B^2 = E[B_c^2]$ and $C_{AB} = E[A_cB_c]$.

To compute the equations (23) and (24) we need the expressions of $E[A]$, $E[B]$, $E[A^2]$, $E[B^2]$ and $E[AB]$.

From (21) and using a classical result we can write:

$$E[A] = (M_1 \otimes E[N])_{(0,0)} \quad \text{and} \quad E[B] = (M_2 \otimes E[N])_{(0,0)} \tag{25}$$

Note that in the above, the expectations are conditional assuming H_s and hence α is deterministic.

The expected value $E[N_s]$ on a given pixel s is simply obtained from the expression of N_s by using equation (7):

$$E[N_s] = E[H_{xs}^2 + H_{ys}^2] = E[H_{xs}^2] + E[H_{ys}^2]$$
$$= C_{xx}(0,0) + C_{yy}(0,0) + E[H_{xs}]^2 + E[H_{ys}]^2 \tag{26}$$

To compute the joint second moments of A and B we first express the product AB as follows (the demonstration is given for $E[AB]$ but the generalization to $E[A^2]$ and $E[B^2]$ is straightforward):

$$AB = \sum_s \sum_t M_1(-s)M_2(-t)N(s)N(t) \tag{27}$$

which yields to:

$$E[AB] = \sum_s \sum_t M_1(-s) M_2(-t) E[N(s)N(t)] \tag{28}$$

Using the same method as for (26) we can compute the joint second moment $E[N_s N_t]$. After some computations, one can express $E[N_s N_t]$ with the following compact relation:

$$E[N_s N_t] = 4V_s^t . M_{st} . V_t + 2Trace[M_{st} . M_{st}] + E[N(s)]E[N(t)] \tag{29}$$

Where $M_{st} = \begin{pmatrix} C_{xx}(s,t) & C_{xy}(s,t) \\ C_{xy}(s,t) & C_{yy}(s,t) \end{pmatrix}$ and $V_i = (H_{xi}, H_{yi})^T$ with $i \in \{s, t\}$.

Re-mapping Animation Parameters Between Multiple Types of Facial Model

Darren Cosker, Steven Roy, Paul L. Rosin, and David Marshall

School of Computer Science, Cardiff University, U.K
D.P.Cosker,Paul.Rosin,Dave.Marshal@cs.cardiff.ac.uk

Abstract. In this paper we describe a method for re-mapping animation parameters between multiple types of facial model for performance
driven animation. A facial performance can be analysed automatically
in terms of a set of facial action trajectories using a modified appearance
model with modes of variation encoding specific facial actions. These parameters can then be used to animate other appearance models, or 3D
facial models. Thus, the animation parameters analysed from the video
performance may be re-used to animate multiple types of facial model.

We demonstrate the effectiveness of our approach by measuring its
ability to successfully extract action-parameters from performances and
by displaying frames from example animations.

1 Introduction and Overview

Facial animation is a popular area of research, and one with numerous challenges.
Creating facial animations with a high-degree of static and dynamic realism is
a difficult task due to the complexity of the face, and its capacity to subtly
communicate different emotions. These are very difficult and time-consuming
to reproduce by an animator. For this reason, research continues to progress in
developing new facial animation methods and improving existing ones. One of
the most popular facial animation methods today is expression mapping, also
known as performance driven animation [7,8,9,1]. In expression mapping, the
face is used an an input device to animate a facial model. This is popular since
it can potentially directly transfer subtle facial actions from the actors face onto
the facial model. This method of animation can also greatly reduce animation
production time.

A common theme in work on expression mapping is that facial parameters only
map between specific types of facial model [6,9,8]. This paper addresses the issue
of re-using facial animation parameters by re-mapping them between multiple
types of facial model. Facial actions along with intensities may be identified from
real video performances using computer vision, parameterised, and used to directly animate video-realistic appearance models with different identities. These
same parameters may also be mapped directly to onto the morph-targets of a
3D facial model to produce 3D facial animation [5]. Thus the facial parameters
may be re-used since they map onto more than one type of facial model.

A. Gagalowicz and W. Philips (Eds.): MIRAGE 2007, LNCS 4418, pp. 365–376, 2007.

Figure 1 gives an overview of our approach. This paper therefore makes the following contributions:

- An approach for expression mapping between different facial appearance models and also between facial appearance models and 3D facial models.
- An approach for extracting meaningful facial action parameters from video performances.
- An approach for creating appearance models with intuitive basis-vectors for use in animation.

Expression mapping between image based models has previously been considered by several authors, e.g. [6,10]. However, in these studies expressions are only transferred between the same type of model, and not between e.g. an image based model and a 3D blend-shape model.

Another such system for image based expression transfer is presented by Zhang *et al* [9]. Our method differs from theirs in several ways. Firstly, our approach represents a persons facial performance as a set of meaningful action parameters, and facial expression transfer is based on applying these parameters to a different facial model. Zhang *et al* transfer expressions via a texture-from-shape algorithm, which calculates sub-facial texture regions on the target face based on transferred shape information from the input performance. Our approach also differs from that of Zhang *et al* in that whereas they incorporate multiple sub-facial models for each person in order to facilitate transfer – each offering a different set of basis vectors – our approach requires only a single set of basis-vectors per person, where these vectors represent information for the entire face.

Zalewski and Gong [8] describe a technique for extracting facial action parameters from real video and then using these to animate a 3D blend-shape facial model. However, their facial parameters concentrate on mapping only full facial expressions. In our work, more specific sub-facial actions may be mapped onto a 3D model as well as full expressions.

This paper is organised as follows. In Section 2 an overview of appearance model construction is given. In Section 3 we describe how to extract meaningful facial parameters from video performances using appearance models, and how to use these parameters to animate other appearance models, or 3D blend-shape facial models. In Section 4 we show animation results, and quantitatively evaluate our appearance model mapping technique. We give conclusions in Section 5.

2   Data Acquisition and Appearance Model Construction

We filmed a male participant using an interlaced digital video camera at 25 fps. Lighting was constant throughout each recording. The participant performed three different facial expressions: *happiness*, *sadness* and *disgust* (see Figure 2). We broke each expression down into a set of individual facial actions. We also added four more actions for individual eye-brow control (see Table 1).

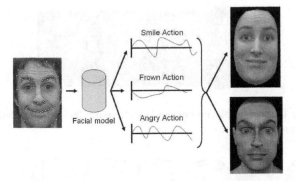

Fig. 1. Given a video performance we track facial features and project image and shape information into our facial model. This produces trajectories of facial action parameters which can be used to animate multiple types of facial model, namely appearance models and 3D facial models. Thus, animation parameters may be reused.

Table 1. Facial Actions

Expression	Actions
Happiness	(1) Surprised Forehead, (2) Smile
Sadness	(3) Sad Forehead, (4) Frown
Disgust	(5) Annoyed Forehead, (6) Nose Wrinkle
Miscellaneous	Left Eye-brow (7) Raise/ (8) Lower, Right Eye-brow (9) Raise/ (10) Lower

We semi-automatically annotated the images in each video performance with 62 landmarks (see Figure 2) using the Downhill Simplex Minimisation (DSM) tracker described in [3]. We then constructed appearance model using the landmarked image data. A brief description of this procedure is now given. For further details, see [2].

We calculate the mean landmark shape vector $\bar{\mathbf{x}}$ and warp each image in the training set to this vector from its original landmark shape $\mathbf{x}$. This provides a shape-free image training set. Performing PCA on this set of image vectors gives $\mathbf{g} = \bar{\mathbf{g}} + \mathbf{P}_g \mathbf{b}_g$ where $\mathbf{g}$ is a texture vector, $\mathbf{P}_g$ are the eigenvectors of the distribution of $\mathbf{g}$, and $\mathbf{b}_g$ is a vector of weights on $\mathbf{P}_g$. Performing PCA on the training set of shape vectors gives the model $\mathbf{x} = \bar{\mathbf{x}} + \mathbf{P}_x \mathbf{b}_x$ where $\mathbf{P}_x$ are the eigenvectors of the distribution of $\mathbf{x}$, and $\mathbf{b}_x$ is a vector of weights on $\mathbf{P}_x$.

We now represent the training set as a distribution of joint shape ($\mathbf{b}_x$) and texture ($\mathbf{b}_g$) weight vectors. Performing PCA on this distribution produces a model where $\mathbf{x}$ and $\mathbf{g}$ may be represented as functions of an appearance parameter $\mathbf{c}$. We write $\mathbf{x} = \bar{\mathbf{x}} + \mathbf{P}_x \mathbf{W}^{-1} \mathbf{Q}_x \mathbf{c}$, and $\mathbf{g} = \bar{\mathbf{g}} + \mathbf{P}_g \mathbf{Q}_g \mathbf{c}$. Here, $\mathbf{Q}_x$ and $\mathbf{Q}_g$ are respective shape and texture parts of the eigenvectors $\mathbf{Q}$ - these eigenvectors belonging to the joint distribution of shape and texture weights. The elements of $\mathbf{c}$ are weights on the basis vectors of $\mathbf{Q}$. Each vector in $\mathbf{Q}$ describes type of

Fig. 2. Example landmark placement and participant facial expressions for *Disgust, Sadness* and *Happiness*

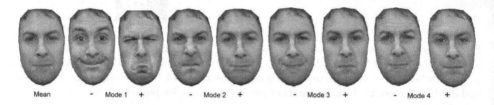

Mean   -   Mode 1   +   -   Mode 2   +   -   Mode 3   +   -   Mode 4   +

Fig. 3. First four modes of variation for our male participant. Note that the modes encode combinations of facial actions.

facial variation. Figure 3 shows the first four modes of variation for the male participant.

3   Expression Mapping

We first describe how we create a new appearance model with parameters for specific facial actions. We then describe how these parameters can be used to animate other other appearance models, or 3D facial models with pre-defined morph-targets.

3.1   Creating Appearance Models with Action Specific Modes

We aim to build a new model with modes of variation controlling the actions in Table 1. One way to achieve this is to create individual appearance models for different sub-facial regions [3]. Since the highest mode of variation should capture the largest proportion of major texture and shape change, then in the case of e.g. modelling the lower part of the face given only images of a smile, then the highest mode of variation should provide a good approximation of that smile. By applying this rule to multiple facial regions we can obtain a set of modes over several sub-facial appearance models which provide our desired modes. We have previously shown this to be the case on several occasions [3]. However, managing multiple sub-facial appearance models becomes cumbersome, and blending these together can produce visual artefacts.

In this paper we describe an alternative approach, and provide a solution which offers all the benefits of using multiple sub-facial appearance models in a single facial appearance model. We break the face into four regions where actions

1, 3 and 5 belong to a forehead region (R_1), actions 2, 3 and 6 belong to a lower face region (R_2), actions 7 and 8 belong to a left eyebrow region (R_3) and actions 9 and 10 belong to a right eyebrow region (R_4). Let $G = (\mathbf{g}_1, \ldots, \mathbf{g}_N)$ be the training set of N shape free facial images. For each region we create a new set of images $R_j^G = (\mathbf{r}_1^G, \ldots, \mathbf{r}_N^G)$. In this set, $\mathbf{r}_i^G$ is constructed by piece-wise affine warping a region from image $\mathbf{g}_i$ over the mean image $\bar{\mathbf{g}}$. The boundaries between the superimposed image region and the mean image are linearly blended using an averaging filter. This removes any obvious joins. Figure 4 defines our four different facial regions, gives example images from each region, and illustrates construction of an artificial image. Images shown in this Figure are shape-free.

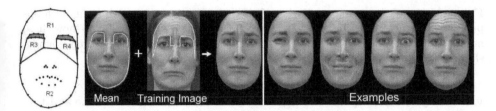

Fig. 4. (Left) There are four facial regions. The grey areas are shared by regions R_1, R_3 and R_4. (Middle) An artificial image is constructed by warping a region from a training image over the mean image. (Right) Example artificial images for actions (Left to Right) 8, 2, 9 and 10.

We now have a new training set of shape-free images $G' = (R_1^G, R_2^G, R_3^G, R_4^G)$ consisting of $4N$ artificial training images. The next task is to create a corresponding training set of artificial shape vectors. Let $X = (\mathbf{x}_1, \ldots, \mathbf{x}_N)$ be the training set of N shape vectors. Again, we define a new set of vectors for each region $R_j^X = (\mathbf{r}_1^X, \ldots, \mathbf{r}_N^X)$. A vector $\mathbf{r}_i^X$ is constructed by calculating offsets between $\mathbf{x}_i$ and $\bar{\mathbf{x}}$ in a specific region, and then adding these to $\bar{\mathbf{x}}$. Figure 5 shows example training vectors superimposed for each region.

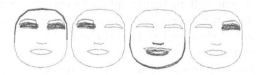

Fig. 5. (Left to Right) Superimposed shape vectors for regions R_1, R_2, R_3 and R_4

We now have a new training set of shape vectors $X' = (R_1^X, R_2^X, R_3^X, R_4^X)$ consisting of $4N$ vectors. Performing PCA on X' and G' we have the new models $\mathbf{x}' = \bar{\mathbf{x}}' + \mathbf{P}'_x \mathbf{W}_x^{-1'} \mathbf{b}'_x$ and $\mathbf{g}' = \bar{\mathbf{g}}' + \mathbf{P}'_g \mathbf{b}'_g$.

A new AAM can be constructed from X' and G', where joint shape and texture information may be represented as a functions of an appearance parameter $\mathbf{c}'$. We define $\mathbf{v}$ as the concatenation of $\mathbf{b}'_x$ and $\mathbf{b}'_g$, and write our model as

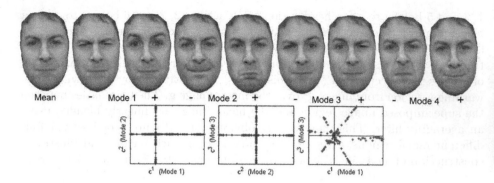

Fig. 6. Modes of appearance variation for the new appearance model, along with appearance parameter distributions visualised in a low dimensional space. Note how these modes capture localised facial variations, as opposed to the standard appearance model shown in Figure 3.

$\mathbf{v} = \bar{\mathbf{v}} + \mathbf{Q}'\mathbf{c}'$, where $\mathbf{Q}'$ are the eigenvectors of the joint artificial shape and texture parameter distribution, and $\bar{\mathbf{v}}$ is the mean concatenated artificial shape and texture parameter. Figure 6 shows the first four modes of appearance model variation for each participant, along with selected vector distributions for elements of $\mathbf{c}'$. Note that the modes of this model represent more localised facial variations than in the previous appearance model, where modes represent combinations of several facial actions at once (Figure 3). Thus this new representation allows us to parametrically control individual facial regions. Also note in this Figure how distributions of appearance parameters (red dots) representing specific facial regions are orthogonal to each other when viewed in this lower-dimensional form.

3.2   Mapping Performances Between Different Appearance Models

When appearance models are constructed for different people, the modes of variation of both models will in nearly all cases encode different types of facial variation, i.e. there will be no one-to-one mappings between the modes of variation in both models with respect to the specific facial actions they contain.

The technique described in the previous section to a great extent allows us to control what variations will be encoded in a particular mode. Therefore, appearance models can be constructed for two different people, and the modes can be biased to encode our desired variations. Given a new facial performance from a person, it can be analysed in terms of the weights it produces on a specific set of modes. This forms a set of continuous parameter trajectories which can be mapped on the modes of variation of a second appearance model. This is how we achieve expression mapping between different appearance models in this work.

We identified modes in the male participants new appearance model relating to the 10 actions specified in Table 1. We then fit this model to a new video performance of the participant. Figure 7 demonstrates the 10 selected action modes along with example action-mode trajectories resulting from fitting the appearance model to the video. Note that some trajectories are given negative values. This relates to the fact that in order to produce the desired action on that particular mode, a negative value is required (this is also shown this way for clarity – if all trajectories were given positive values the figure would be far less clear).

The trajectories are normalised between −1 and 1 by dividing through by their maximum or minimum value. Just by examining the trajectories in Figure 7 it is easy to imagine what the participants video performance would have looked like. This is an advantage of having such an intuitive parameter representation.

We next recorded a new participant using the same set-up described in Section 2. We constructed a new appearance model for this person (using the approach described in Section 3.1), and identified modes for the same 10 actions (see Figure 7). Limits on the values of these modes relate to the maximum and minimum mode-weight values recorded from the training set. Now, given a set of action-mode trajectories from the male participant, an animation for the female participant can be produced by applying these to the corresponding action modes.

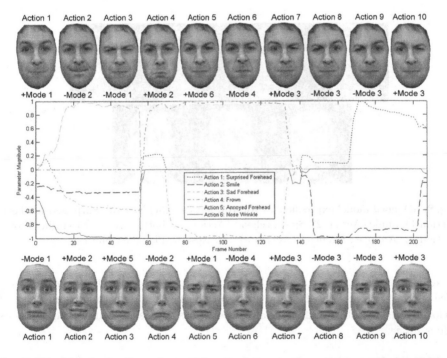

Fig. 7. (Top) Modes for the male participant relating to the actions specified in Table 1. (Middle) A video performance of the male participant represented as a set of continuous action-mode trajectories. (Bottom) Modes for the female participant relating to the actions specified in Table 1. Animations of this persons face can be created by applying the male action-mode trajectories.

3.3   Mapping Between Appearance Models and 3D Facial Models

The model representation described gives us a clear set of facial action trajectories for a persons performance. The next aim is to use these to animate a morph-target based 3D facial model. In such a model, we define a set of facial actions by their peak expression. These act as the morph-targets, and we represent the intensity of these using a set of weights with values between 0 and 1. In practical terms, our morph-targets are just a set of 3D vertex positions making up the desired facial expression. The magnitude of a morph-target is its linear displacement from a neutral expression. Any facial expression in our 3D facial model can therefore be represented as

$$E = N + \sum_{i=1}^{n}((m(i) - N)w(i))$$ (1)

where N is the neutral expression, w is a morph-target weight with a value between 0 and 1, m is a morph-target, and n is the number of morph-targets. Figure 8 shows the neutral expression and 6 morph-targets for our 3D male facial model.

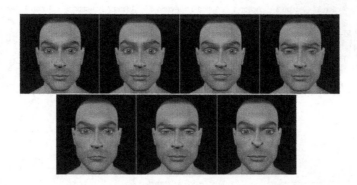

Fig. 8. 3D facial model expressions. (Top-row left to right) Neutral, Surprised-forehead (Action 1), Smile (Action 2), Sad-forehead (Action 3), (bottom-row left to right) Frown (Action 4), Annoyed-forehead (Action 5) and Nose-wrinkle (Action 6).

New animations using this model can be created by fitting a persons appearance model to a facial performance, representing this performance as a set of action-mode trajectories, setting all these values to positive, and using these as values for w.

4   Results

In this Section we first demonstrate animation results before examining our approach from a quantitative perspective.

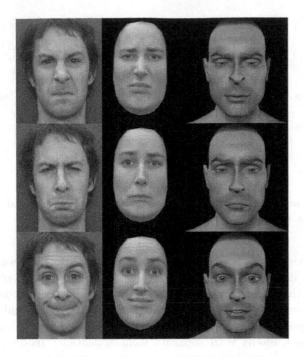

Fig. 9. Mapping expressions from our male participant onto our female participant and a 3D morph-target based facial model

Figure 9 demonstrates expression mapping between our male participant, the new appearance model of our female participant, and our 3D morph-target based model. In our animations, expression transitions are smooth and in perfect synchronisation. We did not smooth the action-mode trajectories captured from our male participant before transfer onto the other facial models, and found that this did not degrade resulting animations. In fact, small changes in the action trajectories often add to the realism of the animations, as these can appear as subtle facial nuances.

For the next part of our evaluation we investigated how well our new method for constructing appearance models encodes isolated facial variations. This is important since it is related to how well our model can recognise facial actions given a facial performance. If the model is poor at representing actions in individual modes, then the action-mode trajectories will be poor representations of the persons performance and the resulting performance driven animation will be less accurate.

Note that in a model with separate appearance models for different sub-facial regions, variations would be entirely confined to a certain region of the face. The following test may therefore also be considered an indirect comparison with a facial model of this kind.

We varied the weight on each action mode of our male appearance model up to its positive or negative limit, produced corresponding facial shape and

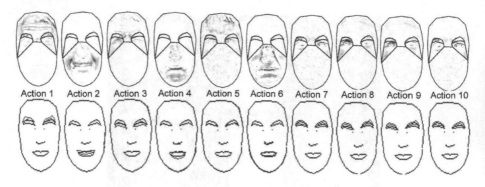

Fig. 10. Differences (for the male participant) between texture and shape vectors produced by our actions and their respective means

texture, and then subtracted the mean shape and texture. The result is shown in Figure 10, and demonstrates how major variations do occur in isolated regions. It also shows that some minor variations also simultaneously occur in other regions. The visual result of this in animations is negligble, and for practical animation purposes it may therefore be said that this new model has comparable performance to a model with separate local appearance models. In fact, the appearance of small residual variations in other parts of the face may in some ways be seen as an advantage over a model with local sub-facial appearance models, since it may be considered unrealistic in the first place to assume the affect of facial actions is localised to a specific facial region.

We further investigated how well our single action-modes encode our separate facial actions using a numerical measure. It is unlikely, even in a model with local facial appearance models, that an entire facial action would be perfectly encoded in a single mode of variation. This would assume that facial actions are linear in motion, when they are not. It is more likely that a single mode will encode a very large proportion of the actions variation, while the rest of the variation will be spread over a small set of other modes. In this next test, we only aim to measure how distinct each of our 10 action-modes are from one another.

We took 10 images from the training set formed in Section 3.1 corresponding to 10 action specific images. Each image consisted of the mean face image, overlaid with a region specific image representing a specific facial action. For example, the image representing the smile action consisted of the mean face overlaid just on region R_2 with a smile image. We formed 10 corresponding action-specific shape vectors in a similar manner.

Projecting this information into our appearance model results in 10 appearance parameter vectors. We can measure the exclusivity of an action with respect to a mode by measuring the orthogonality of these vectors. We take the following measure adapted from [4] where $\mathbf{c}$ is an appearance parameter

$$M(\mathbf{c}_i, \mathbf{c}_j) = \frac{(\mathbf{c}_i \cdot \mathbf{c}_j)^2}{(\mathbf{c}_j \cdot \mathbf{c}_j)(\mathbf{c}_i \cdot \mathbf{c}_i)} \qquad (2)$$

Table 2. Orthogonality between Facial Actions 1 to 10 for our Male Participant. (0 = orthogonal, 1 =non-orthogonal).

	1	2	3	4	5	6	7	8	9	10
1	1	0.153	0.009	0.466	0.205	0	0	0	0.866	0.249
2	0.153	1	0.769	0.006	0.011	0	0	0	0.207	0.004
3	0.009	0.769	1	0.187	0.114	0	0	0	0	0.041
4	0.466	0.006	0.187	1	0.899	0	0	0	0.143	0.019
5	0.205	0.011	0.114	0.899	1	0	0	0	0.009	0.197
6	0	0	0	0	0	1	0.363	0.157	0	0
7	0	0	0	0	0	0.363	1	0.243	0	0
8	0	0	0	0	0	0.157	0.243	1	0	0
9	0.866	0.207	0	0.143	0.009	0	0	0	1	0.565
10	0.249	0.004	0.041	0.019	0.197	0	0	0	0.565	1

This returns a value between 0 and 1, where 0 indicates that the vectors are orthogonal. Table 2 compares the orthogonality of our actions. It can be seen from this result that a great many of the actions are orthogonal. Some actions have a low orthogonality. However, this is because these actions produce variations in the same facial region which can produce changes in the same appearance mode.

In summary, these results show that our method for creating appearance models with action specific modes is successful, and is therefore well suited to producing performance driven animation in the way we have described. The results show that the modes of variation in our models successfully capture facial variations associated with actions when applied to video performances. This means that it is accurate enough to reliably transfer performances onto other facial models.

5   Conclusions and Future Work

We have presented a method for measuring facial actions from a persons performance and mapping this performance onto different types of facial model. Specifically, this mapping is between different appearance models, and between appearance models and 3D morph-target based facial models. We have described how to construct appearance models with action-specific modes in order to record facial actions and represent them as continuous trajectories. We have also shown how these parameters are used for animating the models with respect to different facial actions.

By numerically measuring the orthogonality of our action modes, we have successfully demonstrated that they are well suited to accurately capturing facial actions. This therefore demonstrates the models suitability for performance driven facial animation applications.

One issue that we currently do not address is the transfer of inner mouth detail e.g. for smiles. This would be an interesting experiment, and it may be the case that further basis vector would be required to include this variation. We also do not consider the re-inclusion of head pose variation, and this would be the topic of future work. However, one solution which would part-way address this would be to reinsert the facial animations back into the training footage in a similar way to that described in [3].

References

1. V. Blanz, C. Basso, T. Poggio, and T. Vetter. Reanimating faces in images and video. In *Proc. of EUROGRAPHICS*, 2003.
2. T. Cootes, G. Edwards, and C. Taylor. Active appearance models. *IEEE Trans. PAMI*, 23(6):681–684, 2001.
3. D. Cosker. Animation of a hierarchical image based facial model and perceptual analysis of visual speech. *PhD Thesis, School of Computer Science, Cardiff University*, 2006.
4. P. Gader and M. Khabou. Automatic feature generation for handwritten digit recognition. *IEEE Trans. PAMI*, 18(12):1256–1261, 1996.
5. P. Joshu, W. Tien, M. Desbrun, and F. Pighin. Learning controls for blend shape based realistic facial animation. In *Proc. of Eurographics/SIGGRAPH Symposium on Computer Animation*, 2003.
6. D. Vlasic, M. Brand, H. Pfister, and J. Popovic. Face transfer with multilinear models. *ACM Trans. Graph.*, 24(3):426–433, 2005.
7. L. Williams. Performance driven facial animation. *Computer Graphics*, 24(4):235 – 242, 1990.
8. L. Zalewski and S. Gong. 2d statistical models of facial expressions for realistic 3d avatar animation. In *Proc of IEEE Computer Vision and Pattern Recognition*, volume 2, pages 217 – 222, 2005.
9. Q. Zhang, Z. Liu, B. Guo, D. Terzopoulos, and H. Shum. Geometry-driven photorealistic facial expression synthesis. *IEEE Trans. Visualisation and Computer Graphics*, 12(1):48 – 60, 2006.
10. Z.Liu, Y. Shan, and Z. Zhang. Expressive expression mapping with ratio images. In *Proc. of SIGGRAPH*, pages 271–276, 2001.

Data-Driven Animation of Crowds

Nicolas Courty[1] and Thomas Corpetti[2]

[1] Université de Bretagne-Sud, Laboratoire VALORIA,
56000 Vannes Cedex, France
nicolas.courty@univ-ubs.fr
[2] Université de Haute-Bretagne, Laboratoire COSTEL,
35000 Rennes Cedex, France
thomas.corpetti@uhb.fr

Abstract. In this paper we propose an original method to animate a crowd of virtual beings in a virtual environment. Instead of relying on models to describe the motions of people along time, we suggest to use *a priori* knowledge on the dynamic of the crowd acquired from videos of real crowd situations. In our method this information is expressed as a time-varying motion field which accounts for a continuous flow of people along time. This motion descriptor is obtained through optical flow estimation with a specific second order regularization. Obtained motion fields are then used in a classical fixed step size integration scheme that allows to animate a virtual crowd in real-time. The power of our technique is demonstrated through various examples and possible follow-ups to this work are also described.

1   Introduction

Crowds of people exhibit particular and subtle behaviors whose complexity reflects the complex nature of human beings. While computer simulation of such phenomena have made it possible to reproduce particular and singular crowd configurations, none of them have managed to reproduce, within a generic framework, the typical emergent behaviors observed within a crowd with sufficient details and at a satisfying level. In the context of animation of human-like figures, huge progress have been observed with the use of motion capture. It is now possible to use motions acquired from real performers through a variety of editing and warping operations with substantial benefits in terms of realism in the produced animation. The aim of our technique is to provide such a tool in the context of crowd animation. While other approaches try to track singular pedestrians into the flow of people, our framework is based on the hypotheses that the motions of individuals within the crowd is the expression of a continuous flow that drives the crowd motion. *This assumes that the crowd is dense enough so that pedestrians are considered as markers of an underlying flow.* In this sense, our method is more related to macroscopic simulation models (that try to define an overall structure to the crowd's motions) rather than microscopic models (that define the crowd's motions as an emergent behavior of the sum of individual displacement strategies).

A. Gagalowicz and W. Philips (Eds.): MIRAGE 2007, LNCS 4418, pp. 377–388, 2007.
© Springer-Verlag Berlin Heidelberg 2007

Our methodology relies on an analysis/synthesis scheme which is depicted in Figure 1. First, images are extracted from a video of a real crowd. From all the pairs of successive images a vector field is computed through a motion estimation process. The concatenation of all these vector fields represent a time series which accounts for the displacement of the whole crowd along time. This ends up the analysis part. The synthesis of a new crowd animation is done by advecting particles (the pedestrians) along this time varying flow.

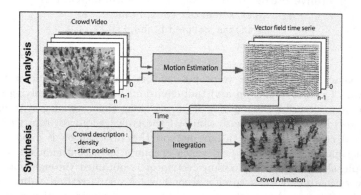

Fig. 1. Overview of the whole process

This paper is divided as follow: section 2 is a state of the art of the different existing approaches in the context of crowd simulation as well as motion estimation. Section 3 deals with the estimator used in our methodology, and section 4 presents the integration of the motion descriptor in a crowd animation controller. The last two sections present results obtained with our method along with a conclusion and perspectives for our work.

2   State of the Art

The idea of using videos as an input to animation system is not new, and has already been succesfully used in the context of, for instance, facial animation [9], character animation from cartoon [8] or animal gaits [14]. Recent works showed example of re-synthesis of fluids flow from real video examples [3]. Simulating crowds from real videos fails into this challenging category of methods. First, it is interesting to understand the limitations of crowd simulation model (first part of this section). We then introduce some general issues about the motion estimation problem.

2.1   Crowd Simulation

Crowd behavior and motion of virtual people have been studied and modeled in computers with different purposes: populating virtual environments, video games, movie production or simulating emergency situations to help the design of buildings and open-spaces. The state of the art in human crowd behavioral modelling is large and can be classified in two main approaches: microscopic and macroscopic models. The models belonging to the first category are those describing the time-space behavior of individual pedestrians whereas the second category are those describing the emergent properties of the crowd.

Microscopic simulation. The simplest models of microscopic simulation are based on cellular automata [6,5]. The social force model was first introduced by Helbing [15]. It consists in expressing the motion of each pedestrian as a result of a combination of *social forces*, that repel/attract pedestrians toward each others. It has been shown that this model generates realistic phenomena as arc formations in exits or increasing evacuation time with increased desired velocities. It has been extended to account for individualities [7] or the presence of toxic gases in the environment [12]. More complex models consider each member of the crowd as autonomous pedestrians endowed with perceptive and cognitive abilities [22,24,23]. Those models exhibit a variety of results depending on the quality of the behavior design.

Macroscopic models. Modelling a crowd composed of discrete individuals may lead to incorrect emergent global behaviors. These difficulties may be avoided by using a continuum formulation [18,26]. Equations using the concepts of fluid mechanics have been derived in order to model such approach of human crowds. Those approaches rely on the assumption that the characteristic distance scale between individuals is much less than the characteristic distance scale of the region in which the individuals move [18]. Hence the density of the crowd has to be taken into account for those models to be pertinent. Finally several hypotheses on the behavior of each members of the crowd lead to partial derivative equations governing the flow of people.

Although crowds are made up of independent individuals with their own objectives and behaviour patterns, the behavior of crowds is widely understood to have collective characteristics which can be described in general terms. Though, macroscopic models may lack of subtleties and often rely on strong hypotheses (notably on density). Our framework propose to capture this global dynamic from real crowd video sequences. This imposes the use of motion estimation techniques.

2.2   Motion Estimation

When a crowd is dense enough, the usual tracking systems like Kalman filters or stochastic filtering [13] will generate large state space that will yield a computationally too expensive problem. It is then necessary to use alternative methods to obtain the information on the dynamics of the crowd in order to characterize its behavior. This section investigates the different ways to obtain some motion descriptors from image sequences. Many families of methods are available to measure a motion information from image sequences. One can cite for instance the parametric methods, the correlation techniques or the optical flow approaches (see [21] for a survey). These latter are known to be the most accurate to address the generic problem of estimating the apparent motion from image sequences (see for instance [27] for some presentations and [2] for comprehensive comparisons with completely different approaches). The idea of using optical flow to estimate crowd motions has recently drawn attention in the context of human activity recognition [1]. The original optical flow is based on the seminal work of Horn & Schunck [16] and is briefly described in the next paragraph.

Optical Flow. The optical flow based on Horn & Schunck consists in the minimization of a global cost function $\mathcal{H}$ composed of two terms. The first one, named "observation term", is derived from a *brightness constancy* assumption and assumes that a given point keeps the same intensity along its trajectory. It is expressed through the well known *optical flow constraint equation* (OFCE):

$$\mathcal{H}_{obs}(E, \mathbf{v}) = \iint_{\Omega} f_1 \left[\nabla E(\mathbf{x}, t) \cdot \mathbf{v}(\mathbf{x}, t) + \frac{\partial E(\mathbf{x}, t)}{\partial t} \right] d\mathbf{x}, \qquad (1)$$

where $\mathbf{v}(\mathbf{x}, t) = (u, v)^T$ is the unknown velocity field at time t and location $\mathbf{x} = (x, y)$ in the image plane Ω, $E(\mathbf{x}, t)$ is the image brightness, viewed for a while as a continuous function.

This first term relies on the assumption that the visible points conserve roughly their intensity in the course of a displacement.

$$\frac{dE}{dt} = \nabla E \cdot \mathbf{v} + \frac{\partial E}{\partial t} \approx 0. \qquad (2)$$

The associated penalty function f_1 is often the L_2 norm. However, better estimates are usually obtained by choosing a "softer" penalty function [4]. Such functions, arising from robust statistics [17], limit the impact of the many locations where the brightness constancy assumption does not hold, such as on occlusion boundaries.

This single (scalar) observation term does not allow to estimate the two components u and v of the velocity. In order to solve this ill-posed problem, it is common to employ an additional smoothness constraint $\mathcal{H}_{reg}$. Usually, this second term enforces a spatial smoothness coherence of the flow field. It relies on a contextual assumption which enforces a spatial smoothness of the solution. This term usually reads:

$$\mathcal{H}_{reg}(\mathbf{v}) = \iint_{\Omega} f_2 \left[|\nabla u(\mathbf{x}, t)| + |\nabla v(\mathbf{x}, t)| \right], \qquad (3)$$

As with the penalty function in the data term, the penalty function f_2 was taken as a quadratic in early studies, but a softer penalty is now preferred in order not to smooth out the natural discontinuities (boundaries, ...) of the velocity field [4,20]. Based on (1) and (3), the estimation of motion can be done by minimizing:

$$\mathcal{H}(E, \mathbf{v}) = \mathcal{H}_{obs}(E, \mathbf{v}) + \alpha \mathcal{H}_{reg}(\mathbf{v})$$

$$= \iint_{\Omega} f_1 \left[\nabla E(\mathbf{x}, t) \cdot \mathbf{v}(\mathbf{x}, t) + \frac{\partial E(\mathbf{x}, t)}{\partial t} \right] d\mathbf{x} +$$

$$\alpha \iint_{\Omega} f_2 \left[|\nabla u(\mathbf{x}, t)| + |\nabla v(\mathbf{x}, t)| \right], \tag{4}$$

where $\alpha > 0$ is a parameter controlling the balance between the smoothness constraint and the global adequacy to the observation assumption.

The minimization of this overall cost function enables to extract the apparent motion field between a pair of images $E(\mathbf{x}, t_1)$ and $E(\mathbf{x}, t_2)$.

Discussion. It has been proved that in many image sequences and especially in fluid-like imagery, these classic assumptions are violated in a number of locations in the image plane. Even if in most of rigid-motion situations, the use of a robust penalty function enables us to recover properly the motion of pathological situations (occluding contours, ...) the usual assumptions are, unfortunately, even less appropriate in fluid imagery.

Some studies have proved that a crowd dense enough has sometimes a behavior that can be explained by some fluid mechanics laws [18]. It is then of primary interest to integrate such prior knowledge in the optical flow (in the observation term or on the regularization constraint, depending on the nature of the physical law to integrate) to obtain a technique devoted to crowd motion. In this paper, we propose to use a smoothing constraint dedicated to the capture of the significant properties of the flow from a fluid mechanics point of view. These properties are the *divergence* (linked to the dispersion of a crowd) and the *vorticity* (also named *curl*) linked to a rotation.

3   Crowd Motion Estimation and Representation

In this section, we present the regularization used in the motion estimator to extract a reliable crowd motion information. For more details on the approach, the reader can refer to [11,10]. Under the assumption that a dense enough crowd has a behaviour that can be modeled with some fluid mechanics laws, one can demonstrate that the usual first-order regularization functional in (3) is not adapted for fluid situations.

By using Euler-Lagrange conditions of optimality, it is indeed readily demonstrated [10] that the standard first-order regularization functional :

$$\mathcal{H}_{reg}(\mathbf{v}) = \iint_{\Omega} |\nabla u(\mathbf{x})|^2 + |\nabla v(\mathbf{x})|^2 d\mathbf{x} \tag{5}$$

is equivalent from the minimization point of view, to the so-called *div-curl* regularization functional [25]:

$$\mathcal{H}_{reg}(\mathbf{v}) = \iint_{\Omega} \left(\mathrm{div}^2 \mathbf{v}(\mathbf{x}) + \mathrm{curl}^2 \mathbf{v}(\mathbf{x}) \right) d\mathbf{x}, \tag{6}$$

where $\mathrm{div}\mathbf{v} = \frac{\partial u}{\partial x} + \frac{\partial v}{\partial y}$ and $\mathrm{curl}\mathbf{v} = \frac{\partial v}{\partial x} - \frac{\partial u}{\partial y}$ are respectively the divergence and the vorticity of the motion field $\mathbf{v} = (u, v)$.

A first-order regularization therefore penalizes the amplitude of both the divergence and the vorticity of the vector field. For a dense crowd motion estimation, this does not seem appropriate since the apparent velocity field normally exhibits compact areas with high values of vorticity and/or divergence. It seems then more appropriate to rely on a second-order div-curl regularization [25]:

$$\mathcal{H}_{reg}(\mathbf{v}) = \iint_{\Omega} \left(|\boldsymbol{\nabla}\mathrm{div}\mathbf{v}(\mathbf{x})|^2 + |\boldsymbol{\nabla}\mathrm{curl}\mathbf{v}(\mathbf{x})|^2 \right) d\mathbf{x}. \tag{7}$$

This regularization tends to preserve the divergence and the vorticity of the motion field $\mathbf{v}$ to estimate. Interested readers may referee to [11] to get precise descriptions on the optimization strategy and on associated numerical implementation issues.

The motion field $\mathbf{v}$ is then the minimum of the following cost function (with $\bullet = (\mathbf{x}, t)$):

$$\mathbf{v}(\bullet) = \min_{\mathbf{v} \in \Omega} \iint_{\Omega} \left\{ f_1 \left[\boldsymbol{\nabla} E(\bullet) \cdot \mathbf{v}(\bullet) + \frac{\partial E(\bullet)}{\partial t} \right] + \alpha \|\boldsymbol{\nabla}\mathrm{div}\mathbf{v}(\bullet)\|^2 + \alpha \|\boldsymbol{\nabla}\mathrm{curl}\mathbf{v}(\bullet)\|^2 \right\} d\mathbf{x}. \tag{8}$$

and the global crowd motion is represented as a time series of such motion fields.

4   Data-Driven Animation of Crowds

Once the time series of motion fields has been computed, it is possible to consider this information as input data for an animation system. Let us first recall that the computed velocities correspond to a velocity *in the image space*, and our goal is to animate individualities *in the virtual world space*. Given the position of such a person in the virtual world, it is possible to get the corresponding position in the image frame along with a camera projection model. Parameters for this projection can be obtained exactly through camera calibration. We have considered as an approximation of this model a simple orthographic projection in the experiments presented in the result sections. This assumption holds whenever the camera is sufficiently far away from the crowd scene. Once this projection has been defined, animating individualities which constitute the crowd amounts to solve the classical following differential equation (with $x(t)$ the position of a person in the image frame at time t) :

$$\frac{\partial x}{\partial t} = v(x(t), t) \tag{9}$$

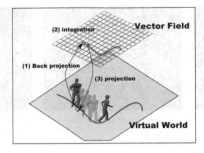

Fig. 2. Motion synthesis from flow field. The position of the crowd's member is projected onto the flow (step 1), the integration is performed in the image frame (step 2) and then the new position is projected back in the vritual world frame (step 3).

equipped with appropriate initial condition $x(0) = x_0$ which stands for the initial positions of the individual in the flow field. In our framework we have used the classical 4-th order Runge Kutta integration scheme, which allows to compute a new position $x(t+1)$ given a fixed timestep with an acceptable accuracy. This new position is then projected back in the virtual world frame. This process is depicted in Figure 2.

Let us finally note that the quality of the generated animation is closely linked with the initial position of the crowd members and their density. We have used in the subsequent results curve sources that create random pedestrians along a hand-designed curve situated in the flow.

5   Results

Our approach was first tested on synthetic crowd sequences to validate the theoritical part of our work. We have also used real crowd sequences to handle real cases. Those results are presented in this section.

5.1   Synthetic Example

The synthetic sequence represents a continuous flow of human beings with an obstacle (a cylinder named $\mathcal{C}$) in the middle of the image. It has been generated using the classical Helbing simulation model [15]. In this situation, the true motion field inside the cylinder $\mathcal{C}$ is known (no motion, *i.e.* $\mathbf{v}(\mathbf{x} \in \mathcal{C}) = 0$). The cost function (8) being defined on the whole image plane, we need to have a particular process to deal with this specific *no-data* area. Actually, since any motion inside the area $\mathcal{C}$ is a reliable candidate (the OFCE (1) is null everywhere), the motion estimation using relation (8) is likely to yield some incoherent results inside and outside the cylinder (due to the regularization term which spreads errors). To cope with this situation, we completely blurred the cylinder area from an image to an other, so that the OFCE constraint is verified nowhere in $\mathcal{C}$. Thanks to the robust estimator f_1 used in (1), this area is not taken into

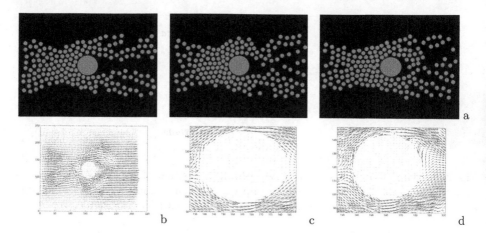

Fig. 3. Estimation of the motion field on the synthetic example; (a): images from the original sequence; (b) the estimated motion field; (c) the motion near the cylinder estimated with a special care of this no-data area and (d) same as (c) but without a specific treatment for the cylinder. One can see that the motion near the cylinder in (d) is not totally coherent.

account by the observation term of the estimation process. Hence, the motions fields estimated outside the cylinder are not disturbed by the ones inside $\mathcal{C}$. This is illustrated in Figure 3. We present an image of the sequence in Figure 3(a), the estimated motion field in Figure 3(b), a zoom of the cylinder area with and without the specific treatment proposed on this particular situation (Figure 3(c) and 3(d) respectively). Some images of the crowd animation synthesis are shown on Figure 4. The animation was generated thanks to a Maya plugin which defines a crowd as a set of particles and performs the synthesis described in section 4. As expected, the virtual crowd is in accordance with the underlying motion and the obstacle is correctly managed. This first example proves the ability of the proposed approach to synthesize a coherent motion from an estimated motion field. Let us now apply this technique to real data.

Fig. 4. Some images of the synthetic crowd animation for 4 different times of the sequence

5.2   Real Data

We present the results obtained on two real sequences. Both data have been acquired with a simple video camera with an MPEG encoder. The resulting images are hence very poor in terms of brightness: this latter is indeed sometimes constant in a squared area. It is important to note that this point is likely to disturb the motion estimation process.

Strike sequence. The first real sequence is a video representing a strike which took place at Vannes in France. All pedestrians are walking on the same direction. Two images of the sequence can be seen on Figure 5 (a) and (b). In Figure 5 (c) and (d), we present the synthetic crowd animation obtained superimposed on the estimated motion field. One can observe that the resulting crowd animation is in accordance with the real pedestrian behaviors. Hence, on this example, our method has the advantage to synthesize correctly the observed phenomena without resorting to usual motion capture techniques. Let us now see the results on a more complicated real sequence.

Shibuya sequence. The second real sequence is a video acquired in the *Shibuya crossroads* in Tokyo, Japan, which is famous for the density of people crossing the streets. Three images of the sequence can be seen on Figure 6 (a-c). This situation is complex since at least two main flows of people in opposite directions are crossing the road. It is important to observe that in this case, the underlying assumptions of our approach (a very dense crowd) are not totally respected. This example is therefore shown to evaluate the limits of our method. In

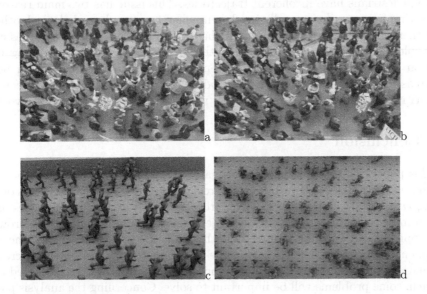

Fig. 5. The strike sequence. (a,b): two images of the sequence; (c,d) the corresponding animation superimposed on the estimated motion field.

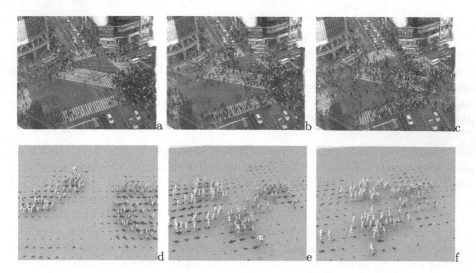

Fig. 6. The Shibuya sequence. (a-c): two images of the sequence; (d-f) the corresponding animation superimposed on the estimated motion field.

Figure 6 (d-f), we present the synthetic crowd animation obtained superimposed on the estimated motion field. One can see on these figures that the two main opposite flows are correctly extracted and synthesised, despite the fact that the initial sequence was very poor in terms of quality and that our initial assumptions were not respected. The generated sequence is relatively realistic. Nevertheless, the intersection of the two groups of people is not correctly managed: some pedestrians have incoherent trajectories. This issue has two main reasons: the estimation process is locally incoherent when two people occlude each other, and there is no temporal continuity in the estimated flow. Two possibilities can be exploited to cope such a situation: the first one consists in improving the motion estimation process through a temporal smoothing of the motion field whereas the second possibility is to introduce a dynamical law in the trajectory reconstruction step. This two key points will be the scope of our further work.

6   Conclusion

In this paper, we have presented a new and orginal method which proposes to animate a virtual dense crowd thanks to real crowd video sequences. This is done using *i)* a specific motion information process applied on the input images and *ii)* an integration part to obtain the trajectories of individualities in the crowd. We applied the presented method on both synthetic and real examples. The experimental part showed the ability of the technique to synthesize reliable crowd animations but also pointed out some limitations. To improve the presented approach, some problems will be important to solve. Concerning the analysis part, the motion estimation process can be improved by introducing more specific spatio-temporal models of continuous crowd behaviours [18]. This can be done using the framework of the optical flow but it can also be relevant to explore the possibilities of the data-assimilation used for instance in meteorology [19]. This constitutes a very exciting challenge for which actually no practical and generic solution exists and stands as a very appealing alternative to tracking systems, too expensive in the context of dense crowds. An other important point would be to specify a motion estimation process for crowds that are not totally dense. Concerning the synthesis part, we aim at enriching existing simulation models by integrating this *a priori* knowledge of the behaviour of the crowd. In this context, the crowd simulation would integrate both dynamical simulation models and observed data from real sequences.

Acknowledgements. The authors wish to thank Amel Achour and Gwendal Jabot for their contributions to the project, and Alvaro Cassinelli for providing us the shibuya video sequences.

References

1. E. Andrade, S. Blunsden, and R. Fisher. Modelling crowd scenes for event detection. In *Int. Conf. on Pattern Recognitiion, ICPR 2006*, pages 175–178, 2006.
2. J. Barron, D. Fleet, and S. Beauchemin. Performance of optical flow techniques. *Int. J. Computer Vision*, 12(1):43–77, 1994.
3. K. Bhat, S. Seitz, J. Hodgins, and P. Khosla. Flow-based video synthesis and editing. *ACM Transactions on Graphics, special issue, Proceedings ACM SIGGRAPH 2004*, 23(3):360–363, 2004.
4. M. Black. Recursive non-linear estimation of discontinuous flow fields. In *Proc. Europ. Conf. Computer Vision*, pages 138–145, Stockholm, Sweden, 1994.
5. V. Blue. Cellular automata microsimulation for modeling bi-directional pedestrian walkways. *Transportation Research, Part B: Methodological*, 35(3):293–312, March 2001.
6. E. Bouvier, E. Cohen, and L. Najman. From crowd simulation to airbag deployment: particle systems, a new paradigm of simulation. *Journal of Electronic Imaging*, 6(1):94–107, January 1997.
7. A. Braun and S. Raupp Musse. Modeling individual behaviors in crowd simulation. In *Proc. of Computer Animation and Social Agents (CASA'03)*, New Jersey, USA, May 2003.
8. C. Bregler, L. Loeb, E. Chuang, and H. Deshpande. Turning to the masters: Motion capturing cartoons. *ACM Transactions on Graphics, special issue, Proceedings ACM SIGGRAPH 2002*, 21(3):320–328, 2002.
9. J. Chai, J. Xiao, and J. Hodgins. Vision-based control of 3d facial animation. In *Eurographics/ACM SIGGRAPH Symposium on Computer Animation*, pages 79–87, Grenoble, France, August 2003.
10. T. Corpetti, D. Heitz, G. Arroyo, E. Mémin, and A. Santa-Cruz. Fluid experimental flow estimation based on an optical-flow scheme. *Experiments in fluids*, 40(1):80–97, 2006.
11. T. Corpetti, E. Mémin, and P. Pérez. Dense estimation of fluid flows. *IEEE Transactions on Pattern Analysis and Machine Intelligence*, 24(3):365–380, March 2002.

12. N. Courty and S. Musse. Simulation of Large Crowds Including Gaseous Phenomena. In *Proc. of IEEE Computer Graphics International 2005*, pages 206–212, New York, USA, June 2005.

13. D. Crisan. Particle filters, a theoretical perspective. In N. de Freitas A. Doucet and N. Gordon, editors, *Sequential Monte-Carlo Methods in Practice*. Springer, 2001.

14. L. Favreau, L. Reveret, C. Depraz, and M.-P. Cani. Animal gaits from video. In *Eurographics/ACM SIGGRAPH Symposium on Computer Animation*, Grenoble, France, August 2004.

15. D. Helbing, I. Farkas, and T. Vicsek. Simulating dynamical features of escape panic. *Nature*, 407(1):487–490, 2000.

16. B. Horn and B. Schunck. Determining optical flow. *Artificial Intelligence*, 17: 185–203, 1981.

17. P. Huber. *Robust Statistics*. John Wiley & Sons, 1981.

18. R. L. Hughes. The flow of human crowds. *Annual revue of Fluid. Mech.*, 20(10): 169–182, 2003.

19. F.X. Le-Dimet and O. Talagrand. Variational algorithms for analysis and assimilation of meteorological observations: theoretical aspects. *Tellus*, pages 97–110, 1986.

20. E. Mémin and P. Pérez. Dense estimation and object-based segmentation of the optical flow with robust techniques. *IEEE Trans. Image Processing*, 7(5):703–719, 1998.

21. A. Mitiche and P. Bouthemy. Computation and analysis of image motion: a synopsis of current problems and methods. *Int. J. Computer Vision*, 19(1):29–55, 1996.

22. S. Raupp Musse and D. Thalmann. Hierarchical model for real time simulation of virtual human crowds. In *IEEE Trans. on Visualization and Computer Graphics*, volume 7(2), pages 152–164. IEEE Computer Society, 2001.

23. W. Shao and D. Terzopoulos. Animating autonomous pedestrians. In *Proc. SIGGRAPH/EG Symposium on Computer Animation (SCA'05)*, pages 19–28, Los Angeles, CA, July 2005.

24. M. Sung, M. Gleicher, and S. Chenney. Scalable behaviors for crowd simulation. *Comput. Graph. Forum*, 23(3):519–528, 2004.

25. D. Suter. Motion estimation and vector splines. In *Proc. Conf. Comp. Vision Pattern Rec.*, pages 939–942, Seattle, USA, June 1994.

26. A. Treuille, S. Cooper, and Z. Popovic. Continuum crowds. *ACM Transactions on Graphics, special issue, Proceedings ACM SIGGRAPH 2006*, 25(3):1160–1168, 2006.

27. J. Weickert and C. Schnörr. A theoretical framework for convex regularizers in PDE-based computation of image motion. *Int. J. of Computer Vision*, 45(3): 245–264, December 2001.

A 3-D Mesh Sequence Coding
Using the Combination of Spatial and Temporal
Wavelet Analysis*

Jae-Won Cho[1,2], Min-Su Kim[1,2], Sébastien Valette[1],
Ho-Youl Jung[2,**], and Rémy Prost[1]

[1] CREATIS, INSA-Lyon, France
{cho, kim, valette, prost}@creatis.insa-lyon.fr
[2] MSP Lab., Univ. of Yeungnam, Korea
Tel.: +82.53.810.3545; Fax: +82.53.810.4742
hoyoul@yu.ac.kr

Abstract. In this paper, we present a wavelet-based progressive compression method for isomorphic 3-D mesh sequence with constant connectivity. Our method reduces the spatial and temporal redundancy by using both spatial and temporal wavelet analysis. To encode geometry information, each mesh frame is decomposed into a base mesh and its spatial wavelet coefficients of each resolution level by spatial wavelet analysis filter bank. The spatially transformed sequence is decomposed into several sub-band signals by temporal wavelet analysis filter bank. The resulting signal is encoded by using an arithmetic coder. Since an isomorphic mesh sequence has the same connectivity over all frames, the connectivity information is encoded only for the first mesh frame. The proposed method enables both progressive representation and lossless compression in a single framework by multi-resolution wavelet analysis with a perfect reconstruction filter bank. Our method is compared with several conventional techniques including our previous work.

Keywords: 3D mesh sequence, lossless compression, lossy compression, progressive transmission, multi-resolution representation, irregular mesh, temporal wavelet analysis, spatial wavelet analysis.

1 Introduction

With the rapid progress of network technology, the demand of 3-D data such as animation, virtual reality and medical image has increased. Polygonal meshes

---

* This work was supported by the Korea Research Foundation Grant funded by the Korean Government (MOEHRD) (KRF-2006-511-D00285), and also supported, in part, by the MIC(Ministry of Information and Communication), Korea, under the ITRC(Information Technology Research Center) support program supervised by the IITA(Institute of Information Technology Advancement) (IITA-2006-(C1090-0603-0002)).
** Corresponding author.

A. Gagalowicz and W. Philips (Eds.): MIRAGE 2007, LNCS 4418, pp. 389–399, 2007.
© Springer-Verlag Berlin Heidelberg 2007

are known as a good representation for 3-D object. It is generally defined by geometry of vertices and their connectivity. To represent an animated 3-D object, a mesh sequence can be used. It consists of successive polygonal meshes. Because it requires enormous bandwidth or capacity in order to transmit or to store, it is important to develop efficient compression techniques for mesh sequence. Since a compression technique for 3-D mesh sequence was introduced by Lengyel [1], there have been several attempts to improve the rate-distortion performance [2,3,4,5,6]. Lengyel [1] proposed a geometry compression method. It segments the original mesh into small rigid body meshes. Each sub-mesh is redefined by affine transform, and then the transform coefficients and the residuals are quantized and encoded. This algorithm uses temporal coherence of rigid body meshes. However, it is difficult to cluster the vertices into the same sub-mesh. Karni and Gotsman [2] proposed a PCA (Principal Component Analysis) based method. They also reduced temporal redundancy by using LPC (Linear Prediction Coding), but it is hard to efficiently work on finer meshes as reported in [5]. In addition, it requires high computational complexity to calculate the eigen vectors. A lossless compression method was presented in [3]. It can simultaneously reduce the temporal redundancy and spatial one by using a space-time replica predictor which can effectively predict the geometry. Some wavelet-based methods have also been introduced [4,5,6]. Payan and Antonini [4] used a temporal wavelet transform to reduce temporal redundancy. They achieved an efficient coding performance by using their optimal quantization scheme, but spatial redundancy was not considered. Guskov and Khodakovsky [5] introduced a progressive compression algorithm. They encoded the difference between the wavelet coefficients of the previous frame and current one. Here, the wavelet coefficients are obtained by using the Burt-Adelson style pyramid scheme. Their method can transmit the original from a coarse mesh to the finest one. However, they could not realize a lossless compression because the wavelet filter does not enable the perfect reconstruction. Recently, Cho et al. [6] presented a wavelet-based progressive compression method. Although the approach was a bit similar with Guskov and Khodakovsky [5], the lossless compression could be realized by using a perfect reconstruction wavelet filter bank.

In this paper, we present a wavelet-based progressive compression method for 3-D mesh sequence. We assume that the number of vertices and their connectivity are fixed, so-called isomorphic mesh sequence. Our method reduces the spatial and temporal redundancy by using spatial and temporal wavelet analysis, respectively. To encode geometry information, each mesh frame is firstly decomposed into a base mesh and its spatial wavelet coefficients of each resolution level by spatial wavelet analysis filter bank. And then, their sequences of temporal direction are once again decomposed into several sub-band signals by temporal wavelet analysis filter bank. We encode the resulting signal by using an arithmetic coder. Because an isomorphic mesh sequence has the same connectivity over all frames, the connectivity information is encoded only for the first mesh frame. The proposed method is based on the wavelet-based multi-resolution analysis which uses a perfect reconstruction filter bank and therefore it enables not only progressive representation but also lossless compression.

The rest of this paper is organized as follows. In Section 2, we briefly review the spatial and temporal wavelet analysis which is adapted in this paper. Section 3 describes the proposed compression scheme. Section 4 shows the compression results in terms of lossless and progressive compressions and comparing with several conventional techniques including our previous work. Finally, we conclude in Section 5.

2   Overview of Spatial and Temporal Wavelet Analysis and Synthesis Techniques

2.1   Spatial Wavelet Analysis and Synthesis

Spatial wavelet-based multi-resolution scheme was firstly introduced by Lounsbery [7]. Fig. 1 shows an example of the spatial wavelet analysis and synthesis processes. The multi-resolution analysis is processed by two filters, A^j and B^j as follows,

$$C^{j-1} = A^j C^j \tag{1}$$

$$D^{j-1} = B^j C^j \tag{2}$$

where, j is the resolution level, and C^j is the $v^j \times 3$ matrix representing the coordinates of the mesh M^j having v^j vertices. A finer mesh M^j is simplified by analysis filter bank to a coarser mesh M^{j-1} and wavelet coefficients D^{j-1} that represent the details. We obtain a hierarchy of meshes from the simplest one M^0, called base mesh, to the original mesh M^J. From the viewpoint of compression, since the probability distribution of spatial wavelet coefficients can be approximated to Laplacian distribution with sharp peak [6], we could achieve an efficient entropy coding. The reconstruction is done by two synthesis filters, P^j and Q^j. It is formulated as,

$$C^j = P^j C^{j-1} + Q^j D^{j-1} \tag{3}$$

Valette and Prost [8] introduced an exact integer analysis and synthesis with the lifting scheme based on Lazy filter bank and Rounding transform [9]. Consequently, this wavelet-based multi-resolution scheme enables us to accomplish a lossless compression. Note that the proposed method uses this modified filter bank for lossy progressive compression and lossless compression. In addition, it solved the major problem of the previous scheme [7] which cannot work on irregular surface mesh. In this paper, we use the spatial analysis and synthesis technique which is introduced in [8].

2.2   Temporal Wavelet Analysis and Synthesis

Temporal wavelet analysis also provides multi-resolution representation of a signal. Fig. 2 shows an example of the temporal wavelet analysis and synthesis

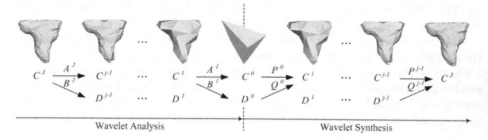

Fig. 1. Spatial wavelet analysis and synthesis processes

processes. In the wavelet analysis process, original signal $x[t]$ is decomposed into low frequency and high frequency band signals by analysis filter bank, $H_L(z)$ and $H_H(z)$. Low frequency and high frequency band signals imply the coarse version of the original signal and its details, respectively. In the wavelet synthesis process, two sub-band signals are transformed into a reconstructed signal $\hat{x}[t]$ by synthesis filter bank, $G_L(z)$ and $G_H(z)$. The probability distribution of temporal wavelet coefficients also can be approximated to Laplacian with sharp peak, and therefore we could expect an efficient entropy coding. To perform an efficient temporal wavelet transform, several analysis and synthesis filter banks have been developed such as Haar (2/2 tap), Le Gall (5/3 tap) and Daubechies (9/7 tap) filter banks. Fig. 3 shows the distribution of wavelet coefficients according to these filters. Here, each standard deviation σ of the distribution is denoted in parentheses. The more the distribution concentrates on zero, the better the coding efficiency can be expected. In this paper, we evaluate the coding efficiency according to these filters in the simulation.

3   Proposed Compression Method

To compress a 3-D mesh sequence, we exploit the spatial and temporal redundancy by using spatial wavelet-based multi-resolution analysis and temporal wavelet analysis techniques. The proposed method enables both progressive representation and lossless compression in a single framework by multi-resolution

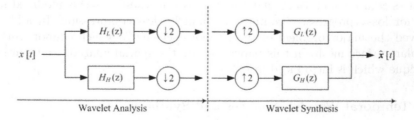

Fig. 2. 2-channel temporal wavelet analysis and synthesis processes

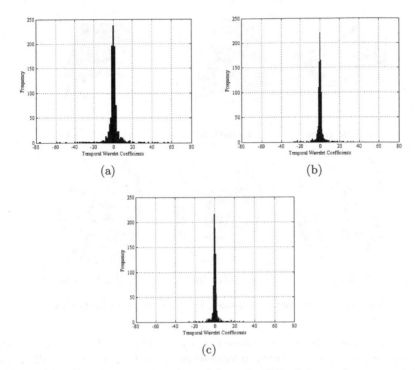

Fig. 3. Distribution of wavelet coefficients of x-axis of first base mesh geometry of Face sequence according to (a) Haar filter($\sigma = 8.32$), (b) Le Gall filter ($\sigma = 4.01$), and (c) Daubechies ($\sigma = 3.40$)

wavelet analysis with a perfect reconstruction filter bank. We encode geometry and connectivity information.

(1) **Geometry coding**

To encode geometry information, each mesh frame is firstly decomposed into a base mesh and its spatial wavelet coefficients of each resolution level by spatial wavelet analysis filter bank. And then, base mesh sequences and spatial wavelet coefficient sequences of temporal direction are once again decomposed into several sub-band signals by temporal wavelet analysis filter bank. We encode the resulting signal by using an arithmetic coder.

(2) **Connectivity coding**

Since an isomorphic mesh sequence has the same connectivity over all frames, the connectivity coding is performed only for the first mesh frame. The connectivity is encoded by the arithmetic coder.

4   Compression Results

Simulation results are carried out on two 3-D irregular triangle mesh sequences, Cow (with 128 frames and 2,904 vertices/frame) and Face (with 1,024 frames and

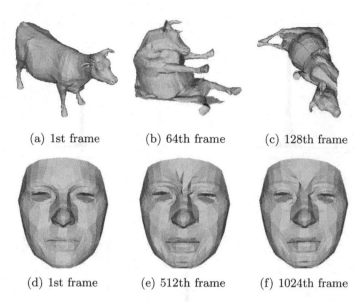

(a) 1st frame   (b) 64th frame   (c) 128th frame

(d) 1st frame   (e) 512th frame   (f) 1024th frame

Fig. 4. Original mesh sequences, (a)-(c) Cow and (d)-(f) Face

539 vertices/frame) which are represented by 12 bits/coordinate. The number of vertices and their connectivity information are not changed over all frames. Fig. 4 shows several frames of the original mesh sequences. The lifted Lazy filter bank for spatial wavelet analysis and synthesis is employed as we mentioned in Section 2.1. For temporal wavelet analysis and synthesis, we use Haar, Le Gall and Daubechies filter banks as we mentioned in Section 2.2. These three filter banks are implemented by lifting scheme. The lossless and progressive lossy compression results of each proposed scheme and the comparisons with conventional techniques are one by one presented in the next sub-sections.

4.1 Lossless Compression

To evaluate the performance of the proposed method, we compare the results with two schemes:

(1) SWA (Spatial Wavelet Analysis) : using only spatial wavelet analysis
    Similar with 3DMC (3-D Mesh Coding) of MPEG (Motion Pictures Experts Group)-4, each mesh frame is decomposed by spatial wavelet analysis filter bank and entropy coded. That is, the temporal coherence is not considered. Table 1 shows the bit-rates (bits/vertex/frame) obtained by the SWA scheme.

(2) SWA + TDC (Temporal Differential Coding) : our previous work[6]
    It encodes the geometry of base mesh, the wavelet coefficients and the connectivity of each resolution level for intra meshes. For inter mesh coding, it encodes the differences of geometry of base meshes and of their wavelet coefficients between adjacent frames by using I, B, and P frame coding scheme

Table 1. The lossless compression result of SWA scheme

Model	Bit-rate
Cow	22.90
Face	30.09

Table 2. The lossless compression result of SWA + TDC scheme

Model	Bit-rate
Cow	13.89
Face	10.95

Table 3. The lossless compression result of the proposed method, SWA + TWA

Temporal Wavelet Decomposition Level	Temporal Wavelet Filter	Model	Bit-rate
1	Haar (2/2 tap)	Cow	17.84
		Face	19.73
	Le Gall (5/3 tap)	Cow	16.30
		Face	18.36
	Daubeches (9/7 tap)	Cow	15.72
		Face	17.81
3	Haar	Cow	15.79
		Face	13.56
	Le Gall	Cow	13.50
		Face	11.36
	Daubechies	Cow	12.71
		Face	10.48
5	Haar	Cow	15.57
		Face	12.35
	Le Gall	Cow	13.31
		Face	10.25
	Daubechies	Cow	12.46
		Face	9.28

which is used in MPEG or H.26x. We compare the new proposed method with IBP frame coding which is the best result of our previous work. Table 2 shows the bit-rates obtained by the SWA + TDC scheme.

(3) SWA + TWA (Temporal Wavelet Analysis) : the proposed method
In simulations, we use three filter banks, Haar, Le Gall and Daubechies filters, for temporal wavelet analysis.

Table. 3 presents the bit-rates according to several temporal wavelet decomposition levels and filter banks. As shown in the table, the coding efficiency is improved when the temporal wavelet decomposition level is higher. It is mainly

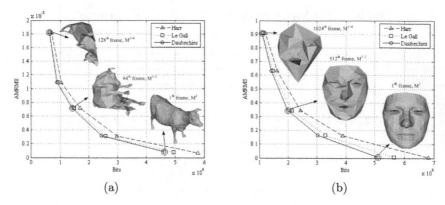

Fig. 5. Rate-distortion curve according to temporal wavelet filter banks, (a) Cow and (b) Face

caused by the fact that higher decomposition level provides more wavelet coefficients. Additionally, Daubechies filter is the most efficient among three filters as mentioned in Section 2.2. The proposed method is more efficient than the SWA scheme. Comparing with the SWA + TDC scheme, the proposed method can be more efficient by controlling the temporal wavelet decomposition level and filter. In case of Le Gall filter and Daubechies filter, when the decomposition level is selected to be higher than five and three, our method has more efficient coding performance, respectively.

4.2   Progressive Compression

To measure the quality of the reconstructed progressive mesh model, we used Metro [10], which provides the forward and backward surface-to-surface RMS (Root Mean Square) errors, $e^f(\mathbf{V}, \mathbf{V}')$ and $e^b(\mathbf{V}', \mathbf{V})$, respectively. We used the maximum value between the two RMS values for each frame, called MRMS

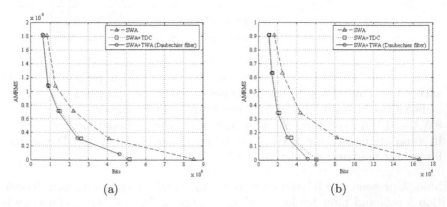

Fig. 6. Rate-distortion curve according to compression methods, (a) Cow and (b) Face

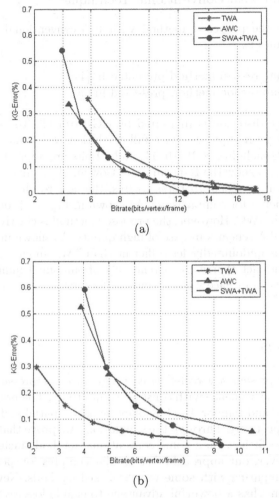

Fig. 7. Rate-distortion curve according to several compression schemes, (a) Cow and (b) Face models

(Maximum RMS). And then, we finally used the average of MRMS for all over the frames, called AMRMS (Average MRMS), as the quality measure.

The proposed method enables a 3-D mesh sequence to be reconstructed as the simplified meshes of each level. Fig. 5(a) and Fig. 5(b) depict the rate-distortion curves of Cow and Face according to temporal wavelet filter banks. Cow and Face models have 17 and 10 of spatial resolution levels, respectively. Here, the results of five highest resolution levels are presented. As shown in Fig. 5, Daubechies filter has the best coding efficiency among three filters. Fig. 6(a) and Fig. 6(b) show the rate-distortion curves according to compression methods. As shown in these figures, the proposed method is more efficient than the previous works.

4.3   Comparison with Conventional Techniques

We also compare the proposed method with two conventional wavelet-based compression schemes :

(1) TWA : the compression method presented in [4]
(2) AWC : the compression method presented in [5]

Here, the visible distorion is measured by KG-Error [2]. To use this metric, the reconstructed mesh sequences with full resolution are employed and various quantization levels including 8, 9, 10, 11, and 12 bits are applied. Fig. 7(a) and Fig. 7(b) respectively show the R-D curves of Cow and Face models according to several compression methods. In these figures, the best results of our proposed technique are dipicted for comparisons. As shown in Fig. 7(a), our method has similar results with AWC. However, the proposed method is clearly more efficient than AWC and TWA schemes in case of high quality. As shown in Fig. 7(b), the proposed scheme is undoubtedly less efficient than TWA in case of Face model. It is caused by the fact that we can relatively obtain small number of spatial wavelet coefficients from Face model, since it does not have many vertices in a frame.

5   Conclusions

In this paper, we present a wavelet-based progressive compression method for isomorphic 3-D mesh sequence with constant connectivity. The proposed method reduces the spatial and temporal redundancy by using spatial and temporal wavelet analysis, respectively. Through the simulations, we prove that the proposed algorithm is more efficient than some conventional methods including our previous work. However, our approache has similar compression performances or is less efficient comparing with some wavelet-based methods. Nevertheless, the proposed algorithms has a powerful advantage to enable lossless to progressive lossy compression for 3-D mesh sequence.

References

1. Lengyel, J.E.: Compression of time-dependent geometry. In: Proceeding of SI3D '99, New York, NY, USA, ACM Press (1999) 89–95
2. Karni, Z., Gotsman, C.: Compression of soft-body animation sequences. Computer and Graphics **28** (2004) 25–34
3. Ibarria, L., Rossignac, J.: Dynapack: space-time compression of the 3d animations of triangle meshes with fixed connectivity. In: SCA '03. (2003) 126–135
4. Payan, F., Antonini, M.: Wavelet-based compression of 3d mesh sequences. In: Proceedings of IEEE ACIDCA-ICMI'2005, Tozeur, Tunisia (2005)
5. Guskov, I., Khodakovsky, A.: Wavelet compression of parametrically coherent mesh sequences. In: Proceedings of SCA '04. (2004) 183–192

6. Cho, J., Kim, M., Valette, S., Jung, H., Prost, R.: 3-d dynamic mesh compression using wavelet-based multiresolution analysis. In: Proceedings of ICIP 2006. (2006) 529–532
7. Lounsbery, M.: Multiresolution Analysis for Surfaces of Arbitrary Topological Type. PhD thesis, Dept. of Computer Science and Engineering, U. of Washington (1994)
8. Valette, S., Prost, R.: Wavelet-based progressive compression scheme for triangle meshes: Wavemesh. IEEE Trans. Visual. Comput. Graphics **10** (2004) 123–129
9. Jung, H., Prost, R.: Lossless subband coding system based on rounding transform. IEEE Trans. Signal Processing **46** (1998) 2535–2540
10. Cignoni, P., Rocchini, C., Scopigno, R.: Metro: Measuring error on simplified surfaces. Computer Graphic Forum **17** (1998) 167–174

Detection of Wilt by Analyzing
Color and Stereo Vision Data of Plant

Shinji Mizuno[1], Keiichi Noda[2], Nobuo Ezaki[2],
Hotaka Takizawa[3], and Shinji Yamamoto[4]

[1] Toyohashi University of Technology, Toyohashi, Aichi, 441-8580 Japan
mizuno@imc.tut.ac.jp
[2] Toba National College of Maritime Technology, Toba, Mie, 517-8501 Japan
{noda, ezaki}@toba-cmt.ac.jp
[3] University of Tsukuba, Tsukuba, Ibaraki, 305-8577 Japan
takizawa@parl.jp
[4] Chukyo University, Toyota, Aichi, 470-0393 Japan
yamamoto@parl.jp

Abstract. The importance of information technology and ubiquitous computing are gained in the agricultural area. A remote monitoring tool, namely Field Servers, is developed and used in recent agricultural industries. The Field Server can handle weather data, measuring and taking photo images for analyzing visualized information. However, image data acquired by the Field Server is not adequately used for automatic control in current systems even though the conditions of plants, pests and thieves can be detected from the images. The purpose of this research is to develop an application which controls peripherals on the basis of features extracted from image data. As our first proposal we developed the farmer support system which pours water to wilting plants automatically. In this system, four indicators are used to detect the wilt of plants that have dense or sparse leaves. Two experiments were employed on using plants which are observed by a Field Server located outside. The experimental results prove that we can detect the wilt of plants by use of the proposed system.

1 Introduction

The importance of information technology and ubiquitous computing are gained in various areas and it is not exceptional in the agricultural area. Large-scale farms have already browsed and managed weather data of the farms in the remote area by using computer administrative system [1, 2], and even relatively small-scale farms including side-work farmers understand the necessity for recording and reviewing the weather data. To meet such situation, a wireless-network-connected weather data measuring instrument, which is called a Field Server [3, 4], is developed and used as a remote monitoring tool (Fig. 1). This Field Server can measure weather data such as temperature, humidity, soil temperature, amount of solar radiation and etc. The Field Server can also obtain images of the farm with mounted camera(s), and control peripherals as well. Distributing Field Servers interconnected by the Ethernet makes the

A. Gagalowicz and W. Philips (Eds.): MIRAGE 2007, LNCS 4418, pp. 400–411, 2007.
© Springer-Verlag Berlin Heidelberg 2007

farm "hotspot". Some systems only using weather data, such as automatic water supply and temperature control by air-conditioner, have been developed [5]. Thus, many systems with an individual function have been in use, and the one with comprehensive function has not been fully developed. The Field Server makes it possible to control interconnected devises if we run an application which controls their functions.

Fig. 1. Field Servers (with a single camera and a stereo camera)

2 Issues and Purposes

The present issues are as follows.

1) Insufficiency of universal applications with the functions of the Field Server such as getting images of plants, measuring weather data, and controlling peripherals.
2) The fact that image data are not adequately used for the automatic control even though the condition of the plants, pests and thieves are detected only from images as in research [6].

Thus, the purpose of this research is to develop an application which controls peripherals on the basis of features extracted from the images. This application, "farmer support system" will assist all the farmers for its convenience.

As our first proposal we have developed supply system, which detects wilting plants and waters them automatically. We propose two methods for plants with dense leaves and plants with sparse leaves.

3 System Configuration and Data Flow

The suggested system consists of a Field Server with watering equipment on the field, and a personal computer (PC) in the user's house. The PC is installed with a main program and an image processing program. The main program calls the image processing program and makes it analyze the plant image. We have developed the main program by LabVIEW [7], which is a useful graphical development environment for signal acquisition and measurement analysis. We have developed the image processing program by Java because of its portability. System configuration and data flow are shown in Fig. 2.

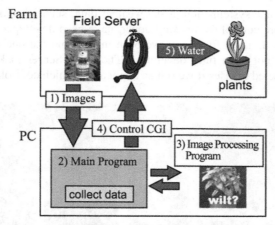

Fig. 2. Basic concept and data flow

We have set network cameras in front of target plants, and measured "wilting" from the photo images. We extracted degrees and areas of leaves regions by using the network cameras. And we defined the degree and the area as "wilting indicator".

In this research, we set a black board behind two "Pentas " as shown in Fig. 3. We defined the left plant as "Plant 1" and the right plant as "Plant 2".

Fig. 3. Target plants "Pentas"

4   Wilt Detection of Plants with Dense Leaves

First, two plants in the image are roughly segmented into green regions for further image processing. We experimented on Pentas and decided the following conditions to extract green regions of Pentas:

$$30 \leq H \leq 100, \tag{1}$$

$$\frac{Re + Gr + Bl}{3} \geq 115, \tag{2}$$

$$\frac{S}{Br} \geq 0.09, \tag{3}$$

where H, Re, Gr, Bl, S and Br represent the values of hue, red, green, blue, saturation and brightness, respectively.

4.1 Extraction of Leaves Region

In this section, we attempt to extract leaves regions as exactly as possible. First, we remove noises in the images that are obtained by a web camera whose resolution is only 300 kilo pixels. Such a low-resolution web camera has an economical advantage, but the obtained images often suffer from noises as shown in Fig. 4(a). To remove the noises, we use the Median Filter that is a kind of image processing. The filter outputs a pixel of median value from each pixel and surrounding 8 neighborhoods on RGB basis. After that, we re-extract green region so as to exclude the pot region and background. Fig. 4(b) shows a result of extraction of leaves regions.

(a) Original.   (b) Leaves.

Fig. 4. Extraction of a leaves region from the original image

4.2 Finding of Target Region for Processing

We make a histogram of the number of pixels of the extracted green regions projected into the X-axis of the images, as shown in Fig. 5(a). We can identify the start point x_1 and the end point x_2 with reference to the X-axis of the several leaves.

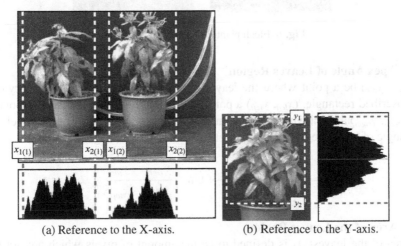

(a) Reference to the X-axis.   (b) Reference to the Y-axis.

Fig. 5. Histogram with reference to the X-axis and the Y-axis

Next, as seen in Fig. 5(b), we make another histogram with reference to a Y-axis for the each region of plants. We define start point as y_1 and end point as y_2 on the Y-axis.

4.3 Detection of Plant Wilt

In this research, we suggest three types of indicator of wilting leaves:

1) The angle of the extracted leaves region at its apex: θ. $\theta_{(a)}$ and $\theta_{(b)}$ in Fig. 6 represent such apex angles.
2) The area of the leaves region: A_1.
3) The area of circumscribed rectangle on the leaves region: A_2.

In the Fig. 6, $\theta_{(b)}$ is smaller than $\theta_{(a)}$ when we compare a flesh plant (a) and a wilting plant (b). Therefore, the indicator θ is thought to be effective as an indicator of the wilting. The indicators A_1 and A_2 are also thought to decrease when the plants get wilting. The details are described below.

Fig. 6. Flesh plant (a) and wilting plant (b)

4.3.1 Apex Angle of Leaves Region

Let (x_{top}, y_{top}) be a point where the leaves region attaches the upper boundary of the circumscribed rectangle, (x_{left}, y_{left}) a point where the region attaches its left boundary and (x_{right}, y_{right}) a point where the region attaches its right boundary, respectively. The apex angle of leaves region: θ is represented as follows (see Fig. 7).

$$\theta = \tan^{-1} \frac{y_{left} - y_{top}}{x_{top} - x_{left}} + \tan^{-1} \frac{y_{right} - y_{top}}{x_{right} - x_{top}} \tag{4}$$

4.3.2 Area of the Leaves Region

The area of the leaves: A_1 is defined to be the amount of pixels which are not black (RGB is not equal to #000000) in the extracted leaves region.

Fig. 7. The apex angle of the leaves region: θ

4.3.3 Area of Circumscribed Rectangle on the Leaves Region

The area of circumscribed rectangle on the leaves: A_2 is defined to be the amount of pixels in the rectangle that circumscribes the extracted region. The circumscribing rectangle is formed by (x_{top}, y_{top}), (x_{left}, y_{left}), (x_{right}, y_{right}) and (x_{bottom}, y_{bottom}) (Fig. 8). The coordinate (x_{bottom}, y_{bottom}) means a point that attaches the rectangle. The rectangular area represents feature quantity, and the area is smaller as its height and width get narrower.

Fig. 8. The circumscribing rectangle formed by 4 points

4.4 Experimental Result

We use two pots of "Pentas" for the experiments. A network camera is mounted in the Field Server, and the camera acquires VGA images on 5 minutes interval from 6:00 to 17:00. Fig. 9, Fig. 10 and Fig. 11 show the results of measurement of the indicators θ, A_1, and A_2, respectively.

We observed the Plant 1 wilting from 6:50 to 7:55 and from 14:15 to 15:55, which correspond to Image No. 11~25 and No. 100~120. We also observed the Plant 2 wilting from 14:15 to 15:55, which correspond to Image No. 100~120. We could find that the value θ of wilting plants decreased more than 10% compared with the value of fresh plants as shown in Fig. 9. The value A_2 also decreased more than 20% when the plants were wilting as shown in Fig. 11. These indicators would be used to detect

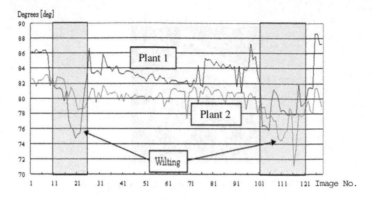

Fig. 9. Transition of the apex angle of leaves region: θ

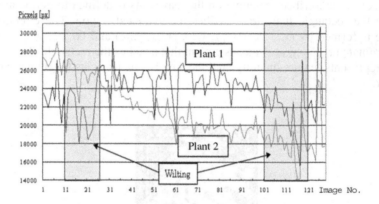

Fig. 10. Transition of the area of the leaves regions: A_1

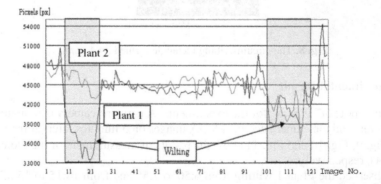

Fig. 11. Transition of the area of the circumscribing rectangles: A_2

wilting of plants. On the other hand, the indicator A_1 changed intensely during the experiment as shown in Fig. 10 and we could not elicit the wilting. We have to extract the green region of the plants more precisely to use this indicator.

5   Wilt Detection of Plants with Sparse Leaves

The method proposed in the former section watches the whole figure of a plant for wilt detection, and it is not suitable for plants with sparse leaves. The three-dimensional information on target plants is quite useful to measure the sizes and shapes of the plants, which help us determine the states of the plants [8]. We reconstruct 3-D leaves using a stereo vision method and measure the declining angles of leaves in a 3-D space. We detect wilt of the plant from the declining angles.

5.1   Extraction of Leaves Region

A pair of cameras is settled so that their vision lines are parallel with each other, and two images are obtained from the cameras. As in the beginning of section 4, we identify and extract green region from these images. We carried out the experiment on "Camellia" (Fig. 13(a)), and used the forms bellow to extract the green regions of the plant:

$$65 < H < 181, \tag{5}$$
$$S > 0.15. \tag{6}$$

The green region includes the leaves and stalks of the plant. To recognize such leaves and stalks individually, they must be separated by applying the knowledge about differences in shape between them. The extraction procedure is as follows:

1) Apply distance transformation to the green regions and generate a distance image.
2) Apply inverse distance transformation to the distance image and generate an inverse distance image (Fig. 12):
   a) Form an influence circle for each pixel. The center of each circle is set on a pixel and its radius is set to the distance value.
   b) Set the distance to all pixels within the influence circle uniformly. Overlapping areas between influence circles are filled with the maximum distance among them.
3) Extract pixels that have higher distance in the inverse distance image and merge them into regions. Such regions are determined to be leaves.

Fig. 13 shows the process of extracting leave regions.

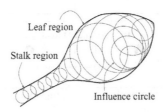

Fig. 12. Recognition of leaves and stalks using influence circles

(a) Target plant "Camellia".   (b) Green regions.   (c) Leaves regions.

Fig. 13. Extracting leaves regions of the target plant

5.2 3-D Data Acquisition by Use of Stereo Vision

We apply an edge-based stereo matching method to the images. In this method, first, the Sobel operator extracts edges from green region images.

A reference area having the edge at its center is established in one image and a searching area is established in the other image (see Fig. 14). The searching area is moved from left to right along the raster direction of the image. At each lateral position, we calculate a correlation value between the pixel values in the areas. The position that maximizes the correlation value is determined. The difference in the lateral position between the reference area and the optimal searching area is called a disparity. In order to avoid mismatching between the areas, we apply the bidirectional matching as shown in Fig. 14. Only if the two disparity values are the same, we adopt

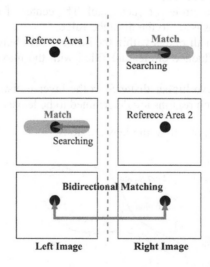

Fig. 14. Bidirectional matching in our edge-based stereo matching method

it. From the disparity, we calculate the 3-D position of the edge by use of the following equation:

$$Z = \frac{B \times f}{d},$$
(7)

where B, f, d and Z represent the base length between the cameras, the focal length of the camera, the disparity value and the depth of the edge, respectively.

5.3 Reconstruction of Leaves

Leaves are represented by a set of 3-D surface patches in this method. To reconstruct such a surface, the Delaunay triangulation is applied to edge data with depth.

The Delaunay triangulation forms surfaces on leaves, but also generates false triangles on stalks and between leaves. Each triangle is checked for overlap with the leaves region at a certain percentage or more. Only triangles meeting this condition remain as leaf surfaces. A set of generated triangles corresponds to one leaf.

5.4 Calculation of Declining Angles of Leaves

The diagonal line of each leaf is decided by choosing a pair of points: $(x_{max1}, y_{max1}, z_{max1})$ and $(x_{max2}, y_{max2}, z_{max2})$, which has the longest distance in the leaf. The declining angle θ between the diagonal line and Y-axis in a 3-D space (Fig. 15) is calculated by the following equation:

$$\theta = \frac{\sqrt{(x_{max1} - x_{max2})^2 + (z_{max1} - z_{max2})^2}}{y_{max1} - y_{max2}}$$
(8)

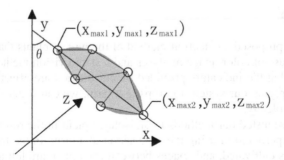

Fig. 15. Definition of declining angle of a leaf: θ in a 3-D space

5.5 Experimental Result

Fig. 16 shows the result of measurement of the declining angles of leaves in the plant. Two arrows in upper part of the graph show they were watered twice. In the graph, we could read out that each leaf's angle θ increases after watering and decreases as

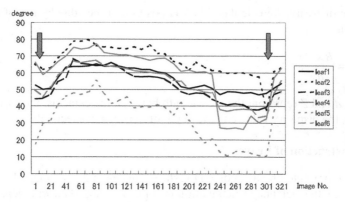

Fig. 16. Transition of the declining angle of the leaves of the plant in a 3-D space

Fig. 17. The farm where we are going to carry out an experiment

time passes. We detected angle variation by wilting and recovering after watering by applying this method like this.

6 Conclusion

In this paper, we proposed a detection method of the wilt of plants that have dense or sparse leaves by use of color image analyses and a stereo vision method. Experimental results show that the indicators provided by our method are effective in detecting plant wilt. By applying our system to crops in a farm, we can water the crops before wilting them completely.

In this paper we tested our methods to an isolated plant in the room. We are going to carry out an experiment of using the field server at a farm. In the farm, one kind of crops (cabbage) is cultivated, and spaces between each plant are left a little as shown in Fig. 17. In this situation our method of extracting leaves regions and detecting plant wilt could be applied by choosing one of plants in the farm as a target and modifying some parameters. However, all farms would not have such a situation.

Our future work is to improve the accuracy in detection of wilting of various plants. We would decide the optimum parameters and thresholds of indicators of wilting for various plants. We would also improve our methods to be able to apply to crowding plants in farms by developing new method such as combining two methods based on 2-D images and 3-D scenes.

References

1. T. Ohtani, K. Sugahara, K. Tanaka, M. Laurenson, T. Watanabe, and S. Umemoto, "Web based IPM system for Japanese pear diseases in Japan. III. Weather data acquisition system to estimate leaf wetness duration and scab infection severity", The 2001 KSPP International Conference and Annual Meeting. Plant Disease Forecast: Information Technology in Plant Pathology. Program and Abstracts 63, 2001.
2. S. Ninomiya, M. Hirafuji, T. Nanseki and T. Kiura, "Present Status and Prospective of Agriculture Grid and Its Implementation", SICE-ICASE International Joint Conference 2006.
3. K. Sasaki, "Progress of Field Server with Image Information and Example of Remote Observation", Keisou, Vol. 45, No. 1, pp. 65-68, 2002.
4. M. Hiratou, "Farm Information Monitoring by Using Field Server", Agriculture And Gardening, Vol. 78, No. 1, pp. 182-188, 2003.
5. W. Choi, M. Dohi and N. Ishizuka, "Development of precision Production Robot for Flower and Vegetable Seeding (Part 1) -Discrimination of Stock Seeding by Image Processing", JOURNAL of the JAPANESE SOCIETY of AGRICULTURAL MACHINERY, Vol. 66, No. 2, pp. 68-75, 2004.
6. A. Tazuke, K. Kamei, S. Okura, Y. Mizutani and K. Shio, "Extraction of Region from Plant Images for the Automatic Detection of Leaf Wilting", Agricultural Information Research, Vol. 11, No. 1, pp. 27-40, 2002.
7. http://www.ni.com/labview/
8. H. Takizawa, N. Ezaki, S. Mizuno and S. Yamamoto "Plant Recognition by Integrating Color and Range Data Obtained Through Stereo Vision", Journal of Advanced Computational Intelligence and Intelligent Informatics, Vol. 9, No. 6, pp. 630-636, 2005.

Human Silhouette Extraction Method Using Region Based Background Subtraction

Jung-Ho Ahn and Hyeran Byun

Dept. of Computer Science, Yonsei University, Seoul, Korea, 126-749
{jungho, hrbyun}@cs.yonsei.ac.kr

Abstract. Background subtraction methods have been used to obtain human silhouettes for gesture and gait recognition. However, background subtraction in pixel units is prone to error which decreases recognition performance significantly. In this paper we propose a novel background subtraction method that extracts foreground objects in region units. Together with the background model, an object's color and movement information are used to obtain the effective region object likelihood. Then an adaptive region decision function determines the object regions. Also, the sequential version of Horprasert's algorithm[2] is presented.

1 Introduction

Background subtraction is a widely used approach for detecting and tracking moving objects in videos from a static camera. Recently background subtraction methods have been used to assist in human behavior analyses such as gesture and gait recognition[4, 10], where accurate human silhouettes are needed to extract the features of human body configuration. However, the human silhouettes obtained by background subtraction are usually not accurate enough for the recognition tasks; in particular, shadows are not properly removed from human silhouettes, as shown in Figure 1(b). Also, when foreground human objects pass background areas with similar colors to those of the human body, background subtraction methods can not give accurate human silhouettes. These problems decrease the recognition performances significantly[5].

Background subtraction has long been an active area of research. For example, Horprasert et al.[2] proposed a robust background subtraction and shadow detection method, which was applied to an object tracking system together with appearance model[6]. The adaptive background subtraction method using Gaussian mixture model[7] was presented and it was applied to foreground analysis with intensity and texture information[8]. Harville [3] extracted the foreground in a joint color-with-depth observation space and many other approaches have been proposed.

Meanwhile we[1] propose an accurate human silhouette extraction method using region based background subtraction, using regions as visual primitives, rather

---

[1] Jung-Ho Ahn moved to the division of Computer & Media Engineering at Kangnam University in March of 2007.

A. Gagalowicz and W. Philips (Eds.): MIRAGE 2007, LNCS 4418, pp. 412–420, 2007.

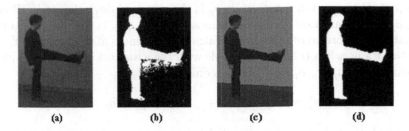

    (a)   (b)   (c)   (d)

Fig. 1. The basic idea for our region based background subtraction method. (a) the original image taken from the 660th frame of the test sequence $JH1$, (b) a binary image that is thresholded in pixel units by using Horprasert's algorithm[2], (c) region units given by the mean shift image segmentation[1], (d) binary image that is thresholded in region units by using the proposed algorithm.

than pixels. Figure 1 illustrates our basic idea. Since the shadowed region is a small part of the wall, it can be ignored. When we evaluate foreground likelihoods in units of image regions, we can recover object boundaries and remove the noises such as shadows. The proposed method is motivated from the visual perceptual grouping principles in still images. The results of the existing approaches, however, do not match human performance in terms of both speed and quality [9]. They have explored bottom-up and top-down models but could not cover the large variability of object shapes. In contrast, our method, which is based on the background subtraction method, can efficiently capture flexible human body shapes in video.

2   Horprasert's Algorithm Revisited

Horprasert et al.[2] proposed a statistical background model that separates brightness from the chromaticity component in a batch mode. The batch mode requires a long training time and a large amount of memory to store the training images while the sequential model does not. Furthermore, a sequential algorithm is of great advantage in practice, especially when cameras can move around and stop to detect foreground objects. In section 2.1, therefore, we modify the Horprasert's algorithm to work in the sequential mode. In section 2.2 the object likelihood of the pixel is presented by modeling the distributions of brightness and chromaticity distortions. Note that the algorithm presented in section 3 can work on not only the background model in this section but also on any other background models.

2.1   Sequential Brightness and Chromaticity Background Model

In Horprasert's background model a pixel p is modeled by 4-tuple of

$$< \mu_p, \sigma_p, a_p, b_p >, \tag{1}$$

where μ_p is the expected color value; σ_p is the standard deviation of RGB color value; a_p is the variation of the brightness distortion; b_p is the variation of the chromaticity distortion of pixel p. We calculate sequences of $< \mu_p^t, \sigma_p^t, a_p^t, b_p^t >$ at every t-th frame when the scene is stable with the assumption that the sequence approximates $< \mu_p, \sigma_p, a_p, b_p >$ as t becomes bigger,

$$< \mu_p^t, \sigma_p^t, a_p^t, b_p^t > \quad \longrightarrow \quad < \mu_p, \sigma_p, a_p, b_p > . \tag{2}$$

If the scene turns to be unstable after Nth frame, we stop computing the sequences and set the model parameter $< \mu_p, \sigma_p, a_p, b_p >$ to be $< \mu_p^N, \sigma_p^N, a_p^N, b_i^N >$.

The sequences are calculated as follows: We define the expectation and standard deviation of the color vector of pixel p as $\mu_p^t = (\mu_r^t(p), \mu_g^t(p), \mu_b^t(p))$ and $\sigma_p^t = (\sigma_r^t(p), \sigma_g^t(p), \sigma_b^t(p))$, respectively, up to the tth frame. For the sequential background training process we calculate μ_p^t and σ_p^t as follows:

$$\mu_i^t(p) = \frac{t-1}{t}\mu_i^{t-1}(p) + \frac{1}{t}C_i^t(p) \tag{3}$$

$$\sigma_i^t(p)^2 = \frac{t-1}{t}\sigma_i^{t-1}(p) + \frac{1}{t}(C_i^t(p) - \mu_i^t(p))^2 \tag{4}$$

where $i = r, g, b$ and $C_p^t = (C_r^t(p), C_g^t(p), C_b^t(p))$ is the observed color of pixel p at the t-th frame. The brightness and chromaticity distortions[2] can be obtained using the temporal mean μ_p^t and standard deviation σ_p^t. The variation of the brightness distortion a_p^t and the chromaticity distortion b_p^t are calculated by

$$(a_p^t)^2 = \frac{t-1}{t}(a_p^{t-1})^2 + \frac{1}{t}(\alpha_p^t - 1)^2, \quad (b_p^t)^2 = \frac{t-1}{t}(b_p^{t-1})^2 + \frac{1}{t}(\gamma_p^t)^2. \tag{5}$$

2.2 Pixel Object Likelihood

Using the background model $< \mu_p, \sigma_p, a_p, b_p >$, we can induce the object likelihood $l(p)$ for each pixel p. The object likelihood is decomposed into brightness and chromaticity likelihoods. The distribution f^b of the brightness distortion α of pixel p can be approximated using normal distribution of mean 1 and variance a_p^2, $\alpha \sim N(1, a_p^2)$. The distribution f^c of chromaticity distortion γ at pixel p can be approximated by one-sided normal distribution of mean 0 and variance b_p^2,

$$f^c(\gamma|p) = \frac{2}{\sqrt{2\pi}b_p} \exp(-\gamma^2/(2b_p^2)), \quad \gamma \geq 0. \tag{6}$$

Assuming that brightness distortion α_p and chromatic distortion γ_p are independent, the *naive* background probability density function f_B of pixel p is given by

$$f_B(C_p|p) = f^b(\alpha_p|p)f^c(\gamma_p|p), \tag{7}$$

---

[2] For the detail explanation of brightness and chromaticity distortion the reader is referred to [2].

(a)   (b)   (c)

Fig. 2. Pixel object likelihoods: (a) image of the 250th frame in test data $JH3$, (b) brightness distortion likelihood $-\log f^b(\alpha_p|p)$, (c) scaled chromaticity distortion likelihood $-\eta \log f^c(\gamma_p|p)$, where $\eta = 5$. The likelihoods are truncated by 255.

where C_p is the RGB color vector of pixel p, and α_p and γ_p are calculated as in [2]. Figure 2 shows that the brightness and chromaticity distortion complement each other, thus our independence assumption can be empirically supported. The pixel object likelihood l of pixel p is given by

$$l(p) = -\log(f^b(\alpha_p|p)) - \eta \log(f^c(\gamma_p|p)), \tag{8}$$

where a constant η is introduced since the chromaticity likelihood is relatively smaller than that of the brightness in practice. Note that $l(p) = -\log(f_B(C_p|p))$ when $\eta = 1$.

3   Region Based Background Subtraction

In this section we present a background subtraction method in region units. To accomplish it, we first perform image segmentation to segment an image into small homogeneous regions. We define $\mathcal{R}^t = \{R_i^t\}_{i\in I^t}$ as the set of the regions at the t-th frame. For computational efficiency we perform it in the bounding box surrounding an object of interest. The way of obtaining the bounding boxes is described in section 4. The information of the object and background colors and previous object positions are fused to determine the object region likelihood. Then, the object silhouette is obtained by the region decision function f_D^t defined on $\mathcal{R}^t$.

3.1   Region Object Likelihood

The region object likelihood $L^t(R_i)$ of region $R_i^t \in \mathcal{R}^t$ is calculated by

$$L^t(R_i) = L_p^t(R_i) + \lambda_1 L_c^t(R_i) + \lambda_2 L_o^t(R_i). \tag{9}$$

In the above equation, $L_p^t(R_i)$ is the *naive* object region likelihood given by the arithmetic mean of the pixel object likelihoods $l(p)$, i.e. $\sum_{p\in R_i^t} l(p)/n_{R_i^t}$, here $n_{R_i^t}$ is the number of pixels in the region R_i^t. The naive region likelihood is not enough especially when some parts of an object are similar in color to the background parts that they occlude, as is shown in Figure 3. To overcome the problem the

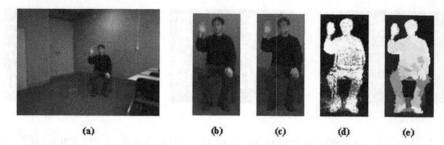

(a)   (b)   (c)   (d)   (e)

Fig. 3. Naive region likelihood. (a) original image of 426th frame in test data $JH3$ with the bounding box, (b) cropped image, (c) mean shift segmentation of the image (a), (d) pixel object likelihoods $l(p)$'s, (e) naive region likelihood $L_p^t(R_i)$ in (9).

foreground color distribution P_f is modeled by a Gaussian mixture in RGB color space, learned from foreground pixels in the previous image frame. Then the object color likelihood $L_c^t(R_i)$ is given by $\sum_{p \in R_i^t} P_f(p)/n_{R_i^t}$. The regularization term $L_o^t(R_i^t)$ is the overlapping ratio of the region R_i^t and is given by $n_{R_i^t}^o/n_{R_i^t}$, where $n_{R_i^t}^o$ is the number of pixels in region R_i^t that belongs to the previous object region. λ_2 is a regularization parameter. If the parameter λ_2 is too large the object silhouette will get overfitted to the previous one. Figure 3 shows the pixel and naive object region likelihoods of an image. Some object regions having lower naive region likelihood was supplemented by L_c^t and L_o^t in Fig. 4 (d).

3.2   Adaptive Region Decision Function

The object segmentation problem can be considered as a labeling problem that assigns each pixel to its label in $\mathcal{L} = \{0, 1\}$, where 0 represents a background and 1 represents an object. In our framework of region based background subtraction, the assignment(or decision) is performed in region units. Therefore the decision function f_D^t of the t-th frame is defined on $\mathcal{R}^t$ and takes its value in $\mathcal{L}$. We define the decision function $f_D^t : \mathcal{R}^t \to \mathcal{L}$ as

$$f_D^t(R_i) = \begin{cases} 1 & \text{if } L^t(R_i^t) > T_{R_i^t}^t - \epsilon \\ 0 & \text{otherwise} \end{cases} \tag{10}$$

where region thresholds $T_{R_i^t}^t$'s are defined as an arithmetic mean of the thresholds T_p^t of pixels in R_i^t, and ϵ is a constant to make sure sufficient lower bound. The pixel threshold T_p^t is determined in the whole image from the previous frame by

$$T_p^t = (T_p^{t-2} + M_p^{t-1})/2. \tag{11}$$

In the above equation, $T_p^0 = T_p^1 = M_p^0 = T_{\min}$ and M_p^{t-1} is the local minimum of the region likelihoods that belongs to object region $\mathcal{O}^{t-1}$ in the $(t-1)$th frame. M_p^{t-1} is calculated by the weighted average of local region object likelihood m_p^{t-1}

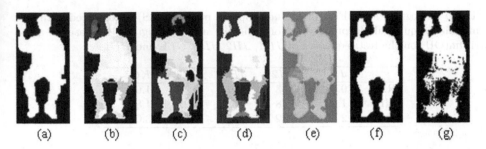

Fig. 4. Segmentation with Region Likelihood. (a) previous object silhouette $\mathcal{O}^{t-1}$ where $t = 426$ in $JH3$, (b) regularization term $L_o^t(R_i^t)$ scaled by 255, (c) object color likelihood $L_c^t(R_i^t)$, (d) region object likelihood $L(R_i^t)$ with $\lambda_1 = 30$ and $\lambda_2 = 30$, truncated by 255. (e) pixel threshold T_p^t in (10), (f) silhouette obtained by the proposed algorithm with $\epsilon=10$, (g) silhouette obtained by the original Horprasert's algorithm[2].

and the pixel object likelihood $l(p)$, i.e. $qm_p^{t-1} + (1 - q)l(p)$ where q is set to 0.7 in the experiments. m_p^{t-1} is given by

$$m_p^{t-1} = \begin{cases} \min_{x \in B(p,r)} \left\{ L^{t-1}(R) | x \in R \subset \mathcal{O}^{t-1}, R \in \mathcal{R}^{t-1} \right\} & \text{if } d(p, \mathcal{O}^{t-1}) < r \\ T_{\min} & \text{otherwise} \end{cases}$$

where $B(p, r)$ is a ball with radius r centered at pixel p, $L^{t-1}(R)$ is the region object likelihood of R at the $(t - 1)$th frame and $d(p, \mathcal{O}^{t-1})$ is the nearest distance from pixel p to the previous object region $\mathcal{O}^{t-1}$. Then we truncate T_p^t's by a constant T_{max} to prevent them from becoming too high. The thresholds vary adaptively so that they are relatively lower in areas having less pixel object likelihoods. The silhouette extraction is completed by morphological opening followed by closing using 1×1 structuring element to make the object contour smooth. Figure 4 shows the likelihoods and compares the results in (f) and (g).

4   Experimental Results

We tested our region based background subtraction method for human silhouette extraction using a static camera indoors. Performance of the proposed method was evaluated with respect to the ground-truth segmentation of every 10th frame in each of five 700 frame test sequences of 320×240 images. The ground-truth data was labeled manually, where each pixel was labeled as object, background or unknown. The unknown label occurred in cases when there were one plus pixel and one minus pixel along the ground-truth object boundaries to mark the mixed pixels. The five test sequences were labeled by $JH1$, $JH2$, $JH3$, $GT1$, $KC1$ with different backgrounds and people. In all sequences one person entered the scene, moved around and assumed natural poses, and the whole body was shown for the gesture recognition.

Table 1. Segmentation Error(%). The proposed method(RBS) is compared with the modified sequential Horprasert's algorithm(MH) and the original Horprasert's algorithm(OH) on the test sequences of $JH1$, $JH2$, $JH3$, $GT1$, and $KC1$.

	$JH1$	$JH2$	$JH3$	$GT1$	$KC1$
RBS	0.39	0.63	0.97	0.75	1.68
MH	1.90	4.68	1.53	1.22	1.89
OH	2.59	5.22	1.67	1.66	3.01

Human Detection. Our human detection method produces the bounding box surrounding a person. We calculated image difference over two frames to identify static backgrounds. If the scene turned unstable we stopped updating the background model. After the frame the foreground regions were obtained in the pixel units by using the background model. The foreground regions of each frame were grouped into connected components. Then the maximal component was assumed to be a human object and its bounding box was obtained. Within the bounding box, a human silhouette was extracted.

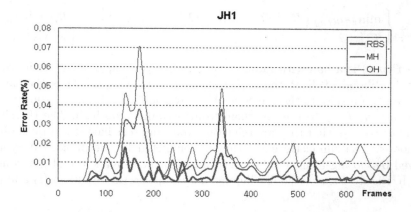

Fig. 5. Segmentation performance in test data $JH1$. The proposed method(RBS) outperforms the original Horprasert's algorithm(OH) and the modified sequential Horprasert's algorithm(MH).

Performance. Segmentation performance of the proposed method was compared with those of Horprasert's original algorithm[2] and the proposed sequential version of Horprasert algorithm described in section 2.1. Table 1 shows the results, where the error rate was calculated within the bounding boxes only ignoring the mixed pixels. The proposed method outperformed the pixelwise background subtraction methods. Interestingly, the sequential version of Horprasert's algorithm performed slightly better than the original one. In the experiments we used the mean shift segmentation method[1] to obtain the regions $\mathcal{R}^t$. The performance of the adaptive method[7] was so poor for the test sequences that we will not report the results. Figure 5 shows the errors at every 10th frame of the

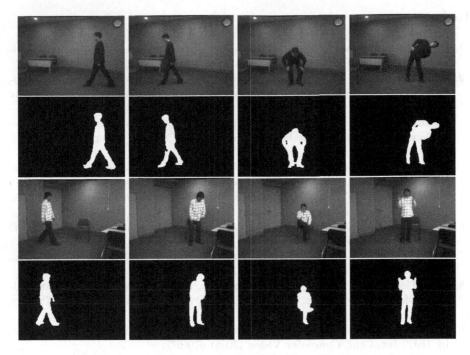

Fig. 6. Examples of human silhouettes extracted by the proposed algorithm. The images are taken from $JH1$ and $GT1$.

$JH1$ test video. Some human silhouette results are shown in Fig. 6. The average running time of our algorithm was 16.8 fps on a 2.8 GHz Pentium IV desktop machine with 1 GB RAM with an average bound box area of 130×100.

5   Conclusions

This paper has addressed the problem of accurate human silhouette extraction in video. We have proposed a novel human silhouette extraction method based on the background subtraction in region units. The proposed algorithm showed very good results on the real sequences and also worked at near real-time speed. The limitation of this approach is that the extracted silhouette quality depends on the region segmentation quality. In the experiments the mean shift segmentation performed best, but it took about 65 percent of the processing time is taken from it. Future research involves developing an efficient image segmentation method to find proper *atomic* regions.

Acknowledgements. This research was supported by the Ministry of Information and Communication, Korea under the Information Technology Research Center support program supervised by the Institute of Information Technology Assessment, IITA-2005-(C1090-0501-0019).

References

1. D. Comaniciu, P. Meer: Mean shift: a robust approach toward feature space analysis: IEEE Trans. Pattern Anal. Mach. Intell. 24(5) (2002) 603-619.
2. T. Horprasert, D. Harwood, L.S. Davis: A statistical approach for real-time robust background subtraction and shadow detection. In: Proc. IEEE Frame Rate Workshop (1999) 1-19.
3. M. Harville: A framework for high-level feedback to adaptive, per-pixel, mixture-of-Gaussian background models. In: Proc. Euro. Conf. on Comp. Vision (2002) 543-560.
4. H. Li, M. Greenspan: Multi-scale gesture recognition from time-varying contours. In: IEEE Int. Conf. Computer Vision (2005) 236-243.
5. Z. Liu, S. Sarkar: Effect of silhouette quality on hard problems in gait recognition. IEEE Trans. Systems, Man, and Cybernetics-Part B 35(2) (2005) 170-183.
6. A. Senior: Tracking people with probabilistic appearance models. In: Proc. IEEE Int. Workshop on PETS, (2002) 48-55.
7. C. Stauffer, W.E.L. Grimson: Learning patterns of activity using real-time tracking. IEEE Trans. Pattern Anal. Mach. Intell. 22 (2000) 747-757.
8. Y.-L. Tian, M. Lu, A. Hampapur: Robust and efficient foreground analysis for real-time video surveillance. In: Proc. IEEE Int. Conf. Computer Vision and Pattern Recognition (2005) 970-975.
9. Z. Tu: An integrated framework for image segmentation and perceptual grouping. In: IEEE Int. Conf. Computer Vision (2005) 670-677.
10. L. Wang, T. Tan, H. Ning, W. Hu: Silhouette analysis-based gait recognition for human identification. IEEE Trans. Pattern Anal. Mach. Intell. 25 (2003) 1505-1518.

Facial Feature Point Extraction Using the Adaptive Mean Shape in Active Shape Model

Hyun-Chul Kim[1], Hyoung-Joon Kim[1], Wonjun Hwang[2],
Seok-Cheol Kee[2], and Whoi-Yul Kim[1]

[1] Department of Electronics and Computer Engineering, Hanyang University,
Haengdang-dong, Seongdong-gu, Seoul, South Korea
{hckim, khjoon}@vision.hanyang.ac.kr, wykim@hanyang.ac.kr
[2] Samsung Advanced Institute of Technology,
Giheung-eup, Yongin-si, Gyeonggi-do, Seoul, Korea
{wj.hwang, sckee}@samsung.com

Abstract. The fixed mean shape that is built from the statistical shape model produces an erroneous feature extraction result when ASM is applied to multi-pose faces. To remedy this problem the mean shape vector which is similar to an input face image is needed. In this paper, we propose the adaptive mean shape to extract facial features accurately for non frontal face. It indicates the mean shape vector that is the most similar to the face form of the input image. Our experimental results show that the proposed method obtains feature point positions with high accuracy and significantly improving the performance of facial feature extraction over and above that of the original ASM.

1 Introduction

The extraction of facial feature point, for example, eyes, nose, mouth corners and others, is an important stage in many facial image interpretation tasks such as face verification, face expression recognition, model based image coding and head pose determination.

Many methods have been developed to extract facial feature point accurately. Most of them generally model two types of information [1]. The first is the local texture around a given feature, for example the pixel values in a small region around an eye. The second is the geometric configuration of a given set of facial features. Many different methods of modelling this shape and texture information present in the human face have been proposed [2-6].

Active Shape Model (ASM) [7] proposed by Cootes *et al.* has been to be a powerful tool for aiding image interpretation and extracting facial feature point. ASM models grey-level texture using local linear template models and the configuration of feature points using a statistical shape model. An iterative search algorithm seeks to improve the match of local feature points and then refine the feature locations according to the best fit of the shape model. Fitting to a large number of facial feature points mitigates the effect of individual erroneous feature detections. However, ASM can only be used only to faithfully model objects whose shape variations are subtle

A. Gagalowicz and W. Philips (Eds.): MIRAGE 2007, LNCS 4418, pp. 421–429, 2007.

and linear [8]. Also ASM has the additional limitation that a good initialisation, one close to the correct solution is required, otherwise it is prone to local minima [1]. Owing to these defects ASM tends to fail easily for multi-pose faces. To solve those problems, many methods have been developed [9-11].

In this work, first we show the problem that occurs when the fixed mean shape vector, which is built from the statistical shape model training, is used to extract feature points of multi-pose faces. Then we find out the reason why it occurs through investigation of the statistical shape model. To prevent from the problem occurring and to accurately extract facial feature point for non frontal face images, we propose the adaptive mean shape. The adaptive mean shape indicates the mean shape vector that has similar form to the input face image. By using the adaptive mean shape instead of the mean shape vector, it modifies the statistical shape model slightly. While the fixed mean shape vector prevent from ASM extracting facial feature point accurately by causing problem in the constrained condition and the shape parameter update procedures of ASM, the adaptive mean shape method allows ASM to perform properly for multi-pose faces. The adaptive mean shape which is the most similar with an input face image is generated using a genetic algorithm [12] among many other optimal algorithms. The objective function of the genetic algorithm consists of the statistical appearance model information [14].

The rest of this paper is organized as follows. In Section 2, we demonstrate the problem that occurs when the fixed mean shape vector is used to extract feature points from multi-pose faces. To remedy this problem, we propose the adaptive mean shape and the detailed algorithm of the proposed method being described in Section 3. Section 4 shows the experimental results for the CMU-PIE [15] face database. Finally, Section 5 offers conclusions.

2   Active Shape Model

ASM consists of building the statistical shape model [7] from a training set and an iterative searching procedure to locate any instance of such shapes in a new image. The statistical shape model is built from a set of shapes using corresponding landmarks. Principle component analysis (PCA) is then used to reduce the dimensionality of the data, such that any shape $\mathbf{x}$ in the training set can be approximated as follows.

$$\mathbf{x} \approx \overline{\mathbf{x}} + \mathbf{Pb} \tag{1}$$

Here $\overline{\mathbf{x}}$ is a mean shape vector, $\mathbf{P}$ is a matrix of eigenvectors and $\mathbf{b}$ is a vector of shape parameters. The variance of the ith parameter across the training set, $\mathbf{P}_i$, is given by the corresponding eigenvalue λ_i. By limiting the parameter $\mathbf{b}_i$ in the range of λ_i, we ensure that the generated shape is similar to those in the original training set [7]. This limit was determined experimentally and generally $\mathbf{b}_i$ is in the range of $\pm 3\sqrt{\lambda_i}$.

For a given new image, the general procedure of ASM that finds where the features lie on the image is as follows. (a) Initialization: the model is initialized according to the mean shape. (b) Points matching: a region of the image around each feature point is examined to find the best nearby match (i.e. by searching along the profile line for the edge locations). (c) Constrained condition: the constraint is applied to the parameters $\mathbf{b}_i$ to ensure that the generated shape is similar to the original training set. So if one element has value outside $\pm 3\sqrt{\lambda_i}$, its value is adjusted artificially so that it may have a value within $\pm 3\sqrt{\lambda_i}$. (d) Shape parameter update: changed shape parameter $\mathbf{b}_i$ is updated to best fit the new found points. These steps are repeated until there is no significant change in the shape parameters [7].

As stated above the general ASM process can be used efficiently for feature point extraction of an object that is immobile or fixed. Thus, it is difficult to expect a good result for multi-pose faces. Fig. 1 shows the results when ASM is applied in two types of facial images. One type is frontal face and the other is side face. Unlike the case with the frontal face, the shape (e) that is fitted to the input image is changed to an undesirable shape (f).

This situation is occurred frequently when ASM is applied in non frontal face image. The reason is that the value of λ_i is not changed despite the facts that the difference between the fitted shape to the input image $\mathbf{x}_f$ and $\overline{\mathbf{x}}$ is great. So most of the shape parameters of $\mathbf{x}_f$ that may include correctly fitted points or incorrectly fitted points are controlled artificially to have a value within $\pm 3\sqrt{\lambda_i}$. By contrast, with a frontal face for which the difference between $\mathbf{x}_f$ and $\overline{\mathbf{x}}$ is small shape (b) is reconstructed correctly as in shape (f).

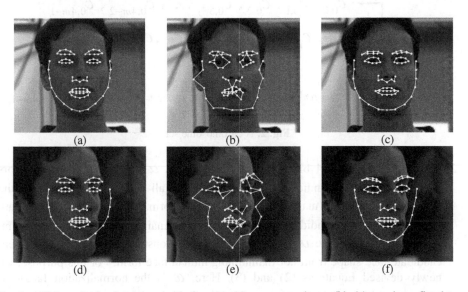

Fig. 1. ASM results for frontal and side face (a), (d) are mean shape, (b), (e) are shape fitted to each input image using local gray information, and (c), (f) are reconstructed shape using statistical shape model

Although the abnormal face shape (e) adjusted to have a human face form (f) owing to the constraint condition, points that may wish to be located on the contour of human face are artificially adjusted so that were moved to the opposite direction. To solve this problem, correctly fitted points must not be adjusted artificially to have a value within $\pm 3\sqrt{\lambda_i}$. This can be done by reducing the gap between $\mathbf{x}_f$ and $\overline{\mathbf{x}}$.

3 Adaptive Mean Shape

In this section, in order to remedy above problem, we propose the adaptive mean shape ($\bar{x}_a$) that is compatible with the face shape of an input image. As stated above several times, because $\bar{x}_a$ is similar to the face shape of the input image, it is able to decrease the difference between x_f and $\bar{x}_a$. So it can specify that most shape parameter elements of x_f have a value within $\pm 3\sqrt{\lambda_i}$. Therefore, ASM can perform the correct process. An approach to achieving the adaptive mean shape is the following.

1. Randomly creates n chromosomes of $4 \times m$ bits length. Here n is the number of the candidate face shape (x_s) to be created, and $s = 0, \cdots, n-1$. m is the number of eigenvector that is used to make candidate face shape. As use more m as the candidate face shape becomes little more detailed human face. $c_{s,t}$ has either the value 0 or 1 and $t = 0, \cdots, 4m-1$. Fig. 2 shows a sample chromosome set.

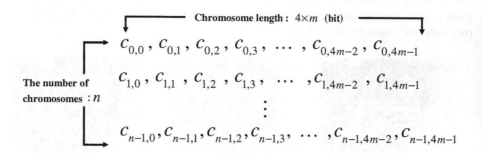

Fig. 2. A chromosome set

2. Create one $\alpha_{s,m}$ per 4 bits of each chromosome. $\alpha_{s,m}$ is used by eigenvectors weight to make the candidate face shape. Here, if all $\alpha_{s,m}$ are inside $\pm 3\sqrt{\lambda_i}$, the candidate face shape maintains a human face form. However, if all $\alpha_{s,m}$ are outside $\pm 3\sqrt{\lambda_i}$, the candidate face shape no longer maintains the human face form. In this paper, we create $\alpha_{s,m}$ so that satisfies the constrained condition to prevent candidate face shape from not maintaining human face form. For this purpose, we newly devised Equations (2) and (3). Here, ω_c is the normalization factor of $\omega_{s,m}$ as and its value is $2^m - 1$.

$$\omega_{s,m} = \sum_{l=4m}^{4m+3} c_{s,l} \cdot 2^{l-4m} \tag{2}$$

$$\alpha_{s,m} = 2\left(\frac{\omega_{s,m}}{\omega_c} \cdot 3\sqrt{|\lambda_m|} \right) - 3\sqrt{|\lambda_m|} \tag{3}$$

When all four chromosomes are 0 $\omega_{s,m}$ becomes 0 and when all four chromosomes are 1 $\omega_{s,m}$ becomes 15. Because $\omega_{s,m}$ has a value in $[0,15]$, consequently $\alpha_{s,m}$ has a value in $\pm 3\sqrt{\lambda_i}$.

3. Compute the total $n \times m$ $\alpha_{s,m}$ using n chromosomes of $4 \times m$ length.
4. Make n-shape vectors ($\mathbf{x}_s$) using equation (4). The $\mathbf{x}_s$ that is created from equation (4) maintains human face form. Because all $\alpha_{s,m}$ that are generated using Equation (3) satisfy the constrained condition.

$$
\mathbf{x}_s = \overline{\mathbf{x}} + \mathbf{P}_m \begin{bmatrix} \alpha_{s,0} \\ \alpha_{s,1} \\ \vdots \\ \alpha_{s,m-1} \\ \alpha_{s,m} \end{bmatrix}
\tag{4}
$$

5. To find out the adaptive mean shape the genetic algorithm is performed using generated candidate face shapes and the objective function in Equation (5). The objective function to estimate the fitness of the $\mathbf{x}_s$, is defined using the statistical appearance model and Mahalanobis distance. As the candidate face shape and the face shape of the input image similar, the objective function has bigger value.

$$
f(\mathbf{x}_s) = \sum_{p=0}^{o-1} \left(\mathbf{g}(x_{s,p}, y_{s,p}) - \overline{\mathbf{g}}_p\right)^{\mathrm{T}} \mathbf{S}_p^{-1} \left(\mathbf{g}(x_{s,p}, y_{s,p}) - \overline{\mathbf{g}}_p\right)
\tag{5}
$$

Here, p is the order of landmark points and o is the total number of landmark points. $(x_{s,p}, y_{s,p})$ denote p^{th} landmark (x,y) at s^{th} candidate face shape. And $\mathbf{g}(x_{s,p}, y_{s,p})$ is a vector that consists of the sampled gray level value along the normal direction of the line that joins two points $(x_{s,p}, y_{s,p}), (x_{s,p+1}, y_{s,p+1})$. $\overline{\mathbf{g}}_p$ is the average vector of the sampled gray level corresponding to p^{th} landmark and $\mathbf{S}_p^{-1}$ is a inverse covariance matrix which is built from the statistical appearance model training.

6. Replace $\overline{\mathbf{x}}_a$ with $\mathbf{x}_s$ that is a finally determined candidate shape according to the convergence condition of genetic algorithm, and then run ASM procedures.

4   Experimental Results

The statistical model training was achieved with various face images taken from the Internet. Face images consisted of frontal faces and non front faces for various people. The number of training images is 318 and the size of the image is 100×120. We labeled 76 landmark points for each image in the training set manually. Fig. 3 (a), (b) show our training images and a face image with 76 landmark points.

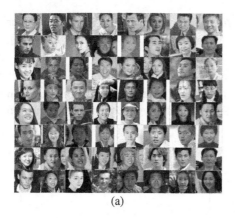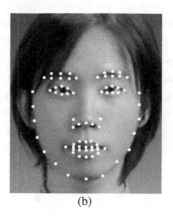

(a)   (b)

Fig. 3. (a) Sample training images (b) Face image with 76 landmark points

We set the chromosome length at 16 bits and used 120 chromosomes for candidate face shapes. The mutation is used as the genetic operator and the tournament selection is used as the method of selection. We set the mutation probability at 0.98 and the tournament selection size at 7. To stop the algorithm a simple stopping criterion, which is to stop after a 60 number of iterations, is used. The above values were determined by a lot of experiments.

Fig. 4 shows the adaptive mean shapes that are made by the proposed method, and we can certainly confirms that the adaptive mean shapes are well correspond with the face form of each input image.

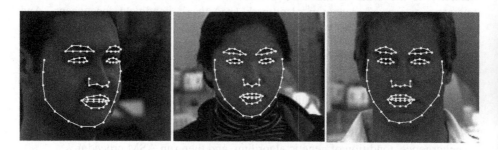

Fig. 4. The adaptive mean shapes corresponding to each input image

Fig. 5 shows the position transition of feature points by the adaptive mean shape method. Here (a) is the adaptive mean shape, (b) is the shape after the model is fitted to the input image, and (c) is shape after the constrained condition and the shape parameter update procedure were done using the adaptive mean shape. When compared (a), (b), and (c) of Fig. 5 with (d), (e), and (f) of Fig. 1, we can see that the correct shape was generated after the constrained condition and the shape parameter update procedure were done unlike the fixed mean shape method.

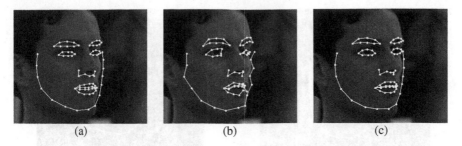

Fig. 5. Position transition of feature points by the adaptive mean shape (a) the adaptive mean shape, (b) fitted shape to an input image, and (c) reconstructed shape using the adaptive mean shape

The search algorithm was tested on an image set known as CMU-PIE. The test data set consisted of a total of 160 images. We used 4 images per each person, as shown in Fig. 6, for about 40 people excepting those who wear glasses.

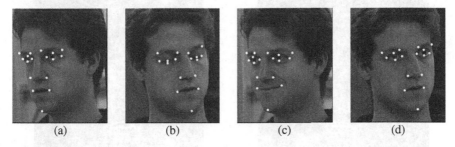

Fig. 6. Selected feature points for purpose of performance test (a) B_W_05, (b) N_W_05, (c) N_W_11, (d) S_W_11

The feature point extraction performance was estimated using the mean position error of the 17 feature points appearing in Fig. 6. The reason why we select 17 feature points among total 76 landmark points is that those 17 points are apt to measure position objectively. Table 1 compares the feature point extraction performance between the adaptive mean shape method (A) and the fixed mean shape method (B). Therefrom we can see that the performance of the adaptive mean shape method is superior to the fixed mean shape method. Fig. 7 shows the results of the feature point extraction.

Table 1. Performance comparison of the feature points extraction

Face pose	B_W_05	N_W_05	N_W_11	S_W_11	Total
Mean position error of (A) (pixel)	2.01	1.51	1.47	1.95	1.735
Mean position error of (B) (pixel)	4.08	5.37	3.54	5.16	4.537

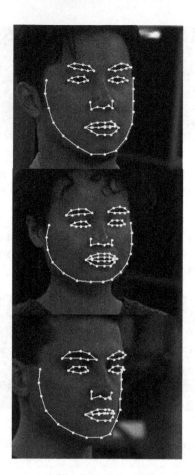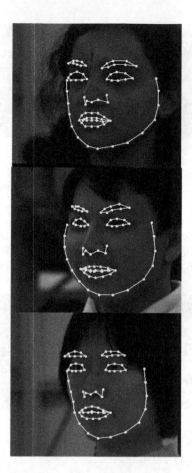

Fig. 7. Results of feature point extractions for non frontal faces

5 Conclusions

In this paper, we first showed the problem that occurs when the fixed mean shape vector is used to extract the feature points for non frontal face. Then, we proposed a robust facial feature extraction method, ASM using the adaptive mean shape. Classical ASM, which used the fixed mean shape, tends to fail easily for non frontal face. Because it adjusted many shape parameters to have a value in $\pm 3\sqrt{\lambda_i}$. In contrast ASM using the adaptive mean shape is able to extract feature points accurately better than the former. In experiment, we compared the feature points extraction performance of two ASM methods, one that uses the fixed mean shape and one that uses the adaptive mean shape. We could see that the performance of the adaptive mean shape method is superior to the performance of the fixed mean shape method. Notably, the feature points extraction problem with regard to the face border line, which was difficult to solve by the fixed mean shape method, was well resolved.

References

1. Cristinacce, D., Cootes, T.: Facial feature detection using adaboost with shape constraints. In 14th British Machine Vision Conference, September (2003) 231-240
2. Burl, M., Leung. T., Perona, P.: Face Localization via shape statistics. In 1st International Workshop on Automatic Face and Gesture Recognition, June (1995) 154-159
3. Wiskott, L., Fellous, J.M., Kruger, N., Von Der Malsburg, C.: Face recognition by elastic bunch graph matching. IEEE Transactions on Pattern Analysis and Machine Intelligence, Vol. 19 (1997) 775-779
4. Cootes, T., Edwards, G. J., Taylor, C. J.: Active appearance models. In 5th European Conference on Computer Vision, Vol. 2 (1998) 484-498
5. Cristinacce, D., Cootes, T.: A comparison of shape constrained facial feature detectors. In 6th International Conference on Automatic Face and Gesture Recognition, (2004) 375-380
6. Cristinacce, D., Cootes, T., Scott, I.: A Multistage Approach to Facial Feature Detection. Proceedings of British Machine Vision Conference 2004, Vol. 1 (2004) 277-286
7. Cootes, T., Taylor, C. J., Cooper, D. H., Graham, J.: Active Shape Models – Their Training and Application. Computer Vision and Image Understanding, Vol. 61 (1995) 38-59
8. Romdhani, S., Gong, S., Psarrou, A.: A multi-view nonlinear active shape model using kernel pca. British Machine Vision Conference, (1999) 483–492
9. Changbo, H., Rogerio, F., Matthew, T.: Active Wavelet Networks for Face Alignment. British Machine Vision Conference, (2003)
10. Reinders, M. J. T., Koch, R. W. C., Gerbrands, J. J.: Locating facial features in image sequences using neural networks. In 2nd International Conference on Automatic Face and Gesture Recognition, (1996) 230-236
11. Graf, H. P., Casotto, E., Ezzat, T.: Face analysis for synthesis of photo-realistic talking heads. In 4th International Conference on Automatic Face and Gesture Recognition, March (2000) 189-194
12. Goldberg, D. E.: Genetic Algorithms in Search, Optimization, and Machine Learning, Addison-Wesley, 1989
13. Goldberg, D. E., Deb, K.: A comparative analysis of selection schemes used in genetic algorithms. In Foundations of Genetic Algorithms, G.J. E. Rawlins, Ed., (1991) 69–93
14. Cootes, T., Taylor, C. J.: Statistical models of appearance for medical image analysis and computer vision. Proceedings of SPIE, Vol. 4322 (2001) 236-248
15. Sim, T., Baker, S., Bast, M., The CMU Pose, Illumination, and Expression (PIE) database of human faces. The Robotics Institute, Carnegie Mellon University, (2001)

Use of Multiple Contexts for Real Time Face Identification

Suman Sedai, Koh Eun Jin, Pankaj Raj Dawadi, and Phill Kyu Rhee

Dept. of Computer Science & Engineering, Inha University
253, Yong-Hyun Dong, Nam-Gu
Incheon, South Korea
{suman,supaguri,pankaj}@im.inha.ac.kr, pkrhee@inha.ac.kr

Abstract. We present the design of face identification system that can run in real time environment. We use multiple contexts to optimize the face recognition performance in real time. Initially different illumination environments are modeled as context using unsupervised learning and accumulated as context knowledge. Optimization parameters for each context are learned using Genetic Algorithm (GA).GA search the optimization parameter so as to minimize the effect of illumination variation. These weight parameters are used during similarity match of face images in real time recognition. Gabor wavelet is used for facial feature representation. Experiment is done using real time face database containing images taken under various illumination conditions. The proposed context aware method has been shown to provide superior performance than the method without using context awareness.

1 Introduction

Face identification is specific case of object recognition. Common appearance of face objects (frontal view) roughly looks similar and small changes make the faces look different from each other. In a traditional feature space, frontal faces will form a dense cluster. In such case recognition is more affected by the environmental factors such as illumination, pose and expression. Therefore, face recognition needs dedicated representations of the images and specific algorithms. Successful approaches include appearance based methods like direct correlation; eigenface and fisher face [1], EBGM [2], Active Appearance Model [3] and discriminant analysis [4]. However most of the systems are highly sensitive to environmental factors during image capture, such as variations in lighting conditions and hence cannot meet the real time constraint. In this paper we present the face recognition system that is especially tolerant of the change of illumination environment suitable for real time. Here we use the context information to minimize the effect of illumination change and optimize the performance during recognition. Our real time system learns the illumination environments and tries to minimize the effect of each environment during the identification process. Three cases are investigated separately, first without using any context, second using single context and thirdly using multiple contexts. In non context case, recognition is done in simple mode without any optimization. In single context case, environment is

A. Gagalowicz and W. Philips (Eds.): MIRAGE 2007, LNCS 4418, pp. 430–439, 2007.
© Springer-Verlag Berlin Heidelberg 2007

learned as a single context and optimization parameter is searched for single context. In multi context case environment is clustered into multiple context and optimization parameters are searched for each context individually. During recognition process context of the test image is identified and optimization parameter belonging to the identified context is used in similarity matching with images in database. Our real time implementation system consists of camera mounted on the 2 GHz personal computer with real time digitizing card and runs on 20 frames per second. The camera is pointed on complex background and when persons appear in front of camera their pictures are captured and compared for previously registered face database image for identification.

2 Gabor Wavelet Based Feature Representation

For the task face recognition in real time scenario we need to find the feature points in face image to generate the feature vector of the image. Furthermore, feature vector is compared to the feature vectors of the face images database to find out the closest match of the given image to images in database. For automatic extraction of facial feature point, mixture of active shape model and gabor jet representation is used and detail technique is discussed in [5]. We locate 16 fiducial points 3 for mouth, 3 for nose, 6 for eyes and 4 for eyebrows as shown in Figure 1. After facial feature points are located then local features at each of the feature point is calculated and finally combined to form the total feature vector of the face image.Gabor wavelet is used to extract the local feature at each point. We use 8 orientation and 8 frequencies of Gabor wavelet at each point, resulting in 64 dimensional vectors for each feature point .Finally we have 1024 dimensional total feature vectors of a face image.

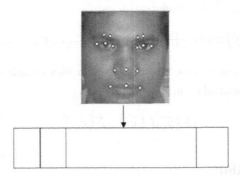

Fig. 1. An example of 16 feature points for face recognition

The proposed face recognition uses Gabor feature vector, which is generated using the Gabor wavelet transform. The kernels show desirable characteristics of spatial locality and orientation selectivity, a suitable choice for face image feature extraction for classification [6]. The Gabor kernels for a facial feature point are defined as follows

$$\psi_{\mu,v}(\vec{x}) = \frac{\left\|(\vec{k})_{\mu,v}\right\|^2}{\sigma^2} \exp\left(-\frac{\left\|(\vec{k})_{\mu,v}\right\|^2 \|(\vec{x})\|^2}{2\sigma^2}\right)\left[\exp\left(i(\vec{k})_{\mu,v}(\vec{x})\right) - \exp\left(-\frac{\sigma^2}{2}\right)\right] \tag{1}$$

where μ and v denote the orientation and dilation of the Gabor kernels, $(\vec{x}) = (x, y)$, $\|\bullet\|$ denotes the norm operator, and the wave vector $(\vec{k})_{\mu,v}$ is defined as follows

$$(\vec{k})_{\mu,v} = \begin{pmatrix} k_v \cos\phi_\mu \\ k_v \sin\phi_\mu \end{pmatrix}, \ k_v = 2^{\frac{-v+2}{2}}, \ \phi_\mu = \pi\frac{\mu}{8}. \tag{2}$$

Gabor wavelet is used at eight different frequencies, $v = 0,...,7$, and eight orientations, $\mu = 0,...,7$. The Gabor wavelet transformation of an image is defined by the convolution of the sub-area of image using a family of Gabor kernels as defined by Eq (3). Let $f(\vec{x})$ be the gray value of a sub-image around pixel $(\vec{x}) = (x, y)$, and the Gabor wavelet transform of the sub-image is defined as follows

$$G_{\mu,v}(\vec{x}) = f(\vec{x}) * \psi_{\mu,v}(\vec{x})$$
$$= \iint f(\alpha, \beta)\psi_{\mu,v}(x - \alpha, y - \beta)d\alpha\,d\beta \tag{3}$$

where $\vec{x} = (x, y)$, and * denotes the convolution operator. Each Gabor kernel $G_{\mu,v}(\vec{x})$ consists of different local, frequency and orientation characteristics at the facial feature point x. Those features are concatenated together to generate a feature vector F for the facial feature point x. The feature vector F of sub-image around fiducial point x is defined as the concatenation of 64 complex coefficients $G_{\mu,v}(\vec{x})$, $\mu = 0,...,7$, $v = 0,...,7$ as follows:

$$F(\vec{x}) = \left(G_{0,0}(\vec{x})^t G_{0,1}(\vec{x})^t ... G_{7,7}(\vec{x})^t\right)^t \tag{4}$$

For N number of fiducial points, the feature vector thus includes all the Gabor transforms at each facial fiducial point $\vec{x}_i$,

$$V = \left(F(\vec{x}_1)F(\vec{x}_2)...F(\vec{x}_N)\right) \tag{5}$$

3 Face Recognition

Given a test face image and a reference face database, the goal of face recognition is to classify test image to one of the image in reference database. The simple classification of feature vector does not overcome the effect of environment on recognition; hence the context information is used to minimize the effect of environment during recognition. First training data is clustered in order to learn the model of illumination conditions. After learning illumination contexts optimal feature representation for each of these context is searched using GA. The optimal feature representation for a context here is the weight value of each feature point that gives maximum recognition rate in the cluster. Combination of weight value of all feature point forms an optimal weight vector for a context. This optimal weight vector is used to measure the weighted distance between the test image vector and training image vector and is discussed in section 3.3.

3.1 Environment Modeling and Identification

The system environment is learned using unsupervised learning technique were illumination is taken as environmental context. Each training face image is scaled as 6 x 6 window and normalized using min-max normalization. 1 x36 dimensional vectors are generated using vertical scanning of image see Fig 2. K Means algorithm [7] is used for context modeling and Euclidian distance [7] metric is used for context identification. An example of different context of face data identified using K-Means is shown Fig. 3. It can be seen that, each cluster consists of group of faces having similar illumination environment.

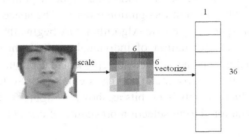

Fig. 2. Face data vectorization in 1x36 dimensions for context modeling

Fig. 3. Sample of Face Images clustered in three illumination contexts

3.2 Optimal Weight Vector Generation for Each Environment

To generate optimal weight vector system undergoes evolutionary learning where, best weight vector $W = [w_1, w_{2...} w_N]$ is searched for each identified context or cluster where N is the number of fiducial points. GA is used to search the best weights for each identified context [8] [9].After several iterations of evolution best sets of weight values for each fiducial point minimizing the classification error is discovered. After evolution, best weight vector is selected for each identified environment as shown in Fig 4. This weight vector is used during similarity measure of two feature vectors.

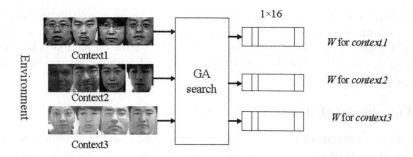

Fig. 4. Optimal weight vector generation for each environment

Environment is clustered into different context (see fig 3,4) by the procedure de-scribed in section 3.1.Then for each context optimal weight vector is found   using the GA. GA finds weight of fiducial point   according to contribution of the fiducial point in recognition process. After search is completed, fiducial points which have higher weight   have more contribution in recognition process. The space of weight vector to be found is the search space of Genetic Algorithm. GA begins the optimization proc-ess by randomly creating population of individuals, called chromosomes. For this purpose binary encoding scheme is used to represent the population of points. For each fiducial point 4 bit chromosome encoding is employed. So total length of chro-mosome for all 16 fiducial points is 64 bits as shown in figure 5. The fitness function used to evaluate population during selection procedure of each GA iteration is shown by equation 6.

$$\eta(W) = \lambda_1 \eta_s(W) + \lambda_2 \eta_g(W) \tag{6}$$

where $\eta_s(W)$ the term for the system correctness, i.e., successful recognition is rate and $\eta_g(W)$ is the term for class generalization. λ_1 and λ_2 are positive parameters that indicate the weight of each term, respectively. W is the chromosome of the popula-tion being evaluated. Figure 5 shows the structure of the chromosome and correspon-dence between each four bit of the chromosome and the weight value w_i of each fidu-cial point.

$$W = [w_0, w_1....w_{15}] \tag{7}$$

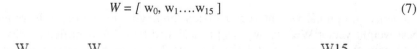

Fig. 5. Structure of chromosome and corresponding weights

Finally the output of learning is the results a set of optimal weights for each context. So the systems recognition performance is the function of optimization parameter W.

3.3 Feature Vector Classification

Classification of the face image can be performed as follows: Feature vector V of image I is extracted as described in section 2. Illumination context c of image I is identified (section 3.1) and optimal weight vector W corresponding to context c is chosen (section 3.2). Similarity score between I and each face image in reference database is then calculated using the feature vectors of images and W using Eq 9. Finally image I is classified to a reference face image in database which gives maximum similarity score .The similarity between the test face image and reference image in database is computed using weighted average cosine similarity   between the test vector and target vector. Here weight W is the optimization parameter discovered by genetic algorithm which is discussed in section 3.2. First similarity score of Gabor vector   is calculated for each corresponding fiducial point in test image and reference image.   Then weighted sum of   similarity scores over all features gives the overall similarity score. Let v_i and u_i be the 64 dimensional Gabor vector generated at ith fiducial point of test image and a reference image in database respectively.

$$v_i = (V_{i,1}, V_{i,2}, \ldots, V_{i,64})$$

$$u_i = (\mu_{i,1}, \mu_{i,2}, \ldots, \mu_{i,64})$$

(8)

Overall similarity between two images is the sum of weighted similarity between each fiducial point of two images. If there are N number of feature points in a face image then, similarity score can be written as

$$S = \frac{\sum_{1}^{N} w_i D(v_i, u_i)}{\sum_{i}^{N} w_i}$$

(9)

where D is the cosine distance between the vector v_i and u_i and the denominator term normalizes the weight parameter so that S is in range 0 and 1.

4   Experimental Setups and Performance Evaluation

The system is evaluated using 240 images data collected over 40 individuals taking 6 trials for each individual under different illumination and slight change in pose and expression. The test set includes various illuminations from different daylight condition. These data were acquired under constant pose but varying illumination because illumination condition is used as context information to optimize the recognition performance. Total number of image is 240 among which 200 images are used as test set and 40 images are used as training set, taking single image per individual for registration. The experiments were carried out off-line in order to keep the condition of re-experiment for comparing   cases below. To compare the effect of illumination context on recognition performance, three cases were compared, non context, single context and multiple contexts. In non context case no optimization parameter is used during recognition. In single context, optimization parameter is calculated taking whole environment as single context, here illumination condition is modeled as single context .In multi context case, illumination environment is clustered in 3 contexts and optimization parameter is calculated for each context separately. During recognition mode context of test image is identified and corresponding optimization parameter is used for recognition.

For each of the case recognition performance, false acceptance rate (FAR) and false rejection rate (FRR) is measured for different identification threshold of similarity. Real time test set is used to measure recognition rate and FRR. FAR measures the rate at which any imposter is accepted by the system.   So imposter data set, containing the images of individuals which are not in training set is used to measure FAR. 1000 images of FERET database is used as imposter set. Equal error rate, point where FRR is equal to FAR is used to compare the performance of the three cases. The lower the error rates better the performance of the system. Figure 6 shows the comparison of FAR vs. FRR for each non-context, single-context and multiple-context cases as shown by three curves. 45 degree line cuts each curve at equal error point. It can be seen that equal error rate for multi context case is 4.9%, single context case is 6.2 % and non-context case is 10.2%.Fig 7 shows the comparison of ROC curve among the three scenarios. It can be seen that for multiple context case error rate is minimum and recognition rate is maximum. The results suggest that multi context case outperforms the non context one.

Table 1.

Method	Contexts	Recognition Rate (%)	Total (%)	Error Rate(%)
Non Context	-	87.8	87.8	10.2
Single Context	-	90.1	90.1	6.2
Multi Context	Context1	91.3	92.7	4.9
	Context2	94.1		
	Context3	92.6		

Experimental results in Table 1 show the recognition success for non-context, single-context and multiple-context scenario. Overall recognition success as high as 92.7% is achieved for multiple context case. Recognition success for single context and non context is found to be 90.1 and 87.8 respectively. Result suggests that recognition performance can be increased and error rates can be decreased by use of context information. Due to its superior performance multiple context based recognition is used in the real time implementation of the system. Figure 9 shows the real time implementation of the system under operation. Operating identification threshold is found by analyzing the error curve as shown in Figure 8. Vertical axis corresponds to

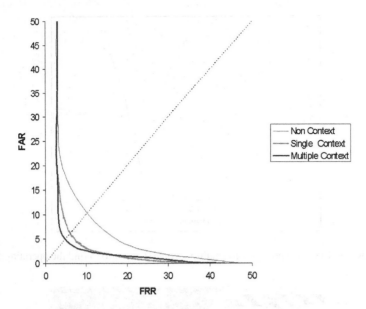

Fig. 6. Comparison of error curve between Multiple Context, Single Context and Non Context scenarios

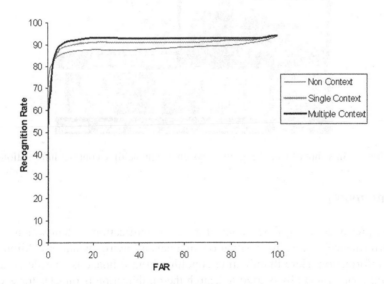

Fig. 7. ROC curve for Multiple Context, Single Context and Non Context scenarios

the error rates and the horizontal axis corresponds to the identification threshold of the similarity. Threshold corresponding to cross point of FAR and FRR is considered as operating threshold for the system.

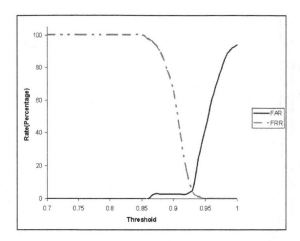

Fig. 8. FAR /FRR vs Threshold plot for multiple context scenario to find the operating threshold

Fig. 9. Snapshot of face recognition system using multiple contexts information

5   Conclusion

We have presented a real-time system for face identification system which can give high performance in real time situation of uneven environmental conditions using context information. Here illumination condition in face image is considered as environmental context and GA is used to search the optimization parameter for each context. Experimental result suggests that optimization parameters maximize the overall recognition performance and reduce the error rates. Use of multiple contexts is compared with the single context and non context scenario. Experimental result shows that using multiple contexts for recognition is better than using single context and without using any context for recognition. Hence in real time implementation of the system, use of multiple contexts is adapted. Hence it can be used in real time outdoor situation where the light source is constantly changing. In future researched will be focused on adding more context information like pose and facial expression for recognition.

References

1. Thomas Heseltine1, Nick Pears, Jim Austin, Zezhi Chen.: Face Recognition: A Comparison of Appearance-Based Approaches. Proc. VIIth Digital Image Computing: Techniques and Applications, 10-12 Dec. 2003, Sydney
2. L. Wiskott, J.-M. Fellous, N. Krueuger, C. von der Malsburg.: Face Recognition by Elastic Bunch Graph Matching, IEEE Trans. on Pattern Analysis and Machine Intelligence, Vol. 19, No. 7, 1997, pp. 776-779
3. T.F. Cootes, K. Walker, C.J. Taylor.: View-Based Active Appearance Models, Proc. of the IEEE International Conference on Automatic Face and Gesture Recognition, 26-30 March 2000, Grenoble, France, pp. 227-232
4. W. Zhao, R. Chellappa, P.J. Phillips.: Subspace Linear Discriminant Analysis for Face Recognition (1999). technical report, Center for Automation Research, University of Maryland, College park.
5. Sanqiang Zhao, Wen Gao, Shiguang Shan, Baocai Yin.: Enhance the Alignment Accuracy of Active Shape Models Using Elastic Graph Matching, Proc. ICBA, pp. 52-58, 2004.
6. Linlin Shen , Li Bai. : A review on Gabor wavelets for face recognition , Pattern Anal Applic (2006) 9:273–292
7. Manian, V.Hernandez, R. Vasquez, R.: Classifier performance for SAR image classification, Geosciences and Remote Sensing Symposium, 2000. Proceedings. IGARSS 2000. IEEE 2000 International.
8. Goldberg, D.E.: Genetic Algorithm in Search, Optimization and Machine Learning. Addison-Wesley Publishing Company, Inc. Reading, Massachusetts. (1989)
9. Xiaoling Wang Hairong Qi.: Face recognition using optimal non-orthogonal wavelet basis evaluated by information complexity, Proceedings, 16th International Conference on Pattern Recognition, 2002
10. Chahab Nastar & Matthias Mitschke.: Real-Time Face Recognition Using Feature Combination, Proceedings of the Third IEEE International Conference on Automatic Face and Gesture Recognition (FG'98) 14-16 April 1998, Nara, Japan.

Computerized Bone Age Assessment
Using DCT and LDA

Hyoung-Joon Kim and Whoi-Yul Kim

Division of Electronics and Computer Engineering, Hanyang University,
17 Haengdang-Dong, Sungdong-Gu, Seoul, 133-791, Korea
khjoon@vision.hanyang.ac.kr, wykim@hanyang.ac.kr

Abstract. This paper presents a computerized bone age assessment method using discrete cosine transform (DCT) and Fisher's linear discriminant analysis (FLD or LDA). Bone age assessment using a radiograph of the left hand is a common procedure in pediatric radiology. In the proposed method, DCT and LDA are applied to the epiphyseal regions segmented from a radiograph of the left hand. The extracted LDA coefficients are compared with features stored in the database, and then the bone age of the given radiograph is estimated. In experiments on 396 radiographs of the left hand collected at Hanyang University Medical Center, the proposed method shows an average error of 0.6 years and an accuracy of 89.71%.

1 Introduction

Bone age (or skeletal age, or skeletal maturity) assessment using a radiograph of the left hand is a common procedure in pediatric radiology. Based on that radiological evidence of skeletal development, bone age is assessed and then compared with the corresponding chronological age. A large discrepancy between these two ages indicates abnormalities in skeletal development. Growth-hormone-related growth diseases, which can include childhood obesity, are issues of increasing concern. Early detection is very important to the treatment of such conditions, and thus bone age assessment has come to the center of public attention.

The two methods most widely used for manual assessment of bone age are the Tanner and Whitehouse (TW2) method [1] and the Greulich and Pyle (GP) method [2]. The GP method, used by over 76% of pediatricians [3], is based on a general comparison with the images in the atlas that corresponds closest with the chronological age of the patient. The TW2 method uses a detailed analysis of each individual bone; owing to its complexity, it is employed by less than 20% of radiologists, even though it yields the more reliable results [4]. Both methods not only are time-consuming but suffer from inconsistencies due to the subjective nature of the analysis as performed by various observers with different levels of training.

Recently, owing to the rapid development of computing power and image processing techniques, many attempts at fully automatic bone age assessment, which can segment regions of interest (ROIs) after removing background to reduce user interaction

A. Gagalowicz and W. Philips (Eds.): MIRAGE 2007, LNCS 4418, pp. 440–448, 2007.

and increase repeatability, have been proposed [4-17]. Those assessment methods usually utilize wrist and phalanx information. Among wrist data, the characteristics of the carpal bones such as their sizes and shapes normally are used [12]. Unfortunately, analysis of carpal bones, due to the nature of the process of their maturity, does not provide accurate and significant information for patients older than 9-12 years of age [12]. By contrast, the methods based on phalangeal analysis use features such as epiphyseal diameter/size, the ratio of epiphyseal diameter to metaphyseal diameter, and/or phalangeal length/shape [4-9, 11, 13-15]. Phalangeal length does not provide any adequate indication of skeletal maturity, and can be used only for the purposes of rough estimation at an early stage of hand image analysis [11]. The most important phalanx data is on the epiphyses. Pietka, one of the pioneers in computerized bone age assessment, well analyzed the characteristics of the epiphyses, such as size and shape, for varying ages [4]. Another approach using the epiphyses for computerized bone age assessment is the principal component analysis (PCA) based method proposed by Jang [16-17]. Instead using the size and shape of the epiphyses, Jang applied PCA on the epiphyseal regions and used those PCA coefficients as features in the assessment of bone age.

In this paper, we present a bone age assessment method using discrete cosine transform (DCT) and Fisher's linear discriminant analysis (FLD or LDA), the application of which to face recognition has shown good performance [18]. The proposed method, similarly to Jang's approach, focuses on nine epiphyseal regions, as shown in Fig. 1. That is, instead of using numeric features such as epiphyseal shape, length, and/or size, we use DCT coefficients computed from the pixel intensity values in an epiphyseal region as features, followed by FLD to make the assessment decision.

The rest of the paper is organized as follows. In Section 2, we demonstrate the proposed bone age assessment method by describing the application of DCT and LDA to nine epiphyseal regions. In Section 3, the experimental results are provided. Finally, concluding remarks are given in Section 4.

2 Bone Age Assessment

To assess bone age, nine epiphyseal regions of interest (EROIs) automatically segmented using Jang's approach [17] are employed. After segmentation, the nine EROIs are aligned by rotation, as shown in Fig. 1. The resolution of aligned EROIs is 200×200 pixels. DCT and LDA are applied in order to estimate the age of each EROI. Finally, the bone age is assessed as the weighted sum of those nine ages.

2.1 Selecting the Discriminative DCT Coefficients

DCT has been widely applied to numerous digital signal processing applications, the most effective of which is data compression. The main merit of DCT is that it is known to be similar to Karhunen-Loeve transform (KLT), which is, from the energy compaction point of view, an optimal transform for signal decorrelation [19]. DCT is applied to an EROI to reduce feature space and thus enable description of the image with only a few coefficients. Since not all DCT coefficients are discriminative features for classification, only those that contribute to discrimination are selected.

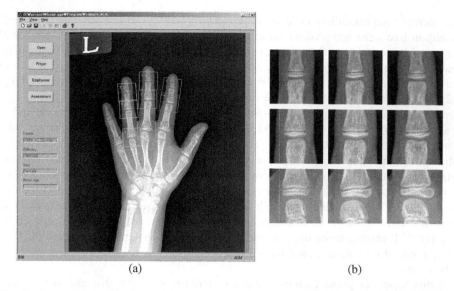

(a)   (b)

Fig. 1. Nine epiphyseal regions of interest (EROIs): (a) a radiograph of the left hand and nine EROIs, (b) Segmented EROIs

Assume, given the training set, that there are N EROIs and c known age stages (w_1, w_2, ..., w_c), where N_i denotes the number of EROIs at an age stage w_i. Before DCT is applied to an EROI, Zero Mean Unit Variance (ZMST) [20] is applied as a preprocessing step to yield an image of zero mean and unit variance. For a EROI image of 200×200 pixels, perform a 2D-DCT [21] on each image according to

$$F(u,v) = \frac{2}{\sqrt{MN}} \alpha(u)\alpha(v) \sum_{x=0}^{M-1}\sum_{y=0}^{N-1} f(x,y)\cos\left[\frac{(2x+1)u\pi}{2M}\right]\cos\left[\frac{(2y+1)v\pi}{2N}\right] \quad (1)$$

where

$$\alpha(w) = \begin{cases} \dfrac{1}{\sqrt{2}} & w = 0 \\ 1 & \text{otherwise.} \end{cases} \quad (2)$$

The between-class variance matrix v_b and the within-class variance matrix v_w are defined as

$$v_b(x,y) = \frac{1}{c}\sum_{i=1}^{c} N_i \left[E_i(x,y) - E(x,y)\right]^2 \quad (3)$$

$$v_w(x,y) = \frac{1}{c}\sum_{i=1}^{c}\left\{\sum_{F\in w_i}\left[F(x,y) - E_i(x,y)\right]^2\right\} \quad (4)$$

where $E_i(x, y)$ and $E(x, y)$ denote the mean value of $F(x, y)$ at an age stage w_i and the total mean value of $F(x, y)$ in the training set, respectively. The matrices of v_b and v_w are different from the between-class scatter matrix and the within-class scatter matrix used in LDA [19, 22], in that v_b and v_w are computed in element-by-element operations. Therefore, we use the term "variance" rather than "scatter."

The discriminant DCT coefficients — strictly speaking, the set of locations S of the discriminant coefficients — are defined as

$$S = \left\{ (x, y) \mid \frac{v_b(x, y)}{v_w(x, y)} > T \right\} \tag{5}$$

where T is the given threshold value. The ratio of $v_b(x, y)$ to $v_w(x, y)$ indicates the degree of the linear separability of the coefficient at location (x, y). The higher the ratio is, the more discriminative the coefficient is. Therefore, we select, as the discriminative features, the coefficients for which the ratio is more than the given threshold T. It is important to the performance and efficiency of bone age assessment to determine an appropriate threshold T. However, the threshold T is experimentally determined at present, there being no rule, as yet, that determines it.

2.2 LDA

LDA is one of the most popular linear projection methods for feature extraction [19, 22]. It is used to find the linear projection of the original vectors from a high-dimensional space to an optimal low-dimensional subspace in which the ratio of the between-class scatter matrix and the within-class scatter matrix is maximized.

After S is determined, the DCT coefficients located in S are represented by a one-dimensional (1D) feature vector. Then, the LDA transform matrix $\mathbf{W}$ is computed using the 1D feature vectors from the training set. Details on LDA can be found in [19] and [22].

2.3 Bone Age Assessment

Since there are nine EROIs segmented from a radiograph of the left hand, there are nine Ss and nine $\mathbf{W}$s after the above-mentioned processes are applied to each EROI of the training set. We represent those by S_i and $\mathbf{W}_i$ for the ith EROI, respectively, where $1 \le i \le 9$.

Given a radiograph of the left hand for testing, DCT is also applied to each of the nine segmented EROIs. On the ith EROI, the DCT coefficients located in S_i are represented by a 1D vector and then projected onto $\mathbf{W}_i$. The projected feature vector is compared to the feature vectors in the database, and the bone age of the ith EROI is estimated according to the smallest distance. Note that Euclidean distance is used as the metric between two feature vectors. Accordingly, for each of nine EROIs, we obtain nine estimated bone ages. For those nine ages, we tested three simple combining rules including the 9-average rule (averaging the nine ages), the 7-average rule (averaging the seven ages excluding the highest and lowest ages among the nine ages), and the median rule (taking the median of the nine ages) in making the final determination.

3   Experimental Results

The proposed method was tested on a dataset composed of 396 radiographs of 93 males and 303 females collected at Hanyang University Medical Center [23]. All of the radiographs were acquired in the DICOM 3.0 standard of $1,950 \times 2,460 \times 12$ bit resolution. Based on the diagnosis of radiologists, the assessed bone ages varied from 2 to 17, as shown in Table 1.

The experiments were performed using the "leaving-one-out" strategy [24], because the number of objects in the dataset was small. To assess the bone age of an object, that object was removed from the dataset and the dimensionality reduction matrices, nine Ss and Ws, were computed. Each of nine EROIs automatically segmented from all of the objects in the dataset, excluding the test object, was projected onto the reduced space by the corresponding S and W. Then, the feature vectors were stored in the database to assess the bone age of the test object.

Table 1. Organization of our dataset

Bone age	Number of objects		
	Male	Female	Total
2	1	8	9
3	3	7	10
4	12	2	14
5	10	2	12
6	6	11	17
7	5	15	20
8	3	24	27
9	6	11	17
10	4	35	39
11	9	50	59
12	5	47	52
13	11	50	61
14	6	17	23
15	5	13	18
16	1	5	6
17	6	6	12
Total	93	303	396

The bone age assessment performance was measured according to the error between the bone age assessed by the proposed method and that assessed by the radiologists. And to compare the performance, we tested Jang's method based on PCA [17] rather than Pietka's method [4]. Pietka did show that bone age and features extracted from EROI are highly correlated [4], but he did not suggest how to assess bone age using those features. Thus his method was not employed in the present experiment.

Figure 3 shows the performances of the proposed method and Jang's method with varying parameters for three combining rules — the 9-average, 7-average, and median rules. The feature dimension (the number of principal LDA components) of the proposed method was set to 15 because there were 16 bone age stages; when there are c

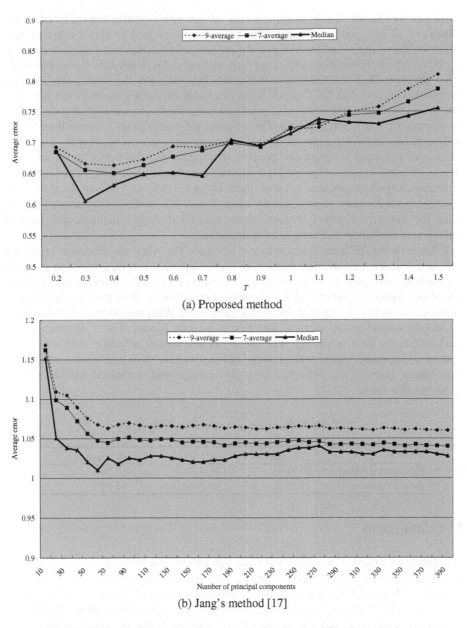

(a) Proposed method

(b) Jang's method [17]

Fig. 3. The performances of the proposed method and Jang's method

Table 2. The best bone age assessment performance

Method	Average error	Variance
Proposed method	0.60	0.40
Jang's method [17]	1.01	1.02

classes to be classified, the maximum rank of the within-scatter matrix in LDA becomes c-1 [22]. Figure 3 indicates that the proposed method produces a higher performance than Jang's method and that the median rule outperforms the other combining rules. The performance of the proposed method tends downward as the threshold T for selecting DCT coefficients is increased. The reason is that increasing T makes the number of selected DCT coefficients too small. In Jang's method, the performance tends upward as the number of principal components is increased, and converges to an error of 1.025 when the number of principal components is more than 90. In both methods, it is important to input the appropriate parameters, that is, T and the number of principal components, because they determine the performance and efficiency of bone age assessment. However, as mentioned earlier, the threshold T is experimentally determined at present, there being no rule, as yet, that determines it. The best performances were obtained when T was 0.3 in the proposed method and when the number of principal components was 60 in Jang's method, and Table 2 summarizes the best performances of both methods.

Table 3 shows the bone age assessment accuracy rate when the allowable errors are 1, 2, and 3 years. Considering that errors within one year can be ignored in practice, our method can assess bone age with an accuracy of 89.71%. Although the accuracy rate of our method is better than Jang's method considering all of the cases in Table 3, improved accuracy is required for real applications. With regard to better accuracy, we should consider two factors. The first is patient gender. Girls' development is markedly faster than boys' [4]. The second is soft tissue influence. Although bony structures are more significant in bone age assessment than soft tissue, soft tissue nonetheless exerts some influence over test results, and we tested EROIs without removing that tissue.

Table 3. Bone age assessment accuracy rate

Method	≤1 year	≤2 years	≤3 years
Proposed method	89.71%	96.81%	97.06%
Jang's method	71.32%	90.93%	95.34%

4 Conclusions

This paper proposed a computerized bone age assessment method using discrete cosine transform (DCT) and Fisher's linear discriminant analysis (FLD or LDA). We applied DCT and LDA on segmented epiphyseal regions of interest (EROIs). First, among the 2D-DCT coefficients, the discriminative coefficients having high linear separability computed from the between-class variance matrix and the within-class variance matrix were selected. Then, LDA was applied to those selected coefficients. The proposed method was applied to nine EROIs of three phalanges. For each EROI, nine bone ages were estimated and three combining rules including the 9-average rule, the 7-average rule, and the median rule were tested in making the final determination. In experiments on 396 radiographs of the left hand collected at Hanyang University Medical Center, the proposed method showed an average error of 0.6 years and an accuracy rate of 89.71% when ignoring the errors within one year.

References

1. Tanner, J. M., Whitehouse, R. H.: Assessment of Skeletal Maturity and Prediction of Adult Height (TW2 Method). Academic Press, London U.K. (1975)
2. Greulich, W. W., Pyle, S. I.: Radiographic Atlas of Skeletal Development of Hand Wrist, 2nd edn. Standford Univ. Press, Stanford CA (1971)
3. Miler, G. R., Levick, R. K., Kay, R.: Assessment of Bone Age: A Comparison of the Greulich and Pyle, and the Tanner and Whitehouse Methods. Clinical Radiology, Vol. 37 (1986) 119–121
4. Pietka, E., Gertych, A., Pospiech, S., Cao, F., Huang, H. K., Gilsanz, V.: Computer-Assisted Bone Age Assessment: Image Preprocessing and Epiphyseal/Metaphyseal ROI Extraction. IEEE Transactions on Medical Imaging, Vol. 20, No. 8 (2001) 715–729
5. Mahmoodi, S. Sharif, B. S., Chester, E. G., Owen, J. P., Lee, R.: Skeletal Growth Estimation Using Radiographic Image Processing and Analysis. IEEE Transaction on Information Technology in Biomedicine, Vol. 4, No. 4 (2000) 292–297
6. Mahmoodi, S. Sharif, B. S., Chester, E. G., Owen, J. P., Lee, R. E. J.: Bayesian Estimation of Growth Age Using Shape and Texture Descriptors. International Conference on Image Processing and its Applications (1999) 489–493
7. Al-Taani, A. T., Ricketts, I. W., Cairns, A. Y.: Classification of Hand Bones for Bone Age Assessment. International Conference on Electronics, Circuits, and Systems, Vol. 2 (1996) 1088–1091
8. Marques Da Silva, A. M., Delgado Olabarriaga, S., Dietrich, C. A., Schmitz, C. A. A.: On Determining a Signature for Skeletal Maturity. Brazilian Symposium on Computer Graphics and Image Processing (2001) 246–251
9. Tristan, A., Arribas, J. I.: A Radius and Ulna Skeletal Age Assessment System. IEEE Workshop on Machine Learning for Signal Processing (2005) 221–226
10. Bocchi, L., Ferrara, F., Nicoletti, I., Valli, G.: An Artificial Neural Network Architecture for Skeletal Age Assessment. International Conference on Image Processing, Vol. 1 (2003) 1077–1080
11. Pietka, E., McNitt-Gray, M. F., Kuo, M. L., Huang, H. K.: Computer-Assisted Phalangeal Analysis in Skeletal Age Assessment. IEEE Transactions on Medical Imaging, Vol. 10, No. 4 (1991) 616–620
12. Pietka, E., Kaabi, L., Kuo, M. L., Huang, H. K.: Feature Extraction in Carpal-Bone Analysis. IEEE Transactions on Medical Imageing, Vol. 12, No. 1 (1993) 44–49
13. Mahmoodi, S. Sharif, B. S., Chester, E. G., Owen, J. P., Lee, R. E. J.: Automated Vision System for Skeletal Age Assessment Using Knowledge Based Techniques. International Conference on Image Processing and its Applications, Vol. 2 (1997) 809–813
14. Chang, C.-H., Hsieh, C.-W., Jong, T.-L., Tiu, C.-M.: A Fully Automatic Computerized Bone Age Assessment Procedure Based on Phalange Ossification Analysis. IPPR Conference on Computer Vision, Graphics and Image Processing (2003) 463–468
15. Niemeijer, M., van Ginneken, B., Maas, C. A., Beek, F. J. A., Viergever, M. A.: Assessing the Skeletal Age From a Hand Radiograph: Automating the Tanner-Whitehouse Method. SPIE Medical Imaging, Vol. 5032 (2003) 1197–1205
16. Jang, S.-H., Hwang, J.-M., Yang, S., Shin, J.-H., Kim, W.-H.: Automatic bone age estimation using eigen analysis of epiphyseal region. Asia pacific paediatric endocrine society, the 3rd biennial scientific meeting (2004) 69
17. Jang, S.-H.: Automatic bone age assessment system using radiographic image processing and pattern analysis technique. Ph.D. Thesis, Hanyang University (2005)

18. Lee, H.-J., Kim, H.-J., Kim, W.-Y.: Face Recognition using Component-Based DCT/LDA. International Workshop on Advanced Image Technology (2005) 25–30
19. Martinez, A. M., Kak, A. C.: PCA versus LDA. IEEE Transactions on Pattern Analysis and Machine Intelligence, Vol. 23, No. 2 (2001) 228–233
20. Kittler, J., Li, Y. P., Matas, J.: On Matching Scores for LDA-based Face Verification. The British Machine Vision Conference (2000) 42–51.
21. Gonzalez, R. C., Woods R. E.: Digital Image Processing, 2nd edn. Prentice Hall, New Jersey (2002)
22. Belhumeur, V., Hespanha, J., Kriegman, D.: Eigenfaces vs. Fisherfaces: Recognition Using Class Specific Linear Projection. IEEE Transactions on Pattern Analysis and Machine Intelligence, Vol. 19, No. 7 (1992) 711–720
23. http://hmct.hanyang.ac.kr/
24. Duda, R., Hart, P.: Pattern classification and scene analysis. Wiley, New York (1973)

Natural Image Matting Based on Neighbor Embedding

Kwang Hee Won, Soon-Yong Park, and Soon Ki Jung

Department of Computer Engineering, Kyungpook National University,
1370 Sankyuk-dong, Buk-gu, Daegu 702-701, South Korea
khwon@vr.knu.ac.kr, {sypark, skjung}@knu.ac.kr

Abstract. In this paper, an automatic technique for natural image matting is proposed. We use visual characteristics of the background and foreground regions for matting. Through the Locally Linear Embedding (LLE) of high-dimensional features, we estimate foreground and background color of unknown pixels. We use gradient information and a hierarchical model to enhance the proposed matting technique. Instead of a user interaction for tri-map generation, we propose an automatic technique that obtains a tri-map using a multi-view camera. A reliability map for the depth of a scene facilitates the generation of a tri-map. It is proven that feature sets obtained from training images can be applied to similar images or video frames.

1 Introduction

Digital image matting extracts embedded foreground objects from a background image by estimating color and opacity values for the foreground elements at each pixel. The opacity value at each pixel is typically called alpha, and the opacity image is referred to as alpha matte. Digital image matting can be used in DVFX (digital video special effects), for instance, to extract the image of actors or objects from a scene and place them into another scene.

Humans can easily distinguish objects from their background even though object colors are similar to those of their background. It is because the human visual system is based on stereo vision; humans can perceive depth information from the disparity between the left and right eyes. The systems also has cells which possess orientation selectivity. Another reason is that human can detect the overlapping of objects by learning. Varying luminance or shadows also help humans in distinguishing objects, but it is not easy to imitate human capabilities in digital image matting.

To separate objects from their natural background image, most image matting methods start from a tri-map, in which each pixel is labeled into one of three categories, foreground, background and unknown. The tri-map may be given by a human user with image-editing tools. To reduce laborious user interaction, automatic keying methods have been developed.

A typical automatic keying method is background subtraction after background modeling [1]. In general, this method cannot extract interested regions

A. Gagalowicz and W. Philips (Eds.): MIRAGE 2007, LNCS 4418, pp. 449–460, 2007.
© Springer-Verlag Berlin Heidelberg 2007

when their colors are similar to the background and is rather vulnerable to light changes. Extra equipment using invisible lights can be used to obtain keying information in real time such as polarized, infrared[2], and thermal images. These methods use a two-camera system and the accurate calibration of the cameras is needed. A specially designed camera, $ZCam^{TM}$ [3] uses the same shooting lens for color and depth information, and it can generate depth keying during live broadcasts. The binary keying mask, obtained from specific devices, should be processed to obtain the alpha matte. Defocus matting [4] uses three different depth-of-field cameras to obtain the alpha matte, but this mathod can be applied to a specific distance only and its output image is darker than real ones due to the beam splitter. In this paper, we employ a multi-view camera system in order to obtain the depth image of a scene, however, instead of using the depth image directly for matting, we introduce a reliability map to obtain a tri-map automatically. By combinations of four digital cameras, we obtain six depth images. A reliability map is generated based on the viewing directions of the cameras and the distances of overlapping depth images.

Natural image matting is to solve the compositing equation (1) for the unknown pixels in a given tri-map.

$$C_i = \alpha_i F_i + (1 - \alpha_i)B_i, \tag{1}$$

where the color of the ith pixel in the input image is a composite of the corresponding foreground color F_i and background color B_i, and α_i is the pixel's foreground opacity or the blending factor. The existing methods normally choose one unknown pixel and calculate the color distributions of the near foreground and background regions. Then, from two distributions and the composite color position in the color space, the blending factor can be estimated [5, 6, 7]. There is a method which transforms the RGB color space to another color space so that it reflects human perception, but the main idea is the same [9].

In this paper we propose a new natural image matting method. It exploits the visual features of the foreground and background regions through Locally Linear Embedding (LLE), which is an unsupervised learning method. The trained features can be applied to similar images or video frames in order to estimate the foreground and background colors of unknown pixels. We give processing orders to each pixel using edge information and the distances from each feature space. The ordering process gives accurate seed information for the next estimation. We also propose a hierarchical scheme in which the estimated pixel opacity on lower resolutions propagates into higher resolutions to improve matting results.

This paper consists of the following: In Section 2, we describe previous research on natural image matting and Locally Linear Embedding. In Section 3, we show a technique that can be used to obtain a reliability map using a multiview camera. In Section 4, we define the natural image matting problem in the manner of Locally Linear Embedding; introduce a neighbor embedding algorithm; and present a hierarchical model to improve the algorithm. We outline the experimental results, conclusions, and future research in Sections 5 and 6.

2   Related Work

Natural image matting calculates the alpha value, F (foreground color) and B (background color) from C (composite color) as already mentioned in equation (1). Due to insufficient information, research regardings reducing background colors has been put forth and research regarding natural images with various background colors has followed.

The methods used to extract the foreground from the background of an image have been divided into two categories; one is the input of simple backgrounds as in a blue,and the other is the input of backgrounds from anywhere in nature (Natral image matting). Mishima [6]'s method is on the former. This method is called blue screen matting due to the use of a blue color background.

Natural image matting usually needs three regions; definitely foreground, definitely background and unknown region. These boundaries, the tri-map, can be obtained by user interaction or automatically. Morgan McGuire *et al.* [4] developed Defocus Matting which does not need user interaction. Tri-maps are acquired using the PSF(point spread func-tion) of each image from the three-differently focused imaging sensors (foreground focused, background focused, pinhole). This method, however, does not work if the background has a low frequency only or if the image is blurred because of fast motion (not because of defocusing).

The image matting method, with user interaction, has been carefully studied. With input images and three separated regions obtained by user interaction, the estimated foreground and background colors of unknown an region and position them along with the composite color onto a color space, in order to calculate the alpha value by projection. According to estimates, Ruzon and Tomasi [7]'s method models F, B and C as Gaussian probability distribution and Chuang [5]'s method models the matting problem using Baye's rule and the output is optimized with a MAP (maximum a priori) sense.

In this paper, we use high-dimensional features and linear weights to reconstruct lower-dimensional features, and foreground and background colors. S.T. Roweis and L.K. Saul [10] proposed Locally Linear Embedding in order to reduce dimensions of high-dimensional feature vectors. They determined the reconstruction weights of each high-dimensional feature from k-closest neighbors under the assumption that the manifold which contained feature vectors was locally linear. They embedded each feature vector with lower dimensions so as to preserve neighbor-relation using their neighbors and corresponding weights. This LLE can be used in dimensionality reduction problems and in other problems which can be solved with unsupervised-learning algorithm.

3   Reliability Map Generation

To generate a tri-map of a scene image automatically, we introduce a reliability map of the image. The scene image is captured from a multi-view camera system which consists of four identical IEEE1394 video cameras. We place the cameras on a slide plate to adjust the baseline between cameras. Optical axes of the four cameras are toed-in so that they converge at about 1m from the cameras. Each camera is calibrated according to the perspective projection model. As shown in Fig. 1, let the left-most camera of the system be C_0, the next one be C_1, and so on. Then we get the perspective projection matrices (PPM) KT_0, KT_1, KT_2, and KT_3. Here K is the internal camera calibration matrix and T_i is the transformation from the world coordinate to each camera coordinate system.

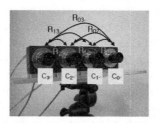

Fig. 1. Multi-view camera system

Total six range images $R_{ij}(x, y)$ are obtained from four cameras. As in Fig. 1, a range image R_{ij} is obtained by a pair of cameras C_i and C_j. To obtain the range image, we apply a SSD(Sum of Squared Difference) based stereo matching technique. From a rectified stereo image pair, we employ a multi-resolution stereo matching technique using the Gaussian pyramid [12]. When there is a pair of stereo image, $g_t^{(l)}$ and $g_t^{(r)}$ for left and right images, which are at t-th level of the pyramid, SSD at image coordinate (x, y) is given as follows:

$$SSD(x, y) = \sum_{k=-m}^{m} \sum_{l=-m}^{m} \{g_t^{(l)}(x, y) - g_t^{(r)}(x + k, y + l)\}^2, \qquad (2)$$

where $(2m + 1)$ is the size of a matching block.

To segment an image into foreground and background regions, we use a new range image which is obtained with respect to a reference camera coordinate system. In addition, we provide a reliability map to facilitate the proposed matting technique to determine if a pixel belongs to foreground, background, or unknown region. To obtain a new range image, six range images are registered to a common coordinate system. Considering the center of the right camera of each stereo pair as the origin of a camera coordinate system, we define three camera coordinate systems O_{c1}, O_{c2}, and O_{c3}. We define O_{c2} as the reference camera coordinate system. Therefore, range image R_{01} is registered to the reference coordinate system by the transformation $T_{21} = T_2 T_1^{-1}$. Similarly, range image R_{23}, R_{13}, and R_{03} are registered to the reference coordinate system by the transformation $T_{23} = T_2 T_3^{-1}$.

To generate a new range image R'_{12} from the point of O_{c2}, six registered range images are merged by using a median filtering technique. Given a 3D point P

in R_{12}, we first find it's correspondences in the other range images. Next, we get the median of the all correspondences and update the point to P'. To speed up the process of correspondence search, we use a point-to-projection technique [13]. As in Figure 2, a 3D point P obtained from C_k is projected to the image plane of C_i to get a 2D point Q.

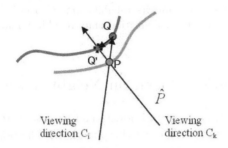

Fig. 2. Point-to-projection approach for correspondence search

To decide the reliability of the new range image R'_{12}, we employ three criteria. The first one is Noverlap which is the number of overlapping range images. With respect to a 3D point in R_{12}, there are maximum five correspondences. If the number of overlapping range images is less than five, it means the number of range images is not enough to generate the new 3D point. Therefore, we reduce the reliability of P'. The second one is the angle between $\hat{P}$ and $\hat{Q}'_{ij}$ which is the point normal at Q'_{ij}. The larger the angle between two vectors, the less the reliability of the new point. It is common that the accuracy of the range images is better when the angle between the viewing direction and the surface normal is close to -180 degree. The third one is σ_Q which is the standard deviation of Q'_{ij}. We combine the three criteria to measure the reliability of a new 3D point. If $N_{overlap}$ is less than 5, σ_Q is multiplied by $5/N_{overlap}$. In addition, its reciprocal and the inner product of vectors $\hat{P}$ and $\hat{Q}'_{ij}$ are added and normalized to get the point reliability. However, the lower bound of the value is set to 0.4. In summary, $S(p)$ the reliability of a point P is determined as follows:

$$
\begin{aligned}
&if(N_{overlap} < 5)\ \sigma_Q = \sigma_Q \times (\tfrac{5}{N_{overlap}}),\\
&if(N_{overlap} = 1)\ S(P) = 0.4,\\
&else \qquad\qquad S(P) = (\sigma_Q^{-1} + \theta_{ij})/2,\ where\ \theta_{ij} = -\hat{P} \cdot \hat{Q}'_{ij}.
\end{aligned}
$$

Fig. 3 shows results of reliability map generation. The second image in the figure shows a new range image generated with respect to C_2. The third image is a segmentation of the input image into foreground and background regions. White area is foreground and the other is background. However the grey level reliability map shows some parts of the segmentation are not reliable because their reliability is very low(dark areas). The pseudo-colored reliability map shows the foreground and background regions more clearly.

Fig. 3. A new range image R'_{12} and its reliability map. From left, input picture from C_2, new depth map R'_{12}, depth segmentation map, reliability map, and pseudo-colored reliability map.

4   Color Estimation Based on Neighbor Embedding

From the image smoothness, an unknown pixel has the characteristics of a near background (or foreground) region if the pixel is not the boundary between the background and the foreground. So we propose an algorithm to find blending factor of the estimated foreground and background colors from unsupervised learning.

4.1   Colors Estimation Using LLE

Using LLE we can embed high-dimensional data to low-dimension with preserving neighbor relationships. Neighbor-preserving helps understanding of high-dimensional data which is represented by low-dimension. LLE preserves neighbor relations in high-dimensions better than projection through PCA(principal component analysis)[10].

We define the colors, luminance and shapes of a small image piece, as the characteristics of a foreground (or background) region, and represent them as a high-dimensional data. Their corresponding low-dimensional data include the color of a specific pixel in the image piece. We choose an unknown pixel which is adjacent to foreground or background region and form the high-dimensional feature from adjacent known region's information and remain the corresponding low-dimensional data as unknown pixel. From high-dimensional feature space, we find k-nearest neighbors and calculate linear weights which can reconstruct this high-dimensional feature. Using this weights and low-dimensional data corresponding to each high-dimensional neighbor, we reconstruct unknown pixel's foreground or background color which is low-dimensional data.

We define high dimensional feature vector of already known region as x_s and its corresponding low dimensional feature vector as y_s. X_s, Y_s are feature vector spaces. X_s and Y_s are defined differently on foreground and background regions. Each region has two types of feature vector. To estimate foreground and background colors for an unknown pixel, we define a target feature vector from one unknown pixel and adjacent three known pixels as x_t and its corresponding low dimensional feature vector with an unknown pixel as y_t. Then the estimation of foreground or background colors of the unknown pixel is defined as follows: given k-nearest neighbors of x_t, we calculate the linear reconstruction weight w_q and the estimated result y_t from their corresponding feature vector y_s.

4.2   Feature Vector and Weight Matrix

To construct X_s from already known regions we define characteristics of each region as their pixels' color, luminance, relative position and global position. Using these characteristics we form feature vectors as shown in Fig. 4.

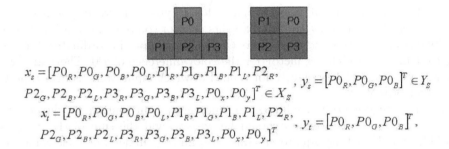

$$x_s = [P0_R, P0_G, P0_B, P0_L, P1_R, P1_G, P1_B, P1_L, P2_R,$$
$$P2_G, P2_B, P2_L, P3_R, P3_G, P3_B, P3_L, P0_x, P0_y]^T \in X_s$$
$$, \quad y_s = [P0_R, P0_G, P0_B]^T \in Y_s$$

$$x_t = [P0_R, P0_G, P0_B, P0_L, P1_R, P1_G, P1_B, P1_L, P2_R,$$
$$P2_G, P2_B, P2_L, P3_R, P3_G, P3_B, P3_L, P0_x, P0_y]^T$$
$$, \quad y_t = [P0_R, P0_G, P0_B]^T,$$

Fig. 4. High dimensional feature vector x_s has eighteen elements constructed from foreground or background region, and y_s is its corresponding low dimensional vector. We form x_t from the estimated colors of the pixels $P1$, $P2$, $P3$, and the composite color of the pixel $P0$. By embedding x_t into low dimensional vector, we can get y_t, the foreground or background color of the unknown pixel.

These feature vectors represent color distribution of the image pieces in the pre-defined distance from the unknown regions. There are two kinds of feature space constructed from foreground and background regions. In each space, there are also two types of features, T-type and *Block*-type. When we estimate foreground or background color of an unknown pixel, we first form x_t from the pixel and its adjacent unknown or already estimated pixels. After that we find k-nearest neighbors of x_t from X_s. We use weighted Euclidean distance for the distance measure between two vectors as follows:

$$d^2 = (x_t - x_s)^T W (x_t - x_s). \tag{3}$$

In equation (3), we use a weight matrix W due to the different weighting scales for color components and luminance, and the different relative pixel distances between $P0$ and their near pixels $P1$, $P2$ and $P3$. The weighting scale of luminance is three times of that of color components. The weighting scale of the pixels $P_i (i = 1, 2, 3)$ is defined as the inverse of the distance to $P0$ in the image coordinate.

$$
W_1 = \begin{pmatrix} \begin{matrix} w_s \times I \\ & 0.71 \times I & & 0 \\ & & I \\ & 0 & & 0.71 \times I \\ & & & & O \end{matrix} \end{pmatrix}, \quad W_2 = \begin{pmatrix} \begin{matrix} w_s \times I \\ & I & & 0 \\ & & 0.71 \times I \\ & 0 & & I \\ & & & & O \end{matrix} \end{pmatrix},
$$

$$
I_{4\times4} = \begin{pmatrix} w_r \\ & w_g \\ & & w_b \\ & & & w_l \end{pmatrix}, \quad O_{2\times2} = \begin{pmatrix} w_x \\ & w_y \end{pmatrix}. \tag{4}
$$

where W_1 and W_2 are the weight matrix for T-type and $Block$-type features, respectively. The matrix I contains weights of color components and luminance on its diagonal entries and the matrix O contains the pixel coordinates. We use w_s to define the weighting factor for the color difference of $P0$. There are two values of w_s in our algorithm, 1 for a pixel of which alpha value is near 0 or 1, and 0 for otherwise.

From these k-nearest neighbors, we find linear combination weights w_q to reconstruct x_t. These weights should be positive and the sum of the weights should be 1. In a least squares manner, we find w_q under two constraints as follows:

$$
\epsilon = \left\| x_t - \sum w_q x_s^p \right\|^2, \text{ where } w_q \geq 0 \text{ and } \sum w_q = 1. \tag{5}
$$

To solve constrained least squares in equation (5), we use C. L. Lawson and R. J. Hanson's algorithm[17] for the first constraint and S. T. Roweis and L. K. Saul[10]'s suggestion for the second constraint. From each w_q and y_s, we get y_t, the foreground or background color of unknown pixel. The total process of foreground or background color estimation of the unknown pixels is like this:

Step 1. En-queue all pixels on inner and outer boundary of unknown region to the priority-queue.

Step 2. De-queue one pixel from the priority-queue and form the target feature vector x_t from all possible direction as shown in Fig. 5. Use composite color for unknown pixel $P0$.

Step 3. Find x_t in each feature space with weight $w_s = 1.0$ if it has a neighbor feature, this pixel is one of the foreground(or background) pixels. Update nearby pixels with their distance from the closest neighbor on their feature sets and en-queue them to priority-queue.

Step 4. If there is no close feature in the feature sets with weight $w_s = 1.0$, then find k-nearest neighbors with $w_s = 0.0$ from X_s and calculate their linear combination weights.

Step 5. With the k-nearest neighbors and their combination weights, get y_t for all possible direction as shown in Fig. 5 and choose one of them (or blend them) as a foreground(or background) color of the unknown pixel $P0$.

Step 6. If there are unknown pixels which we can proceed, adjacent to the estimated pixel, then en-queue them to the priority-queue.

Step 7. Repeat **Step 2** to **Step 6** until the queue is empty.

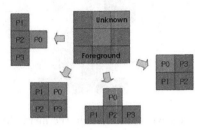

Fig. 5. One unknown pixel can be estimated from mostly eight directions. The unknown pixel $P0$ is estimated from possible four directions. Then we choose the best $P0$'s color among the results or take $P0$ from weighted sum of each result.

In the above steps, the priority of the current pixel is defined with the image gradient direction and the priorities of adjacent pixels which are processed previously. The priority determines the processing order so that the estimation proceeds along the tangential direction of the gradient. It is because similar luminance has similar foreground or background color. If an adjacent pixel is estimated accurately, then the current pixel can be estimated more precisely. In addition, we use the distance of the closest neighbors to measure the similarity to each feature space. After this foreground and background color estimation of unknown pixels, we calculate alpha value using Chuang's projection [5].

4.3 Hierarchical Model

Typical matting methods have their own optimization techniques to prevent wrong estimation. When they estimate the alpha value of a pixel, they guess colors several times from the clustered color pairs in order to reduce wrong estimations. In contrast, we use image gradients and distances from the feature spaces. In addition, we use a hierarchical model so as to avoid accumulation error. The main idea is to make the unknown region narrower. We remove some unknown parts from the higher level (low resolution) and then propagate them to the lower level (high resolution). We get one pixel in the higher level from nine pixels in the lower level. The next pixel in the higher level is then obtained from nine pixels again with three pixels overlapping in the lower level as in Fig. 6.

In the higher level, we search the two nearest feature vectors for each unknown pixel, on the background and foreground feature spaces. If one of the nearest feature vectors is near and another is far from the unknown pixel, we determine the label of the pixel as foreground or background. If the pixel is determined to be the foreground (or background) in the higher level, the corresponding nine pixels in the lower level are also labeled as being in the foreground (or background).

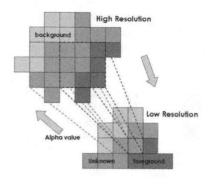

Fig. 6. An unknown reduction via the hierarchical model

5   Experimental Results

To obtain a tri-map of a scene image, we segment the pseudo-colored reliability map into three regions. If the pixel color is pure blue or red, it is decided as a background or foreground region. Otherwise we define it as an unknown region. Then we obtain a matte from the input image and its tri-map. Fig. 7 shows the results of our approach. The obtained alpha matte shows details of target object boundary even though a input image has very complex background textures. We compared our result with Global Poisson matting in Fig. 8. The Global Poisson Matting supposes that the background and foreground regions of an input image are smooth. So, this method produces artifects on the resulting alpha matte with input image which has complex background or foreground regions. Our approach produces better results with input images which have complex background(or foreground) regions. Fig. 9 shows the results from two similar input images. We applied the feature sets of the first image to the third image. In the case of wide

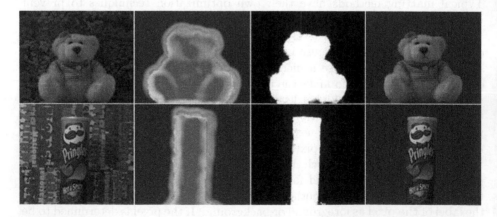

Fig. 7. From left, input image, pseudo-colored reliability map, alpha matte, and extracted foreground image

Fig. 8. From left, input image, manual tri-map, alpha matte(our approach), extracted foreground image(our approach), alpha matte(Global Poisson matting) and extracted foreground image(Global Poisson matting)

Fig. 9. Two similar test images and their alpha mattes. The feature space of the first image is applied to the third image.

Fig. 10. From left, the input lighthouse obtained from [5], the alpha matte result with random order, the result with the proposed order, extracted foreground image(random order, proposed order)

unknown regions, the order of estimation is important. Fig. 10 illustrates the effect of estimation orders in our method. For the input lighthouse image and the tri-map from [5], the alpha matte result with random priority, is worse than that of the proposed method. It means that the processing order in the gradient tangential direction has more stable estimates and object edges are preserved more precisely as you can see in Fig. 10.

6 Conclusion and Future Work

We have proposed a natural image matting algorithm. To obtain the tri-map automatically, we compute the reliability map from a multi-view camera system. For the natural image matting, we adopted LLE based learning to obtain the feature space of the foreground and background regions. The feature space obtained from a scene will be applied to the similar scene without the feature learning step so that our approach is applicable to the video matting. Furthermore, we proposed a hierarchical scheme to reduce the unknown regions. The proposed method had a good result in the complex background scene.

In the future, we will investigate a technique to obtain a discrete depth map instead of full range depth map. The discrete depth map will facilitate to obtain the reliability map faster than the current approach. In addition, we will compare the proposed method with the previous work and enhance it to have the near real-time performance.

Acknowledgement

This work was supported by the Dual Use Technology Center (DUTC) projects through ARVision Inc.

References

[1] Christopher Wren, Ali Azarbayejani, Trevor Darrell, Alex Pentland : Pfinder: Real-Time Tracking of the Human Body. IEEE Trans. Pattern Analysis and Machine Intelligence. Vol. 19(7) (1997) 780-785
[2] S.-Y. Lee, I.-J. Kim, S.C. Ahn, H.-G. Kim : Active Segmentation for Immersive Live Avatar. Electronics Letters, Vol. 40. (2004) 1257-1258
[3] Ronen Gvili, Amir Kaplan, Eyal Ofek, Giora Yahav : Depth Keying, Proceedings of SPIE Electronic Imaging (2003) 564-574
[4] Morgan McGuire, Wojciech Matusik, hanspeter Pfister, John F. Hughes, Fredo Durand : Defocus Video Matting. ACM Transactions on Graphics(Proceedings of ACM SIGGRAPH 2005), Vol. 24. (2005) 567-576
[5] Y. Y. Chuang, B. Curless, Salesin, R. Szelisji : A Bayesian Approach to Digital Matting. Proceedings of CVPR2001, (Dec 2001) 264-271
[6] T. Mitsunaga, T. Yokoyama, T. Totsuka : Autokey : Human Assisted Key Extraction. Proceedings of ACM SIGGRAPH 95, (Aug 1995) 265-272
[7] M. Ruzon, C. Tomasi : Alpha Estimation in Natural Images. Proceedings of CVPR2000, (Jun 2000) 18-25
[8] Jian Sun, Jiaya Jia, Chi-Keung Tang, Heung-Yeung Shum : Poisson Matting. ACM Trans-actions on Graphics (Proceedings of the SIGGRAPH 2004), Vol. 23(3). (2004) 315-321
[9] Yung-Yu Chuang, Aseem Agarwala, Brian Curless, David Salesin, Richard Szeliski : Video Matting of Complex Scenes. ACM Transactions on Graphics (Proceedings of ACM SIGGRAPH 2002), Vol. 21(3). (2002) 243-248
[10] S. T. Roweis, L. K. Saul : Nonlinear Dimensionality Reduction by Locally Linear Embedding. Science, Vol. 290(5500). (2000) 2323-2326
[11] C. L. Lawson, R. J. Hanson : Solving Least Squares Problems. PrenticeHall, (1974)
[12] P. J. Burt: The Laplacian Pyramid as a Compact Image Code. IEEE Transactions on Communications, Vol. 31(4). (1983) 532-540
[13] S. Y. Park M. Subbarao : An Accurate and Fast Point-to-Plane Registration Technique. Pattern Recognition Letter, Vol. 24(16). (Dec 2003) 2967-2976

Epipolar Geometry Via Rectification of Spherical Images

Jun Fujiki[1], Akihiko Torii[2], and Shotaro Akaho[1]

[1] National Institute of Advanced Industrial Science and Technology,
Umezono, Tsukuba-shi, Ibaraki 305-8568, Japan
jun-fujiki@aist.go.jp
[2] Center for Machine Perception, Department of Cybernetics
Faculty of Elec. Eng., Czech Technical University in Prague,
Karlovo nám. 13, 121 35 Prague, Czech Republic

Abstract. For computation of the epipolar geometry from central-omni-directional images, the use of the spherical camera model is essential. This is because the central-omnidirectional cameras are universally expressed as the spherical camera model when the intrinsic parameters of the cameras are calibrated. Geometrically, for corresponding points between two spherical images, there exists the same epipolar constraint as the conventional pinhole-camera model. Therefore, it is possible to use the conventional eight-point algorithm for recovering camera motion and 3D objects from two spherical images. In this paper, using the geometric properties on rotation of the spheres, we propose a method of the accurate computation based on the rectification of the spherical-camera images via the conventional eight-point algorithm.

1 Introduction

Recovering camera motion and 3D objects from images is studied as a fundamental problem in the field of computer vision. For recovering the 3D information, the epipolar geometry [5,8] is well-established based on the conventional pinhole-camera model with the perspective projection. On the other hand, as the large field-of-view cameras [3], central-catadioptric cameras [1,2] and central-dioptric cameras [10] have been developed and analyzed their camera models geometrically. We call these cameras central-omnidirectional cameras. Since these central-omnidirectional cameras are constructed with a mirror or a refractor, the camera models are different from the conventional pinhole-camera model. For estimating intrinsic parameters of the central-omnidirectional cameras, it is required to re-establish the epipolar geometry [9,6,10]. After the calibration of the intrinsic parameters, these cameras are universally modeled as the spherical camera with the spherical perspective projection [10,6]. In this paper, we establish a method for the numerically accurate computation of the epipolar geometry from two spherical images, which are images on a unit sphere.

In the pinhole-camera model with the perspective projection, a point on the planar image is expressed using the homogeneous coordinates. In the spherical-camera model with the spherical-perspective projection, a point on the spherical

A. Gagalowicz and W. Philips (Eds.): MIRAGE 2007, LNCS 4418, pp. 461–471, 2007.
© Springer-Verlag Berlin Heidelberg 2007

image is expressed using the spherical coordinates. When the camera coordinates of the pinhole and spherical cameras are at the equivalent geometrical configuration, the points on each image specify the same points in 3D space up to scale. Since the epipolar constraint does not depend on the scale, there exists the same epipolar constraint between the spherical-camera model and the pinhole-camera model [4]. Therefore, it is possible to use the conventional eight-point algorithm for solving the epipolar geometry from two spherical images as described in Section 3.

On the other hand, using the geometrical properties of spheres, we achieve a method based on the rectification of the spherical-camera images. Rotating each camera coordinate with related to the epipole, it is possible to simplify the mathematical expression of point correspondences among spherical images. This is because there exists a rotation which transforms the epipole of the first camera to the north pole. There also exists a rotation which transforms the epipole of the second camera to the south pole. These rotational transformations are called **rectification** of the spherical images[1]. After the rectification, the corresponding points between two spherical images should lie on the same longitude when there is no noise. This geometric property enables us to derive a method for improving accuracy of computation of the epipolar geometry based on the iterative rectification as described in Section 4.

One of the significant advantages of using the spherical camera model is that two spherical images potentially generates many corresponding points since these images can share the large region in 3D space compared to the conventional pinhole-camera images. Furthermore, the corresponding points are probabilistically distributed in the large area on the spherical images. We verify through numerical examples in Section 6 that these advantages improve the accuracy of the estimation of epipoles.

2   Notations

2.1   Colatitude and Longitude of Points on a Unit Sphere

Setting $\boldsymbol{x} = (x, y, z)^\top = (\sin\phi\cos\psi, \sin\phi\sin\psi, \cos\phi)^\top$ to be a point on a unit sphere, the colatitude and longitude of the point $\boldsymbol{x}$ are expressed by ϕ ($0 \leq \phi \leq \pi$) and ψ ($-\pi \leq \psi \leq \pi$) in the polar coordinates. The relationship between $\boldsymbol{x}$ and (ϕ, ψ) is expressed as follows:

$$\phi = \cos^{-1} z, \quad \psi = \operatorname{sgn}(y) \times \cos^{-1} \frac{x}{\sqrt{x^2 + y^2}}. \tag{1}$$

When the colatitude $\phi = 0$, the point is the north pole expressed as $\boldsymbol{\mathcal{N}} = (0, 0, 1)^\top$ in the three-dimensional coordinates.

---

[1] In the pinhole camera images, the rectification is expressed by the projective transformation.

2.2 Exterior Product as a Linear Transformation

The exterior product of the unit vectors a and x is denoted as $a \times x = [a]_\times x$
where $[a]_\times = \begin{pmatrix} 0 & -a_3 & a_2 \\ a_3 & 0 & -a_1 \\ -a_2 & a_1 & 0 \end{pmatrix}$ is an antisymmetric matrix.

2.3 Rotation Matrices

On a unit sphere, the transformation of a point a to the other point b is expressed by the rotation along the geodesic between a and b such that

$$R(a \to b) = I_3 + [a \times b]_\times + \frac{1 - a^T b}{||a \times b||^2}[a \times b]_\times^2.$$

The axis of the rotation is defined by $a \times b$. Note that, for a point $a = (a_1, a_2, a_3)^T$ on a unit sphere and the north pole $b = \mathcal{N}$,

$$R(a \to \mathcal{N}) = \frac{1}{1 + a_3} \begin{pmatrix} 1 + a_3 - a_1^2 & -a_1 a_2 & -a_1(1 + a_3) \\ -a_1 a_2 & 1 + a_3 - a_2^2 & -a_2(1 + a_3) \\ a_1(1 + a_3) & a_2(1 + a_3) & a_3(1 + a_3) \end{pmatrix}. \quad (2)$$

The **Rodrigues' rotation formula** denotes an infinitesimal rotation

$$R(n, d\omega) = I_3 + [n]_\times (d\omega)$$

where $d\omega$ is the angle of rotation around the axis n. Under this infinitesimal rotation, the motion quantity of a point x on the unit sphere is defined as

$$\frac{\partial x}{\partial \omega} = [n]_\times x = (-n_3 y + n_2 z, n_3 x - n_1 z, -n_2 x + n_1 y)^T. \quad (3)$$

3 Epipolar Geometry for Spherical Camera Model

3.1 Spherical Camera Model

We set X_p and z_p to be the p-th point in 3D space expressed in the spherical-camera coordinates and the p-th point on a unit sphere in the spherical-image coordinates[2]. The spherical perspective projection is expressed as $z_p = \frac{1}{||X_p||} X_p$ as shown in Fig. 1.

In this spherical camera model, the north pole $\mathcal{N}$ is the intersection between the optical axis and the unit sphere. The colatitude ϕ_p and longitude ψ_p of the point z_p on the unit sphere is also expressed in the polar coordinates using the relationship defined in Section 2.1. Therefore, the point z_p in the spherical-image coordinates and the colatitude ϕ_p and longitude ψ_p always satisfy the relationship

$$z_p = (\sin \phi_p \cos \psi_p, \sin \phi_p \sin \psi_p, \cos \phi_p)^T. \quad (4)$$

---

[2] Note that the radius of a sphere is set to 1 without loss of generality.

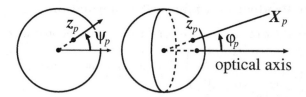

Fig. 1. spherical-camera coordinates. Left: relationship between a point z_p on the unit sphere and its longitude. Right: relationship between a point z_p in the unit sphere and its colatitude.

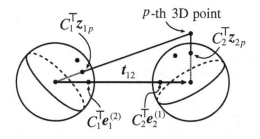

Fig. 2. Epipolar geometry for spherical cameras

3.2 Epipolar Geometry for Spherical Camera

Let z_{1p} and z_{2p} be the p-th corresponding points in the first and second spherical-image coordinates, respectively. The matrices C_1 and C_2 express the rotation from the first and second spherical-camera coordinates to the world coordinates, respectively. For the points z_{1p} and z_{2p} of the spherical images, there exists the epipolar constraint such that

$$z_{1p}^{\top} E_{12} z_{2p} = 0 \tag{5}$$

where

$$E_{12} = C_1 [t_{12}]_\times C_2^{\top}, \tag{6}$$

as same as the one in the pinhole-camera images [4]. In the same manner of the pinhole camera model, we call the matrix E_{12} and Eq. (5) as the **essential matrix** and the **epipolar equation**, respectively.

When we select a point z_{1p} in the first image, the equation $(z_{1p}^{\top} E_{12})z = 0$ draws a great circle on the second spherical image. This great circle is called the **epipolar great circle**. For the point z_{2p} in the second spherical image corresponding to the point z_{1p} in the first image, there exists the equation $(z_{1p}^{\top} E_{12})z_{2p} = 0$. Therefore, the point z_{2p} lies on the great circle in the second spherical image. The point which satisfies the equation $E_{12} e_2^{(1)} = 0$ is the **epipole** on the second image. This epipole $e_2^{(1)}$ denotes the center of the first camera. In the same manner, the point which satisfies the equation $e_1^{(2)\top} E_{12} = 0$ is the epipole on the first image. This epipole $e_1^{(2)}$ denotes the center of the second camera. Furthermore, the epipoles are expressed as

$$e_1^{(2)} = \pm \frac{1}{||t_{12}||} C_1 t_{12}, \quad e_2^{(1)} = \mp \frac{1}{||t_{12}||} C_2 t_{12}. \tag{7}$$

4 Epipolar Geometry Computation Via Rectification of Spherical Images

4.1 Rectification for Spherical Images

We define the rotation matrix R_1 which transforms the epipole $e_1^{(2)}$ in the first spherical image to the north pole. The rotation matrix also transforms the longitude of a randomly selected point in the first spherical image to be zero. The relationship between the point z_{1p} in the first spherical image and the point x_{1p} in the rotated spherical image is expressed as $x_{1p} = R_1 z_{1p}$. In the same manner, we define the rotation matrix R_2 which transforms the epipole $e_2^{(1)}$ in the second spherical image to the south pole. The rotation matrix also transforms the longitude of a randomly selected point in the second spherical image to be zero. The relationship between the point z_{2p} in the first spherical image and the point x_{2p} in the rotated spherical image is expressed as $x_{2p} = R_2 z_{2p}$. These transformations are the rectification for the spherical images as shown in Fig. 3.

After the rectification, x_{1p} and x_{2p} has the same longitude. Then x_{1p}, x_{2p} and $\mathcal{N}$ lie on the same plane. Therefore,

$$\det (\begin{matrix} x_{1p} & x_{2p} & \mathcal{N} \end{matrix}) = x_{1p}^\top [\mathcal{N}]_\times x_{2p} = 0. \tag{8}$$

This implies the epipolar equation after the rectification.

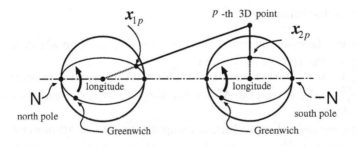

Fig. 3. Epipolar geometry by longitude

4.2   Epipolar Geometry Computed by Solving the Minimization Problem

Let z_p be a point on a spherical image and e be the epipole on the spherical image. Then, let R be the rotation which rectifies the longitude of the point z_p to be zero and the epipole e to be the north pole $\mathcal{N}$. The relationship between the point z_p on the spherical image and the point x_p on the rectified image is expressed as $x_p = Rz_p$. The colatitude ϕ_p and longitude ψ_p of the point x_p are $\phi_p = \cos^{-1} z_p$ and $\psi_p = \text{sgn}\,(y_p) \times \cos^{-1} \frac{x_p}{\sqrt{x_p^2 + y_p^2}}$.

We define α_p as the longitude of a point randomly selected from corresponding points in the rectified spherical image. The difference between the longitude ψ_p of x_p and the longitude α_p is computed as $|\psi_p - \alpha_p|$. We define the energy function

$$J = \frac{1}{2} \sum_{p=1}^{P} (\psi_p - \alpha_p)^2. \tag{9}$$

The energy function J is minimized using the steepest decent method. The partial differentiation of J is computed as

$$\frac{\partial J}{\partial \omega} = \sum_{p=1}^{P} (\psi_p - \alpha_p) \frac{\partial \psi_p}{\partial \omega} = \sum_{p=1}^{P} \frac{\psi_p - \alpha_p}{1 - z_p^2} (-x_p z_p, \ -y_p z_p, \ 1 - z_p^2) n.$$

The direction of the steepest descent is defined as the rotation around the axis m such that

$$m = -\sum_{p=1}^{P} \frac{\psi_p - \alpha_p}{1 - z_p^2} (x_p z_p, \ y_p z_p, \ z_p^2 - 1)^\top. \tag{10}$$

Setting n to be the normalized vector of m, the steepest decent method updates the epipole, the points on the spherical image and the rotation matrix such that

$$R^{\text{new}} = R(n, \Delta\omega) R^{\text{old}}, \quad x_p^{\text{new}} = R^{\text{new}} z_p, \quad e_p^{\text{new}} = (R^{\text{new}})^\top \mathcal{N}. \tag{11}$$

where $\Delta\omega$ is the angle of rotation.

5   Algorithms

5.1   Initial Estimation

(1) Estimate the essential matrix E_{12} using the eight-point algorithm.
(2) Compute the epipole $\pm e_1^{(2)}$ and $\pm e_2^{(1)}$.
(3) Compute the rotation matrix R_1. This rotation matrix transforms the epipole $e_1^{(2)}$ to the north pole $\mathcal{N}$ and the longitude of a randomly selected point z_{1q} to be zero.
(4) On the second spherical image, compute the two rotation matrix $R_2^{(\pm)}$ for the epipoles $\pm e_2^{(1)}$, respectively, since there exists two possible selections of the north pole. For each rotation matrix and epipole, we compute the energies J_+ and J_- using Eq. (9). If $J_+ < J_-$, we select $+e_2^{(1)}$ and $R_2^{(+)}$ as $e_2^{(1)}$ and R_2, and vice versa.

5.2   Estimation of Epipoles Based on Rectification

(1) Set the initial state and compute $\boldsymbol{x}_{ip} = R_i \boldsymbol{z}_{ip}$ $(i = 1, 2)$.
(2) Using the steepest descent method, rectify the second image to the first image based on the coordinates of the first spherical image.
  (a) Compute the longitude α_{1p} from $\boldsymbol{x}_{1p}$
  (b) Compute the colatitude ϕ_{2p} and the longitude ψ_{2p} from $\boldsymbol{x}_{2p}$.
  (c) Compute $\boldsymbol{n}$ using the steepest descent method
  (d) Set $\Delta\omega$ and compute $R(\boldsymbol{n}, \Delta\omega)$.
  (e) Update the data defined in Eq. (11).
(3) Rectify the first image to the second image by the steepest descent method on the coordinates of the second spherical image.
(4) Repeat (2) and (3) for a given number of iteration.
(5) After the convergence, the rotation matrices becomes the estimation of R_1 and R_2. The essential matrix is finally computed as $E_{12} = R_1^\top [\mathcal{N}]_\times R_2$.

6   Numerical Experiments

6.1   Generation of Synthetic Data

We generate points in 3D space and points on spherical images as follows.

- We generate points in 3D space in the cube whose center of gravity is at the origin of the world coordinate systems. The points in 3D space are randomly generated based on the uniform distribution.
- The points in 3D space are projected onto points $\boldsymbol{z}_{1p}$ and $\boldsymbol{z}_{2p}$ on the spherical images of the cameras $\boldsymbol{c}_1$ and $\boldsymbol{c}_2$.
- For each point $\boldsymbol{z}_p$ on the spherical image, we add noise and transform to the point $\boldsymbol{z}'_p$ such that

$$\boldsymbol{z}'_p := R(\boldsymbol{z}_p \to \mathcal{N})^\top R(\boldsymbol{t}_\epsilon \to \mathcal{N})^\top R(\boldsymbol{z}_p \to \mathcal{N}) \boldsymbol{z}_p,$$

where $R(\boldsymbol{a} \to \boldsymbol{b})$ is defined in Eq. (2) and $\boldsymbol{t}_\epsilon$ is a point on a unit sphere randomly generated based on the uniform distribution. For the colatitude ϕ_ϵ and longitude ψ_ϵ of the point $\boldsymbol{t}_\epsilon$, we define the range of the distribution of $\boldsymbol{t}_\epsilon$ such that $0 \le \phi_\epsilon \le \epsilon$ and $-\pi \le \psi_\epsilon \le \pi$.

6.2   Design of Experiments

The principle procedure of an experiment consist of the following three steps,

(1) Generate data as defined in Section 6.1.
(2) Perform the initial estimation and compute the error d_8^t.
(3) Perform the rectification-based estimation the error d_R^t.

We repeat this procedure T times for statistical evaluation.

In each procedure, we compute the error using angles between epipoles. After the initial estimation, we compute the angle between the initial epipole e_I and the ground truth e_G such that $d_8^t = |\cos^{-1}(e_I^\top e_G)|$. Furthermore, we define the standard error of the eight-point algorithm as $d_8 = \frac{1}{T}\sum_{t=1}^{T} d_8^t$. In the same manner, we compute the angle between the epipole e_R computed by our rectification-based method and the ground truth e_G such that $d_R^t = |\cos^{-1}(e_R^\top e_G)|$. We also define the standard error of the rectification-based method as $d_R = \frac{1}{T}\sum_{t=1}^{T} d_R^t$.

Throughout the experiments, the parameters are defined as the first camera $c_1 = (4,0,0)^\top$, the second camera $c_2 = (-4,0,0)^\top$ and the rotation of the first camera $R_1 = I$. Furthermore, the iteration is $T = 1000$, the edge of the cube is 40 and the noise variance of a point on a spherical image is $\epsilon = 0.01$.

6.3   Evaluation w.r.t. Changes of Numbers of Correspondences

Figure 4 shows the results of the numerical experiments in which the number of 3D points P is increased from 12 to 240 with the interval 8. The rotation of the second camera is fixed to $R_2 = I$. Therefore, there always exists the P corresponding points on the two spherical images. Figures 4 (a) and (c) show the

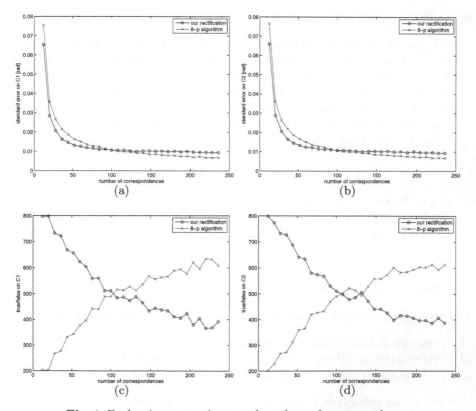

Fig. 4. Evaluation w.r.t. changes of numbers of correspondences

results w.r.t. the first camera C_1. Figures 4 (b) and (d) show the results w.r.t. the second camera C_2. In Figs. (a) and (b), the standard errors of the eight-point algorithm are plotted with dashed lines and cross "+" dots. The standard errors of our rectification-based method are plotted with solid lines and circular "o" dots. In Figs. (c) and (d), the plots with dashed lines and cross "+" dots show the numbers of the procedures if $d_8^t < d_R^t$ in the T times iteration. The plots with solid lines and circular "o" dots show the numbers of the procedures if $d_R^t < d_8^t$ in the T times iteration. We can observe that our rectification-based method shows positive results while the numbers of corresponding points are less than 120 approximately.

6.4   Evaluation w.r.t. Changes of Region Shared by Two Cameras

Figure 5 shows the results of the numerical experiments in which the second camera coordinates are rotated around y-axis from zero to π with the interval $\pi/12$. The the number of data P is fixed to 50. Therefore, according to the increase of the rotation, the region shared in the two spherical images is decreased. When the rotation is over $10\pi/12$, there do not exist enough corresponding points.

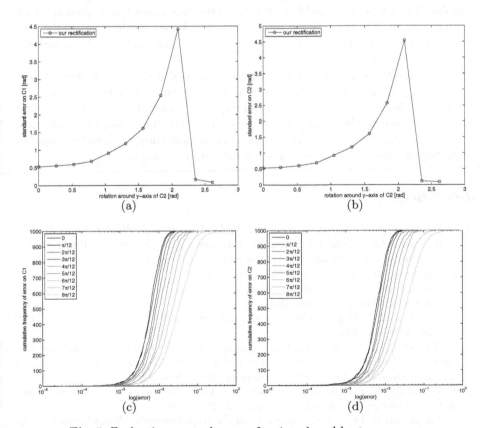

Fig. 5. Evaluation w.r.t. changes of region shared by two cameras

Figures 5 (a) and (c) show the results w.r.t. the first camera C_1. Figures 5 (b) and (d) show the results w.r.t. the second camera C_2. In Figs. 5 (a) and (b), the standard errors of our rectification-based method are plotted with solid lines and circular "o" dots. In Figs. 5 (c) and (d), the curves show the cumulative frequency distributions of errors in each rotation. According to the increase of the gray-level intensity of curves, the region shared in the two spherical images is increased. For example, the black and lightest-gray curves denote zero and $8\pi/12$ rotation around y-axis of the second camera coordinates. We can naturally observe that the accuracy of the estimation of the epipoles is increased when the region shared in the two spherical images is increased.

7   Discussions and Concluding Remarks

In the spherical camera model, the rectification transforms the epipoles of the first and second cameras to the north and south poles, respectively. Then, the corresponding points between two spherical images should lie on the same longitude. Using this geometric property, we established the method for improving accuracy of computation of the epipolar geometry. In the sense of geometry, all epipolar planes which are yielded by pairs of corresponding points pass through a single line in 3D space. Since our rectification-based method naturally uses this geometrical constraint, the epipoles are estimated numerically accurately for spherical images.

In the results of numerical experiments, we clarified the numbers of corresponding points which are required for the accurate computation using our rectification-based method. Our method requires less numbers of corresponding points compared to the eight-point algorithm. Furthermore, since the spherical cameras can naturally share a large region in common, the epipoles are computed accurately compared to the use of small field-of-view images.

References

1. S. Baker and S. K. Nayar. A theory of single-viewpoint catadioptric image formation. *International Journal of Computer Vision*, vol. 35(2), pp. 175–196, 1999.
2. J. P. Barreto and K. Daniilidis. Unifying image plane liftings for central catadioptric and dioptric cameras. In *OMNIVIS '04*, pp. 151–162, 2004.
3. R. Benosman and S. B. Kang, editors. *Panoramic Vision: Sensors, Theory, Applications*. Springer-Verlag, 2001.
4. P. Chang and M. Hebert, Omni-directional structure from motion, In *OMNIVIS '00*, pp. 127–133, 2000.
5. O. Faugeras, Q. T. Luong, and T. Papadopoulou. *The Geometry of Multiple Images: The Laws That Govern The Formation of Images of A Scene and Some of Their Applications*. MIT Press, Cambridge, MA, USA, 2001.
6. C. Geyer and K. Daniilidis, Catadioptric projective geometry. *International Journal of Computer Vision*, vol. 45(3), pp. 223–243, 2001.
7. C. Geyer and K. Daniilidis, Properties of the catadioptric fundamental matrix, In *ECCV '02*, vol. 2, pp. 140–154, 2002.

8. R. Hartley and A. Zisserman. *Multiple view geometry in computer vision.* Cambridge University, Cambridge, 2nd edition, 2003.
9. T. Svoboda and T.Pajdla. Epipolar Geometry for Central Catadioptric Cameras. *International Journal of Computer Vision,* vol. 49(1), pp. 23–37, 2002.
10. X. Ying and Z. Hu. Can we consider central catadioptric cameras and fisheye cameras within a unified imaging model. In *ECCV '04,* vol. 1, pp. 442–455, 2004.

Parallel Implementation of Elastic Grid Matching Using Cellular Neural Networks

Krzysztof Ślot[1], Piotr Korbel[2], Hyongsuk Kim[3], Malrey Lee[4], and Suhong Ko[3]

[1] Institute of Electronics, Technical University of Lodz, Wolczanska 211/215, 90-924 Lodz and Academy of Humanities and Economics, Lodz, Poland
kslot@p.lodz.pl
[2] Institute of Electronics, Technical University of Lodz, Poland
pkorbel@p.lodz.pl
[3] Division of Electronics and Information Engineering, Chonbuk National University, 561-756 Chonju, Republic of Korea
hskim@chonbuk.ac.kr
[4] Research Center of Industrial Technology, School of Electronics and Information Engineering, Chonbuk National University, Republic of Korea
mrlee@chonbuk.ac.kr

Abstract. The following paper presents a method that allows for a parallel implementation of the most computationally expensive element of the deformable template paradigm, which is a grid-matching procedure. Cellular Neural Network Universal Machine has been selected as a framework for the task realization. A basic idea of deformable grid matching is to guide node location updates in a way that minimizes dissimilarity between an image and grid-recorded information, and that ensures minimum grid deformations. The proposed method provides a parallel implementation of this general concept and includes a novel approach to grid's elasticity modeling. The method has been experimentally verified using two different analog hardware environments, yielding high execution speeds and satisfactory processing accuracy.

1 Introduction

A concept of image analysis by means of deformable templates (also referred to as deformable grids or prototypes) [1] belongs to a category of template matching-based object recognition strategies and is derived from the active-contour paradigm [2]. A deformable template is a class prototype, represented by an array of elastically connected and appropriately preset nodes, which interact with an image under analysis and with each other. Although deformable templates are potentially attractive for the purpose of recognition of nonlinearly deformed objects, high computational demands of a grid-matching procedure limit practical applications of the concept. A possible way to alleviate this drawback is to consider parallel processing architectures as a grid-matching framework, with an emphasis on paradigms that offer a low cost of the algorithm's execution. In particular, parallel processors integrated with optical sensors (often referred to

A. Gagalowicz and W. Philips (Eds.): MIRAGE 2007, LNCS 4418, pp. 472–481, 2007.

as 'smart' optical sensors) could be considered as a tool for the algorithm execution. A delegation of complex processing tasks from a central processing unit to image acquisition stages, could significantly improve performance of vision systems, driven by multiple, distributed optical inputs.

The following paper presents a method of deformable template matching implementation by means of a Cellular Neural Network Universal Machine [3] (abbreviated henceforth CNN UM). CNN UM paradigm combines an ultra-fast execution of several image processing operations with a simplicity of an underlying hardware. CNN UM is a regular array of locally connected, neuron-like processing elements (called *cells*) with local information storage capabilities. A function of a network is determined by spatially-invariant cell coupling rules. Although CNN UM has universal capabilities (in a Turing sense), problem solving algorithms need to be appropriately adapted to specific constraints of the paradigm to ensure their efficient execution. The proposed method expresses deformable template matching process in a CNN UM-tailored manner, by providing appropriate ways for data representation and for parallel modeling of basic grid's node-driving mechanisms: image-grid interactions and elastic internode bindings. The method has been verified using two different parallel image-processing environments: CNN-UM analog implementation (ACE chips) [3] and an analog, general-purpose cellular processor (SCAMP chip) [4]. Both types of processors are integrated with optical sensor arrays and are considered to be potential smart sensor frameworks. An execution time of the proposed algorithm is at the order of milliseconds (for ACE chips) and dozens of milliseconds (for the SCAMP chip), regardless of a size of a grid considered in processing, with approximately 5% accuracy (SCAMP chip).

The paper has the following structure. A brief outline of two basic concepts underlying the proposed method - the deformable template paradigm and the Cellular Neural Network Universal Machine - has been presented in Section 2. The introduced algorithm for CNN UM implementation of deformable grid matching has been described in Section 3. Finally, experimental evaluation of the proposed method has been provided in Section 4.

2 Deformable Templates and Cellular Neural Networks

Object recognition with deformable templates involves matching of deformable grid-encoded class prototypes followed by an assessment of grid-matching results. Deformable template matching is a process of confronting information embedded at grid's nodes with image properties present at current node locations [1]. In case of a mismatch, nodes are pulled towards better matching regions. Grid deformations that result from node displacements are counteracted by elastic node interactions, which are intended to preserve grid's initial topology. An assessment of these interactions requires quantification of local grid deformations. This can be done using Lagrangean strain tensors or Cauchy-Green deformation tensors [5]), however, it is commonly simplified using various geometrical approaches [6].

Node location updates continue until the both node-driving mechanisms - grid-image dissimilarity and elastic node interactions - get balanced. An outcome of deformable template matching is commonly expressed by computing final grid deformations and the resulting image-grid similarity. Since modeling of node displacement dynamics is complex, grid-matching procedure, and consequently, object recognition, is computationally expensive.

Deformable template matching is a spatially-invariant process, based on local information. These two properties are key elements of the CNN UM paradigm. CNN UM architecture is specialized for image processing - each network cell is topologically assigned to an image pixel. CNN UM cells are neuron-like elements that nonlinearly transform weighted sums of inputs. In case of existing CNN-UM VLSI implementations [7], [8], [9] cells are interconnected only within their nearest neighborhood. Since a cell-coupling rule is spatially-invariant, a complete description of interactions among CNN processors is specified through a small set of weighting coefficients, which is called *a template*. An operation of a network is a function of a template. A multitude of various templates that allow for performing different elementary image processing tasks, have been proposed so far [10]. CNN UM cells have local storage capabilities, so that complex sequences of elementary transformations, called *analogic algorithms* can be performed on initial network's information. In addition, each CNN UM cell can be individually included or excluded from processing, which provides a mechanism for implementing conditional instructions.

CNN UM based image processing can be extremely fast, providing that one can design an efficient analogic algorithm for a given task realization and that it runs on an actual hardware (e.g. simple geometrical shape recognition can be performed at a rate of a few thousand frames per second [9]). An objective of the reported research was to develop a CNN UM algorithm that provides fast execution of a deformable template matching. To accomplish this goal, basic ideas of the original algorithm had to be restated into a form that well suits capabilities and constraints of CNN UM processing.

3   A Description of the Algorithm

Parallel CNN operation requires all data that are being processed to be arranged in a form of two-dimensional arrays (maps) that match network's topology. Input information for grid matching comprises an image, which is to be analyzed, and a deformable template. Deformable prototype-related data include information on current node locations and prototype samples that are stored at grid's nodes. To represent this information in a CNN-convenient form, logical association between deformable template nodes and CNN cells are made using two different maps (Fig. 1). The first one - a binary map, referred to as L-map - is used to indicate current node locations. Any cell that is pointed by a non-zero entry of this map becomes a node and is a focus of subsequent image processing steps. The second map (referred to as V-map) contains class' prototype samples, which are stored at the entries that correspond to current node locations.

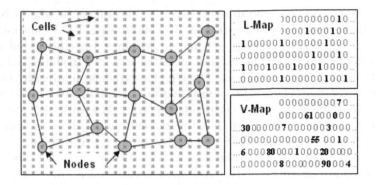

Fig. 1. Deformable template nodes and CNN cells (left) and prototype information coding (right)

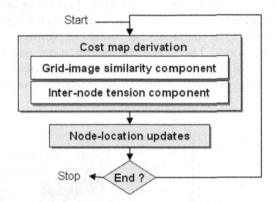

Fig. 2. Block diagram of the proposed method

A general idea of the proposed grid matching implementation is to construct a cost map that reflects both grid-image similarity and inter-node tensions, and next, to use this map for guiding node-location updates (Fig. 2). Nodes are iteratively moved to these CNN cells within a current neighborhood, which are assigned with the minimum cost. A displacement of a node means a change in locations of the corresponding entries in both L-map and V-map. Since both cost map components depend on node locations, the cost map needs to be iteratively recreated.

3.1 Cost Map Derivation

Cost map construction involves two phases, aimed at evaluation of the two node-driving mechanisms. The first component of a cost map accounts for grid-image similarity. The similarity is assessed by computing an absolute value of a difference between node-recorded information and image properties at nodes' vicinity.

The corresponding CNN procedure utilizes an application of standard CNN templates [10] and is summarized in Fig. 3. To comply with VLSI implementation constraints, node displacements are limited within a 1-neighborhood of their current locations, so a meaningful portion of the cost map includes 3×3 regions, centered at current node locations. These regions are initialized with gray-levels stored at the V-map using eight-step procedure, which involves horizontal and vertical shift operations controlled by L-map entries. The constructed patchwork image is subtracted from the analyzed image and an absolute value of the result is computed using two CNN operations: zero-level thresholding, aimed at negative cell output detection, and a selective inversion of the detected entries.

The second component of the cost map accounts for grid's elastic interactions. The required two-dimensional cost function should characterize node candidate-locations according to induced levels of grid's deformation. Existing ways of evaluating of local distortions [5], do not fit well within CNN computational framework. Therefore, to enable efficient, CNN-based inter-node tension modeling, a new approach has been developed. The major premise of the proposed elasticity-modeling method is an observation that locations of nodes of a non-distorted regular grid coincide with centers of Voronoi regions, which are generated by these nodes. Therefore, grid deformation reduction could be accomplished by Voronoi region center-wise displacements of all offset nodes. This idea has been implemented using a two-phase procedure presented schematically in Fig. 4.

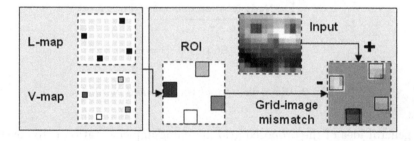

Fig. 3. Derivation of grid-image dissimilarity cost component (ROI denotes regions of interest for mismatch evaluation)

An objective of the first phase of the procedure is to find Voronoi region boundaries and then, to localize Voronoi region centers. Since Voronoi region boundaries group elements that are equidistant to nearest nodes, they can be extracted by iterative thinning (i.e. by finding a skeleton) of a binary image, initialized appropriately at node locations (Fig. 4a). To find centers of the extracted Voronoi regions, one can execute another image thinning procedure, which begins with an inverted result of the previous processing step and collapses convex binary regions into their central elements.

An objective of the second phase of the procedure is to assign all region elements with a cost that increases as one departs from a region's center (Fig. 4b).

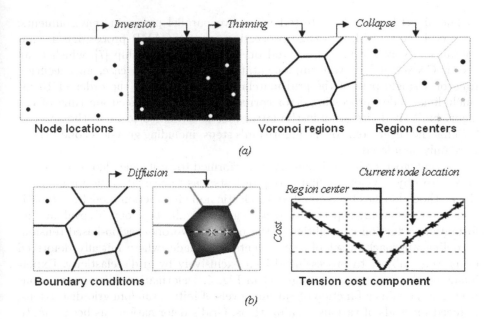

Fig. 4. Derivation of grid tension-related cost component: derivation of Voronoi regions and their centers (a), cost function component (shown for the central Voronoi region), with a plot of tension-related cost distribution along the marked cross-section

Given Voronoi region boundaries and their centers, this can be done by an execution of a CNN diffusion template [10], with boundary conditions fixed at the maximum for region boundaries and fixed at zero for centers. As a result, every element of a region is assigned with a cost that increases as one moves outwards region's center.

A cost function that is used in for guiding node location updates is a weighted sum of both of the presented cost components. A procedure used for displacing nodes involves a search for minima of the cost function, performed within 3×3 neighborhoods centered at current node locations.

4   Experimental Evaluation of the Proposed Method

An execution of the proposed CNN UM algorithm involves a repetition of a sequence of standard CNN templates [10], an appropriate selection of cells that are to be active at various phases of the procedure and a temporary storage of intermediate, analog and binary results. At majority of steps of the algorithm, no more than four local analog and eight binary memories per cell are required, which matches resources allocated to a cell in existing hardware CNN implementations [4], [7], [8]. The operations used throughout the algorithm include: horizontal and vertical shifts as well as inversions (for the grid-image mismatch evaluation phase), thinning and diffusion (for elasticity modeling), and minima-selection and shifts (for new node location assessment and node displacements).

The algorithm has been tested using two parallel processing environments: a general purpose SIMD image processing array (SCAMP processor) [4] that contains 128 by 128 processors and on 64 by 64 ACE4k chip [7], which is an actual CNN-UM hardware implementation. In the former case, an execution time of a single pass of the grid-matching procedure is at the order of 15 ms (including analog processing error-correction steps). An execution time of the algorithm's single iteration in the latter case is estimated to be at the order of 0.75 ms (however, some of the algorithm's steps, including gray-level operations, were only simulated).

Two categories of experiments were performed to verify the algorithm's operation. An objective of the first group of tests was to evaluate a performance of the method that has been adopted for elastic node interaction modeling. Elastic node interactions are expected to restore grid's regular topology. To evaluate deformation reduction capabilities of the proposed Voronoi region-based tension-modeling approach, a set of experiments was made, where initially deformed grids were subject to processing driven exclusively by grid's elasticity. Experiment results have been summarized in Fig. 5. Deformation compensation has been evaluated as a function of varying levels of initial, random grid distortions, induced for grids of various organizations. Grid's deformation has been quantified as a normalized sum of local mismatches between an expected node location (which is an average of its four nearest neighbors) and an actual node location:

$$\Phi = \frac{1}{MN} \sum_{i=1}^{M} \sum_{j=1}^{N} |4\mathbf{r}_{i,j} - \mathbf{r}_{i-1,j} - \mathbf{r}_{i+1,j} - \mathbf{r}_{i,j-1} - \mathbf{r}_{i,j+1}| \tag{1}$$

Three different organizations of a rectangular $M \times M$ grid ($M = 8, M = 10$ and $M = 14$) were considered. The proposed approach for elastic interaction modeling works fine unless neighboring nodes do not form vertices of a parallelogram. Since such node arrangements occur sporadically if boundary grid's nodes are fixed, the proposed procedure yields good deformation compensation. Initial grid deformations featuring average absolute node displacements ranging from two to four pixels per node, are reduced to an average of 0.66 pixel per node after an execution of the procedure.

The second set of experiments was aimed at evaluating of grid matching accuracy. To assess grid's capability to adapt to limited object distortions, a set of grid matching procedures, using distorted versions of reference objects as inputs, was executed. Object distortions were introduced as local, affine image geometry transformations that occur at random locations and at random magnitudes. To emphasize image-grid similarity assessment, after a completion of a grid matching procedure, additional k−steps ($k = 1...dg/4$, where dg is an initial inter-node distance) were performed with elastic node interactions set to zero.

Sample experiment results are summarized in Fig. 6. A deformable template was constructed based on a reference image shown in Fig. 6a (top-left) by sampling this image at regular intervals (top right). The template was then used for processing of deformed versions of the reference object (sample images I1 and I2 are shown at the bottom part of Fig. 6a). At each step of the matching

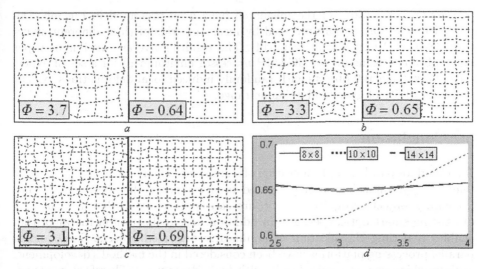

Fig. 5. Deformation compensation examples for 8-by-8 (a), 10-by-10 (b) and 14-by-14 grids (c); deformation compensation plots for three different grids and local initial average node displacements ranging from 2.5 two 4 pixels (d)

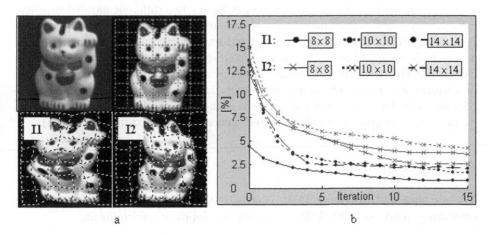

Fig. 6. Reference object and its sampling for deformable template construction, along with grid-matching results for two deformed versions of the reference object (a); grid-image similarity evolution plots for I1 and I2 images for three different grid organizations (b)

procedure, a grid-image dissimilarity measure was computed as a sum of absolute values of gray-level differences between node information and corresponding image information:

$$\Gamma = \frac{1}{MN} \sum_{i=1}^{M} \sum_{j=1}^{N} |f(\mathbf{r}_{i,j}) - n_{i,j}| \qquad (2)$$

Temporal evolutions of the mismatch have been presented in Fig. 6b. Deformed images have been processed by means of grids of three different structures (8-by-8, 10-by-10 and 14-by-14). The resulting average dissimilarity per node, obtained using analog SCAMP processor environment for a set of experiments involving 100 objects with randomly induced local deformations, was at the order of 5% of gray-level dynamic range.

5   Conclusion

A method for parallel implementation of a grid-matching phase of the deformable template paradigm has been presented in the paper. It has been shown that a complex object recognition procedure can be executed within a framework of existing smart optical sensors. In addition, fast realization of the algorithm enables real time classification of nonlinearly deformed objects. Since analog parallel processing platforms have been considered in the method's development, grid-matching can be realized only with limited accuracy. Therefore, a coarse, fast object classification is perceived as a potential application of the proposed approach.

One need to emphasize that the proposed algorithm has not been optimized for an execution on a particular hardware platform - two different parallel processing environments were employed for its execution. Therefore, several platform-specific modifications can be introduced to further increase its performance (such as e.g. resistive grid-based diffusion realization, which is available for CNN UM chips). Another direction of further research is a development of more efficient procedures for several of algorithm's steps (for example, convexity of Voronoi regions could be exploited for derivation of more efficient boundary and center extraction procedures than the adopted, general skeletonization algorithm).

Acknowledgment

The authors wish to thank Prof. Piotr Dudek (University of Manchester) for providing an access to SCAMP processor development environment.

References

1. Jain, A.K., Zhong, Y., Lakshmanan, S.: Object Matching Using Deformable Templates. IEEE Transactions on PAMI, Vol. 18, No. 3, 1996, 267-278.
2. Kass M., Witkin A., Terzopoulos D.: Snakes: Active Contour Models, International Journal of Computer Vision, Vol. 1, No. 4, 1998, 321-331.
3. Roska, T., Chua, L.O.: The CNN Universal Machine: An Analogic Array Computer. IEEE Transactions on Circuits and Systems-II., vol. 40, 163-173.
4. Dudek P., Carey S.J.: General-purpose 128128 SIMD processor array with integrated image sensor, Electronic Letters, Vol. 42, No. 12, 2006.
5. Symon, Keith.: 'Mechanics', Addison-Wesley, 1971

6. Szczypinski, P.M., Materka, A.: Object tracking and recognition using deformable grid with geometrical templates. Proc. of Int. Conference on Signals and Electronic Systems ICSES 2000, Poland, 169-174.
7. Linan, G., Espejo, S., Dominguez-Castro, R., Rodriguez-Vazquez, A.: ACE4K: An analog I/O visual microprocessor chip with 7-bit analog accuracy. International Journal of Circuit Theory and Applications, Vol. 30, 89-116.
8. Linan, G., Dominguez-Castro, R., Espejo, S., Rodriguez-Vazquez, A.: ACE16K: an Advanced Focal-Plane Analog Programmable Processor. Proceedings of ESS-CIRC'2001, Austria, 201-204.
9. Zarandy A., Rekeczky C.: Bi-i: a Standalone Ultra High Speed Cellular Vision System, IEEE Circuits and Systems Magazine, Second Quarter 2005.
10. Image Processing Library Reference Manual v. 3.2, AnaLogic Computers Ltd., Budapeszt, 2004

Automatic Segmentation of Natural Scene Images Based on Chromatic and Achromatic Components

Jonghyun Park, Hyosun Yoon, and Gueesang Lee

Dept. of Computer Science, Chonnam National University, Korea
{jhpark,hsy,gslee}@chonnam.ac.kr

Abstract. This paper presents a simple method for segmenting text image on the basis of color components. It is shown how segmentation can benefit from splitting color signals into chromatic and achromatic components and separately smoothing them by proposed clustering method. We analyze and compare the performance of several color components in terms of segmentation of the text regions from color natural scenes. We also perform a fast 1-dimensional k-means clustering algorithm. Therefore we can perform accurate object segmentation using both H and I components. And then, the effectiveness and reliability of proposed method are demonstrated through various natural scene images. The experimental results have proven that the proposed method is effective.

1 Introduction

Natural scenes contain a wealth of information. Text information in a natural scene is quite useful since it can convey a very important meaning. Nowadays, we easily accumulate natural scene images by PDA (personal digital assistant), mobile phone, and robot vision systems; equipped multimedia with diverse systems as a digital camera has been widespread. It is natural that the demand for automatic detection and recognition of the text region from these images has been increased. Detecting a text region generally consists of two processes; the first is segmenting the text region from the natural scene, and then recognizing the text region. The quality of segmentation of the text regions affects the whole performance directly. In this research, we are interested in segmenting the text region of the natural scene fast.

The methods of text region segmentation can be classified into region-based, texture-based, and edge-based [1]. Using the region-based method, it is difficult to obtain precise segmentation region for natural scene images that the contrast of light is not uniform since the similarity of color and brightness in the same text region are assumed [2],[3],[4]. Texture-based method is proper for complicated images [5],[6], but it is not good method because of heavy computation. The edge-based algorithms need a heavy post-processing to merge the sub-regions of a character, which is caused from the variation of light [10],[15]. Prototype systems for sign translation have been developed for handheld device and for personal computers [7],[8],[9],[10],[11],[16]. The PDA-based sign translator developed in [8] presents users the translated sign from Chinese to English. Works related to segmentation of text regions are in [17]. The previous works can be classified in terms of color space based on segmentation

A. Gagalowicz and W. Philips (Eds.): MIRAGE 2007, LNCS 4418, pp. 482–493, 2007.

method. RGB space was used in [7],[8],[9],[16] and works [8] were based on RGB and HSI spaces. Diverse segmentation methods were used, such as edge detection [8],[10],[16], Gaussian mixture model [8],[16], color quantization [10], binarization method [9], and histogram-based color clustering [11].

We analyze and compare the performance of several color components in terms of segmentation of text regions of color natural scene images in Section 2. Applications on mobile terminals are targeted in the paper. Thus, heavy computation should be avoided. It is proved experimentally that 1-dimensional k-means algorithm based on HSI space is viable to text region segmentation of the color natural scene. Section 3 describes a fast segmentation method. 500 natural images supplied from ICDAR were used for comparison among five color components. The experimental results are presented in Section 4, and conclusion and future work are described in Section 5.

2 Analysis of Natural Scene and Color Components

Color natural scenes of ICDAR database [23] with the text region were analyzed to identify characteristics of the text region of color natural scenes. Our observations can be summarized as follows.

- Visually, text regions have uniform color by achromatic or chromatic. In an ICDAR database, 90% out of images show this characteristic.
- The difference between text and background regions is large value in either intensity or hue.
- Text regions are affected by illumination noise such as highlights, shadows, and shades.

Text images include various characteristics. One difficulty lies in the variety of text; it varies in font, size, and orientation. The second problem is found in the images whose texts are damaged by highlights. In Fig. 1, (a) and (b) show the case. The rapid change of light in Fig. 1(c) and (e) is also commonly seen in natural scene images. It is much more difficult to segment text regions on the surface of a convex object like Fig. 1(f). Similar intensities between text and backgrounds shown in Fig. 1(g) and (h) cause some problems that can be an incitement to study.

Image segmentation is a bottleneck for image processing and computer vision. Most segmentation algorithms only deal with gray scale images. A color can be represented by several color formats such as RGB, YUV, YIQ, and HSI [14]. Previous works have segmented text regions based on either only one space or combining a space depending on the goal of application. The works [7],[16],[17] are related to segmentation based on RGB space. However, RGB representation does not coincide with the vision psychology of human eyes and there is a high correlation among its three components, although it's convenient for display devices. It is difficult to choose the best model to work well for text segmentation of color natural scenes since each model has merit and demerit. The performance of each color representation depends on the image's feature, the goal and the method. Therefore, the combination of at least two representations has been used normally; the approaches based on RGB and HSI representations [8], a color quantization method based on RGB representation [10], and the hybrid method using color quantization and edge detection based on RGB space [17].

Fig. 1. Various color natural scene images containing the text region from ICDAR database

The combination method based on RGB representation needs a complex post-processing although its performance is increased. C. Zhang and P. Wang proposed a new algorithm segmenting color images in HSI space [19]. HSI color representation is compatible with the vision psychology of human eyes, and its three components are relatively independent. Distortion from light effect makes segmenting text regions of color natural scene much more difficult as previously mentioned. It is difficult to segment text regions of a natural scene by only intensity because of broken, erosion and expansion of the character. We empirically conclude that HSI space is better than the other representations RGB, YUV, YIQ and show that the hue component is robust to highlights, shading, and shadows in our experiment.

3   Clustering-Based Text Segmentation

3.1   Selection of Color Features in Natural Images

In general, images of including text have achromatic as well as chromatic regions. In text image case, one object is mainly classified in either perceptually chromatic or achromatic region. Using only the hue component for segmentation can be unstable in achromatic regions. In such regions, it is more appropriate to use intensity for segmentation. This section details a decision function for classifying a pixel as chromatic or achromatic such that the appropriate feature (HUE or INTENSITY) is used in segmentation. In [26], S. Sural et. al. used the saturation value to determine the relative dominance of hue and intensity. Thresholding on saturation, however, is not illumination invariant. When a chromatic region is illuminated brightly, the saturation value in the region is likely to be low compared to the same chromatic region with lower illumination. The low saturation incorrectly indicates an achromatic region. We propose an alternative decision function in RGB space that is independent of illumination. Instead of thresholding on saturation, we derive a chromaticity measure based on the sum of differences of R(red), G(green), and B(blue) components at each pixel $(\mathbf{x}, \mathbf{y})$ in RGB space.

$$\mathbf{F}(\mathbf{x}, \mathbf{y}) = (|R(x, y) - G(x, y)| + |G(x, y) - B(x, y)| + |R(x, y) - G(x, y)|)/3 \qquad (1)$$

From our experimental observation, the smaller the sum, the closer the related position is to the achromatic regions. The level of chromaticity is proportional to $\mathbf{F}(\mathbf{x}, \mathbf{y})$ in (1). A threshold value $\mathbf{TH} = 20$ is used to classify a pixel with RGB components in the range [0-255]. Values below $\mathbf{TH}$ are classified as being achromatic and analyzed using the intensity component in HSI space. The remaining pixels are chromatic, and analyzed using the hue component as shown in Fig. 2. Hue and intensity values are defined in different ranges. The selected color features are used in clustering-based algorithm for segmenting text.

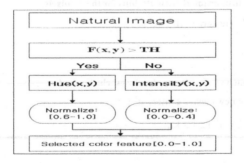

Fig. 2. Proposed method for selecting color components in HSI space

3.2 Fast Clustering Algorithm

The k-means the clustering algorithm is applied to each component hue and intensity to perform segmentation of the text region fast [19]. Table 1 illustrates the k-means clustering algorithm. It has the complexity $O(nkdl)$ where n is the number of pixels, d is the number of dimensions, k is the number of clusters, and l is the number of loops. Since we use each of the color components separately, d is 1. So the time complexity is $O(nkl)$. In addition, by operating on histogram space the time complexity could be reduced drastically. Table 2 shows the modified algorithm. In the line 7, new cluster center is computed by

$$u_i^l = \frac{1}{N} \sum_{b \in B[i]} H[b] * b \qquad (2)$$

where B[i] represents the set of bins assigned to the *i-th* cluster by line 6. Now the time complexity is $O(mkl)$. Since a color component is usually quantized into 256 levels, m may be regarded as content 256. Hue space is not Euclidean space, and it is a 2π cyclic space. A new definition of distance in the cyclic hue space that was proposed by C. Zhang and P. Wang is used in this paper [19]. The center point of a cluster is computed by the definition of center point proposed by them.

Table 1. k-means clustering algorithm

1.   **Initialize k cluster center, $u_i^0 \leq i \leq k$;**
2. $l = 0$;
3.   **REPEAT {**
4. $l = l+1$;
5.   **Assign each of n pixels to the closest cluster center;**
6.   **Computer new cluster center, u_i^l;**
7.   **} until $(u_i^{l-1} = u_i^l, 1 \leq i \leq k)$;**

Table 2. k-means clustering algorithm operating on histogram space

1. **Computer histogram H with m bins for the n pixels;**
2. **Initialize k cluster, $u_i^0, 1 \leq i \leq k$;**
3. **l=0;**
4. **REPEAT {**
5.   **l=l+1;**
6.   **Assign each of m bins to the closest cluster center;**
7.   **Compute new cluster center, u_i^l;**
8. **} until $(u_i^{l-1} = u_i^l, 1 \leq i \leq k)$;**

The *k*-means clustering algorithm requires the number of clusters to be known beforehand. The number of clusters is not only the most important factor for the quality of clustering algorithm, but also increasing the complexity of the problem segmenting text region in the next post-processing step. The number that is less than the proper number of clusters makes the text region blurred, and a character is divided into multiple segments in the case that the number is more than one. Many approaches to solve the problem have been proposed over the years [20],[21],[22]. S. Ray and R. H. Turi [21] proposed the new cluster validity measure based on intra-cluster and inter-cluster distance measures in equation (3) and (4), respectively. We use the validity measure to determine the number of clusters.

$$intra = \frac{1}{N} \sum_{i=1}^{k} \sum_{x \in C_i} \| x - u_i \| \qquad (3)$$

where N is the number of pixels in the image, k is the number of clusters, u_i is the cluster center, and C_i is the i-th cluster.

$$inter = \min \| u_i - u_j \|, \quad 1 \leq i, \ j \leq k \ and \ i \neq j \tag{4}$$

$$\textbf{validity} = intra/inter \tag{5}$$

Using the validity measurement in (5), our text segmentation algorithm can be described as Table 3. And then, we describe two different k-means clustering algorithms using Table 3 because intensity values are linear and hue values are characterized with the cyclic property as shown in Fig. 3.

Table 3. Validity measurement for text segmentation

1. for(k = 2; k < max_mumber_of_cluster; k++) {
2.   Apply the algorithm II by letting number of clusters to be k ;
3.   Compute the validity measure in (5), v_k ;
4. }
5. k' = arg max v_k ;
    Using k' th clustering result for each of n pixels in the color image, assign region label, if the pixel belongs to i th cluster, assign the pixel to i th cluster

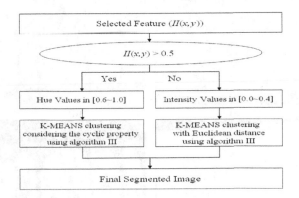

Fig. 3. Our segmentation scheme using k-means clustering algorithm

4 Experimental Results

The method is implemented by Visual C++ on the system of Windows XP-2000. The specifications of hardware consist of 1GHz dual CPU and 512MB memory. Experiments have been performed on all color natural scene images supported from an ICDAR database, which consist of 501 images containing text regions for testing and for learning [23],[24]. It includes diverse images, such as simple, complex, and distorted images, and the sizes and distribution of color of natural scene images are various. The images based on RGB representation are converted into HSI space. Fig. 4 contains examples of natural scene images whose text regions are rather uniform. In this case, experimental results indicate that segmentation by proposed produces a good result. Fig. 5 is the cases containing text regions of varying distortion for light change. Fig. 5(b) shows the segmented results using intensity component. The result is not good because it dose not segment text regions. In Fig. 5(c), we perform using EDISON system proposed by [27]. In this case, text regions of "BUS" and "TIMES" regions are divided with many regions though text region have homogeneous color components. But segmenting results based on proposed method are good in the text regions as shown in Fig. 5(d).

Fig. 6 indicates the outcome of either the images that there is no change of intensity between text and background regions in Fig 6(a) and (b) or the ones that are affected by highlights in Fig. 6(c). We confirm the same facts. The first fact is that the segmentation based on proposed method is robust for the cases of highlighted natural

Fig. 4. The natural scene images with uniform intensity:(a) and (b) are original images, (c) and (d) are text segmentations with the H component, (e) and (f)are the results proposed method

scene images although there are many separated regions on characters. Second, is that segmenting text region based on intensity causes the division and blurring of the character since it is very sensitive to variations of intensity.

Fig. 5. The natural scene with varying intensity: (a) input image, (b) segmentation result with the I component, (c) segmentation result by proposed method, (d) segmentation result by EDISON

The experimental result in Table 4, which shows that the I component dominate over other components, is performed to examine which component is dominant. We subjectively determine what is good, middle, and bad in a subjective way; a good case is that the text region is almost detected, a middle case is that 30% of the text region is lost, and a bad case is when the text region lost more than 50%. The input images and the corresponding results are presented in Fig. 7 for credibility of the results of Table 4. Additionally the fact that the green component is good to segment the text region of color natural scene is acknowledged according to the result. The

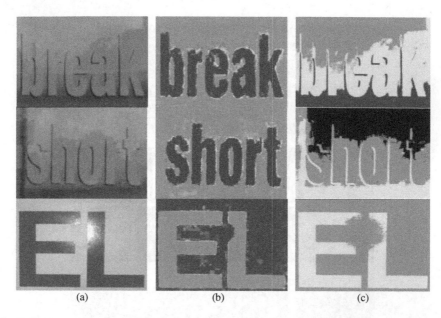

(a)   (b)   (c)

Fig. 6. Text segmentation of the images with the distortion of intensity: (a) input image, (b) proposed method, (c) intensity

processing time is a very important factor for the efficiency of an algorithm running on mobile devices. The running time of our method is a millisecond level as presented in Table 5. From the experimental results, the following result is drawn: the method using H and I components can efficiently segment text regions in natural scene image, especially, hue component shows robust to highlights, shading, and shadows.

Table 4. Segmentation result of 501 images of ICDAR database

	R	G	B	H	I	PM
Good	37	43	29	14	46	48
Middle	39	34	35	26	32	35
Bad	24	23	36	60	22	17

*PM : proposed method

Table 5. Processing time of clustering

	Image Size	Hue	Intensity	PM
Fig. 1(b)	640*480	0.001	0.015	0.5
Fig. 1(d)	640*480	0.016	0.001	0.5
Fig. 1(h)	640*480	0.015	0.046	0.5
Fig. 1(a)	1280*960	0.047	0.047	0.9
Fig. 1(c)	1280*480	0.047	0.049	0.9

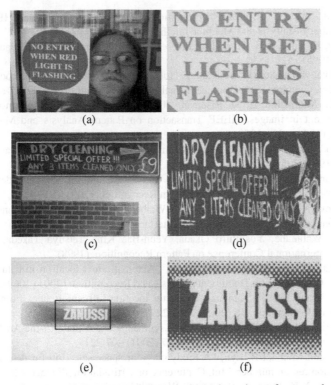

Fig. 7. The input images and the corresponding result: (a) is an input for a good case, (b) is the result of (a), (c) is an input for a middle case, (d) is the result of (c), (e) is input for a bad case, and (f) is the result of (e)

5   Conclusion

The performances of five components R, G, B, H, S, and I are analyzed and compared in terms of segmentation of text regions in color natural scene images. We conclude that the I component is dominant among the other components, but the hue component is better than the I component for the color natural scene image whose text region is highlighted. One dimensional k-means clustering algorithm is applied to HSI space to reduce the processing time. The method of selecting initial conditions is proposed to improve the performance of segmentation. Experimental results of natural scene images of ICDAR show that the performance and computational time of the method are enough for a mobile device. As we can see, segmentation using hue and intensity component works well when the one with intensity might fail.

References

1. D. Chen, H. Bourlard, J.P. Thiran, "Text identification in complex background using SVM," Proc. of the Int. Conf. on Computer Vision and Pattern Recognition, 2 (2001) 621-626

2. J. Ohya, A. Shio, S. Aksmatsu, "Recognition characters in scene images," IEEE Transaction on Pattern Analysis and Machine Intelligence, 16 (1994) 214-220
3. Y. Zhong, K. Karu, A.K. Jain, "Locating text in complex color images," Pattern Recognition, 28 (1995) 1523-1536
4. K. Sobottka, H. Bunke, H. Kronenberg, "Identification of text on colored book and journal covers," Int. Conference on Document Analysis and Recognition, (1999) 57-63
5. V. Wu, R. Manmatha, E. M. Riseman, "Textfinder: An automatic system to detect and recognize text in images," IEEE Transaction on Pattern Analysis and Machine Intelligence, 20 (1999) 1224-1229
6. K. Jain and B. Yu, "Automatic text location in images and video frames," Pattern Recognition, 31 (1998) 2055-2076
7. Ismail Haritaoglu, "Scene text extraction and translation for handheld devices," IEEE Conference on Computer Vision and Pattern Recognition, (2001) 408-413
8. Jing Zhang, Xilin Chen, Jie Yang, Alex Waibel, "A PDA-based sign translator," IEEE International Conference on Multimodal Interfaces, (2002) 217-222
9. Yasuhiko Watanabe, Yoshihiro Okada, Yeun-Bae Kim, Tetsuya Takeda, "Translation camera," International Conference on Pattern Recognition (1998)
10. Chuang Li, Xiaoqing Ding, Youshou Wu, "Automatic text location in natural scene images," Int. Conference on Document Analysis and Recognition, (2001) 1069-1073
11. Kongqiao Wang, Jari A. Kangas, "Character location in scene images from digital camera," Pattern Recognition, 36 (2003) 2287-2299
12. L. Lucchese and S.K. Mitra, "Color image segmentation: A State-of-the-Art Survey," Pro. of the Indian National Science Academy, 67 (2001) 207-221
13. Ping Guo and Michael R. Lyu, "A Study on color space selection for determining image segmentation region number," Int. Conference on Artificial Intelligence, (2000) 1127-1132
14. H.D. Cheng, X.H. Jiang, Y. Sun, Jingli Wang, "Color image segmentation: Advances and Prospects," Pattern Recognition, 34 (2001) 2259-2281
15. Jiang Gao, Jie Yang, "An adaptive algorithm for text detection from natural scenes," Int. Conference Computer Vision and Pattern Recognition, 2 (2001) 84-89
16. Xuewen Wang, Xiaoqing Ding, Changsong Liu, "Character extraction and recognition in natural scene image," Int. Conference on Document Analysis and Recognition, (2001) 1084-1088
17. Hao Wang, "Automatic character location and segmentation in color scene images," International Conference on Image Analysis and Processing, (2001) 2-7
18. R.O. Duda, P.E. Hart, and D.G.Stork, Pattern Classification, Wiley-Interscience, (2001)
19. C. Zhang and P. Wang, "A new method of color image segmentation based on intensity and hue clustering," Int. Conference on Pattern Recognition, 3 (2000) 3617-3621
20. James C. Bezdek and Nikhil R. Pal, "Some new indexes of cluster validity," IEEE Transactions on Systems, MAN, AND Cybernetics-Part B: Cybernetics, 28 (1998) 301-315
21. Siddheswar Ray and Rose H. Turi, "Determination of number of clusters in K-means clustering and application in colour image segmentation," International Conference on Advances in Pattern Recognition and Digital Techniques, (1999) 27-29
22. Jianqing Liu and Yee-Hong Yang, "Multiresolution color image segmentation," IEEE Tran. on Pattern Analysis and Machine Intelligence, 16 (1994) 689-700
23. http://www.essex.ac.uk/ese/icdar2003/index.htm
24. S.M. Lucas, A. Panaretos, L. Sosa, A. Tang, S. Wong and R. Young, "ICDAR2003 robust reading competitions," Int. conference on Document Analysis and Recognition, (2003) 682-687

25. Sing-Tze Bow, Pattern Recognition and Image Processing, Marcel Dekker, (2002)
26. S. Sural, G. Qian, and S. Pramanik, "Segmentation and histogram generation using the hsv color space for image retrieval," IEEE Int. Conf. on Image Processing, 2 (2002) 589-592
27. D. Comaniciu and P. Meer, Mean shift: A Robust approach towards feature space analysis," IEEE Transactions on Pattern Analysis and Machine Intelligence, 24 (2001) 1-18

3D Model-Based Tracking of the Human Body in Monocular Gray-Level Images

Bogdan Kwolek

Rzeszów University of Technology
W. Pola 2, 35-959 Rzeszów, Poland
bkwolek@prz.rzeszow.pl

Abstract. This paper presents a model-based approach to monocular tracking of human body using a non-calibrated camera. The tracking in monocular images is realized using a particle filter and an articulated 3D model with a cylinder-based representation of the body. In modeling the visual appearance of the person we employ appearance-adaptive models. The predominant orientation of the gradient combined with ridge cues provides strong orientation responses in the observation model of the particle filter. The phase that is measured using the Gabor filter contributes towards strong localization of the body limbs. The potential of our approach is demonstrated by tracking of the human body on real videos.

1 Introduction

Accurate and reliable tracking of three-dimensional human body is an important problem. It is particular substantial for service robots that should understand and predict the behavior of humans' beings in their vicinity. Although there exist several methods to perform 3D body tracking [1][2][3], there is still a need to improve the accuracy and reliability of such systems.

The method we utilize in our work relies on a 3D-2D matching between 3D features of a generic human model and corresponding 2D features extracted in a monocular image sequence. Given a 3D object model, the pose estimation problem can be defined as recovering and tracking the model parameters that include translation, rotation, and joint angles, so that the back-projected 3D model primitives match the 2D image features which have been extracted through an image analysis. Extracting 3D body configurations from monocular and uncalibrated video sequences is coupled with complex modeling as well as difficulties related to feature extraction. The process of extraction of the features in a cluttered scene and their matching to a self-occluding body model is an inherently complex task. The non-observable states are due to motions of body segments towards or away from the camera. The ambiguity, non-linearity, and non-observability make the posterior likelihoods over human pose space multi-modal and ill-conditioned. Efficient locating the body features for the 3D-2D matching during estimating the pose of the human body is therefore an important problem.

A. Gagalowicz and W. Philips (Eds.): MIRAGE 2007, LNCS 4418, pp. 494–505, 2007.

This work is motivated by necessity of equipment of mobile robot with basic capabilities of understanding and predicting some human behaviors. A service robot that does not understand people behavior might be dangerous to people and environment in a situation that has not been forecasted by a designer. Such understanding capability is therefore a basic prerequisite for service robots.

In this work, we focus on real-time estimating the pose of the upper body using a monocular and uncalibrated camera and a 3D model of human body. The tracking of the 3D model is realized using a kernel particle filter. By using such a filter we avoid the need for a huge number of particles to represent the probability distributions in high dimensional state space [4]. To accomplish strong localization of the body parts we utilize phase that is measured on the basis of Gabor filter responses. By using it our intent is to provide an alternative to edge and ridge cues when they are unreliable, and to supplement them if they are. In order to distinguish the person from the cluttered background effectively we employ appearance-adaptive models. The ridge cue that is combined with predominant orientation of the gradient in a window surrounding the feature provides strong orientation responses in the observation model. In this context, the novelty of our approach lies in the introduction of phase measured via the Gabor filter, predominant orientation as well as adaptive appearance models which results in an observation model with better localization of the limbs.

The paper is organized as follows. Next Section contains an overview of related work. Section 3. is devoted to a short presentation of the bases of probabilistic tracking. The image processing is described in Section 4. We then describe the components and details of the system. We present and discuss experimental results in Section 6. The paper concludes with a summary in the last Section.

2 Related Work

One of the first applications to track a human body in real-time using a single camera is the PFINDER system [5]. The applied body model is rather coarse and tracking provides only information about the position of head, hands and feet. Tracking of a human in 3D with limited computational resources on a mobile robot was described by Kortenkamp et al. [1]. This approach used depth information from a stereo camera to track a 3D body model. The work [6] employs an articulated 3D body model built on truncated cones and a cost function-based on edge and silhouette information. The images have been acquired using 3 calibrated cameras in scenarios with a black background. The experiments have been conducted with 4000 particles using an annealing particle filter. The computation times of this system are far from real-time. Similarly to mentioned work the multiple cameras are often employed to cope with body self-occlusions [7][8][9]. Some of the mentioned above approaches construct a probabilistic model of the body [5][7], whereas other approaches are based on a body model [6][9]. Using a body model only few authors have addressed the problem of 3D body tracking on the basis of uncalibrated monocular cameras [4][6][10][11][12].

3 Particle Filtering

Particle filter is an inference technique for estimating the *posterior* distribution $p(\mathbf{x}_t \mid \mathbf{z}_{1:t})$ for the object state $\mathbf{x}_t$ at time t given a sequence of observations $\mathbf{z}_{1:t}$. For nonlinear models, multi-modal, non-Gaussian or any combination of these models the particle filter provides a Monte Carlo solution to the recursive filtering equation $p(\mathbf{x}_t \mid \mathbf{z}_{1:t}) \propto p(\mathbf{z}_t \mid \mathbf{x}_t) \int p(\mathbf{x}_t \mid \mathbf{x}_{t-1}) \, p(\mathbf{x}_{t-1} \mid \mathbf{z}_{1:t-1}) d\mathbf{x}_{t-1}$. With this recursion we calculate the *posterior* distribution, given a dynamic model $p(\mathbf{x}_t \mid \mathbf{x}_{t-1})$ describing the state evolution and an observation model $p(\mathbf{z}_t \mid \mathbf{x}_t)$ describing the likelihood that a state $\mathbf{x}_t$ causes the measurement $\mathbf{z}_t$.

The main idea of particle filtering is to represent the probability distribution by a set of weighted particles $S = \{(\mathbf{x}_t^{(n)}, \pi_t^{(n)}) \mid n = 1, ..., N\}$ evolving over time on the basis of simulation-updating scheme. The resampling selects with higher probability particles that have a high likelihood associated with them, while preserving the asymptotic approximation of the particle-based posterior representation. Sequential Importance Sampling (SIR) is the basic algorithm with resampling applied at every time step. The prior $p(\mathbf{x}_t \mid \mathbf{x}_{t-1}^{(n)})$ is used as the importance density for drawing samples. Within the SIR scheme the weighting equation takes the form $\pi_t^{(n)} \propto p(\mathbf{z}_t \mid \mathbf{x}_t^{(n)})$. This simplification gives a variant of a well-known particle filter in computer vision, CONDENSATION [13]. Since the optimal importance density relies on both the present observation $\mathbf{z}_t$ and previous state $\mathbf{x}_{t-1}$ which are not considered in such a scheme, the SIR-based sampling is not too effective.

4 Image Processing

At the beginning of this section, we show how low-level features for determining the limb orientation are computed. Gabor filter will be presented as the second topic. A description of appearance modeling ends this section.

4.1 Low-Level Features

The edge is employed in comparison of the gradient angle with the limb angle β resulting from the 3D model. The gradient is computed at the position in the image plane, where the edge of the considered limb is projected. The orientation of the whole limb can be determined by averaging over the feature orientations laying on the projected cylinder. The model is generated in a variety of possible configurations and overlaid on the image to find the true body pose. The ridge detection is based on the LoG filter. The variance of the Gaussian can be chosen such that the feature of interest is highlighted. Therefore the ridge cues are employed to find in the image the elongated structures of a specified thickness. The response of the ridge cue depends on the size of the limb at the image and thus it strongly depends on the distance of the limb to the camera. On the basis of the estimated distance of the limb to the camera the appropriate level in the

Gaussian pyramid is chosen to obtain the suitable responses of the ridge filter. The steered response is calculated by applying an interpolation formula to the second partial derivatives d:

$$f_R(\beta) = \left| \sin^2 \beta \, d_{xx} + \cos^2 \beta \, d_{yy} - 2 \sin \beta \, \cos \beta \, d_{xy} \right| - \\ \left| \cos^2 \beta \, d_{xx} + \sin^2 \beta \, d_{yy} + 2 \sin \beta \, \cos \beta \, d_{xy} \right| . \tag{1}$$

4.2   Predominant Orientation of the Feature

The orientation of a feature is assumed as the predominant orientation of the gradient in a window around the considered feature. The predominant orientation is calculated as the quadratically interpolated maximum of the histogram of the gradient orientations within a window around the feature. The histogram is weighted both by the magnitude of the gradient and a Gaussian window centered on the feature. Before determining the maximum the histogram is smoothed by a moving average filter. In addition, each local maximum with a value above 0.8% of the global maxium is retained.

4.3   Gabor Filter

The choice of Gabor filter responses is biologically motivated since they model the response of human visual cortical cells [14]. Gabor filters extract the orientation-dependent frequency contents, i.e. edge like features. The main advantage of Gabor wavelets is that they allow analysis of signals at different scales, or resolution, and further they accommodate frequency and position simultaneously. Gabor filters remove most of variation in lighting and contrast. They are also robust against shifts and small object deformations. The Gabor wavelet is essentially a sinewave modulated by a Gaussian envelope. The 2-D kernel of Gabor filter is defined in the following manner [15]:

$$f(x, y, \theta_k, \lambda) = \exp\left[-\frac{1}{2} \left\{ \frac{R_1^2}{\sigma_x^2} + \frac{R_2^2}{\sigma_y^2} \right\} \right] \exp\left\{ i \frac{2\pi R_1}{\lambda} \right\} \tag{2}$$

where $R_1 = x\cos\theta_k + y\sin\theta_k$ and $R_2 = -x\sin\theta_k + y\cos\theta_k$, σ_x and σ_y are the standard deviations of the Gaussian envelope along the x and y dimensions, λ and θ_k are the wavelength and orientation of the sinusoidal plane wave, respectively. The spread of the Gaussian envelope is defined in terms of the wavelength λ. θ_k is defined by $\theta_k = \frac{\pi(k-1)}{n}$, $k = 1, 2, ..., n$, where n denotes the number of orientations that are taken into account. For example, when $n = 4$, four values of orientation θ_k are used: 0°, 45°, 90°, and 135°.

A Gabor filter response is achieved by convolving the filter kernel given by (2) with an image. The response of the filter for sampling point (x, y) is as follows:

$$g(x, y, \theta_k, \lambda) = \sum_{u=-(N-x)}^{N-x-1} \sum_{v=-(N-y)}^{N-y-1} I(x + u, y + v) f(u, v, \theta_k, \lambda) \tag{3}$$

where $I(x, y)$ denotes a $N \times N$ grayscale image.

In this work four different orientations and four different wavelengths have been utilized, see Fig. 1. The Gabor filter responses were used to locally measure the phase. In contrast to work [16] we are not interested in determining the highest score for the features being in the correspondence, but in determining a weighting factor to express degree of similarity between potential matches. The simplest way to achieve this goal is to use a Gabor filter with orientation θ and scale λ to extract the phase $\phi_{\theta,\lambda}$ of features i and j and then to compare the considered features according to: $\exp\left(-\mid\phi_{\theta,\lambda}(i)-\phi_{\theta,\lambda}(j)\mid\right)$. Using the phase of all filters we obtain the following correspondence measure:

$$G_{ij} = c\prod_{\theta,\lambda}\exp\left(-\mid\phi_{\theta,\lambda}(i)-\phi_{\theta,\lambda}(j)\mid\right) \tag{4}$$

where c is a normalization constant ensuring that G_{ij} varies between 0 and 1.

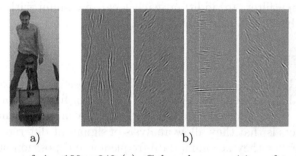

a)   b)

Fig. 1. Test image of size 100×240 (a). Gabor decomposition of test image at four different orientations and for real channels (b).

Figure 2 demonstrates pairs of images with some phase-based matching results. Left images in each pair depict the locations at the corners of the projected model that have been employed in matching, whereas the right images depict coherence probability between pixels at marked locations and image pixels from Fig. 1a. The images illustrate the Gabor wavelet's capability to match coherent image structures in subsequent frames during human model tracking.

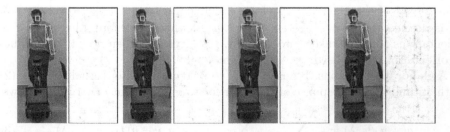

Fig. 2. Searching for pixel coherence using Gabor filter responses. Left images in the pair demonstrate the locations of pixels undergoing matching, the right ones are probability images expressing coherence between the marked pixel and image at Fig. 1a.

4.4 Visual Appearance Modeling Using Adaptive Models

Our intensity-based appearance model was inspired by work [17] which proposed the model $\mathcal{WSL}$ consisting of three components. The Wandering-Stable-Lost components are employed to track an object while adapting to slowly changing appearance and providing robustness to partial occlusions. During model adaptation each $\mathcal{WSL}$ component votes according to its level of stability. The method has been shown to yield reliable tracking of human faces.

By the usage of 3D human model in this method we can provide and additional support for handling self-occlusions and therefore restrict the adaptation of parametric model to visible pixels. In our approach the model that is assigned to a single data observation d_t consists of three components, namely, the W-component expressing the two-frame variations, the S-component characterizing the stable structure within all previous observations and C-component representing a constant object template. The model represents thus the appearances existing in all observations up to time $t-1$. It is a mixture of Gaussians with centers $\{\mu_{i,t} \mid i = w, s, c\}$ and their corresponding variances $\{\sigma^2_{i,t} \mid i = w, s, c\}$ and mixing probabilities $\mathbf{m}_t = \{m_{i,t} \mid i = w, s, c\}$. The mixture probability density for a new data d_t conditioned on the past observations can be expressed by

$$p(d_t|d_{t-1}, \mu_{s,t-1}, \sigma^2_{s,t-1}, \mathbf{m}_{t-1}) = m_{w,t-1}p_w(d_t|\mu_{w,t-1}, \sigma^2_w) +$$
$$m_{s,t-1}p_s(d_t|\mu_{s,t-1}, \sigma^2_{s,t-1}) + m_{c,t-1}p_c(d_t|\mu_{c,0}, \sigma^2_c). \tag{5}$$

In wandering term the mean is the observation d_{t-1} from the previous frame and the variance is fixed at σ^2_w. The stable component $p_s(d_t|\mu_{s,t-1}, \sigma^2_{s,t-1})$ is intended to express the appearance properties that are relatively stable in time. A Gaussian density function with slowly accommodated parameters $\mu_{s,t-1}, \sigma^2_{s,t-1}$ captures the behavior of such temporally stable image observations. The fixed component accounts for data expressing the similarity with initial object appearance. The mean is the observation d_0 from the initial frame and the variance is fixed at σ^2_c

Similarly to [17] we assume that with respect to the contributions to current appearance the previous data observations are forgotten according to exponential function. The update of the current appearance model A_{t-1} to A_t is done using the on-line EM algorithm. The posterior ownership probabilities $\{o_{i,t} \mid i = w, s, c\}$ forming a distribution (with $\sum_i o_{i,t}(d_t) = 1$) are computed in E-step for each data d_t as follows:

$$o_{i,t}(d_t) = m_{i,t-1}p_i(d_t|\mu_{i,t-1}, \sigma^2_{i,t-1}) \mid i = w, s, c, \tag{6}$$

Then the mixing probabilities are updated using an accommodation factor α according to:

$$m_{i,t} = \alpha o_{i,t} + (1 - \alpha)m_{i,t-1} \mid i = w, s, c. \tag{7}$$

The higher the α value, the faster the model adapts to the new data. During the M-step the ML estimates of the mean and variance are computed using the moments of the past observations. The first and the second-moment images are computed recursively in the following manner:

$$M_t^{(p)} = \alpha d_t^j o_{s,t}(d_t) + (1 - \alpha)M_{t-1}^{(p)} \mid p = 1, 2. \tag{8}$$

In the last step the mixture centers and the variances are updated as follows:

$$\mu_{s,t} = \frac{M_t^{(1)}}{m_{s,t}}, \quad \mu_{w,t} = d_{t-1}, \quad \mu_{c,t} = d_0,$$

$$\sigma_s^2 = \frac{M_t^{(2)}}{m_{s,t}} - \mu_{s,t}^2, \quad \sigma_{w,t}^2 = \sigma_{w,0}^2, \quad \sigma_{c,t}^2 = \sigma_{c,0}^2. \tag{9}$$

In order to initialize the model the initial moment images are set using the following formulas: $M_0^{(1)} = m_{s,0}d_0$ and $M_0^{(2)} = m_{s,0}(\sigma_{s,0}^2 + d_0^2)$.

To demonstrate the usefulness of the adaptive appearance models in tracking we performed various experiments on freely available test sequences. Figure 3 depicts some tracking results that were obtained on PETS-ICVS 2003 test sequence. The original images 768 pixels wide and 576 high have been converted to size of 320×240 by subsampling (consisting in selecting odd pixels in only odd lines) and bicubic based image scaling. Inference was performed using 50 particles and CONDENSATION algorithm. The observation likelihood was calculated according to the following equation:

$$p(\mathbf{z}_t \mid \mathbf{x}_t) = \prod_{j=1}^{M} \sum_{i=w,s,c} \frac{m_{i,t}(j)}{\sqrt{2\pi\sigma_{i,t}^2(j)}} \exp\left[-\frac{d_t(j) - \mu_{i,t}(j)}{2\sigma_{i,t}^2(j)} \right], \tag{10}$$

where d_t denotes the value of gray pixel, M is the number of pixels, and $i = w, s, c$. The samples are propagated on the basis of a dynamic model $\mathbf{x}_t = \mathbf{x}_{t-1} + w_t$, where $\mathbf{x}_t = \{x, y\}$ and w_t is a multivariate Gaussian random variable. The size of face pattern in this sequence is comparable to the size of face pattern from Fig. 1a. We can observe that despite the fixed size of the object template the method enables reliable tracking of the face. The cycle time of the tracking at P IV 2.4 GHz is approximately 0.014 sec.

+10   +50   +100 +150 +180 +190 +200 +220 +230 +240   +250 +270 +300 +325 +350 +370

Fig. 3. Face tracking using adaptive appearance models (top row). The tracking starts at frame #11000 and the images from left to right depict some tracking results in frames #11010, #10050, etc. Next rows present the evolution of the mean of stable (middle row) and wandering (bottom row) components during tracking.

Figure 4. illustrates how the mixing probabilities at two locations (x=7, y=10 and x=9, y=10) in the window of the tracker evolve over time. The static size template is not subject to drifting and algorithm adapts to changing appearances of the face. The mixing probabilities change something more in the second part of the sequence, i.e. starting at frame #11000 + 200, see also Fig. 3.

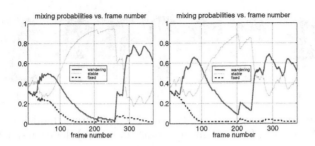

Fig. 4. Mixing probabilities versus frame number

5   3D Body Tracking

Modeling the appearance of humans will be presented as the first topic in this section. The observation and motion models will be presented afterwards.

5.1   Modeling the Visual Appearance of Humans

We use an articulated 3D body model composed of cylinders with ellipsoid cross sections [10][4]. Such representation gives best outcomes when the cylinder is observed by a camera from the side. The more the cylinder axis is parallel to the optical axis of the camera, e.g. arm pointing directly into the camera, the more the pose estimation is inaccurate. A given pose configuration is determined by the relative joint angles between connected limbs and the position and orientation of the torso. The kinematic structure is completed by individual joint angle limits, which model the physical constraints of the human body. A typical model of an upper body with two arms has 13 degrees of freedom. The 3D body model is back-projected into the image plane through a pinhole-camera model. This yields an approximate representation of the 3D body model in the image plane consisting of 2D polygons for each limb. The model is generated in a variety of possible configurations and overlaid on the image plane to find the true body pose.

Given three coordinates and three angles determining the pose of the torso we employed a simple cylindrical model depicted in Fig. 5a to re-render the object texture into the requested object pose. Using such re-rendered images and the adaptive appearance models we can compute the observation likelihoods. In our approach the re-rendering is only applied to torso, see Fig. 5c, but for demonstrational purposes we utilize face images to show the usefulness of re-rendering in template matching, see Fig. 5b. The images from bottom row in Fig. 5b depict some re-rendered faces to frontal pose. These images demonstrate that the usage of such simple cylindrical model consisting of only 12 triangles can lead to better object representation for object matching based on a model containing an initial template. In particular, we can observe that the re-rendered face from the fifth bottom image in Fig. 5b would give a high similarity score in case of comparison with the frontal face template.

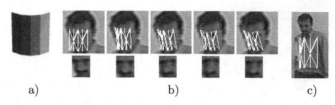

a)   b)   c)

Fig. 5. 3D cylindrical face/torso model (a). The cylindrical model overlaid on face images (b) and torso (c). Bottom images in the column (b) depict re-rendered images.

5.2   Motion and Observation Model

One way to model the transition of the state is using a random walk which can be described by

$$\mathbf{x}_{t+1} = \mathbf{x}_t + \eta, \tag{11}$$

where $\eta \sim N(0, \nu^2)$, and ν^2 is typically learned from training sequences. The reason for not using a specific motion model in the particle filter is that we want to track general human motions.

Assuming that the cues and limbs are independent the observation model takes the form:

$$p(\mathbf{z}_t \mid \mathbf{x}_t) = \prod_{i=1}^{L} \prod_{k=r,a,g,d} p(i, k), \tag{12}$$

where L denotes number of cylinders in the 3D model, r represents ridge, a stands for adaptive appearance model, g accounts for phase, d is dominant orientation and $p(i, k)$ denotes the likelihood of the whole limb i for cue k. The likelihood is calculated on the basis of the following Gaussian weighting: $p(\mathbf{z}^C \mid \mathbf{x}) = (\sqrt{2\pi}\sigma)^{-1} e^{-\frac{1-\rho}{2\sigma^2}}$, where ρ denotes the response of the filter for the considered cue. The filter responses are calculated on the basis of techniques described in Section 4.

To exploit the structure of the probability density distribution and to reduce the number of particles an iterative mode-seeking via the mean-shift is employed. The density distribution is estimated through placing a kernel function on each particle and then shifting the particles to high weight areas [4].

6   Experiments

To test the proposed method of 3D body tracking in monocular images we performed several experiments on real images. Experiments demonstrated that through the tracking of the human legs the robot is able to detect collisions. We have also looked at how the system tracks the upper body. The lower arms are one of the hardest body parts to track because in comparison with legs they are smaller and move faster. The modeling their motion is harder. In contrast, the face has more features and textures than the legs and arms and can be tracked easily.

During computation of likelihoods we utilize various combinations of cues. The ridge cues as well as dominant orientations are not utilized in computation of likelihoods of torso, face and hands. The torso and face are tracked in conjuction. The phase is computed using the fast method [18] at four points of the lower arm cylinders. The dominant orientation is extracted at 20 points, whereas the ridge at 30 points of each cylinder.

In order to show the stability of our approach to images with complex background, we have performed experiments in a typical home/office environment. Figure 6 shows some tracking results. The person depicted at this figure is wearing a green shirt and is standing in front of plants. The color of the wall in the background is similar to color of human skin. The mentioned above figure illustrates the behavior of the algorithm in such conditions. The tracking has been done using the kernel particle filter doing 3 mean-shift iterations and built on 200 particles. The adaptive appearance models were employed in computation of the likelihoods of torso, face and lower arms. Other experiments demonstrated that this algorithm allows the tracking of the human body in cluttered environments if no large self-occlusions occur.

The algorithm can estimate a direction of pointing towards an object using only 110 particles and doing 2-3 mean shift iterations. Using such settings the algorithm calculates the estimate of 3D hand position at a frame rate about 8 Hz. A configuration of the algorithm with 500 and even 250 particles gives repeatable results. The algorithm was tested on images of size 320x240 acquired

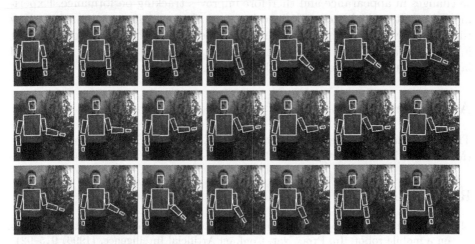

Fig. 6. Tracking of the upper body using gray and monocular images. Every 10th frame from the sequence is depicted.

by EVI-D31 color camera. A typical laptop computer equipped with 2.4 GHz Pentium IV is utilized to run the C/C++ software under Windows control.

Initial experiments demonstrate that a proposal distribution in form of a Gaussian that is generated on the basis of the face position estimated in advance by a particle filter can lead to shorter computation time. In particular, this particle filter can perform the tracking of the face using smaller number of particles in comparison with the 3D tracker. Such configuration of the system can be used in many scenarios with a person facing the camera. Comparing the appearance-based cues with color we found that the former provides better results. The dominant orientation gives better estimates in comparison to edges. The overall performance of the system built on adaptive appearance models and dominant orientation is better in comparison to a configuration of system based on color and edges. We expect a prior model of body motion can likely improve robustness of the system further. Color images would provide additional information in stabilization of the tracker. But determining which image features are most informative requires more research. The initialization of the tracking algorithm is done manually before starting the tracking. An occlusion test is performed, particularly with respect to pixels for which the Gabor filter responses are calculated.

7   Conclusions

We have presented a model-based approach for monocular tracking of the human body using a non-calibrated camera. By employing ridge, dominant orientation, phase and appearance the proposed method can estimate the pose of the upper body using a monocular and uncalibrated camera. The proposed combination of cues leads to higher performance of the system and better quality of tracking. Once the human body is being tracked, the appearance model adapts according to changes in appearance and therefore improves tracking performance. Experimental results, which were obtained in a typical home/office environment show the feasibility of our approach to estimate the pose of the upper body against a complex background. The resulting system runs in real-time on a standard laptop computer installed on a real mobile agent.

Acknowledgment

This work has been supported by Polish Ministry of Education and Science (MNSzW) within the projects 3 T11C 057 30 and N206 019 31/2664.

References

1. Kortenkamp, D., Huber, E., Bonasso, R.P.: Recognizing and interpreting gestures on a mobile robot. In: Proc. Nat. Conf. on Artificial Intelligence. (1996) 915–921
2. Cham, T., Rehg, J.: A multiple hypothesis approach to figure tracking. In: Int. Conf. on Computer Vision and Patt. Recognition. (1999) 239–245

3. Deutscher, J., Reid, I.: Articulated body motion capture by stochastic search. Int. J. Comput. Vision **61** (2005) 185–205
4. Fritsch, J., Schmidt, J., Kwolek, B.: Kernel particle filter for real-time 3d body tracking in monocular color images. In: IEEE Int. Conf. on Face and Gesture Rec., Southampton, UK, IEEE Computer Society Press (2006) 567–572
5. Wren, C., Azarbayejani, A., Darrell, T., Pentland, A.: Pfinder: Real-time tracking of the human body. IEEE Trans. on Pattern Analysis and Machine Intelligence **19** (1997) 780–785
6. Deutscher, J., Blake, A., Reid, I.: Articulated body motion capture by annealed particle filtering. In: IEEE Int. Conf. on Pattern Recognition. (2000) 126–133
7. Sigal, L., Bhatia, S., Roth, S., Black, M.J., Isard, M.: Tracking loose-limbed people. In: IEEE Int. Conf. on Computer Vision and Pattern Recognition. (2004) vol. 1, 421–428
8. Rosales, R., Siddiqui, M., Alon, J., Sclaroff, S.: Estimating 3d body pose using uncalibrated cameras. In: Int. Conf. on Computer Vision and Pattern Recognition. (2001) 821–827
9. Kehl, R., Bray, M., Gool, L.V.: Markerless full body tracking by integrating multiple cues. In: ICCV Workshop on Modeling People and Human Interaction, Beijing, China (2005)
10. Sidenbladh, H., Black, M., Fleet, D.: Stochastic tracking of 3d human figures using 2d image motion. In: European Conference on Computer Vision. (2000) 702–718
11. Sminchisescu, C., Triggs, B.: Mapping minima and transitions of visual models. In: European Conference on Computer Vision, Copenhagen (2002)
12. Urtasum, R., Fleet, D.J., Fua, P.: Monocular 3-d tracking of the golf swing. In: IEEE Int. Conf. on Computer Vision and Pattern Recognition. (2005) vol. 2, 932–938
13. Isard, M., Blake, A.: Condensation - conditional density propagation for visual tracking. Int. J. of Computer Vision **29** (1998) 5–28
14. Jones, J., Palemer, L.: An evaluation of the two dimensional gabor filter model of simple receptive fields in cat striate cortex. Journal of Neurophysiology **58** (1987) 1233–1258
15. Nixon, M., Aguado, A.: Feature extraction and image processing. Newnes, Oxford, Boston (2002)
16. Fleet, D.: Disparity from local weighted phase-correlation. In: Proc. IEEE Int. Conf. on System Man and Cybernetics (SMC). (1994) 46–48
17. Jepson, A.D., Fleet, D.J., El-Maraghi, T.: Robust on-line appearance models for visual tracking. PAMI **25** (2003) 1296–1311
18. Nestares, O., Navarro, R., Portilla, J., Tabernero, A.: Efficient spatial-domain implementation of a multiscale image representation based on gabor functions. J. Electronic Imaging **7** (1998) 166–173

Measurement of the Position of the Overhead Electric-Railway Line Using the Stereo Images

Hyun-Chul Kim[1], Yeul-Min Baek[1], Sun-Gi Kim[1], Jong-Guk Park[2], and Whoi-Yul Kim[1]

[1] Department of Electronics and Computer Engineering, Hanyang University, Haengdang-dong, Seongdong-gu, Seoul, South Korea
hckim@vision.hanyang.ac.kr, ymbaek@vision.hanyang.ac.kr, sungi@yuravision.co.kr, wykim@hanyang.ac.kr
[2] 2iSYS, Geumjung-dong, Gunpo, Gyeonggi-Do, South Korea
pjk@2isys.com

Abstract. In this paper, we propose a method that measures the height and stagger of an overhead electric-railway line using the stereo images. Two 1624×1236 pixel area scanner CCD cameras are used. To quickly and accurately extract, from a photographed image, the area of the overhead line on which the line laser is shone, we consider the established fact that the overhead line is the lowest among the electric wires. And to precisely measure the height and stagger in low resolution, sub-pixel and line fitting methods are used. Also, because of the different pixel resolution of the camera according to the overhead line position, we compensate the measurement result through camera calibration. We aimed for a measurement accuracy of 1mm error and indeed our experimental results show that the proposed method achieves that.

1 Introduction

An overhead line is used to transmit electrical energy from the energy supply point to an electric train. As the electric train passes under the overhead line, one or more current collection devices on the roof of the train make contact with the wire. To achieve good high-speed current collection and to run the train both quickly and safely, it is necessary to keep the overhead line geometry within defined limits throughout the length of the line. Therefore, it is necessary to accurately measure and maintain the height and stagger of the overhead line.

Over the last 40 years, numerous Overhead line Geometry Measurement systems have been developed to accurately determine the height and stagger of the overhead line with respect to the track [2-4]. Those systems may be broadly classified as manual or automatic, contact or non-contact, and portable or vehicle-borne [1]. The latest technologies are capable of measuring the height and stagger to a high accuracy within 5mm. However, such devices are constructed of many parts, their manufacture is thus very expensive, and their operation and control is difficult. Therefore, a new method, one that solves those problem and measures to a high accuracy, is required.

A. Gagalowicz and W. Philips (Eds.): MIRAGE 2007, LNCS 4418, pp. 506–515, 2007.

In this paper, we propose a method that measures the height and stagger of an overhead electric-railway line using the stereo images. We use two 1624×1236 pixel area scanner CCD cameras to take a photograph. To mark the position of the overhead line that to be measured, a line laser positioned 500mm away from the straight line that joins the two cameras is used. To easily and accurately segment, from stereo images, the area of the overhead line onto which the laser is shone, we consider the established fact that the overhead line is lowest among the electric wires. Given that the pixel resolution of those two cameras is not sufficient to achieve the desired 1mm-error measurement accuracy, sub-pixel and line fitting methods are used. The sub-pixel method is used to determine the center coordinates of the area of the overhead line onto which the laser can be shone more precisely. The line fitting method is used to compensate incorrect height and stagger measurement resulting from various external causes. Finally, the measurement result is compensated again, because the camera's pixel resolution differs according to the height and stagger of the overhead line.

The rest of this paper is organized as follows. In Section 2, we introduce the proposed method to measure the height and stagger of the overhead line. Section 3 shows the experimental results for the test stereo images. Finally, Section 4 presents conclusions.

2   Measurement of the Height and Stagger

Usually, it is possible to accurately measure the distance of an object from the camera plane, which procedure does not require equipment other than a pair of digital cameras of known field stop diameter and focal length [3]. However, to do this, it is necessary to determine the exact position of the object in the stereo images. Various methods [4], [5], [7] of demonstrably good performance have been developed to find the position of the object. By applying those methods to our measurement algorithm, we can calculate the overhead line's height and stagger using only the pair of digital cameras.

In our study, a line laser was used to mark the position of the overhead line to be measured. And, to determine the position of the object in the stereo images, the fact that the overhead line is lowest among the electric wires was used instead of applying [4], [5], [7]. Because the execution time of the above stereo matching methods is not sufficiently fast in our application.

Our measurement algorithm consists of (a) Gaussian filtering, (b) segmentation of the laser area of the overhead line, (c) calculation of the center coordinates, (d) line fitting for the center coordinates, (e) calculation of the height and stagger, (f) compensation of the height and stagger, and (g) line fitting for the height and stagger.

2.1   Gaussian Filtering

As preprocessing, two-dimensional(2D) discrete Gaussian filtering [6] is applied to an input image. Gaussian filtering is used principally to merge the divided laser regions according to the photographic circumstances(e.g. weather, flying bugs). 2D discrete Gaussian filtering is defined as:

$$I'(x, y) = \sum_{m=0}^{M-1}\sum_{n=0}^{N-1} I(m,n)G(m+x,n+y) \tag{1}$$

Here, I' is the output intensity, I is the original intensity and G is the 2D Gaussian function of $M \times N$ size. G is defined as:

$$G(x, y) = qe^{\left(\frac{-(x^2+y^2)}{c^2}\right)} \tag{2}$$

where q is determined in order to normaliz the Gaussian function by

$$\int\int qe^{\left(\frac{-(x^2+y^2)}{c^2}\right)} dxdy = 1 \tag{3}$$

and c is the scale that determines the size of the neighborhood.

Figure 1 shows a zoom-in image of the area of the overhead line onto which the laser is shone. As shown, the laser area is non-uniform because of the properties of the laser and the difference of the camera's pixel resolution. And if the photographic circumstances are bad, an image like that shown in Figure 1 (b) results.

(a)   (b)

Fig. 1. Enlarged laser area of the overhead line

2.2 Segmentation of the Laser Area of the Overhead Line

As stated above, the overhead line is the lowest among the electric wires. Therefore, the area of the overhead line onto which the laser is shone always exists at the highest position in the photographed image, and can be segmented easily from that image. The steps by which the laser area of the overhead line is segmented are as follows.

(a) Convert a gray scale input image into a binary image and set the binarization threshold value to 100.

(b) Apply the labeling [6], [11] algorithm to the binary image. If the size of an labeled area is smaller than 25 or larger than 45, that area is treated as noise because usually the laser area of the overhead line has a size of 30~40.

(c) Calculate the approximate center coordinates of each labeled area.

(d) Sort the y-axis value of the approximated center coordinates in descending order.

(e) Select the area that has the smallest y-axis value. Here, if three areas have close values, select all three areas as the laser area of the overhead line, because a total of three overhead lines can appear at the same time on South Korean electric railways.

(f) Determine a pair of laser areas corresponding to a same overhead line among the segmented areas by referring to the before and next input images.

2.3 Calculation of the Center Coordinates

The pixel resolution of our camera for an overhead line at 5m height is about 4mm. This order of pixel resolution, when the height calculation is performed according to the pixel unit, renders it difficult to achieve the target accuracy of 1mm error. In order to solve this problem, a sub-pixel method is used.

The sub-pixel methods generally are classified into two types. One type is based on the edge [7-8] and the other type is based on the center of gravity [9-10]. The former type does not work well when the subject of photography is not fixed. Therefore, in this work, the sub-pixel method based on the center of gravity was used to calculate the center coordinates, which are defined as:

$$(x_c, y_c) = \left(\frac{\sum\limits_{x,y\in\Omega} w(x,y)x}{\sum\limits_{x,y\in\Omega} w(x,y)}, \frac{\sum\limits_{x,y\in\Omega} w(x,y)y}{\sum\limits_{x,y\in\Omega} w(x,y)} \right) \tag{4}$$

Here, Ω denotes the set used to calculate the center of gravity, and $w(x,y)$ is the pixel intensity at (x,y).

2.4 Line Fitting for the Center Coordinates

Although the center coordinates of the laser area of the overhead line, with the sub-pixel method, are calculated more precisely than with the pixel resolution, incorrect coordinates owing to the insufficient resolution or external physical impact nonetheless can be calculated. To solve this problem the line fitting method is used. Because the overhead line is a continuous object, effectively maintains the variation of the height and stagger over short distance.

The Weighted Least Square Method [12] is used with the line fitting method, and it decreases the effect of noise by giving small weight. It is defined as equation 5, and Figure 2 shows the line fitting process.

$$error_w = \sum_i w_i \left(Y_i - \hat{Y}_i \right)^2 = \sum_i w_i \left(Y_i - (a + bX_i) \right)^2 \tag{5}$$

Here, Y_i is the original center coordinates and $\overline{Y}_i$ is the center coordinates adjusted by the line fitting method.

$$w_i = \begin{cases} 1 & if\ r < c \\ c/r & otherwise \end{cases} \tag{6}$$

where w_i is the Huber weight [12], r is the distance between the data point and the line and c is the threshold value.

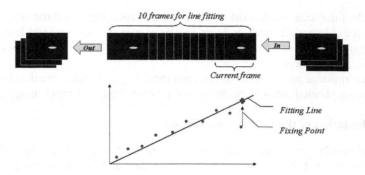

Fig. 2. Line fitting processing

2.5   Calculation of the Height and Stagger

The overhead line's height and stagger is calculated using equation (7) and it can be derived easily using the trigonometric ratio, as shown in Figure 3.

$$h(height) = \frac{L \cdot f}{dl + dr}, \quad s(stagger) = \frac{h \cdot dl - f(dl + 0.5L)}{f} \tag{7}$$

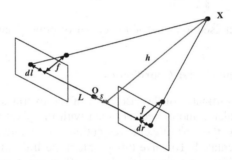

Fig. 3. Geometric relations between two cameras and an object

2.6   Compensation of the Height and Stagger

Although the actual height of p_1 and p_2 is equal, if the stagger of p_1 and p_2 differ, the measured heights are not the same. Likewise, if the height of p_1 and p_2 differ, the measured staggers are not the same, not even if the actual staggers of p_1 and p_2 are equal. The reason this problem occurs is that the pixel resolution of the camera differs according to the height and stagger of the overhead line. Therefore, the measured height and stagger should be compensated, considering the pixel resolution according to the height and stagger.

Usually, compensation coefficients have values that differ according to the height and stagger. However, those values were almost equal in close-proximity positions. We experimentally confirmed that the compensation coefficients had almost the same value for a proximity within 100mm. Thus, we divided the total moving range of the overhead line to the height direction into 9, to the stagger direction into 7, and calculated the compensation coefficients in each divided region($R_{i,j}$). To compensate the result, four coefficients($\alpha_i, \beta_j, c_i, d_j$) were used, which were determined by minimizing the MSE(mean square error) between the value measured by the proposed method and the actual value.

$$h' = \alpha_i \cdot h + c_i \qquad i = 0,1...,6,7$$
$$s' = \beta_j \cdot s + d_j \qquad j = 0,1...,7,8$$

(8)

Here, h', s' is the compensated height and stagger, respectively. Next we had to determine whether compensation coefficients should be applied for h, s, which determination was made by choosing the compensation coefficients that minimize the Euclidean distance between the h, s and h'', s''. Here, h'', s'' is the height and stagger corresponding to the $R_{i,j}$ and measured by the proposed method.

2.7 Line Fitting for the Height and Stagger

The line fitting method is used to again correct the height and stagger, as the final process. Its purpose and procedure is the same as in line fitting for the center coordinates except the fact that an input is the measured height and stagger.

3 Experimental Results

Figure 4 shows our measurement system. It consists of two 1624×1236 pixel area scanner CCD cameras and one line laser of 660nm wavelength and 100mW power. The interference optical filter was installed in front of the camera lens in order to receive only the laser's wavelength. The distance between the two cameras is 1500mm, and the distance between the camera and the line laser is 500mm. The reason we used the high power laser was to achieve a good image in the daytime. Although we used the interference optical filter to receive only the laser's wavelength, the sun emits equal wavelength to that of the laser. Therefore, if the power of the laser is low, it is difficult to receive the laser's wavelength and to achieve a good image like that shown in Figure 5 (a). Figure 5 shows two images, one photographed in the daytime and the other photographed at night.

Figure 6 (a) shows the result of the application of the labeling algorithm to the image in Figure 5 (a). A total of six areas are labeled, and two of those were selected as the overhead line area because they were far from the other areas and had a very close y-axis value

The segmentation task was easy for the night image but difficult for the day image, because the day image could not be converted into a binary image like that in Figure 5 (a). The reason is that the gray level[230,255] of the background(sky) and the gray level[240,255] of the laser are similar as shown in Figure 5 (b). Therefore, the day image required additional work to segment the laser area of the overhead line. To solve this problem, we used Hough transform [6]. First we applied Hough transform

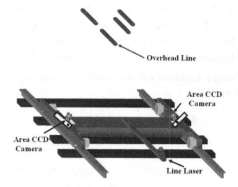

Fig. 4. System of the measurement device

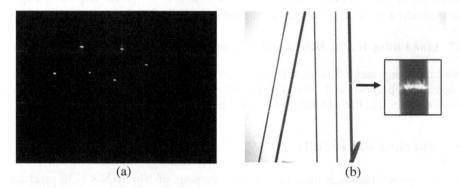

Fig. 5. Photographed image (a) at night, (b) in the daytime

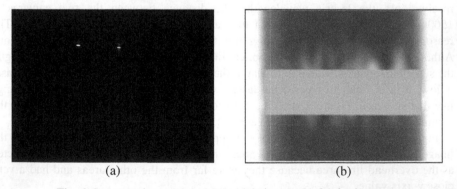

Fig. 6. Segmentation result in (a) the night image, (b) the day image

to the day image and found the straight lines corresponding to the overhead line. Then we searched the laser area along those straight lines. Figure 6 (b) shows the segmentation result for the day image. The segmentation region is displayed in the rectangle that has the gray level of 183.

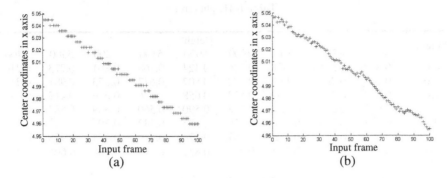

Fig. 7. Result of center coordinate calculation by (a) pixel, (b) sub-pixel

Figure 7 shows the result of the center coordinates calculation by pixel unit and sub-pixel unit. As the input frame grew, the actual stagger of the overhead line was moved by 1mm. To perform and to verify following accuracy experiments, the actual height and stagger were measured by a straight-line laser ruler with 1mm precision. The accuracy of the center coordinates calculation was improved greatly by using the sub-pixel method, as shown in Figure 7 (b). Figure 7 (b) has the form of the line function, in contrast to Figure 7 (a), which has the form of the step function.

Figure 8 (a) shows the difference between the actual value and the value measured by the proposed method. Here, the difference indicates a measurement error. The number of the input was set to 5 to perform the line fitting for the center coordinates and for the height and stagger. The plus-sign line denotes the measured height, and the dot line denotes the actual height. An experiment increasing the overhead line's height by 1mm was performed. The maximum measurement error of the height and stagger measurement was 0.8mm, 0.15mm. As stated above, the slope of the actual height and the slope of the measured height differ, as shown in Figure 8 (a). Therefore, we compensated the measured height and stagger considering the pixel resolution according to the height and stagger. Figure 8 (b) shows the compensated results. The average errors of the height and stagger were reduced to each 0.1mm, 0.15mm. Tables 1 and 2 show the results for the movement of the height and stagger

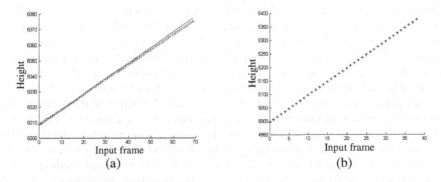

Fig. 8. Measured height (a) and compensated height (b)

Table 1. Height error

Stagger	Height								
	4600	4700	4800	4900	5000	5100	5200	5300	5400
-300	0.879	0.555	0.474	0.246	0.424	0.768	0.861	0.773	0.210
-200	0.246	0.204	0.113	0.472	0.807	0.647	0.873	0.981	0.213
-100	0.338	0.522	0.730	0.553	0.658	0.126	0.666	0.419	0.270
0	0.632	0.243	0.524	0.718	0.590	0.560	0.889	0.584	0.323
100	0.123	0.973	0.301	0.320	0.374	0.382	0.301	0.142	0.481
200	0.981	0.511	0.382	0.657	0.474	0.419	0.424	0.978	0.711
300	0.457	0.323	0.100	0.677	0.831	0.017	0.068	0.605	0.412

Table 2. Stagger error

Height	Stagger						
	300	200	100	0	-100	-200	-300
4600	0.231	0.145	0.583	0.470	0.961	0.434	0.230
4700	0.894	0.098	0.641	0.328	0.167	0.785	0.872
4800	0.554	0.717	0.309	0.415	0.733	0.523	0.910
4900	0.349	0.625	0.777	0.259	0.897	0.647	0.673
5000	0.874	0.119	0.210	0.352	0.125	0.335	0.816
5100	0.228	0.415	0.156	0.991	0.778	0.498	0.517
5200	0.109	0.911	0.202	0.618	0.328	0.523	0.882
5300	0.081	0.284	0.918	0.635	0.319	0.971	0.817
5400	0.972	0.357	0.468	0.738	0.297	0.652	0.715

of the overhead wire by 100mm each. In this experiment, line fitting for the center coordinates was not used. A total of 6 experiments were performed to measure the error. The arithmetic mean error for the height was 0.500238mm and the arithmetic mean error for the stagger was 0.530762mm.

4 Conclusions

In this paper, we proposed a method that measures the height and stagger of an overhead line using the stereo image. Although we aimed for a measurement accuracy of 1mm error, the camera's pixel resolution was insufficient. To solve this problem and to measure accurately in low resolution, we used the sub-pixel and line fitting methods. The sub-pixel method was used to determine the center coordinates of the laser area of the overhead line more precisely. The line fitting method was used to correct the inaccurate measurements resulting the insufficient pixel resolution or external physical impact. Also, we compensated the measurement result, because the camera's pixel resolution differs according to the actual position of the overhead line. Experimental results showed that the proposed method was accurate within an error of 1mm, and we confirmed that the method produced good results in daytime. Also we passed the official test provided by Korea Railroad Research Institute. The test was performed comparing the measured results by the proposed method and by MITUTOYO Beyond-Crysta C121210 with 0.1 μm precision, and to pass the test, the difference of the measured results should be within 1mm.

Acknowledgements

This work was supported by the New Product Development Project in 2005 of South Korea Small and Medium Business Administration, and the Brain Korea 21 Project in 2007.

References

1. Fararooy, S., Mari, C.: Review of railway overhead line geometry measurement systems. IEE Current Collections for High Speed Trains Seminar, (1998) 4/1-4/4
2. Franca, J.G.D.M., Gazziro, M.A., Ide, A.N., Saito, J.H.: A 3D scanning system based on laser triangulation and variable field of view. IEEE International Conference on Image Processing, Vol. 1 (2005) 424-428
3. Tjandranegara, E., Lu., Y.H.: Distance estimation algorithm for stereo pair images. TR-ECE-05-10 (2005)
4. Dhond, U.R., Aggarwal, J.K.: Structure from stereo: a review. IEEE Tansactions on System, Man, and Cybernetics, Vol. 19 (1989) 1489-1510
5. Scharstein, D., Szeliski, R.: A Taxonomy and Evaluation of Dense Two-Frame Stereo Correspondence Algorithms International l J. Computer Vision, Vol. 47 (2002) 7-42
6. Gonzalez, R. C.: Digital Image Processing, Prentice-Hall (2002)
7. van Assen, H.C., Egmont-Petersen, M., Reiber, J.H.C.: Accurate Object Localization in Gray Level Images Using the Center of Gravity Measure: Accuracy Versus Precision. IEEE Transaction on Image Processing, Vol. 11, No. 12 (2002)
8. Patwardhan, A.: Subpixel position measurement using 1D, 2D and 3D centroid algorithms with emphasis on applications in confocal microscopy. Journal of Microscopy (1997)
9. Kim, T.H., Moon, Y.Sh., Han, C.S.: An efficient method of estimating edge location with subpixel accuracy in noisy images. Proceedings of the IEEE Region 10 Conference, Vol. 1 (1999) 589-592
10. Lee, C.K., So, W.C.: A fast edge detector with sub-pixel accuracy. Proceedings of the 1992 International Conference on Industrial Electronics, Vol. 2 (1992) 710-715
11. Park, J.M., Looney, C.G, Chen, H.C.: Fast Connected Component Labeling Algorithm Using A Divide and Conquer Technique. CATA 2000 Conference on Computer and Their Applications (2000) 373-376
12. Huber, P.J.: Robust Statistics. Wiley, New York (1981)

Hand Shape Recognition by Hand Shape Scaling, Weight Magnifying and Finger Geometry Comparison

Ching-Liang Su

Department of Industrial Engineering and Technology Management
Da Yeh University
112 Shan-Jeau Road, Da-Tsuen, Chang-Hua, Taiwan 51505
Tel.: 886-4-851-1888 ex 4121; Fax: 886-4-851-1270
cls2@mail.dyu.edu.tw

Abstract. This study uses object-extracting technique to extract thumb, index, middle, ring, and small fingers. The algorithm developed in this study can locate the precise locations of fingertips and finger-to-finger-valleys. The extracted fingers contain many useful geometry features. One can use these features to identify fingers. The geometry descriptor is used to transfer geometry features of fingers to another feature-domains. Fingers are scaled to allow fingers possess more salient features. Finger is also magnified by the basis of "distance multiplying gray level". After finger magnifying, finger will possess more salient feature. Image subtraction is used to examine the difference of the two fingers.

Keywords: Finger shape information extraction, image phase matching, identification intelligence.

1 Introduction

In the past twenty years, researchers have devoted much attention to identify the hand images. This past works have included hand geometry [1,2,4,5,12,15, 16,17,18], middle finger crease pattern matching [6], various finger size measurements [7,14], various finger lateral view size measurements [14], vein pattern [9], eigenpalm [10], implicit polynomials [13], algebraic invariants [13], Karen invariant computation [13], line interception and slope comparisons [19], control point selection [8,19], coarse to fine strategy [3], B Spline [11], watershed transform [9], HMM [16].

In this study, the new technique is used to extract thumb, index, middle, ring, and small fingers. Geometry descriptor is used to transfer geometry features of finger to another feature domain. The techniques of image inflation and magnification are used to allow finger possesses more salient features. Image subtraction is used to examine the difference of two fingers.

This report consists of four sections. Section 2 extracts finger images. Section 3 describes geometry descriptor and subtraction. Section 4 concludes this report.

A. Gagalowicz and W. Philips (Eds.): MIRAGE 2007, LNCS 4418, pp. 516–524, 2007.
© Springer-Verlag Berlin Heidelberg 2007

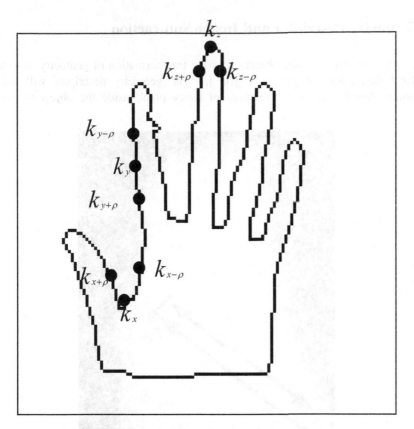

Fig. 1. Show positions of various feature points

2 Extract the Fingers

In figure 1 K_x represents thumb-index-fingers-valley, K_y represents pixel between thumb-index-fingers-valley and index fingertip, and K_z represents the middle fingertip. From figure 1, one can find the distance between ($K_{x+\rho}$ and $K_{x-\rho}$) is shorter than the distance between ($K_{y+\rho}$ and $K_{y-\rho}$) and the distance between ($K_{z+\rho}$ and $K_{z-\rho}$) is shorter than the distance between ($K_{y+\rho}$ and $K_{y-\rho}$). In equation 1, $K_{n-\rho}$ represents the (n-ρ)th pixel residing in the hand-edge. Response energy Energy(K_n) is weighted by the distance of two points $K_{n+\rho}$ and $K_{n-\rho}$. As checking figure 1, one can find Energy(K_n) should have less value when K_n is fingertip or finger-to-finger valley. In this study, ρ is set to 10. By this process, one can extract fingertips and finger-to-finger-valleys. Furthermore, one can extract thumb, index, middle, ring, and small fingers. Since fingertip and finger-roots might cause some errors during finger-recognition process, fingertips and finger-roots are truncated.

$$Energy(k_n) \underset{n=1}{\overset{PalmOutlinePixelNumber-\rho}{=}} \underset{n=1}{\overset{PalmOutlinePixelNumber-\rho}{Distance}} \parallel (k_{n-\rho}) \; ^{to} \; (k_{n+\rho}) \parallel \qquad (1)$$

3   Geometry Descriptor and Image Subtraction

For every pixel g(i, j) in the object, after the transformation of geometry descriptor, the final destination of g(i, j) is $g(i_f, j_f)$. The geometry descriptor will transfer and interpolate the geometry features of every pixel inside the object to another

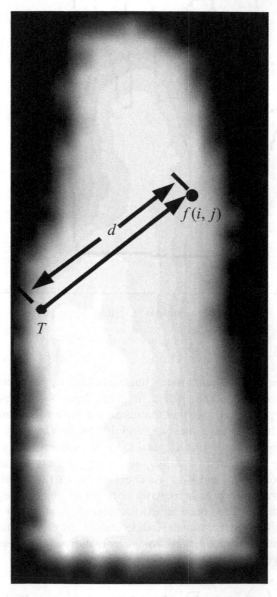

Fig. 2. The distance between points T and f(i, j) is d

feature-domain. After the transformation, the original geometry feature of finger will be preserved. In the new feature-domain, every object will have same straight orientation and the centroid of every object is aligned to position $(64,64)$. After this, one can perform image subtraction. Equation 2 shows the scheme of the geometry descriptor. In equation 2, "θ" represents orientation of object and "*Centroid*" represents centroid of object. By using equations 3, 4, and 5, one can find parameter "θ". In equations 3 and 4, $i_{distance}$ represents the i-distance of a specific pixel g(i, j) to centroid, $j_{distance}$ represents the j-distance of a specific pixel g(i, j) to centroid, and $Weight_{ij}$ represents gray level of a specific pixel g(i, j).

In this study, in order to allow fingers to possess more salient features, one also "magnifies" the fingers to various magnitudes. The magnified fingers are named "distance-weighted fingers". One can obtain the "magnified" fingers by processing the following steps:

Assume one existing pixel T, $T \in$ finger image, and assume $f(i, j)$ is the gray level of one specific pixel located on position (i, j), and also assume $f(i, j) \in$ finger image. One uses the symbol $\|T - f(i, j)\|$ to represent the distance between points T and $f(i, j)$. One denotes it as d. The construction of points T, $f(i, j)$, and d is shown in figure 2. The left picture in figure 3 shows the picture before performing image magnifying and the right picture in figure 3 shows after magnifying. As the previous discussion, assume one existing pixel T, $T \in$ finger image and T is in the left side image in figure 3. One can use the formula in equation 6 to transfer pixel T to T'. The relationship of T to T' is shown in figure 3.

In this study, the image subtraction is used to examine the difference of two fingers. The image subtractions are shown in figures 4, 5, and 6. By calculating the difference of the subtracted-result, one can recognize different fingers.

$$(i, j, \theta, Centroid) \implies (i_f, j_f) \tag{2}$$

$$\text{Geometry}$$
$$\text{Descriptor}$$

$$Var1 = \sum_{j=1}^{N}\sum_{i=1}^{N}(i_{dis\tan ce})^2 \cdot Weight_{ij} - \sum_{j=1}^{N}\sum_{i=1}^{N}(j_{dis\tan ce})^2 \cdot Weight_{ij} \tag{3}$$

$$Var2 = \sum_{j=1}^{N}\sum_{i=1}^{N} 2 \cdot i_{dis\tan ce} \cdot j_{dis\tan ce} \cdot Weight_{ij} \tag{4}$$

$$\theta = \cfrac{Sin^{-1}\cfrac{\displaystyle\sum_{j=1}^{N}\sum_{i=1}^{N}2\cdot i_{dis\tan ce}\cdot j_{dis\tan ce}\cdot Weight_{ij}}{\sqrt{Var2^2 + Var1^2}}}{2} \tag{5}$$

$$T^{'} = \sum_{\forall f(i,j)\in finger}\sum \|T - f(i,j)\| * f(i,j) \tag{6}$$

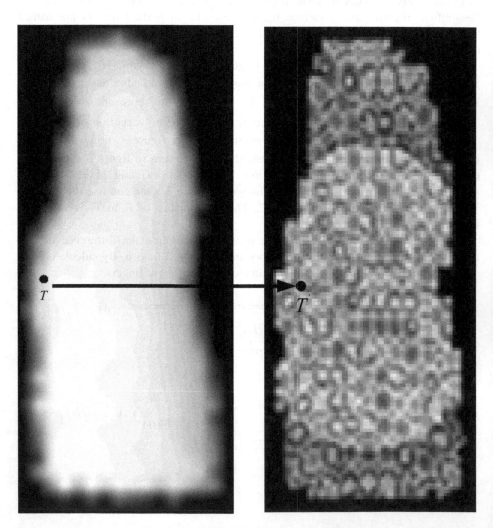

Fig. 3. Images before and after magnifying

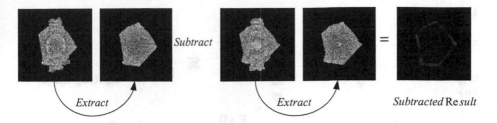

Fig. 4. Image subtraction of different orientations and positions

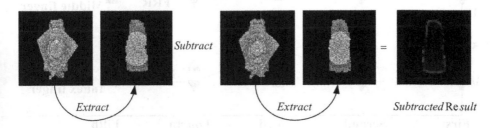

Fig. 5. Image subtraction of different orientations and positions

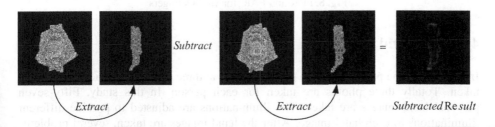

Fig. 6. Image-subtraction of different orientations and positions

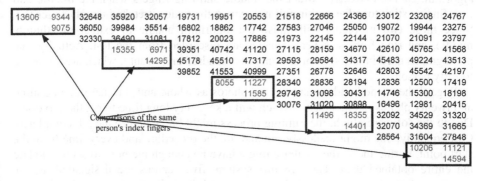

Fig. 7. Comparison data

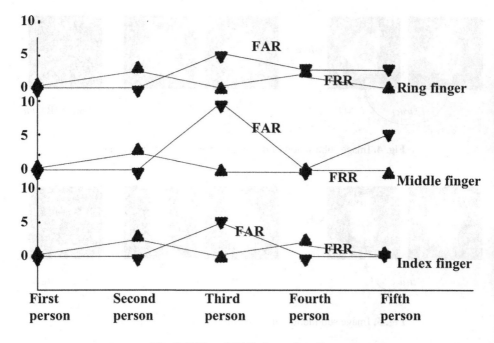

Fig. 8. FRR and FAR for various fingers

4 Results and Conclusion

In this study, one person needs to place his hand at three different positions for photos taken. Totally three photos are taken for each person. In this study, Fifty-seven persons' hand-images are taken. The illuminations are adjusted to provide different illuminations to each hand image. After the hand images are taken, several problems are found in the hand images – the middle and the ring fingers of several people hands are stick together or the thumb and the index fingers are stretching too wide. The algorithm cannot correctly extract the middle and ring fingers when the middle and ring fingers stick together and it will not extract the wider stretched thumb finger too. Since these two problems will cause the algorithm unable to extract the thumb, middle, and ring fingers, several images are discarded from the test. Actually, the photographs used in this system are only one hundred and twenty, which are belonged to forty persons.

Regard these one hundred and twenty photos as whole and run these one hundred and twenty photos in one batch – which will take a very long time to get the job done. Due to the software glitch, the running process might break before the job completed. Consequently, one might endlessly run and run the procedure and every time from the start point. Furthermore, the database might have no enough memory to accommodate the entire obtained data. Thus, in this system, five persons are designated as one group, i.e. five people are regarded as a group and these five persons are tested in one step. Since one person has been taken three different photos, totally fifteen photos are tested in each step. As mentioned earlier, in this system, there are forty persons participating the test. Thus, the system will totally run eight different batches. Totally, one hundred and twenty photographs are tested. For each photograph, the following steps are performed – (1) hand edge is found, (2) fingers are extracted separately, (3) geometry descriptor is performed, (4) image is shifted and rotated, (5) image is magnified, (6) genuine and imposter comparisons are conducted. To each group, one finger is compared against the other 14 fingers. Totally, one hundred and five comparisons are conducted to test the accuracy of the algorithm. Within those one hundred and five comparisons, fifteen comparisons are genuine comparison. The other ninety comparisons are imposter comparisons. In this study, there are eight different test batches. Thus, there are 120 genuine tests and 720 imposter tests. Figure 7 shows partial comparison data. The data inside the rectangular boxes is the subtraction result of genuine fingers. The other data, which is not surrounded by the rectangular boxes, show the subtracted results of imposter fingers. Figure 8 shows FAR and FRR of various finger comparisons.

Acknowledgement. National Science Council, Taiwan, supported this work under grant NSC 95-2221-E-212-003.

References

1. Editorial, "Hand-based biometrics," Biometric Technology Today, Volume 11, Issue 7, July 2003, Pages 9-11
2. Karen O Egiazarian, S. Gonzalez Pestana, "Hand shape identification using neural networks," The International Society for Optical Engineering, v 4667, 2002, p 440-448
3. Chin-Chuan Han, "A hand-based personal authentication using a coarse-to-fine strategy," Image and Vision Computing, Volume 22, 2004, pp 909–918
4. Chin-Chuan Han, Hsu-Liang Cheng, Chih-Lung Lin and Kuo-Chin Fan, "Personal authentication using palm-print features," Pattern Recognition, 36, 2003, pp 371-381
5. Bing He, Zheng-Ding Qiu, Dong-Mei Sun "Secure authentication system incorporating hand shapes verification and cryptography techniques," IEEE Region 10 Annual International Conference, Proceedings/TENCON, v 1, 2002, p 156-159
6. D. G. Joshi, Y. V. Rao, S. Kar, V. Kumar, "Computer vision based approach to personal identification using finger crease pattern," Pattern Recognition, 31, 1998, pp 15-22
7. Ajay Kumar, David C. M. Wong, Helen C. Shen, "Personal Verification Using Palmprint and Hand Geometry Biometric," Lecture Notes in Computer Science, Springer-Verlag Heidelberg, Volume 2688, 2003, pp 668-678
8. Wenxin Lia, David Zhang, and Zhuoqun Xub, "Image alignment based on invariant features for palmprint identification," Signal Processing: Image Communication, Volume 18, Issue 5, May 2003, Pages 373-379
9. Chih-Lung Lin and Kuo-Chin Fan, "Biometric Verification Using Thermal Images of Palm-Dorsa Vein Patterns," IEEE TRANSACTIONS ON CIRCUITS AND SYSTEMS FOR VIDEO TECHNOLOGY, VOL. 14, NO. 2, FEBRUARY 2004
10. Guangming Lua, David Zhang, and Kuanquan Wanga, "Palmprint recognition using eigenpalms features," Pattern Recognition Letter, Volume 24, Issues 9-10, June 2003, Pages 1463-1467

11. YingLiang Ma, Frank Pollick and W. Terry Hewitt, "Using B-Spline Curves for Hand Recognition," Proceedings of the 17th International Conference on Pattern Recognition (ICPR'04), 2004
12. Aya Mitome and Rokuya Ishii, "A Comparison of Hand Shape Recognition Algorithms," The 29th Annual Conference of the IEEE Industrial Electronics Society, Nov 2-6 2003
13. Cenker Oden, Aytul Ercil, and Burak Buke, "Combining implicit polynomials and geometric features for hand recognition," Pattern Recognition Letter, Volume 24, Issue 13, September 2003, Pages 2145-2152
14. R. Sanchez-Reillo, Sanchez-Avila, and Gonzales-Marcos, "Biometric identification through hand geometry measurements," IEEE Trans Pattern Anal Mach Intell, Volume 22, No. 10, 2000, Pages 1168-1171
15. Ching-Liang Su, "Technique for Person's Identification: Using the Extracted Index Finger Image to Identify Individuals," Journal of Intelligent and Robotic Systems, Netherlands, July 2003, pp. 337-354, vol. 37, No. 3
16. Dong-Mei Sun, Zheng-Ding Qiu "Automated hand shape verification using HMM," the 7th International Conference on Signal Processing Proceedings (ICSP'04), 2004, p 2274-2277
17. Wei Xionga, Kar-Ann Toha, Wei-Yun Yaua, and Xudong Jiangb, "Model-guided deformable hand shape recognition without positioning aids," Pattern Recognition, Volume 38, 2005, Pages 1651 –1664
18. Wei Xiong, Changsheng Xu, and Sim Heng Ong, "PEG-FREE HUMAN HAND SHAPE ANALYSIS AND RECOGNITION," ICASSP, 2005, Pages 77 –80
19. Jane You, Wenxin Li, and David Zhang, "Hierarchical palmprint identification via multiple feature extraction," Pattern Recognition, Volume 35, Issue 4, April 2002, Pages 847-859

Volumetric Bias Correction

Edoardo Ardizzone, Roberto Pirrone, Salvatore La Bua, and Orazio Gambino

Universita' degli Studi di Palermo
DINFO - Dipartimento di Ingegneria Informatica
viale delle Scienze - Edificio 6 - Terzo piano
90128 Palermo
{ardizzon,pirrone}@unipa.it, slabua@gmail.com, gambino@csai.unipa.it

Abstract. This paper presents a method to suppress the bias artifact, also known as RF-inhomogeneity, in Magnetic Resonance Imaging
(MRI). This artifact produces illumination variations due to magnetic
field fluctuations of the device. In the latest years many works have been
devoted to face this problem. In this work we present the 3D version of
a new approach to bias correction, which is called Exponential Entropy
Driven Homomorphic Unsharp Masking ($E^2D - HUM$). This technique
has been already presented by some of the authors for the 2D case only.
The description of the whole method is detailed, and some experimental
results are reported.

1 Introduction

The RF-inhomogeneity, also called bias artifact, is an interesting research topic in
Magnetic Resonance Imaging (MRI). Bias corrupted MR images exhibit strong
brightness variations so that voxel's grey levels change spatially also inside the
same tissue. Statistical estimations of the corruption to restore the images have
been proposed in [8][4][19]. Some methods[11][13] need a special probe inserted
into the device to capture the image representing the artifact so that the image
is restored using this estimation with a homomorphic-like method. These techniques move from [12] which applies the Homomorphic Unsharp Masking (HUM)
method and continued by [14], but they don't perform a volumetric approach.
Some of the methods cited above have been compared in [18]. We propose a fully
3D approach to bias correction in a MR volume, and we called it Exponential
Entropy Driven Homomorphic Unsharp Masking ($E^2D - HUM$). Our technique
is an evolution of the HUM method proposed by Guillemaud [10]. In our work,
an accurate region segmentation is performed to avoid some typical artifacts
introduced by the homomorphic filter. Moreover, we obtain automatically the
cutoff frequency of the filter: this is a typical drawback when using the homomorphic approach. $E^2D - HUM$ doesn't require any a priori hypothesis about
the tissues under investigation, and it performs well regardless the MR spectrum (T1, T2, PD, FLAIR ...). The experimentation of this article is focused on
some T1-weighted image volume of the knee because it is the most common MR
modality used, but it is not a limitation. Moreover, the hardware configuration

A. Gagalowicz and W. Philips (Eds.): MIRAGE 2007, LNCS 4418, pp. 525–533, 2007.
© Springer-Verlag Berlin Heidelberg 2007

of low magnetic field MR devices specialized in lower limbs particularly affected
by this artifact is prone to generate a considerable bias artifact, due to the use of
surface coils. Because most of the method cited above are oriented to brain MRI,
also results on brain are presented. The paper is arranged as follows: Section 2
describes the 3D version of E^2D-HUM and the related theoretical background,
Section 3 shows the improvement of the presented method with regards to the
inter-slice brightness variations arising when a bias correction technique is applied separately to each slice and not to the entire volume, Sections 4 describes
the measures employed to validate the effectiveness of the method and shows
some experimental results that have been compared with the well known SPM
technique [5]. This can be considered a state-of-the-art approach to the bias
correction. Section 5 reports some conclusions.

2   3D $E^2D - HUM$

The presented method moves from $E^2D - HUM$ algorithm [1] for MR images.
Here this algorithm is extended to volumes. The degradation model of a volume
affected by RF-inhomogeneity shows that the artifact is multiplicative:

$$I(x, y, z) = I_{corrected}(x, y, z) \cdot B(x, y, z) \tag{1}$$

where $I(x, y, z)$ is the voxel intensity of the corrupted volume whose coordinates are x, y, z; $I_{corrected}(x, y, z)$ is the intensity of the uncorrupted volume and
$B(x, y, z)$ is the intensity of the artifact. For all the following formulas, the x, y, z
coordinates will be omitted. A natural logarithm function ln can be applied to
both members of 1 to transform the multiplicative model into an addictive one:

$$I_{\log} = \ln(I) = \ln(I_{corrected}) + \ln(B) \tag{2}$$

In this way a linear filtering can be applied. The bias artifact B corrupts the
illumination signal located at low frequencies of the Fourier spectrum, while the
high frequencies aren't altered. This is a classical luminance/reflectance model
suited to the application of the homomorphic filter. To separate low frequencies from high ones, a high pass filtering can be performed on the $I_{\log}$ and an
exponential function is computed on the result, achieving the classic homomorphic filter. But if a strong edge is present in the image, like the one between
foreground and background of a medical volume, luminance peaks arise on the
boundaries between the two zones. The Guillemaud filter prevent this problem.
A toy problem has been prepared to compare the Guillemaud filter with a homomorphic one. A 32x32x32 volume has been filled with values 120 and 128 for
each part and has been padded by zero voxels obtaining a 63x63x63 volume. A
bias artifact has been simulated multiplying the closest harmonics to the DC
component by 4. Fig.1 shows a slice taken from the original and corrupted volume along with the 2D 1/2 representation of their grey levels. The figure also
shows the effect of the homomorphic filter and Guillemaud one. The luminance
peaks effect can be seen very well on both images while they are absent in the
Guillemaud result.

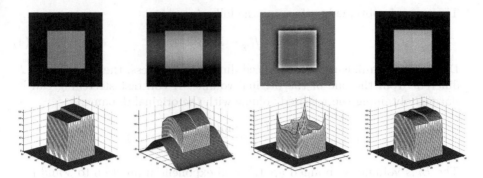

Fig. 1. The first row shows a slice taken respectively from the following volumes: original, corrupted, after homomorphic filtering, after Guillemaud filtering. The experiments are performed with $D_0 = 0.1$. The second row shows their 2D 1/2 representation.

2.1   The 3D Guillemaud Filter

Guillemaud [10]proposed a method to avoid the problem mentioned before in MRI for the 2D case and here the 3D extension is presented for a complete volume. According to the Guillemaud approach, a 3D Region of Interest (ROI) is a binary volume which identifies only the foreground voxels, so that the ln function in 2 is applied only on the foreground :

$$I_{\log}^* = \{\ln I : ROI = 1\}$$

Here the high pass filter is accomplished subtracting the result of the low pass filtering, which estimates the artifact. The result of the low pass filtering will be used also in the next section. The low pass filtering is performed using the 3D version of the Butterworth filter whose Frequency Impulsive Response is:

$$H = \frac{1}{1 + \left(\frac{D(u,v,w)}{D_0} \right)^{2n}}$$

where $D(u, v, w)$ is the euclidian distance from the origin of the frequency domain, n is the filter order and D_0 is the cutoff frequency. The order of the filter must be set to 1, so that the well known ringing artifact can't appear. The filter is applied to $I_{\log}^*$ obtaining $\hat{I}$:

$$\hat{I} = FFT^{-1} \left[H \cdot FFT \left(I_{\log}^* \right) \right]$$

The same filtering is applied to the 3D ROI:

$$\widehat{ROI} = FFT^{-1} \left[H \cdot FFT \left(ROI \right) \right]$$

The ln-transformed version of the $Bias$ image is obtained dividing pixel-by-pixel the magnitude of $\hat{I}$ and $\widehat{ROI}$:

$$\ln(Bias) = \frac{\left\| \hat{I} \right\|}{\left\| \widehat{ROI} \right\|} \tag{3}$$

$$I^* = exp(I^*_{\log} - \ln(Bias)) \tag{4}$$

Due to the non-linearities introduced during the process, the dynamics of I^* is different from the one of the original volume. A contrast stretching can be performed obtaining the restored volume with the original dynamic:

$$I_{corrected} = \frac{I^* - \min(I^*)}{\max(I^*) - \min(I^*)} \cdot \max(I) \tag{5}$$

The *Bias* volume is obtained applying an exponential function to 3 and performing the same contrast stretching showed in 5. Even if the ROI selection prevents the luminance peaks on the external volume boundary, it cannot avoid some overshoots along the boundaries between those sub-volumes corresponding to tissues with very different brightness. This is the case of muscles surrounded by fat. We propose a more careful procedure to obtain the ROI. Once a restored volume has been obtained using the Guillemaud ROI, a fuzzy c-means [2] segmentation is performed using three clusters. We choose three clusters to distinguish between dark, medium and bright grey levels. The new ROI is obtained merging the voxels pertaining to the medium and bright class. Fig.2 reports a comparison of the behavior of the filter with the Guillemaud ROI and using our selection. White arrows indicate the presence of luminance peaks that are completely corrected in our approach.

2.2   The Volumetric Cutoff Frequency D_0

It's hard to find the right value of this parameter to prevent a certain amount of luminance to be removed from the restored image. There are no approaches

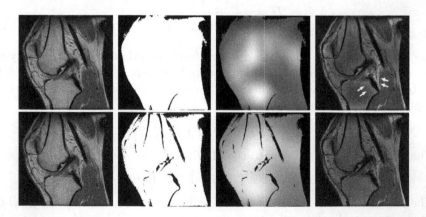

Fig. 2. Results using Guillemuad ROI (first row) and new ROI selection(second row). From left-to-right: original image, selected region, estimated bias and restored image. The white arrows show the luminance peaks introduced by the filter using the Guillemaud ROI.

dealing with an automatic estimation of the cutoff frequency in the literature devoted to MRI. The core of $E^2D - HUM$ is the Guillemaud filter and an entropy based method automatically computes the cutoff frequency. Here the 3D version of this method is also given. The corrupted volume contains more information than an uncorrupted one: the useful information and the one of the artifact. The Guillemaud filter attenuates the low frequencies of the corrupted volume while the ones of the *Bias* image are enhanced of the same amount, so that this process can be considered an information transfer between the volumes. The amount of information moved from the corrupted volume to the Bias one becomes bigger and bigger while increasing the cutoff frequency. The problem consists in finding a criterion for placing the cutoff frequency to move a sufficient information away from the corrupted volume. A classical information measure is the Shannon Entropy (SE) [15] computed on the grey value of each voxel. The plot of the Bias volume entropy versus an increasing value of the cutoff frequency shows an increasing of this function, according to the considerations said before. In correspondence of the low frequencies the most part of the information moved away from the corrupted volume is made by the artifact so the slope of the curve is steep, as shown in fig3. After this transient phase, the curve appears flat because all the information placed at the high frequencies is related to the tissues luminance. We can choose to place D_0 at the end of the transient phase. Due to its shape the curve can be modelled using an exponential function:

$$y(x) = k_1 + k_2 e^{-\frac{x}{\tau}} \tag{6}$$

Eq.6 is the capacitance charge function where the end of transient phase is obtained at 5τ, so that D_0 can be obtained using this approximation. The model is fitted on the curve using a Nelder-Mead algorithm [3]which minimizes the following objective function:

$$E = \frac{1}{2} \sum_{i=1}^{n} \left[k_1 + k_2 \cdot e^{-\frac{x(i)}{\tau}} - SE\left[x(i)\right] \right]^2$$

here $SE\left[x(i)\right]$ are the entropy values computed for each cf sample $x(i)$.The initial conditions can be set as follows: k_1 is the final value of the model in the

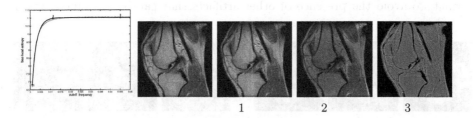

Fig. 3. The local entropy diagram and the superimposed exponential model, original image and the restored ones obtained with the cutoff frequencies corresponding to the point on the diagram. The point 2 is selected by $E^2D \quad HUM$.

flat region and can be set to mean of the last ten entropy values; due to the profile of the function, k_2 can be set to -1; τ can be set to the minimum of the frequency range, because has to increase. Three points on the curve are sampled in fig.3 and show the filtering obtained using the respective cutoff frequencies, justifying the proposed approach.

3   Inter-slice Variations

When a multi-slice acquisition is performed, the excitation of the slices must be carefully applied. In fact, adjacent slices produce inter-slice variations caused by cross-talk between them, even if the excitation is interleaved. To avoid this undesirable phenomenon, the time between excitation of adjacent slices can be increased or special slice-selective acquisition sequences can be employed [6]. Of course, these particular treatments can be implemented by the radiologist only during the medical examination. Once the images are acquired, only a software solution can be implemented. Some techniques reported in the literature for bias correction are not able to suppress the inter-slice variations. Rapid variations are badly corrected by N3 [4] while FMI [9] isn't able to remove the smooth ones, as shown in the paper of Likar et al. [15]. If the 2D version of $E^2D - HUM$ were applied on each slice of a volume, the average luminance would be different from a slice to another. This happens for two reasons: a different cutoff frequency is found for each slice and the cutoff frequency along the 3rd dimension isn't defined. Our approach uses a 3D filtering kernel that processes the bias along all the directions. Fig.4 shows this result. Here two slices are shown that have been reconstructed respectively on the transversal and the coronal plane. In other words the slices are both orthogonal to the plane of acquisition (the sagittal one). The figure shows the inter-slice brightness variations that are enhanced by the application of the 2D $E^2D - HUM$, while the 3D version of the filter significantly reduces this artifact. Fig.5 shows a 3D reconstruction of the artifact plotting iso-level contours for each slice.

4   Experimental Setup

The method has been applied on several volumes decoded from DICOM files format, to avoid the presence of other artifacts that can be introduced by an

Fig. 4. For each group of images, from left to right: original, 2D correction of each slice, 3D $E^2D - HUM$ restored image. Left group shows a transversal plane reconstruction, the other one the coronal plane.

optical scanner acquisition. The device is an ESAOTE ARTOSCAN C with a magnetic field intensity of 0.18 Tesla. The dataset consists in multi-slice acquisitions of knees on sagittal plane each composed by 87 T1-weighted images. The volumes have been acquired with the following parameters: Spin Echo sequence, Repetition time (980 ms), Echo time (26 ms), Slice thickness (1mm), Flip Angle (90). The useful resolution of FOV is 256x256 pixels with 12 bit of pixel depth. In order to validate the choice of D_0, we introduce two measures. The former is the coefficient of variation cv that is used to measures the non-uniformity intensity of a region, the latter is the coefficient of contrast and it measures the contrast between two adjacent tissues. They are defined as follows:

$$cv(zone) = \frac{\sigma(zone)}{\mu(zone)} \qquad cc(zone_1, zone_2) = \frac{\mu(zone_1)}{\mu(zone_2)}$$

where σ and μ are, respectively, the standard deviation and the mean of gray values in the region under examination. A region affected by bias artifact exhibits a higher cv than a normal one. Table 1 reports that in general 3D $E^2D - HUM$ has lowest cv both the original value and the one obtained using SPM2. The coefficient of contrast (cc), which consists in the ratio between the mean values μ of two adjacent zones, has been introduced to check the loss of contrast in the restored volume. In fact, a normal consequence of the bias reducing is a loss of contrast among the tissues; this fact compromises the tissue identification during a visual inspection. Both the measures require homogenous regions, so a handmade segmentation has been performed on a volume by an orthopedic physician to identify the tissues for each slice. Even though the Table 2 shows that cc is in general lower than SPM2, but the values are around of 150%, which is still good.

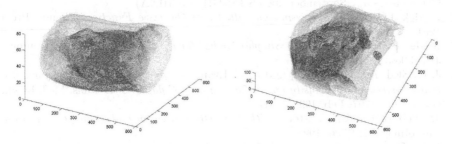

Fig. 5. Slice contours of the Bias artifact

5   Conclusions and Future Work

An automatic method to suppress RF-inhomogeneity in MR image volumes has been presented. It doesn't require any hypothesis both on the tissues and on the artifact shape. A semi-automatic version of our filter can be implemented, so that the physician can select the value of D_0, according to her visual preferences. Even tough in this paper it is applied on a knee volume, $E^2D - HUM$ can be applied to whatever anatomical region due to its general purpose designing. Most of the cited paper are devoted to brain MRI and they don't care of other body parts. It's worth noticing that the 3D nature of the approach allows the filter to reduce also the inter-slice brightness variations. In this way it is possible to obtain a good restoration also when we create a slice by sectioning the volume along an orthogonal plane with respect to the acquisition one. In general the bias artifact has an anisotropic nature due to the non uniform displacement of the magnetic coils with respect to the patient. We are currently working on a 2D anisotropic $E^2D - HUM$, and we plan to derive an anisotropic kernel also in the 3D case.

TABLE 1 - COEFFICIENTS OF VARIATION

TISSUES	ORIGINAL	3D E²D-HUM	SPM
A_Genu	0,408	0,4013	0,4006
C_Femoralis	0,5588	0,5229	0,5657
C_MedTibialis	0,5029	0,5257	0,5056
Femur	0,2126	0,2021	0,2108
InfrapatellarFB	0,3237	0,3227	0,335
L_CollatTibiale	0,6208	0,48	0,613
L_CrucifPost	0,5488	0,5301	0,5472
M_GastrocnMed	0,2448	0,2461	0,2744
M_Gracilis	0,5636	0,4849	0,5104
M_Sartorius	0,3759	0,2984	0,3236
M_Semimembr	0,4499	0,3989	0,402
M_Semitend	0,7473	0,7947	0,7426
M_VastusMed	0,4403	0,3589	0,3711
MeniscusMed	0,7094	0,5398	0,709
TM_Adductoris	0,6434	0,6066	0,6326
TM_Gracilis	0,6041	0,5125	0,6192
TM_Semitend	0,7552	0,6871	0,7669
Tibia	0,2118	0,2254	0,2189
V_Saphena	0,4853	0,4683	0,4542

M: Muscle - C: Cartilage - L: Ligament - TM: Tendon/Muscle V: Vein

TABLE 2 - COEFFICIENTS OF CONTRAST

TISSUES	ORIGINAL	3D E²D-HUM	SPM2
M_Sartorius - M_Gracilis	1,4187	1,0913	1,2104
M_Semimembr - M_Semitend	2,4984	1,8653	1,8283
Femur - C_Femoralis	2,7058	2,3233	2,5499
Femur - L_CollatTibiale	4,0819	3,4817	4,0956
L_CollatTibiale - C_Femoralis	1,5086	1,4986	1,6062
MeniscusMed - C_Femoralis	2,3770	1,8837	2,4376
MeniscusMed - C_MedTibialis	3,8202	2,9226	3,7321
C_MedTibialis - Tibia	1,5135	1,5349	1,5148

M: Muscle - C: Cartilage

References

1. Ardizzone, E.; Pirrone ,R. and Gambino, O. :*Exponential Entropy Driven HUM on Knee MR Images* Proc. OF IEEE XXVII Engineering in Medicine and Biology Conference - 4/7 September 2005 SHANGHAI (CHINA)
2. Bezdek J.C. :*Pattern Recognition with Fuzzy Objective Function.* Plenum Press 1981.
3. Nelder, J. A. and Mead, R. *A Simplex Method for Function Minimization.* Comput. J. 7, 308-313, 1965.
4. J. G. Sled, A. P. Zijdenbos, and A. C. Evans. *A nonparametric method for automatic correction of intensity nonuniformity in MRI data.* IEEE Trans. Med. Imag., vol. 17, pp. 8797, Feb. 1998. MRI
5. J. Ashburner and K. Friston. *MRI sensitivity correction and tissue classification.* NeuroImage, 7: S706, 1998.
6. Y De Deene. *Fundamentals of MRI measurements for gel dosimetry.* Journal of Physics: Conference Series 3 (2004) 87114.
7. B. Johnston, M. S. Atkins, B. Mackiewich, Member and M. Anderson. *Segmentation of Multide Sclerosis Lesions in Intensity Corrected Multispectral MRI.* IEEE Transaction On Medical Imaging, vol. 15, no. 2, April 1996
8. Styner, M.; Brechbuhler, C.; Szckely, G.; Gerig, G.: Parametric estimate of intensity inhomogeneities applied to MRI Medical Imaging. IEEE Transactions on Medical Imaging **22** (2000)153-165
9. E. A. Vokurka, N. A. Thacker, and A. Jackson. *A fast model independent method for automatic correction of intensity nonuniformity in MRI data.* J. Magn. Reson. Imag., vol. 10, pp. 550562, 1999.

10. Guillemaud, R.: Uniformity Correction with Homomorphic filtering on Region of Interest. IEEE International Conference on Image Processing **2** (1998) 872–875
11. Dawant B.M.; Zijdenbos A.P.; Margolin R.A.: Correction of Intensity Variations in MR Images for Computer-Aided Tissue Classification. IEEE Transactions on Medical Imaging **12** (1993) 770–781
12. Axel L.; Costantini J.; Listerud J.: Intensity Correction in Surface Coil MR Imaging. American Journal on Roentgenology **148** (1987) 418–420
13. Tincher M.; Meyer C.R.; Gupta R.; Williams D.M.: Polynomial Modelling and Reduction of RF Body Coil Spatial Inhomogeneity in MRI. IEEE Transactions on Medical Imaging **12** (1993) 361–365
14. Brinkmann B. H. , Manduca A. and Robb R. A.: Optimized Homomorphic Unsharp Masking for MR Greyscale Inhomogeneity Correction. IEEE Transactions on Medical Imaging. **17** (1998) 161–171
15. Likar B.; Viergever M.A.; Pernus F.: Retrospective Correction of MR Intensity Inhomogeneity by Information Minimization. IEEE Transactions on Medical Imaging **20** (2001) 1398–1410
16. Kwan R.K.S.; Evans A.C.; Pike G.B.: MRI simulation-based evaluation of image-processing and classification methods. IEEE Transactions on Medical Imaging. (1999) 18(11):1085–1097.
17. Kwan R.K.S.; Evans A.C.; Pike G.B.: An Extensible MRI Simulator for Post-Processing Evaluation. Visualization in Biomedical Computing (VBC'96). Lecture Notes in Computer Science, vol. 1131. Springer-Verlag, (1996) 135–140.
18. Arnold JB; Liow J-S; Schaper KS; Stern JJ; Sled JG; Shattuck DW; Worth AJ; Cohen MS; Leahy RM; Mazziotta JC; Rottenberg DA. Quantitative and Qualitive Evaluation of Six Algorithms for Correcting Intensity Non-Uniformity Effects. Neuroimage (2001) 13(5) 931–943.
19. Christian Brechbuhler, Guido Gerig, and Gabor Szekely, Compensation of spatial inhomogeneity in MRI based on a multi-valued image model and a parametric bias estimate, Visualization in Biomedical Computing Proc. VBC'96, Lecture Notes in Computer Science, No. 1131, Springer, pp. 141-146, Sept. 1996

Object Tracking with Particle Filter Using Color Information

Peihua Li[1] and Haijing Wang[2]

[1] School of Comp. Sci. and Tech., Heilongjiang University, China, 150080
peihualj@hotmail.com
[2] School of Comp. Sci. and Tech., Harbin Institute of Technology, China, 150080

Abstract. Color-based particle filter for object tracking has been an active research topic in recent years. Despite great efforts of many researchers, there still remains to be solved the problem of contradiction between efficiency and robustness. The paper makes an attempt to partially solve this problem. Firstly, the *Integral Histogram Image* is introduced by which histogram of any rectangle region can be computed at negligible cost. However, straightforward application of the Integral Histogram Images causes the problem of "curse of dimensionality". In addition, traditional histogram is inefficient and inaccurate. Thus we propose to adaptively determine histogram bins based on K-Means clustering, which can represent color distribution of object more compactly and accurately with as a small number of bins. Thanks to the Integral Histogram Images and the clustering based color histogram, we finally achieve a fast and robust particle filter algorithm for object tracking. Experiments show that the performance of the algorithm is encouraging.

Keywords: Image sequence, object tracking, image processing.

1 Introduction

Color-based Particle Filter algorithm [3,5,6,10,11,12] that can handle nonlinear and/or no-Guassian tracking problem has received great attention in recent years. The basic idea of the particle filter is that the posterior density is recursively approximated by a set of discrete samples (called particles) with associated weights. Due to its Monte Carlo simulation property, the algorithm requires in general a large number of particles to represent well the posterior density of the object state [1,2], which results in high computational cost. Despite the great efforts devoted to color based particle filter, there still remains to be solved the problem of contradiction between efficiency and robustness.

1.1 The Problem in Color-Based Particle Filter

In color-based particle filter framework, a great number of histograms need to be calculated of rectangle regions with different size and position overlapping each other [3,5,6,10]. Though one histogram can be computed efficiently via lookup

A. Gagalowicz and W. Philips (Eds.): MIRAGE 2007, LNCS 4418, pp. 534–541, 2007.

table, large numbers of histograms of overlapping regions are very inefficient and time-consuming. Fig. 1 highlights this analysis, where one frame in a video clip is shown for face tracking based on particle filter, each blue dashed rectangle representing a particle and indicating a possible face location. Most rectangle regions overlap each other, and thus computation of histograms corresponding to these rectangles involve lots of repeated operations.

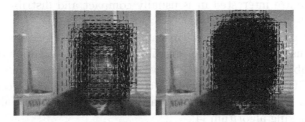

Fig. 1. Histograms of overlapping regions need to be computed repeatedly. The left figure shows 100 particles, and the right figure shows 500 particles, each blue dashed rectangle indicating one particle.

1.2 The Strategy of the Researchers

Thus to make the algorithms more efficient, researchers have to represent coarsely the color information of the target so that evaluation of one particle as fast as possible, and use as little as possible the total number of particles (e.g. 100). Perez et al. [6] used the histogram of a joint uniform 10x10 bins in HS space plus a separate uniform 10 bins in V Space. Nummiaro et al. [5] represented object distribution with weighted color histogram of uniform 8x8x8 bins in RGB color space. In [10], either the means and standard variances of independent color channels or less than 8 bins histogram in normalized RG space were used. The above work obviously fails to take full advantage of ample color information of the object.

1.3 Our Strategy

We presented a straightforward method to compute histogram very efficiently by introducing a concept of *Integral Histogram Image* [8], motivated by the the work of [13]. This way, the redundant computation of histograms for images may be avoided. An Integral Histogram Image can be constructed through one pass of the original image, by which histogram of any size of rectangle region can be computed with $4d$ array index operations, where d is the number of histogram bins. Note that Porikli [7] independently presented the concept of *Integral Histogram*, quite similar to our *Integral Histogram Image*.

Unfortunately, due to the problem of "curse of dimensionality", it is impossible for us to apply the Integral Image to real-time tracking. Take for example a typical image of 384x288 pixels, a histogram of 16x16x16 bins are is to describe color distribution, the memory and the number of array index operations needed will amount to 1728M and 4.5x10^8 (roughly 5 seconds on our laptop with Pentium 4 2.2GHz CPU). Even if the Integral Histogram Image were available on the above occasion, from which evaluation of one rectangle region takes 16384 array index operations, even larger than that conventional computation of the histogram takes. In addition, uniform histogram binning, which induces histogram bins by partitioning the whole color space (RGB, HSV etc.) into uniform rectangular tesselations, is inefficient and not accurate, because of the well-known fact that object color we are interested in is usually compact and distributed in a small region in multi-channel color space.

We thus introduce clustering algorithms to adaptively partition color space, which enables us to represent color distribution of the object with the histogram of a small number of bins. In this way, we achieve benefits of overcoming "curse of dimensionality" and of representing color distribution more compactly and accurately. The Integral Histogram Image is then applied to Kalman particle filter based tracking algorithm [4].

2   The Proposed Algorithm

2.1   Construction of Integral Histogram Image

Given a $p \times q$ image, the corresponding Integral Histogram Image I is $(p+1) \times (q+1)$ arrays of length d (dimension of histogram). The Integral Histogram Image $I_{x,y}[u]$ at location (x, y) corresponds to the number of pixels that falls within the u-th bin above and to the left of (x, y) in the image:

$$I_{x,y}[u] = \sum_{x' \leq x, y' \leq y} \delta(x', y'), \ u = 1, \ldots, d \tag{1}$$

where $\delta(x', y') = 1$ if the pixel at location (x', y') belongs to the u-th bin of histogram; otherwise $\delta(x', y') = 0$. Using the following pair of recurrences:

$$i_{x,y}[u] = i_{x,y-1}[u] + \delta(x, y)$$
$$I_{x,y}[u] = I_{x-1,y}[u] + i_{x,y}[u], u = 1, \ldots, d \tag{2}$$

where $i_{x,0}[u] = 0$ for any x and u, the Integral Histogram Image can be computed in one pass over the original image.

Given any rectangle, its histogram $p_u(u = 1, \ldots, d)$ can be determined in $4d$ array references (see Fig. 2 and Eq. (3)) with Integral Histogram Image for $u = 1, \ldots, d$:

$$p[u] = I_{x+w,y+h}[u] - I_{x+w,y}[u] - I_{x,y+h}[u] + I_{x,y}[u] \tag{3}$$

where $I_{x,0}[u] = I_{0,y}[u] = 0$, w and h are the width and height of the rectangle respectively.

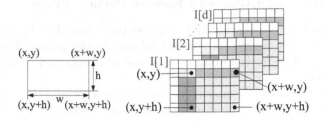

Fig. 2. Construction of Integral Histogram Image. Left figure is a rectangle with width w and height h, and on the right each image plane corresponds to Integral Histogram Image of one bin.

2.2 K-Means Clustering to Determine Bin Ranges

In the paper we employ K-Means clustering algorithm to determine adaptively non-uniform histogram bins. For each cluster, we get the pixel farthest to that cluster center and use this pixel to determine corresponding bin ranges (nonuniform rectangles for two dimensions or super-rectangle for higher dimensions). Adjacent rectangles (or super-rectangles) may have small overlapping regions. For a pixel within such an overlapping region we determine its identity by computing its distance to relevant cluster centers and selecting the cluster with minimum distance.

Fig. 3 presents an example of adaptive determination of histogram bins. Fig. 3(a) is a reference image of a human face, the color distribution of which in HS color space (V-component characterizing chrominance is discarded) is shown in Fig. 3(b), where we can see color is very compact and distributed only in some small regions of the whole HS color space. Fig. 3(c) shows clustering result (d=64) in which pixels in the reference face image belonging to the same cluster are labelled with the same color. We finally get non-uniform histogram bins as shown in 3(d), where pixels belonging to the same bin are labelled with the same color.

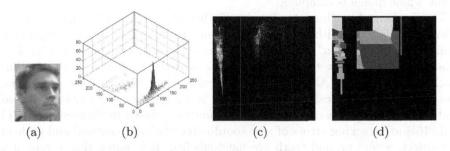

(a)   (b)   (c)   (d)

Fig. 3. Adaptive determination of histogram bins. Explanation please see text.

2.3   Tracking Algorithm with Kalman Particle Filter

The reference shape is represented by a rectangle described by a quadratic B-Spline curve with a double knot at each of four control points. The rectangle is allowed to translate freely in image plane and to change width and height with the same scale.

The object dynamics is modelled as a random walk $p(\mathbf{x}_k|\mathbf{x}_{k-1})$, where $\mathbf{x}_k$ is system state at time k. The dissimilarity between color distribution of target $\mathbf{q} = \{q_u\}_{u=1,\cdots,d}$ and that of candidate $\mathbf{p}(\mathbf{x}_k) = \{p_u(\mathbf{x}_k)\}_{u=1,\cdots,d}$ is measured based on Bhattacharyya distance $d(\mathbf{q}, \mathbf{p}(\mathbf{x}_k)) = (1 - \Sigma_{u=1}^{m} \sqrt{p_u(\mathbf{x}_k)}\sqrt{q_u})^{\frac{1}{2}}$. The measurement density is defined as:

$$\pi(\mathbf{y}_k|\mathbf{x}_k) = \frac{1}{\sqrt{2\pi}\sigma} \exp -\frac{d^2(\mathbf{q}, \mathbf{p}(\mathbf{x}_k))}{2\sigma^2} \qquad (4)$$

The Kalman partile filter [4], which has benefit of steering discrete samples to the most probable regions and thus can get more accurate results, is used to track object.

3   Experiments and Discussion

The algorithm is written with C++ on a laptop with 2.2GHz mobile Pentium CPU and 1G Memory. Initialization of the algorithm is automated with face detection algorithm [8] in the first experiment, or manually labelled in the second experiment.

3.1   Single Object Tracking

The first image sequence comprises 603 frames with image size of 256x192 pixels, which involves agile motion of a human face, short period of occlusion, illumination changes and distraction similar to skin color[1]. Among different color spaces, HSV color space with V-component discarded neglecting luminance information that gets the best result is used. On this occasion, the Integral Histogram Image of the whole image is computed.

The tracking algorithm introduced in [5] (hereafter called "Old Algorithm" for reference simplicity) with 8x8=64 bins is compared with our proposed algorithm (called "New Algorithm") with 8 bins (8 clusters), as shown in Fig. 4. Fig. 4(a) shows average tracking time versus number of particles. It is seen clearly that tracking time of Old Algorithm is much more than that of New Algorithm, and increases dramatically with gradually larger number of particles, whereas that of New Algorithm remains negligible increase. Shown in Figures 4(b), 4(c) and 4(d) are tracking errors of x, y coordinates of object centroid and scale of the object, where ground truth are hand-labelled. It is noted that errors of x coordinate and scale of the Old Algorithm are a little less than those of the New

---

[1] Dr. S. Birchfield is acknowledged for providing the test sequence.

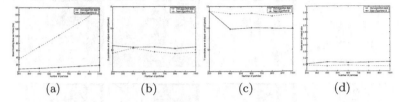

| (a) | (b) | (c) | (d) |

Fig. 4. Comparisons of tracking time and errors between the algorithm in [5](the Old Algorithm) and the proposed algorithm (the New Algorithm)

Fig. 5. Some of typical tracking results with the proposed algorithm

algorithm, while error of y coordinate of the Old Algorithm is larger than that of the New one. Overall for this image sequence the performances of the two algorithms are comparable, meanwhile the proposed algorithm takes very little time. Some typical results using our algorithm are shown in Fig. 5.

3.2 Multiple Object Tracking

The second experiment is conducted on a video sequence named "ThreePast-Shop2cor.mpg" (frames 535 to 900 with image size of 384x288), publicly available at http://homepages.inf.ed.ac.uk/rbf/CAVIAR/. The challenging point in the experiment is that the clothes of the second and third subjects have very similar color, and during frames 790 to 860 a fourth person enters the field of view from the right and occludes the three sequentially.

Thanks to spatio-temporal continuity, it is unnecessary for us compute the Integral Histogram Image of the whole image. Thus in this experiment, tracking area is focused on a sufficiently large region surrounding the object (three times of the size of the object) and its Integral Histogram Image is calculated.

We use three separate trackers to follow the three subjects respectively, using 16 bins (clusters) in RGB space and 1000 particles. The proposed algorithm can track stably the three persons throughout the sequence, except that after frame 840, the third tracker is lost and locks erroneously on the second subject. The reason of this failure is that the color of that subject does not bear resemblance

Fig. 6. Some of tracking results using the proposed algorithm with 16 bins and 1000 particles. From left to right, top to bottom are frames 535 590, 642, 756,789, 837, 888 and 900.

at all to the reference color due to illumination changes. Some typical results are show in Fig. 6.

The algorithm presented in [5] is also used to follow the three subjects with 16x16x16 bins in RGB space and 200 particles. The first tracker can follow the subject with red cloth during the whole clip. However, from frames 637 to 673 and 742 to 768, the other two trackers are often confused and locked on to the erroneous objects. The third tracker is lost and never recovers since frame 786.

The average tracking time per frame is 40ms for the proposed algorithm and 150ms for the old algorithm.

4   Conclusions

Particle filter is a powerful algorithm to deal with non-linear and/or non-Gaussian problem. However high computational load often prevents its real-time implementation off the shelf. Most traditional algorithms try to improve computational efficiency however at the cost of coarsely representing object color and decreasing the number of particles, thus risking being unable to well represent posterior distribution and tracking failure.

By presenting the *Integral Histogram Image* and adaptive histogram based on K-Means clustering, we get an effective and efficient color based particle filter for object tracking. The computational cost of the algorithm increases very little as the number of particles, which is an important property for both theoretical and experimental research show that with increase of particle number, the convergence and accurateness of particle filter are much more possibly ensured [1,2]. Future work is concerned with how to adaptively determine the number of cluster numbers, and a combination of color with other image cues to deal with much more challenging scenarios.

Acknowledgment

The work was supported by the National Natural Science Foundation of China (NSFC) under Grant Number 60505006 and 60673110 and Natural Science

Foundation of Heilongjiang Province (F200512), supported in part by Science and Technology Research Project of Educational Bureau of Heilongjiang Province (1151G033), the Scientific Research Foundation for the Returned Overseas Chinese Scholars, State Education Ministry, the Excellent Scientific Research Project for the Returned Overseas Scholars, Ministry of Personnel of China, Science and Technology Innovation Research Project (2006RFLXG030) of Harbin Sci. & Tech. Bureau, Postdoctoral Fund for Scientific Research of Heilongjiang Province (LHK-04093).

References

1. Doucet, A., Godsill, S., Andrieu, C.: On Sequential Monte Carlo Sampling Methods for Bayesian Filtering. Statistics and Computing, 10(3) (2000) 197–208
2. Isard, M., Blake, A.: Condensation-Conditional Density Propagation for Visual Tracking. Int. J. of Computer Vision, 29(1) (1998) 5–28
3. Kwolek, B.: Stereovision-Based Head Tracking Using Color and Ellipse Fitting in a Particle Filter. Proc. Eur. Conf. on Comp. Vis. Springer-Verlag, Berlin Heidelberg (2004) 192–204
4. Li, P., Zhang, T., Pece, A.E.C.: Visual Contour Tracking Based on Particle Filters. Image and Vision Computing, 21(1) (2003) 111–123
5. Nummiaro, K., Koller-Meier, E.B., Van Gool, L.: An Adaptive Color-based Particle Filter. Image and Vision Computing, 21(1) (2003) 100–110
6. Pérez P., Hue C., Vermaak J. and Gangnet M.: Color-based Probabilistic Tracking. Proc. Eur. Conf. on Comp. Vis. Springer-Verlag, Berlin Heidelberg (2002) 661–675.
7. Porikli, F.: Integral Histogram: a Fast Way to Extract Histograms in Cartesian Spaces. Proc. IEEE conf. on Comp. Vis. and Patt. Recog. (2005) 829–836
8. Wang, H., Li, P., Zhang, T.: Proposal of Novel Histogram Features for Face Detection. Int. Conf. On Advances in Pattern Recognition. Bath, United Kingdom (2005) 334–343
9. Wang, J, Chen, X., Gao, W.: Online Selecting Discriminative Tracking Features Using Particle Filter. Proc. IEEE Conf. on Comp. Vis. and Patt. Recog. (2005) 1037–1042
10. Wu, Y., Huang, T.: Robust Visual Tracking by Integrating Multiple Cues Based on Co-inference Learning. Int. J. of Computer Vision, 58(1) (2004) 55–71
11. Yang, C., Duraiswami, R., Davis L.S.: Fast Multiple Object Tracking via a Hierarchical Particle Filter. Proc. IEEE Conf. on Comp. Vis. Beijing (2005) 212–219
12. Town, C.P., Moran, S.J.: Robust Fusion of Colour Appearance Models for Object Tracking. Proc. British Machine Vision Conference (2004)
13. Viola, P., Jones, M.: Rapid Object Detection Using a Boosted Cascade of Simple Features. Proc. IEEE conf. on Comp. Vis. and Patt. Recog. (2001) 511–518

Fitting Subdivision Surface Models to Noisy and Incomplete 3-D Data

Spela Ivekovic and Emanuele Trucco

Heriot-Watt University, Riccarton, Edinburgh EH14 4AS, UK
{sil,e.trucco}@hw.ac.uk

Abstract. We describe an algorithm for fitting a Catmull-Clark subdivision surface model to an unstructured, incomplete and noisy data set. We complete the large missing data regions with the *a-priori* shape information and produce a smooth, compact and structured data description. The result can be used for further data manipulation, compression, or visualisation. Our fitting algorithm uses a *quasi-interpolation* technique which manipulates the base mesh of the subdivision model to achieve better approximation. We extend the approach designed for scientific visualisation and animation to deal with incomplete and noisy data and preserve prior shape constraints where data is missing. We illustrate the algorithm on range and stereo data with a set of different subdivision models and demonstrate the applicability of the method to the problem of novel view synthesis from incomplete stereo data.

1   Introduction

Fitting subdivision surfaces to unstructured high-quality range data has received considerable attention in the area of Computer Graphics. Subdivision surface models present a convenient tool for approximation of data with arbitrary topology to a high level of detail and naturally lend themselves to almost any shape deformation which makes them an ideal modelling technique for computer animation and visualisation.

In this paper we use subdivision surface models for post-processing noisy and incomplete data, much more common in Computer Vision. Instead of a visually appealing model, our goal is to provide a fairly simple model smoothing the noisy raw data, filling in large regions of missing data with the available prior information and providing a compact, complete and noise free description for further data manipulation.

We base our model fitting algorithm on the quasi-interpolation approach [14] originally developed for scientific visualisation and animation. Our algorithm is a modification of [14] which extends the use of quasi-interpolation to noisy and incomplete data. We illustrate the potential of the method on high-quality, incomplete range data and noisy stereo data with a set of different subdivision models. The applicability of the method to the problem of novel view synthesis is demonstrated by post-processing raw disparity data and using the complete disparity data description to synthesise high quality novel views.

This paper is structured as follows. We first describe the related work in Section 2, followed by a brief overview of the subdivision surfaces in Section 3 and description of the original quasi-interpolation method used in [14] in Section 4. Our version of the

A. Gagalowicz and W. Philips (Eds.): MIRAGE 2007, LNCS 4418, pp. 542–554, 2007.
© Springer-Verlag Berlin Heidelberg 2007

fitting algorithm is presented in Section 5 and the experimental results are described in Section 6. We present the conclusions in Section 7.

2   Related Work

In Computer Graphics, a lot of research effort has already been devoted to geometric modelling with subdivision surfaces [6,20,25]. They are now an established tool for geometric modelling and animation and have in most cases successfully replaced traditional modelling with NURBS surfaces. They have been used commercially by animation studios such as Pixar [17] and Blue Sky [2]. Fitting subdivision surfaces to unstructured range data for the purpose of modelling and animation has also been addressed by various researchers in the Computer Graphics area [4,8,12,13,14,19,23].

Unlike in Computer Graphics, models used in Computer Vision are typically very simple and problem specific. When modelling a human body, for example, the generic models can be anything from conic sections [7], superquadric ellipsoids [21], to implicit surfaces [18], more detailed mesh models [22] and volumetric models [15].

In Computer Vision, working with visually appealing models is not the most important issue. This is very likely one of the reasons why subdivision surfaces, perceived mainly as a Computer Graphics technique, do not seem to have established their role as a useful modelling tool yet. To the best of our knowledge, the only attempts to use the subdivision surfaces for a Computer Vision related problem are human body pose estimation with subdivision surfaces [11] and using subdivision surfaces for reconstruction from noisy 3-D data [9].

The aim of the work described in this paper is very similar to that in [9]. Unlike [9] we use a quadrilateral mesh as a base mesh for subdivision and therefore also use a different subdivision method (Catmull-Clark instead of Loop subdivision) providing an alternative to the approach described in [9]. Our fitting algorithm does not involve an optimisation for model parameters but is instead an explicit iterative approximation process which can be stopped at any level of detail sufficient to solve the problem.

Like [9], we highlight the modelling potential of subdivision surfaces and present them as a viable alternative to other modelling approaches currently in use in Computer Vision. They are a very simple and yet very powerful modelling tool that can inherently be used on various levels of detail, deformed to various extremes and visualised as a traditional polygonal mesh model. Their multiresolutional nature lends itself to a wide variety of problems including modelling, reconstruction, compression, visualisation and animation.

3   Subdivision Surfaces

Subdivision surfaces were introduced in 1978 by Catmull and Clark [3] and Doo and Sabin [5]. The algorithm for modelling smooth 3-D objects starts with a coarse polyhedron p_0 approximating the shape of the desired object. This coarse model can then be refined using subdivision rules to produce increasingly faceted approximations to the associated smooth shape. If these rules are represented by the operator S, this process has the form [24]

$$p^k = Sp^{k-1}. \tag{1}$$

Applying S to an initial model p^0 yields a sequence of polygonal models $p^1, p^2, \ldots$. The rules comprising S specify how the polygonal faces of p^{k-1} are split, as well as how the vertices of p^k are positioned in terms of the vertices p^{k-1}. If these rules are chosen carefully, the limit of this process is a smooth surface p^∞ that approximates the coarse model p^0.

Depending on the type of the mesh describing the coarse polyhedron, different rules are applied to produce the smooth surface. The two basic and most frequently used subdivision methods are *Loop* subdivision, for triangular meshes, and *Catmull-Clark* subdivision, for quadrilateral meshes. A detailed description of both can be found in [24]. These two subdivision schemes are applicable generally as an arbitrary mesh can be reduced to a triangular or quadrilateral mesh after one subdivision pass.

4 Quasi-interpolation

The use of quasi-interpolation for subdivision surface fitting was first suggested by Litke et al. in [14]. The basic idea behind quasi-interpolation is to use local, weighted averages of samples of the desired surface as control points. No solution of global linear systems with an a priori fixed set of coefficients is required. Quasi-interpolation has an optimal order of convergence on regular meshes, making it asymptotically as good as least-squares [14].

Summarising [14], it is instructive to first illustrate the quasi-interpolation operator on the univariate approximation problem. Let us assume that samples of a sufficiently smooth function f are given which we would like to approximate with a uniform cubic spline curve. The solution is to find values of control points for an optimal cubic spline with knots at the integers. The least-squares solution would be to set up a linear system whose size is proportional to the number of knots and solve it for the control point values. Instead of solving a global system, the quasi-interpolation operator can be applied locally as follows:

$$p_i = -\frac{1}{6}f(i-1) + \frac{4}{3}f(i) - \frac{1}{6}f(i+1), \quad \forall i \in \mathbb{Z}, \tag{2}$$

where p_i is the control point at the knot i. Although this quasi-interpolant is a local operator, it is an exact interpolant whenever f is a cubic polynomial [14].

The univariate limit stencil with weights for cubic B-splines can be written as $L = (1/6, 4/6, 1, 6)$. Writing the identity stencil as $I = (0, 1, 0)$, we can derive the quasi-interpolation stencil Q as $Q = 2I - L$:

$$\left(-\frac{1}{6}, \frac{4}{3}, -\frac{1}{6}\right) = (0, 2, 0) - \left(\frac{1}{6}, \frac{4}{6}, \frac{1}{6}\right). \tag{3}$$

The stencil is applied to the mesh by centering it on the mesh vertex currently being updated and using the remaining weights on its 1-neighbourhood. The rule for constructing quasi-interpolation stencils from cubic B-spline limit stencils can be simply extended to a bivariate case on a regular mesh by means of the tensor product:

$$L = \frac{1}{36} \begin{bmatrix} 1 & 4 & 1 \\ 4 & 16 & 4 \\ 1 & 4 & 1 \end{bmatrix} \quad I = \begin{bmatrix} 0 & 0 & 0 \\ 0 & 1 & 0 \\ 0 & 0 & 0 \end{bmatrix} \quad Q = 2I - L = \frac{1}{36} \begin{bmatrix} -1 & -4 & -1 \\ -4 & 56 & -4 \\ -1 & -4 & -1 \end{bmatrix}, \quad (4)$$

where L is a limit stencil for a bicubic B-spline. Given that limit stencils L are known for all popular subdivision rules such as creases, boundaries, etc., the formula $Q = 2I - L$ is simply extended to the irregular mesh case by substituting L with the appropriate limit stencil. A more detailed description of quasi-interpolation can be found in [14].

5 The Surface Fitting Algorithm

The input to our fitting algorithm is the base mesh $\mathcal{B}_0$ of a subdivision model and an unstructured set of M data points $\{P_j\}$, $j = 1 \ldots M$. We assume that the correspondences between the data and the model surface are established during the fitting process.

First a few words about the terminology. The base mesh $\mathcal{B}_0$ is the coarse mesh which, when subdivided infinitely many times, takes on the shape of the smooth subdivision surface, the *limit surface* $\mathcal{S}^\infty$:

$$\mathcal{S}^\infty = \lim_{n \to \infty} S^n \mathcal{B}_0, \quad (5)$$

where S is the subdivision operator. In practice, it suffices to subdivide the base mesh a finite number of times to obtain an acceptable approximation of the limit surface which we will denote by $\tilde{\mathcal{S}}^\infty$:

$$\tilde{\mathcal{S}}^\infty = S^N \mathcal{B}_0, \quad where \quad N < \infty. \quad (6)$$

In all our experiments we set $N = 3$, and, when referring to our fitting algorithm, the limit surface $\tilde{\mathcal{S}}_i^\infty$ denotes the base mesh $\mathcal{B}_i$ subdivided 3 times. Every vertex of the base mesh $b_k \in \mathcal{B}_0$ has its limit position on the limit surface, denoted by $v_k^\infty = \lim_{n \to \infty} S^n b_k$, where $k = 1 \ldots K$ and K is the number of base mesh vertices.

The fitting process consists of two stages: the initialisation stage, where the base mesh is deformed while its density remains unchanged, and the fitting loop, where the base mesh is repeatedly subdivided and deformed until satisfactory approximation is achieved. We describe the algorithm in more detail in the sequel.

5.1 The Algorithm

Our fitting algorithm can be summarised as follows.

1. Initialisation: $(i = 0)$
   (a) Generate the limit surface of the initial base mesh $\tilde{\mathcal{S}}_0^\infty$
   (b) Establish correspondences between $\tilde{v}_0^\infty$ and the data points $\{P_j\}$
   (c) Apply the quasi-interpolation operator Q to all vertices of the base mesh for which the correspondences are available

2. Loop: ($i = i + 1$, repeat until satisfactory approximation is achieved)
   (a) Once uniformly subdivide the base mesh: $\mathcal{B}_i = S^1 \mathcal{B}_{i-1}$
   (b) Generate the limit surface of the new base mesh $\tilde{S}_i^\infty$
   (c) Establish correspondences between $\tilde{v}_i^\infty$ and the data points $\{P_j\}$
   (d) Apply the quasi-interpolation operator to all vertices of the base mesh for which the correspondences are available

Notice that the vertices of the base mesh for which no correspondences could be found remain unchanged during the quasi-interpolation step. In this way, the parts of the model corresponding to missing data regions simply converge towards the predefined limit surface dictated by the model and complete the missing data with the prior shape information.

A nice property of our method is that we start with a very simple and coarse base mesh and gradually increase its density and add more detail. In this way, unlike [9], we avoid the need for a regularisation factor to enforce consistent mesh deformation, as this is naturally achieved through the fitting process itself.

In comparison with [14], we avoid the adaptive subdivision of the base mesh and instead subdivide uniformly. This might seem an unusual choice, however there are several good reasons for it:

- With noisy data it is very important to begin with a simple low-density mesh and gradually proceed towards the details. We want to preserve control over the behaviour of the surface in the regions where no data is available. Continuously uniformly subdividing the base mesh regardless of the existence of correspondences guarantees that the parts of the model which do not deform due to missing data eventually converge towards the predefined shape, achieving model-based interpolation of complex shapes.
- We want to allow for possible incremental fitting to the data, i.e., we want to be able to backtrack to the original base mesh and update it with new data as it becomes available. Keeping the subdivision process uniform makes the process of updating the mesh by working down the subdivision tree relatively straightforward, as only the vertex positions change while the mesh connectivity remains the same.
- Last but not least, we want to keep the fitting method simple and easy to reproduce. Adaptive subdivision involves paying attention to a number of ways in which the mesh connectivity must change to bridge the gaps between the faces on different levels of subdivision and deciding where to subdivide adaptively requires a much more thorough assessment of the quality-of-fit which is not of the utmost importance when dealing with very noisy data.

6   Experiments

In our experiments we used two different data sets. The first, range data of the Julius Caesar head statue, provided courtesy of INRIA by the AIM@SHAPE Shape Repository [1], was used to study the behaviour and capabilities of the method. The second, noisy and incomplete wide-baseline stereo data of the upper human body was used to demonstrate a potential application of the fitting method to the problem of novel view synthesis. We describe experiments with both data sets in the following sections.

6.1   Range Data

The range data of the Julius Caesar head statue used for the first set of experiments is illustrated in Figure 1. The reason for choosing this particular data set is two-fold. Firstly, the data on the back of the head is missing, which allows us to test how well we can complete the missing data with an *a priori* shape. Secondly, the data is accurate enough to allow for an informative quality-of-fit assessment by measuring the distance of the surface from the data as the fit evolves.

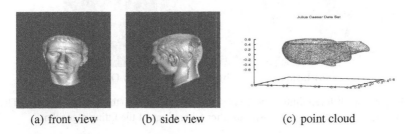

(a) front view   (b) side view   (c) point cloud

Fig. 1. (a,b) Julius Caesar range data set. (c) The data set is originally provided as a mesh model, however, for the purpose of our fitting experiment we ignore the mesh connectivity information and only use the mesh vertices as a raw data point cloud containing 19572 points.

In order to illustrate the potential of the method, we performed several experiments using different subdivision surface models. The sensitivity of the method to the initial conditions was assessed using a simple sphere subdivision surface and varying its position and mesh density. A simple head model was then used to test how a more informative *a-priori* shape improves the visual quality of the fit. A slightly more sophisticated head model was used to demonstrate how the vertex placement in the starting mesh influences the convergence speed and the visual quality of the fit. We describe all these experiments in more detail in the following sections.

Sphere Model and Varying Initial Conditions. In this set of experiments we use a simple sphere model in order to test the sensitivity of the method to the distance and relative position of the initial model with respect to the data. We scaled the sphere to fit inside the data, as close as possible to the data, and around the data. The three initial positions are illustrated in the upper row of Figure 2. We iterated the main loop of the fitting algorithm five times for each of the three initial positions to achieve a very good resemblance between the model surface and the data. The final results are shown in the lower row of Figure 2. Visually, the results do not differ much and all achieve a very good resemblance in 5 iterations. Error analysis (Figure 3) reveals that each of the fits achieved the goal in a slightly different way. The error metric adopted for this analysis is defined below. The iterations in Figure 3 are labelled from -1 to 5 to differentiate between the initialisation stage of the algorithm and the fitting loop. The iteration -1 illustrates the starting point of the fit and iteration 0 describes the model after the initialisation step. Iterations 1-5 repeat the main loop of the fitting algorithm. The thresholds used to establish the correspondences between the model and the data must be much larger in the first two iterations to successfully attract the model to the

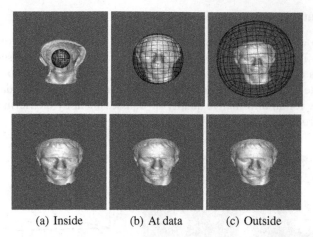

(a) Inside   (b) At data   (c) Outside

Fig. 2. Upper row: different initial sphere positions with respect to the data. Lower row: The final results for the three initial sphere positions after 5 iterations of the fitting algorithm.

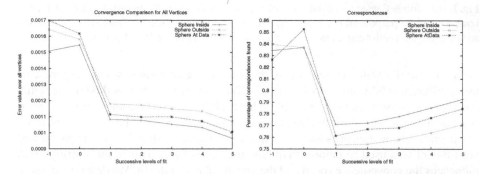

Fig. 3. The behaviour of the fitting process for three different starting points. Left: Error function convergence. Right: Percentage of correspondences found on every level of the fit.

data. After that, the threshold values can be reduced and, in our experiments, linearly decrease with every iteration which explains the sudden change in the behaviour of the error function from iteration 0 to iteration 1.

The error function evaluates the RMS distance between the model surface and the data where correspondences were successfully established and weighs the result by the percentage of vertices for which the correspondences were not found:

$$E = \frac{N_{nc}}{N} \sqrt{\frac{1}{N_c} \sum_{i=1}^{N_c} (v_i - p_{v_i})^2},$$ (7)

where v_i is a limit surface vertex, p_{v_i} is the corresponding data point, N is the total number of vertices in the limit surface, N_c is the number of vertices for which correspondences were established and N_{nc} is the number of limit surface vertices without correspondences.

As shown in Figure 3, the initial position of the model does have some influence on the convergence behaviour of the fitting process. The smallest sphere does best in terms of error convergence as well as in the number of correspondences found. As it is the smallest, it can be placed in the centre of the head where it is surrounded by the majority of the data which it samples very densely and the most important correspondences are found very early in the fitting process.

As the first experiment favoured the smallest and densest sphere, we performed another experiment investigating how the density of the starting base mesh influences the behaviour of the fit. We chose the sphere model scaled to fit the data from the previous experiment and modified it to obtain two additional levels of density as shown in Figure 4. For reasons of computational complexity and for fair comparison, we used 5 iterations of the algorithm on the lowest density model, 4 iterations on the medium one and 3 iterations on the highest density model. In this way all three models had the same base mesh density at the final level and could be compared more fairly. Figure 5 illustrates

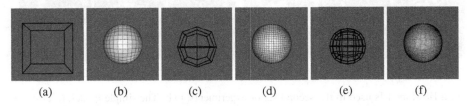

(a)   (b)   (c)   (d)   (e)   (f)

Fig. 4. Initial sphere model with an increasingly dense mesh. (a,b) lowest density base mesh and corresponding subdivision model; (b,c) medium density base mesh and corresponding subdivision model; (d,e) highest density and corresponding subdivision model.

the behaviour of each model. The error plot over all vertices shows that the model with a denser base mesh achieves the same quality of the fit in fewer iterations as it samples the data in more detail, establishes more correspondences and recovers the detail faster. All three models achieve comparable fit quality if allowed to iterate to the same level of base mesh complexity. This is a useful property if an approximation on several levels of detail is required. The two more dense models have a very similar performance which also indicates that there is a limit to the useful mesh density.

Head Model. In this experiment we show how we can use a more informative prior shape to complete large regions of missing data with our fitting algorithm. Our aim is to keep the model as simple as possible and test how much simplicity we can get away with. We first fit a very basic head and neck model (see Figure 6) and then show how strategically placed control points of the base mesh improve the overall fit quality and convergence. Results of the fit with the basic head model are shown in Figure 7. Although the shape of this model is much more informative than the sphere, the basic model turns out to be too simple to convincingly model the head. While performing experiments with this model, we realised that it made a noticeable difference if the important data points were sampled first, i.e., the nose, ears and other more significant parts of the data set. We therefore constructed another base mesh for the generic head and neck model, which contained control points exactly where the important data points

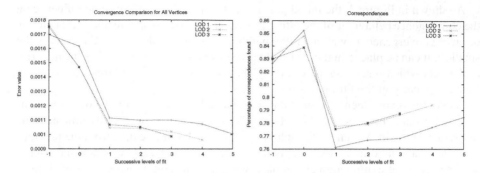

Fig. 5. Behaviour of the fit for three different model mesh densities. Left: Error function convergence. Right: Percentage of correspondences found at every level.

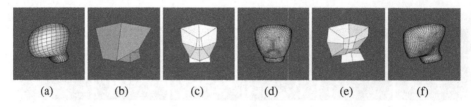

Fig. 6. Head models used in the second set of experiments. (a,b) The simple model, (c-f) strategically placed control points.

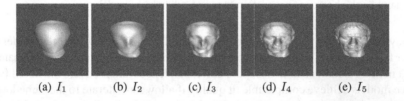

(a) I_1 (b) I_2 (c) I_3 (d) I_4 (e) I_5

Fig. 7. The fitting stages with the basic head model (Figure 6(a)). I_i denotes the iteration of the fitting algorithm.

were expected to be (see Figure 6). This proved a much more successful approach (Figure 8). As a side effect of constructing a new, slightly denser, base mesh, we also created a much more convincing head shape which very nicely completes the missing back data (see Figure 8). These experiments show that it is important to use a generic model with control points placed at strategic positions. As the fitting is performed hierarchically, it makes sense to "schedule" the correspondence search to some extent, i.e., force the most important correspondences to be established very early in the fitting process. This would not be such a big issue if the correspondences were established manually and in advance, however, since we are aiming at a fully automatic process, the base mesh vertex placement is an important consideration.

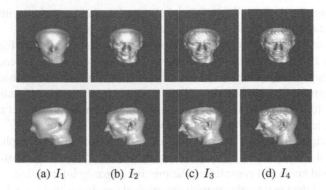

(a) I_1 (b) I_2 (c) I_3 (d) I_4

Fig. 8. Upper row: The fitting stages with the model where control points have been placed in strategic positions. Lower row: view from the side to show the complete model even where data is missing.

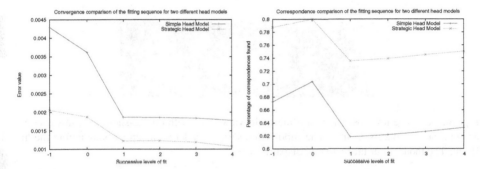

Fig. 9. Comparison of the convergence for two different head models. The model with the base mesh designed to have vertices at strategic positions performs better. Left: Error function convergence Right: percentage of correspondences found at every level.

6.2 Stereo Data

To illustrate the applicability of our fitting algorithm to noisy and incomplete data sets typical of Computer Vision, we performed experiments on stereo data obtained from a multi-view video sequence (Figure 11). The data was generated with a stereo correspondence search algorithm based on pyramid correlation.

An example of a problem which highly depends on the quality of the stereo data is the image-based novel view synthesis. The more accurate and complete the disparity data for the original pair of views, the better the synthesised novel view, however, the complexity of the surface makes simple interpolation approaches unusable [10].

Figure 10 (left) shows the wide-baseline camera setup used to acquire the test images. In comparison with range data, fitting to stereo data is a much more demanding problem as the data is sparse and noisy, as can be seen from example disparity maps (see Figure 11). The aim of the fitting process is not to produce a visually pleasing result with a high level of detail, but instead to complete the sparse data with an *a-priori* shape information containing low level of detail and remove the outliers.

We used a very simple generic subdivision model of the upper body (Figure 10 centre) which we fit directly to the raw disparity data. Before the model could be fit to the data, the upper body pose had to be estimated. This was achieved using the Particle Swarm Optimisation method described in [11]. After the pose estimation step, the model was fit to the data using our fitting algorithm from Section 5 and then used to generate complete disparity maps for novel view synthesis (Figure 11).

Figure 10 (right) illustrates the model after the fit. Notice that the emphasis was not on modelling the data to a high level of detail but instead on discriminating between reliable data and noise and completing the missing disparity information.

The results of the view synthesis with the original raw disparity data and the disparity data obtained from the model after the fit are shown in Figure 11. The complete disparity data clearly improves the result of the view synthesis with the subdivision model providing the missing information necessary to complete the synthesis.

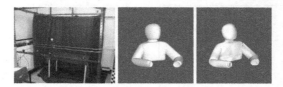

Fig. 10. Left: The low cost wide-baseline multi-view setup with off-the-shelf webcams used to acquire the test images. Centre: The subdivision surface model of the upper body before the fit. Right: The model after fitting to raw disparity data.

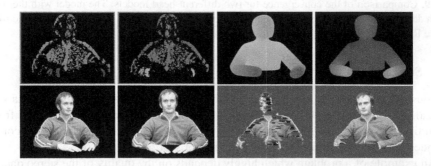

Fig. 11. Upper row: Original disparity map (left-right and right-left) as produced by the correspondence search algorithm and disparity map generated from the model after it was fit to the disparity data. Lower row: The original views, the novel view synthesised with the original disparity map and the model-generated disparity map. The original two cameras were positioned to the left and in front of the test subject and the synthetic camera was placed to the right of the test subject. The hands are not visible in the synthesised view as we do not model them with our simple upper-body model.

7 Conclusion

We have presented an iterative method for fitting the Catmull-Clark subdivision surface models to unorganised and noisy data with large missing regions using quasi-interpolation. The effectiveness of the method was demonstrated with a number of experiments on high quality range data and noisy stereo data. Our method is fully automatic, simple, quick and easy to implement and hopefully highlights some of the potential of using subdivision surfaces for modelling applications in Computer Vision.

References

1. A.I.M.A.T.S.H.A.P.E.: http://www.aim-at-shape.net
2. www.blueskystudios.com
3. Catmull, E., Clark, J.: Recursively generated b-spline surfaces on arbitrary topological meshes. Computer Aided Design, 10, 1978
4. Cheng, K.-S. D., Wang, W., Qin, H., Wong K.-Y. K., Yang, H., Liu, Y.: Fitting subdivision surfaces to unorganized point data using SDM. Pacific Conference on Computer Graphics and Applications 2004, 16 – 24
5. Doo, D., Sabin, M.: Analysis of the behaviour of recursive division surfaces near extraordinary points. Computer Aided Design, 10, 1978
6. DeRose, T., Kass, M., Truong, T.: Subdivision surfaces in character animation. Proceedings of SIGGRAPH 1998, New York, USA, 85 – 94
7. Deutscher, J., Blake, A., Reid, I.: Articulated body motion capture by annealed particle filtering. IEEE International Conference on Computer Vision and Pattern Recognition 2000
8. Hoppe, H., DeRose, T., Duchamp, T., McDonals, J., Stuetzle, W.: Surface reconstruction from unorganised points. Computer Graphics, 26(2): 71–78, 1992
9. Ilić, S.: Using Subdivision Surfaces for 3-D Reconstruction from Noisy Data. Deform - Workshop on Image Registration in Deformable Environments, Edinburgh, UK, 2006, 1 – 10
10. Ivekovic, S., Trucco, E.: Dense Wide-Baseline Disparities from Conventional Stereo for Immersive Videoconferencing. ICPR 2004, Volume 4, 921 – 924
11. Ivekovic, S., Trucco, E.: Human Body Pose Estimation with PSO. IEEE World Congress on Computational Intelligence 2006, Vancouver, Canada
12. Jeong, W. K., Kim, C. H.: Direct reconstruction of displaced subdivision surface from unorganised points. Pacific Conference on Computer Graphics and Applications, 160 – 169, 2001
13. Jeong, W. K., Kähler, K., Haber, J., Seidel, H.-P.: Automatic Generation of Subdivision Surface Head Models from Point Cloud Data. Graphics Interface 2002
14. Litke, N., Levin, A., Schröder, P.: Fitting Subdivision Surfaces. IEEE Visualization (2001), 319 – 324
15. Mikic, I., Trivedi, M., Hunter, E., Cosman, P.: Human Body Model Acquisition and Tracking Using Voxel Data, International Journal on Computer Vision, 53(3): 199–223, July 2003
16. Niyogi, S. A., Adelson, E. H.: Analyzing and Recognizing Walking Figures in XYT. IEEE Conference on Computer Vision and Pattern Recognition 1994, 469 – 474
17. www.pixar.com
18. Plänkers, R., Fua, P.: Articulated Soft Objects for Video-based Body Modeling. ICCV 2001, Vancouver, Canada
19. Scheib, V., Haber, J., Lin, M. C., Seidel, H.-P.: Efficient fitting and rendering of large scattered data sets using subdivision surfaces. Computer Graphics Forum 21(3) 2002

20. Schröder, P.: Subdivision as a fundamental building block of digital geometry processing algorithms. Journal of Computational and Applied Mathematics, 149, 2002
21. Sminchisescu, C., Triggs, B.: Covariance Scaled Sampling for Monocular 3D Body Tracking. CVPR 2001, 447–454
22. Starck, J., Hilton, A.: Model-Based Multiple View Reconstruction of People, ICCV 2003
23. Suzuki, H., Takeuchi, S., Kimura, F., Kanai, T.: Subdivision surface fitting to a range of points. IEEE Computer Society Pacific Conference on Computer Graphics and Applications, pp 158, 1999
24. Warren, J., Schaeffer, S.: A factored approach to subdivision surfaces. Computer Graphics and Applications 24 (2004)
25. Zorin, D., Schröder, P., DeRose, T., Kobbelt, L., Levin, A., Sweldens, W.: Subdivision for modeling and animation. SIGGRAPH 2000 Course notes

Classification of Facial Expressions Using K-Nearest Neighbor Classifier

Abu Sayeed Md. Sohail[1] and Prabir Bhattacharya[2]

[1] Department of Computer Science and Software Engineering, Concordia University
1455 de Maisonneuve Blvd. West, Montreal, Quebec H3G 1M8, Canada
a_sohai@encs.concordia.ca
[2] Concordia Institute for Information Systems Engineering, Concordia University
1515 St. Catherine West, Montreal, Quebec H3G 2W1, Canada
prabir@ciise.concordia.ca

Abstract. In this paper, we have presented a fully automatic technique for detection and classification of the six basic facial expressions from nearly frontal
face images. Facial expressions are communicated by subtle changes in one or
more discrete features such as tightening the lips, raising the eyebrows, opening
and closing of eyes or certain combinations of them. These discrete features can
be identified through monitoring the changes in muscles movement (Action
Units) located near about the regions of mouth, eyes and eyebrows. In this
work, we have used eleven feature points that represent and identify the principle muscle actions as well as provide measurements of the discrete features responsible for each of the six basic human emotions. A multi-detector approach
of facial feature point localization has been utilized for identifying these points
of interests from the contours of facial components such as eyes, eyebrows and
mouth. Feature vector composed of eleven features is then obtained by calculating the degree of displacement of these eleven feature points from a non-
changeable rigid point. Finally, the obtained feature sets are used for training a
K-Nearest Neighbor Classifier so that it can classify facial expressions when
given to it in the form of a feature set. The developed Automatic Facial Expression Classifier has been tested on a publicly available facial expression database
and on an average 90.76% successful classification rate has been achieved.

1 Introduction

Facial expression is a visible manifestation of the affective state, cognitive activity,
intention, personality and psychopathology of a person that plays a communicative
role in interpersonal relations [1]. According to Mehrabian [2], the verbal part of a
message contributes only for 7% to the effect of the message as a whole; the vocal
part contributes 38%, while facial expression of the speaker contributes for 55% to
the effect of the spoken message. This implies that the facial expressions form the
major modality in human communication and can play an important role wherever
humans interact with machines. Automatic recognition of facial expressions may act
as a component of both natural human-machine interfaces [3] and its variation known

A. Gagalowicz and W. Philips (Eds.): MIRAGE 2007, LNCS 4418, pp. 555–566, 2007.

as perceptual interfaces [4]. This can also be a possible application domain in behavioral science or medicine for automated analysis of human facial expressions.

Although humans can recognize facial expressions virtually without error or delay, reliable and fully automated expression recognition by machine is still a challenge. Automated systems for facial expression recognition usually take the form of a sequential configuration of processing blocks which adheres to a classical pattern recognition model [5]. The main blocks of such a system as identified by Chibelushi et al. [6] are: image acquisition, pre-processing, feature extraction, classification, and post-processing.

In this paper, we have presented a fully automatic technique for detection and classification of the six basic facial expressions from static face images namely, anger, disgust, fear, happiness, sadness and surprise as defined by Ekman [7]. The subsequent discussion of this paper has been organized into the following six sections: Section II outlines the related works in this field. Discussion about the features used in this work for representing facial expressions has been provided in Section III. Section IV elaborates the technique of obtaining feature set for each of the six facial expressions through detecting the eleven feature points. Section V gives an overview of the K-Nearest Neighbor Classification technique. Experimental results along with discussion on the performance of the system have been provided in Section VI and finally, Section VII concludes the paper.

2   Related Works

Due to its importance for application domains in human behavior interpretation and the human-computer interface, the automatic analysis and classification of facial expression has attracted the interest of many computer vision researchers. Since the mid 70s, different approaches have been proposed for automatic classification of facial expression from either static images or image sequences. Cottrell and Metcalfe [8] used a three layer back-propagation neural network for classifying facial expressions. They used features from the whole face by manually selecting the face region and normalizing it to 64×64 pixels. A pyramid-like feed-forward neural network has been used by Rahardja et al. [9] for classifying six basic facial expressions from hand-drawn face image. Their system can classify expressions successfully from the images of training data set but performance of their system on unknown data set is not reported. Kobayashi and Hara [10] used features obtained from 30 facial characteristics points to train their 60×100×100×6 neural network for classifying facial expression and achieved a success rate of 80%. Vanger et al. [11] proposed a system for classifying facial expressions using neural network by creating a prototype index for each of the emotion category through averaging all eye and mouth parts of 60 utilized static images. The claimed success rate for their system is 70%. Essa and Pentland [12] used an optical flow computation based 3D mesh model technique to track the muscle movement of face. Facial expressions were classified in their work using alternative similarity measurement. Hidden Markov Model based facial expression classifier was developed by Lien et al. [13] where tracking of feature points were performed using dense optical flow and edge detection. Pantic and Rothkrantz [14] performed rule-based classification of facial expressions by extracting features through geometric measurement among the landmarks located on the contours of eyebrows, eyes, nostrils, mouth and chin. Feng et al. [15] proposed a technique where local binary pattern has been used to represent a facial image and classification of facial expressions has been performed by linear programming technique.

As can be inferred from the literature review, most of the previous works depend greatly on manual initialization of the landmark points or facial regions used for representing facial expressions as well as for feature extraction. In this work, we have attempted to eliminate this problem by automatic detection of the used landmark points. Besides this, a small subset of the previously used landmark points has been utilized in this work that has less tendency of being failed during the detection process and thus contributes significantly in improving the performance of the facial expression classifier.

3 Features for Facial Expression Classification

To enable a machine learning technique to learn as well as to classify the patterns of facial expressions successfully, salient properties of the facial expression have to be passed through it as features during both the learning and classification stages. Although each part of human face somehow contributes in producing the non verbal facial expressions, participation of certain face regions are stronger comparative to that of the others. These regions are the eyebrows, eyes and mouth. In this work of detection and classification of human facial expressions, we have considered only the features that are concentrated around these regions.

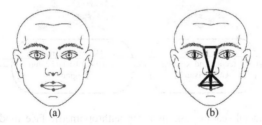

Fig. 1. (a) Feature points used for capturing the facial actions (Action Units) (b) distances that have been used as features by the K-NN classifier for classifying facial expression

Considering the technique of how humans perceive emotions from the face of other humans, we have selected total eleven points (Fig. 1.a) on human face that can detect the movement of eyebrows, eyelids and mouth providing useful information about the involved action units (AU). A set of eleven measurements are performed among these eleven feature points to estimate the level (strength) of activation of the triggered action units using midpoints of nostrils as the base point (Fig. 1.b). This set $\{D_1, D_2, D_3, D_4, D_5, D_6, D_7, D_8, D_9, D_{10}, D_{11}\}$ represents one of the six basic human emotions and is used as a set of feature by the classifier for training as well as classifying facial

Table 1. Description of the distances used as features by the K-Nearest Neighbor classifier for classifying facial expression

Distance	Description of Distances Used as Features
D_1 and D_2	Distance of the right and left eyebrow inner corners from the mid point of nostrils
D_3	Distance between the inner corners of right and left eyebrows
D_4 and D_5	Distance between the mid points of the upper and lower eyelids of left and right eyes
D_6 and D_7	Distance of the right and left mouth corners from the mid point of the nostrils
D_8 and D_9	Distance of the mid upper lip and mid lower lip from the mid point of the nostrils
D_{10}	Distance between the mid points of upper and lower lips
D_{11}	Distance between right and left mouth corners

expressions. Brief description of the measurements, used for generating feature set of facial expressions, is given in Table-1.

4 Detection of Feature Points and Obtaining the Feature Vector

The task of feature point extraction has been performed in two separate stages. At the first stage, feature regions of human faces are isolated using an anthropometric face model based technique specified in [16].

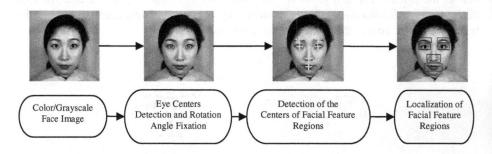

| Color/Grayscale Face Image | Eye Centers Detection and Rotation Angle Fixation | Detection of the Centers of Facial Feature Regions | Localization of Facial Feature Regions |

Fig. 2. Detection of facial feature regions using anthropometric face model based technique. Eye centers are detected first. Location of other facial feature regions are then identified and isolated using distance between two eye centers as the principle parameter of measurement.

In this method, centers of the two eyes are first identified using a generalized framework for robust, real-time object detection [17]. Eye, eyebrow and mouth regions of the face images are then isolated using the distance between two eye centers as the principal parameter of measurement. Results of applying the facial feature regions localization technique over a face image is given in Fig. 2.

During the second stage, a hybrid image processing technique is applied over these isolated feature regions for detecting the specific eleven feature points (Figure 1.a). Feature set, representing a specific facial expression is then obtained using Euclidian distance based measurement performed among these feature points (Table-1).

4.1 Facial Feature Point Detection

Searching for the eleven facial feature points is done separately within each of the areas returned by the facial feature region identifier [16]. Steps constituting the searching process for identifying the eleven feature points are described below:

4.1.1 Mid Upper and Lower Eyelid Detection

The eye region is composed of dark upper eyelid with eyelash, lower eyelid, pupil, bright sclera and the skin region that surrounds the eye. The most continuous and non deformable part of the eye region is the upper eyelid, because both pupil and sclera change their shape with various possible situations of eyes, especially when the eye is closed or partially closed due to various facial expressions. So, inner and outer eye corners are determined first by analyzing the shape of the upper eyelid, and are used later on for locating the mid upper and mid lower eyelid. To avoid the erroneous detection of the eye feature points, discontinuity in upper eyelid region must be avoided. It can be done by changing the illumination of the upper eyelid so that it differs significantly from the surrounding region. This has been carried out by saturating the intensity values of all the pixels towards zero that constitutes the lower 50% of the image intensity cumulative distribution (Fig. 3.b). The adjusted image is then converted to binary one (Fig. 3.c) using the threshold value obtained from the following iterative procedure [18].

1. Pick an initial threshold value, t
2. Calculate the two mean intensity values from the histogram (m_1 and m_2) using the pixels' intensity values that fall below and above the threshold t.
3. Calculate new threshold. $t_{new} = (m_1 + m_2) / 2$.
4. If the threshold has stabilized $(t = t_{new})$, this is the appropriate threshold level. Otherwise, t become t_{new} and reiterate from step 2.

Contour that covers the largest area is then isolated (Fig. 3.d) using the 8-connected contour following algorithm specified in [19]. For right eye, the inner eye corner is the right most point of the contour and outer eye corner is the leftmost point of the contour (Fig. 3.e). For left eye, right most point over the contour becomes the inner corner and leftmost point becomes the outer corner. The whole eye contour region is then divided vertically into three equal parts and searching for the upper and lower mid eyelid is then done within the mid division. For each value of x coordinate $\{x_1, x_2, x_3,...,x_n\}$ that falls within this mid division, there will be two values of y coordinate: one from the upper portion of the eye contour $\{y_{11}, y_{12}, y_{13},...,y_{1n}\}$ and another from the lower portion of the eye contour $\{y_{21}, y_{22}, y_{23},...,y_{2n}\}$. Distance between each pair of points $\{(x_i, y_{1i}), (x_i, y_{2i})\}$ is then calculated. The maximum distance, calculated from the two points that are closest to the midpoint of inner and outer eye corner, is considered as the amount of eye opening and provides the mid points of the upper lower eyelids respectively (Fig. 3.f).

(a)   (b)   (c)   (d)   (e)   (f)

Fig. 3. Mid upper and lower eyelid detection (a) eye region (b) intensity adjustment (c) binarization (d) isolated eye contour (e) inner and outer eye corner detection (f) detected mid points of the upper and lower eyelids

4.1.2 Detection of Inner Eyebrow Corners

Aside from the dark colored eyebrow, eyebrow regions also contains relatively bright skin portion. Sometimes, this region is also partially occulted with hair. Since dark pixels are considered as background in digital imaging technology, the original image is complemented to convert the eyebrow region as the foreground object and rest as the background (Fig. 4.b).

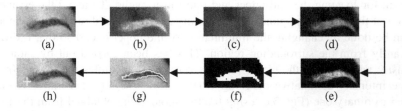

(a)   (b)   (c)   (d)

(h)   (g)   (f)   (e)

Fig. 4. Inner eyebrow corners detection (a) eyebrow region (b) complemented eyebrow image (c) estimated background (d) background subtraction (e) intensity adjustment (f) binary eyebrow region (g) eyebrow contour (h) detected inner eyebrow corner

Morphological image opening operation is then performed over the complemented image with a disk shaped structuring element of 10 pixel radius for obtaining the background illumination (Fig. 4.c). The estimated background is then subtracted from the complemented image to have a comparatively brighter eyebrow over a uniform dark background (Fig. 4.d). Intensity of the resultant image is then adjusted on the basis of the pixels' cumulative distribution to increase the discrimination between the foreground and background (Fig. 4.e). Binary version of this adjusted image (Fig. 4.f) is obtained by thresholding it using Otsu's method [20] and all the available contours of the binary image are detected using the 8-connected contour following algorithm specified in [19]. The eyebrow contour, which is usually the largest one, is then identified by calculating the area covered by each contour (Fig. 4.g). For left eyebrow, the point on the contour having the minimum values along x and y coordinates simultaneously is considered as the inner eyebrow corner. Similarly, for the right eyebrow, point on the eye contour that has the maximum values along x axis and minimum value along y axis simultaneously is considered as the inner eyebrow corner (Fig. 4.h).

4.1.3 Detection of the Midpoint of Nostrils

Nostrils of a nose region are the two circular or parabolic objects having the darkest intensity (Fig. 5.a). For detecting the centre points of nostrils, separation of this dark part from the nose region is performed by filtering it using a Laplacian of Gaussian (LoG) as the filter. The 2-D LoG function centered on zero and with Gaussian standard deviation σ has the form:

$$LoG(x, y) = -\frac{1}{\pi\sigma^4}\left[1 - \frac{x^2 + y^2}{2\sigma^2}\right]e^{-\left(\frac{x^2+y^2}{2\sigma^2}\right)}$$

The LoG operator calculates the second spatial derivative of an image. This means that in areas where the image has a constant intensity (*i.e.* where the intensity gradient is zero), the LoG response will be zero. In the vicinity of a change in intensity, however, the LoG response will be positive on the darker side, and negative on the lighter side.

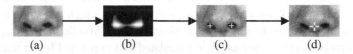

(a)   (b)   (c)   (d)

Fig. 5. Detection of the midpoint of nostrils from isolated nose region (a) isolated nose region (b) filtered by LoG (c) detected nostrils (d) midpoint of nostrils

This means that at a reasonably sharp edge between two regions of uniform but different intensities, the LoG response will be zero at a long distance from the edge as well as positive just to the one side of the edge and negative to the other side. As a result, intensity of the filtered binary image gets complemented and changes the nostrils as the brightest part of the image (Figure 5.b). Searching for the local maximal peak is then performed on the filtered image to obtain the centre points of the nostrils. To make the nostril detection technique independent of the image size, the whole process is repeated varying the filter size starting from 10 pixel, until the number of peaks of local maxima is reduced to two (Figure 5.c). Midpoints of the nostrils are then calculated by averaging the coordinate values of the identified nostrils (Figure 5.d).

4.1.4 Feature Point Detection from Mouth

The simplest case of mouth feature points detection occurs when mouth is normally closed. However, complexities are added to this process by situations like when mouth is wide open or teeth are visible between upper and lower lips due to laughter or any other expression. These two situations provides additional dark and bright region respectively in the mouth contour and makes the feature point detention process quite complex.

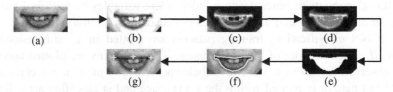

(a)   (b)   (c)   (d)

(g)   (f)   (e)

Fig. 6. Feature point detection from mouth region (a) isolated mouth region (b) intensity adjustment (c) complemented mouth region (d) filled image (e) binary mouth region (f) detected mouth contour (g) detected feature points from mouth region

To handle these problems, contrast stretching on the basis of the cumulative distribution of the pixels is performed on the image for saturating the upper half fraction of the image pixels towards higher intensity value. As a result, lips and other darker region become darker while the skin region becomes comparatively brighter providing a clear separation boundary between the foreground and background (Fig. 6.b). A flood fill operation is then performed over the complemented image to fill-up the wholes of mouth region (Fig. 6.d). After this, the resultant image is converted to its binary version using the threshold value obtained by the procedure given in [18]. All the contours are then identified applying the 8-connected contour following algorithm specified in [19] and mouth contour is isolated as the contour having the largest area (Fig. 6.f). The right mouth corner is then identified as a point over the mouth contour having the minimum x coordinate value, and the point which has the maximum x coordinate values is considered as the left mouth corner. Middle point (X_{mid}, Y_{mid}) of the left and right mouth corner are then calculated and upper and lower mid points of mouth are obtained by finding the two specific points over the mouth contour which has the same x coordinate as that of (X_{mid}, Y_{mid}) but minimum and maximum y coordinates respectively.

4.2 Obtaining the Feature Vector

Once all the eleven feature points are detected, a set of eleven measurements (Table 1) is performed over these points to obtain the feature vector that represents a specific facial expression. The obtained feature vector(s) is/are then fed into the facial expression classification system for training as well as classification of the represented unknown facial expression.

5 Overview of K-NN Classifier

K-Nearest Neighbors (K-NN) is a well-known and widely used instance-based classification algorithm [21], [22]. The basic idea behind this classification paradigm is to compute the similarity between a test object and all the objects in the training set, select the k most similar training set objects, and determine the class of the test object based on the classes of this k nearest neighbors. One of the advantages of K-NN is that it is well suited for multi-modal classes as its classification decision is based on a small neighborhood of similar objects. As a result, even if the target class is multi-modal (i.e., consists of objects whose independent variables have different characteristics for different subsets), it can still lead to good classification accuracy.

In K-NN classification, training patterns are plotted in d dimensional space, where d is the number of features present. These patterns are plotted according to their observed feature values and are labeled according to their known class. An unlabelled test pattern is plotted within the same space and is classified according to the most frequently occurring class among its k most similar training patterns; its nearest neighbors. The most common similarity measure for K-NN classification is the Euclidian distance metric, defined between feature vectors $\vec{x}$ and $\vec{y}$ as:

$$euc(\vec{x}, \vec{y}) = \sqrt{\sum_{i=1}^{f}(x_i - y_i)^2}$$

where, f represents the number of features used to represent each pattern. Smaller distance values represent greater similarity. Classification occurs after identifying the k most similar training points to a query point. Rather than using a standard voting scheme, the algorithm used here assigns class labels to query points using a weighted scheme based upon each neighbor's proximity to the query point [23]. Let d be a distance measure, and $x_1, x_2, x,...,x_k$ be the k nearest neighbors of x arranged in increasing order of $d(x_i,x)$. So x_1 is the first nearest neighbor of x. Dudani [23] proposes to assign a weight w_i to the i-th nearest neighbor x_i defined as:

$$w_i = \begin{cases} \frac{d(x_k,x)-d(x_i,x)}{d(x_k,x)-d(x_1,x)}, & \text{if } d(x_k,x) \neq d(x_1,x) \\ 1, & \text{if } d(x_k,x) = d(x_1,x) \end{cases}$$

Pattern x is assigned to the class for which the weights of the representatives among the k nearest neighbors sum to the greatest value. This rule was shown to yield lower error rates by Dudani [23] than those obtained using the voting K-NN rule.

6 Experimental Results

As specified earlier, K-Nearest Neighbor (K-NN) technique has been used for the recognition part of our Automatic Facial Expression Classification System. Performing experimentation with different values of k, we have observed that $k = 3$ is the best choice for our work. The developed Automatic Facial Expression Classifier has been tested using the Japanese Female Facial Expression (JAFFE) Database [24]. This publicly available database contains 213 images each representing 7 different facial expressions (6 basic facial expressions + 1 neutral) posed by 10 Japanese female models. Each image of this database was rated on 7 emotion adjectives by 60 Japanese subjects. "Leave-One-Out" criteria has been maintained in training the classifier and for each subject, six feature vectors calculated from the image of each of the six basic facial expressions, were used during the training session. The remaining images, that were left unused during the training session, have been used to verify the performance of the Automatic Facial Expression Classification System and on an average, successful recognition rate of 90.76% have been achieved. Performance of the K-NN based Automatic Facial Expression Classifier has also been compared with that of the two other classifiers namely Back-propagation Neural Network Classifier and Naive Bayes Classifier. Obtained results are summarized in Table 2.

Table 2. Accuracy of the automatic facial expression classifier in classifying facial expression

	Recognition Accuracy (%) on JAFFE Database		
Expression	K-NN (K=3)	Neural Network	Naive Bayes Classifier
Anger	88.58	82.48	84.27
Disgust	86.75	79.45	82.84
Fear	84.52	76.74	80.58
Happiness	96.14	89.45	89.26
Sad	89.93	79.67	72.64
Surprise	98.66	91.32	94.69
Average	90.76	83.19	84.05

7 Conclusion

We have discussed the development technique of an automatic facial expression classification system that incorporates a hybrid image processing based facial feature point detection method along with K-Nearest Neighbor algorithm as classifier. As shown in the experimental results, the system performs better when K-NN is used as classifier rather than Neural Network or Naive Bayes Classifier and provides an average successful recognition rate of 90.76%. Use of only eleven feature points has enabled the system to be computationally time effective compared to the other systems that works by identifying more feature points. Beside this, incorporation of the anthropometric model based facial feature regions localization technique [16] has further reduced the computational time of our system by confining the search space of he eleven feature points. Since aggregation of emotional information in human-computer interfaces allows much more natural and efficient interaction paradigms to be established, we believe that the developed automatic facial expression classifier can play an increasing role in building effective and intelligent multimodal interfaces for next generation.

Acknowledgement

The authors wish to thank the corresponding authority of the JAFFE database for releasing necessary permission regarding its use in this research. This work was supported in part by grants from the NSERC and the Canada Research Chair Foundation.

References

1. Donato, G., Bartlett, M.S., Hager, J.C., Ekman, P., Sejnowski, T.J.: Classifying Facial Actions. IEEE Trans. Pattern Analysis and Machine Intelligence, Vol. 21, No. 10 (1999) 974–989
2. Mehrabian, A.: Communication without Words. Psychology Today, Vol. 2, No. 4 (1968) 53–56

3. Van Dam, A.: Beyond WIMP. IEEE Computer Graphics and Applications, Vol. 20, No. 1 (2000) 50–51
4. Pentland, A.: Looking at People: Sensing for Ubiquitous and Wearable Computing. IEEE Trans. Pattern Analysis and Machine Intelligence, Vol. 22, No. 1 (2005) 107–119
5. Jain, A.K., Duin, R.P.W., Mao, J.: Statistical Pattern Recognition: A Review. IEEE Trans. Pattern Analysis and Machine Intelligence, Vol. 22, No. 1 (2000) 4–37
6. Chibelushi, C.C., Bourel, F.: Facial Expression Recognition: A Brief Tutorial Overview. Available Online at:
   "http://homepages.inf.ed.ac.uk/rbf/CVonline/LOCAL_COPIES/CHIBELUSHI1/CCC_FB _FacExprRecCVonline.pdf"
7. Ekman, P., Friesen, W.V.: Unmasking the Face. Prentice Hall, New Jersey (1975)
8. Cottrell, G.W., Metcalfe, J.: EMPATH: Face, Emotion, Gender Recognition Using Holons. Advances in Neural Information Processing Systems, Vol. 3 (1991) 564–571
9. Rahardja, A., Sowmya, A., Wilson, W.H.: A Neural Network Approach to Component Versus Holistic Recognition of Facial Expression in Images. Intelligent Robots and Computer Vision X: Algorithms and Techniques, Vol. 1607 (1991) 62–70
10. Kobayashi H., Hara, F.: Recognition of Mixed Facial Expressions and Their Strength by a Neural Network. In: IEEE International Conference on Acoustic, Speech and Signal Processing (1992)1495–1498
11. Vanger, P., Honlinger, R., Haken, H.: Applications of Synergetics in Decoding Facial Expression of Emotion. In: IEEE International Conference on Automatic Face and Gesture Recognition (1995) 24–29
12. Essa, I. A., Pentland, A. P.: Coding, Analysis, Interpretation and Recognition of Facial Expressions. IEEE Trans. Pattern Analysis and Machine Intelligence, Vol. 19, no. 7 (1997) 757–763
13. Lien, J.J., Kanade, T., Cohn, J.F., Li, C.C.: Automated Facial Expression Recognition Based on FACS Action Units. In: Third IEEE International Conference on Automatic Face and Gesture Recognition (1998) 390–395
14. Pantic, M., Rothkrantz, L.J.M.: An Expert System for Multiple Emotional Classification of Facial Expressions. In: 11th IEEE International Conference on Tools with Artificial Intelligence (1999) 113–120
15. Feng, X., Pietikainen, M., Hadid, A.: Facial Expression Recognition with Local Binary Patterns and Linear Programming. IEEE Trans. Pattern Recognition and Image Analysis, Vol. 15, No. 2, (2005) 546–548
16. Sohail, A.S.M., Bhattacharya, P.: Localization of Facial Feature Regions Using Anthropometric Face Model. In: First International Conference on Multidisciplinary Information Sciences and Technologies (2006)
17. Fasel, I., Fortenberry, B., and Movellan, J. R.: A Generative Framework for Real Time Object Detection and Classification. Computer Vision and Image Understanding, Vol. 98, (2005) 182–210
18. Efford, N.: Digital Image Processing: A Practical Introduction Using Java. Addison-Wesley, Essex (2000)
19. Ritter, G.X., Wilson, J.N.: Handbook of Computer Vision Algorithms in Image Algebra. CRC Press, Boca Raton, USA (1996)
20. Otsu, N.: A Threshold Selection Method from Gray Level Histograms. IEEE Trans. Systems, Man, and Cybernetics, Vol. 9, No. 1 (1979) 62–66
21. Dasarathy, B.V. (eds.): Nearest Neighbor: Pattern Classification Techniques (Nn Norms: Nn Pattern Classification Techniques). IEEE Computer Society Press (1991)

22. Wettschereck, D., Aha, D., and Mohri, T.: A Review and Empirical Evaluation of Feature-weighting Methods for a Class of Lazy Learning Algorithms. Artificial Intelligence Review, Vol. 11 (1997) 273–314
23. Dudani, S.A.: The Distance-weighted K-Nearest-Neighbor Rule. IEEE Transaction on Systems, Man and Cybernetics, Vol. 6 (1976) 325–327
24. Lyons, J., Akamatsu, S., Kamachi, M., and Gyoba, J.: Coding Facial Expressions with Gabor Wavelets. In: Third IEEE International Conference on Automatic Face and Gesture-Recognition (1998) 200–205

Cortical Bone Classification
by
Local Context Analysis

Sebastiano Battiato[1], Giovanni M. Farinella[1], Gaetano Impoco[1],
Orazio Garretto[2], and Carmelo Privitera[2]

[1] Computer Science Department, University of Catania, Catania, Italy
{battiato, gfarinella, impoco}@dmi.unict.it
http://www.dmi.unict.it/ iplab/
[2] Radiology Department, Vittorio Emanuele Hospital, Catania, Italy

Abstract. Digital 3D models of patients' organs or tissues are often
needed for surgical planning and outcome evaluation, or to select prostheses adapted to patients' anatomy. Tissue classification is one of the
hardest problems in automatic model generation from raw data. The
existing solutions do not give reliable estimates of the accuracy of the
resulting model. We propose a simple generative model using Gaussian
Mixture Models (GMMs) to describe the likelihood functions involved
in the computation of posterior probabilities. Multiscale feature descriptors are used to exploit the surrounding context of each element to be
classified. Supervised learning is carried out using datasets manually annotated by expert radiologists. 3D models are generated from the binary
volumetric models, obtained by labelling cortical bone pixels according
to maximal likelihoods.

1 Introduction and Motivation

The rapid technological advances in digital medical imaging devices have brought
the attention of various medical communities to computer-assisted diagnosis.

One of the trends of modern surgery is computer-aided pre-operative planning
and post-operative outcome evaluation. Digital models of the interested organs
or tissues can be of great value both to predict and to evaluate the outcome of
an operation. In particular, planning and evaluation often involve the creation
of a model from patient-specific data, acquired by means of CT, MRI, and so on.
3D models of human body parts can be also useful for selecting perfectly-fitting
prostheses e.g., for knee replacement [1] (using FEM stress analysis) and plastic
surgery [2] (by means of ad-hoc geometric measurements).

Unfortunately, due to the limitations of current imaging devices the acquired
data is often noisy. Moreover, in most technologies the ranges of data values of
different tissues often overlap. This is especially true for soft tissues and trabecular bone in aged patients, where osteoporosis degenerates the bone density
and thus the intensity of the bone is decreased (see Figure 1). Thus, data values cannot be uniquely associated with specific tissues i.e., the data cannot be

A. Gagalowicz and W. Philips (Eds.): MIRAGE 2007, LNCS 4418, pp. 567–578, 2007.
© Springer-Verlag Berlin Heidelberg 2007

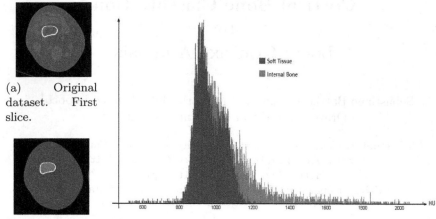

(a)   Original
dataset.   First
slice.

(b) Manual la-
belling of the
first slice.

(c) Distribution of HU values for soft tissue and trabecular bone of a dataset.

Fig. 1. A CT scan of a 80-years-old patient, affected by osteoporosis and arthrosis. A manual labelling is also shown together with the relative distribution of *Hounsfeld Units* (HU) values of two tissue classes: *soft tissue* and *trabecular bone* (not used in our experiments).

partitioned using *Hounsfeld Units* (HU) values alone. This rules out global as well as local thresholding techniques. Moreover, defining a similarity function between neighbouring pixels is hard, since the same tissues often have uneven values in different positions. Hence, region-growing, or edge detection algorithms are unable to effectively cope with this data.

Although a large variety of segmentation methods have been developed for medical image processing, ad-hoc solution are often preferred especially to properly detect complex structures, such as vessel, brain, or skeletal structures. In [3] a multi-step approach for 3D bone segmentation of CT data is presented. It combines a simple thresholding strategy with a 3D region growing followed by a refining step taking into account anatomically oriented boundary adjustment. The involved factors are in general of high complexity and require extreme accuracy. Moreover, the discriminative thresholds for tissues are chosen by experience, without any statistical justification. A computerised system, called *MedEdit* is presented in [4] to help surgeons in operation planning by making use of a Finite Element Analysis (FEA) program to measure and compare the effects of the modifications involved in skeletal injury operations. A seeded region growing techniques enriched with a suitable fuzzy heuristics is used for segmentation purposes. In our case, the CT data are acquired from old patients, which means that the bone density is lower than average. Since the intensity values in CT data are directly related to the tissue density, the low bone density is reflected in low intensity values for the affected parts. This makes the classification task more challenging. In addition to this, it is difficult to automatically separate adjoining bones and regard them as different objects due to the limited spatial resolution of CT datasets. This is a requirement in the segmentation process, though, where the goal is to generate patient-specific models. Model-based approaches are needed as suggested in [5] and [6] even if there is no availability of reliable anatomical models.

Almost all previous works produce in some cases effective 3D reconstructions but without providing a reliable measure of uncertainty of the output. This is a serious drawback in applications that require an error measure, such as mechanical simulations [1]. Finally, and most important, segmentation algorithm group pixels into regions but do not label regions as being part of a semantic region or another. Hence, they lack a real classification mechanism.

In [7] a statistically-founded approach is used to infer the percentage of different tissues within each voxel due to the *partial volume* effect. Each voxel is modelled as a mixture of contributions from different tissues. They search for the tissue mixture that maximises the posterior probability. However, rather than labelling real data to compute HU distributions, they assume that the HU values of each tissue class are normally distributed. Our collected data show that this assumption does not hold for the knee region (Figure 1(c)). A learning procedure is clearly needed to build a reliable classification system.

Another statistical approach to bone segmentation from X-ray data is presented in [5]. However, as stated by the authors themselves, it is a largely immature work.

In this paper, we address the problem of classifying CT data in order to extract cortical bone structures. A simple generative model is used to classify the pixels belonging to a CT dataset into two classes: cortical bone, other. The likelihood functions involved in the computation of posterior probabilities are modelled by Gaussian Mixture Models (GMM), and are learned in a supervised way from manually-labelled data using the Expectation-Maximisation (EM) algorithm. Our approach shares some similarities with Lu et al.'s [7]. Anyway, while they model voxels as mixtures of contributions from different tissues, we use a single label for each pixel. This may look like a simplification, since our model cannot capture the intrinsic partial volume (PV) effects of the data. However, this choice is justified by the fact that there is no straightforward manual labelling procedure for supervised learning models. Basically, one can ask radiologists to give a single classification for each pixel (crisp classification), not to guess the percentage of a pixel occupied by a certain tissue (fuzzy classification).

The learned model is used to assign a probability to each pixel to belong to a certain class. A *Maximum A-posteriori Probability* (MAP) rule is used to get a crisp classification. The user can enforce a threshold on these probabilities to bound the classification uncertainty. A binary volumetric model is generated by labelling cortical bone voxels with low uncertainty. This model, in turn, can be used to build a mesh model of cortical bones using the well-known Marching Cubes algorithm [8]. The learning model can be easily extended to include a wider range of tissue classes by gathering and labelling more data. Results are presented for knee joint data.

2   Classification Model

Since our model is intended to be used for surgical planning, one of our main objectives is bounding the classification uncertainty. This is a good property because it is intuitive and is easily related to background knowledge of medical experts. Basically, one would say that she would accept the output of segmentation if the algorithm is p-percent sure about the result. Hence, we would classify only the pixels whose probability of belonging to a certain class is above a user-defined threshold, and leave the others unclassified.

2.1   Model

Suppose we want to partition our data into N different classes. We denote with c_k the k-th class. Let us define a number of feature functions $F_1(.), \ldots, F_M(.)$ on the pixel domain. We use a simple generative approach [9] to learn the model for the posterior probability $P(c_k|F_1(z), \ldots, F_M(z))$ for each pixel z. We model the likelihoods $P(F_1(z), \ldots, F_M(z)|c_k)$ using GMMs (one for each class). Manually-annotated training datasets are used to learn the likelihoods, using the EM algorithm. We assume that the priors $P(c_k)$ are uniformly distributed. One might argue that these probabilities are different for each class and that we can compute them from our training sets by counting the number of pixels in each class. Anyway, too many uncontrolled elements can affect the percentage of bone pixels over the total volume, such as biological factors (e.g., age, sex, osteoporosis), and machine setup parameters (e.g., percentage of patient bone contained into the imaged volume). Hence, equiprobability of the priors $P(c_k)$ is a reasonable choice. Assuming equiprobable priors, by the Bayes' theorem we get

$$P(c_k|F_1(z), \ldots, F_M(z))) = \frac{P(F_1(z), \ldots, F_M(z)|c_k)}{\sum_k P(F_1(z), \ldots, F_M(z)|c_k)} \tag{1}$$

where the evidence can be expressed in terms of likelihood functions alone.

Once we get the posterior probabilities $\hat{p}_k(z) = P(c_k|F_1(z), \ldots, F_M(z)))$, we partition the CT data using a MAP classification rule. In particular, for each pixel z the most probable labelling is

$$C(z) = \arg \max_{c_k} [\hat{p}_k(z)] \tag{2}$$

with associated probability $\hat{p}_C(z) = \max[\hat{p}_k(z)]$. In our application [1], it is preferable to be conservative employing a strict rejection rule to retain only very probable classifications. Thus, we accept this classification if $\hat{p}_C(z) \geq \varepsilon$, where ε is a user-defined threshold which bounds the classification uncertainty. If we restrict to two classes, c_1 and c_2, and to a single feature $F_1(z)$ for the sake of visualisation, our simple rejection option can be depicted using the diagram in Figure 2.

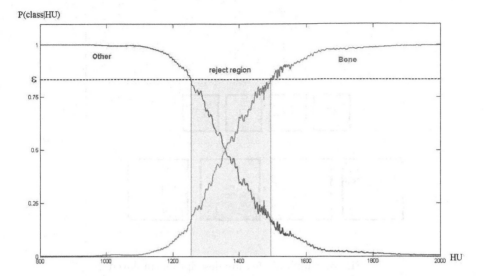

Fig. 2. Rejection rule. Probability distributions for two classes (*cortical bone* and *other*), conditioned by the HU value (our simplest feature). The threshold ε is used for rejection of low-probability classifications (see text). The shadowed region depicts the rejection interval.

2.2 Local Context Features

As pointed out in Section 1, the HU values of pixels do not suffice to get a robust classification. Pixel values can be affected by noise which rules out simple pixel-wise partitioning methods. According to [10], there are four sources of noise in CT images: physics-based artifacts, patient-based artifacts, scanner-based artifacts, and helical and multisection artifacts. Although the effect of some of these artefacts can be reduced or compensated, it can still strongly affect the acquired data. Moreover, the distributions HU values of different classes can largely overlap (Figure 1) especially for aged patients or for patients affected by osteoporosis or arthrosis. For this reason, we employ a more robust pixel analysis by looking at the neighbourhood, which can give useful information to estimate the probability of pixels to belong to a certain class, given their surrounding context. Hence, we employ a set of features at different scales to capture the variability of HU values in the surrounding context of a pixel.

For each scale s, we employ a $s \times s$ window centred around the interest pixel. We define $v_s = (F_{s,N}(.), F_{s,E}(.), F_{s,S}(.), F_{s,W}(.))$ as the mean of the HU values for four regions in the surrounding window: North (N), East (E), South (S), and West (W) (see Figure 3). In our implementation, we use the HU value of the interest pixel together with the feature vectors v_s.

We choose these features to selectively evaluate the surrounding context of a pixel in four directions. Being independent from orientation, circular features

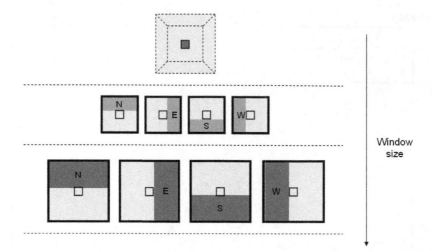

Fig. 3. Multiscale feature descriptors employed

Table 1. Parameter settings used for the acquisition of the knee CT data employed in our experiments

Parameter	Value	
Exposure	200	Sv
kVp	140	kiloVolt
Slice thickness	1.3	mm
Slice spacing	0.6	mm
Slice resolution	512×512	pixels
Number of slices	70–140	

would bring less useful information. We also use simple mean instead of more complex distance weighings since distance is accounted for using multiple scales.

Due to the dimension of feature windows, especially in larger scales, a special treatment should be reserved to border pixels. Anyway, we do not bother about image borders since in our application interest pixels always lie in the central area of CT scans.

3   Experimental Procedure

The simple model presented in Section 2 has been tested on knee CT data. Nine knee datasets were imaged at the Radiology Department of the Vittorio Emanuele Hospital in Catania. The data were captured by means of a Multidetector CT Scanning (MDCT) device in spiral mode, using the acquisition parameters reported in Table 1. The age of the patients ranged from 70 to 80 years and all of them suffer from osteoporosis and arthrosis. This choice is motivated by the fact that this is one of the most difficult cases (due both to age and to severe osteoporosis and arthrosis) and the most widespread in the clinical cases of knee replacement surgery, which is our main interest [1]. The acquired data was then manually labelled by expert radiologists of the Vittorio Emanuele Hospital. 75% of the labelled data were used for learning, and the remaining were employed for testing.

3.1   Labelling Procedure

In order to simplify the labelling phase, we segmented the CT data using the SRM algorithm [11,12]. Namely, labelling *superpixels* (i.e., pixel patches with homogeneous properties [13]) is much easier and faster than working with single pixels. We extended SRM to cope with 3D datasets. Basically, we insert in the couple pixel table couple of corresponding pixels of neighbouring slices, besides those in the same slice. Since inter-slice distance is usually much greater than pixel size, we weighted the priority of pixel couples by their physical distance. In principle, couple statistics should be collected for the whole dataset since regions might span the whole dataset along the scanning direction. However, this is quite computationally demanding, due to its memory requirements. Hence we segment each slice using only a small window of neighbouring slices. Although any window dimension can be used, we found that in practice using three slices is the best tradeoff between quality (the result is very similar to those obtained with larger windows) and computational burden. The rationale behind the use

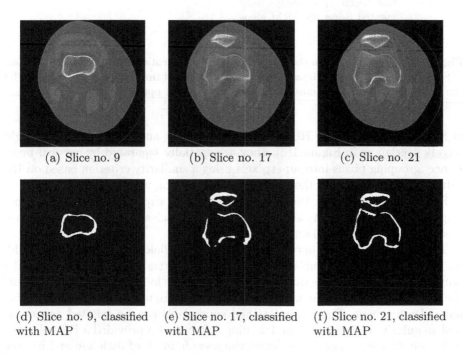

    (a) Slice no. 9   (b) Slice no. 17   (c) Slice no. 21

(d) Slice no. 9, classified   (e) Slice no. 17, classified   (f) Slice no. 21, classified
with MAP   with MAP   with MAP

Fig. 4. Examples of three slices classified with MAP

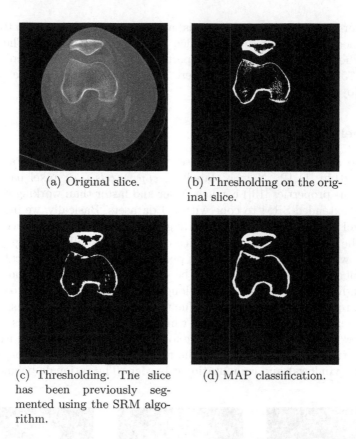

(a) Original slice.   (b) Thresholding on the original slice.

(c) Thresholding. The slice has been previously segmented using the SRM algorithm.   (d) MAP classification.

Fig. 5. Comparison between the proposed MAP classification and simple thresholding of Slice no. 21 of the same dataset as Figure 4. A global threshold has been chosen for the whole dataset, and optimised by hand by an expert operator.

of SRM is that while the HU values of soft tissues and trabecular bone might largely overlap as in Figure 1(c), they are spatially separated by cortical bone. Hence, grouping pixels into superpixels using a similarity criterion based on HU value is safe and enriches the pixel value information with spatial context.

For labelling purposes, the user can select only superpixels as a whole, not single pixels. Hence, during learning the pixels in each superpixel share the same label. Classification is run on a pixel basis.

The labelling proceeds in two steps. First, the radiologists set three thresholds on HU values: background/soft tissue, soft tissue/trabecular bone, trabecular bone/cortical bone. These threshold are selected by looking at a single slice and then are propagated to the whole datasets. They are used as a basis for further manual refinement. Then, misclassified superpixels can be selected separately and singularly re-classified. The labelling software also provided a HU tolerance when selecting superpixels. However, the users found it of little use and its concept tricky to understand. Hence, we excluded it. In order to make the labelling

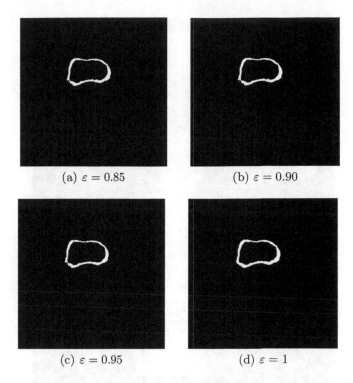

(a) $\varepsilon = 0.85$ (b) $\varepsilon = 0.90$

(c) $\varepsilon = 0.95$ (d) $\varepsilon = 1$

Fig. 6. Comparison between the classification with different values of ε. Slice no. 9 of the same test dataset as Figure 4 is used.

environment more familiar to the radiologists, we show three panels containing the original slice, its segmented version (used to select superpixels), and the current annotation.

For the time being, only two classes are discriminated: *cortical bone* and *other*. However, the presented model can be easily extended to include a wider range of tissue classes by gathering and labelling more data. However, due to the lack of fast labelling methods and label propagation procedures, collecting a sufficient amount of labelled data can be prohibitive. We are currently investigating labelling propagation procedures to alleviate the burden of manual annotation.

3.2 Model Parameters and Learning Procedure

In our experiments we use the features $v_s = (F_{s,N}(.), F_{s,E}(.), F_{s,S}(.), F_{s,W}(.))$ described in Section 2 with $s \in \{5, 15, 45, 135, 151\}$, and the HU value of the interest pixel.

We model the likelihoods involved in our classification framework using GMMs

$$P(F_1(z), \ldots, F_M(z)|c_k) = \sum_{i=1}^{M} \pi_i G(F_1(z), \ldots, F_M(z), \mu_i, \Sigma_i) \qquad (3)$$

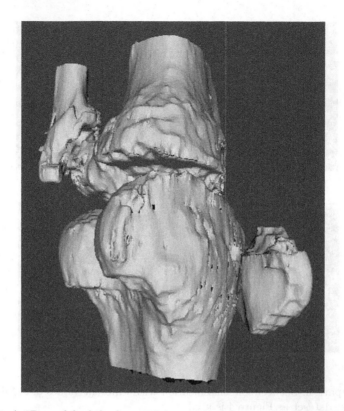

Fig. 7. A 3D model of the knee joint generated from a classified CT dataset

Manually-annotated training datasets are used to learn the likelihoods using the Expectation Maximisation algorithm [9] (20 iterations). In particular, we learn $P(F_1(z), \ldots, F_M(z)|bone)$ using 100 Gaussians ($M = 100$) and $M = 150$ for $c_k \neq bone$. The k-means algorithm was used to determine the initial centres μ_i. The initial priors π_i were computed from the proportion of examples belonging to each cluster. The initial covariance matrices Σ_i were calculated as the sample covariance of the points associated with the corresponding centres.

3.3   Results

Figure 4 shows the result of MAP classification (i.e., $\varepsilon = 1$) on three slices from a test dataset (slice no. 9, 17, 21 over 70 total slices). For the sake of comparison, the same results are compared with simple thresholding in Figure 5. A global threshold has been chosen for the whole dataset, and optimised by hand by an expert operator. Due to the lack of space, only one of the worst cases (Slice no. 21) is shown for comparison. Although different thresholds could be chosen for each slice, it would be too much human-intensive. Moreover, global thresholds on the HU values alone cannot do a good job, as already pointed out. Using smarter thresholding techniques does not lead to significant improvements because they miss important features, lacking a robust classification mechanism. This simple experiment highlights the advantage of using a simple classification rather than thresholding on HU values.

In order to test the influence of the reject rule on the final result, we classified our test datasets using $\varepsilon \in \{0.85, 0.90, 0.95, 1\}$. A slice of the same test dataset is shown in Figure 6. Clearly, there is no noticeable difference between the results. Hence, the result is not strongly affected by the choice of ε.

Figure 7 shows a 3D mesh model of the knee joint generated (by means of the Marching Cubes [8] algorithm) from a CT dataset in which the cortical bone has been classified using the proposed method.

4   Future Work

We have presented a method to classify cortical bone pixels from CT scans, employing a simple generative model. Manually-labelled data are used to learn the posterior probability of two classes of tissues: *cortical bone* and *other*. Classification is carried out using multiscale features and a MAP criterion. A rejection rule is used to bound classification uncertainty. 3D mesh models are generated from classified datasets.

The proposed method can be easily extended to cope with more classes, provided that more labelled data is available. In order to gather more data, we are currently run a systematic acquisition and labelling campaign on aged patients affected by osteoporosis or arthritis.

The proposed model will be extended by using superpixels rather than pixels for classification. We expect that discrimination will be improved when working with more than two classes. Computation will be speed up as well.

References

1. Battiato, S., Bosco, C., Farinella, G.M., Impoco, G.: 3D CT segmentation for clinical evaluation of knee prosthesis operations. In: Proceedings of the Fourth Eurographics Italian Chapter Conference. (2006)
2. Farinella, G.M., Impoco, G., Gallo, G., Spoto, S., Catanuto, G., Nava, M.: Objective outcome evaluation of breast surgery. Lecture Notes in Computer Science **4190/2006** (2006)
3. Kang, Y., Engelke, K., Kalender, W.A.: A new accurate and precise 3-D segmentation method for skeletal structures in volumetric CT data. IEEE Transactions on Medical Imaging **22** (2003) 586–598
4. Ollé, K., Erdőhelyi, B., Halmai, C., Kuba, A.: MedEdit: A computer assisted planning and simulation system for orthopedic-trauma surgery. In: 8th Central European Seminar on Computer Graphics Conference Proceedings. (2004)
5. Tzacheva, A., El-Kwae, E., Kellam, J.: Model-based bone segmentation from digital X-ray images. In: Proceedings of the Second Joint EMBS/BMES and IEEE Engineering in Medicine and Biology. (2002)
6. Pettersson, J., Knutsson, H., Borga, M.: Automatic hip bone segmentation using non-rigid registration. In: Proceedings of the IEEE International Conference on Pattern Recognition. (2006)

7. Lu, H., Liang, Z., Li, B., Li, X., Meng, J., Liu, X.: Mixture-based bone segmentation and its application in computer aided diagnosis and treatment planning. In: Proceedings of the Third International Conference on Image and Graphics (ICIG'04), Washington, DC, USA, IEEE Computer Society (2004) 507–510
8. Lorensen, W.E., Cline, H.E.: Marching cubes: A high resolution 3D surface construction algorithm. In: ACM Computer Graphics (SIGGRAPH 87 Proceedings). Volume 21. (1987) 163–170
9. Bishop, C.M.: Pattern Recognition and Machine Learning. Springer (2006)
10. Barrett, J.F., Keat, N.: Artifacts in CT: recognition and avoidance. Radiographics 24 (2004) 16791691
11. Nock, R., Nielsen, F.: Statistical region merging. IEEE Transactions on Pattern Analysis and Machine Intelligence 26 (2004) 1452–1458
12. Nock, R., Nielsen, F.: Semi-supervised statistical region refinement for color image segmentation. Pattern Recognition 38 (2005) 835–846
13. Ren, X., Malik, J.: Learning a classification model for segmentation. In: ICCV '03: Proceedings of the Ninth IEEE International Conference on Computer Vision. (2003)

Line Segment Based Watershed Segmentation

Johan De Bock and Wilfried Philips

Dep. TELIN/TW07, Ghent University
Sint-Pietersnieuwstraat 41, B-9000 Ghent, Belgium
jdebock@telin.UGent.be

Abstract. In this paper we present an overview of our novel line segment based watershed segmentation algorithm. Most of the existing watershed algorithms use the region label image as the main data structure for its ease of use. These type of watershed algorithms have a relatively large memory footprint and need unbounded memory access. For our new watershed algorithm we replaced the traditional region label image with a data structure that stores the regions in linked line segments. Consequently, the new algorithm has a much smaller memory footprint. Using the new data structure also makes it possible to create an efficient algorithm that only needs one scan over the input image and that only needs the last 3 lines and a small part of the data structure in memory.

1   Introduction

Image segmentation is the process of partitioning a digital image in meaningful segments, i.e. segments that show a certain degree of homogeneity. This can be homogeneity of any type, such as intensity, color, texture or higher level objects. It is crucial in a number of applications, such as image coding, tracking, content-based image retrieval and object recognition. The image segmentation concept can be translated to many techniques, the technique we will discuss is the watershed segmentation. It is a well-known low-level image segmentation technique. It can be attributed properties of both edge directed and region directed segmentation classes. First we generate an edge indication image, i.e. an image with for each pixel a value that indicates the probability of an edge going through the pixel in question. In case of intensity segmentation, the edge indication image can be created by calculating the norm of the gradient vector at each pixel position. Then the watershed algorithm will try to find the homogeneous closed regions by using the edge indication image as input. The watershed algorithm achieves this by regarding the edge indication image as a topographic landscape in which "valleys" correspond to the interior of segments, whereas the "mountains" correspond to the boundaries of segments. The watershed algorithm derives the "mountain rims" from the landscape and those mountain rims then delineate the segments in the image.

Watershed algorithms can be divided in two classes depending on the method that is used to extract the mountain rims from the topographic landscape. The first class contains the flooding watershed algorithms. These type of watershed

A. Gagalowicz and W. Philips (Eds.): MIRAGE 2007, LNCS 4418, pp. 579–586, 2007.

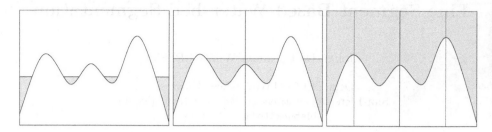

Fig. 1. Chronological stages in the flooding process

algorithms extract the mountain rims by gradually flooding the landscape. The points where the waterfronts meet each other constitute the mountain rims. This process is displayed chronologically in Fig. 1. The classic example of this class is the discrete Vincent-Soille flooding watershed algorithm [1]. The second class contains the rainfalling watershed algorithms. The algorithm discussed in this paper belongs to this class. Other examples of this class are the algorithm described in [2] and our previous algorithms [3,4]. In Sect. 2 we will describe the general layout of a rainfalling watershed algorithm. In Sect. 3 we will explain our line segment based rainfalling watershed algorithm. We will give a detailed report on the execution times of the algorithm for different parameters and for both natural and artificial images in Sect. 4. Finally we will draw some conclusions in Sect. 5.

2   General Layout of a Rainfalling Watershed Algorithm

As the name partly reveals, a rainfalling watershed algorithm exploits a different concept (compared to the flooding watershed) to extract the mountain rims. For each point on the topographic landscape an algorithm tracks the path that a virtual droplet of water would follow if it would fall on the landscape at that point. All droplets or points that flow to the same local minimum constitute a segment. This concept is depicted in Fig. 2 for the two-dimensional case. The lowest mountains (weakest edges) can be suppressed by drowning them. All the mountains below a certain drowning threshold will not be taken into account. This is shown in Fig. 3.

In the implementation, the rainfalling concept is carried out by calculating the steepest descent direction for each pixel. The directions are limited to the pixels neighboring the central pixel. A visualization of the steepest descent directions for a small part of an image is given in Fig. 4. The pixels marked with a circle in the middle are pixels from where there is no descent possible. Hence, they are the local minima of the topographic landscape. The pixels with a topographic height lower than the drowning threshold will also be marked as local minima. A steepest descent direction from one to another pixel is depicted as an arrow, a segment between two circles designates two connected local minima pixels. Both these arrows and segments will be called "connections" in this paper. One

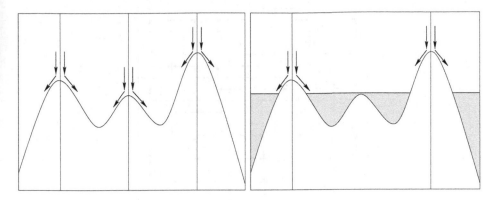

Fig. 2. Rainfalling concept   **Fig. 3.** Drowning threshold

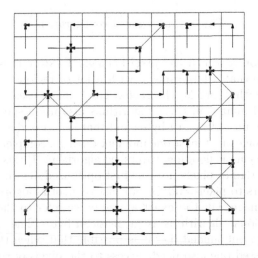

Fig. 4. Steepest descent directions and local minima

group of pixels that is connected must now make up one segment. We used 4-neighborhood for the steepest descent calculations and 8-neighborhood for determining the minima. Experimental results showed that this combination produces the least oversegmented image out of all 4 possible combinations. All the results presented in this paper are produced with this combination.

3 Description of the Line Segment Based Rainfalling Watershed Algorithm

The traditional rainfalling and flooding watershed algorithms use the region label image as the main data structure during the algorithm and also as the output of the algorithm. A region label image is an image with for each pixel

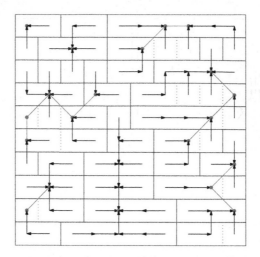

Fig. 5. Line segment configuration

a label of the region to which the pixel belongs. To store these labels one uses 4 bytes to be sure that a large image with a lot of regions can be segmented. So for an image with n pixels, the region label image uses up $4n$ bytes. Next to the region label image, all these algorithms also use a specific internal data structure that uses up at least $4n$ bytes and that is accessed at the same time as the region label image on at least one moment during a complete execution of the algorithm. For the classic flooding watershed algorithm [1] this specific structure is an array of pointers to pixels, for our first optimized algorithm [3] this is also an array of pointers to pixels and for our fast sequential algorithm [4] this is an additional label image. For the exact amounts we refer to the original papers. In total the traditional algorithms use at least $8n$ bytes. The memory access for these algorithms is unbounded, i.e. it is possible that when the bottom row of an image is processed one also needs access to the pixels of the top row (worst case). One can not limit the memory access to the last few already processed lines. For the classic flooding watershed algorithm this unbounded access can be noticed during the sorting step and during the spatially "random" filling of the region label image based on increasing topographic height, for example when both at the top and at the bottom there is a pixel at the same height. For our previous algorithms this unbounded access can be noticed during the tracking of the steepest descent paths, for example when there is a path that goes all the way from bottom to top.

In our line segment based watershed algorithm we replaced the traditional region label image with a data structure that stores the regions in linked line segments [5]. This makes it possible to create an efficient algorithm that uses considerably less memory, that only needs one scan over the input image and that only needs access to the last 3 processed lines. A line segment is an interval of pixels on a certain row of the image. The final configuration of line segments for the steepest descent directions shown in Fig. 4 is depicted in Fig. 5. A line

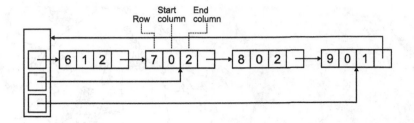

Fig. 6. Example region descriptor, linking line segments together

segment contains its row, start column and end column (all 2 bytes). It also contains a pointer to another line segment (4 bytes). These pointers are used to link all the line segments belonging to one region together with a region descriptor. The region descriptor for the region in the bottom left corner of Fig. 5 is displayed in Fig. 6. A region descriptor contains a pointer to the first line segment, a pointer to the last line segment and a pointer to one of the middle line segments of a region (12 bytes). The last line segment of a region descriptor always points to the region descriptor itself. Finally a data structure with r regions and l line segments will take up $12r + 10l$ bytes.

Now we will describe the general steps of the line segment based watershed algorithm. We assume that the rows 0 to $i - 1$ are already processed.

- Calculate the steepest descent directions of row i.
- Repeat the following steps until the end of the row is reached.
    • Look for a "continuous run" of horizontal connections and create a new line segment from this run, i.e. as long as there is a horizontal connection between the current and the next pixel, keep extending the current line segment with an extra pixel.
    • Look for connections with the line segments of row $i - 1$. More specific, check for vertical and diagonal connections that connect the current line segment with any of the line segments of the previous row.
        * No connections. Create a new region descriptor and add the current line segment.
        * One connection. Add the current line segment to the respective region descriptor.
        * Two or more connections with line segments of distinct region descriptors. Merge the respective region descriptors and add the current line segment.
    • Determine the next line segment.
- Process the next row.

To conclude the description we will sum up some important remarks:

- The merging of two region descriptors is done by interleaving the start to middle and middle to end parts of both region descriptors.

Fig. 7. PEPPERS 512x512, segmented with $rdt = 0.001$

- The region descriptor to which a line segment belongs is found by going to the next line segment in the linked list until one reaches the pointer to the region descriptor. The execution time lost on this search is very limited because this search is only initiated for the line segments of the previous row and those are always kept in the middle to end part of a region descriptor (together with the line segments of the current row).
- If the current line segment will be added to the region descriptor where the previous line segment was added to then we can extent the previous line segment with the current line segment instead of just adding the current line segment. This situation is visualized by the vertical dotted lines in Fig. 5. This check can be done with no penalty in execution time and it will severely reduce the total amount of line segments. In the realistic example we will give later on, it reduced the amount of line segments from 67138 to 39092, about 58%.

4   Results

The segmentation results are theoretically identical to our previous algorithms when using the same neighborhoods. To still give an example of how a typical low-level watershed segmentation result looks like, we tested our line segment based watershed algorithm on the standard test image PEPPERS 512x512 with a relative drowning threshold of 0.001 (the relative drowning threshold rdt is the absolute drowning threshold divided by the maximum topographic height). For a more detailed analysis of the segmentation results we refer to our previous papers on the subject [3,4]. The segmentation result is shown in Fig. 7. The line segment based watershed algorithm produced 2354 regions and 39092 line segments and thus used 419168 bytes. This is 20% of what a region label image based technique

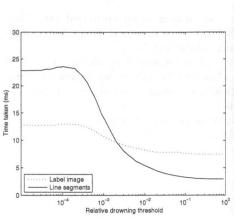

Fig. 8. Execution times   **Fig. 9.** Connected components test pattern

would use. To show that the line segment based watershed algorithm is still competitive speed-wise despite the higher complexity we compared it to our fast region label image based technique [4]. Both algorithms were implemented in C, compiled with gcc 3.4.2 with optimization parameter -O3 and run on one core of an Intel Core 2 Duo T7400 2.16 GHz. The execution times are shown in Fig. 8. For low drowning thresholds it is not much slower and for very high thresholds it is even faster than the label image based algorithm. Our new algorithm is also a bit faster for the complex connected components test image displayed in Fig. 9, 5.9 ms vs 7.9 ms. These type of artificial images have very little pixels above the drowning threshold and almost no steepest descent calculations have to be done, thus the running time is completely dominated by the parts that have to merge the connected minima.

5 Conclusions

We have developed a line segment based watershed segmentation algorithm that uses considerably less memory than the traditional region label image based watershed algorithms and that is very competitive speed-wise. The memory access is also limited to the last 3 processed lines. Future work will be the construction of a 3D version of this algorithm and the investigation if the complexity of the algorithm can be reduced.

References

1. Vincent, L., Soille, P.: Watersheds in digital spaces: An efficient algorithm based on immersion simulations. IEEE Transactions on Pattern Analysis and Machine Intelligence **13** (1991) 583–598

2. Beucher, S.: Segmentation d'images et morphologie mathématique. PhD thesis, School of Mines (1990)
3. De Smet, P., Pires, R.: Implementation and analysis of an optimized rainfalling watershed algorithm. In: Proc. Electronic Imaging, Science and Technology, Image and Video Communications and Processing. (2000) 759–766
4. De Bock, J., De Smet, P., Philips, W.: A fast sequential rainfalling watershed segmentation algorithm. In: Advanced Concepts for Intelligent Vision Systems, 7th international conference, Antwerp, Belgium. Volume 3708 of Lecture notes in computer science., Springer (2005) 477–484
5. Philips, W.: Weakly separable segmented image coding: Theory, results and implementation aspects. Technical report, ELIS (1996)

A New Content-Based Image Retrieval Approach Based on Pattern Orientation Histogram

Abolfazl Lakdashti[1,2,3] and M.Shahram Moin[2]

[1] Computer Group, Islamic Azad Univ./ Sari Branch, Mazandaran, Iran
[2] Multimedia Research Group, IT Faculty, Iran Telecom Research Center
(ITRC),Tehran, Iran
[3] Computer Group, Islamic Azad Univ./ Science and Research Branch, Tehran, Iran
{lakdashti, Moin}@itrc.ac.ir

Abstract. This paper presents a new content based image retrieval approach based on histogram of pattern orientations, namely pattern orientation histogram (POH) method. POH represents the spatial distribution of five different pattern orientations: vertical, horizontal, diagonal down/left, diagonal down/right and non-orientation. In this method, a given image is first divided into image-blocks and frequency of each type of patterns is determined in each image-block. Then local pattern histograms for each of these image-blocks are computed. As a result, local pattern histograms are obtained for each image. We compared our method with one of the texture descriptors MPEG-7 standard. Experimental results demonstrate that POH leads to better precision and recall rates than edge histogram descriptor (EHD) of MPEG-7 standard for search and retrieval of digital imagery.

Keywords: content-based image retrieval, MPEG-7 descriptors, image databases.

1 Introduction

During the present decade, Content-based image retrieval is one the most important and interesting research areas in information systems. Managing and transmitting a huge number of images in internet and image databases needs more efficient and faster algorithms and tools. Image similarity measurement is one of the most important aspects in a large image database for efficient search and retrieval to find the best match for a user query. In this way, well-known techniques such as color histogram [1], texture descriptors [2], color Correlogram [3] and international standard MPEG-7 (set of descriptors for color, texture and shape)[6] have been developed. Image retrieval performance and accuracy in all presented methods have different strengths and weaknesses. Performance evaluation of a given technique in content based image retrieval is often difficult, because, up to now, there is no common measuring criterion and benchmark testing data set for comparing different methods. However, one of the aims of

A. Gagalowicz and W. Philips (Eds.): MIRAGE 2007, LNCS 4418, pp. 587–595, 2007.

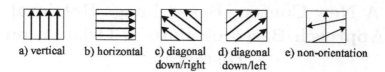

a) vertical   b) horizontal   c) diagonal   d) diagonal   e) non-orientation
                                down/right   down/left

Fig. 1. Five types of pattern orientations

our work is to develop an efficient and precise method for content based image retrieval; i.e. a method which can extract the indexing feature simply from the block patterns. Block based approaches in content based retrieval index images using feature extraction techniques are applied into image blocks. These features consist of color [4], [5], edge [9], texture [5] and or combination of them [5]. Block size depends on the type of feature, pixel correlations rate, and type of application.

This paper proposes a new non-edge based image retrieval technique using pattern orientations in spatial domain, so called Pattern Orientation Histogram (POH). POH represents distribution of five types of pattern from each image and produces 80 bins histogram. Patterns are classified into five categories based on their orientation: vertical, horizontal, diagonal down/left, diagonal down/right and non-orientation(Figure 1). In this method, first, each image is divided into 4×4 (16) non-overlapping and equal-sized partitions called image-block. Then, each image-block is segmented into sub-blocks and pattern orientations are extracted from each sub-block. Pattern orientations are detected using signal energy rate of sub-blocks. Local histograms are computed from each image-block with five bins, where each bin presents frequency of one of the five patterns in each image-block. Therefore, with 16 image-blocks in original image and five bins for each image-block, we obtain a histogram containing 80 bins. Then, histogram bin values are normalized in [0, 1]. The normalized histogram is quantized with 3 bits per bin, which codebook quantizer is reported in [9]. Extracted feature vector can be used in similarity image retrieval systems.

We compared our method with Edge Histogram Descriptor (EHD) of MPEG-7 [9] using a color natural image data set selected from Corel Photos Collection. Assessment measures for comparing results are recall and precision rates. Experimental results show that the proposed method (POH) yields better performance than the EHD of MPEG-7 standard.

This paper is organized as follows. Section 2 presents pattern orientation histogram extraction method. Pattern orientation detection in each sub-block is explained in section 3. Experimental results on Corel Collection photos are shown in section 4. Final section contains the conclusions.

2   Pattern Orientation Histogram

Histogram is an efficient model for representing features of an image such as color, texture and edge. Histogram is invariant to image rotation, scaling and translation. Due to these properties, the histogram is useful for image search and

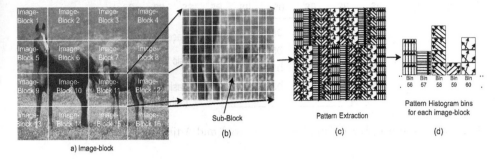

a) Image-block

Sub-Block
(b)

Pattern Extraction
(c)

Pattern Histogram bins
for each image-block
(d)

Fig. 2. Concepts of (a) image-block, (b) sub-block, (c) pattern extraction from each sub-block into image-block and (d) pattern histogram (local) bins for each image-block with five types of patterns

retrieval applications [7],[8]. This paper introduces a new block based approach called pattern orientation histogram (POH) for image indexing and retrieval. As we mentioned in the last section, the POH uses spatial distribution of five types of block orientation or direction in each local area from original image. First, we partition the original image into 4×4 non-overlapping image-blocks. Thus, we obtain 16 equal-sized image-blocks from original image, as shown in Figure 2. We then generate the histogram of block patterns distribution for each image-block with five bins. Block patterns of image-blocks are classified into five types: vertical, horizontal, diagonal down/left, diagonal down/right and non-orientation. Therefore, the histogram for each image-block shows the frequency of occurrence of 5 types of block patterns in the corresponding image-block. As a result, each local histogram contains 5 bins corresponding to one of 5 pattern types. And, since there are 16 image-blocks in each image, the final histogram contains $5 \times 16 = 80$ bins. Each bin in 80-bins histogram has two concepts: position and block pattern orientation type. For instance, the bin for the vertical type block pattern in the image-block 4 in Figure 2 represents the frequency of the vertical block patterns in top-right local region of the image. It is located in the sixteenth place in 80-bins histogram. Final histogram is obtained by scanning 16 image-blocks row by row. Within each sub-block, block pattern types are arranged in the following order: vertical, horizontal, diagonal down/left, diagonal down/right and non-orientation.

In next step, histogram bin values are normalized, because histogram bins should be compared with each other. For normalization, number of occurred patterns for each bin is divided by the total number of sub-blocks. Finally the histogram bin values are nonlinearly quantized to minimize the overall number of bits.

3   Patterns Orientation Detection

In this section, we explain the procedure of extracting a pattern orientation type from a sub-block. Since the POH operates on distribution of four oriented

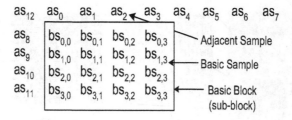

Fig. 3. Basic-Block, Basic-Samples ($bs_{00} - bs_{33}$) and Adjacent-Samples. ($as_0 - as_{12}$).

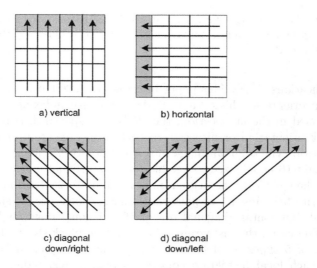

Fig. 4. Four types of the pattern modes

patterns, as well as non-orientation pattern, pattern detection method should be based on sub-blocks as a basic element for block based pattern detection[10].

First, we extract sub-block patterns based on their orientation, which could be vertical, horizontal, diagonal down/left, diagonal down/right and non-orientation (Figure 1). Consider the following definitions as shown in Figure 3.

1. Basic-block: $n \times n$ sub-block, basic unit for pattern extraction.
2. Basic-sample: each element (pixel) inside a basic-block ($bs_{00} - bs_{33}$).
3. Adjacent sample: samples located above and at left side of a basic block ($as_0 - as_{12}$).

Using these definitions, we extract four features from each basic-block as follows:

1. Vertical feature: each basic-sample into a column is subtracted from its corresponding adjacent-sample, as shown in Figure 4.a. The sum of the obtained values in basic block gives the vertical feature.

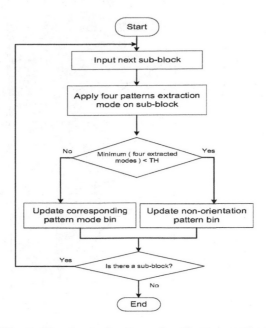

Fig. 5. Flowchart of pattern classification method

2. Horizontal feature: each basic-sample into a row is subtracted from its corresponding adjacent-sample, as shown in Figure 4.b. Like the last case, summation of obtained values is called horizontal feature.
3. Diagonal down/right feature: each basic-sample into a diagonal arrow is subtracted from its corresponding adjacent-sample located at the end of the same arrow, as shown in Figure 4.c. Summation of obtained values is called ddr-feature.
4. Diagonal down/left feature: each basic-sample into a position; located at lower part of the basic-block intersected by a diagonal line, is subtracted in a manner applied to past three modes. Other samples are subtracted from the mean of adjacent-samples of each corresponding diagonal line, as shown in Figure 4.d. Like previous mode, the summation of obtained values is called ddl-feature.

As shown in Figure 5, at the next step, these extracted features are compared, in order to determine the pattern mode(Equation (1)).The minimum value is compared with a predetermined threshold, if it is higher than this threshold, the pattern mode corresponds to the selected feature. Otherwise, the pattern mode is labeled as non-orientation.

$$Min\{\text{vertical-feature, horizontal-feature, ddr-feature, ddl-feature}\} < T_{pattern}$$
$$(1)$$

The best threshold value is determined experimentally and in our simulation, the value of 22 is assigned to this parameter.

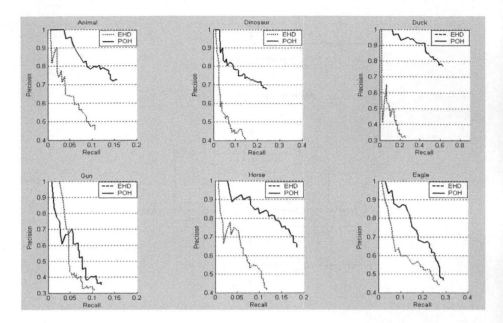

Fig. 6. The retrieval performances of POH and EHD methods for 30 queries with 50 returned images

4   Experimental Results

In this section, we present experimental results obtained from POH method and it is compared with EHD from MPEG-7 standard[9].

4.1   Image Database

We have selected 7100 color images of Corel Photos Collection as image database. This database includes different classes of natural images such as: birds, flowers, polar, jungle, texture, sport, sunset, sea waves, animals, gun, mountain, portrait, mine, natural scene, lion, Africa, fashion. In each class, there are images with different imaging conditions such as rotation, scaling, color, translation and illumination.

Subsequently, we have selected 35 images from different classes of this database as image queries including animal, gun, eagle, duck, dinosaur and farm. For the purpose of performance evaluation, we need to characterize the type of relevance between image queries and images in database. Relevance score are as follows: 1 if both belong to the same class, 0.5 if they are partially relevant, and 0 otherwise.

4.2   Performance Evaluation Criterion

Precision and recall are well-known criteria for retrieval performance evaluation [11]. In this paper, the performance of the retrieval methods is measured

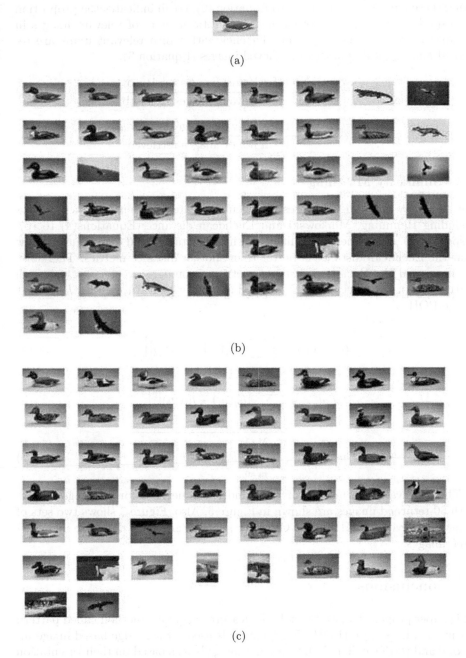

(a)

(b)

(c)

Fig. 7. (a) Query image. (b) and (c) instances top 50 retrieved images by different methods from an image database containing 7100 images. The first image on the top left corner is the query image and succeeding images are retrieved in the raster scan order according to their similarity to the query image. (b) EHD method. (c) POH method.

using these measures. According to Equation (2), recall indicates the proportion of desired results that are returned among total number of relevant images in database. Precision measures the efficiency with which relevant items are returned among total number of retrieved images (Equation 3).

$$Recall = \frac{\text{No. of relevant images retrieved}}{\text{Total no. of relevant images in database}} \tag{2}$$

$$Precision = \frac{\text{No. of relevant images retrieved}}{\text{Total no. of images retrieved}} \tag{3}$$

4.3 Similarity Matching

For similarity matching purposes we calculated three different distance metrics including Hamming, Minkowski and Euclidean distances(Equations(4) to (6), respectively). Experimental results in our image database and query images show that the Euclidean distance is better than another distance metrics. Therefore, we have used the Euclidean distance metric to compare two images, one with feature vector h_q(query image POH) and another with feature vector h_t (target image POH).

$$Ham.d_{q,t} = \Big[\sum_{m=0}^{M-1} \big|h_q(m) - h_t(m)\big| \Big] \tag{4}$$

$$Min.d_{q,t}^r = \Big[\sum_{m=0}^{M-1} \big|h_q(m) - h_t(m)\big|^r \Big]^{\frac{1}{r}} \tag{5}$$

$$Euc.d_{q,t} = \sqrt{\Big[\sum_{m=0}^{M-1} \big|h_q(m) - h_t(m)\big|^2 \Big]} \tag{6}$$

The retrieval performances of POH and EHD methods for 30 image queries with 50 returned images are shown in Figure 6. Also, Figure 7 shows two sets of images retrieved by EHD and POH methods from an image database including 7100 images.

5   Conclusions

This paper proposed a new block based feature extraction method called pattern orientation histogram (POH). This feature is used for non-edge based image indexing and retrieval. The POH classifies image blacks based on their orientation and then calculates the histogram of different orientation, making features used in similarity matching step. The proposed algorithm is compared with EHD of MPEG-7 texture descriptor. Experimental results show that our method produces better results than EHD in all conditions including histogram bit rate, image queries, image database and quantization table.

References

1. Swain M.J., Ballard D.H., Color Indexing, *Int. Journal of Computer Vision*, vol. 7-1, (1991) 11-32.
2. Manjunath B.S., Ma W.Y., Texture Features for Browsing and Retrieval of image Data, *IEEE Trans on PAMI*, vol. 18, no. 8, Aug. (1996) 837-842.
3. Huang J., Kumar S., Mitra M., Zhu W., Zabih R., Image Indexing Using Color Correlograms, *In Proc. IEEE Comp. Soc. Conf. Comp. Vis. and Patt. Rec.*, (1997)762-768.
4. Nezamabadi-pour H., Kabir E., Image retrieval using histograms of uni-color and bi-color blocks and directional changes in intensity gradient,*Pattern Recognition Letters*, vol. 25, no. 14, (2004) 1547-1557.
5. Guoping Qiu, Color Image Indexing Using BTC, *IEEE Transactios on image processing*, vol. 12, no. 1, (2003) 93-101.
6. Chang S.F., Sikora T., Purl A., "Overview of the MPEG-7 standard", *IEEE Trans. Circuits and Systems for Video Technology*, vol. 11, no. 6 ,(2001) 688-695.
7. Jain A.K., Vailaya A., Image Retrieval Using Color and Shape, *Pattern Recognition, Elsevier Science*, vol. 29, no. 8, (1996) 1233-1244.
8. Manjunath B. S., Ohm J.R., Vasudevan V.V., Yamada A., Color and Texture Descriptors, *IEEE Trans On Circuits And Systems For Video Technology.*, vol. 11, no. 6, (2001).
9. Won C. S., Park D.K., Park S., Efficient Use of MPEG-7 Edge Histogram Descriptor, *ETRI Journal*, vol. 24, no. 1, (2002) 23-30.
10. Wiegand T., Sullivan, Bjntegaard G.J., Luthra G., An Overview of the H.264/AVC video coding standard, *IEEE Trans on Circuits and Systems for Video Tech*, vol. 13, no. 12, (2003) 560- 576.
11. Castelli V., Bergman L. D., *Image Databases: Search and Retrieval of Digital Imagery*, John Wiley Pub.,(2001).

A Robust Eye Detection Method in Facial Region

Sung-Uk Jung and Jang-Hee Yoo

ETRI-Information Security Research Division
161 Gajeong-Dong, Yuseong-Gu, Daejeon 305-700, S. Korea
{brcastle, jhy}@etri.re.kr

Abstract. We describe a novel eye detection method that is robust to the obstacles such as surrounding illumination, hair, and eye glasses. The obstacles above a face image are constraints to detect eye position. These constraints affect the performance of the face applications such as face recognition, gaze tracking, and video indexing systems. To overcome this problem, the proposed method for eye detection consists of three steps. First, the self quotient images are applied to the face images by rectifying illumination. Then, unnecessary pixels for eye detection are removed by using the symmetry object filter. Next, the eye candidates are extracted by using the gradient descent which is a simple and a fast computing method. Finally, the classifier, which has trained by using AdaBoost algorithm, selects the eyes from all of the eye candidates. The usefulness of the proposed method has been demonstrated in an embedded system with the eye detection performance.

Keywords: Face Recognition, Eye Detection, SQI, SOF.

1 Introduction

Eye detection is a basic and an important process in the human computer interation field such as gaze tracking, face recognition, video indexing and so on [1][2]. Especially, in the application systems related to human face, precise eye detection affects on the performance of the systems. Because these systems use normalized face to extract the features based on eye position. Recently, face detection technique became mature so that the eye detection is started after the face image is obtained. There are two major approaches to eye detection in face recognition.

The first is appearance-based approach which uses face and eye patterns. In this approach, Jee et al. [3] detect face and eyes in case that the eye objects are isolated from other face objects and fairs using classifier which trained using SVM (Support Vector Machine). Ma et al. [4] find face region with face classifier using AdaBoost algorithm and divide a face image into two parts in which contain left and right eye. In each part, they detect an eye candidate using the eye classifiers [5]. Ichikawa et al. [6] also use trained classifiers for each face components using AdaBoost algorithm. They detect face components independently and detect the face based on detection results.

A. Gagalowicz and W. Philips (Eds.): MIRAGE 2007, LNCS 4418, pp. 596–606, 2007.
© Springer-Verlag Berlin Heidelberg 2007

An alternative approach is knowledge-based approach which uses prior information such as shape, position and intensity of eyes. Among the knowledge-based approach, Li et al. [7] detect the face features using multi-template ASM (Active Shape Model). There are two local templates for eyes, four local templates for mouth and the rests for the whole face. Wang and Yin [8] interpret gray values as three dimensions and detect eye position. The position of eyes is likely to locate in lowest region in 3D (three dimensional) curve. Tan et al. [9] detect precise eye position using deformable template. They first detect eyes using two independent templates and then verify the eyes using the energy function between the templates.

Generally, the appearance-based approach is robust to the occlusions due to use the training images. However, it is hard to get the precise eye positions, if we only train eye images, the application systems may have a lower performance because the information of eye patterns has fewer than that of the face pattern. In the case of knowledge-based approach, it can be detected the eye region using relatively simple methods, but it need posterior verification process.

In this paper, we propose a novel method of eye detection which applies to real world application using the above two approaches. The simplest and fastest eye detection method can be used gray profiles in the case of the non-constrained environment where there is proper illumination, untextured background, no occlusion, not wearing glasses and so on. However, in the real world, the factors mentioned here take effect. Therefore, in our system, first, we do preprocessing to rectify illumination and to minimize the effect of hair and glasses. Next, using the profile of gray image, we find the eye candidates. Finally, we detect the eye position through the eye verification process using statistical method.

The remainder of this paper is organized as follows: Section 2 describes the overall structure of the eye detector, Section 3 explains the preprocessing method to be robust to illumination and occlusion. Section 4 and 5 shows the eye candidate extraction and verification method using the 3D gray profile and AdaBoost algorithm. Section 6 presents the simulation and the experiment results, and shows feasibility of the proposed eye detector. In Section 7, we finally conclude our study.

2   Overall Structure

Figure 1 shows the overall structure of the eye detection system. When the face image is obtained by the face detector, the system rectifies illumination effect using SQI (Self Quotient Image) [10]. Then, the system removes the pixels which are unnecessary of eye detection such as hair and eye glasses using a novel method of SOF (Symmetry Object Filter). The SOF has been built according to each SQI processed image. The high symmetry region has high value in the SOF filtered image such as eyes, mouth and eyebrow. So, these objects remain in SOF filtered image. The eye candidates are extracted through the eye candidate process. Initially in the eye candidate process, 3D curves are obtained to perform Gaussian filtering to SOF filtered image. From the curves we can extract the eye candidates using the gradient descent algorithm because the position of eyes is likely to locate in the lowest region in 3D curve. Finally, using the strong classifier trained by AdaBoost algorithm we decide the eye positions.

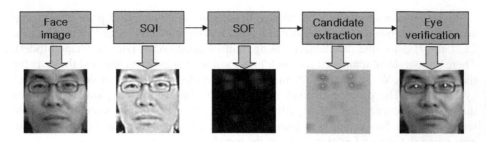

Fig. 1. Overall structure of the eye detection system

3   Preprocessing

We use 3D gray curve to extract the eye candidates. The method is a fast and a simple way in eye detection. Besides that, it can detect precise eye position. However, the problem in this method is an effect of illumination, hair, and eye glasses. The illumination effects on gray intensity, hair and eye glasses make it difficulty to detect a precise eye position. Therefore, input face image needs to be preprocessed. In this section, we describe SQI process to rectify illumination and SOF process to reduce unnecessary pixels to detect eyes.

3.1   SQI (Self Quotient Image)

In the SQI, Q is described in Eq. (1). SQI can be thought as a sort of high pass filter [10].

$$Q = \frac{I}{\hat{I}} = \frac{I}{F * I} \tag{1}$$

where $\hat{I}$ is the low frequency image of the original image, F is the Gaussian kernel.

$$G = \frac{1}{2\pi\sigma^2} e^{-\frac{(i^2+j^2)}{2\sigma}} \tag{2}$$

$$\tau = Mean(I_{\Omega}) \tag{3}$$

$$W(i,j) = \begin{cases} 0 & I(i,j) < \tau \\ 1 & otherwise \end{cases} \tag{4}$$

$$F(i,j) = W(i,j)G(i,j) \tag{5}$$

where Ω is the kernel size, $I(i,j)$ is the intensity, $F(i,j)$ is the Gaussian kernel , and $W(i,j)$ is the weight in (i,j).

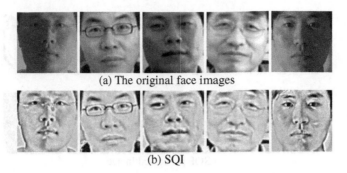

(a) The original face images

(b) SQI

Fig. 2. The face image and Self Quotient Image

The weight of filter, which applies to each matrix component independently, has 0 when the intensity of pixels is lower than the mean of filtering region (τ), otherwise 1. Gaussian kernel (F) is obtained by the multiplication between weight (W) and Gaussian filter (G). Fig. 2 shows the original images and the illumination rectified images. The face images in Fig. 2(a) have a lighting variation. In Fig. 2(b) show the lighting variation is unchanged, and the chrematistics of face is remaining.

3.2 SQF (Symmetry Object Filter)

GST (Generalized Symmetry Transform) [11] is a method of estimating the symmetry without prior shape information of object. In the GST, magnitude of the symmetry in a pixel is estimated by the weighted sum between functions which express the distance and the phase of the gradients around pixels. This method can be used to find eye position. However, it has much calculation and can not get a precise eye position. So, in out system, we use SOF (Symmetry Object Filter) which modifies GST and use it as a noise filter which filters the non-eye parts. The gradient and phase for a pixel can be expressed by

$$\nabla I_p = \left(\frac{\partial I_p}{\partial x}, \frac{\partial I_p}{\partial y} \right) \tag{6}$$

$$\theta_p = \tan^{-1} \frac{\partial I_p / \partial y}{\partial I_p / \partial x}. \tag{7}$$

Then, the magnitude of the symmetry, $M_\sigma(p)$ in a pixel, p, is described by

$$M_\sigma(p) = \sum_{(q,r)\in\Gamma(p)} h(q,r)a_p a_r \tag{8}$$

where $\Gamma(p)=\{(q,r)|(q+r)/2 =p\}$, $a_p=\| \nabla I_p \|$, $a_q = \| \nabla I_q \|$.

$$h(q,r) = \begin{cases} 1 & \theta_p < \|\theta_{threshold}\| \\ 0 & otherwise \end{cases} \tag{9}$$

where $\theta_{threshold}$ is the threshold phase of the gradients.

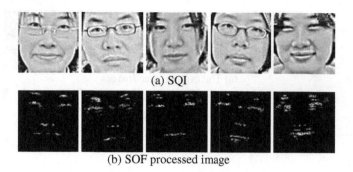

(a) SQI

(b) SOF processed image

Fig. 3. The SQI and SOF image

Equation (8) expresses the SOF. The SOF can be described by the multiplication between the magnitude of around the pixel, p and the function of gradient phases. We can detect fixed size objects depended on the range of $\Gamma(p)$. Here, we assume that the face size is known, so, using the general ratio between the size of face and eyes, the eye objects can be discernable. After SOF processing, $M_\sigma(p)$ has low value except around the symmetric regions. To use this characteristic as a filter, we normalize the SOF processed data, then, multiply it by SQI processing image independently. The process make better image to detect eye position because it can reduce the effect of hair and glasses. Fig. 3 shows the result of the SQI processed image and the SOF processed image. As shown in Fig. 3, the SOF can remove the region of eye glasses and hair from the face region even though the hair and the eye glasses occlude the eye region. However, we can use the SOF directly to do filtering, because the result of the SOF is the value of the specific position and located in face image sparsely. So, we do Gaussian filtering to the result of the SOF. The result of the SOF represents the highest values in the highest symmetry part. Therefore, the highest symmetry position may be considered as the centre of eyes. However, it does not consider another important clue of eye detection; intensity. So, in case of only using the SOF, it can not detect the precise eye position. In this paper, we use the result of the SOF as eye filter to detect the approximate eye candidate region. Fig. 4(a) shows the SQI processed

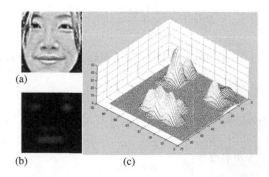

(a)

(b)   (c)

Fig. 4. SOF filtering. (a) SQI, (b) SOF, (c) 3D curve of SOF.

image and Fig. 4(b) is SOF of the SQI processed image. Fig. 4(c) is the 3D curve of Fig. 4(b). As shown in Fig. 4(c), the region except the region of eyes, nose and mouth is filtered.

4 Eye Candidate Extraction

This section shows the process to find the eye candidates using the pre-processed image. When the pre-processed image is considered as a 3D curve, the intensity of the eye region is likely to be lower than the rest of face region. To find the eye candidates using this characteristic, first, we perform Gaussian filtering to the pro-processed image, so that the smoothened 3D curve is obtained. In the curve, we extract all the local minimums using the method of the gradient descent algorithm [12]. The local minimums are the final eye candidates.

The gradient descent algorithm is following:

1) initialize a, threshold θ, $\eta(\bullet)$, $k \leftarrow 0$
2) do $k \leftarrow 1$
3) $a \leftarrow a - \eta(k)\nabla f(a)$
4) Until $|\eta(k)\nabla f(a)| < \theta$

where a is the solution vector, $f(\bullet)$ is the 3D eye profile, $\eta(\bullet)$ is the weighting function.

Gradient descent algorithm is an optimization algorithm that approaches a local minimum of a function by taking steps proportional to the negative of the gradient of the function at the current point. If instead one takes steps proportional to the gradient, one approaches a local maximum of that function. Fig.3 shows the process

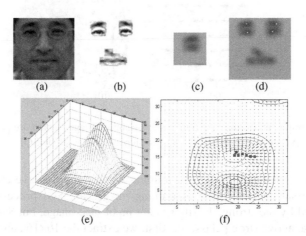

(a)   (b)   (c)   (d)

(e)   (f)

Fig. 5. Face images, 3D curve and contour of left eye. (a) original face image, (b) SOF filtered image, (c) approximated left eye image, (d) result of the eye candidates process, (e) 3D curve of left eye image, (f) result of the gradient descent algorithm for the test point.

for finding the eye candidate from the original image. The original image shown in Fig. 5(a) is filtered by SOF and Gaussian function (filter size 9×9, σ=3.0). Then, the approximate eye image, which has the left and right eye one at a time by dividing the image by 4 parts, is extracted. Accordingly, the eye candidates can be extracted by the method of the gradient descent.

Fig. 5(d) is the result of eye candidate process. There are four eye candidates; two for eyes and two for eye brows. Fig. 5(e) shows the three dimensional view of Fig. 5(c). Fig. 5(f) shows the result of applying any vector to Fig. 5(c) using the gradient descent algorithm. The small rectangle in the figure is the point where the orientation has changed. Fig. 5(f) shows the trace convergence to the local minimum.

5 Eye Verification

In the previous section, the process for extracting the left and right eye candidates is described. This section describes the eye verification process. To reduce the invalid eye candidates, we used the strong eye classifier, which is trained by Viloa's AdaBoost training methods [3]. AdaBoost is a simple learning algorithm that selects a small set of weak classifiers from the large number of potential features. In our system, a variant of AdaBoost is used to prove eye position. Using the training data which consist of total 1,100 left and right eye images in 16×16 pixels, we construct the strong eye classifier which is the weight sum of 30 week classifiers. Even through the less information of eye patterns than that of face, it can be sufficient for the eye detector to distinguish the valid eye candidates from the rest of them.

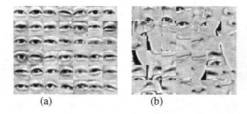

        (a)   (b)

Fig. 6. The training set. (a) the 16x16 pixels eye training images which are processed by SQI, (b) the 16x16 pixels non-eye training images which are processed by SQI.

Fig. 6 shows samples of the eye training images and non-eye training images to construct the strong classifier. All training images are SQI processed images. The image applied by the strong classifier is not input face image, but SQI processed face image. To use above strong classifier, first, we extract the 16×16 sub-windows around each eye candidates during reducing the size of SQI face image. The reason why we use image pyramid is to be robust to different eye size. Then, we insert the sub-windows to the strong classifier. Eyes can be determined by the eye candidates which has the maximum value.

6 Experiment Results

Fig. 7 shows the embedded system which estimates the performance of eye detector. It use 32bit 400MHz ARM9 core and has TFT LCD which display the result of eye detection. The operation system in the embedded system is the embedded Linux.

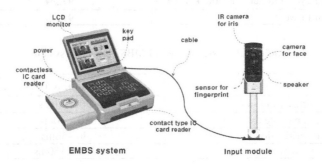

Fig. 7. EMBS (ETRI Multi-modal Biometric System)

6.1 ETRI Face Databases

The test database for experimenting the eye detection consists of a total of 1,100 frontal images cropped in 64×64 pixels selected from our face database where there are total of 55 people (21 males, 24 females). The database has not only normal frontal face images, but also slightly rotated face images in plane and out of plane, as well as faces with eye glasses and facial hair. Fig. 8 shows the samples of ETRI database.

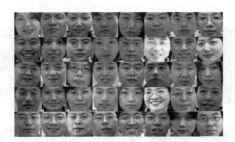

Fig. 8. The samples of ETRI face database

6.2 Detection Rate Comparison

We compare the rate of our system with other systems; labeling eye detection system and SVM eye verification system. The former labels the face image and interprets the labeled object to find the eyes. The latter has uses SVM with RBF (Radial Basis Function) kernel as eye verification step. Table 1 shows the result of the eye detection rate. The comparison result is that the label system has lower detection rate. Because the system can not detect the eyes from the face images where there are eye glasses

Table 1. Comparison of the rate of eye detection with labeling method

	Eye detection rate for ETRI DB (64×64 pixels)
Labeling	60.36%
Labeling + SVM	92.5%
Our eye candidate method + SVM	97.5%
Our method	99.2%

Table 2. Processing time in EMBS embedded system

	Processing time (64×64 pixels)
Pre-processing step	50 ~ 70 ms
Eye candidate extraction step	20 ~ 30ms
Eye verification step	30 ~50ms
Total processing time	100 ~ 150ms

and eye occlusion with the hair. The detection rate of the system which uses our eye candidate step and SVM is higher than the system which uses labeling method and SVM. Also, comparing with our eye candidate method and SVM, our method shows almost same detection rate.

6.3 Processing Time and Eye Detection Results

We use lookup table and approximation method in the eye detection algorithm to execute it in the embedded system. Table 2 shows the processing time for each eye detection step. Pre-processing step including SQI, SOF and Gaussian filtering takes

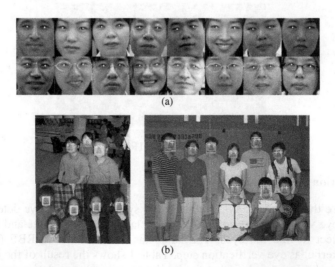

(a)

(b)

Fig. 9. The experiment results. (a) the result for single-face images, (b) the result of multiple-face images.

50 ~ 70 ms for a 64×64 pixels face image. The processing time of eye candidate extraction step depends on the number of test points to find local minimum in the gradient descent method. We use 20 test points for each eye image. Eye verification step takes 30 ~50 ms to verify the eye position using the classifier trained by AdaBoost.

Figure 9 demonstrates some image examples and the corresponding eye and face detection results. In Fig. 9, the rectangle box is the experiment result using Viola's face detector. Once the face is detected, the eye detector tries to detect the eye position around the region of the face. The white cross line is located in the eye positions.

7   Conclusions

We have described a method of eye detection using the strong pre-processing method including the fast eye candidate extraction and verification. We used SQI to minimize illumination effect and SOF to reduce unnecessary region to detect eyes. Besides that, eye candidate extraction method based on the 3D curve could make the system to detect a precise eye positions. In eye verification step, we used the strong classifier which was trained by the eye samples using AdaBoost algorithm. We also compared our method with other methods, and showing that the rate of eye detection was better than that of other methods.

References

1. LEE, J. Ho.: Automatic Video Management System Using Face Recognition and MPEG-7 Visual Descriptors. ETRI Journal. 27(6). (2005) 806-809
2. Hwang, T.H., Cho, S.I., Park, J. H., Choi, K. H.: Object Tracking for a Video Sequence from a Moving Vehicle: A Multi-modal Approach. ETRI Journal. 28(3). (2006) 367-370
3. Jee, H. K., Lee, K. H., Pan, S. B.: Eye and Face Detection using SVM. In Proc. of Int. Conf. on Intelligent Sensors, Sensor Networks and Information Processing. (2004) 577-580
4. Ma,Y., Ding, X., Wang, Z., Wang, N.:Robust Precise Eye Location Under Probabilistic Framework, In Proc. of Int. Conf. on Automatic Face and Gesture Recognition. (2004) 339-344
5. Viola, P., Jones, M.: Rapid Object Detection using a Boosted Cascade of Simple Features, In Proc. of IEEE Int. Conf. on Computer Vision and Pattern Recognition. (2001) 511-518
6. Ichikawa, K., Mita, T., Hori, O.: Component-based Robust Face Detection using AdaBoost and Decision Tree, In Proc. of Int. Conf. on Automatic Face and Gesture Recognition. (2006) 413-418
7. Li, Y., Lai, J. H., Yuen, P. C.: Multi-template ASM Method for Feature Points Detection of Facial Image with Diverse Expressions, In Proc. of Int. Conf. on Automatic Face and Gesture Recognition. (2006) 435-440
8. Wang, J., Yin, L.: Eye Detection Under Unconstrained Background by the Terrain Feature, In Proc. of Int. Conf. on Multimedia and Expo. (2005) 1528-1531

9. Tan, H., Zhang, Y. J., Li, R.: Robust Eye Extraction Using Deformable Template and Feature Tracking Ability, In Proc. of Int. Conf. on Information and Communications Security. (2003) 1747-1751
10. Wang, H., Li, S. Z., Wang, Y.: Face Recognition under Varying Lighting Condition Using Self Quotient Image, In Proc. of Int. Conf. on Automatic Face and Gesture Recognition. (2004) 819-824
11. Reisfeld, D., Wolfson, H., Yeshurun, Y.: Context Free Attentional Operators: the Generalized Symmetry Transform, Int. Journal of Computer Vision. **14**(3). (1995)119-130
12. Duda, R. O., Hart, P. E., Stork, D. G.: Pattern Classification, 2nd eds, A Wiley-Interscience Publication. (2001)

Accuracy Improvement of Lung Cancer Detection Based on Spatial Statistical Analysis of Thoracic CT Scans

Hotaka Takizawa[1], Shinji Yamamoto[2], and Tsuyoshi Shiina[1]

[1] University of Tsukuba, 305-8573, Japan
takizawa@cs.tsukuba.ac.jp
http://www.pr.cs.tsukuba.ac.jp/~takizawa
[2] Chukyo University, 470-0393, Japan

Abstract. This paper describes a novel discrimination method of lung cancers based on statistical analysis of thoracic computed tomography (CT) scans. Our previous Computer-Aided Diagnosis (CAD) system can detect lung cancers from CT scans, but, at the same time, yields many false positives. In order to reduce the false positives, the method proposed in the present paper uses a relationship between lung cancers, false positives and image information on CT scans. The trend of variation of the relationships is acquired through statistical analysis of a set of CT scans prepared for training. In testing, by use of the trend, the method predicts the appearance of lung cancers and false positives in a CT scan, and improves the accuracy of the previous CAD system by modifying the system's output based on the prediction. The method is applied to 218 actual thoracic CT scans with 386 actual lung cancers. Receiver operating characteristic (ROC) analysis is used to evaluate the results. The area under the ROC curve (Az) is statistically significantly improved from 0.918 to 0.931.

Keywords: Detection of lung cancers, Thoracic CT scans, Computer-aided diagnosis, Statistical analysis, Spatial relationship.

1 Introduction

Lung cancer is the most common cause of death among all cancers worldwide [1]. To cope with this serious problem, mass screening for lung cancer has been widely performed by simple X-ray films with sputum cytological tests. However, it is known that the accuracy of this method is not sufficient for early detection of lung cancer [2]. Therefore, we proposed a lung cancer screening system by CT for mass screening [3]. This system improves the accuracy of the cancer detection considerably [4], but has one problem that the number of the images is increased to over 30 slice cross sections per patient from 1 X-ray film. It is very difficult for a radiologist to interpret all the images in a limited time. In order to make the system more practical, it is necessary to develop a CAD system that automatically detects pathologic candidate regions suspected to contain lung

A. Gagalowicz and W. Philips (Eds.): MIRAGE 2007, LNCS 4418, pp. 607–617, 2007.

cancers in thoracic CT scans, and informs radiologists about the positions of the nodule candidates in scans as *a second opinion*.

Extensive research has been dedicated to automated detection of lung cancers in thoracic CT scans. Two-dimensional [5] and three-dimensional [6] image filters based on the mathematical morphology theorem are conventional approaches. Hessian-based image filter [7] can enhance blob-shaped regions and ridge-shaped ones individually. In [8], a multiple-thresholding technique was used to detect lung cancers. Lee, *et al.* [9] reported a template-matching method using nodular models with Gaussian distribution as reference images to CT scans. These methods were often used for initial detection of lung cancers, and were intentionally adjusted to minimize the number of misdetection. Consequently, they yielded many false positives that correspond to normal pulmonary structures (such as blood vessels) that are mistakenly identified as lung cancers.

In order to reduce such false positives, discrimination methods between lung cancers and false positives have been also developed. Many rule-based methods followed by feature analysis were proposed [10,11]. Suzuki, *et al.* [12] suppressed false positives by using voxel values in regions of interest as input for a novel artificial neural network [13]. Kawata, *et al.* [14] classified lung cancers based on differences in shape indexes, which were computed from two principal curvatures of intensity profiles in images, between lung cancers and false positives. McCulloch, *et al.* [15] discriminated between lung cancers and false positives by applying the Bayesian theorem to image features such as step-edges obtained by the Canny edge detector. In the work [16], we recognized lung cancers by use of the Markov random field that is composed of three-dimensional geometrical models representing lung cancers and blood vessels [17]. In another work [18], we identified lung cancers based on the subspace method where subspaces are formed by intensity values in regions of interest. These methods used image information only on a local area including a nodule candidate, and ignored information on other outer areas in a CT scan. However, the appearance of lung cancers and false positives would be related with image information not only on the local area but also on the outer areas. We should pay attention to relationships between lung cancers, false positives and image information on the whole scan.

Generally, the poses of human bodies are mostly fixed in thoracic CT scans taken for mass screening. The statistical analysis of such pose-fixed CT scans tells us two important properties of CT scans. One is that the spatial distributions of appearance frequencies of lung cancers and false positives are not uniform. In a lung, some areas would cause more lung cancers and false positives, whereas the others would cause less them. The other is that the frequency distributions depend on image features extracted from each area of a CT scan. By making the most of such spatial relationships between lung cancers, false positives and image features, we can get more effective hints for determining whether or not each nodule candidate is an actual lung cancer.

In the present paper, we formulate a relationship between the appearance frequency of lung cancers, that of false positives and the values of image features in each area of a CT scan, and acquire the trend of variation of the relationships through statistical analysis of a set of CT scans prepared for training. In the testing phase, by use of the variation trend, we predict how many lung cancers and false positives would appear in each area of a CT scan, and then improve the accuracy of our previous CAD system by modifying its output based on the prediction.

2   Formulation of Spatial Relationship

In order to formulate the spatial relationship effectively, we introduce a three-dimensional (3-D) lattice system that forms a rectangular solid that is composed of smaller rectangular solids, which are called *cells*. The larger rectangular solid is settled so as to circumscribe a lung region extracted from a CT scan. Fig.1 depicts an example of a 3-D lattice system for a lung. In this paper, the appearance frequency of lung cancers, that of false positives and image feature values are collectively called *attributes*. Each attribute is defined to be possessed by a cell in which the attribute is obtained.

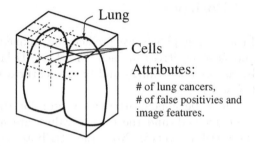

Fig. 1. 3-D lattice system for a lung

Let $a^s_{(c,i)}$ be the i-th attribute obtained in the c-th cell in the s-th CT scan for training, where $i = 1, 2, \cdots, I$, $c = 1, 2, \cdots, C$, and $s = 1, 2, \cdots, S$. For simplicity, we define $a^s_{(c,1)}$ to be the frequency of lung cancers, $a^s_{(c,2)}$ to be the frequency of false positives and $a^s_{(c,i)}$ ($i \geq 3$) to be image feature values. For each CT scan, we construct one attribute vector:

$$
\boldsymbol{a}^s = \Big(a^s_{(1,1)}, a^s_{(1,2)}, \cdots, a^s_{(1,I)},
$$
$$
a^s_{(2,1)}, a^s_{(2,2)}, \cdots, a^s_{(2,I)},
$$
$$
\cdots,
$$
$$
a^s_{(C,1)}, a^s_{(C,2)}, \cdots, a^s_{(C,I)} \Big)^T. \tag{1}
$$

From a set of attribute vectors $\boldsymbol{a}^1, \boldsymbol{a}^2, \cdots, \boldsymbol{a}^S$, the mean vector $\bar{\boldsymbol{a}}$ and covariance matrix $\Sigma_{\boldsymbol{a}}$ are calculated. Let $\lambda^1, \lambda^2, \cdots$ denote the eigen values of $\Sigma_{\boldsymbol{a}}$ and $\boldsymbol{u}^1, \boldsymbol{u}^2, \cdots$ their eigen vectors, where $\lambda^1 \geq \lambda^2 \geq \cdots$ and each $\boldsymbol{u}^k$ corresponds to

λ^k. An eigen space formed by $\boldsymbol{u}^1, \boldsymbol{u}^2, \cdots, \boldsymbol{u}^Q$ ($Q << C \cdot (I - 2)$) represents the trend of variation of the spatial relationships between attributes. An arbitrary point on the eigen space is represented by

$$a = \bar{a} + U\boldsymbol{\alpha}, \tag{2}$$

where

$$U = (\boldsymbol{u}^1 | \boldsymbol{u}^2 | \cdots | \boldsymbol{u}^Q) \tag{3}$$
$$\boldsymbol{\alpha} = (\alpha^1, \alpha^2, \cdots, \alpha^Q)^T. \tag{4}$$

The $\boldsymbol{\alpha}$ is a coefficient vector.

3 Prediction of Appearance of Lung Cancers and False Positives

In a testing phase, we predict the frequencies of appearance of lung cancers and false positives in each cell of a 3-D lattice system for a sample CT scan by use of both Eq.(2) and image features that are extracted from the sample CT scan.

Let $\boldsymbol{x}$ be a new attribute vector for the sample CT scan. Image features are extracted, and the feature values are set to the corresponding elements of the attribute vector. Now, the attributes concerning image features, i.e. $x_{(1,3)}$, $x_{(1,4)}, \cdots, x_{(1,I)}, x_{(2,3)}, \cdots, x_{(C,I)}$ ($I \geq 3$), are obtained, whereas $x_{(1,1)}, x_{(1,2)}$, $x_{(2,1)}, \cdots, x_{(2,I)}$ are not determined yet. The most promising prediction for the undetermined attributes is employed by the c- and i-th element values ($i = 1$ or 2) of the following attribute vector:

$$\tilde{\boldsymbol{x}} = \bar{a} + U\boldsymbol{\alpha}^*, \tag{5}$$

where

$$\boldsymbol{\alpha}^* = \arg\min_{\boldsymbol{\alpha}} \left\{ \sum_c \sum_{i \neq 1,2} \left\{ \boldsymbol{x}_{(c,i)} - [\bar{a} + U\boldsymbol{\alpha}]_{(c,i)} \right\}^2 \right\}. \tag{6}$$

In Eq.(6), $[\cdot]_{(c,i)}$ means the c- and i-th element value of a vector.

4 Accuracy Improvement Based on Prediction

Many CAD systems would detect a nodule candidate with the level of confidence that the nodule candidate is an actual lung cancers. If you cannot obtain such a confidence level from your CAD system, you can use, for example, 1 and 0 that correspond to an actual lung cancer and a false positive, respectively. In this section, we improve the accuracy of a previously proposed CAD system by modifying the confidence levels with the predicted frequencies of lung cancers and false positives.

Suppose that J nodule candidates are detected from the sample CT scan by the previous CAD system. Let L_j be the previous confidence level of the j-th nodule candidate, which is supposed to be in the $c(j)$-th cell of a 3-D lattice system for the sample CT scan. The following modification is applied to the L_j:

$$\hat{L}_j = \omega_0 \cdot L_j + \omega_1 \cdot \tilde{x}_{(c(j),1)} - \omega_2 \cdot \tilde{x}_{(c(j),2)}, \tag{7}$$

where ω_0, ω_1 and ω_2 are coefficient values. The $\tilde{x}_{(c(j),1)}$ and $\tilde{x}_{(c(j),2)}$ are the predicted frequencies of lung cancers and false positives, respectively, that are obtained by Eq.(5). For accuracy improvement, we use $\hat{L}_j$ as a new confidence level instead of the L_j.

5   Experiment

5.1   Materials and Conditions

In this experiment, we use 218 actual thoracic CT scans with 386 actual lung cancers. They are low-dose CT scans, and one slice cross section contains 512×512 pixels. The 109 CT scans are used for training and the others are used for testing. We apply our previous CAD system to the CT scans, and detect 361 lung cancers and 201497 false positives with confidence levels.

We use a 3-D lattice system that is composed of $15 \times 15 \times 10$ cells. The parameters, Q, ω_0, ω_1 and ω_2, are experimentally defined to be 10, 1, 0.001 and 0.02, respectively. We use the following two image features for this experiment.

Lung Region Occupancy. In many CAD systems, a lung region extracted from a CT scan is used only to restrict the searching area for lung cancers. In the proposed method, the information related to the lung region is directly used to detect lung cancers. Here, a label "lung" is attached to the voxels in a lung region extracted from a CT scan by use of a threshold-based extraction method. The *lung region occupancy* is defined to be the ratio of the amount of the lung-labeled voxels in a cell (see Fig.2) to the amount of the whole voxels in the cell.

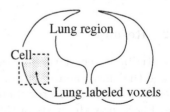

Fig. 2. The dotted region indicates lung-labeled voxels in the cell

Blood Vessel Radius. Our preliminary study [19] tells us that the 64% of false positives arise from blood vessels in a lung. To reduce such false positives, we use a relationship between the appearance frequency of false positives and the

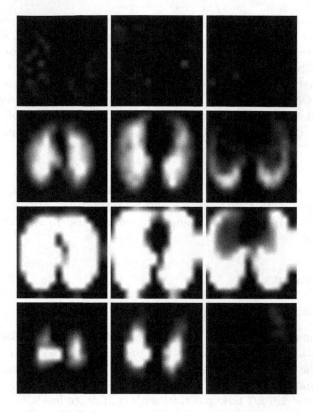

Fig. 3. The mean attribute vector computed from the 109 CT scans for training

features of blood vessel regions. In [19], the regions are extracted by a threshold-based extraction method, and the radii of the blood vessels are measured by applying the distance transform operation to the extracted regions. The *blood vessel radius* is defined to be the maximum radius value in each cell.

5.2   Results

An attribute vector can be visually observed by converting the vector to an image that has the attribute values as its pixel values. Fig.3 show the parts of the mean attribute vector computed from the 109 CT scans for training. Fig.4 and Fig.5 show the parts of the first, second and third eigen vectors of the 109 CT scans, respectively. In these figure, the first, second, third and fourth rows correspond to the frequency of lung cancers, that of false positives and the two features described in Sec.5.1, respectively. The first, second and third columns correspond to the third, sixth and ninth cross sections of the 3-D lattice system, respectively. The mean vector demonstrates that the spatial distributions of appearance frequencies of lung cancers and false positives are not uniform.

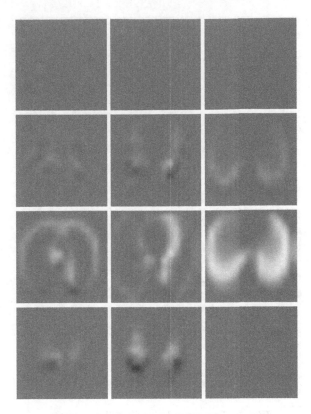

Fig. 4. The first eigen attribute vector

The eigen vectors prove that there are relationships between lung cancers, false positives and image features.

Fig.6 shows ROC curves yielded by the following three methods:

1. our previous method [16,18],
2. the newly proposed method only,
3. the new method combined with the previous method.

The ω_1 and ω_2 in Eq.(7) are set to be 0 in the previous method, and the ω_0 is set to be 0 in the newly proposed method. In the combined method, the ωs are set to be the values that are described in Sec.5.1. Their Az values are 0.918, 0.809 and 0.931, respectively. The accuracy of the new method only is less than that of the previous method. However, by combining the new method with the previous method, the accuracy is statistically significantly improved ($p < 0.01$).

Fig.7 shows a slice cross section of a thoracic CT scan. From the slice image, our previous CAD system detects one actual lung cancer and thirty-two false positives. The arrow "A" indicates the lung cancer and the others examples of

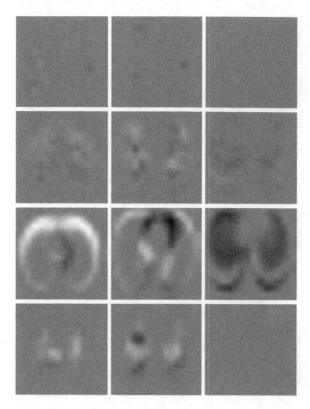

Fig. 5. The second eigen attribute vector

Table 1. The confidence levels of the lung cancers ("A") and false positives ("B" ∼ "E") in Fig.7

	the previous method	the new method only	the combined method
A	2.475×10^{-2}	$+0.033 \times 10^{-2}$	2.508×10^{-2}
B	3.07×10^{-2}	-0.69×10^{-2}	2.38×10^{-2}
C	2.83×10^{-2}	-0.90×10^{-2}	1.93×10^{-2}
D	2.57×10^{-2}	-0.66×10^{-2}	1.91×10^{-2}
E	4.08×10^{-2}	-0.29×10^{-2}	3.79×10^{-2}

the false positives. Table 1 lists their confidence levels that are obtained by the three methods. The previous method cannot distinguish the lung cancer from the false positives. By using the new method, the confidence level of the lung cancer is increased, and those of false positives are decreased. Consequently, the combined method can correctly discriminate between the lung cancer and the false positives "B" ∼ "D" by use of its new confidence levels. Although the confidence level of the false positive "E" can be decreased by the new method, it

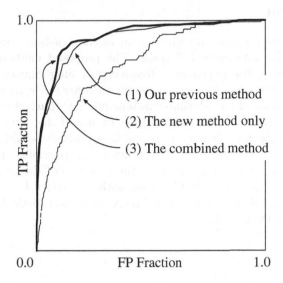

Fig. 6. The ROC curves of (1) our previous method, (2) the new method only and (3) the combined method

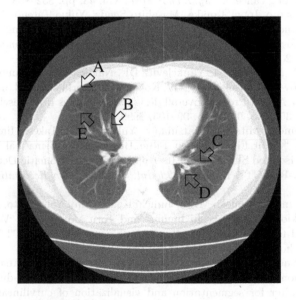

Fig. 7. A sample thoracic CT scan. The arrow "A" indicates an actual lung cancer and the others false positives.

would still remain as a false positive. The nodule candidate "E" is small, hence its misjudgement. Furthermore, the spot comprising the nodule candidate tends to be not so in favor of false positives.

6   Conclusion

This paper describes a novel discrimination method of lung cancers based on statistical analysis of thoracic CT scans. The proposed method formulates a relationship between the appearance frequency of lung cancers, that of false positives and the values of image features in each area of a thoracic CT scan. The trend of variation of the relationships is acquired through statistical analysis of a set of CT scans for training. In testing, by use of the variation trend, the method predicts how many lung cancers and false positives would appear in each area of a CT scan, and improves the accuracy of our previously proposed CAD system by modifying its output based on the prediction. The proposed method is applied to 218 actual thoracic CT scans with 386 actual lung cancers. ROC analysis is used to evaluate the method. The Az value is statistically significantly improved from 0.918 to 0.931.

References

1. H.K.Weir. "Annual report to the nation on the status of cancer,1975–2000". *Journal National Cancer Institute*, Vol. 95, No. 17, pp. 1276–1299, 2003.
2. T.Tanaka, K.Yuta, and Y.Kobayashi. "A study of false-negative case in mass-screening of lung cancer". *Jay.J.Thor.Med.*, Vol. 43, pp. 832–838, 1984.
3. Shinji Yamamoto, Ippei Tanaka, Masahiro Senda, Yukio Tateno, Takeshi Iinuma, Toru Matsumoto, and Mitsuomi Matsumoto. "Image Processing for Computer-Aided Diagnosis of Lung Cancer by CT(LSCT)". *Systems and Computers in Japan*, Vol. 25, No. 2, pp. 67–80, 1994.
4. Henschke CI, McCauley DI, Yankelevitz DF, Naidich DP, McGuinness G, Miettinen OS, Libby DM, Pasmantier MW, Koizumi J, Altorki NK, and Smith JP. "Early Lung Cancer Action Project: overall design and findings from baseline screening". *Lancet*, Vol. 354, No. 9173, pp. 99–105, 1999.
5. Shinji Yamamoto, Mitsuomi Matsumoto, Yukio Tateno, Takeshi Iinuma, and Toru Matshmoto. "Quoit Filter: A New Filter Based on Mathematical Morphology to Extract the Isolated Shadow, and Its Application to Automatic Detection of Lung Cancer in X-Ray CT". In *Proc. 13th Int. Conf. Pattern Recognition II*, pp. 3–7, 1996.
6. Toshiaki Okumura, Tomoko Miwa, Junichi Kako, Shinji Yamamoto, Mitsuomi Matsumoto, Yukio Tateno, Takeshi Iinuma, and Toru Matshmoto. "Variable NQuoit filter applied for automatic detection of lung cancer by X-ray CT". In *Computer Assisted Radiology and Surgery(CAR98)*, pp. 242–247, 1998.
7. Yoshinobu Sato, Shin Nakajima, Nobuyuki Shiraga, Hideki Atsumi, Shigeyuki Yoshida, Thomas Koller, Guido Gerig, and Ron Kiknis. "Three-dimensional multiscale line filter for segmentation and visualization of curvilinear structures in medical images". *Medical Image Analysis*, Vol. 2, No. 2, pp. 143–168, 1998.
8. Maryellen L. Giger, Kyongtae T. Bae, and Heber MacMahon. "Computerized detection of pulmonary nodules in CT images". *Investigative Radiology*, Vol. 29, No. 4, pp. 459–465, 1994.
9. Yongbum Lee, Takeshi Hara, Hiroshi Fujita, Shigeki Itoh, and Takeo Ishigaki. "Automated Detection of Pulmonary Nodules in Helical CT Images Based on an Improved Template-Matching Technique". *IEEE Transactions on Medical Imaging*, Vol. 20, No. 7, pp. 595–604, 2001.

10. Michael F. McNitt-Gray, Nathaniel Wyckoff, Eric M. Hart, James W. Sayre, Jonathan G. Goldin, and Denise R. Aberle. "Computer-Aided Techniques to Characterize Solitary Pulmonary Nodules Imaged on CT". In *Computer-Aided Diagnosis in Medical Imaging*, pp. 101–106. Elsevier, 1999.
11. Samuel.G.Armato III, Maryellen.L.Giger, Catberine.J.Moran, Kunio Doi, and Heber MacMahon. "Computerized detection of lung nodules on CT scans". *RadioGraphics*, Vol. 19, No. 5, pp. 1303–1311, 1999.
12. K.Suzuki, S.G.Armato, F.Li, S.Sone, and K.Doi. "Massive training artificial neural network (MTANN) for reduction of false positives in computerized detection of lung nodules in low-dose computed tomography". *Medical Physics*, Vol. 30, No. 7, pp. 1602–1617, 2003.
13. Kenji Suzuki, Isao Horiba, and Noboru Sugie. "Neural Edge Enhancer for Supervised Edge Enhancement from Noisy Images". *IEEE Transaction on Pattern Analysis and Machine Intelligence*, Vol. 25, No. 12, pp. 1582–1596, 2003.
14. Y.Kawata, N.Niki, H.Ohmatsu, R.Kakinuma, K.Eguchi, M.Kaneko, and N.Moriyama. "Quantitative surface characterization of pulmonary nodules based on thin-section CT images". *IEEE Transaction Nuclear Science*, Vol. 45, pp. 2132–2138, 1998.
15. Colin C. McCulloch, Robert A. Kaucic, Paulo R.S.Mendonca, Deborah J. Walter, and Ricardo S. Avila. "Model-Based Detection of Lung Nodules in Computed Tomography Exams". *Academic Radiology*, Vol. 11, pp. 258–266, 2004.
16. Hotaka Takizawa, Shinji Yamamoto, Tohru Nakagawa, Tohru Matsumoto, Yukio Tateno, Takeshi Iinuma, and Mitsuomi Matsumoto. "Recognition of Lung Nodule Shadows from Chest X-ray CT Images Using 3D Markov Random Field Models". *Systems and Computers in Japan*, Vol. 35, No. 8, pp. 1401–1412, 2004.
17. Hotaka Takizawa and Shinji Yamamoto. "Construction Method of Three-dimensional Deformable Template Models for Tree-shaped Organs". *IEICE Transactions on Information and Systems*, Vol. E89-D-II, No. 1, pp. 326–331, 2006.
18. Gentaro Fukano, Yoshihiko Nakamura, Hotaka Takizawa, Shinji Mizuno, Shinji Yamamoto, Kunio Doi, Shigehiko Katsuragawa, Tohru Matsumoto, Yukio Tateno, and Takeshi Iinuma. "Eigen Image Recognition of Pulmonary Nodules from Thoracic CT Images by Use of Subspace Method". *IEICE Transactions on Information and Systems*, Vol. E88-D-II, No. 6, pp. 1273–1283, 2005.
19. Gentaro Fukano, Hotaka Takizawa, Kanae Shigemoto, Shinji Yamamoto, Tohru Matsumoto, Yukio Tateno, Takeshi Iinuma, and Mitsuomi Matsumoto. "Recognition method of lung nodules using blood vessel extraction techniques and 3D object models". In *Proc. of Society of Photo-Optical Instrumentation Engineers, Medical Imaging 2003*, pp. 190–198, 2003.

Author Index

Lecture Notes in Computer Science

For information about Vols. 1–4327

please contact your bookseller or Springer